Writing with POWER

Contributing Author
Joyce Senn

Senior Consultants
Constance Weaver
Peter Smagorinsky

Language

Composition

21st Century Skills

Perfection Learning®

Editorial

Editorial Director	Carol Francis
Executive Editor	Jim Strickler
Editorial Team	Gay Russell-Dempsey, Terry Ofner, Kate Winzenburg, Sue Thies, Andrea Stark, Paula Reece

Design

Art Director	Randy Messer
Design Team	Tobi Cunningham, Deborah Bell, Emily Greazel, Mike Aspengren, Jane Wonderlin, Dea Marks, Lori Zircher, Jill Kimpston
Illustration/Diagrams	Mike Aspengren, Sue Cornelison
Image Research	Anjanette Houghtaling

Joyce Senn taught both middle and high school before putting her experience and love of language to work in her distinguished career as educational consultant and author. Specializing in grammar, Senn was a pioneer in textbook publishing in her use of themed activities, helping to provide a context for once-isolated grammar, usage, and mechanics practice. Senn's other publications include the acclaimed children's reference book *Quotations for Kids* (Millbrook Press, 1999) and *Information Literacy: Educating Children for the 21st Century* (with Patricia Breivik, National Education Association, 2nd Ed., 1998).

Special thanks to Joan McElroy, Ph.D., for contributions to the research strand of *Writing with Power*, and to David Kulieke, English instructor and consultant, for his review of the grammar, usage, and mechanics chapters.

Copyright © 2012
by Perfection Learning® Corporation
1000 North Second Avenue
P.O. Box 500
Logan, Iowa 51546-0500
Tel: 1-800-831-4190 • Fax: 1-800-543-2745
perfectionlearning.com

3 4 5 6 7 RRD 16 15 14

ISBN 13: 978-1-61563-628-0
ISBN 10: 1-61563-628-5

Senior Consultants

Peter Smagorinsky wrote the activities that form the project-centered "structured process approach" to teaching writing at the heart of the composition units of *Writing with Power*. A high school English teacher for fourteen years, Smagorinsky has also taught in the English Education programs at the University of Oklahoma (1990-1998) and University of Georgia (1998-present). In addition to numerous articles, he has published books through Heinemann (*Teaching English by Design*, 2007, and *The Dynamics of Writing Instruction: A Structured Process Approach for the Composition Teacher in the Middle and High School,* with Larry Johannessen, Elizabeth Kahn, and Thomas McCann, 2010); through Teacher's College Press (*Research on Composition: Multiple Perspectives on Two Decades of Change*, ed., 2006); through Cambridge University Press (*Vygotskian Perspectives on Literacy Research: Constructing Meaning through Collaborative Inquiry*, with Carol D. Lee, 2000); and through the National Council of Teachers of English (NCTE) Press (*Standards in Practice, Grades 9–12*, 1996). For NCTE, he also chaired the Research Forum, co-edited *Research in the Teaching of English*, co-chaired the Assembly for Research, chaired the Standing Committee on Research, chaired the Research Foundation, and served as President of the National Conference on Research in Language and Literacy.

Constance Weaver developed the "power" concept and features for *Writing with Power,* identifying strategies for using grammatical options to add power to writing and thinking as well as developing the "Power Rules," beginning with ten "must know" conventions for success in school and the workplace and expanding into features more relevant for advanced writers. Weaver has shaped English education for more than thirty years, illuminating the relationship between grammar and writing and providing practical, effective teaching guidance, from her earliest works on the subject, the best-selling *Grammar for Teachers* (NCTE, 1979) and the widely acclaimed *Teaching Grammar in Context* (Boynton/Cook, 1996), to her most recent *Grammar Plan Book* (Heinemann, 2007) and *Grammar to Enrich and Enhance Writing* (with Jonathan Bush, Heinemann, 2008). She has also long been a leader in literacy and reading. Her book *Reading Process and Practice* (Heinemann, 1988) is authoritative in its field. In 1996, Weaver was honored by the Michigan Council of Teachers of English with the Charles C. Fries award for outstanding leadership in English education. Weaver is the Heckert Professor of Reading and Writing at Miami University, Oxford, Ohio, and Professor Emerita of English at Western Michigan University, Kalamazoo.

National Advisory Panel

Writing with Power was developed under the guidance of outstanding educators—teachers, curriculum specialists, and supervisors—whose experience helped ensure that the program design was implemented in a practical, engaging way for every classroom.

Middle School

DeVeria A. Berry
Curriculum Specialist
Frank T. Simpson-Waverly School
Hartford Public Schools
Hartford, Connecticut

Marylou Curley-Flores
Curriculum Specialist
Reading/Language Arts
Curriculum and Instruction
San Antonio Independent School District
San Antonio, Texas

Karen Guajardo
Curriculum Specialist
Reading/English Language Arts
Curriculum and Instruction
San Antonio Independent School District
San Antonio, Texas

Tina DelGiodice
English Teacher/Staff Developer (retired)
Jersey City Public Schools
Jersey City, New Jersey

Julie Hines-Lyman
Curriculum Coach
Agassiz Elementary School
Chicago Public Schools
Chicago, Illinois

Marcia W. Punsalan
Language Arts Department Chair
Clay High School
Oregon City Schools
Oregon, Ohio

Melanie Pogue Semore
Director of Upper School
Harding Academy
Memphis, Tennessee

High School

Nathan H. Busse
English Language Arts Teacher
Fox Tech High School
San Antonio Independent School DIstrict
San Antonio, Texas

Joyce Griggs
Instructional Specialist
Peoria Unified School District
Peoria, Arizona

Jill Haltom
English Language Arts/Reading Director
Coppell Independent School District
Coppell, Texas

Lynn Hugerich
Retired English Supervisor
Secaucus Public School District
Secaucus, New Jersey

Linda M. Moore, M.Ed.
English Instructor
Coppell High School
Coppell Independent School District
Coppell, Texas

Debora Stonich
Secondary Curriculum Coordinator of
English Language Arts
McKinney Independent School District
McKinney, Texas

Student Contributors

Writing with Power proudly and gratefully presents the work of the following students, whose writing samples—from effective opening sentences to in-depth literary analyses—show so clearly the power of writing.

From Lucyle Collins Middle School
Fort Worth, Texas
Marbella Maldonado
Victor Ramirez

From Evanston Township High School
Evanston, Illinois
Morgan Nicholls

From Sunrise Mountain High School
Peoria, Arizona
Griffin Burns

From Canton South High School
Canton, Ohio
Cody Collins
Marti Doerschuk
Reanna Eckroad
Erica Gallon
Lindsay Kerr
Elise Miller
Katie Smith
Natalie Volpe

CONTENTS IN BRIEF

COMPOSITION

Common Core State Standards Focus

W.5 With some guidance and support from peers and adults, develop and strengthen writing as needed by planning, revising, editing, rewriting, or trying a new approach, focusing on how well purpose and audience have been addressed.

W.4 Produce clear and coherent writing in which the development, organization, and style are appropriate to task, purpose, and audience.

**Common Core
State Standards Focus**

W.2 (b) Develop the topic with relevant, well-chosen facts, definitions, concrete details, quotations, or other information and examples.

COMPOSITION

UNIT 2 Purposes of Writing

Common Core State Standards Focus

W.2 (a) Introduce a topic clearly, previewing what is to follow; organize ideas, concepts, and information into broader categories; include formatting (e.g., headings), graphics (e.g., charts, tables), and multimedia when useful to aiding comprehension.

W.3 Write narratives to develop real or imagined experiences or events using effective technique, relevant descriptive details, and well-structured event sequences.

**Common Core
State Standards Focus**

W.3 (d) Use precise words and phrases, relevant descriptive details, and sensory language to capture the action and convey experiences and events.

COMPOSITION

Common Core
State Standards Focus

W.3 Write narratives to develop real or imagined experiences or events using effective technique, relevant descriptive details, and well-structured event sequences.

W.2 Write informative/explanatory texts to examine a topic and convey ideas, concepts, and information through the selection, organization, and analysis of relevant content.

**Common Core
State Standards Focus**

W.1 Write arguments to
support claims with clear
reasons and relevant
evidence.

COMPOSITION

Common Core
State Standards Focus

W.9: Draw evidence from literary or informational texts to support analysis, reflection, and research.

Common Core State Standards Focus

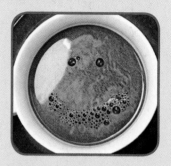

W.8 Gather relevant information from multiple print and digital sources, using search terms effectively; assess the credibility and accuracy of each source; and quote or paraphrase the data and conclusions of others while avoiding plagiarism and following a standard format for citation.

COMPOSITION

Common Core State Standards Focus

W.7 Conduct short research projects to answer a question (including a self-generated question), drawing on several sources and generating additional related, focused questions that allow for multiple avenues of exploration.

Guide to 21st Century School and Workplace Skills

Common Core State Standards Focus

SL.1 Engage effectively in a range of collaborative discussions (one-on-one, in groups, and teacher-led) with diverse partners on grade 8 topics, texts, and issues, building on others' ideas and expressing their own clearly.

COMPOSITION

Common Core State Standards Focus

L.4 Determine or clarify the meaning of unknown and multiple-meaning words or phrases based on grade 8 reading and content, choosing flexibly from a range of strategies.

SL.6 Adapt speech to a variety of contexts and tasks, demonstrating command of formal English when indicated or appropriate.

Common Core
State Standards Focus

W.6 Use technology,
including the Internet, to
produce and publish writing
and present the relationships
between information and
ideas efficiently as well as to
interact and collaborate with
others.

GRAMMAR

Common Core State Standards Focus

L.3 Use knowledge of language and its conventions when writing, speaking, reading, or listening.

Common Core
State Standards Focus

L.1 Demonstrate command of the conventions of standard English grammar and usage when writing or speaking.

GRAMMAR

**Common Core
State Standards Focus**

L.3 Use knowledge of
language and its conventions
when writing, speaking,
reading, or listening.

**Common Core
State Standards Focus**

L.1 Demonstrate command of the conventions of standard English grammar and usage when writing or speaking.

GRAMMAR

Common Core State Standards Focus

L.1 (a) Explain the function of verbals (gerunds, participles, infinitives) in general and their function in particular sentences.

Common Core
State Standards Focus

W.1 (c) Use words, phrases, and clauses to create cohesion and clarify the relationships among claim(s), counterclaims, reasons, and evidence.

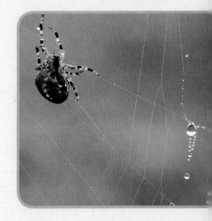

GRAMMAR

UNIT 5 Usage

Common Core State Standards Focus

L.1 (d) Recognize and correct inappropriate shifts in verb voice and mood.

L.1 (b) Form and use verbs in the active and passive voice.

**Common Core
State Standards Focus**

L.1 Demonstrate command
of the conventions of
standard English grammar
and usage when writing or
speaking.

GRAMMAR

**Common Core
State Standards Focus**

W.3 (d) Use precise words and phrases, relevant descriptive details, and sensory language to capture the action and convey experiences and events.

Common Core State Standards Focus

L.3 Use knowledge of language and its conventions when writing, speaking, reading, or listening.

GRAMMAR

Common Core State Standards Focus

L.1 Demonstrate command of the conventions of standard English grammar and usage when writing or speaking.

30 Other Punctuation

Common Core State Standards Focus

L.2 Demonstrate command of the conventions of standard English capitalization, punctuation, and spelling when writing.

GRAMMAR

Common Core State Standards Focus

L.2 (a) Use punctuation (comma, ellipsis, dash) to indicate a pause or break.

L.2 (b) Spell correctly.

Writing with POWER

Language
Composition
21st Century Skills

Perfection Learning®

Unit 1

Style and Structure of Writing

Like other crafts, writing calls for using the right tools for the right job. Writers learning their craft might sometimes reach for the writing equivalent of a hammer when a screwdriver is actually the better tool for the job. Fortunately, most people learn the craft of writing in school, where they are surrounded by a community of writers—their classmates and teacher. In such a community, each mistake is an opportunity to learn, and everyone benefits from the learning.

Writing is a craft. . . . You learn by doing, by making mistakes and then seeing where you went wrong. —*Jeffrey A. Carver*

CHAPTER 1

A Community of Writers

This **program** is called *Writing with Power.* Its goal is to help you develop powerful writing and necessary and useful communication skills for success in the 21st century. You may ask, What does it mean to write with power? Why would language and communication in the 21st century be any different from language and communication in earlier times? This chapter will provide the answers and lay the foundation for the writing instruction and activities presented in future chapters.

Writing with Power

You read texts every day. You can usually distinguish one that has been written with power from one that has not. Such writing usually

- demonstrates the **six traits** of good writing
- uses **language in varied, interesting ways** to show relationships and provide details
- follows the **conventions** appropriate for the purpose, occasion, audience, and genre

This program will help you to write with power and enable you to accomplish your goals through your writing.

 ## The Six Traits

IDEAS

Strong writing includes a clear idea, message, or theme. Writers add strong and lively details that help explain or support the substance of their writing. Powerful writing helps you focus your thinking so that readers can easily follow what you are trying to say.

ORGANIZATION

Well-organized writing typically has a clear beginning, middle, and ending. It presents details in a logical order by using the transitional words and phrases listed in the chart below.

WRITING PURPOSE	ORGANIZATIONAL PATTERNS	COMMON TRANSITIONS
Expository (to explain or inform)	Order of importance	*First, next, most important*
	Comparison/contrast	*Similarly, in contrast, on the other hand*
	Cause/effect	*As a result, for that reason, because*
Narrative (to tell a real or imaginary story)	Chronological (time) order	*First, yesterday, the next day, last year, next, until*
Descriptive	Spatial (location) order	*At the top, near the middle, to the right, on the other side, next to, behind*
Persuasive	Order of importance	*The most important, equally important, in addition, also, in fact*

VOICE

Voice is what gives your writing a unique personality and message and provides a personal way of expressing ideas. Your writing voice should meet the expectations for the situation. For example, you would use different voices to write a solemn poem on the occasion of a beloved pet's death and to write a note of congratulations to a friend who has won an award. The following chart identifies appropriate voices for different writing occasions.

WRITING PURPOSE	WHAT THE WRITER'S VOICE SHOULD CONVEY
Expository and argumentative writing	Genuine interest in the subject, often including personal insights about why the subject is important to the writer and what the reader might expect to gain from it; respect for differing viewpoints; confidence without swagger
Descriptive and narrative writing	A genuine, not phony, personality; often some personal statements that show a willingness to trust readers with ideas you may find sensitive

WORD CHOICE

You can capture your readers' attention by using specific, lively, and natural sounding language appropriate to the situation. Use active-voice verbs (see pages 697–698), precise nouns and modifiers, and colorful and figurative language (see pages 186–187) that meet the expectations of your readers. (You will learn more about word choice in Chapter 2.)

SENTENCE FLUENCY

Your sentences flow smoothly together when you employ transitions, repeated words, and pronouns that refer back to an earlier word. These devices enable sentences to connect fluidly to one another, creating **internal coherence.** They also help support **external coherence,** the smooth, logical flow from one paragraph to the next. Most writers go back and revise some parts of their writing so that readers can follow their thinking as easily and clearly as possible. To help your readers grasp your points, you may need to add transitions, repeat a key word, or replace a word with a pronoun, a synonym, or a substitute. (You will learn more about sentence fluency in Chapter 2.)

CONVENTIONS

Writing that communicates effectively is generally free of problems with spelling, capitalization, punctuation, and word choice. Paragraph breaks occur where you change topics, and sentences follow appropriate rules for grammar and usage. Writing that adheres to these principles can make a strong positive impression on readers. If you use inappropriate writing conventions, you may confuse your readers. (You will learn more about some of the most important conventions on pages 8–10.)

② The Power of Language

There are so many available words and sentence structures that you could conceivably construct sentences of infinite variety. Simple pictures can communicate an idea such as "Fatima emptied the dishwasher," but language can add detail, meaning, subtlety, and feeling to that idea in seemingly endless ways: "Fatima was exhausted when she got home after running in the track meet but knew that she still had to do her chore of emptying the dishwasher. She opened the dishwasher door, creaking along with it, and reached slowly for the first plate. She sluggishly removed it and put it in the cabinet. She continued unloading in this way, seemingly in slow motion, removing every last dish and utensil before crawling up to her room and into bed."

Fluent writers generate power through their careful language use. For this reason, each composition chapter in this program includes a warm-up activity called "The Power of Language." These activities help you learn how to create interesting and varied sentence patterns to help you express your thoughts persuasively. Most language strategies have two names. The first identifies the language concept. The second name, after the colon, reflects its purpose or function. The "Power of Language" strategies in this book are:

- Prepositional Phrases: Scene Setters, page 49
- Parallelism: The Power of 3s, page 78
- Fluency: Let It Flow, page 97
- Dashes: Dash It All, page 120
- Adjectives: What Kind?, page 139
- Appositives: Who or What?, page 165
- Colorful Verbs: In Living Color, page 202
- Clauses: Tip the Scale, page 237
- Participial Phrases: Getting into the Action, page 266
- Adverbial Clauses: Scene Setters, page 320

Using these strategies will help you transform your writing from "Fatima emptied the dishwasher" to an endless variety of detailed, interesting, and original expressions, giving your language significant *power*.

Learning Tip

With a partner, take the simple sentence "Fatima emptied the dishwasher" and use your language power to expand it with details and subtlety of meaning. Share your revised sentence with the rest of the class.

CHAPTER 1

③ The Power Rules

Your use of language can help you get where you want to go. Your language—the words, their arrangement in your sentences, the rules you follow—indicates your membership in a social group. You speak comfortably with your family and friends. Depending on the people who surround you, you might have learned to say, "You can't have no more" or you might have learned to say "You can't have any more." Your speech usually sounds like the language used by the people you spend time with or hope to spend time with. This speech is the language of power of the people you are with most often. You use it comfortably, and it feels natural to you.

However, your everyday speech is not necessarily the language of power in other situations. In some areas of society, "mainstream English" or Standard English—the language used in many workplaces—is expected. Its conventions may depart from the speech you use with your family and friends. However, if you hope to succeed in school, college, or a profession, you benefit from learning the language of power used by people in those settings. The speech and writing conventions you follow are therefore not absolutely right or wrong. However, if you are addressing an audience of parents, either in writing or at a podium on stage, you would use language conventions appropriate to that somewhat formal setting.

English professors and employers believe that certain patterns of language use create more negative impressions than others. Since these errors can influence how people perceive you, you should learn how to edit your writing so that it meets the standards for formal occasions. The list below identifies ten of the most important conventions to master. Check for these Power Rules whenever you edit.

EDITING FOR MAINSTREAM CONVENTIONS: THE POWER RULES

1. Use only one negative form for a single negative idea. (See page 773.)

Before Editing	After Editing
You don't have *nothing*.	You don't have *anything*.
I didn't do *nothing*.	I didn't do *anything*.

2. Use mainstream past tense forms of regular and irregular verbs. (See pages 674–682.) You might try to recite and memorize the parts of the most common irregular verbs.

Before Editing	After Editing
I *play* that song two minutes ago.	I *played* that song two minutes ago.
We *was* chilling.	We *were* chilling.
Consuelo *come* to the game last night.	Consuelo *came* to the game last night.
Y'all should have *went* home.	Y'all should have *gone* home.
They *done brung* me to the concert.	They *brought* me to the concert.

3. Use verbs that agree with the subject. (See pages 736–740.)

Before Editing

Shamique usually *clean* her plate.
The cat and the dog *gets* along well.
Either the chipmunks or the squirrel *eat* the walnut.
Neither the biscuit nor the muffins *is finished* baking.

After Editing

Shamique usually *cleans* her plate.
The cat and the dog *get* along well.
Either the chipmunks or the squirrel *eats* the walnut.
Neither the biscuit nor the muffins *are finished* baking.

4. Use subject forms of pronouns in subject position. Use object forms of pronouns in object position. (See pages 712–716.)

Before Editing

Her and her backpack are inseparable.
Him and his problems are none of my business.
Her and *me* had lunch at Murray's Deli.

After Editing

She and her backpack are inseparable.
He and his problems are none of my business.
She and *I* had lunch at Murray's Deli.

5. Use standard ways to make nouns possessive. (See pages 878–880.)

Before Editing

Who is the *dogs* owner?
Who broke the *cars* window?
Horace mounted the *horses* back.
Both *dogs* barking kept me awake.

After Editing

Who is the *dog's* owner?
Who broke the *car's* window?
Horace mounted the *horse's* back.
Both *dogs'* barking kept me awake.

6. Use a consistent verb tense except when a change is clearly necessary. (See pages 689–696.)

Before Editing

The bell *rings* when the class ended.
After the boring movie, I *yawn* and gave it thumbs down.

After Editing

The bell *rang* when the class ended.
After the boring movie, I *yawned* and gave it thumbs down.

7. Use sentence fragments only the way professional writers do, after the sentence they refer to and usually to emphasize a point. Fix all sentence fragments that occur before the sentence they refer to and ones that occur in the middle of a sentence. (See page 656.)

Before Editing

Today. I will ace the test.
Trying to build a boat. *While sailing it is hard.* So we try to build it ahead of time.
I released the healed robin into the wild. *The reason being that I wanted it to be free.*

After Editing

Today, I will ace the test.
Trying to build a boat *while sailing it is hard, so* we try to build it ahead of time.
I released the healed robin into the wild *because I wanted it to be free.*

8. **Use the best conjunction and/or punctuation for the meaning when connecting two sentences. Revise run-on sentences.** (See pages 662–663.)

Before Editing	After Editing
We turned on the faucet, brown water came out.	*When we turned on the faucet,* brown water came out.
I went to summer school, I didn't go on vacation.	I went to summer school, *so* I didn't go on vacation.
Preston ironed his shirt, he polished his shoes.	Preston ironed his shirt, *and* he polished his shoes.

9. **Use the contraction *'ve* (not *of*) when the correct word is *have*, or use the full word *have*. Use *supposed* instead of *suppose* and *used* instead of *use* when appropriate.** (See pages 786–791.)

Before Editing	After Editing
They should *of* elected me president.	They should *have* elected me president.
We might *of* underestimated her ability.	We might *have* underestimated her ability.
The banana would *of* tasted better if we hadn't let it turn brown.	The banana would *have* tasted better If we hadn't let it turn brown.
We were *suppose* to turn off the lights.	We were *supposed* to turn off the lights.
Pedro *use* to be wasteful, but he now recycles his cans and bottles.	Pedro *used* to be wasteful, but he now recycles his cans and bottles.

10. **For sound-alikes and certain words that sound almost alike, choose the word with your intended meaning.** (See pages 782–791.)

Before Editing	After Editing
We are going *too* quit watching so much TV. (*too* means "also" or "in addition")	We are going *to* quit watching so much TV. (*to* is part of the infinitive form of the verb *to quit*)
I will put *to* slices of tofu on each sandwich. (*to* means "in the direction of")	I will put *two* slices of tofu on each sandwich. (*two* is a number)
Was that *you're* seat I took? (*you're* is a contraction of *you are*)	Was that *your* seat I took? (*your* is the possessive form of *you*)
They're idea is worth considering. (*they're* is a contraction of *they are*)	*Their* idea is worth considering. (*their* is the possessive form of *they*)
I'd like the table placed *their*. (*their* is the possessive form of *they*)	I'd like the table placed *there*. (*there* means "in that place")
Its a shame I ran out of zucchini. (*its* is the possessive form of *it*)	*It's* a shame I ran out of zucchini. (*it's* is a contraction of *it is*)

When working with hard copy, writers often use the following proofreading symbols to indicate where they need to make changes when they edit. These symbols help writers know where their writing should be revised to follow the Power Rules.

PROOFREADING SYMBOLS

∧	insert	We ~~completed~~ an journey. *went on* *eventful*
∧	insert comma	Meg enjoys hiking, skiing and skating.
⊙	insert period	Gary took the bus to Atlanta⊙
ɣ	delete	Refer ~~back~~ to your notes.
¶	new paragraph	¶ Finally Balboa saw the Pacific.
no ¶	no paragraph	no ¶ The dachshund trotted away.
. . .	let it stand	I appreciated her ~~sincere~~ honesty.
#	add space	She will beback in a moment.
◡	close up	The airplane waited on the runway.
↔	transpose	They only have two dollars left.
≡	capital letter	We later moved to the south.
/	lowercase letter	His favorite subject was Science.
SP	spell out	I ate 2 oranges.
⌄" ⌄"	insert quotes	I hope you can join us, said my brother.
=	insert hyphen	I attended a schoolrelated event.
⌄'	insert apostrophe	The ravenous dog ate the cats food.
⟳	move copy	I usually on Fridays go to the movies.

Learning Tip

Write the following sentence on a piece of paper, just as it's written here.

Ernesto said said he wouldbe late to Practice.

Add proofreading symbols to show corrections. Compare your work with a partner's. Did you find the same errors and mark them in the same way?

4 Writing in the 21st Century

You likely have expertise in 21st century writing. Like most teenagers, you probably send about 100 text messages every day. You spend an hour or more a day on the Internet, often on a social networking Web site. You blog to share your opinions and respond to other people's blogs and social networking sites. For this writing, you probably follow unique conventions. You upload photos, videos, and music files, and people often respond to them. You "talk" with friends in chat rooms and with instant messaging software, often carrying on several conversations at the same time.

You also write in school. You answer essay questions on tests, write papers for English, produce research reports in social studies, and write for other classes.

Outside school, you may write spoken word poems that you intend to perform, keep a journal, make shopping lists, and keep records of things you collect.

THE RIGHT KIND OF WRITING?

With all these kinds of writing, what is the "right" way to write?

There is no single way to write that is "right" for every occasion. The right way to write is the way that's appropriate for the situation, your reasons for writing, and the expectations of your readers. In other words, writing should be "in tune" with what is appropriate for the situation.

GLOBAL INTERACTIONS

Technology makes it possible for you to stay connected with other people. Life today has a global character: The Internet allows you to buy goods from around the world, phone calls in the U.S. are answered by service employees in India and other distant places, and a machine may be assembled from parts produced in dozens of different countries.

Those who live in this wired world benefit from **creative thinking** and the ability to **work cooperatively with others,** including people from different cultures. Life in the 21st century also involves **critical thinking,** logical reasoning, and effective **problem solving, often in more than one language.** You will need to know how to communicate, often through **technology** that enables you to find and evaluate information. Writing can help you develop all of those skills and prepare you to live a satisfying life in the 21st century.

> ### Learning Tip
> For one day, keep a log of how many times you write, and under what circumstances. Include text messaging. Compare your log to those of your classmates and look for patterns.

Collaborating Through the Writing Process

When they think of writing, many people envision a writer toiling away in solitude. Of course, some parts of the writing process are accomplished alone. Most people, however, write collaboratively. This book, for instance, was not written by one person, but by a number of people contributing different sections and revising one another's work so that it appears smooth to you, the readers. Behind this program there is also a team of edtors who orchestrate the whole process, not only giving individual writers feedback but making sure that the whole is more than the sum of its parts. For the writing in this program, you and your classmates will create and participate in a **community of writers** and work in **collaboration** throughout the writing process, often in groups of three to four students.

Prewriting: Getting Started

STRATEGIES FOR FINDING A SUBJECT

A good subject is one that will truly interest you and your readers. The following strategies will help you discover ideas for writing.

Taking an Inventory of Personal Interests One way to find a writing subject is to focus on topics that are most familiar to you. Try the technique of self-interview. Ask yourself questions like the following and write the answers:

- What subjects do I know a lot about?
- What are my hobbies?
- What unusual experiences have I had?

Keeping a Journal A **journal** is a daily notebook in which you record your thoughts, feelings, and observations. Your teacher might ask you to keep a writing journal of responses to stories, poems, and other literature. Date each entry. You may write about whatever is on your mind, or you may look through this book or any other for ideas.

Reading, Interviewing, Discussing Use the following strategies to develop ideas for subjects. In each case, take notes to remember the ideas that surfaced.

Strategies for Thinking of Subjects

- Do some background reading on general topics that interest you. If you are interested in popular music, for example, find some recent articles to read in the library or on the Internet.
- Interview someone who knows more about a subject than you do.
- Discuss subjects of mutual interest with classmates, friends, and/or family to find interesting and fresh angles on a subject.

Keeping a Learning Log A Learning Log is a section of your journal where you can write down ideas or information about math, science, history, health, or any other subject that interests you. You can use it to capture what you know about a subject and what you still need or want to learn about it. You can also record your progress as a writer there.

CHOOSING AND LIMITING A SUBJECT

How can you use the prewriting work you have done so far to find a good subject? The following guidelines will help.

Guidelines for Choosing a Subject

- Choose a subject that genuinely interests you.
- Choose a subject that will interest your readers.
- Choose a subject that you know something about or can research with reasonable effort.

The subject you choose may be very broad. Subjects such as "sports" or "school" are too general to cover completely in a single composition. Focusing on a detail or smaller aspect of the subject can help you narrow the scope of your search and make your writing more concise. To limit your subject, use the following strategies.

Strategies for Limiting a Subject

- Focus on one person or one example that represents the subject.
- Limit your subject to a specific time or place.
- Focus on a particular event or person.
- Choose one effect or one purpose of your subject.

Consider the subject of sports. The following model shows how this broad subject can be limited.

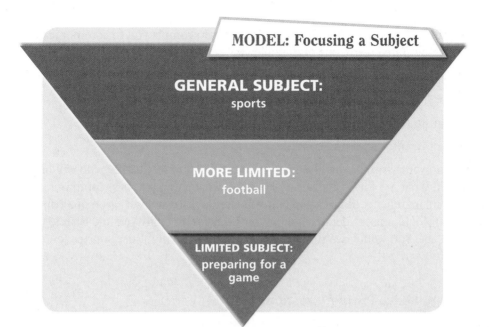

MODEL: Focusing a Subject

GENERAL SUBJECT:
sports

MORE LIMITED:
football

LIMITED SUBJECT:
preparing for a game

CONSIDERING YOUR PURPOSE, OCCASION, AUDIENCE, AND GENRE

Purpose is your reason for writing or speaking. For example, the purpose of an article in a computer magazine may be to explain how a software program works or to inform readers about a new laptop model. The purpose of a campaign letter from a political candidate may be to persuade people to vote a certain way. The purpose of a children's story may be to entertain or amuse. The purpose of an entry in a personal diary may be to express and reflect. The following chart shows common purposes for writing and the forms that different kinds of writing can take.

WRITING PURPOSES	POSSIBLE FORMS
Expository to **explain** or **inform;** to focus on your subject matter and audience	**Factual writing** scientific essay, research paper, business letter, summary, descriptive essay, historical narrative, news story
Creative (literary) to **create;** to focus on making imaginative use of language and ideas	**Entertaining writing** short story, novel, play, poem, dialogue
Persuasive to **persuade;** to focus on changing your readers' minds or getting them to act in a certain way	**Convincing writing** letter to the editor, argumentative essay, movie or book review, critical essay (literary analysis), advertisement
Self-expressive to **express** and **reflect** on your thoughts and feelings	**Personal writing** journal entry, personal narrative, reflective essay, personal letter

Occasion is your motivation for writing. It's what prompts you to communicate, and it usually can be stated using one of the following sentences.

- I feel a need to write for my own satisfaction.
- I have been asked to write this by [name a person].
- I want to write an entry for [name a publication].
- I want to enter a writing contest.

As you plan your writing, you also need to remember the **audience** who will be reading your work. What are their interests and concerns? How can you best communicate to this particular audience? For example, if you were writing a description of a trip you had taken, you would present details in a different way for an eight-year-old than for someone your own age. You would use simpler language, and you might use shorter sentences and more pictures.

HERE'S HOW

Audience Profile Questions

- Who will be reading my work?
- How old are they? Are they adults? teenagers? children?
- What do I want the audience to know about my subject?
- What background do they have in the subject?
- What interests and opinions might they have?
- Are there any words or terms I should define for them?

Your writing will also be influenced by the **genre,** or form of writing, you choose. (See the chart on the previous page for a listing of common forms or genres of writing.) Each genre has characteristics that make it different from the others, and readers expect these characteristics to be present. If you are reading a play, for example, you expect that there will be dialogue and stage directions. If instead you find long descriptive passages, you wouldn't know what to make of it. In the same way, if are writing a thank-you note to an aunt for a gift certificate to a skating rink, she will expect certain characteristics—a greeting, a body, a closing. If instead she finds that you have sent her a bulleted list of reasons you like the gift, without an opening or closing, she is likely to be mystified, even though you are still writing about the gift. Later, when you revise, you will check again to make sure your writing addresses the needs of the genre.

Collaboration in Action

Prewriting

David, Alysha, Kiki, and Ted are in a writing group together. It's their first writing activity of the year. They are supposed to come up with a topic and choose the purpose and audience for their writing. Here's how their discussion might go:

David: Okay, what do we do now?

Kiki: We're supposed to think of things to write about.

David: Please. I can't write. I'm sore from football practice.

Alysha: Why don't you write about football?

David: Hmm... Could I do that?

Alysha: The assignment is to write about a topic of your choice, so I assume so.

Ted: Yeah, write about football. In fact... I think I will too.

Kiki: Well, just "football" isn't specific enough. And don't pick me for your audience.

Ted: So what *about* football then?

David: Well, I think I'm going to write about getting ready for a game. My audience will be Ms. Cruz, because she always gives us homework and doesn't understand how much intensity I bring to my preparation for a game.

Ted: Makes sense.

Talking and listening help David focus his thoughts and start to get a good subject. After the group finishes talking about his topic, they have a similar conversation about the subjects Alysha, Kiki, and Ted will write about.

Collaboration Practice

Meet with a small group for 10 minutes. Use what you have learned to try to come up with a good writing topic for each member.

2 Prewriting: From Ideas to a Plan

DEVELOPING A SUBJECT

After you have chosen and limited your subject—and you have considered your audience and purpose—you should collect specific details that develop your writing. Supporting details are the facts, examples, incidents, reasons, or other specific points that back up your ideas. Following are some strategies for developing supporting details.

Brainstorming **Brainstorming** is the process of writing everything that comes to mind when thinking about a particular subject. Once you have chosen and limited a subject, brainstorming can help you discover details when you work with a group or partner. Sometimes, one idea will lead to another or result in a new subject or perspective.

Collaborating: Guidelines for Brainstorming

- Set a time limit, such as 15 minutes.
- Write the subject on a piece of paper and assign one group member to record ideas.
- Brainstorm for details—facts, examples, reasons, connections, and associations.
- Build on the ideas of other group members. Add or modify the ideas until they can be used as supporting details.
- Keep your mind open and avoid criticizing others.

You can learn more about cooperative learning on page 416.

When you have finished brainstorming, you should get a copy of all the supporting details from the group recorder. Select details that support your subject or use the details to generate new ideas.

Clustering **Clustering** is a visual form of brainstorming in which you not only jot down details as you think of them, but also make connections among those details. A cluster can look like a wheel. At the hub, or center, is your subject. Each idea that supports or explains your subject is connected to the hub by a line, like a spoke in a wheel. Sometimes supporting ideas become hubs of their own, with new spokes coming out of them. David, the student who was writing about preparing for a game, created the following cluster.

With a partner, use brainstorming, clustering, or inquiring to develop ideas for a topic of your choice. Share your work with the rest of the class.

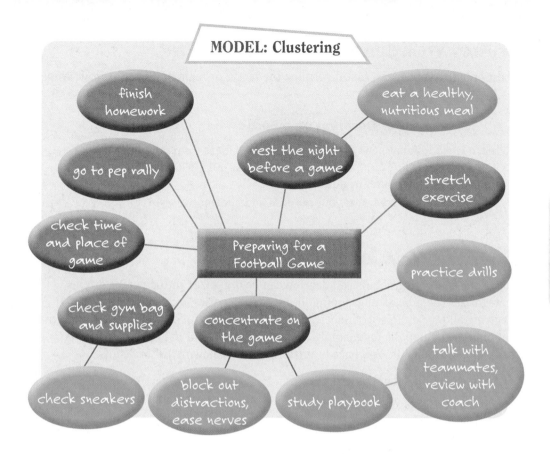

MODEL: Clustering

- finish homework
- eat a healthy, nutritious meal
- rest the night before a game
- go to pep rally
- stretch exercise
- check time and place of game
- **Preparing for a Football Game**
- practice drills
- check gym bag and supplies
- concentrate on the game
- talk with teammates, review with coach
- check sneakers
- block out distractions, ease nerves
- study playbook

Inquiring Another strategy for exploring a subject is to ask yourself questions concerning that subject. *Who, what, where, when, why,* and *how* questions can provide answers and help generate ideas that are helpful in developing details. The following model shows how one writer used inquiring to develop details on the subject "studying insects."

MODEL: Inquiring

Subject: Studying Insects

Who	are some of the experts in the field of studying insects?
What	specific details do people look for when they study insects?
What	tools are used?
Where	are the best places to look for insects?
When	did people first begin to study insects?
How	are insects captured, named, and observed?
Why	is gaining knowledge about insects helpful to people?

FOCUSING YOUR SUBJECT

To best organize your ideas, first determine the focus, or main points, of your writing.

Guidelines for Deciding on a Focus

- Look over your details. Can you draw meaningful ideas from some or all of the details? If so, the ideas could be the focus of your writing.
- Choose a main idea that intrigues you.
- Choose a main idea that suits your purpose and audience.

CLASSIFYING YOUR DETAILS

Many of the supporting details you develop can be organized into different groups or categories. The process of grouping ideas into categories is called **classifying.** Classifying allows you to see connections among details or information that at first may seem unrelated. Suppose, for example, you are writing about the opportunities your school offers to students. You have brainstormed the following list of details.

- basketball teams for boys and girls
- variety of classes students can take
- intramural program in sports
- tutoring available in all subjects

The first step in classifying is to ask whether any of the details are alike. When you look closely at the list of your school's opportunities, you can see that two of the details are alike in that they relate to sports. You can also see that the remaining two details are alike in that they relate to studying and learning. By looking for similarities, you have discovered two large groupings into which these details can be classified.

SPORTS OPPORTUNITIES	STUDYING AND LEARNING OPPORTUNITIES
• basketball teams for boys and girls • intramural program in sports	• variety of classes students can take • tutoring available in all subjects

ORDERING YOUR DETAILS

Once you have classified your details, you need to place them in an order that will not only support your subject, but also help you achieve your purpose and make sense to your readers.

WAYS TO ORGANIZE DETAILS

Types of Order	Definition	Examples
Chronological	the order in which events occur	story, explanation, history, biography, drama
Spatial	location or physical arrangement	description (top to bottom, near to far, left to right, etc.)
Order of Importance	degree of importance, size, or interest	persuasive writing, description, evaluations, explanations
Logical	Logical progression, one detail growing out of another	classifications, definitions, comparison and contrast

Choose the type of order most appropriate to your writing purpose. For example, if you were writing to persuade, you might choose to use order of importance, whereas if you were to write about a past vacation or trip, you might choose to use chronological or spatial order.

Following is a list of details compiled by a student who is writing about training for a relay race.

MODEL: Ordering Details

Before running
- get plenty of rest
- maintain a healthful diet
- stretch and exercise your muscles
- wear suitable clothes, good running shoes
- practice holding onto the baton
- practice handing off the baton
- be strategic about who runs first and who runs last

Running the race
- stay in the designated handoff area
- look straight ahead
- try to keep your muscles relaxed

③ Drafting

Drafting is the stage in writing where all your ideas from prewriting are put into complete sentences, forming an introduction, a body, and conclusion. Your first draft is just a rough sketch that allows you to see how your details and ideas fit on paper. You will most likely have to write several complete drafts. The following strategies will help you prepare a first draft.

Strategies for Drafting

- Write an introduction that will capture the reader's interest and express your main idea.
- After you write your introduction, use your organized prewriting notes as a guide. Depart from those notes, however, when a good idea occurs to you.
- Write fairly quickly without worrying about spelling or phrasing. You will have the opportunity to go back and fix your writing when you revise.
- Stop frequently and read aloud what you have written. This practice will help you move logically from one thought to the next.
- Return to the prewriting stage whenever you find that you need to clarify your thinking. You can always stop and freewrite, brainstorm, or cluster to collect more ideas.
- Write a conclusion that drives home the main point of the composition.

David wrote the following draft on the subject of preparing for a football game. Notice that he did not take the time to correct mistakes. The errors will be corrected later.

MODEL: Unedited First Draft

I am often asked how us players prepare for a big game. One thing is having team meetings, these help build team spirit and make you want to do good for all the other players. The fans are also counting on you. It also helps to concentrate only on the game and the game plan. If you let your mind wander, you can forget or make a mistake on a important play. Team meetings also help you get all the plays straight. Even more important, though, is the long, hard practice you put in all season long nothing can take the place of practice. Practice makes perfect. Maybe the most important thing is visualizing, or picturing, victory or a big play. That's how we prepare for a big game.

Drafting a Title When you have written a complete draft of your composition, take some time to come up with a title for it. Whichever title you create, you should try to choose one that captures your reader's interest and suggests the main idea of your composition.

 **Revising**

Following are some strategies you can use to improve your draft. If you answer *no* to any of the questions in the first column, you can try the fixes suggested in the second.

STRATEGIES	QUICK FIXES
Check for Clarity and Creativity • Are your ideas interesting, fresh, and original, rather than ones that people have heard over and over? • Does the text satisfy its purpose?	• Insert a personal experience or example. • Think of an unlikely comparison between your subject and something else. • Talk with others to get ideas.
Elaborate by Adding Details • Does your writing seem fully developed? • Are your ideas fully supported? • Have you used details that would help bring a scene or idea to life for a reader?	• Use one of the prewriting strategies on pages 13–16 to come up with lively elaborations. • Get into the action with participial phrases (page 266), tell who or what with appositives (page 165), add scene setters (pages 49 and 320), and/or add adjectives (page 139) and other descriptive words. • Show, don't tell. • Take a mental snapshot of a scene and write what you see.
Rearrange Out-of-Order Items • Check the organization of your words, sentences, and ideas. Does one idea lead logically into another?	• Use your word processor to rearrange and reorganize your sentences or paragraphs so the reader can easily follow your thoughts. • Use transitions to show the relationships between ideas.
Delete Unnecessary Words or Details • Does every detail in your draft really relate to your controlling idea?	• Delete, or remove, them. Also delete any extra or unneeded words and repetitive sentences.
Substitute Words and Sentences • Are all parts of your draft clear enough for a reader to follow easily? • Are your words lively and precise?	• Ask a "test reader" to tell you where you need to provide more or clearer information. • For a dull, general word, find a richer and more vivid synonym.

CHAPTER 1

A rubric like the one below can help you determine what you need to do to improve your draft. You can also use it to evaluate the work of your writing-group partners. Each row focuses on a specific aspect of writing. Each column describes a different level of quality, with the highest quality traits labeled 4.

Ideas	**4** The main idea is clear. Plenty of details such as facts, examples, and anecdotes provide support.	**3** The main idea is clear. There is enough support for the main idea to back it up adequately.	**2** The main idea could be clearer. There are some supporting details, but more details would be helpful.	**1** The main idea statement is missing or unclear. Few examples and facts are provided in support.
Organization	**4** The organization is clear with abundant transitions.	**3** A few ideas seem out of place or transitions are missing.	**2** Many ideas seem out of place and transitions are missing.	**1** The organization is unclear and hard to follow.
Voice	**4** The voice sounds natural, engaging, and unique.	**3** The voice sounds natural and engaging.	**2** The voice sounds mostly natural but is weak.	**1** The voice sounds mostly unnatural and is weak.
Word Choice	**4** Words are specific, powerful, and appropriate to the task.	**3** Words are specific and language is appropriate.	**2** Some words are too general and/or misleading.	**1** Most words are overly general and imprecise.
Sentence Fluency	**4** Varied sentences flow smoothly.	**3** Most sentences are varied and flow smoothly.	**2** Some sentences are varied but some are choppy.	**1** Sentences are not varied and are choppy.
Conventions	**4** Punctuation, usage, and spelling are correct. The Power Rules are all followed.	**3** Punctuation, usage, and spelling are mainly correct, and Power Rules are all followed.	**2** Some punctuation, usage, and spelling are incorrect, but all Power Rules are followed.	**1** There are many errors and at least one failure to follow a Power Rule.

Using a Checklist

A checklist like the one below is another tool for improving a draft.

 Evaluation Checklist for Revising

✓ Did you clearly state your main idea? (pages 91–92)

✓ Does your text have a strong introduction, body, and conclusion? (pages 96–99)

✓ Did you support your main idea with enough details? (page 90)

✓ Do your details show instead of merely tell what you want to say? (pages 47–48)

✓ Did you present your ideas in a logical order? (page 21)

✓ Do any of your sentences stray from the main idea? (pages 20–21)

✓ Are your ideas clearly explained? (page 92)

✓ Are your words specific? (page 45)

✓ Are any words or ideas repeated unnecessarily? (page 61)

✓ Are your sentences varied and smoothly connected? (page 63)

✓ Is the purpose of your text clear? (pages 15–16)

✓ Is your writing suited to your audience? (pages 15–16)

✓ Is your title effective? (page 22)

Word Processor Help

Your word processor can help in the revising stage. In addition to the usual Cut and Paste commands, you can use the Undo command to make a change in your draft from the earlier version. The Undo command reverses whatever action you have most recently taken.

Or suppose you named your main character "Jim" in the first draft of a short story and then, while revising, decide you want to name him "Bob" instead. You can do this with ease by using the global search-and-replace function of your word processing software. Pull down the Edit menu and click Replace. Do this for words, phrases, or even punctuation marks that you want to change throughout an entire story.

CONFERENCING

You have been **conferencing,** meeting with others to share ideas or identify and solve problems, throughout the writing process. Conferencing is especially helpful during revising when weaknesses in the writing can be addressed. However, offering even constructive criticism isn't easy. Yet you don't help your writing group members if you are not honest with them. Be positive and specific and praise as well as critique.

HERE'S HOW Guidelines for Conferencing

Guidelines for the Writer

- List some questions for your peer. What aspects of your work most concern you?
- Try to be grateful for your critic's candor rather than being upset or defensive. Keep in mind that the criticism you are getting is well intended.

Guidelines for the Critic

- Read your partner's work carefully. What does the writer promise to do in this text? Does he or she succeed?
- Point out strengths as well as weaknesses.
- Start your comments by saying something positive like, "Your opening really captured my interest."
- Be specific. Refer to a specific word, sentence, or section when you comment.
- Be sensitive to your partner's feelings. Phrase your criticisms as questions. You might say, "Do you think your details might be stronger if… ?"

Collaboration in Action

Revising

David's writing group has already discussed Alysha's, Kiki's, and Ted's drafts. They made notes on their papers about where they could make improvements based on their peers' feedback. Now it is David's turn to have his paper discussed:

David: So, what do y'all think of what I've got so far?

Alysha: I like what you say, but you could say it better.

Kiki: Yeah, you say, "Practice makes perfect." That's a cliché. Try to say something original, like, "To get my game to the top, I need to make the most of each practice to perfect my technique and get the conditioning I need when the game matters most."

David: And you said you didn't want to be in my audience.

Kiki: That's what I do in soccer, so it must work for football.

David: All right. What else?

Ted: Well, you start to tell about the meetings, but you don't say much. I think you should talk more about the meetings.

David: Okay, that's good, I can use that. What else?

Alysha: It seems to me that you jump around from one thing to the next. What are your main points?

David: (Reads over paper) Well team meetings is one. Practice, and then visualizing victory.

Alysha: So the stuff about each of those points needs to be all together. And I'm not sure the comment about the fans even belongs at all.

David: I'll think about that, thanks.

Collaboration Practice

Choose a paper you are working on or have completed previously and make one copy for each member of your group. Conference with one another to improve your drafts.

Here is how David revised his composition.

MODEL: Unedited Revised Composition

I am often asked how us football players prepare for a big game. One important part of preparing is having team meetings, these help build team spirit and make you want to do your best for all the your teammates. Team meetings also help you get your plays straight. It also helps to concentrate only on the game and the game plan If you let your mind wander, you can make a mistake on a important play. Team meetings also help you get all the plays straight. Even more important though, are the long hours of hard practice you put in all season long. Nothing can take the place of practice making sure that you know what to do on each play. Maybe the most important thing is visualizing, or picturing, victory or a big play. You have to picture yourself making an interception or tackling a runner or else you won't suceed. That's how we prepare for a big game.

Learning Tip

Choose a composition you have already completed or one that is still in process. Use the revision strategies on page 23 to make at least three improvements to your paper. Evaluate the paper with the rubric and checklist on pages 24–25.

USING FEEDBACK FROM YOUR TEACHER

Your teacher is a member of the community of writers and an excellent collaborator. He or she is probably with you for each stage of the writing process. The chart shows different ways your teacher can provide feedback and how you can use that feedback to improve your writing.

TEACHER FEEDBACK	HOW TO USE FEEDBACK
During prewriting your teacher might • meet briefly with you to discuss and approve your topic • suggest ways you might gather information and other supporting materials • comment on your organization	You can use this feedback to improve your work by • rethinking if necessary to come up with a sharply focused topic • following the suggestions with an open mind • experimenting with different organizational patterns
During drafting your teacher might • move from desk to desk to offer suggestions on your process of drafting (for example, continually going back and rereading what you've written) • offer suggestions or concerns about a direction your draft seems to be taking	You can use this feedback to improve your work by • trying out the suggestions, even if they are uncomfortable at first • saving your work and then coming back to it with a fresh eye to try to see the concerns your teacher raised • asking questions if you don't understand the concerns your teacher has
During revising your teacher might • meet with you to go over some issues face to face • make written comments on your work about ideas, organization, and flow	You can use this feedback to improve your work by • making a good effort to change the things you discussed • using the comments as positive guides rather than negative criticisms
During editing your teacher might • identify errors • offer mini-lessons on challenging points	You can use this feedback to improve your work by • making corrections and adding items to your personalized checklist
During publishing your teacher might • give you presentation ideas • help you reach your audience	You can use this feedback to improve your work by • gaining confidence in sharing your work with readers and being willing to take risks

⑤ Editing and Publishing

EDITING FOR WORDINESS: EDITING STAR

Products such as clothes dryers are certified by The Environmental Protection Agency to ensure "energy star" efficiency. Products that are marked with an energy star are guaranteed to get the same results as similar products that require more energy. The less power required to get the job done, the more energy-efficient the product is.

You should use word power, like other kinds of energy, efficiently. The fewer words needed to get the job done, the more energy-efficient the writing is. In the following two examples, note how much stronger the efficient version is.

Word Guzzler   Mr. Franklin determined that his whiskers needed to be removed from the surface of his face, and so he removed from its storage drawer the implement that he used to shave.

Fuel Efficient   Mr. Franklin saw that he needed a shave, so he got out his razor.

Throughout the composition chapters in this book, you will see the language arts version of the energy star logo: the editing star. It will accompany a brief activity to remind you to cut out wordiness.

USING A GENERAL EDITING CHECKLIST

When you edit you should go over your work at least three times, each time looking for a different kind of problem. For example, the focus of one reading might be misspellings. During another reading, focus on usage errors, such as subject-verb agreement. The last reading can be reserved for identifying and fixing errors in punctuation or capitalization. The following **Editing Checklist** will help you.

> ✔ **Editing Checklist**
>
> ✓ Are sentences free of errors in grammar and usage?
> ✓ Did you punctuate each sentence correctly?
> ✓ Did you spell each word correctly?
> ✓ Did you use capital letters where needed?
> ✓ Did you indent paragraphs as needed?

CREATING A PERSONALIZED EDITING CHECKLIST

As you work through the editing stage, reserve a section in your journal to use as a Personalized Editing Checklist. Write one of the following headings on every other page: Grammar Problems, Usage Problems, Spelling Problems, and Mechanical Problems. Use these pages to record your errors. Add to this checklist throughout the year and refer to it each time you edit your writing.

PROOFREADING

Proofreading is the process of carefully rereading one's work and marking corrections in grammar, usage, spelling, and mechanics using the proofreading marks on page 11. The following techniques may help.

Proofreading Techniques

- Focus on one line at a time.
- Exchange your work with a partner and check each other's work.
- Read your writing aloud, very slowly.
- Use a dictionary and a writer's handbook to check spelling, grammar, usage, and mechanics.

Here is how David used proofreading symbols to do a first-pass edit for his revised draft.

I am often asked how us ^football players prepare for a big game. One ~~thing~~ important part of preparing is having team meetings, these help build team spirit and make you want to do ~~good~~ your best for all ~~the other players~~ your teammates. The fans are also counting on you. It also helps to concentrate only on the game and the game plan. If you let your mind wander, you can ~~forget or~~ make a mistake on a important play. (Team meetings also help you get all the plays straight.) Even more important, though, ~~is~~ are the long, hours of hard practice you put in all season ~~long~~. nothing can take the place of practice. for making sure that you know what to do on each play. ~~Practice makes perfect.~~ Maybe the most important thing is visualizing, or picturing, victory or a big play. You have to picture yourself making an interception or tackling a runner or else you won't suceed. That's how we prepare for a big game.

Later, David exchanged papers with Alysha and she helped him correct the remaining errors (see page 33).

PUBLISHING

Following are just a few ways you could share your writing.

Publishing Options

In School

- Read your work aloud to a small group in your class.
- Display your final draft on a bulletin board in your classroom or school library.
- Read your work aloud to your class or present it in the form of a radio program or video presentation.
- Create a class library and media center to which you submit your work. The class media center could be a collection of folders or files devoted to different types of student writing and media presentations.
- Create a class anthology to which every student contributes. Share your anthology with other classes.
- Submit your work to your school literary magazine, newspaper, or yearbook.

Outside School

- Submit your written work to a newspaper or magazine.
- Share your work with an interested professional.
- Present your work to an appropriate community group.
- Send a video based on your written work to a local cable-television station.
- Enter your work in a local, state, or national writing contest.

Using Standard Manuscript Form The appearance of your composition may be almost as important as its content. A marked-up paper with inconsistent margins is difficult to read. A neat, legible paper, however, makes a positive impression on your reader. Use the following guidelines for standard manuscript form to help you prepare your final draft. The model that follows the guidelines shows how the writer used these guidelines to prepare his final draft on preparing for a game.

Standard Manuscript Form

- Use standard 8½-by-11-inch white paper. Use one side of the paper only.
- If handwriting, use black or blue ink. If using a word-processing program or typing, use a black ink cartridge or black typewriter ribbon and double-space the lines.
- Leave a 1.25-inch margin at the left and right. The left margin must be even. The right margin should be as even as possible.
- Put your name, the course title, the name of your teacher, and the date in the upper right-hand corner of the first page. Follow your teacher's specific guidelines for headings and margins.
- Center the title of your composition two lines below the date. Do not underline or put quotation marks around your title.
- If using a word-processing program or typing, skip four lines between the title and the first paragraph. If handwriting, skip two lines.
- If using a word-processing program or typing, indent the first line of each paragraph five spaces. If handwriting, indent the first line of each paragraph 1 inch.
- Leave a 1-inch margin at the bottom of all pages.
- Starting on page 2, number each page in the upper right-hand corner. Begin the first line 1 inch from the top. Word-processing programs allow you to insert page numbers.

CHAPTER 1

MODEL: Final Draft

1 inch

David Byrne
English: Ms. Weymouth
September 13, 2015

2 lines

Preparing for a Game

4 lines

    I am often asked how we football players prepare for a big game. One important part of preparing is having team meetings. These help build team spirit and make you want to do your best for all your teammates. Team meetings also help you get the plays straight. It also helps to concentrate only on the game and the game plan. If you let your mind wander, you can make a mistake on an important play. Even more important are the long hours of hard practice you put in all season. Nothing can take the place of practice for making sure that each player knows exactly what to do on each play. Maybe the most important thing, though, is visualizing, or picturing, victory or a big play. You have to picture yourself making an interception or tackling a runner or else you won't succeed. That is how we prepare for a big game.

1.25 inches

1 inch

KEEPING A WRITER'S PORTFOLIO

Saving your written work—short stories, poems, plays, or other completed works—is a good way to keep track of your development as a writer.

The portfolio displays your progress as a writer and your ability to express yourself on a broad range of topics and in many different styles. When you add to your portfolio, be sure to include the date of your entry and a summary of the piece.

Guidelines for Including Work in Your Portfolio

- Date each piece of writing so that you can see where it fits into your progress.
- Write a note to yourself about why you included each piece—what you believe it shows about you as a writer.
- Unfinished works may be included if they demonstrate something meaningful about you as a writer.

TIME OUT TO REFLECT

How would you describe yourself as a writer? What are your strengths? What would you like to improve? How do you think the experience of working with your peers will affect your writing? Write answers to these questions in the Learning Log section of your journal. At the end of the term, you can look back to measure your growth.

Timed Writing: On Your Own

There are times in school, such as during testing, when you will not be able to benefit from collaboration. The more you collaborate when you can, however, the less alone you will feel in those situations. You will no doubt remember things your writing partners have said during your group meetings and use them in your solo writing. For example, you might catch yourself writing a word or phrase that your group members thought was overused and too general. Or you might remember that time after time, your group members reminded you to use transitions to connect ideas. Use these memories to help you do your very best on timed writing tasks.

The following chart shows the stages of a timed writing experience. In each, imagine what your writing partners would be saying to help you.

Working Through Timed Writing Tasks

- Begin by understanding the task. Read the prompt carefully. Identify the key words in the directions: they will tell you what kind of writing to produce. Ask yourself what your audience—the examiners—will be looking for, and try to provide it.
- Think about the time you have for the test and make a budget. Leave the most time for drafting, but build in time for planning and revising as well.
- Plan your writing by jotting down ideas, making lists, or using any other format that helps you (such as a cluster diagram). When you have good ideas to work with, arrange them in a logical order.
- Think through how to begin your writing. Begin drafting when you know what your main idea will be and you have ideas for introducing it.
- Use your notes to draft the body of your work.
- Remember what you have learned about strong conclusions and write a good ending to your work.
- Read over your work. If something seems confusing or out of place, fix it.
- Check your work for errors in grammar, usage, mechanics, and spelling. Try to remember the mistakes you have made in the past so that you can avoid them.

Like everything else, writing under time pressure gets easier with practice. Each composition chapter in this book ends with a timed writing activity that you can use to practice.

You can learn more about preparing for timed writing experiences on pages 374–375.

CHAPTER 2

Developing Your Writing Style

Your writing style is the distinctive way you express yourself through the words you choose and the way you shape your sentences.

Writing is choice and exploration. As a writer you choose words, phrases, and sentence structures to communicate your ideas. Your choices create your writing style.

Writing Project *Story*

You Have the Right to Remain Incompetent *Use vivid words and varied sentences to create a story by completing the following project.*

Think Through Writing Many strange things happen. Following are brief outlines of real stories of incompetent criminals. Choose one and write a more detailed story built on the basic premise.

- A burglar drilled through the outside wall of a bank but missed the room with the safe deposit boxes and wound up instead in a restroom.

- A man was preparing to leave for a costume party, dressed as Thor, the Norse god of thunder, who always had an enormous hammer in hand. A burglar entered through a window just as "Thor" was leaving and found himself face-to-face with the Thunder God. The robber scampered back out the window, slid down a sloped roof, landed on the ground, and ran like crazy.

- A man tried to rob a fast-food restaurant armed only with a tree branch. A 56-year-old employee grabbed a broom and engaged him in a stick fight until the robber dropped his branch and ran off, whereupon he was arrested.

- A man was hospitalized after he used a front-end loader to steal an ATM. He drove to the edge of a 50-foot embankment and tried to drop the machine and break it open. But instead, he, the loader, and the ATM all crashed to the bottom.

Talk About It In your writing group, discuss the stories you developed. What details did you fill in? How did these details help the author tell an interesting story?

Read About It In the following selection, author Natalie Goldberg talks about a yogi in India who ate a car over the period of one year. See how she uses her imagination to generate questions and scenarios about how a writer might fill in the details of this seemingly odd news story.

MODEL: Creative How-To Text

From *Writing Down the Bones*

Man Eats Car

Natalie Goldberg

There was an article in the newspaper several years ago—I did not read it, it was told to me—about a yogi in India who ate a car. Not all at once, but slowly over a year's time. Now, I like a story like that. How much weight did he gain? How old was he? Did he have a full set of teeth? Even the carburetor, the steering wheel, the radio? What make was the car? Did he drink the oil?

> A startling anecdote, or story, grabs readers' attention from the very start.

I told this story to a group of third-graders in Owatonna, Minnesota. They were sitting on the tile blue carpet in front of me. The students looked confused and asked the most obvious question, "Why did he eat a car?," and then they commented, "Ugh!" But there was one bristling, brown-eyed student, who will be my friend forever, who just looked at me and burst into tremendous laughter, and I began laughing too. It was fantastic! A man had eaten a car! Right from the beginning there is no logic in it. It is absurd.

> Goldberg writes in first-person style, using the pronoun *I* and writing from her own point of view.

> Details about the student make the scene easy to picture.

In a sense, this is how we should write. Not asking "Why?," not delicately picking among candies (or spark plugs), but voraciously, letting our minds eat up everything and spewing it out on paper with great energy. We shouldn't think, "This is a good subject for writing." "This we shouldn't talk about." Writing is everything, unconditional. There is no separation between writing, life, and the mind. If you think big enough to let people eat cars, you will be able to see that ants are elephants and men are women. You will be able to see the transparency of all forms so that all separations disappear.

Goldberg avoids general statements and uses lively, specific examples.

This is what metaphor is. It is not saying that an ant is like an elephant. Perhaps; both are alive. No. Metaphor is saying the ant is an elephant. Now, logically speaking, I know there is a difference. If you put elephants and ants before me, I believe that every time I will correctly identify the elephant and the ant. So metaphor must come from a very different place than that of the logical, intelligent mind. It comes from a place that is very courageous, willing to step out of our preconceived ways of seeing things and open so large that it can see the oneness in an ant and in an elephant.

Goldberg varies her sentence patterns to keep the text flowing.

But don't worry about metaphors. Don't think, "I have to write metaphors to sound literary." First of all, don't be literary. Metaphors cannot be forced. If all of you does not believe that the elephant and the ant are one at the moment you write it, it will sound false. If all of you does believe it, there are some who might consider you crazy; but it's better to be crazy than false. But how do you make your mind believe it and write metaphor?

Don't "make" your mind do anything. Simply step out of the way and record your thoughts as they roll through you. Writing practice softens the heart and mind, helps to keep us flexible so that rigid distinctions between apples and milk, tigers and celery, disappear. We can step through moons right into bears. You will take leaps naturally if you follow your thoughts, because the mind spontaneously takes great leaps. You know. Have you ever been able to just stay with one thought for very long? Another one arises.

Fresh expressions breathe life into the writing.

Your mind is leaping, your writing will leap, but it won't be artificial. It will reflect the nature of first thoughts, the way we see the world when we are free from prejudice and can see the underlying principles. We are all connected. Metaphor knows this and therefore is religious. There is no separation between ants and elephants. All boundaries disappear, as though we were looking through rain or squinting our eyes at city lights.

These details appeal to the senses.

Respond in Writing In your journal, compare your process of writing to that described by Goldberg. How do you go about writing imaginatively?

Develop Your Own Tools for Creativity Work with your classmates to understand the creative process.

Small Groups: In small groups, discuss your method for writing creatively. What processes do you use to create a story that is driven by your imagination?

Whole Class: Make a master chart of all of the ideas generated by the small groups, and use these ideas for further discussion of how to generate an interesting imaginative text.

Write About It You will next develop your story of an incompetent criminal into a longer piece. Your goal is to write an imaginative story that holds reader interest by creating an engaging story line that includes interesting characters and well-paced action. Your writing might use any of the following possible topics, audiences, and forms.

Possible Topics	Possible Audiences	Possible Forms
• a burglar drilling into the bank restroom • a thief robbing someone dressed as Thor • a man robbing a restaurant with a tree branch • a man stealing an ATM with a frontloader	• incompetent criminals • the police • a prison warden and guards • owners of businesses • the editor of a fiction anthology	• story posted on a Web site • entry in a creative writing competition • submission to a literary magazine • one-act play

As you make choices in your writing and develop your style, you will also be developing your writing voice. (See page 6.) **Voice** is the quality in writing that makes it sound as if there is a real and unique person behind the words. A writing voice is like a speaking voice. You speak in one way to your little sister, another to your dog, and yet another to your grandmother. In the same way, the voice you use as a writer will change according to your writing purpose and audience. A social studies report and text messages to your friends, for example, would call for different voices.

WRITING PURPOSE	WHAT THE WRITER'S VOICE SHOULD CONVEY
To provide information and/or persuade people	Genuine interest in the subject, often including personal insights about why the subject is important to the writer and what the reader might expect to gain from it; respect for differing viewpoints; confidence without swagger.
To describe a subject clearly and/or tell a real or imaginary story	A genuine, not phony, personality; often some personal statements that show a willingness to trust readers with sensitive ideas.

No matter what the purpose, however, a writer's voice should be engaging and genuine. The following rubric shows the traits of more and less successful writing voices.

Voice Rubric

4 The voice is engaging throughout. It sounds natural and unique.	3 The voice is engaging almost always. It usually sounds natural and unique.	2 Sometimes the voice doesn't connect with the reader. Parts may not sound natural or unique.	1 The voice does not make a connection with the reader and there's little sense of a unique person.

PROJECT PREP   *Analyzing*   *Voice*

With a partner, take turns reading the excerpt from Goldberg's text. When you have finished, identify her writing purpose. Then try to describe her writing voice. Based on her writing voice, how do you picture her? Does her voice seem well suited to her purpose? Finally, identify the words and expressions that led you to "hear" Goldberg's voice as you did. Use the above rubric to evaluate it. Summarize your discussion to share with the class.

Understanding the Varieties of English

Although English is one language, there are variations in pronunciation, usage, and meanings. As you find your writing voice, you will be drawing on the variation you have heard spoken around you as you have been growing up.

1 American Dialects

The English language is made up of almost a million words, and it is spoken in many different countries around the world. Not all English-speaking people speak the language in the same way. Even across our own country, because of the rich mix of people, there are differences in the way words are pronounced from place to place. These different ways of speaking are called **dialects.** Americans tend to speak two kinds of dialects: regional dialects and ethnic dialects. Dialects can be different from one another in vocabulary, pronunciation, and even grammar. Of course, not all people from a certain place or ethnic group speak in the same way. People who live close to each other or have similar backgrounds, though, tend to share similar ways of speaking.

REGIONAL DIALECTS

People from one part of the same country tend to speak alike. In the United States, English varies among three main regional dialects: Eastern, Southern, and General American. For example, New Englanders are said to speak with a twang, dropping some *r's* ("pahk the cah" for "park the car") and Southerners with a drawl. Each of these dialects may contain many subdialects. In western Oklahoma, for instance, a common insect may be called a *snake doctor*, while in other places in the United States it is known as a *dragonfly*. The language of New Orleans known as Cajun derived from eighteenth-century Canadian settlers who spoke Acadian French. Words such as *bogus, jive,* and *hip* worked their way into the Southern dialect through African Americans. Dialects add color and richness to language.

ETHNIC DIALECTS

A person's cultural background can also be a factor in how he or she speaks. A variety of English spoken by a large number of members of a particular ethnic group is called an **ethnic dialect.** Some of the most widely spoken ethnic dialects in the United States are black, Hispanic, and Asian-influenced English.

Ethnic dialects have a great influence on the general American vocabulary in that they often add new words, meanings, and pronunciations. (See pages 379–380 for a list of words that were added to the English language from other languages and cultures.) These words became part of our language in part because members of various ethnic groups immigrated to America and introduced words from their own languages and experiences into the English language through ethnic dialects.

● Practice Your Skills

Identifying Dialects

Different people use different words for the same thing. With a small group of classmates, discuss the words you use for items in your home and how you pronounce them. For example, do you say *sofa, lounge, davenport, couch,* or *settee*? Do you say *soda, pop,* or *tonic*? Do you carry a *pail* or a *bucket*? Are the words and pronunciations you use the same words and pronunciations that you hear spoken on television?

PROJECT PREP   *Elaborating*   Dialect

Consider adding dialect features to the text you are working on. For the incompetent criminal story, for example, use the strategies for creative thinking that you generated during your earlier discussions to write a new, more detailed and elaborate draft of your story. In this draft, try to make the story as complete as possible, but don't worry if some details are not fully fleshed out. When you think of your narrator and other characters, consider whether the person might speak in a particularly noticeable dialect, and try to include some of those dialect features to enhance the style of your story.

2 Standard and Nonstandard American English

Standard American English is the most widely used and accepted form of English. It is the variety of English used in newspapers, scholarly writings, and in most nonfiction books. It is the formal kind of English that is expected in your schoolwork and in most business situations. This is not to say that other forms of English are wrong, just that different forms are appropriate to different situations. Using Standard English helps people of different regions and cultures to communicate clearly with one another.

Nonstandard American English is English that does not follow the rules and guidelines of Standard American English. It is not incorrect or wrong, but simply language that is inappropriate in certain situations, with some audiences, or on occasions where Standard English is expected. Nonstandard English is the variety of English you probably use when speaking to friends and family members or when you write fiction, journal entries, or personal letters. It has a conversational tone and is very informal.

COLLOQUIALISMS

English has a number of informal expressions called **colloquialisms.** These are appropriate for informal writing and conversation but not for formal writing.

An **idiom** is an informal phrase or expression that has a meaning different from what the words suggest in their usual meanings. Since idioms do not mean what they seem to mean, avoid them when writing for a large general audience so you won't be misunderstood.

Writing Tip

Use Standard English when writing for school and for a large general audience.

Idioms	
	Antonio has had **a chip on his shoulder** since he lost the game. (a grievance)
	Ella **got a taste of her own medicine** when Saundra shared her secret. (felt mistreated in the same way she had mistreated others)
	Salvatore and his brother are **cut from the same cloth.** (very much alike)
	Rajshree had studied so hard that she found the Constitution test to be a **piece of cake.** (easy)
	The boy band turned out to be a **flash in the pan.** (something that started out promising but didn't amount to anything in the long run)

SLANG

Slang consists of English expressions that are developed and used by particular groups. For example, teenagers often come up with their own slang expressions. Such expressions are highly colorful, exaggerated, and often humorous.

> **Slang Expressions**   That new movie was really **sick.** (great)
>
> I'm going to **chill** with Manny. (relax)

● Practice Your Skills

Identifying Informal Language

Each sentence below contains informal language. Rewrite each sentence using formal English.

1. Let's stop and grab some grub before the movie.

2. She leaped at the chance to go to the concert.

3. My mom keeps bugging me to clean my room.

4. The library has tons of books on space travel.

5. I'm not gonna go to the park with them on Sunday.

6. There are lots of things to do at the amusement park.

7. A rainy summer day can be a bummer.

8. That's a really cool pair of pants.

9. The band's last song brought the house down.

JARGON

Jargon is specialized vocabulary used by a particular group of people. It is usually shared among group members who engage in the same activity or profession. For example, photographers use the word *zoom*, meaning "to move the camera's lens in toward the subject." The word *zoom* might not be understood to have that meaning outside a group of photographers.

Jargon can be useful when you are speaking to a group of people who are sure to understand it. It should not be used, however, when you are speaking to or writing for a general audience who may not be familiar with a specialized meaning.

> **PROJECT PREP** *Evaluating* *Peer Response*
>
> In your writing group, discuss the language choices of each writer. If informal or colloquial language is used, does it serve the story well? Are there any places where a character's language seems inappropriate and needs to be changed? Take notes to use in producing a revision of your work.

Choosing Vivid Words

Readers need something concrete to support their understanding of a passage. Vivid words that communicate exactly what you mean will give your readers a firm footing.

1 Specific Words

Read the following movie reviews. Which one gives you a better idea of the film?

> The movie was very good. The actors were good. The special effects were great. The story was interesting.

> *Star Base* is thrillingly entertaining. The young cast performed sensitively. The special effects were dazzling. The story throbbed with action and conflict and concluded with a surprise ending.

The first review uses only general words. Since general words can mean different things to different people, they do not communicate precisely. The second review replaces the general words with specific words that call precise images to mind.

● Practice Your Skills

Revising with Specific Words

The following paragraph contains too many general words. On separate paper, revise the paragraph, substituting specific words for each word that is underlined.

Summer Camp

Every year I go to camp. The people plan many things for us to do. On nature walks we sometimes see a deer running for cover. Once a day we can pair up and take boats out on the lake. The rules require partners because going swimming or boating without a companion is bad. The counselors teach us how to make a fire and put it out. At night we sometimes cook marshmallows over the embers. After two weeks in the woods, I return home feeling good.

PROJECT PREP Making Choices *Narrator*

Consider the best way to present your text. For the incompetent criminal project, for example, discuss in your writing group who might best tell each writer's story. The incompetent criminal? A person he meets in the story? A bystander? An all-knowing narrator? Take notes from your discussion to use as you draft. Also decide what that narrator does and does not know, see, hear, and suspect, and decide how that narrator sees the world, speaks, and thinks. Make a list of specific words your narrator might use.

In the Media

Tourist Brochure

All forms of advertising have a target audience that they are trying to reach. Whether it is a toy commercial geared to children or a billboard intended for middle-aged men, each advertisement is created with particular groups in mind. The words, pictures, and colors used are all chosen for a specific intended effect: to interest the targeted consumer.

In targeting consumers so specifically, advertisers work hard to find the right words and images that will attract people. A sports car speeding around curves makes the car seem exciting. A picture of a meadow full of flowers on a shampoo bottle makes the shampoo seem natural and wholesome. A positive slogan suggests that anything is possible if you have the right athletic shoes. Advertisers find out what is important to the people they are selling to and then create ads that promise to deliver those qualities—excitement, wholesomeness, or other endless possibilities.

Media Activity

Suppose you are on the city council for the city or town in which you live. You need to attract tourists to your town and are creating a brochure toward that end.

- Working in groups, brainstorm a list of attractions in your town.

- Target a brochure to each of the following audiences: football fans, poets, and naturalists.

- Feature the same attractions from your list for each group, but change what you emphasize about each attraction to appeal to your target audience.

How does your brochure change depending on what group you are targeting?

2 Appealing to the Senses

Your experiences are based on what you see, hear, smell, taste, or touch. You can share these experiences in writing by using words that appeal to your readers' senses. Compare the following two sentences.

Josie felt sad.

Josie slumped in the big, overstuffed chair, resting her downcast head on her fist and sighing.

The first sentence **tells** a reader that Josie is sad. The second sentence **shows** the sadness. A reader can see Josie's posture and hear her sighing. These sensory details communicate more clearly than does the adjective *sad* in the first sentence.

Take time during the prewriting stage to think of vivid sensory details you will be able to use in your composition. Clustering and brainstorming will help you come up with details that will appeal to your readers' senses. The following cluster shows a number of sensory words that could be used to describe a peach.

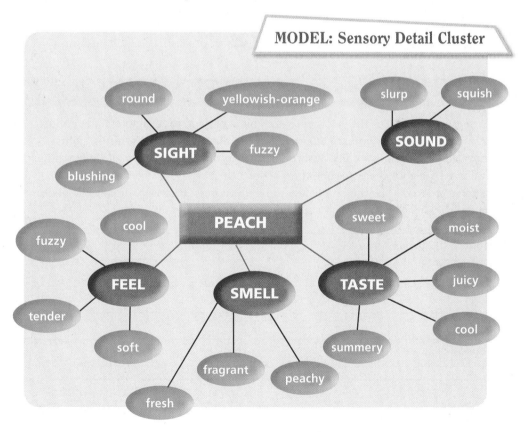

MODEL: Sensory Detail Cluster

● Practice Your Skills

Revising Using Sensory Detail

Rewrite each of the following sentences. Use details that appeal to the senses.

| Example | Bill was happy. |
| Possible Answer | Bill whistled as he raced home. |

1. My dog is beautiful.

2. Katrina was angry.

3. The pancake breakfast was delicious.

4. Mary seemed nervous.

● Practice Your Skills

Describing with Sensory Words

Think of a food that you really like and make a cluster like the one on page 47. Write as many sensory words as you can to describe the food. When you have finished, use your cluster to write five sentences that describe the food without naming it. Then exchange papers with a classmate. Try to guess the kind of food your partner has described.

PROJECT PREP Brainstorming Sensory Details

Add sensory details. For the incompetent criminal project, for example, think about the setting of the story you are telling. What are the sounds, smells, tastes, sights, and touch sensations in a bank washroom? During the drilling of a wall? In any other location where your character goes into action? On a separate sheet of paper, make a graphic organizer like the one below to help you harvest sensory details you might include in your story. Then write a new draft adding the details.

Sight	
Smell	
Taste	
Touch	
Sound	

The Power of Language ⚡

Prepositional Phrases: Scene Setters

One way to add sensory details to sentences is to use prepositional phrases. A prepositional phrase is a group of words made up of a preposition, its object, and any words that describe the object. Compare the following sentences.

Without Prepositional Phrases	I told this story. They were sitting.
With Prepositional Phrases	I told this story *to a group of third-graders in Owatonna, Minnesota.* They were sitting *on the tile blue carpet in front of me.*

The phrases *to a group, of third-graders, in Owatonna, Minnesota, on the tile blue carpet, in front,* and *of me* add meaningful and descriptive details to the sentences.

Placing prepositional phrases before a sentence provides variety and also helps to set the scene.

Common Order	I told this story **to a group of third-graders in Owatonna, Minnesota.** They were sitting **on the tile blue carpet in front of me.**
Variation and Scene Setter	**In Owatonna, Minnesota, to a group of third-graders sitting on the tile blue carpet in front of me,** I told this story.

Try It Yourself

Use the sentences above as models for writing sentences with prepositional phrases. Write an example of the common order and variation in order for each. If possible, write sentences on your project topic and include them in your draft. Later, check your draft for places where you can add prepositional phrases.

Punctuation Tip

Put a comma after a prepositional phrase of four words or more that begins a sentence.

③ Tired Words and Clichés

A **tired word** is a word that has been so overused that it has been drained of meaning. Take, for example, the word *wonderful*. This word literally means "full of wonder." Now, through overuse, the word means "good."

A **cliché** is a tired expression. These are also bland and powerless because of overuse. Some examples of clichés follow.

CLICHÉS		
good as gold	rich as Midas	cold as ice
heavy as a rock	light as a feather	bright and early

Speakers often use tired words and clichés. In casual conversations, people call sunsets "pretty," movies "fabulous," and sweaters "cute." They say a baby is "cute as a button." None of these words convey precise information, however.

Writing Tip

Avoid **tired words and clichés.** Without them, your writing will be fresh, precise, and interesting to read.

PROJECT PREP *Evaluating* **Details**

Return to your writing group with the new draft. Discuss each writer's draft, with a focus on improving it if necessary. Are there any details missing that make the action hard to follow? Take notes on where you might elaborate by adding details or events that would make the story more interesting, humorous, insightful, or better in any other way. Did you use any tired words or clichés? Eliminate them and replace them with fresh and vivid language, including figures of speech. (See pages 45–50 and 183–186.)

Denotations and Connotations

The **denotation** of a word means the specific definition of a word—the definition you will find in the dictionary. However, sometimes through usage a word takes on additional meaning that often conveys a judgment; this is the **connotation** of a word. For example, although *lazy* and *idle* have similar denotative meanings, they have very different connotative meanings. *Lazy* has come to mean "not willing to work," while *idle* means "not working." The difference in connotative meanings of words is important to consider when choosing vocabulary to use in writing.

● **Practice Your Skills**

Identifying Denotations and Connotations

Read the following list of words. Each pair shares a denotative meaning. What do you think the connotative meaning is for each word?

1. thrifty; stingy

2. nosy; curious

3. decline; reject

4. childish; playful

5. mature; aged

6. historic; old

7. economical; cheap

8. picky; selective

9. dark; unlit

10. scrawny; thin

CHAPTER 2

Writing Tip

The **connotation** of a word can have an emotional impact; as a writer, you should be aware of this impact and choose words with the connotation you intend.

PROJECT PREP *Evaluating* **Connotations**

In your writing group, focus again on the author's language choices. Do the words selected have connotations that are appropriate to the tone or feeling the writer is trying to create? Mark your manuscript in any places where you could revise the language to create a more consistent tone and mood for your story. (See page 177 for more on mood.) Also use literary strategies, such as figurative language, and devices such as parallelism to enhance the style of your story.

Evaluate your word choice with the following rubric.

4 Words are specific and powerful, rich in sensory images.	3 Words are specific and some words appeal to the senses.	2 Some words are overly general and/or tired.	1 Most words are overly general and tired.
• I used Standard English if required. • I used Nonstandard English, with colloquialisms, if appropriate. • I used words with connotations that match my intended meaning. • I used fresh, not tired words. • I used words with punch and sparkle that appeal to the senses of sight, sound, touch, smell, and taste.	• I was aware of differences between Standard and Nonstandard English and made reasonable choices. • My word choice conveys my meaning but may not have sparkle and punch. • I made a good effort to appeal to the senses but now see where I might have done more.	• I was not always aware of differences between Standard and Nonstandard English and made some choices that might confuse a reader. • I still need to work on finding the best, most specific word to give sparkle and punch to my writing. • I used a few tired expressions. • I appealed to only one or two senses.	• I was not aware of differences between Standard and Nonstandard English and made some confusing choices. • Few of my words are as specific and vivid as they need to be. • I used many tired expressions. • I didn't really appeal to the senses.

PROJECT PREP *Evaluating* **Using a Rubric**

Use these strategies according to the rating you give yourself:
4 Keep up the good work!
3 Learn from what you did well: how can you apply that throughout your story?
2 Work with a peer to get ideas for improving word choice.
1 Work with a peer, and read your favorite writer to see how he or she uses words.

Creating Sentence Variety

A good mix of sentence types and structures will help keep your readers interested.

1 Sentence Combining Strategies

Sentence combining is one way to vary the patterns of your sentences. You can simply eliminate unnecessary parts of one sentence while adding its essential details to another, or you can use coordinating and subordinating words to join sentences.

COMBINING WITH SPECIFIC DETAILS

One good strategy for creating sentence variety is to combine specific details from short, choppy sentences into one interesting sentence. Study the following example.

| Choppy Sentences | The robot squeaked. The robot was metallic. It squeaked continually. It squeaked at its hinges. |
| Combined Sentence | The metallic robot squeaked continually at its hinges. |

If your combined sentence contains two or more adjectives in a row, remember to separate the adjectives with commas. Study the following example.

| Choppy Sentences | The museum has a robot. It is metallic. It is squeaky. |
| Combined Sentence | The museum has a metallic, squeaky robot. |

● Practice Your Skills

Combining Sentences with Specific Details

Combine each group of short sentences into one longer one.

1. The *Viking* spacecraft was a robot. It was enormous. It was sophisticated.
2. It was sent on a mission. The mission was to the surface of Mars.
3. *Viking* relayed information. The information went to Earth.
4. It also took photographs. They were of the surface of Mars. The surface was red and dusty.
5. *Viking* had instruments aboard. The instruments were complex. They were for measuring Marsquakes.
6. Over a period of years, *Viking* sent back information. The information was useful.

COMBINING BY COORDINATING

You can also combine choppy sentences by **coordinating,** or linking ideas of equal importance. Use the coordinating conjunctions *and, but, or,* and *yet* to combine subjects, to combine verbs, and to combine parts of sentences.

Choppy	Two huge tusks are one characteristic of the walrus. A mustached upper lip is another characteristic.
Combined Subjects	Two huge tusks and a mustached upper lip are characteristics of the walrus.
Choppy	Scientists have observed the walrus for many years. Scientists still have much to learn.
Combined Verbs	Scientists have observed the walrus for many years but still have much to learn.
Choppy	The walrus is a powerful member of the seal family. The walrus is timid.
Combined Parts of Sentences	The walrus is a powerful yet timid member of the seal family.

● Practice Your Skills

Combining Sentences by Coordinating Sentence Parts

On separate paper, revise the paragraph below to get rid of clumsiness and repetition. Combine sentence parts by coordinating. Use the words *and, but, or,* or *yet* to combine the sentences. The first sentence is done for you.

Walruses

Scientists have observed the walrus for many years. Scientists have
recorded much information. They differ from seals in many ways. The air
sacs in its neck make the walrus unique. Its huge tusks make it unique. The
inflatable air sacs help keep the walrus's head above water. These air sacs
allow the walrus to take a nap in the ocean. Their huge ivory tusks serve
as helpful tools in the ice. These long, curved teeth can become dangerous
weapons during a fight. The walrus is a timid animal. It will fight for the
protection of its young. Many mysteries about these fascinating sea animals
have been solved. Scientists still have much to learn about them.

The Language of Power *Agreement*

Power Rule: Use verbs that agree with the subject.
(See pages 736–740.)

See It in Action A singular subject and a plural subject require different forms of the verb. Look at these examples based on the text of "Man Eats Car."

Singular Subject and Correct Verb	Your <u>mind</u> **is** leaping.
Plural Subject and Correct Verb	Their <u>minds</u> **are** leaping.

You have learned that combining sentences by creating compound subjects is one way to help your writing flow. When you use this strategy, be sure your subjects and verb agree. When you use *and* to join ideas, you will create a plural subject, as in the first example below. When you use *or, nor, either...or,* and *neither...nor,* the subject closest to the verb is the one that must agree with the verb.

Compound subjects joined with *and*	<u>Ants, elephants, moons,</u> *and* <u>bears</u> **are** equal in the writer's mind.
Compound subjects joined with *or, nor, either, neither*	*Neither* the celery <u>stalks</u> *nor* the <u>moonbeam</u> **walks** upright except in writing.

Remember It Record this rule and these examples in the Power Rule section of your Personalized Editing Checklist.

Use It Exchange papers with a partner. Find any compound subjects in your partner's writing. For any you find, check to see if they follow the agreement conventions explained above. If not, point them out so your partner can make changes.

Think Critically

Comparing

Goldberg writes, "Metaphor is saying the ant is an elephant." A **metaphor** is one kind of *figure of speech* that shows comparisons. Another is a simile. A **simile** uses the word *like* or *as* to show the comparison. A third is **personification,** which implies a comparison by giving human qualities and abilities to a nonhuman subject. Some of the most original thinking you can do is to find similarities between two things that are different in most ways.

Metaphor	The moon is a pearl in the velvet night sky.
Simile	His eyes are like lasers.
Personification	The moon held hands with Venus.

The two things being compared are alike in only one way. The moon and pearl are alike because they are both shining white spheres. The eyes and lasers are alike because of their piercing quality. The nearness of the moon to Venus is like the nearness of people holding hands.

Thinking Practice

Write two poems comparing two subjects that are mainly different. First, think of the subjects you will compare. In the first poem, use figures of speech to make your comparison. Pay attention to such poetic techniques as rhyme and meter (see pages 183–185). In the second poem, try to express your comparison using graphic elements, such as the shape of the poem on the page. The following poem by e. e. cummings implies a comparison between loneliness and a falling leaf and expresses that visually. Share your poems with the rest of the class.

a leaf falls loneliness

l(a

le
af
fa
ll

s)
one
l

iness

COMBINING BY SUBORDINATING

If the ideas in two short sentences are of unequal importance, you can combine them by **subordinating.** This technique turns one of the sentences into a clause that becomes part of another sentence. The following are some subordinating words.

SUBORDINATING WORDS		
who	after	if
which	although	because
that	unless	until

● Practice Your Skills

Combining Sentences by Subordinating

In the following paragraph, each pair of choppy sentences can be improved through combining by subordinating. Use the subordinating word in parentheses to create the combined sentence. Use commas where needed.

Example   Lifting an eyebrow may show disbelief. It may also show surprise. (although)

Answer   Although lifting an eyebrow may show disbelief, it may also show surprise.

Body Language

(1) You can learn a lot about people's feelings. You study their body language. (if) (2) Shrugging the shoulders can mean a lack of knowledge. Shrugging the shoulders is a common body signal. (that) (3) The head houses memory. Many people touch their foreheads to show forgetfulness. (because) (4) You are sitting alone at a cafeteria table. Your eyes can signal to a new arrival that you want to be left alone. (if) (5) You look down. The new arrival will assume you want some company and conversation. (unless)

PROJECT PREP *Evaluating* *Sentence Fluency*

In your writing group, look at the flow of sentences in each writer's work. Do the sentences make grammatical sense? Are they varied and smoothly flowing? Are they an appropriate length and complexity for the situation? Mark your manuscript with your peers' feedback so you can make adjustments as needed.

② Sentence Beginnings

You have learned how to use sentence combining to vary the length and structure of your sentences. Another way to add variety to your writing is to begin your sentences in different ways.

The most natural way to begin a sentence is with the subject. For variety, experiment with other sentence beginnings.

Subject	Chi Cheng was a very fast runner in her high school days.
Phrase	In her high school days, Chi Cheng was a very fast runner.

The following sentences show just a few of the ways you can begin your sentences.

Prepositional Phrase	At the age of 16, she represented Taiwan in the 1960 Olympics.
Adjective	Steadfast, she kept up her running even though she hurt her leg during the second Olympic match.
Adverb	Altogether Cheng broke or matched seven world records during the next five years.

● Practice Your Skills

Varying Sentence Beginnings

Add variety to the following passage by beginning each sentence with either an adverb or a prepositional phrase. Remember to follow the rules for using commas with introductory elements. (See pages 832–834.)

Writing Tip

Vary sentence beginnings by moving phrases from the end to the beginning.

Example	William J. Watson went to work for the National Cash Register Company in 1894.
Answer	In 1894, William J. Watson went to work for the National Cash Register Company.

1. Watson sold many, many machines for National Cash Register Company.
2. Watson became the sales manager of the National Cash Register Company at 35 years of age.
3. Watson left NCR and became president of the Computer-Tabulating-Recording-Company after five years.

4. Watson worked tirelessly year after year to build up the struggling company.
5. Watson changed the company's name to International Business Machines (IBM) before long to reflect its growing foreign business.
6. IBM grew steadily under Watson's direction.
7. One reason for the company's huge success was undoubtedly Watson's belief in the value of expert sales people.
8. Watson stressed the importance of careful thought for his workers by printing up signs that said "THINK."

PROJECT PREP *Revising* *Using Feedback*

Using the feedback from your writing group, revise your draft so that it provides readers with a satisfying experience and tells the story in the clear, focused way you intend for it to be told.

Writing Concise Sentences

When you shop, you want the most value for your dollar. When you write, you want the most value for each word you use. Avoid bulky writing. Be economical when you write.

RAMBLING SENTENCES

One cause of bulky writing is throwing too many ideas into one sentence. The result, called a rambling sentence, is hard to read and difficult to understand.

> **Rambling Sentence**
>
> About seven million people in the United States do not eat meat, but they find protein in other types of food, and they combine certain kinds of food, such as rice and beans, to make sure they eat complete proteins, or they sometimes eat such dairy products as cheese, milk, and yogurt for protein.
>
> **Revised Sentences**
>
> About seven million people in the United States do not eat meat. Instead, they find protein in other types of food. They also combine certain kinds of food, such as rice and beans, to make sure they eat complete proteins. Others eat such dairy products as cheese, milk, and yogurt for protein.

● **Practice Your Skills**

Revising Rambling Sentences

On a separate sheet of paper, revise the following paragraph to eliminate the rambling sentences.

Dusty Skies

Sunlight passing through and reflecting dust particles explains the sometimes brilliant colors we see in the sky, and one of the sources of this dust is volcanic explosion, and a single blast can send tons of dust into the air. Another source of dust is the ocean, from which salt is sprayed and then evaporated into salty dust, and plants also give off billions of grains of pollen and spores. Dust particles by the ton also enter Earth's atmosphere from outer space, but no one knows exactly where these come from. Around the house dust looks gray and dingy, but in the skies dust glimmers with some of the most beautiful colors ever seen.

REPETITION

Sometimes without thinking you may repeat an idea unnecessarily. As you revise check your sentences to be sure you have not included unnecessary words and phrases.

Repetitive	I resolved to try again and not give up.
Concise	I resolved to try again.
Repetitive	Sam's face looked pale and colorless.
Concise	Sam's face looked pale.
Repetitive	The famished guests waited hungrily to eat.
Concise	The guests waited hungrily to eat.

editing ☆

Streamline the following passage by eliminating the repetition.

It's a true fact that people who get up by 7 A.M. in the morning feel most energetic at 9:00 A.M. when they feel their most energy.

EMPTY EXPRESSIONS

Empty expressions are wasted words that add no meaning to a sentence. Notice how they can be deleted or replaced when you revise.

Empty	What I mean is, I learned a difficult lesson.
Concise	I learned a difficult lesson.
Empty	The Girl Scouts met their fund-raising goal due to the fact that cookie sales were high.
Concise	The Girl Scouts met their fund-raising goal because cookie sales were high.

Revising to Eliminate Unnecessary Words

Pets and Health

Pets are good for more than just fun and good times. As a matter of fact, stroking an animal can even reduce blood pressure. People who own dogs also exercise more regularly because they take their dogs for walks, which gives the people exercise too. Because of the fact that pets help sick people recover from their illness, pets are sometimes even brought to hospitals. There is this natural bond that forms between humans and pet animals, and due to this fact senior citizens should be allowed to have pets in their housing.

PROJECT PREP *Editing* **Conventions**

Exchange papers with a writing partner and provide final suggestions. Pay special attention to such conventions as capitalization, spelling, punctuation, and usage, and check to be sure there are no Power Rule errors. Use your partner's feedback to make any necessary corrections.

Using a Fluency Rubric

Evaluate your fluency with the following rubric.

4 Sentences are varied in length and structure. Every sentence matters.	3 Sentences are mostly varied in length and structure. A few words and sentences seem unnecessary.	2 Many sentences are the same in length and structure. A number of words and sentences seem unnecessary.	1 Most sentences are the same in length and structure. A number of words and sentences seem unnecessary.
• I combined short, choppy sentences into varied, longer ones. • I used coordinating and subordinating conjunctions to improve the flow and show the relationship of ideas. • I started my sentences in a variety of ways, not always with the subject first. • I avoided rambling sentences.	• I combined some short, choppy sentences into varied, longer ones, but in a few places there is still some choppiness. • I sometimes used coordinating and subordinating conjunctions to improve the flow and show the relationship of ideas. • I started most of my sentences in a variety of ways, not always with the subject first. • I avoided rambling sentences.	• A few parts of my work flow, but there is still choppiness. • I used a few conjunctions to improve the flow and show relationships, but I see now that I could have used more. • Many of my sentences start the same way, with the subject. • Several of my sentences ramble or contain unnecessary information.	• I didn't quite achieve a flow. My writing seems to start and stop. • I didn't often combine ideas into one sentence to improve the flow and show relationships. • Most of my sentences start the same way, with the subject. • Many of my sentences ramble or contain unnecessary information.

PROJECT PREP Evaluating *Using a Rubric*

Use these strategies according to the rating you have given yourself:

4 Keep up the good work!

3 Learn from what you did well: how can you apply that throughout your scene?

2 Work with a peer to get ideas for improving fluency.

1 Work with a peer, and read your favorite writer to see how he or she achieves fluency.

When you are satisfied with your text, publish it in one of the ways suggested on page 32 or through another appropriate medium such as a class anthology.

Writing Lab

Project Corner

Get Visual Make a Storyboard

In your writing group, select one story from among those written and create a **storyboard** for a television show or video game based on the story. (See pages 438–443 for more information on visual representation.)

Act It Out Create a Play

In your writing group, select one story from among those written and produce a short **play** based on the action. (See pages 174–180 for help on creating a script.)

Experiment
Change Points of View

Tell the same story from the **perspective of a different character.** How would the narration change? How would the original narrator be viewed by this new speaker? What details would change based on this different point of view? How would the language change with a different narrator telling the story?

Experiment Try a Different Form

Review the suggested project forms on page 39. Think about how your project would be different if it were in one of those forms you didn't use or another that you can think of. Choose a part of your project and rewrite it in that **new form.** Write a brief paragraph explaining the changes you had to make.

In Everyday Life

Postcard to a Friend

1. Your father has recently taken a knitting course and is proud of his new ability—so proud that he has knitted matching sweaters for you and your sister. Unfortunately, the sweaters look hideous. Nevertheless, you and your sister wore them to school yesterday because you appreciate his effort. ***Write a postcard*** to a friend at another school describing the sweaters in vivid detail. Appeal to all five senses—sight, smell, sound, touch, and taste—in this description. Use specific details and include at least one comparison in your description.

In Everyday Life Poster for a Picnic

2. Your neighborhood is having its annual block party, and you are on the publicity committee. In previous years the committee has had trouble getting people to come to the party. This year the publicity committee is putting all its energy into a poster with an appealing photograph of people having fun at last year's party. ***Write the text for the committee's poster*** aimed at persuading your neighbors to attend the party. List the main events of the party and describe them using sensory language and specific details. Be sure to vary your sentence structure by beginning your sentences in different ways.

Timed Writing ⏱ Improving Style

3. Twenty general words and phrases are underlined in the passage below. Revise the passage by replacing each general word or phrase with a specific noun, verb, adjective, or adverb. In addition, vary the sentences by combining specific details and using conjunctions and subordinate clauses. You have 15 minutes to complete your work.

> The <u>day</u> was <u>bright</u> outside. The sun was <u>shining</u>. The <u>birds</u> were <u>singing</u>. I <u>walked</u> along, <u>thinking</u> of all the <u>things</u> I was going to do that <u>day</u>. <u>In the afternoon</u> I was <u>going</u> to a <u>game</u> with my sister, and then we were <u>going</u> <u>out to eat</u>. That night <u>there</u> was a <u>party</u> at <u>this one boy's</u> house. But before all that I had to <u>do</u> this <u>school project</u> that involved some complicated <u>things</u>. So even though the day was <u>nice</u>, I could not really <u>enjoy</u> it.

Writing Well-Structured Paragraphs

A paragraph is a group of related sentences that present and develop one main idea.

Paragraphs take a variety of forms, as the following examples show.

- **A paragraph in an e-mail to a friend** begins by saying that you played a great soccer game, moves on to describe some of the plays you made, and ends by saying you hope you will play just as well next time.

- **A paragraph in the instructions you wrote for your dog sitter** begins by stating that your dog gets walked four times a day, continues by explaining where to find the leash and describing your dog's favorite route, and concludes by explaining that your dog gets a biscuit when she returns from her walk.

- **A paragraph summarizing a science experiment** begins with a hypothesis, describes the experiment and the evidence, and then evaluates the hypothesis on the basis of the evidence.

- **A paragraph in a school newspaper** explains that the school basketball team lost because of the misguided effort of a player who tried too hard to be a star.

Writing Project  Narrative

Be Yourself **Complete the following project to write a narrative paragraph about an experience that taught you the importance of being yourself.**

Think Through Writing One way people learn and grow is to try to be like others they admire. Sometimes, though, when they try to impress others, their efforts to be like someone they admire might backfire. Write about a time when you or someone you know tried too hard to be like someone else but instead of impressing people ended up seeming phony or silly.

Talk About It In your writing group, discuss the experience you wrote about and why people try to impress others and sometimes fail. Be as specific as you can and include as many details in your discussion as possible.

Read About It In the following selection, author Richard Lederer makes an argument that writers should use short words rather than long words. As you read, think about what motive people might have for using big words.

MODEL: Clear Paragraphs

From *The Miracle of Language*

The Case for Short Words

Richard Lederer

When you speak and write, there is no law that says you have to use big words. Short words are as good as long ones, and short, old words—like *sun* and *grass* and *home*—are best of all. A lot of small words, more than you might think, can meet your needs with a strength, grace, and charm that large words do not have.

> The introductory paragraph lays out the main idea.

Big words can make the way dark for those who read what you write and hear what you say. Small words cast their clear light on big things—night and day, love and hate, war and peace, and life and death. Big words at times seem strange to the eye and the ear and the mind and the heart. Small words are the ones we seem to have known from the time we were born, like the hearth fire that warms the home.

> This paragraph is structured to alternate between a sentence about big words to a sentence about small words.

Short words are bright like sparks that glow in the night, prompt like the dawn that greets the day, sharp like the blade of a knife, hot like salt tears that scald the cheek, quick like moths that flit from flame to flame, and terse like the dart and sting of a bee.

> All the similes in this paragraph help the reader get a sense of the emotional impact short words can have.

Here is a sound rule: Use small, old words where you can. If a long word says just what you want to say, do not fear to use it. But know that our tongue is rich in crisp, brisk, swift, short words. Make them the spine and the heart of what you speak and write. Short words are like fast friends. They will not let you down.

> The concluding paragraph sums up the author's views and makes a strong case for using small words.

Respond in Writing Write about Lederer's argument in favor of small rather than big words. Do you agree with him? Why or why not? If he's right, why do so many people try to use big words?

Develop Your Own Insights Work with your classmates to develop an understanding of efforts to impress people and why they sometimes fail.

Small Groups: In small groups, discuss in greater detail the experiences you have written about. Use the following graphic organizer to catalog your insights. A few starter ideas are provided for you.

Things people do to try to impress others	Reasons people have for impressing others
—use big words	—get attention

Whole Class: Make a master chart of all of the ideas generated by the small groups, and use these ideas to help you write in greater detail about your experience.

Write About It You will next write a paragraph about a time when you or someone you know did not follow the advice "Be yourself." You will focus on what the person did, what motive the person had, what the result was, and what, if anything, the person learned from the experience. Your writing might address any of the following topics and audiences and take any of the listed forms.

Possible Topics	Possible Audiences	Possible Forms
• a personal experience with trying but failing to impress others • an experience of someone else who tried and failed to impress others • examples of celebrities trying to impress people • examples of characters in movies, books, or on TV trying but failing to impress others	• friends on your social network site • parents • teachers • a person younger than you	• a narrative paragraph • a poem • a blog • a song

Paragraph Structure

A paragraph is a unit of thought. It can be part of a long composition, as in the reading about short words on page 67, or it can stand alone as a short composition, complete within itself. However it is used, a paragraph always sticks to one main idea—the general point the paragraph is trying to make.

Most paragraphs that stand alone consist of three main types of sentences: the **topic sentence,** the **supporting sentences,** and the **concluding sentence.** Each type of sentence performs a special function in a paragraph. Review the chart below.

STRUCTURE OF A PARAGRAPH	
Topic Sentence	states the main idea
Supporting Sentences	expand on the main idea with specific facts, examples, details, or reasons
Concluding Sentence	provides a strong ending

In the paragraph below, notice how all the other sentences relate directly to the main idea stated in the topic sentence.

MODEL: Paragraph Structure

The Man Who Rode the Thunder

Marine pilot William Rankin made history in 1959 when he survived a nine-mile fall from the sky. Over Norfolk, Virginia, Rankin had engine trouble and had to eject himself from his plane. After he had fallen for about eight minutes, his parachute opened perfectly. To his dismay, however, he found himself in the middle of a thunderstorm. The strong winds kept driving him up instead of down toward the earth. For forty minutes Rankin was tossed by fierce winds and surrounded by blasts of thunder and sheets of lightning. Finally he reached the ground, frostbitten and injured, but alive. Soon after, newspapers all around the world honored "the man who rode the thunder."

Topic Sentence

Supporting Sentences

Concluding Sentence

1 Writing a Topic Sentence

The topic sentence is usually more general than the other sentences in a paragraph. It may be at the beginning, at the end, or in the middle of a paragraph. The purpose of the topic sentence is to focus the reader's attention on the main idea.

The **topic sentence** states the main idea of the paragraph.

Although a topic sentence is usually more general than the other sentences, it also serves to limit a paragraph to one specific subject. The following paragraph begins with a very general sentence. The second sentence, which is the topic sentence, limits the broad subject to one specific aspect.

MODEL: Topic Sentence

The Emperor's Feet

The bitterly cold climate of Antarctica is hostile to many forms of life. Even the emperor penguin, which thrives in the cold, has had to develop unusual — Topic Sentence
behaviors to hatch a chick. If an egg were allowed to touch the frozen ground, the developing chick inside would not survive. To protect the chick, the male penguin carries the egg on his feet, tucking it under the feathers on his body. For two months, while the female penguin is away storing food in her belly, the male goes nowhere without the egg on his feet. Cuddled securely in the male's warmth, the chick can survive until hatching. At that time the mother returns and takes over the care of her newborn chick. Even then the down-covered chick needs its mother's feet and feathers to shield it from the frigid weather of Antarctica.

CHAPTER 3

● Practice Your Skills

Choosing a Topic Sentence

Read each paragraph. Choose the sentence that would be the best topic sentence.

1. *Moving People*

> A city train system can move 60,000 people an hour on each line. Expressways can manage only about 2,000 cars an hour in each lane. If the average number of passengers in each car is one and a half, the total number of people moved is only 3,000 an hour in each lane. Rapid transit systems, then, can move 20 times more people in the same amount of space.

  a. More and more people are riding subways.
  b. Many cities are encouraging people to join car pools in order to cut down on traffic.
  c. Rapid transit systems are more efficient than expressways in moving great numbers of people.

2. *Breaking the Sound Barrier*

> On October 14, 1947, test pilot Chuck Yeager was ready to fly a new jet to see if it could travel faster than the speed of sound. Until then many people had believed that a plane would be destroyed if it tried to go faster than the speed of sound. Yeager took off confidently. Before long a thunderous blast was heard. The sound barrier had been broken, and Yeager brought the plane down safely.

  a. The day the sound barrier was broken was a milestone in aviation history.
  b. When a plane accelerates beyond the speed of sound, a loud roar can be heard.
  c. High-speed jet transport is taken for granted today.

Writing Topic Sentences

Write one other possible topic sentence for each
paragraph in the preceding activity.

PROJECT PREP *Prewriting* *Sketching*

In your writing group, sketch out the points you wish to make in your composition.
For the paragraph on impressing others, you can use a graphic organizer like the one
below to help you organize your thoughts.

> **Main Idea:**
>
> > **Supporting Details**
> > What the person did:
> > Why the person did it:
> > The outcome:
>
> > **Concluding Idea**
> > Lesson learned:

When you have finished, write a topic sentence for your paragraph. Share it with the
members of your writing group and discuss what makes a topic sentence effective.
Rework your sentence after your group meeting if appropriate.

Think Critically

Generalizing

The topic sentence you write in a paragraph is a kind of generalization. A **generalization** is an overall idea that explains specific facts, examples, or instances. You have been forming generalizations all your life. For example, the first time you roller-skated over a crack in the sidewalk, you may have fallen down. Without previous experience, you might not know that there is a relationship between the crack in the sidewalk and losing your balance. Then you begin to notice that your friends sometimes fall when they try to go over a crack. Maybe you try it again and fall again. By this time you might conclude from your experience that skating over cracks is dangerous. That general idea guides you to avoid big sidewalk cracks.

The general idea in a paragraph is the topic sentence. Its purpose is to explain the specific facts, examples, or instances you relate in the rest of the paragraph. As a general statement, it clarifies the details by stating a broad idea that connects them.

Thinking Practice

Read the following facts. Then write a general statement that connects them in a meaningful way.

- Many breakfast cereals contain sugar.
- People often add even more sugar.
- Sugar adds calories but no nutrients.
- Excess calories lead to unhealthy weight gain.
- Sugar promotes tooth decay.

> ### Writing Tip
>
> Check the topic sentence in your paragraph to make sure it expresses the most meaningful **generalization** possible from the specifics you include.

② Writing Supporting Sentences

Supporting sentences make up the body of a paragraph. Their purpose is to back up the main idea in the topic sentence with specific information.

Supporting sentences explain, prove, or elaborate on a topic sentence with specific details, facts, examples, or reasons. They also provide answers to questions that readers might have about the topic sentence. Read the following topic sentence. Think of questions that you would expect the supporting sentences to answer.

Topic Sentence   People who lived in pioneer days would never have believed that world news could be received as quickly as it is today.

Most readers would probably want to know how news traveled during pioneer days and how news travels today. The supporting sentences answer these questions. They provide facts and examples that relate to the main idea.

MODEL: Supporting Sentences

Changes in News Communication

People who lived in pioneer days would never have believed that world news could be received as quickly as it is today. In early days newspapers were often several months old by the time they reached a settlement. Letters were carried by travelers who happened to be going in the right direction and often were received months after they were sent, or not at all. Today by radio, television, newspapers, and the Internet, we get world news almost at once. Letters are carried to distant countries overnight. It is hard to believe that such changes have taken place in less than 100 years.

— Topic Sentence

— Supporting Sentences

— Concluding Sentence

PROJECT PREP *Drafting* *Supporting Sentences*

Draft the body of your paragraph. For the paragraph on trying to impress others, refer back to the sketch you made and use the details you listed in the middle section to draft your supporting sentences.

③ Checking for Unity and Coherence

A paragraph has **unity**, or focus, when all of the supporting sentences relate directly to the main idea. Paragraphs without unity include unrelated ideas that distract readers from the main point. Suppose you are writing a paragraph about tricks your dog can do. In the process of writing, you can sometimes lose your focus. You may be led to include other details about your dog, such as where and when you got him, or what his favorite foods are. Although these relate to your dog generally, they probably do not belong in a paragraph about the tricks your dog can do.

● Practice Your Skills

Deleting Unrelated Ideas

In the following paragraph, two sentences do not relate directly to the topic sentence. Write these sentences. Then write a statement that tells why you believe the additional two sentences do not support the main idea.

Achieve **unity** by making sure all the supporting sentences relate directly to the topic sentence.

Medic Alert Saves Lives

The Medic Alert bracelet was designed to help people with medical problems in emergency situations. If the wearer of the bracelet is unconscious or otherwise unable to talk, the bracelet can tell medical workers what they need to know about the patient. On the back of the Medic Alert bracelet are listed the patient's medical problem, an identification number, and an emergency number. The Red Cross offers classes in emergency techniques. By dialing this telephone number, the medical workers can find out about the patient's special condition from a computer. Computers are also used by doctors to help make diagnoses. Knowing the patient's medical background can help the workers decide which treatment to provide and what kind of medication to give. In an emergency, a Medic Alert bracelet can become a lifesaver.

Coherence in a paragraph is the quality that makes each sentence seem connected to all the others. One way to achieve coherence is to present ideas in a logical order. Another way is to use transitions. **Transitions** are words and phrases that show how ideas are related.

Achieve **coherence** by presenting ideas in logical order and using transitional words and phrases.

The following chart shows some common types of logical order and the transitions often used with them.

TRANSITIONS FOR DIFFERENT TYPES OF ORDER		
Types of Order	Definition	Transitions
Chronological	The order in which events occur	first, second, third, before, after, next, on Tuesday, later, finally
Spatial	Location or physical arrangement	left, right, in front of, behind, next to, to the south of
Order of Importance	Degree of importance, size, or interest	first, finally, in addition, smallest, largest, more/most important

Chronological order is used with events or stories to tell what happened first, next, and so on. It is also used when giving directions or the steps in a process.
Spatial order is used in descriptions to show how objects are related in location.
Order of importance is often used in paragraphs that explain or persuade.

● **Practice Your Skills**

Improving Paragraph Coherence

This paragraph lacks transitions. It also presents some details out of order. On a separate sheet of paper, revise the paragraph to improve its coherence.

Spotting Fire Engines

Since fire engines must rush to arrive at a fire, all possible warning measures must be used to alert other drivers. Firefighters in Detroit, Newark, and Kansas City have lime-yellow fire trucks. Their accident rate is less than half that of firefighters in other cities where red fire engines are used. The siren is a warning measure. It is probably other drivers' first clue that an emergency vehicle is approaching. The flashing light is a warning device. Very important in spotting a fire engine is its color. Although red trucks are the tradition, lime-yellow fire trucks may ultimately prove to be safer.

PROJECT PREP *Revising* *Unity and Coherence*

Return to your writing group and share your first draft with your writing partners. For each writer, make suggestions to ensure that the paragraphs are coherent and clearly support the topic sentence. Make notes on your paragraph about what you can improve.

The Power of Language ⚡

Parallelism: The Power of 3s

You have seen that one way to emphasize important points is to use order of importance. Another is to use parallelism. **Parallelism** is the same kind of word or group of words, grammatically speaking, in a series of three or more. Read aloud the following sentence from Lederer's essay on small words. Notice the parallelism of the highlighted constructions.

> Short words are bright like sparks that glow in the night, prompt like the dawn that greets the day, sharp like the blade of a knife, hot like salt tears that scald the cheek, quick like moths that flit from flame to flame, and terse like the dart and sting of a bee.

Why do you think Lederer chose to write all these comparisons in sequence, beginning each with the same kind of construction? What effect does this parallelism have on you as a reader?"

Here is another example of parallelism. This one is from *The House on Mango Street* by Sandra Cisneros (see pages 111–112).

> They always told us that one day we would move into a house, a real house that would be ours for always so we wouldn't have to move each year. And our house would have running water and pipes that worked. And inside would have real stairs, not hallway stairs, but stairs inside like the houses on T.V. And we'd have a basement and at least three washrooms so when we took a bath we wouldn't have to tell everybody.

By the sheer force of repetition, parallelism leaves a strong impression on a reader and makes some ideas stand out more than others.

Try It Yourself

Use the sentences above as models for writing sentences with parallel elements. Use the first as a model for writing a sentence about something you like a lot— watermelon on a hot summer's day, or the thrill of attending a baseball game. Use the second to write a series of sentences about something you want very much. If possible, write sentences on your project topic and include them in your draft. Later, check your draft for other places where parallelism would be effective.

Punctuation Tip

Use commas to separate items in a series. Use a comma before the final item and the word *and*.

Writing a Concluding Sentence

Every good composition has a clear beginning, middle, and ending. In a single paragraph, the concluding sentence serves as the ending. It wraps up the ideas and makes the reader feel that the message is complete.

A **concluding sentence** adds a strong ending to a paragraph by summarizing, referring to the main idea, or adding an insight.

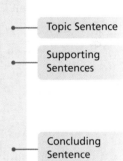

MODEL: Concluding Sentence

Solving the Rubik's Cube

Students at the University of Illinois invented the final answer to solving the Rubik's Cube. Their invention is Robbie Rubik, a robot that can solve the cube in two-tenths of a second. Robbie's computer works very fast, but his mechanical hands work much slower. It takes Robbie about five to six minutes to make the 75 to 160 twists and turns needed to unscramble a cube. Despite slow hand movements, Robbie can still solve the puzzle faster than any of its human inventors.

Topic Sentence

Supporting Sentences

Concluding Sentence

 PROJECT PREP *Drafting* *Concluding Sentence*

Review your sketch and reread your composition. Draft a concluding sentence that provides a strong ending. Then use the feedback from your writing group to prepare a new draft of your paragraph. In this draft, in addition to shaping up the ideas of the paper, make sure to polish the whole presentation by correcting any errors in form you have made.

TIME OUT TO
REFLECT

What makes a good ending? Look back over other things you have written and find a conclusion you especially like. Why is it effective? Make a note for your Learning Log about what you've learned about strong endings.

In the Media

Movie Review

Movie reviews can be excellent examples of well-structured writing because, like strong paragraphs, they tend to follow a predictable pattern. Movie reviews first tell you what the movie is about without giving away the ending. Then they point out aspects of the film that the reviewer felt either worked or did not. They might also discuss the actors' performances or the way the movie was filmed or edited. Often movie reviews will conclude with an overall evaluation that can be crucial in persuading people whether they should see a movie or not.

Media Activity

Choose a movie from the media center or rent one from a video store. Watch the movie, and then write a movie review.

Give a basic plot description. Be very careful not to give too much away or even to hint at some event that should remain a secret to the audience. Then use the following guidelines to help you.

Guidelines for Movie Criticism

- Was the movie fast-paced or slow?
- What lighting or camera angles were used? Were they effective?
- Were the actors' performances moving? Why or why not?
- How did the setting affect the feeling of the movie?
- Was the script well written? Did you believe what people were saying?
- Describe the use of special effects.

The last few sentences of the review should sum up your overall evaluation of the movie in a way that lets the readers know if they should see it. Share your review with your classmates.

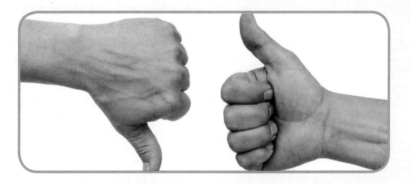

Writing Well-Structured Paragraphs

The Language of Power   *Run-ons*

Power Rule: Use the best conjunction and/or punctuation for the meaning when connecting two sentences. Revise run-on sentences. (See pages 662–663.)

See It in Action Richard Lederer ends his essay with two short, punchy sentences.

> Short words are like fast friends. They will not let you down.

When drafting, you might be tempted to write those sentences this way:

> Short words are like fast friends, they will not let you down.

However, when two independent clauses are joined by a comma without a conjunction such as *but* or *and,* the result is a comma splice—one kind of run-on sentence. You can fix this problem in one of three ways: 1) change the comma to a period and begin the next sentence with a capital letter, as Lederer did; 2) insert a conjunction between the comma and the first word of the second independent clause; or 3) replace the comma with a semicolon.

Remember It Record this rule and these examples and fixes in the Power Rule section of your Personalized Editing Checklist.

Use It Exchange papers with a partner. Check each comma to be sure that it is not joining two independent clauses without a conjunction. Fix any in your own paragraph that you or your partner finds.

PROJECT PREP   Editing and Publishing   *A Final Look*

1. Look over your paragraph one more time. Does each element in your paragraph accomplish its purpose? (See the chart on page 69 for the purpose of each kind of sentence in a paragraph.) Does your paragraph have unity and coherence? Have you avoided mistakes in usage and mechanics?

2. Return to your writing group. With your partners, think of ways you could publish your paragraphs. With your teacher's permission, carry out your publishing plans.

Writing Lab

Project Corner

Make It Visual
Hamburger with the Works

Paragraphs have been represented by many different graphic organizers. One you might know is the hamburger. The top of the bun is the topic sentence; the meat with all the trimmings is the body of the paragraph; and the bottom of the bun is the concluding sentence. With a small group, **create your own original visual representation** of a paragraph. Help prepare a display of all the different visuals your class comes up with.

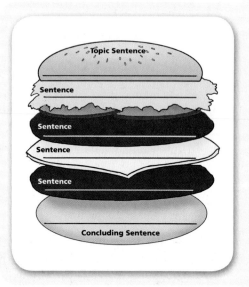

Investigate Further The Pilcrow

With a partner, learn what you can about the **history of the *pilcrow*, the paragraph sign.** Write a paragraph explaining how it was originally used and how its use changed through the ages.

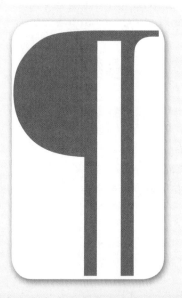

Experiment Try a Different Form

Review the suggested project forms on page 68. Think about how your project would be different if it were in one of those forms you didn't use or another that you can think of. **Try rewriting it in that new form.** Then write a brief paragraph explaining the changes you had to make for the new form.

In Everyday Life
Persuasive E-mail to a Friend

1. Your friend who lives in Texas is trying to decide between taking a guitar class or acting in the drama club's productions after school. You have been a member of both groups at different times but have enjoyed drama more. Knowing your friend's interests, you think she will probably enjoy the drama group, too. **Write an e-mail** to your friend, persuading her in one paragraph to join the drama group. Make sure you include a topic sentence, supporting sentences, and a concluding sentence. (For information on persuasive writing, see pages 220–247.)

For Oral Communication Brief Report

2. Your class has returned from a trip to zoo. The teacher has asked each student to give a presentation to the rest of the class describing the animal he or she found most interesting. **Write a one-paragraph report** about your choice. Research your animal if necessary. Elaborate fully in the body of your paragraph so your classmates learn as much as possible about your animal, but be sure you have a clear focus. Practice delivering your presentation before actually giving your speech. (For information on giving a speech, see pages 421–422.)

Timed Writing 🕐 How-To Paragraph

3. An online magazine and Web site called Techno Wizard is looking for submissions for a new project called "How to Do Just About Anything." Write a paragraph to send to Techno Wizard in which you explain how to do a specific activity. It can be playing a sport or game, creating a craft project, building a model or a Web site, or performing an experiment. Present your information in a clear, logical manner with smooth transitions. Be sure to organize your thoughts and sentences so that they flow smoothly and make sense. You have 20 minutes to complete your work. (For help with budgeting time, see pages 374–375.)

Before You Write Consider the following questions: What is the subject? What is the occasion? Who is the audience? What is the purpose?

After You Write Evaluate your work using the six-trait evaluation form on page 24.

CHAPTER 4

Writing Effective Compositions

A composition presents and develops one main idea in three or more paragraphs.

Writing a good composition is something of an art. It takes practice, dedication, and enthusiasm. Compositions will be required in all areas of study throughout your academic career—and possibly beyond. In history class you may be asked to write a composition about the system of checks and balances employed by the U. S. government. In science class, you may have to write a composition explaining the life cycle of a moth. Knowing how to write a strong composition will serve you well. Below are other examples of compositions you may be called upon to write.

- **As a reporter, you write about a class trip** for the readers of your school newspaper.
- **When applying as a volunteer, you write an essay** about why you want to tutor struggling students.
- **To win a set of tablets for your classroom, you and your friends work together on an explanation** of how the class will use the tablets.
- **To broaden your cultural experiences, you and your classmates write a proposal** for a foreign-exchange program.

Writing Project   *Personal Narrative*

I Remember . . . Write a story about an elementary school event that remains vivid in your memory.

Think Through Writing Think about something that happened in elementary school that stands out sharply in your mind. What was this event? How did it unfold? How did it end? Write descriptively about this event.

Talk About It In your writing group, discuss the events you have written about. What are the emotions involved? How well are they conveyed?

Read About It In the passage that follows, Annie Dillard describes a moth cocoon that hatched in her elementary school class. Think about the details she includes in her description that help you relive the experience along with her.

"The Fixed"

From

Pilgrim at Tinker Creek

Annie Dillard

Once, when I was ten or eleven years old, my friend Judy brought in a Polyphemus moth cocoon. It was January; there were doily snowflakes taped to the schoolroom panes. The teacher kept the cocoon in her desk all morning and brought it out when we were getting restless before recess. In a book we found what the adult moth would look like; it would be beautiful. With a wingspread of up to six inches, the Polyphemus is one of the few huge American silk moths, much larger than, say, a giant or tiger swallowtail butterfly. The moth's enormous wings are velveted in a rich, warm brown, and edged in bands of blue and pink delicate as a watercolor wash. A startling "eyespot," immense, and deep blue melding to an almost translucent yellow, luxuriates in the center of each hind wing. The effect is one of a masculine splendor foreign to the butterflies, a fragility unfurled[1] to strength. The Polyphemus moth in the picture looked like a mighty wraith,[2] a beating essence of the hard-wood forest, alien-skinned and brown, with spread, blind eyes. This was the giant moth packed in the faded cocoon. We closed the book and turned to the cocoon. It was an oak leaf sewn into a plump oval bundle; Judy had found it loose in a pile of frozen leaves.

> This paragraph sets the scene and offers a rich description of the moth.

> While Dillard's purpose is to convey a memory, she also provides information. The detailed information helps readers come to know the moth very well and develop some feelings for it.

We passed the cocoon around; it was heavy. As we held it in our hands, the creature within warmed and squirmed. We were delighted, and wrapped it tighter in our fists. The pupa began to jerk violently, in heart-stopping knocks. Who's there? I can still feel those thumps, urgent through a muffling of spun silk and leaf, urgent through the swaddling of many years, against the curve of my palm. We kept passing it around. When it came to me again it was hot as a bun; it jumped half out of my hand. The teacher intervened. She put it, still heaving and banging, in the ubiquitous Mason jar.

> An equally descriptive, paragraph, this one draws the reader into the activity.

---

1 **unfurled:** Opened or spread out; unrolled.

2 **wraith:** An apparition or ghost.

It was coming. There was no stopping it now, January or not. One end of the cocoon dampened and gradually frayed in a furious battle. The whole cocoon twisted and slapped around in the bottom of the jar. The teacher fades, the classmates fade, I fade: I don't remember anything but that thing's struggle to be a moth or die trying. It emerged at last, a sodden crumple. It was a male; his long antennae were thickly plumed, as wide as his fat abdomen. His body was very thick, over an inch long, and deeply furred. A gray, furlike plush covered his head; a long, tan furlike hair hung from his wide thorax over his brown-furred, segmented abdomen. His multijointed legs, pale and powerful, were shaggy as a bear's. He stood still, but he breathed.

Here, the author creates tension through her descriptions.

He couldn't spread his wings. There was no room. The chemical that coated his wings like varnish, stiffening them permanently, dried, and hardened his wings as they were. He was a monster in a Mason jar. Those huge wings stuck on his back in a torture of random pleats and folds, wrinkled as a dirty tissue, rigid as leather. They made a single nightmare clump still wracked with useless, frantic convulsions.

Which description in this paragraph do you find most compelling?

The next thing I remember, it was recess. The school was in Shadyside, a busy residential part of Pittsburgh. Everyone was playing dodgeball in the fenced playground or racing around the concrete schoolyard by the swings. Next to the playground a long delivery drive sloped downhill to the sidewalk and street. Someone—it must have been the teacher—had let the moth out. I was standing in the driveway, alone, stock-still, but shivering. Someone had given the Polyphemus moth his freedom, and he was walking away.

The next thing I remember serves as a transition to the next part of the story.

He heaved himself down the asphalt driveway by infinite degrees, unwavering. His hideous crumpled wings lay glued and rucked on his back, perfectly still now, like a collapsed tent. The bell rang twice; I had to go. The moth was receding down the driveway, dragging on. I went; I ran inside. The Polyphemus moth is still crawling down the driveway, crawling down the driveway hunched, crawling down the driveway on six furred feet, forever.

How does the end make you feel? How has Dillard helped create that feeling in you?

Respond in Writing Write an answer to the questions raised in the sidenote next to the final paragraph.

Develop Your Own Ideas Work with your classmates to develop ideas to assist you in writing about your own memory from elementary school.

Small Groups: In your writing group, use a chart like the one below to organize ways in which you and your writing partners have written about your elementary school experiences. Two examples are given.

The Experience	Emotions Felt	Sensory Details
• winning a major sports event	• joy, pride, accomplishment	• cheering of crowd, laughter, tears, sunshine, sweat
• the death of a pet	• sadness, anger, confusion	• soft fur, tears, sobs, darkness, rain

Whole Class: Make a master chart of all of the emotions and sensory details generated in the small group discussions. Refer to this chart for ideas as you work on your narrative.

Write About It You will next write a narrative about a memorable experience you had in elementary school. The following chart lists possible topics, audiences, and forms for your writing:

Possible Topics and Examples	Possible Audiences	Possible Forms
• a story about a conflict • a story about a friend • a story about things you learned • a story about a misunderstanding • a story about an unusual event	• your classmates • the teacher you had that year • the school principal • the student council	• a letter requesting a change in school rules • a story for your journal • a story for the school yearbook • a narrative submitted to a teen magazine

By now you've had some success writing paragraphs. The process of writing a composition is not very different from that of writing a paragraph. Like paragraphs, compositions written on subjects of sincere interest to you are usually the most successful. The strategies that follow will help you find a good subject.

❶ Choosing and Limiting a Subject

Choosing a subject you care about is an important prewriting activity. If you choose a subject you are not genuinely interested in, your composition will lack fire. If you care about your subject, however, your writing will crackle with interest.

GETTING IDEAS FLOWING

Use freewriting, clustering, brainstorming, or any of the other strategies from pages 13–16 to explore your interests and knowledge in search of a subject you can develop into a composition. After exploring your interests, home in on and refine the one that seems most promising for developing into a composition.

REFINING YOUR SUBJECT

Three factors are especially important in refining a subject: your purpose, your audience, and the genre you will use to convey your ideas. To clarify your **purpose,** ask yourself "Do I want to provide information? Do I want to persuade my readers or do I want to entertain them?" To clarify your **audience,** develop an audience profile to help you understand your readers' knowledge, attitudes, and beliefs. To clarify your **genre,** ask yourself, "What form is best to convey my ideas? An essay? A narrative? An editorial? Readers have certain expectations of each genre, so being aware of genre will help you give your readers what they expect.

FOCUSING ON YOUR SUBJECT

To determine a good subject, list several possible focus points that would suit your purpose and audience and that would be appropriate for your chosen genre. **Focus points** are smaller, more limited topics contained within your general subject. If you had decided to write about the sport of snorkeling, for example, you might list the focus points on the following page.

Subject	snorkeling (underwater exploring)
Purpose	to explain
Audience	people who are interested in the sport but do not know much about it
Focus Points	what equipment is needed
	how to control breathing and clear snorkel
	the things someone can see while snorkeling
	how to make different kinds of surface dives

Any one of the four focus points above would be a suitably limited subject for a short composition.

Steps for Limiting a Composition Subject

- Decide on the purpose of your composition: to create, to express, to inform or explain, or to persuade.
- Think about who your audience (readers) will be.
- Choose the best genre for your subject, purpose, and audience.
- List focus points that suit your purpose, audience, and genre and choose one as your limited subject.

PROJECT PREP *Prewriting* *Limited Subject*

In your writing group, discuss each writer's subject. Can it be developed with interesting and perceptive details? Is it suitably limited? Is the focus clearly defined? Based on your discussions with your writing group and classmates, write a new version of your narrative about an elementary-school memory.

❷ Listing Supporting Details

During the writing process, you move back and forth between letting your thoughts run freely and controlling what you write. First, you brainstorm. Next, you narrow your subject. The next stage, listing supporting details, calls for letting your ideas run freely again. Your supporting details will depend on your purpose for writing, as the chart below shows.

SUPPORTING DETAILS IN A COMPOSITION	
Purpose	**Kinds of Details**
To inform	details relating cause and effect or likenesses and differences
To explain	facts, examples, reasons
To give directions	steps in a process
To persuade	reasons, based on fact, to support an opinion or claim
To create	details that develop characters and incidents

BRAINSTORMING

You develop details by freewriting and clustering, or you could discuss your subject or research it in the library or media center. You could also come up with supporting details by brainstorming. Write down everything that comes to mind when you think about your subject. One idea will lead to another.

Limited Subject	Things to Do While Snorkeling
Brainstorming Ideas	master basic snorkeling techniques
	feed fish
	fish will eat bread or cheese
	carry the food in a bag you can close
	collect shells
	shells are sometimes hidden in sea grasses
	take pictures
	need waterproof camera equipment
	watch for dangerous animals that could be hiding nearby

PROJECT PREP *Brainstorming* *Developing Details*

In your writing group, brainstorm about the event each of you plans to write about. Discuss the conditions that affected the event. What was the setting? Who was involved? How did the events play out? What was the outcome and why was it so memorable? Help each writer develop ideas about the importance of this event.

③ Developing the Main Idea

In each stage of the writing process, your ideas become increasingly clear. After brainstorming, you probably have a clearer understanding of your subject than you did before. By this time you probably know enough about your subject to formulate your **thesis statement**—the sentence expressing your theme, or main idea.

To formulate your thesis statement, try to express your limited subject in a complete sentence. Looking over your brainstorming notes will help you know how to develop that sentence.

The writer who brainstormed about snorkeling reviewed his brainstorming notes and limited subject and came up with the following thesis statement.

> **Thesis Statement**　After mastering basic techniques, a snorkeler can find lots of things to do underwater.

This thesis statement will probably change somewhat as the writer continues writing. For now, it serves as a focus—this is the information he wants to impart to his reader. All other details in the composition will be anchored to this main idea.

A solid and interesting main idea is worth the time and trouble it may take to formulate it. The best main ideas are those that can be explored in depth and that interest you enough to think creatively and informatively about them.

Using the idea rubric on the next page, consider whether or not the idea you have for your own composition is worthy of earning you a 4.

Idea Rubric

4 Ideas are presented and developed in depth.	3 Most ideas are presented and developed with insight.	2 Many ideas are not well developed.	1 Most ideas are not well developed.
• I developed each idea thoroughly and used specific details. • My presentation of ideas was original. • I made meaningful connections among ideas. • I took some risks to make my writing come alive.	• I developed most ideas thoroughly with some specific details. • My presentation of some ideas was thoughtful. • I made some connections among ideas. • I played it safe and did not put much of myself into the composition.	• I tried to develop ideas but was more general than specific. • I listed rather than developed ideas. • I made few connections among ideas. • I left a few things out but I think my meaning comes across.	• Most of my ideas are overly general. • I did not develop my ideas. • I did not try to connect ideas. • I left some important things out so my meaning wasn't really clear.

Look at the last item in the first column about taking risks. What does it mean to take a risk in writing? Review the brainstorming notes about snorkeling on page 90. They are solid ideas that can be used to build a solid composition—no risk there. But what if these details were also part of the list?

- weightlessness
- shimmering colors
- cool water on skin

These details might seem somewhat risky because they are not strictly essential to the thesis statement the writer developed. Yet they could help create an engaging setting that could make all the difference between a pretty good composition and a *very* good composition.

PROJECT PREP *Prewriting* *Developing the Main Idea*

In your writing group, help each writer develop a main idea or thesis statement. What is the theme that runs through the narrative? Is it the consequences of bullying, or the trials and rewards of doing the right thing? Help each writer identify the theme for the narrative and to express it in a thesis statement. Also make suggestions to each writer about how he or she might take risks to lift the composition to a new level.

④ Arranging Details in Logical Order

After brainstorming, arrange your ideas in a logical order.

TYPES OF ORDER	
Chronological	Items are arranged in time order.
Spatial	Items are arranged in location order.
Importance or Degree	Items are arranged in order of least to most or most to least important.
Sequential	Steps in a process are arranged in their proper sequence.

As you group your ideas, you may find that some do not fit in neatly. Save these for possible use later. Notice the order of the notes about things to do while snorkeling.

Least Difficult
feed fish
fish will eat bread or cheese
carry the food in a bag you can close

Next in Difficulty
collect shells
shells are sometimes hidden in sea grasses
watch for dangerous animals that could be hiding nearby

Most Difficult
take pictures
need waterproof camera equipment

Use Elsewhere?
mastering basic snorkeling techniques

PROJECT PREP *Prewriting* *Organizing*

Organize your supporting details in the most logical order you can. Make an outline or a graphic organizer to represent the organizational strategy you will use. Share your plan with your writing group members and ask for feedback. Might there be other, better ways to organize the ideas?

editing ☆

In the following sentence, items are arranged in logical order, but the sentence is too wordy. Make it more readable.

My very most favorite seashells are the blushing fanlike pink scallop; the smooth, shiny bright oval cowrie; and the mighty spiral-shaped conch that makes a big sound if you blow it with all your might, using all your air.

Think Critically

Inferring

Inferring means using your reasoning powers to draw a meaningful conclusion, or inference, from given information or situations. A sound inference should be stated in the introduction of your composition.

You are making inferences all the time, probably without realizing it. For example, if you text a friend and get no response, you may infer that your friend is too busy to answer. You have used specific information—the fact that your friend has not replied to your text—and drawn a conclusion from it. Is your conclusion necessarily true? No. Maybe your friend is annoyed with your text messages and prefers not to answer. Maybe your friend has been restricted from texting for a few days.

A good inference accounts for as many details as possible. For example, if you texted and got no reply, and then saw your friend texting after school, you would have a piece of evidence to back up the inference that your friend might be displeased with you.

Thinking Practice

Decide which of the following could be inferred from the specific information provided on pages 89–93 about snorkeling. After each statement, explain why it can or cannot be inferred from the details.

1. Snorkeling is easy.
2. Snorkeling is for professionals only.
3. Snorkeling carries some risks.
4. So many people are snorkeling today that the underwater wildlife is disturbed.
5. Snorkeling requires special equipment.

When your outline or notes are organized, you are ready to begin the second stage of the writing process—drafting. Remember that your goal is to turn your prewriting notes into an actual composition in which sentences and paragraphs flow smoothly, with transitions connecting one sentence or paragraph neatly to the next.

Like paragraphs, compositions have three main parts. In the following composition, the three main parts are labeled at the right.

CHAPTER 4

MODEL: Composition

Messages into Space

Two space missions from recent years are carrying our messages into interstellar space. *Pioneer 10* is carrying a plaque with a drawing of a man and a woman plus some information about Earth and its inhabitants. *Voyager* is carrying a "cosmic LP," a two-hour phonograph record. Encoded on the record are photographs, diagrams, and drawings that represent life on this planet. It also contains greetings from Earth spoken in 53 languages, musical selections, sounds of our animal life, the roar of the surf, the cry of a baby, and the soft thump of the human heartbeat. Thirty-two thousand years will pass before *Pioneer 10* draws close to a star. After that approach a million years will go by before there is another close approach, and still another million years will elapse before a third occurs.

Because of the emptiness of interstellar space, the spacecraft's ancient hulk will probably never be seen by alien eyes. In fact, the messages aboard the *Pioneer* and *Voyager* spacecraft were composed with little hope that anyone would ever discover them. They were only bottles thrown in a cosmic ocean, a symbol of our deep desire to communicate with a civilization other than our own.

Millions of years from now, those messages will still be journeying through the universe. They may never be found. They will, however, be a solid piece of evidence that a tiny inhabited planet exists, or once existed, in the suburbs of a small galaxy with the odd name *Milky Way*.

— Margaret Poynter and Michael J. Klein, *Cosmic Quest*

Main Idea

Introduction: Provides many specific details about the messages

Words like also and in fact and pronouns such as those provide internal and external coherence.

Body: Interprets the details from the first paragraph

Conclusion: Adds a strong ending

① The Introduction of a Composition

A good introduction should arouse the reader's interest and make the reader want to know more. It should also state clearly the main idea of the composition.

HERE'S HOW

Strategies for Writing an Introduction

- Capture the reader's attention with an interesting fact, detail, incident, or description.
- Give background information if needed.
- Include a sentence expressing the main idea or thesis.
- Do not include empty expressions, such as *This composition will be about* . . . .

In the following introduction on the subject of snorkeling, the sentence stating the main idea is highlighted.

MODEL: Introduction

Imagine the feeling of suddenly having all of your weight lifted from you. You glide along almost without effort. You feel the coolness of water around you. You see the brilliant colors of fish swimming past you, and the sounds of the world outside are muffled. These are just a few of the pleasures of snorkeling. For those who have mastered the basic techniques, however, the pleasures are even greater. Instead of simply gliding and observing, an experienced snorkeler can keep busy underwater with several interesting activities.

PROJECT PREP *Drafting* *Introduction*

Use your prewriting notes to help you draft the introduction to your narrative. Consider the following:

- How can you capture a reader's attention?
- What details might you include to take a risk and stray from the strictly expected?
- What background information, if any, should you provide?
- What is the best way to express your thesis statement?
- How can you make every word count?

Share your draft and write down suggestions from your group.

The Power of Language⚡

Fluency: Let It Flow

You have learned various ways of adding content and detail to your sentences, and using grammatical options to add style and voice to your writing. To make your paragraphs flow invitingly and achieve fluency, you need to add another strategy into your mix. That strategy is varying the length and structure of your sentences.

Notice the sentence variety in the following passage from "The Fixed" by Annie Dillard. The subject of each sentence is highlighted to show how much the placement of the subject varies from sentence to sentence.

> Once, when I was ten or eleven years old, my friend Judy brought in a Polyphemus moth cocoon. It was January; there were doily snowflakes taped to the schoolroom panes. The teacher kept the cocoon in her desk all morning and brought it out when we were getting restless before recess. In a book we found what the adult moth would look like; it would be beautiful. With a wingspread of up to six inches, the Polyphemus is one of the few huge American silk moths, much larger than, say, a giant or tiger swallowtail butterfly.

Only in a few sentences is the subject at the beginning. In others it comes after an adverb, or a subordinate clause, or a prepositional phrase. The length of the sentences is also varied. The longest sentence (the last one) has 29 words; the shortest (the second sentence) has fewer than half that number, 12.

When you read that passage you don't have to ask yourself where the subjects are or how many words a sentence contains to know that it flows smoothly. When you write, however, if you are aware of the factors that help create flow, you can produce fluent writing.

Punctuation Tip

Use a comma after certain introductory elements in a sentence. (See pages 832–834.)

Try It Yourself

Write a passage of about five sentences on your project topic. Use different colored highlighters to see how you started your sentences. If you have only one color, revise until you have at least three.

Also count the number of words in each sentence. If they are all about the same, look for ways to vary their length to achieve a smoother flow.

② The Body of a Composition

Keep your reader in mind as you write the body of your composition. Try to make your message as clear as possible. Use your prewriting outline and notes to create complete, varied sentences with vivid details. Use transitions to connect your thoughts smoothly.

Notice how each transition below (printed in **bold** type) smoothly connects two topics or sections to each other. Refer to pages 122 and 140 for a list of transitions.

MODEL: Body

One of the easiest and most enjoyable underwater activities is feeding fish. Fish particularly like bread or cheese. If you want to feed fish, carry the food in a bag you can close. **In that way** you can keep hungry fish from swimming inside your food bag. **Another** activity, shell collecting, requires slightly **more** skill. A good shell collector must know where to look for shells that might be hidden in grasses on the seafloor. He or she must also recognize dangerous animals that might be hiding near the shells. **A third activity,** taking pictures underwater, requires the **most** skill and equipment. The camera and gear must all be made specially for working underwater.

PROJECT PREP *Drafting* *Body Paragraphs*

Draft the body of your composition. Make sure it is logically organized with appropriate supporting details. Also check to make sure that it has unity, that all the ideas relate to the main idea with no extra information. Then share your draft with your writing group for feedback.

③ The Conclusion of a Composition

A conclusion to a composition is like a farewell. It wraps up the ideas in the composition and provides a strong ending.

MODEL: Conclusion

Almost anything you do while snorkeling is a pleasure. The nearness to sea creatures, the beauty of a coral reef, and the feel of the water all add up to an unforgettable experience. When you actually interact with the life below by feeding fish, collecting empty shells, or taking action pictures, you will feel even more a part of the mysterious sea.

Use the guidelines below when writing a conclusion.

Writing a Conclusion

A strong concluding paragraph

- emphasizes the main idea without restating it exactly.
- may refer to ideas in the introduction.
- does not introduce a completely new idea.
- does not use such empty expressions as *I have just told you about . . .* or *Now you know about . . . .*

You may want to end your composition by stating a lesson you learned or by issuing a warning. Or you may want to show how your subject can apply to other areas as well. Sometimes you may want to end with a thought-provoking question or quotation.

Writing a Title A title should give the reader an idea of what the composition will be about and make your reader curious enough to want to read the entire composition. (See pages 811–814 for information on capitalization of titles.)

PROJECT PREP   *Drafting*   Conclusion

Draft your conclusion. Then, In your writing group, discuss how each writer's story ends. Does it have a clear resolution? Is it like Annie Dillard's story, where the story concludes as an image that carries over to the present without revealing the fate of the moth? What is the best way for each writer's story to end?

Make sure your composition fulfills its purpose, addresses your audience appropriately, and reflects the features of the chosen genre. Then use the checklist for further revision.

 Evaluation Checklist for Revising

Checking Your Composition

✓ Do you have an interesting introduction that states the main idea or thesis of the composition? (page 96)

✓ Do all your sentences relate to the main idea? In other words, does your composition have unity? (pages 75–77)

✓ Are your ideas arranged logically with transitions? In other words, is your composition coherent? (pages 75–77)

✓ Do you have a strong conclusion? (pages 79 and 99)

Checking Your Paragraphs

✓ Does each paragraph in the body of your composition have a topic sentence? (pages 70–73)

✓ Is each paragraph unified? (pages 75–76)

✓ Is each paragraph coherent? (pages 75–76)

Checking Your Sentences and Words

✓ Did you eliminate short, choppy sentences by combining related sentences? (pages 53–57)

✓ Did you vary the length and beginnings of your sentences? (pages 58–59)

✓ Did you eliminate rambling sentences? (page 60)

✓ Are your sentences free of repetition and empty expressions? (pages 61–62)

✓ Are your words fresh and precise? (pages 45–50)

PROJECT PREP **Revising** *Using Feedback and a Checklist*

Use feedback from your peers and the checklist above to revise your composition. Start by checking the composition as a whole and make any needed changes. Then read it a second time, this time checking and revising your paragraphs. Read it a third time, this time focusing on style, voice, and tone. Make any needed revisions.

As you revise your writing, use the rubric on the next page to evaluate the structure and organization of your story. Make changes as needed.

Using an Organizational Rubric

4 Ideas progress smoothly and the organizational strategies clarify meaning.	3 Most ideas progress smoothly and the organizational strategies are clear.	2 Some ideas progress smoothly but the organizational pattern is not consistent.	1 Few ideas progress smoothly and there is no clear organization.
• I stated the main idea creatively in the introduction and captured attention. • I used the best organizational pattern to present the supporting paragraphs. • My conclusion was strong and the composition feels complete. • My paragraphs and sentences flowed smoothly from one into another. • I used transitions to keep the order clear.	• I stated the main idea in the introduction and captured attention. • I used an appropriate organizational pattern to present the supporting paragraphs. • My conclusion helped make the composition feel complete. • Most but not all of my paragraphs and sentences flowed smoothly from one into another. • I used some transitions to keep the order clear.	• I stated the main idea in the introduction but did not capture attention. • I used an appropriate organizational pattern to present the supporting paragraphs but had some things out of order. • My conclusion provided an ending but it did not feel strong. • I repeated some ideas unnecessarily. • I could have used more transitions to keep the order clear.	• I did not state my main idea clearly. • I did not use an organizational pattern. • I did not provide a clear ending. • I repeated some things and also had some things out of order or not related to the topic. • I did not use many transitions, so the order was hard to follow.

PROJECT PREP *Revising* *Internal and External Coherence*

In your writing group, review the description of internal and external coherence on page 6. Then using the rubric above, evaluate the internal and external coherence of each composition. Point to at least three specific words or phrases that help achieve both kinds of coherence. Make revisions if your composition lacks coherence.

When you are satisfied with your ideas and organization, you are ready to check your composition carefully for errors. Use the proofreading symbols on page 11 when you edit.

The Language of **Power**   *Verb Tense*

Power Rule: Use a consistent verb tense except when change is clearly necessary. (See pages 689–696.)

See It in Action In the following example, Dillard uses mainly past tense as she recalls her memorable experience with a moth. Notice, though, that in the second sentence she switches to present tense as she mentions an ongoing action (things fade from memory). She returns to past tense in the second part of that final sentence because she picks up the memory again.

> The whole cocoon twisted and slapped around in the bottom of the jar. The teacher fades, the classmates fade, I fade: I don't remember anything but that thing's struggle to be a moth or die trying. It emerged at last, a sodden crumple.

Remember It Record this rule and example in the Power Rule section of your Personalized Editing Checklist. Note that the example is a case in which a tense shift *is* necessary.

Use It Read over your writing to make sure you do not shift tenses incorrectly.

PROJECT PREP **Editing** *Checking Conventions*

Exchange papers with a writing partner and read one another's compositions. Look for possible errors, especially those related to the Power Rules and any other last minute items that need changing. Based on your partner's feedback, prepare a final polished version of your composition.

When you prepare to publish your composition, its appearance can be almost as important as its content. A paper with uneven margins and words crossed out or crowded together is difficult to read. A neat paper, however, can help you convey your message and make a positive impression on your reader.

 Publishing Checklist

✓ Have I included all editorial feedback in this final copy?
✓ Does my final copy meet the standards of my audience?
✓ Can I get feedback from my audience in order to further improve my story?
✓ Did I use capital letters where needed?
✓ Is my final copy neatly prepared and ready for publication?

PROJECT PREP *Publishing* *Share Your Work*

Publish your finished story in the genre you chose (see pages 15–16) or through another appropriate medium. For example, you might find a place on the Internet asking for personal writing by students that will allow you to contribute your story. You might also contribute your story to a magazine whose audience is comprised of people interested in your subject or to a local newspaper.

CHAPTER 4

In the Media

Television Cartoons

Thinking about your audience is an important part of any communication—oral, written, or visual. Cartoons, for example, are produced for several different audiences. Once viewed as children's entertainment, animation has become popular with all age groups. Cartoons often reflect the culture in which they are created. Cartoons on television, particularly those on prime time, often deal in surprising depth with serious subjects in a lighthearted way. These cartoons are more than just entertainment for young people. They regularly comment on and explore the culture of the audience.

Media Activity

Select a cartoon that appears on television and, if possible, record several episodes. As you watch, take notes on any aspect of American culture that the show presents. What is the action of the plot? How do characters react to it? Is the setting rural? Urban? Watch once again with the sound off. What messages are strictly visual?

Once you have done some research, write a paragraph evaluating cartoons as a statement about culture. Answer the following questions in your paragraph.

- What is the actual subject of the cartoon? Is it simply presenting the antics of animals or superheroes, or is it offering bigger ideas?

- What happens in the cartoon itself? Give a brief description of the plot. What, if anything, does the cartoon say about life in America today?

Share your paragraph about cartoons with your classmates.

Types of Composition

You have already learned that a writer's purpose is a key element in shaping the final text. Writers can have a variety of purposes for writing (see page 15), but four are especially common.

FOUR COMMON WRITING PURPOSES

- **To tell a story.** This kind of writing is called narrative writing.
- **To describe.** Descriptive writing is often used within writing for a larger purpose.
- **To explain or inform.** This kind of writing is called expository writing.
- **To persuade.** Persuasive writing can take many forms--essays, editorials, even documentaries.

The chapters in the next unit will cover these different kinds of writing as well as creative writing and writing about literature.

● Practice Your Skills

Identifying Writing Purposes

After each of the following thesis statements, write *narrative, descriptive, expository,* or *persuasive* to indicate the purpose of the text.

1. The photosynthesis process has three main stages.

2. My 10th birthday was my favorite, because the day was full of surprises.

3. To promote a sense of community involvement, our school should require 20 hours of community service as a graduation requirement.

4. The girl's room was decorated in a most unusual way.

5. Taking good photographs requires a few basic skills.

Learning Tip

Think of three compositions you have written in your school years. What was the writing purpose of each? In your Learning Log, write a brief paragraph explaining their different purposes and also explaining what writing techniques you might use for one purpose but not for another.

Writing Lab

Project Corner

Change Perspectives
Publisher's Rewrite

Writers submitting a story to a publisher are sometimes asked to **rewrite some aspect of the story.** Suppose the publisher asked you to rewrite the story of your memorable event from someone else's perspective—perhaps another person who was involved or just an impartial bystander. How would you go about writing this new version? What might you learn in the process? Write a portion of the narrative from another point of view.

Collaborate and Create   Write a Sequel

With a partner, **write a sequel** to another student's story. What might have happened following the events described? On what do you base the events that you imagine happening?

Get Technical   Write a Prequel

Use a screen-writing computer program to **write a film scene** that is the prequel to another student's story. What might have happened before the events described? On what do you base the events that you imagine happening? When your scene is written, cast the parts and film the scene. Share it with the class.

In the Workplace
Magazine Article

1. You work at the local telephone company. Your boss has asked you to write for other employees about your experience with a customer who tried to pay his telephone bill with a truckload of carrots. *Write a composition* for the company magazine about your experience with the carrot-paying customer. Consider the audience of the magazine as you write. Provide a beginning that will capture reader's attention. Use specific details when describing the customer and the event. Include dialogue and make sure you tell how the situation was resolved.

For Oral Communication Descriptive Presentation

2. As the set designer for a community theater, you have been asked to come up with a plan for a design of the theater company's latest production—*Romeo and Juliet's Excellent Adventure.* You need to present your ideas orally to producers before you begin sketching out your plans. *Write a composition* describing the set of *Romeo and Juliet's Excellent Adventure.* Include sensory words and specific details in your description. Use spatial order to arrange your details into a logical order. Present the description to your class, who will act as the producers of the play.

Timed Writing ⏱ Show and Tell

3. You are helping your pesky little brother with his homework when he remembers that his first-grade class is holding show-and-tell tomorrow. Since he looks up to you so much, he wants to bring in a picture of you. Write a composition about yourself for your brother to read when he shows your picture. As you write, remember the age of your audience as well as the occasion. Focus your subject and include an introduction that will capture the audience's attention. Remember to include lively details and use precise wording in your composition. Vary sentence beginnings to give the composition an interesting structure. Your conclusion should leave the audience with a memorable image. You have 20 minutes to complete your work. (For help budgeting time, see pages 35 and 374-375.)

Before You Write Consider the following questions: What is the subject? What is the occasion? Who is the audience? What is the purpose?

After You Write Evaluate your work using the six-trait evaluation form on page 24.

Unit 2

Purposes of Writing

Writers can have many different purposes—from recording their most private thoughts in their diaries to composing a stirring call for action to right a public wrong. Hemingway's story, "The Battler," shown in manuscript on the next page, began with thoughts and feelings put on paper for the purpose of writing fiction. Whatever their purpose, however, writers would do well to try to achieve Hemingway's broader aim: to put thoughts and feelings on paper in the best and simplest way.

They all bust their hands on me," th... ttle
..." They couldn't hurt me"
He looked at Nick.
"Set down," he said "Want to eat?"
"Sure" ~~struck~~ Nick said "I'm hungry"
Sisters, the man said, "Call me Ad"
"Sure"
Sisters, the man little man said "I'm not right"
"What's the matter?"
"I'm crazy"
He put on his cap Nick felt like laughing
"You're all right," he said
"No I'm not. I'm crazy. Listen, you ever been crazy?"
"No," Nick said "How does it get you?"
"I don't know" Ad said "When you... you don't know about it. You know it's got hold of you?"
"No."
"I'm Ad Francis."
"... Come on take it," the man said "D..."

My aim is to put down on paper what I see and what I feel in the best and simplest way. —Ernest Hemingway

CHAPTER **5**

Personal Writing

Narrative writing tells a real or imaginary story that has a clear beginning, middle, and end.

Whenever your purpose in writing is to tell what happened, you will be writing a narrative. A **personal narrative,** a story based on personal experience, is one kind of narrative writing.

Here are just a few examples of the ways in which narrative writing is used to relay thoughts, feelings, and events.

- **A presidential candidate makes a speech** to convince voters that her background has shaped her for this important office.

- **Your grandmother writes you an e-mail** telling you how much your visit means to her.

- **A filmmaker makes a documentary** on the real-life stories of hurricane survivors.

- **You keep a journal** of your amazing experiences exploring the mountains of Peru.

Writing Project   *Personal Narrative*

Home Sweet Home   *Write a personal narrative that reflects your feelings about home by completing the following project.*

Think Through Writing   To you, what and where is home? Is it a house? Is it a group of people? Is it a neighborhood or town? Think about what you consider to be "home" and write about it freely. Don't worry about grammar, punctuation, or spelling for now; rather, just get your ideas out on paper.

Talk About It   In your writing group, discuss the writing you have done. What characterizes home to the people in your group?

Read About It   In the following memoir, Sandra Cisneros writes about the many houses her family has occupied. Think about her essay in light of your own writing about what you consider to be "home."

From

The House on Mango Street

Sandra Cisneros

We didn't always live on Mango Street. Before that we lived on Loomis on the third floor, and before that we lived on Keeler. Before Keeler it was Paulina, and before that I can't remember. But what I remember most is moving a lot. Each time it seemed there'd be one more of us. By the time we got to Mango Street we were six— Mama, Papa, Carlos, Kiki, my sister Nenny and me.

The house on Mango Street is ours, and we don't have to pay rent to anybody, or share the yard with the people downstairs, or be careful not to make too much noise, and there isn't a landlord banging on the ceiling with a broom. But even so, it's not the house we'd thought we'd get.

We had to leave the flat on Loomis quick. The water pipes broke and the landlord wouldn't fix them because the house was too old. We had to leave fast. We were using the washroom next door and carrying water over in empty milk gallons. That's why Mama and Papa looked for a house, and that's why we moved into the house on Mango Street, far away, on the other side of town.

They always told us that one day we would move into a house, a real house that would be ours for always so we wouldn't have to move each year. And our house would have running water and pipes that worked. And inside would have real stairs, not hallway stairs, but stairs inside like the houses on T.V. And we'd have a basement and at least three washrooms so when we took a bath we wouldn't have to tell everybody. Our house would be white with trees around it, a great big yard and grass growing without a fence. This was the house Papa talked about when he held a lottery ticket and this was the house Mama dreamed up in the stories she told us before we went to bed.

But the house on Mango Street is not the way they told it at all. It's small and red with tight steps in the front and windows so small you'd think they were

---

Sidebar annotations:

In telling this story from her past, Cisneros uses first-person point of view. This perspective lets her reflect on her experiences as she relates them.

In this paragraph and the next, Cisneros supplies lots of details that appeal to the senses.

This paragraph explains the events that set the story in motion.

Readers get the feeling from the way Cisneros writes that maybe their dream house would never become a reality. Her use of the word *would* indicates uncertainty. Uncertainty helps create tension and suspense in the story.

holding their breath. Bricks are crumbling in places, and the front door is so swollen you have to push hard to get in. There is no front yard, only four little elms the city planted by the curb. Out back is a small garage for the car we don't own yet and a small yard that looks smaller between two buildings on either side. There are stairs in our house but they're ordinary hallway stairs, and the house has only one washroom. Everybody has to share a bedroom—Mama and Papa, Carlos and Kiki, me and Nenny.

> This paragraph resolves the uncertainty and the reader sees the house as it really is.

Once when we were living on Loomis, a nun from my school passed by and saw me playing out front. The laundromat downstairs had been boarded up because it had been robbed two days before and the owner had painted on the wood YES WE'RE OPEN so as not to lose business.

Where do you live? she asked.

> Dialogue helps move the story along.

There, I said pointing to the third floor.

You live *there*?

There. I had to look to where she pointed—the third floor, the paint peeling, wooden bars Papa had nailed on the windows so we wouldn't fall out. You live *there*? The way she said it made me feel like nothing. *There*. I lived *there*. I nodded.

> Cisneros reflects on her experiences and their consequences. The nun's response made her sure she wanted to have a house of her own, but not like the one on Mango Street.

I knew then I had to have a house. A real house. One I could point to. But this isn't it. The house on Mango Street isn't it. For the time being, Mama says. Temporary, says Papa. But I know how those things go.

Respond in Writing Respond to Cisneros's writing about where she has lived. What to her is home? How does it compare to your own conception of home? Write at least three points of comparison.

Develop Your Own Ideas Work with your classmates to develop ideas for stories that will help you explain your sense of "home."

Small Groups: In your writing group, discuss some possible stories based on your personal experiences that come to mind when you think about the essence of "home."

Whole Class: Make a master chart of all of the story ideas generated by the small groups. Choose a few and discuss what point each might make about how the writer feels about home. Here are a few possible overall ideas about home:

- Home feels like home only when all family members are present.
- I didn't appreciate home until I was away from it for three weeks one summer.
- Home is wherever my mother/father is.
- Your first home always feels like your "real" home.

Write About It You will next write a focused narrative about the place you call home. The following chart provides possible topics, audiences, and forms for your writing.

Possible Topics and Examples	Possible Audiences	Possible Forms
• moving out of a house you have lived in all your life • making a decision or behaving in a certain way that had an effect on your family • realizing that your feeling of home depends on one person in particular • understanding the consequences of a family interaction	• other people from your home • people who have never met you or your family • someone you are bringing home to meet the family • people In your neighborhood	• a letter • a memoir • a magazine article • a script for a video about your home

The following narrative describes a woman's visit to the Serengeti, a large wildlife preserve in northern Tanzania. Notice how the story unfolds event by event.

MODEL: Narrative

A Surprise Visitor

My nights in camp were often exciting. I could hear lions prowling around. I even came to recognize the voices of most of them. Once I awoke to hear lapping noises. Being half asleep, I listened for some time before I realized that a lioness was inside my tent drinking out of my basin. I shouted at her to go away, which finally she did. I reported this incident to the park warden. He told me that lions of the Serengeti were known occasionally to go into tents and take a look around to see what was going on. I shall never forget the night that nothing but a table stood between me and Africa.

— Joy Adamson, *Forever Free*

Beginning: Sets scene and makes a general statement

Middle: Tells story event by event

Ending: Imparts importance of experience

Each part of a narrative, whether a paragraph or an essay, helps tell a story.

STRUCTURE OF A NARRATIVE

- The **beginning** engages and orients the reader by establishing a context and introducing a narrator.
- The **middle** tells a story that unfolds logically and naturally and answers the questions *Who? What? Where? Why? When?* and *How?*
- The **ending** shows the outcome and often interprets or reflects on the experience.

PROJECT PREP *Analyzing* **Structure**

In your writing group, look over your first writing once again. Analyze your and your partners' writing to determine any structure that may be there. Discuss what each writer would need to do to compose a well-structured event sequence.

Think Critically

Imagining

When you write a narrative, you can tell a true story like the one Joy Adamson told about her surprise visitor. By using the skill of imagining, however, you can also write a narrative about events that *could* have happened but did not. **Imagining** means creating new situations and events out of your memory and experience. Through imagining you can enter new worlds and take your reader with you. Edgar Allan Poe, author of "The Raven" and many other stories and poems about the dark side of life, knew the power of the imagination. He wrote: "If you cannot conveniently tumble out of a balloon, or be swallowed up in an earthquake, or get stuck fast in a chimney, you will have to be contented with simply imagining some similar misadventure."

Thinking Practice

Look at the picture on this page. Use your imagination to answer one of the following questions through freewriting. Save your ideas in case you would like to use them in developing an imaginative narrative.

- Imagine you are one of the people in the cage. How did you get there? What are you doing? Why are you doing it? How do you get back to safety?
- Imagine you are one of the polar bears in the picture. What do you make of this thing and the creatures in it? How do you feel about it? How do you respond?

1 Reflecting on Experience

During the prewriting stage, your mind should be free to wander as you search your memories for possible subjects for narratives. This is the time to take the opportunity to jot down any ideas that come to mind, using prewriting techniques such as brainstorming, clustering, and freewriting to help get ideas flowing. Before long you will find that you have a good subject for a personal narrative. You may find the following sources helpful in jogging your memory.

IDEA SOURCES FOR SUBJECTS OF PERSONAL NARRATIVES

letters	family stories
photographs	favorite things
souvenirs or mementos	albums or scrapbooks

When you are experiencing events, you may be too close to them to see their significance. Later, however, you may be able to understand their meaning and importance. When you reexamine an experience to interpret its meaning, you might begin by completing a checklist like the one on the next page. A student writing about his volunteer work at the hospital checked the following items to help him interpret the importance of the experience.

Checklist for Interpreting Experience

Experience: I delivered toys to children at the local hospital.

This experience is important to me now because it
   helped me see something in a new way.
   ✓ changed the way I felt about helping others.
   ✓ changed the way I felt about myself.

I will always remember this experience because it
   strongly affected my emotions.
   ✓ gave me new knowledge or understanding.
   had important consequences.
This experience is worth writing about because
   it will touch many readers.
   it is unique or extraordinary.
   ✓ writing will help me to understand it better.

Interpretation: This event boosted my self-confidence. It was the first time I realized how good it felt to help others. I became a better person because of it.

PROJECT PREP   *Interpreting* *Focus*

1. Using your work so far and your discussions and reading, develop an idea for a personal narrative about an event that is memorable and worth writing about. What is the story you want to tell? What is its focus? For example, what overall idea would it convey about home?

2. Complete a checklist like the one above to help you interpret the experience.

3. Share your ideas with your writing group. Give one another feedback for writing.

4. Write a rough draft of your narrative based on feedback and your own judgment.

editing ☆

During prewriting, when you are not paying too much attention to surface details, you may find yourself writing wordy sentences with unnecessary repetition. Look back over your draft and eliminate any wordiness you find.

❷ First-Person and Third-Person Narratives

In personal narratives, the person telling the story is a character in the story. In this type of narrative, the first person pronouns *I, we, me, us, my,* and *our* are used. These narratives are called **first-person narratives.**

> ### MODEL: First-Person Narrative
>
> Mike and **I** were just packing away **our** gear after a successful day of fishing when the trouble began. As storm clouds started to gather, **we** headed for the shore. Suddenly . . . .

Some narratives do not involve the writer at all. Writers telling a story about other people will refer to them using third-person pronouns. These stories are called **third-person narratives.**

> ### MODEL: Third-Person Narrative
>
> The boys were just packing away **their** gear after a successful day of fishing when the trouble began. As storm clouds started to gather, **they** headed for shore. Suddenly . . . .

PROJECT PREP *Discussing* *Narrative Voice*

In your writing group, consider the voice of the narrator in each writer's story. What emotions, perspective, knowledge, interests, and other factors are evident from the narrative voice? Do you get a good sense of who the author Is and how the author feels about home, for example? For each author, provide suggestions on how to make the narrative voice consistent and in line with the personality he or she wishes to convey through the writing. Keep notes for when you write a second draft.

Writing Tip

As you plan your narrative, decide which **point of view** suits your story and then use it consistently.

③ Chronological Order

Most narrative paragraphs are arranged in **chronological order.** In chronological order, or time order, events are arranged in the order in which they happened.

You can use a chart like the one below to help you arrange your details in chronological order, or you could use a timeline. You might start by writing what happened first and what happened last and then fill in the remaining details in order.

Subject	power blackout caused by electrical storm
What happened first	last Tuesday severe thunderstorm occurred at 9:20 P.M.
What happened next	power out in six-block area near my home
What happened next	workers from power company began tracing problem immediately
What happened next	located a power line that had been hit by lightning
What happened last	workers restored the power a little after midnight

● Practice Your Skills

Arranging Events in Chronological Order

Write the subject. Then list the events in chronological order.

Subject	auditioning for the school musical
Events	being called to audition
	rehearsing for weeks to master the songs for the part I wanted
	signing up for the audition
	searching for my name on the list of people who made the cast
	seeing my name next to the part I wanted

PROJECT PREP *Analyzing* Organization

In your writing group, focus on each author's arrangement of events. If the order of the narrative is chronological, do you get a clear sense of the flow from one event to the next? If the narrative has gaps that affect your reading, help the writer understand what is missing or what descriptions get in the way of the narrative flow. Suggest ways to improve the flow. Keep notes for when you write a second draft.

The Power of Language ⚡

Dashes: Dash It All

A personal narrative can be formal or informal. The excerpt from *The House on Mango Street* is informal. Cisneros seems eager to be familiar and somewhat casual with the reader. Using dashes (see pages 902–903), she adds a touch of informality to her personal narrative.

> By the time we got to Mango Street we were six—Mama, Papa, Carlos, Kiki, my sister Nenny and me.
>
> I had to look to where she pointed—the third floor, the paint peeling, wooden bars Papa had nailed on the windows so we wouldn't fall out.

Dashes have sometimes been thought to serve about the same purpose as parentheses or commas. As the examples above show, however, a single dash can be used, sparingly, to create an abrupt break between most of a sentence and something the writer wants to emphasize at the end.

A pair of dashes can be used to set off something in the middle of a sentence. Here is an example from "Man Eats Car" on pages 37–38.

> There was an article in the newspaper several years ago—I did not read it, it was told to me—about a yogi in India who ate a car.

Try It Yourself

Write three sentences similar to those above. Two of your sentences should have a dash preceding and emphasizing the important material that ends the sentence. One should have dashes setting off text in the middle of a sentence. Look for opportunities to use dashes in your writing, both as you draft and as you revise.

Punctuation Tip

To create a dash on the computer, type two hyphens, with no space before and none after. The computer may convert these to the kind of dash you see in published writing, which is a single line.

Writing the first draft of your personal narrative is a matter of transforming your prewriting work into a coherent text with a clearly defined focus. As with other kinds of paragraphs, your narrative paragraph should include a topic sentence, a body, and a concluding sentence. Keep your readers' interests in mind as you write.

1 Setting the Scene

Start your narrative by introducing the main idea, the event you plan to write about. Look over your prewriting notes and try to express your main idea in one sentence. Avoid "This narrative will be about . . ." or "In this narrative I will . . ." Use the opening to present the focus of your narrative.

The opening sentences in the narrative paragraph below set the scene and define the focus. They also engage and orient readers by establishing a context and introducing the narrator.

MODEL: Setting the Scene

Anything but Trotting

I had often dreamed of riding a horse. I imagined myself sailing smoothly along, horse and rider as one. This was my day! Here I was, perched on top of a beautiful gray horse. Everything was fine. The lead horse led us slowly down the forest path. We came to a clearing and the horses broke into a canter, a smooth and easy-to-ride gait. They sped into a gallop, a thunderous pace that was surprisingly easy to ride. Everything went fine until the lead horse started to trot and my dream of riding smoothly vanished. I was bouncing wildly and could hardly catch my breath. After minutes that seemed like hours, the lead horse finally headed back to the stable at a slow walk. I knew very well what it meant to be saddle sore. The only place I wanted to be for the next few days was in a very soft chair.

PROJECT PREP   *Evaluating*   Setting

In your writing group, focus on how each author begins the narrative. Can you picture the setting clearly? Help each writer set the scene for the narrative by asking questions about details that might help readers get a good sense of the location for the narrative. Keep notes for when you write your second draft.

CHAPTER 5

2 Transitions

Presenting your ideas in chronological order will help your readers follow the events in narrative writing. Use transitional words and phrases to make sure that the order is clear. **Transitions** are words and phrases that show how ideas are related. In chronological order, transitions show the event sequence clearly and signal shifts in time.

The following transitions are useful in showing chronological order in narrative writing.

TRANSITIONS FOR CHRONOLOGICAL ORDER			
after	during	afterward	immediately
later	until	just as	while
next	first	meanwhile	then
when	second	suddenly	the next day
before	at last	finally	after a while

Following is a version of the paragraph that you read on page 121. This version, however, contains transitions, which appear in **bold** type.

MODEL: Transitions

I had often dreamed of riding a horse, of sailing smoothly as if horse and rider were one. **Today** was my day. Here I was perched on top of a huge gray horse. **At first** everything was fine. The horses in my group were walking slowly down the forest path. **Before long** we came to a clearing and the horses broke into a canter, a smooth and easy-to-ride gait. **Then** the lead horse sped into a gallop, a thunderous gait that was surprisingly easy to ride. Everything went fine **for the rest of the morning** until the lead horse started to trot. **With the first** trot, my dream of horse and rider as one vanished. I was bouncing wildly and could hardly catch my breath. **After** minutes that seemed like hours, we **finally** headed back to the stable at a slow walk. **By then** I knew very well what it meant to be saddle sore. The only place I wanted to be **for the next few days** was in a very soft chair.

PROJECT PREP *Revising* **Transitions**

In your writing group, help each author provide transitions to keep one event in the narrative flowing smoothly into the next. Keep notes for your second draft.

Revising a personal narrative involves attention to three important points.

- Have you developed your personal narrative with precise words and phrases, relevant descriptive details, and sensory language?
- Have you made your ideas and feelings clear?
- Have you maintained a consistent voice?

1 Checking for Development of Ideas

Make sure you have included enough specific supporting details for your reader to clearly see and hear what you want to share. Use the following strategies.

Strategies for Development of ideas

Events	Close your eyes and visualize the experience you are writing about. Write down the details that you "see" in your mind's eye.
People	Visualize each person you are writing about. Visualize the head and face of each person and slowly move down to the feet. Write down details as you "see" them.
Places	Visualize the place you are describing. Visualize that place from left to right and from top to bottom, as well as from the foreground to the background.
Feelings	Imagine reliving the experience that you are writing about. As you relive the experience, focus on your thoughts and feelings.

Practice Your Skills

Revising for Adequate Development

Revise the following paragraph by adding details that would help readers visualize or understand the experience.

> I got off of my bike to look at the bird. It was on the ground, under a plant. It flapped its wings and tried to scare me away as soon as I started to approach it. I was surprised that a bird would try to scare a person away, but that's exactly what it did.

PROJECT PREP *Revising* Development of Ideas

Based on the feedback you've gotten from your writing group, write a second draft of your narrative, with attention to sensory details, the setting of the story, and a smooth flow. Are there places where dashes would be effective? Also, begin to pay attention to spelling, grammar, and punctuation so that readers can easily follow your story.

2 Checking for Unity, Coherence, and Clarity

A paragraph in which all of the sentences support the main idea has **unity.** A paragraph with **coherence** is well organized and tightly written. A paragraph with **clarity** is easy to understand and is enjoyable to read. The following checklist will help you improve the unity, coherence, and clarity of your personal narrative.

 Evaluation Checklist for Revising

Checking Your Narrative

✓ Does your narrative fulfill its purpose? (page 110)

✓ Is your narrative appropriate for your audience and occasion? (page 113)

✓ Does your story have all the features of the narrative genre? (pages 15–16 and 113–114)

✓ Does the beginning engage and orient readers by establishing a context and introducing a narrator? (pages 114 and 121)

✓ Does the body tell a story that unfolds naturally and logically event by event and answer the questions *Who? What? Where? Why? When?* and *How?* (page 122)

✓ Does each paragraph support the main idea in some way, giving it unity? (page 124)

✓ Do the words you've used reflect your distinctive writing style and connect with the reader?

✓ Does your narrative have an organizational strategy with appropriate transitions to give it clarity and signal shifts in time? (page 122)

✓ Did you use first person if you are a character in the story? Did you use third person if your story is about something that happened to someone else? (page 118)

✓ Does your conclusion follow from and reflect on the narrated experience? (page 114)

Checking Your Sentences

✓ Did you combine related sentences to avoid choppy sentences? (pages 53–57)

✓ Did you vary the length and beginnings of your sentences? (pages 58–59)

✓ Did you write concise sentences? (pages 60–63)

Checking Your Words

✓ Did you use precise, specific words? (pages 45–50)

✓ Did you use words that appeal to the senses? (pages 47–49)

PROJECT PREP *Revising* **Using a Checklist**

Exchange papers with a writing partner and read one another's narratives with the checklist items in mind. Make suggestions to help the author prepare the most effective version of the story possible.

CHAPTER 5

As you revised your personal narrative, you looked for ways to help your reader clearly see and hear what you wanted to share. You also checked for development of ideas, clarity, and consistency of tone. Now you are ready to edit, or polish, your writing.

The Language of **Power** *Pronouns*

Power Rule: Use subject forms of pronouns in subject position. Use object forms of pronouns in object position. (See pages 712–716.)

See It in Action In the following example, the object pronoun *me* is used unconventionally in a subject position.

Object pronoun used as subject	Nenny and me shared a room in the house.
Edited	Nenny and I shared a room in the house.

A good way to check correct pronoun use is to use *only* the pronoun with the verb. You would not say, "Me shared a room with...," so you know *I* must be correct.

Object pronoun used as subject	My parents could hear Nenny and I laughing at night.
Edited	My parents could hear Nenny and me laughing at night.

Again, you would not say, "My parents could hear *I*," so you know *me* must be right.

Remember It Record this rule and these examples in the Power Rule section of your Personalized Editing Checklist.

Use It Read through your narrative to make sure you have used pronouns correctly. Strip away any other parts of the subject or object to test your choice.

PROJECT PREP **Editing** *Conventions*

Exchange papers with a writing partner and check one another's narratives for any problems in grammar, usage, punctuation, or spelling. Pay special attention to the Power Rules (see pages 8–11).

Use an evaluation form like the one below to measure a personal narrative.

Ideas	4 The topic and details convey the meaning of the experience to the intended audience and fulfill the intended purpose.	3 The topic and details convey the meaning of the experience to the intended audience and attempt to fulfill the intended purpose.	2 The topic and details do not convey the meaning of the experience to the intended audience nor fulfill the purpose.	1 The topic and details do not convey the meaning of the experience and fail to address the audience and fulfill the purpose.
Organization	4 The organization is very clear; the details are logically organized, with nothing out of place.	3 The organization is mostly clear, but a few ideas seem out of place or transitions are missing.	2 Many ideas seem out of place and transitions are missing. The introduction, body, and conclusion are weak.	1 The organization is hard to follow. The introduction, body, and conclusion are weak.
Voice	4 The voice sounds natural, engaging, and personal.	3 The voice sounds natural, and personal.	2 The voice sounds mostly unnatural with a few exceptions.	1 The voice sounds mostly unnatural.
Word Choice	4 Words are vivid, specific, and powerful. The writing is rich in sensory words.	3 Words are vivid and specific with some words that appeal to the senses.	2 Some words are overly general.	1 Most words are overly general.
Sentence Fluency	4 Varied sentences flow smoothly. Transitions are used effectively.	3 Most of the sentences are varied and flow smoothly. Transitions help coherence.	2 Sentences are not varied, and some are choppy. Few transitions are present.	1 Sentences are not varied and are choppy. There are very few transitions.
Conventions	4 Punctuation, usage, and spelling are correct. The Power Rules are all followed.	3 There are only a few errors in conventions. The Power Rules are all followed.	2 There are a number of errors in conventions, but all Power Rules are followed.	1 There are many errors and at least one failure to follow a Power Rule.

You may decide to complete the writing process by sharing your writing with someone who was part of your experience or may have an interest in it.

PROJECT PREP Publishing Sharing Your Work

1. Based on the feedback from your writing partner, prepare a final draft of your narrative about home. If you chose one of the forms listed on page 113 for your published work, meet with others in your class to discuss the publishing conventions of that form. For example, if you chose to write a letter, does your finished work have all the elements of a letter? If you chose to write a script for a video, in what ways did you need to adjust your narrative to fit the form? How might you have done that better?

2. When you are satisfied that you have polished it as well as you can, publish your work through your chosen medium. If you wrote a letter, for example, share It with other people from the place you consider home so they can appreciate your feelings.

TIME OUT TO **REFLECT**

Meet with your writing group. Discuss what you learned from the experience of writing a personal narrative about writing and about yourself.

CHAPTER 5

Writing Lab

Project Corner

Think Creatively
Change Perspectives

Retell your narrative from another character's perspective. What changes when the story is told from another point of view?

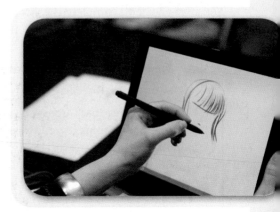

Connect across Cultures Read On

Read at least one memoir of a childhood by an author from a culture different from yours. Think about the author's conception of "home" in light of what you have written and discussed with your classmates and look for similarities and differences.

Get Artistic Try a Different Medium

Tell your story through an artistic medium, such as a drawing, painting, sculpture, story soundtrack, or other art form. What is gained and lost through your expression in a different form?

In Everyday Life
Narrative Friendly Letter

1. Your cousin is a city dweller. You live on a goat farm in a town with one stoplight. Your mother has invited your cousin to spend the summer with your family. You are worried that she might be bored and not fit into life on the farm. *Write a friendly letter* to your cousin preparing her for country life. Describe a "day in the life" of a country dweller. Use as much detail as possible to give your cousin an idea of what to expect. (You can find information on writing friendly letters on pages 400–401.)

In the Workplace Journal Entry

2. You have recently been promoted to head of the design department at the advertising company where you work. You are so excited that you can barely restrain yourself from jumping up and down on your desk and shouting out all of your ideas for the next big advertising campaign. *Write a journal entry* that relates the day you found out about your big promotion. Use vivid details and be sure to arrange them in a logical and coherent order. (You can find information on writing journal entries on pages 13–15.)

Timed Writing ⏱ Reflective Narrative Letter

3. You are a member of the school band and have earned a reputation as a top-notch tuba player. Last weekend the band played at the school's first football game of the season. The first half of the game passed uneventfully, but in the last half of the game, nearly everything went wrong! The scene was such a disaster that you have decided to write a reflective letter to your friend Bill to tell him about the events of the night. Write the letter to Bill that describes the episode at the football game. Decide whether to make the narrative hilarious or horrible. Put the events in chronological order and use first person point of view, with a topic sentence and concluding sentence for each paragraph. Remember to use specific and colorful details in describing the disaster and be sure to use transitions to help your narrative flow smoothly. You have 15 minutes to complete your work.

Before You Write Consider the following questions: What is the subject? What is the occasion? Who is the audience? What is the purpose?

After You Write Evaluate your work using the six-trait evaluation form on page 126.

Descriptive Writing

Descriptive writing uses words to create a vivid picture of a person, an object, or a scene.

Below are some examples of places where you might find descriptive writing in your daily life.

- **A coin collector creates a classified ad** to sell coins.
- **A travel agent creates a colorful brochure** describing a new package tour.
- **A journalist describes the latest fashions** appearing in the stores that season.
- **A detective observes and writes down every detail** to re-create the scene of a crime.
- **An author describes a giant that appears in her book** so the illustrator can begin work.

Writing Project

Think Big **Follow the directions below to write a description of an imaginary and very big pet.**

Think Through Writing Imagine that you have an enormous pet. It could be any sort of animal, from flea to rhinoceros, from unicorn to flying pig. But it is big. What would it look like? How would it act? How would you play with it? How would it help you? Let your imagination go and write about this large pet; do not let reality get in the way of your description.

Talk About It In your writing group, discuss the writing you have done. What sorts of animals have you written about? What are their powers? How does this animal interact with people and other animals? How would you describe the animals physically? Use as much detail as possible.

Read About It In the following selection, author Sterling North describes his gigantic St. Bernard dog. Think about how his interactions with his dog Wowser compare to your imaginary relationship with the pet you have written about. This selection begins with the arrival of a young raccoon into the narrator's life.

From

Rascal

Sterling North

It was in May, 1918, that a new friend and companion came into my life: a character, a personality, and a ring-tailed wonder. He weighed less than one pound when I discovered him, a furry ball of utter dependence and awakening curiosity, unweaned and defenseless. Wowser and I were immediately protective. We would have fought any boy or dog in town who sought to harm him.

Wowser was an exceptionally intelligent and responsible watchdog, guarding our house and lawns and gardens and all my pets. But because of his vast size—one hundred and seventy pounds of muscled grace and elegance—he seldom had to resort to any violence. He could shake any dog on the block as a terrier shakes a rat. Wowser never started a fight, but after being challenged, badgered, and insulted, he eventually would turn his worried face and great sad eyes upon his tormentor, and more in sorrow than in anger, grab the intruder by the scruff of the neck, and toss him into the gutter.

The opening paragraph describes a tiny raccoon and offers a picture of Wowser's protectiveness.

Details of Wowser's size are worked smoothly into the account of how he guarded the boy's home.

Vivid description of one of Wowser's actions helps readers get to know him well.

Wowser was an affectionate, perpetually hungry Saint Bernard. Like most dogs of his breed he drooled a little. In the house he had to lie with his muzzle on a bath towel, his eyes downcast as though in slight disgrace. Pat Delaney, a saloonkeeper who lived a couple of blocks up the street, said that Saint Bernards drool for the best of all possible reasons. He explained that in the Alps these noble dogs set forth every winter day, with little kegs of brandy strapped beneath their chins, to rescue wayfarers lost in the snowdrifts. Generations of carrying the brandy, of which they have never tasted so much as a blessed drop, have made them so thirsty that they continuously drool. The trait has now become hereditary, Pat said, and whole litters of bright and thirsty little Saint Bernards are born drooling for brandy.

The details make this scene of Wowser resting his head on a bath towel easy to picture.

On this pleasant afternoon in May, Wowser and I started up First Street toward Crescent Drive where a semicircle of late Victorian houses enjoyed a hilltop view. Northward lay miles of meadows, groves of trees, a winding stream, and the best duck and muskrat marsh in Rock County. As we turned down a country lane past Bardeen's orchard and vineyard, the signature of spring was everywhere: violets and anemones in the grass; the apple trees in promising bud along the bough.

This description of the area incudes many specific sights. It is arranged in spatial order and words like "northward" and "ahead" help guide the reader's eye through the scene.

Ahead lay some of the most productive walnut and hickory trees I had ever looted, a good swimming hole in the creek, and, in one bit of forest, a real curiosity—a phosphorescent stump which gleamed at night with foxfire, as luminescent as all the lightning bugs in the world—ghostly and terrifying to boys who saw it for the first time. It scared me witless as I came home one evening from fishing. So I made it a point to bring my friends that way on other evenings, not wishing to be selfish about my pleasures.

Respond in Writing Write about Sterling North's description of Wowser. How clearly can you picture Sterling and his dog? What details in the writing are helpful to you in imagining what they look like?

Develop Your Own Ideas Work with your classmates to develop ideas to assist you in writing a clear description of your imaginary pet.

Small Groups: Make a graphic organizer like the one below. In small groups, use it to chart the sorts of descriptions that you have generated so far to describe your imaginary pet.

Physical appearance	Types of actions the pet is capable of	How you interact with the pet	Why the pet is loyal to you and protects you

Whole Class: Make a master chart of all of the ideas generated by the small groups. As you work on your projects, refer to the chart for ways to describe your gigantic animal friends.

Write About It You will next write a description of your imaginary pet, using the following possible topics, audiences, and forms.

Possible Topics and Examples	Possible Audiences	Possible Forms
• an animal that is large in real life, such as an elephant • an enlarged version of a real animal, such as a toad the size of a truck • an enlarged version of a real animal, with special features or powers added, such as a fire-breathing, elephant-sized turtle • an enlarged mythical beast, such as a thunderbird the size of a house • an extinct creature, such as a mastodon • an animal that you make up entirely	• your parents, guardians, or other significant adults • people who want to harm you • people who are interested in having a pet just like yours • other owners of gigantic pets • people who visit your home	• an owner's manual • a tribute • a magazine article • a warning sign posted outside the pet's cage • a myth • a pet adoption description

Elements of Descriptive Writing

Like all good writing, effective descriptive paragraphs and essays have worthy ideas, plenty of support to back them up, a clear organization, and fluency in moving from one point to the next.

1 Descriptive Structure

Whether a single, stand-alone paragraph or a multi-paragraph essay, descriptive writing has a recognizable structure. The following chart shows how each part helps to complete the picture.

STRUCTURE OF A DESCRIPTIVE TEXT

- The **introduction** (or **topic sentence**, in a paragraph) identifies the subject and often suggests an overall tone, impression, or generalization.

- The **body** supplies specific details that appeal to the senses to bring the subject to life.

- The **conclusion** (or **concluding sentence**, in a paragraph) **s**ummarizes the subject or leaves a strong impression.

The following paragraph paints a dynamic picture.

MODEL: Descriptive Paragraph

The Jack Gore Baygall

The Jack Gore Baygall is a junglelike region about three miles wide and four miles long. Sunlight filters through one-hundred-foot-tall tupelos and cypresses, reaching the thick undergrowth in eerie green shafts. By night the sounds of animals moving, calling, warning others of their kind, fill the recesses of the baygall. It is the home of alligators, otters, beavers, hawks, owls, roadrunners, snakes, fox squirrels, and whitetail deer. Oaks growing out of the muck to heights of 135 feet sprouted from acorns in the days when America was only a British colony. The Jack Gore Baygall is a wild piece of the Big Thicket National Preserve.

— Howard Peacock, *The Big Thicket of Texas*

Topic Sentence

Supporting sentences with specific details

Concluding Sentence

The topic sentence of this paragraph gives the reader a clue about the kind of place the Jack Gore Baygall is: "a junglelike region." The descriptions of the eerie shafts of sunlight and the nighttime sounds of animals support this overall impression. The concluding sentence summarizes the impression by calling this area a "wild piece" of land.

● **Practice Your Skills**

Writing Descriptive Topic Sentences

For each subject, write a topic sentence that conveys an overall feeling.

Example	a swimming pool
Possible Answer	The empty pool looked forsaken with the dead leaves and branches lying at its bottom.

1. a wolf   **6.** a baby

2. the night sky   **7.** a hayride

3. a carnival   **8.** your kitchen

4. a grandparent   **9.** a fancy cake

5. a forest   **10.** a spaceship

PROJECT PREP *Evaluating* **Structure**

With your writing group, evaluate the structure of what you have written. Chances are it is not very tightly organized because you were just doing exploratory writing. For each writer, make suggestions about how to now provide a clear structure. Based on your group's feedback, make revisions.

2 Specific Details and Sensory Words

In descriptive writing, you state your overall impression of the subject. Your supporting details should then help your readers see what you see.

As you read the following descriptive paragraph, look for specific details and words that appeal to the senses.

> **Writing Tip**
>
> Use **specific details** and **sensory words** to bring your description to life.

MODEL: Specific Details and Sensory Words

The Square Dance

Stepping into the school auditorium on Tuesday nights is like traveling through time to the colorful days of the frontier barn dance. On the stage at the front of the hall, musicians in overalls and red bandanas stomp out the tunes for the dances. The middle of the floor creaks under the weight of the twirling dancers in their squares. The colors of the women's full skirts blur into a mosaic as partners swing around and around. From the back of the hall, the smells of popcorn being made in the kitchen tell the dancers that a break is coming up. Within minutes the tables set up along the back of the hall will be brimming with pitchers of ice-cold lemonade and bowls of popcorn. For a few short minutes, the dancers will cool off, but before long they will be back on the floor, reliving the fun of old-time dancing.

The topic sentence expresses an overall impression.

Specific sounds, sights, smells, and tastes provide the supporting details.

The concluding sentence provides a strong ending and refers back to an idea in the topic sentence.

Think Critically

Observing

When developing intense sensory details for descriptive writing, you can call on your skills of **observation.** Observing something is different from simply seeing it. When you observe a scene, you notice not only separate things that make it up, but also the relationships among those things. For example, while at the beach, you might see water lapping at the shore and sunbathers on blankets. With focused observation you may also be aware of the striking contrast between the natural landscape of water, sky, and sand, and the numerous objects such as boats, planes, and people that cover it. Careful observation allows the separate details of the scene—the seagulls, the wind and waves, the smells of suntan lotion—to form a whole, complete picture in your mind.

Thinking Practice

Use a chart like the one below to record your observations about a scene of your choosing. Share your chart with a partner and describe in detail what you observed.

SENSE	OBSERVATIONS
Sight	sand, colorful beach blankets
Touch	hot sand, hot sun, cool water
Sound	birds, lapping waves, wind, music
Smell	suntan lotion, sea air, sizzling hot dogs
Taste	salty water, lemonade

● Practice Your Skills

Identifying Sensory Details

List all the details in the paragraph on page 136 that appeal to the five senses: sight, sound, taste, smell, and touch.

Developing Sensory Details

Choose five of the following subjects. Under each one, write five sensory details you could use in a description.

1. Thanksgiving   **6.** a workshop

2. a wedding   **7.** a mountain lake

3. a football game   **8.** a newborn kitten

4. an old book   **9.** a run-down car

5. a horse   **10.** a pickle

PROJECT PREP   *Evaluating*   Details

In your writing group, help each author describe his or her subject according to the senses. What does it look, smell, sound, taste, and feel like? For each author, help to think of ways in which the subject could be described in greater detail. Don't simply announce a sense, as in, "My pet Chinese Phoenix has bad breath." Rather, use your imagination to fill your readers' senses, as in, "Each of the nine heads of my pet Chinese Phoenix breathes in a different flavor: licorice, lavender, compost heap, dumpster, mocha java, sour milk, rotten egg, lilac, and rubbing alcohol." Based on the feedback you get, make revisions to your description.

The Power of Language ⚡

Adjectives: What Kind?

A single descriptive word can sometimes speak volumes about a character, a place, a mood, or an event. In the following excerpt from *Rascal*, note how the author uses adjectives to intensify the action. **Adjectives** are words that modify nouns and pronouns and that answer the question "What kind?"

> But we couldn't have been more surprised when a **furious** mother raccoon exploded from her lair screaming her rage and dismay. Wowser nearly fell over backward to avoid the **flying** claws and **slashing little** teeth. A moment later the **big** raccoon had racked her way up a **slender** oak tree.

Here are more examples from *Rascal*.

Vague	He turned and looked at the raccoon. (The reader cannot relate to how Wowser is feeling.)
Vivid	After being challenged, badgered, and insulted, he eventually would turn his worried face and great sad eyes upon his tormentor. (The reader can relate to Wowser's anxiety and sadness—human qualities.)
Vague	Wowser was a dog. (What kind of dog?)
Vivid	Wowser was an affectionate, perpetually hungry Saint Bernard.

In the examples above, the adjectives come before the noun. An adjective can also come after a linking verb, modifying the subject of a sentence.

> Big words at times seem strange to the eye and the ear and the mind and the heart.

Sometimes, an entire group of words acts as an adjective, modifying a noun.

> I was standing on the driveway, alone, stock still, but shivering.

Try It Yourself

Find some sentences you have written that are vague or uninteresting. Try adding some adjectives to make your sentences vivid or exciting.

> **Punctuation Tip**
>
> If you use three adjectives in a series, separate them with commas, and put a comma before the final *and*.

③ Spatial Order and Transitions

One way to organize the details in a description is spatial, or location, order. Transitions used with spatial order tell how the details are related in space. They are like pointers that lead a reader's eye from spot to spot.

Spatial order arranges details according to their location. **Transitions** show the relationship of the details.

The following chart shows four directions commonly used with spatial order and some transitions associated with each one.

SPATIAL ORDER	TRANSITIONS
near to far (or reverse)	close by, beyond, around, farther, across, behind, in the distance
top to bottom (or reverse)	at the top, in the middle, lower, below, at the bottom, above, higher
side to side	at the left (right), in the middle, next to, at one end, to the west
inside to outside (or reverse)	within, in the center, on the inside (outside), the next layer

The following descriptive paragraph arranges details from top to bottom.

MODEL: Spatial Order

Yoda's Face

Every detail in the face of Yoda, the Jedi master in *The Empire Strikes Back*, suggests his wisdom and intelligence. His green body is dwarfed by his huge head. His high forehead gives the impression of a large, busy brain. **Beneath** his forehead his expressive eyes show both disappointment and hope at his young pupil's progress. His huge pointed ears that reach **the same level** as his eyes show his ability to take in sounds that others would miss. **Below** his eyes, a smallish nose twitches in response to events around him. **At the bottom** of his face, a mouth that knows how to stay shut reveals his ability to concentrate. At first sight, Yoda may appear ugly, but as you see his great intelligence at work, his face begins to show the wisdom of the Jedi masters.

Identifying Types of Spatial Order

Identify the type of spatial order used by writing *top to bottom, side to side, near to far,* or *outside to inside.*

1. The Animal Shelter

As I looked at the row of puppies, I wanted to adopt them all. In a cage to my left was a single black puppy, peacefully curled up with her nose warmed by her tail. Next to her was a litter of twelve-week-old beagle puppies, playfully pawing the cage and yelping with excitement. In the cage directly in front of me were two white, fluffy pups with wildly wagging tails. To my right, in the biggest cage, were a mother dog and her litter of four-week-old puppies who would stay with her for another month before being adopted. How would I ever choose?

2. The Piñata

Piñatas are a tradition at parties in my family. The piñata is a papier-mâché form, often in the shape of a burro, that is colorful on the outside and filled with surprises inside. The outside of the piñata is covered with brightly colored short strips of paper to suggest a burro's hair. Inside the piñata is a hollow space filled with small presents such as yo-yos, balls, twirlers, and other trinkets. The piñata is hung by twine from the ceiling. Near the end of the party, guests take turns hitting the piñata with a stick, eagerly waiting for it to split and the presents to come tumbling down.

3. My Sister Gwen

My five-year-old sister Gwen looks as mischievous as she usually is. A stubborn cowlick rises out of her sandy-colored hair, imitating Gwen's own strong will. Her bangs are cut straight across her forehead, but somehow they always seem to part in a funny spot on the left side. Her blue eyes always flash with humor when she tells a joke, while her long curly eyelashes give her an innocent look she sometimes hides behind. Gwen's cheeks are usually flushed, mainly because of her energetic dashing around the house and yard. Her delicate lips are often turned up in a tricky smile. Gwen looks like one of the family, but her own impish personality always shines through.

CHAPTER 6

PROJECT PREP   *Revising*   *Organization*

In your writing group, discuss ways to present the details in your description so that readers can follow them clearly. What is the most effective order of presentation for the details of your description? Help each author determine an appropriate order for the information in the description. Make revisions based on the suggestions you receive.

In the Media

Sound Bites

You may have heard about sound bites, but what are they exactly? A **sound bite** is a short audio or video clip that has been extracted from a larger piece of footage and used by television or radio stations to capture the interest of the viewer. A sound bite is used to summarize the most sensational or interesting ideas from a speech or interview. Often it is a phrase used by a public figure. For example, when former President George Bush indicated in the early 1990s that he would never raise taxes, he said, "Read my lips, no new taxes." This became a sound bite. Today the news media are in constant competition for our attention, and sound bites are used more and more to grab the viewer or listener and to get them to watch a news program, log on to a Web site, or listen to the radio.

Media Activity

Make an audio or video recording of yourself or a partner describing something you see every day, on your way to school, in your classroom, or at home. Be sure to discuss as many details of the object as you can. Then listen to or watch the recording to find a phrase or sentence you or your partner used that somehow sums up the object. If you can edit the tape, create your own sound bite. Play it for the class and ask them to tell you what it brings to mind.

Using a Six-Trait Rubric: Descriptive Writing

Strong descriptive writing has the traits identified in the first column. Use this rubric to evaluate descriptive writing.

Ideas	4 The text conveys an overall tone with abundant vivid details and is well suited to the purpose and audience.	3 The text conveys an overall tone with ample details and suits the purpose and audience.	2 The text conveys an overall tone with some vivid details and suits the purpose and audience.	1 The text does not convey an overall tone and fails to suit the purpose and audience.
Organization	4 The organization is clear with abundant transitions.	3 A few ideas seem out of place or transitions are missing.	2 Many ideas seem out of place and transitions are missing.	1 The organization is unclear and hard to follow.
Voice	4 The voice sounds natural, engaging, and personal.	3 The voice sounds natural and personal.	2 The voice sounds mostly unnatural with a few exceptions.	1 The voice sounds mostly unnatural.
Word Choice	4 Words are specific and powerful, rich in sensory images and figures of speech.	3 Words are specific and some words appeal to the senses.	2 Some words are overly general.	1 Most words are overly general.
Sentence Fluency	4 Varied sentences flow smoothly.	3 Most sentences are varied and flow smoothly.	2 Some sentences are varied but some are choppy.	1 Sentences are not varied and are choppy.
Conventions	4 Punctuation, usage, and spelling are correct. The Power Rules are all followed.	3 Punctuation, usage, and spelling are mainly correct and Power Rules are all followed.	2 Some punctuation, usage, and spelling are incorrect but all Power Rules are followed.	1 There are many errors and at least one failure to follow a Power Rule.

You can review all the Power Rules on pages 8–11.

The following checklist will also remind you of the elements of good descriptive writing.

 Evaluation Checklist for Revising

Checking Your Writing Overall
- ✓ Does your introduction identify the subject and suggest a tone and general impression of it? (pages 134–135)
- ✓ Do your supporting details bring your description to life? (pages 134 and 136)
- ✓ Does your composition have unity? (pages 75–76)
- ✓ Are your details in either spatial order or another logical order? (pages 76 and 93)
- ✓ Did you use transitions to give your writing coherence? (pages 75–76)
- ✓ Does your conclusion summarize the overall impression of the subject and provide a strong ending? (page 79)

Checking Sentences
- ✓ Did you combine related sentences to avoid too many short, choppy sentences in a row? (pages 53–57)
- ✓ Did you vary the beginnings of your sentences? (pages 58–59)
- ✓ Did you avoid rambling sentences? (page 60)
- ✓ Did you avoid repetition and empty expressions? (pages 61–62)

Checking Words
- ✓ Did you use specific, lively words? (pages 45–52)
- ✓ Did you use words that appeal to the senses? (pages 47–49)

editing

As always, look over your writing to be sure you have expressed yourself in as few words as possible. For practice at eliminating unnecessary words, edit the following sentence.

In my comfortable bed, I smell the familiar smell of the fragrance of the detergent my mom uses to wash the sheets, the point being that I feel so comfortable and relaxed in my bed.

The Language of Power  Suppose v. Supposed

Power Rule: Use the contraction *'ve* (not *of*) when the correct word is *have,* or use the full word *have.* Use *supposed* instead of *suppose* and *used* instead of *use* when appropriate. (See pages 789–791.)

See It in Action Confusing *suppose to* for *supposed to* would be understandable, because when spoken they often sound the same. In writing, though, confusions like that would be distracting to readers and would weaken the writing. In *Rascal,* North keeps his readers focused by assuring there are no distractions.

> You're supposed to catch her when she falls in the hazel brush.

Remember It Record this rule and example in the Power Rule section of your Personalized Editing Checklist.

Use It Read through your descriptive composition and make sure you have not used *suppose to* instead of *supposed to.* Also check for *use to* instead of *used to* and for *of* instead of *have* in such constructions as "He could *have* (not *of*) flown away."

CHAPTER 6

PROJECT PREP — Polishing / Final Draft

Exchange papers with a partner from your writing group and give each other final feedback using the rubric on page 143 and the checklist on page 144 as evaluation tools. Use your partner's suggestions to prepare a final, polished version of your description, checking for conventions as you prepare your work. Publish your description in the form you chose (see page 133) or another appropriate medium, such as a Web-based collection of writing about mythical beasts.

TIME OUT TO REFLECT In your Learning Log, write briefly about what you have learned about writing descriptions. How have you improved as a writer because of these activities? How have your peers helped you? How can you apply what you've learned to other writing projects?

Writing Lab

Project Corner

Think Critically
Classify

Take all of the pets created by all class members and **create a taxonomy** from them. A *taxonomy* is a scheme of classification broken down into Kingdom, Phylum, Class, Order, Family, Genus, and Species. How could you classify the animals in a chart that relates the various animals according to these categories?

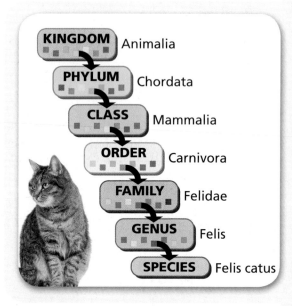

KINGDOM — Animalia
PHYLUM — Chordata
CLASS — Mammalia
ORDER — Carnivora
FAMILY — Felidae
GENUS — Felis
SPECIES — Felis catus

Think Creatively
Make a Game

Plan a video game based on the characters created by you and the other members of your writing group. What would a game featuring all of the gigantic pets look like? What would be the goal of playing It? How would a player use the animals? How would they interact? Would they cooperate or compete? Write up rules and share your game idea with the rest of the class.

Experiment Change Genres

Create a narrative based on your description in which you and the pet go on an adventure. How would the details you included in your description figure into a story that centers on you and your pet?

In Everyday Life
E-mail Message

1. Your family has decided to host an exchange student from Kenya named Sulia. The agency that runs the exchange program has asked you for a short e-mail message with specific details about your family, school, and community. They will pass on your description to Sulia and send you her comments about her family, school, and village in Kenya. *Write an e-mail* to Sulia explaining what makes your "homeland" unique. Include specific details and sensory words to create a vivid picture. Brainstorm for ideas first, and edit your message for coherence. (You can find information on writing e-mail messages on pages 451–455.)

In Academic Areas Informal Note

2. The year is 3508, and you are a scientist at Lunar State University. You are visiting Earth on a field trip and you have found the ruins of an ancient city from the early 2000s. Your boss has asked you for a brief update on your discovery. Among the ruins, you see a household object, such as an iron, a telephone, a television, or a personal computer. Although you pick up the object and observe it closely, you have no idea what it is or how it was used. *Write an informal note* to your boss describing your relic. Use sensory words and specific details to help your boss imagine the object.

Timed Writing 🕐 Family Profile

3. Your grandfather wants to create a family history book starting with a short profile, or description, of each living family member. He has asked you to describe someone in your family. You may choose your mother, father, brother, sister, cousin, aunt, uncle, or grandparent. List the person's characteristics or traits. Then limit your subject to one aspect of the person. Use your notes to draft a one-paragraph profile. Provide a clear structure for your profile and use specific details, sensory words, and transitions. You have 15 minutes to complete your work. (For help budgeting time, see pages 35 and 374-375.)

Before You Write Consider the following questions: What is the situation? What is the occasion? Who is the audience? What is the purpose?

After You Write Evaluate your work using the six-trait evaluation rubric on page 143.

Descriptive Writing Workshops

Writing a description is like making a movie. Like a set designer, you must create striking visual images. Like a sound operator, you must include sounds that go along with the scene. Finally, like a director, you must put all the details together to create an overall impression. Through prewriting, drafting, revising, and editing you will be able to shape your words into a moving picture.

1 Describing a Person

PREWRITING

When you are deciding on a subject to write about, pick someone you know. A friend, neighbor, or family member would be a good choice for the subject of a description. Limit your description to an aspect that you consider unique to that individual. You may wish to consider the following questions:

- What are your subject's facial features?
- What are your subject's facial expressions?
- What is your subject's hair like?
- How old is your subject?
- What kind of clothing does your subject like to wear?
- What is your subject's posture like?

Look through some photographs and choose a picture of a friend or a member of your family. Then develop a list of details, such as facial features, facial expression, hair, clothing, and posture. Arrange your details in a logical order.

DRAFTING

Without mentioning your subject's name, write a description of the friend or family member exactly as he or she appears in the photograph. Your purpose is to describe the person's appearance so well that other members of your family will be able to recognize who it is.

REVISING AND EDITING

Ask someone who knows your subject well to review your description. Ask your reviewer these questions: *Are you able to name the person I have described? What clues helped you to decide who it is? What other details might I have included?* Use the **Evaluation Checklist for Revising** on page 144 and the feedback from your reviewer to revise your work. When you are happy with your latest revision, spend some time polishing it. During the editing stage, carefully go over your paragraph, looking for any errors.

2 Creating and Describing a Scene

PREWRITING

The items listed below appeal to the sense of smell. Think of a scene that goes along with each one. Then write freely about each item using the questions that follow. After writing, draw a sketch of each scene.

pine	popcorn	campfire	hay	soap

1. What sights go along with this smell?
2. What sounds would I hear when I smell this?
3. What tastes, if any, go with this smell?
4. What might appeal to my sense of touch?

DRAFTING

Choose one item from the list. Use your freewriting notes and your sketch to write a descriptive paragraph that creates your scene in words. Be sure to include details that appeal to at least four of the five senses.

REVISING AND EDITING

Take turns reading your descriptive paragraphs out loud with a partner. When it is your turn to listen, take note of the words and phrases you hear that appeal to your senses. Are there enough sensory words to create a vivid picture? Share your comments with your partner. Use your partner's comments and your own judgment to revise your paragraph. When you are satified with your draft, edit it for usage, mechanics, and spelling. Check carefully to make sure you followed all the Power Rules.

CHAPTER 7

Creative Writing

Creative writing takes many forms. In addition to stories, authors may choose to write plays, poems, movie scripts, songs, or comic strips. Creative writing does not have to be serious; it can be humorous, tragic, suspenseful, or whimsical. Whatever you can imagine, you can create.

Here are some examples of ways creative writing is used in daily life.

- **The creator of a comic strip writes humorously** about life in his neighborhood.
- **A poet uses poetic forms** to tell about a visit to a new country.
- **Comedians write funny sketches** about current events.
- **A songwriter uses rhyming lyrics and music** to tell about a beautiful autumn afternoon.
- **A short story author writes** about an event that is interpreted differently by the onlookers.
- **A playwright writes** a drama about pioneers seeking a new life for various reasons.

Writing Project — Imaginative Story

Point of View Write an imaginative story about two people who view an event differently and the conflict that results.

Think Through Writing Consider a situation in which two people view something that happened completely differently. It could be a situation you have some knowledge of or it could be entirely imagined. Think about why two individuals might have different impressions of the same event. Examine whether their age, gender, social situation, or other issues might influence their perception. Write freely about a situation that comes to mind, providing as many details as you can, and without worrying about grammar, spelling, or punctuation.

Talk About It In your writing group, discuss the different perspectives you have described. How do the two perspectives differ? In what way are they alike? Compare the two people involved, and discuss reasons for their perspectives.

Read About It In the following selection, author Langston Hughes tells a story that begins with a confrontation and then takes a surprising twist. Think about his characters in light of the situation you have begun to investigate in your writing.

MODEL: Short Story

Thank You, M'am

She was a large woman with a large purse that had everything in it but hammer and nails. It had a long strap and she carried it slung across her shoulder. It was about eleven o'clock at night, and she was walking alone, when a boy ran up behind her and tried to snatch her purse. The strap broke with the single tug the boy gave it from behind. But the boy's weight, and the weight of the purse combined, caused him to lose his balance so, instead of taking off full blast as he had hoped, the boy fell on his back on the sidewalk, and his legs flew up. The large woman simply turned around and kicked him right square in his blue-jeaned sitter. Then she reached down, picked the boy up by his shirt front, and shook him until his teeth rattled.

After that the woman said, "Pick up my pocketbook, boy, and give it here."

She still held him. But she bent down enough to permit him to stoop and pick up her purse. Then she said, "Now ain't you ashamed of yourself?"

Firmly gripped by his shirt front, the boy said, "Yes'm."

The woman said, "What did you want to do it for?"

The boy said, "I didn't aim to."

She said, "You a lie!"

By that time two or three people passed, stopped, turned to look, and some stood watching.

"If I turn you loose, will you run?" asked the woman.

"Yes'm," said the boy.

"Then I won't turn you loose," said the woman. She did not release him.

"I'm very sorry, lady, I'm sorry," whispered the boy.

"Um-hum! And your face is dirty. I got a great mind to wash your face for you. Ain't you got nobody home to tell you to wash your face?"

"No'm," said the boy.

"Then it will get washed this evening," said the large woman starting up the street, dragging the frightened boy behind her.

He looked as if he were fourteen or fifteen, frail and willow-wild, in tennis shoes and blue jeans.

The woman said, "You ought to be my son. I would teach you right from wrong. Least I can do right now is to wash your face. Are you hungry?"

"No'm," said the being-dragged boy. "I just want you to turn me loose."

"Was I bothering you when I turned that corner?" asked the woman.

"No'm"

"But you put yourself in contact with *me*," said the woman. "If you think that contact is not going to last awhile, you got another thought coming. When I get through with you, sir, you are going to remember Mrs. Luella Bates Washington Jones."

Sweat popped out on the boy's face and he began to struggle. Mrs. Jones stopped, jerked him around in front of her, put a half nelson about his neck, and continued to drag him up the street. When she got to her door, she dragged the boy inside, down a hall, and into a large kitchenette-furnished room at the rear of the house. She switched on the light and left the door open. The boy could hear other roomers laughing and talking in the large house. Some of their doors were opened, too, so he knew he and the woman were not alone. The woman still had him by the neck in the middle of her room.

She said, "What is your name?"

"Roger," answered the boy.

"Then, Roger, you go to that sink and wash your face," said the woman, whereupon she turned him loose—at last. Roger looked at the door—looked at the woman—looked at the door—*and went to the sink*.

"Let the water run until it gets warm," she said. "Here's a clean towel."

"You gonna take me to jail?" asked the boy, bending over the sink.

"Not with that face, I would not take you nowhere," said the woman. "Here I am trying to get home to cook me a bite to eat and you snatch my pocketbook! Maybe you ain't been to your supper either, late as it be. Have you?"

"There's nobody home at my house," said the boy.

"Then we'll eat," said the woman. "I believe you're hungry—or been hungry—to try to snatch my pocketbook."

"I wanted a pair of blue suede shoes," said the boy.

"Well, you didn't have to snatch *my* pocketbook to get some suede shoes," said Mrs. Luella Bates Washington Jones. "You could of asked me."

"M'am?"

The water dripping from his face, the boy looked at her. There was a long pause. A very long pause. After he had dried his face and not knowing what else to do dried it again, the boy turned around, wondering what next. The door was open. He could make a dash for it down the hall. He could run, run, run, run, *run!*

The woman was sitting on the daybed. After a while she said, "I were young once and I wanted things I could not get."

There was another long pause. The boy's mouth opened. Then he frowned, but not knowing he frowned.

The woman said, "Um-hum! You thought I was going to say *but*, didn't you? You thought I was going to say, *but I didn't snatch people's pocketbooks.* Well, I wasn't going to say that." Pause. Silence. "I have done things, too, which I would not tell you, son—neither tell God, if he didn't already know. So you set down while I fix us something to eat. You might run that comb through your hair so you will look presentable."

In another corner of the room behind a screen was a gas plate and an icebox. Mrs. Jones got up and went behind the screen. The woman did not watch the boy to see if he was going to run now, nor did she watch her purse which she left behind her on the daybed. But the boy took care to sit on the far side of the room where he thought she could easily see him out of the corner of her eye, if she wanted to. He did not trust the woman not to trust him. And he did not want to be mistrusted now.

"Do you need somebody to go to the store," asked the boy, "maybe to get some milk or something?"

"Don't believe I do," said the woman, "unless you just want sweet milk yourself. I was going to make cocoa out of this canned milk I got here."

"That will be fine," said the boy.

She heated some lima beans and ham she had in the icebox, made the cocoa, and set the table. The woman did not ask the boy anything about where he lived, or his folks, or anything else that would embarrass him. Instead as they ate, she told him about her job in a hotel beauty shop that stayed open late, what the work was like, and how all kinds of women came in and out, blondes, redheads, and brunettes. Then she cut him a half of her ten-cent cake.

"Eat some more, son," she said.

When they were finished eating she got up and said, "Now, here, take this ten dollars and buy yourself some blue suede shoes. And next time, do not make the mistake of latching on to *my* pocketbook *nor nobody else's*—because shoes come by devilish like that will burn your feet. I got to get my rest now. But I wish you would behave yourself, son, from here on in."

She led him down the hall to the front door and opened it. "Good night! Behave yourself, boy!" she said, looking out into the street.

The boy wanted to say something else other than, "Thank you, m'am," to Mrs. Luella Bates Washington Jones, but he couldn't do so as he turned at the barren stoop and looked back at the large woman in the door. He barely managed to say, "Thank you," before she shut the door. And he never saw her again.

Respond in Writing Write freely about how you perceived the perspectives of each of the characters as the story begins. Then write about how their perspectives might have changed during their lunch, and later. What do you think is different in their perspectives after the boy leaves Mrs. Jones?

Develop Your Own Story Ideas Work with your classmates to develop ideas for an imaginative story about two characters who see things from different perspectives.

Small Groups: Discuss the writing you have done. Answer the following questions to help think of details for each author's story.

Questions for Thinking of Details
• Where will the story take place? How might this affect the story?
• What is the nature of the situation that is viewed differently by the two main characters?
• How is the situation viewed by one of the two characters?
• How is the situation viewed by the other main character?
• How, if at all, will the different perceptions be resolved in the story?
• How does the action move the story along?

Whole Class: Make a master chart of all of the ideas generated by the small groups to compare the differences in perspectives of the two characters and the problems that may arise as a consequence.

Write About It You will next write a short story about two people who view the same event in different ways. You might choose from any of the topics, audiences, and forms in the chart below.

Possible Topics and Examples	Possible Audiences	Possible Forms
• two people witness an accident and each describes what happened differently	• parents	• a short story
	• teenagers	• a narrative poem
• two friends interpret the remarks of a third friend very differently	• a teacher	• a television or movie script
	• a judge	• a graphic novel
• two people on opposite sides of an issue see the issue in very different ways		
• a police officer and a citizen view a situation from very different perspectives		

Analyzing a Story

A **short story** is a fictional account of characters facing a conflict or problem.

Your purpose in writing a short story is to entertain and perhaps enlighten your reader (and yourself). You will use your narrative skills and your descriptive skills as you write. As the narrative unfolds, you will describe the characters, situation, and surroundings in order for the reader to gain a clear picture of what is happening.

Learn more about narrative and descriptive writing on pages 110–129 and 130–149.

ELEMENTS OF A SHORT STORY

All short stories have three main parts: The beginning introduces the characters and the problem or conflict. The writer provides all the background information that readers need to understand the story right from the beginning. Readers find out where the story takes place, who the main characters are, and what problem, or **conflict,** the main character has to face or overcome.

The middle of the story develops the **plot;** that is, the writer tells what happens (usually in the order it happens) as a result of the conflict and how the characters react to those events.

As the conflict develops, the action rises until it hits its highest level, the **climax.** The climax involves a dramatic event that is the high point of the story. The ending of the story tells the outcome, or **resolution,** of the central conflict.

Plot and Central Conflict The plot is the story's core. It tells what happens as the characters meet and struggle to resolve the conflict. This conflict can come from within a character, such as a conflict of conscience; between characters, such as a conflict between friends; or between characters and the outside world, such as a struggle against the forces of nature. After resolving the conflict (or explaining why it remains unresolved), the story ends.

Characters Most short stories focus on one main character who has or faces the conflict, or on two main characters whose relationship is often the source of the conflict. The other characters in the story—the minor, or supporting, characters—either help or hinder the main character in resolving the crisis. In the best short stories, characters are colorful, authentic, and memorable to readers in some way. Authors develop characters through narration, description, dialogue, and setting.

Setting The **setting** of a story is where the action takes place. It is like the scenery and props on a stage set. The setting also includes the time during which the story occurs. An author will often create settings that match the character's feelings or reflect his or her place in society.

Mood The **mood** of the story is the atmosphere created by the author's descriptions. Mood is also defined as the way you feel when you are reading the story. The mood of "Thank You, Ma'm" might be described as positive, even humorous.

Narrator The person who tells the story is the **narrator.** Readers see the events of a story through the eyes of the narrator, or from the narrator's **point of view.** When the point of view is first person, the narrator is involved in the events of the story and refers to himself or herself using the pronoun *I.* A third-person narrator is an observer, relating events that happen to the characters and sometimes the characters' thoughts and feelings as well.

The chart below shows the important elements most short stories should have.

SHORT STORY ELEMENTS	
Narrator	the person telling the story; either first person (if the person telling the story is a participant) or third person (if the person is telling about what happened to others)
Setting	the time and place in which the story takes place
Characters	the people, animals, or others involved in the story
Conflict	the problem at the heart of the story
Triggering Event	the event that starts the story rolling
Climax	the point in the story when the conflict or problem is most serious
Resolution	how the problem or conflict is solved
Dialogue	words spoken by the characters
Description	writing that helps the reader see, hear, feel, taste, or smell what is happening

Theme Most short stories have a **theme,** or main idea. Often the theme is an idea or message about life, society, or human nature. The outcome of the story may then imply some lesson or moral about the theme, or it may affirm some meaningful observation or conclusion about life. However, some short stories aim chiefly to inform, surprise, or entertain readers rather than to convey a message.

WRITING OUTSTANDING STORIES

If all stories have the same elements, what makes some better than others? Look at the chart on the next page for the qualities of outstanding stories. Keep them in mind as you write your stories.

Writing an Outstanding Story

- Create interesting, "3-D" characters, showing their unique personalities through dialogue, actions, thoughts, and feelings.

- Create a believable, easy-to-imagine setting, rich in details that appeal to the senses.

- Base your story on an engaging plot, one that keeps the reader wanting to read on to find out what happens next.

- Pace your story skillfully. Don't let the action of the story get bogged down in unnecessary information.

- Put your words to work for you. Pack your story with style and energy by using such literary devices as similes, metaphors, and other figures of speech.

- Show your attitude toward your characters and storyline through the tone you establish.

Practice Your Skills

Analyzing a Short Story

Reread "Thank you, M'am" on pages 151–153. Then write answers to the following items.

1. What is the setting of this narrative?

2. Who are the characters in the story? Describe them.

3. Is the narrator a character in the story?

4. What is the conflict or problem in this story?

5. In your own words, summarize the events in this story.

6. Choose one sentence of description from the story and write it down.

PROJECT PREP *Evaluating* *Story Sketch*

Based on the discussions you have had with your classmates, your reading of "Thank You, Ma'm," and the charts on these pages, sketch out the imaginative story you will write. Turn a piece of 8 ½" by 11" paper sideways and make three columns. In the first column, write the elements in a short story, using the chart on the previous page as a guide. In the second column, write ideas for your own story next to each of the elements in the first column. In the third column, write the details that will help make your plot, setting, characters, and literary style outstanding. Share your chart with your writing group for feedback.

Think Critically

Predicting

A good short story writer gives readers information that will enable them to logically predict what might be coming next. **Predicting** means using available information to foretell a future outcome. Before football games, for example, sports announcers often make predictions about who will win the game based on what they know about the players, their drive to win, past successes and failures, and injuries that may give one team an advantage over another. The only worthwhile predictions are those based on available information.

As readers, you probably make predictions more often than you realize. On what do you base your predictions? You base them on such things as other stories you have read, similar situations you are aware of, and your own life experiences. You also base your predictions on the details, or clues, in the work you are reading—the clues planted by the author. Good writers know they can shape their readers' expectations with well-chosen details.

Thinking Practice

Explore your ability to make predictions by reading a story that appears later in this book, "Checkouts" by Cynthia Rylant, on pages 249–251. Stop reading after the eighth paragraph. Then write your impressions of the story so far and briefly tell the situation. Using information in the story and your past reading experiences, predict how the story will end. Then finish reading the story. Afterward return to your prediction and, in writing, tell whether or not your prediction came true. If it did come true, explain how you came to that conclusion. If it did not come true, explain what elements in the story led you to believe that it would.

1 Developing the Key Elements

When choosing a subject, search your memory and imagination for experiences that stand out as interesting or important. Then use them as the basis for establishing characters, plot, setting, and point of view.

SKETCHING INTERESTING CHARACTERS

Characters thrust into a puzzling, threatening, or desperate situation can make a good basis for a story. You might create a story character by mixing together details of yourself and other people, such as the determined way you approach challenges, the way your third-grade teacher walked, the color of your best friend's hair, and the laugh of your Great-Aunt Matilda. Below are sketches of the characters created by Langston Hughes in "Thank you, M'am." Notice how the descriptions include both physical and personality traits.

EXAMPLE: Character Sketches

Luella Bates Washington Jones	Urban, large, physically strong, stern, intimidating, kind, no-nonsense, uses *ain't* in speech, hardworking, works in a hotel beauty shop, middle-aged, may have a "past"
Roger	Urban, skinny, fourteen or fifteen, speech reflects urban street culture, probably poor and feeling defeated, desperately wants blue-suede shoes, a good kid inside

Interesting characters, like interesting people, are complex. They have a past that has helped shape them into the characters they are at the beginning of a story. Something in that same past, however, may also help them undergo a change as the story progresses and come out of the story a somewhat different person.

As you read the following beginning of a short story, note how much you learn about the mother from only a few well-chosen details. How would you describe her?

CHAPTER 7

STUDENT MODEL: *Interesting Character*

Tying her sparkly shoelaces, Rosie imagined all the fun that she was going to have playing with her best friend, Crystal, on that fine Saturday morning. Rosie hurried to eat the breakfast her mom had made for her.

"Rosie, honey, I made your favorite breakfast! Smilin' pancakes and scrambled eggs with ketchup in a zigzag pattern."

Lisa, Rosie's mom, had wakened to a horrible dream. She had dreamed about losing Rosie in a car accident. So to make herself feel better, she made her daughter that fabulous breakfast.

Marbella Maldonado, Lucyle Collins Middle School, Fort Worth, Texas

BUILDING AN ENGAGING PLOT

Ideas for your plot can come from anywhere: something you've read, a dream you had, a friend's experience. The following strategies may stimulate your imagination.

Strategies for Developing Your Plot

- Brainstorm for a list of story ideas based on conflicts you have read about, thought about, or experienced firsthand. Then use clustering or inquiring to develop plot details. For each conflict you think of, identify the triggering event and describe the resolution or outcome.
- Scan newspaper headlines and news items for an event you could build into a fictional story.
- Think of conflicts or events in history—including your family history and local history—that might be interesting to develop in fiction writing.
- Observe people and events in your life. Sometimes even small events or snatches of conversation will suggest a conflict on which to build a plot. An argument that you overheard at the coffee shop could become the basis of a story.

Characters and plot merge in the heart of a story, the conflict. The chart on the next page can help you develop the conflict creatively by exploring the characters' motivations and ability to change.

Strategies for Developing the Conflict

1. Introduce the event that triggers the conflict. Make the source of the conflict clear.

   From within a character   the desire to change one's circumstances

   From the outside world   an accident, a phone call, a letter

2. Develop details describing the nature of the conflict.

   Conflict with self   one's conscience

   Conflict with others   friend, family, enemies, strangers

   Conflict with circumstances   illness, disease, disability, loss, assault

3. Develop details about the characters' struggles to resolve the conflict.

   Within a character   fears or other emotions

   In the outside world   other characters, society

4. Develop details showing how the conflict is resolved.

   Obstacles overcome   new wisdom, success or satisfaction

   Obstacles not overcome   acceptance of shortcomings, decision to try again

Writing Tip

You might want to create a story map, which gives an overview of your story's plot from start to finish. Write a sentence explaining each major event from the beginning to the end of the story.

CREATING A BELIEVABLE SETTING

You've established your plot, conflict, and characters. Now you can work on creating a believable setting. First determine the location and time of your story. Then elaborate on the setting with details that will bring it to life. Notice how the details on the following page give the setting a vivid mood in "Thank you, M'am."

SETTING OF "THANK YOU, M'AM"	
Where	**When**
city	evening
a quiet street	recent past
a rooming house	11:00 P.M.
large kitchenette-furnished room	probably summer

CHOOSING A POINT OF VIEW

Every story has a narrator, the person whose written "voice" is telling the story. Readers see the story unfolding through the eyes, or **point of view,** of the narrator. If the narrator takes part in the story, the narrative is said to have a **first-person** point of view. If the narrator tells what happens to others and is not a character in the story, the narrative has a **third-person** point of view.

Writing Tip

Use the first-person point of view if the narrator is a character in the story. Use the third-person point of view if the narrator is telling what happened to others.

Compare the two story openers below. Both introduce the same narrative. Each, however, is told from a different point of view. Notice the different pronouns used in each.

EXAMPLE: Points of View

First Person
Last year, on an early spring evening, **I** was looking forward to having the house to **myself. My** parents were going out to dinner, and **my** younger sister was staying overnight at a friend's house. For about four hours, **I** would be alone in the house. **I** could play **my** CDs as loudly as **I** wanted.

Third Person
Last year, on an early spring evening, **Mark** was looking forward to having the house to **himself. His** parents were going out to dinner, and **his** younger sister was staying overnight at a friend's house. For about four hours, **he** would be alone in the house. **He** could play **his** CDs as loudly as **he** wanted.

Each point of view has certain advantages. Because the first-person point of view involves a narrator who is a part of and comments on the action, the reader gets an intimate, firsthand look at the story. However, the first-person narrator may withhold information based on his or her own prejudices, so the reader must be aware of that. The third-person point of view gives the writer great flexibility. Using third person, the writer can reveal the thoughts and feelings of all the characters in the story. Additionally, events happening simultaneously in different places can be revealed.

PROJECT PREP *Prewriting* Key Story Elements

1. Write sketches of your characters and read them to your writing group members. Ask for your group's response: Do they get a clear picture of each character? Are there details of each character's appearance that would help readers envision the person? Are there clues that suggest how a character might change, or resist changing, as the story progresses?

2. Using your group's feedback about the characters, develop a map for your imaginative story. Indicate the central conflict and each event, from the beginning of the story to the end, and write a sentence explaining each major event.

3. Focus next on the setting of your story. Where would the characters come into contact? What characterizes the physical setting of their meeting? What sensory details can you use to create a suitable mood for their encounter? Make another graphic organizer showing your ideas for a setting.

4. Finally, imagine how your story would read if it were told from the point of view of one of your main characters or the other, or from a third person's viewpoint. Choose the point of view you think will work best.

5. Share all your ideas with your writing group. Offer comments and suggestions to each writer on how he or she might create more interesting characters, a more engaging plot, a more believable setting, or a more appropriate point of view. Keep notes of your group's feedback to use when you draft your story.

2 Ordering Events

After you have your basic story elements in place, visualize all the events you will write about in the order in which they will happen, called **chronological order.** This order helps readers follow the events as they rise to their climax and are resolved at the end. You may decide to rearrange this order later, but the order you use in your first draft will at least help you keep track of the events you plan to include. You may want to use the following questions to help you list all the separate events in your story in the proper order.

Listing Events in Chronological Order

- What happens to start the story rolling?
- What happens next? Next? Next?
- What is the climax of the story?
- What finally happens to resolve the conflict?
- How does the story end?

List all the events in your story in chronological order. Include the event that starts the story in motion, the climax of the story, the resolution of the conflict, and the outcome. You might want to use index cards or sticky notes and write one event in the story on each paper. That way you can easily rearrange the events to put them in just the order you want.

PROJECT PREP   *Prewriting*   *Order of Events*

Arrange the events of your plot in chronological order. Then, in your writing group, talk through the story. Tell it out loud and make sure that the order of events seems clear to your writing group partners. Make any adjustments in your ordering that might improve the unfolding of the story.

The Power of Language ⚡

Appositives: Who or What?

You can enhance the style of your creative writing by adding details that elaborate on the people, places, or things you are exploring. As you draft, you can add such details in the form of appositive phrases. An **appositive phrase** is a noun or pronoun phrase that identifies or adds identifying information to a preceding noun, usually a person, place, or thing. (See pages 592–594.) The following sentence from *The Fixed* by Annie Dillard (pages 85–86) contains an appositive phrase at the end that describes the appearance of a moth emerging from a cocoon. Notice that the appositive phrase is set off by a comma.

Appositive Phrase   It emerged at last, a sodden crumple.

In the example below from *Rascal* by Sterling North (pages 131–132), the appositive phrase adds identifying information about a character in a story. Here the phrase comes in the middle of the sentence. Notice that commas separate the appositive phrase from the rest of the sentence.

Appositive Phrase   Pat Delaney, a saloonkeeper who lived a couple of blocks up the street, said that Saint Bernards drool for the best of all possible reasons.

Try It Yourself

Try writing one sentence with each of the above structures on your project topic. Use the resulting sentences in your draft if you can, and try creating other similar sentences. You can always add more details with appositives when you revise.

> ### Punctuation Tip
>
> Use two commas to enclose an appositive in the middle of a sentence. Use one comma to separate an appositive from the rest of the sentence when it appears at the end.

Writing a Short Story **Drafting**

Good stories draw readers into the action and make them feel involved. Before you begin writing your short story, think about what you enjoy most as you read stories. Do you like characters with whom you can identify? Do you like a lot of action, humor, or suspense?

As you work on the first draft of your short story, keep your audience in mind. Add details that will make your narrative more interesting to readers and leave out unnecessary details that slow down the **pace** of the story or lead your readers to false predictions. Use the following strategies, which are specific to fiction writing, to draft your story.

Strategies for Drafting a Short Story

- Use vivid language and interesting details to introduce the characters and the central conflict.
- Use sensory details to create a mood.
- Use background details to set the time and place of the story and to capture your readers' interest.
- Aim for originality in your writing by avoiding stereotypes and by using vivid words to bring the story to life.
- Start the plot early in the story by introducing the triggering event.
- Reveal the characters and unfold the plot through a combination of description; narration, or action; and dialogue.
- Maintain a clear and consistent point of view.
- Pace your story by including only those events that have a direct bearing on the plot and the central conflict.
- Connect the events in your story by showing how each event in the plot relates naturally and logically to the central conflict.
- Use chronological order and transitions to show the passing of time and to build up tension.
- End your story in a way that makes the outcome clear and that reflects on the narrated experiences.

USING DIALOGUE

When you write the actual words that the characters speak, the characters spring to life. A conversation between characters in a story is called **dialogue.** Reread the dialogue in "Yes, Ma'm." Notice how natural it sounds, and how much it tells you about each speaker.

EXAMPLES: Using Dialogue

To present the central conflict	. . . a boy ran up . . . and tried to snatch her purse. . . . "Now ain't you ashamed of yourself?" . . . "Yes'm." The woman said, "What did you want to do it for?" The boy said, "I didn't aim to." She said, "You a lie!"
To reveal thoughts	The woman said, "You ought to be my son. I would teach you right from wrong. Least I can do right now is to wash your face. Are you hungry?"
To advance the plot	"You gonna take me to jail?" asked the boy . . . "Not with that face, I would not take you nowhere," said the woman. "Here I am trying to get home to cook me a bite to eat and you snatch my pocketbook! Maybe you ain't been to your supper either, late as it be. Have you?" "There's nobody home at my house," said the boy. "Then we'll eat," said the woman.
To express the climax	"Now, here, take this ten dollars and buy yourself some blue suede shoes. And next time, do not make the mistake of latching on to *my* pocketbook *nor nobody else's*—because shoes come by devilish like that will burn your feet.
To express the resolution	The boy wanted to say something else other than, "Thank you, ma'am," to Mrs. Luella Bates Washington Jones, but he couldn't do so. . . . He barely managed to say, "Thank you," before she shut the door.

● Practice Your Skills

Writing Dialogue

Imagine each of the following situations. Then select one of the situations or another of your choice and write a dialogue about 10 lines long between the characters. You may want to review the correct form for writing dialogue on the preceding pages.

1. The postal carrier brings you a box from an unknown address.

2. Your parents tell you they are unhappy with your recent behavior.

3. You disagree with a friend about a political issue.

4. You are babysitting for the first time for a six-year-old with attitude.

5. A driver turns a corner and nearly runs you over as you ride your bike.

ENHANCING THE PLOT

One of the great pleasures of reading is the sense of being swept up in a story. You may feel anxious as you read, fearing trouble ahead for the main character. You may be intrigued by missing pieces in the story that are only revealed in unexpected places or unexpected order. These feelings are the result of the writer's skill in using devices to enhance the plot and keep the reader turning the pages. Try using these devices to add excitement and flavor to your plot.

DEVICES FOR ENHANCING THE PLOT

Flashback	an event from the past that is presented out of order and interrupts the chronological order
Foreshadowing	clues that help the reader anticipate what is to come
Story within a Story	a story that is told during the telling of another story
Subplot	a secondary plot line that reinforces the main plot line
Juxtaposition	placing two normally unrelated events, characters, or words next to one another to create a surprise effect

editing ☆

The following sentences are an attempt to use foreshadowing, but too much information is given. Revise the passage, deleting unnecessary words and excess information.

Meg stood at the murky water's edge. She looked across the water and saw the sparkling harbor of Snug Island. The waves seemed to beckon sweetly to her to slip in the water. If only she could swim. She would dive in and pull herself along to the distant shore. Or would she drown? No, she would swim!

PROJECT PREP *Drafting* *Dialogue and Plot Techniques*

After reviewing all your prewriting work and feedback about character, setting, plot, and narrator, write the first draft of the short story you have been developing. Work in dialogue that sounds realistic and that advances the plot. Use such literary strategies and devices as figurative language, flashback, and juxtaposition to enhance your style. Use peer conferencing to test your ideas or to get help with trouble spots. Keep writing until you have a workable first draft.

In the Media

Evaluating Performances

Some literary works are wonderful when they are performed. This process can in fact help the audience understand the work more fully. Books on tape, poetry readings on the radio, and literary television shows attract faithful audiences.

How can you tell if a performance is effective? Here is a list of criteria that may help you evaluate artistic performances.

Criteria for Evaluating Performances

✓ Does the performance move you?

✓ Does the performance make confusing parts clearer?

✓ Do the performers communicate using their bodies as well as voices?

✓ Do the performers use vocal variety to express the work's underlying meanings?

✓ Does the performance use the stage effectively, with variety of pacing and use of space?

✓ Are camera angles, lighting, sequencing, and music used effectively? How do they contribute to the overall effect?

Media Activity

Use the criteria above to evaluate the following:

- A poem such as "Like Scales" on pages 184–185 or another of your choice that you perform for your class.

- A short story read on the radio. Check your National Public Radio station for story broadcasts.

- A video presentation of a literary work.

Share your evaluation with your classmates.

Most writers agree that their first drafts are good starting points but rarely good enough ending points. Usually the effort of just getting your ideas down in a smooth, flowing form takes all your concentration when drafting. Once your draft is on paper, however, you can stand back from it and concentrate on improving it. Use the checklist below.

Evaluation Checklist for Revising

✓ Does the beginning of your story describe the setting, engage and orient readers, introduce characters, and include the triggering event? (page 166)

✓ Does the middle develop the plot by making the central conflict clear and by using transition words to keep the action moving? (pages 160–161)

✓ Are events in the plot arranged in chronological order or in an order that makes the chronology of events clear? (pages 164 and 166)

✓ Does the story build until the action reaches a climax? (page 168)

✓ Did you use such narrative techniques as dialogue, pacing, description, and reflection to keep the story moving and bring your characters to life? (pages 166–167)

✓ Does the ending show how the conflict was resolved and follow from the narrated experience? (pages 155 and 166)

✓ Did you choose an appropriate point of view and stick to it throughout the story? (pages 162–163)

✓ Does the story have a theme or express your reasons for writing it? Does it accomplish your specific purpose for creative writing? (pages 155–156)

✓ Did you use various techniques to enhance the style and tone? (pages 156–157 and 168)

PROJECT PREP Revising Using a Checklist

Pair off in your writing group and exchange papers. Use the checklist above to evaluate your partner's story. Revise your work based on your partner's feedback. Write a new draft of your story. In this version, in addition to your development of the setting, characters, and events of the story, make sure that your grammar, punctuation, and spelling are correct so that your readers will not be distracted.

When you are satisfied with your short story, read through one more time for errors in grammar, spelling, usage, and mechanics. As you edit, check for commonly misspelled words such as *their, they're,* and *there.* (See **A Writer's Glossary of Usage** on pages 782–791 for more commonly misused words.) Also make sure you have always used complete sentences.

PUNCTUATING DIALOGUE

When writing dialogue you show a person's exact words with quotation marks. The following example shows how dialogue should look on the page.

> The woman said, "You ought to be my son. I would teach you right from wrong. Least I can do right now is to wash your face. Are you hungry?"
>
> "No'm," said the being-dragged boy. "I just want you to turn me loose."

The following guidelines will help you present clear dialogue.

Guidelines for Using Dialogue

- Use quotation marks to enclose a person's words.
- Capitalize the first word of a direct quotation.
- Use a comma to separate a direct quotation from a speaker tag, such as *the woman said* or *he replied.*
- Place punctuation inside the closing quotation marks when the end of the quotation comes at the end of the sentence.
- When writing dialogue, begin a new paragraph each time the speaker changes.

A direct quotation can appear before or after a speaker tag. A speaker tag can also interrupt a direct quotation. The quotation marks enclose only the speaker's words.

Editing Checklist

✓ Have you used a new paragraph for each change of speaker?
✓ Have you enclosed exact quotes in quotation marks?
✓ Have you used commas to separate direct quotations from speaker tags?

The Language of **Power**   *Negatives*

Power Rule: Use only one negative form for a single negative idea. (See page 773.)

See It in Action In formal writing, two negative words should not be used to express the same idea.

Double Negative	She doesn't know nothing about the surprise party.
Correct Negative	She doesn't know anything about the surprise party.
Double Negative	He doesn't have no money.
Correct Negative	He doesn't have any money.

In short stories and other creative writing, authors often use double negatives in dialogue to reflect a character's dialect. Here are some examples from *Thank You, M'am.*

"Ain't you got nobody home to tell you to wash your face?"

"Not with that face, I would not take you nowhere."

Remember It Record this rule and example in the Power Rule section of your Personalized Editing Checklist.

Use It Read through your short story and check that you have not used double negatives unless you are using them in dialogue to reflect a character's speech patterns.

PROJECT PREP *Editing* *Checking Conventions*

In your writing group, exchange papers and edit your peer's story. Discuss the issues that came up and help one another fix any problems in grammar, spelling, and punctuation.

CHAPTER 7

Ideas	**4** The plot, setting, characters, and dialogue are original and creative.	**3** The plot, setting, characters, and dialogue are effective.	**2** Most aspects of the plot, setting, characters, and dialogue are effective.	**1** Most aspects of the plot, setting, characters, and dialogue are ineffective.
Organization	**4** The organization is clear with abundant transitions.	**3** A few events or ideas seem out of place or transitions are missing.	**2** Many events seem out of place and transitions are missing.	**1** The order of events is unclear and hard to follow.
Voice	**4** The narrator's voice sounds natural and the point of view is effective.	**3** The narrator's voice sounds mostly natural and the point of view is effective.	**2** The narrator's voice sounds unnatural at times and the point of view seems forced.	**1** The narrator's voice sounds mostly unnatural and the point of view is forced and ineffective.
Word Choice	**4** Specific words and sensory images help readers picture characters and setting.	**3** Words are specific and some words appeal to the senses to help readers picture characters and setting.	**2** Some words are overly general and do not bring characters or setting into focus.	**1** Most words are overly general and do not bring characters or setting into focus.
Sentence Fluency	**4** Varied sentences flow smoothly and dialogue reflects characters.	**3** Most sentences are varied and flow smoothly, and dialogue reflects characters.	**2** Some sentences are choppy and dialogue seems forced.	**1** Sentences are choppy and not varied, and dialogue seems forced or is missing.
Conventions	**4** Conventions are correct and Power Rules are followed except for effect.	**3** Conventions are mainly correct and Power Rules are followed except for effect.	**2** Some conventions are incorrect but Power Rules are followed except for effect.	**1** There are many errors and at least one accidental failure to follow a Power Rule.

PROJECT PREP *Evaluating* *Editing and Publishing*

Use the six-trait rubric to evaluate your story. Submit it to your teacher and make changes in response to his or her feedback. You may want to create a class anthology of your stories.

A play is a special form of creative writing. It differs from a short story because it is performed. Like the short story, however, it employs character, setting, and plot.

A **play** is a piece of writing intended to be performed on a stage by actors.

Modern playwrights provide the dialogue in a script along with stage directions that supply additional information. **Stage directions** indicate the movement, position, or vocal range of an actor (sometimes even the sound effects and lighting needed).

The following scene is from one of William Shakespeare's most famous plays, *Romeo and Juliet*. In this scene, Juliet, a girl from a wealthy family, anxiously asks her nurse for news of her loved one, Romeo. (In Shakespeare's time, a nurse was like a nanny.) As you read the scene, imagine how you would say the dialogue. Does the language give you clues to the characters? What can you tell about the relationship between Juliet and her nurse from the way they speak to one another?

> **MODEL: Play Scene**

from *Romeo and Juliet*

Juliet: The clock struck nine when I did send the nurse;
In half an hour she promised to return.
Perchance she cannot meet him. That's not so.
O, she is lame! Love's heralds should be thoughts
which ten times faster glide than the sun's beams
Driving back shadows over low'ring hills.
Therefor do nimble-pinioned doves draw love,
And therefor hath the wind-swift Cupid wings.
Now is the sun upon the highmost hill
Of the day's journey, and from nine till twelve
Is three long hours; yet she is not come.
Had she affections and warm youthful blood,
She would be as swift in motion as a ball;
My words will bandy her to my sweet love,
And his to me.

Given the lines he gives her, what do you think Shakespeare's attitude was toward Juliet? How can you tell?

But old folks, many feign as they were dead—
Unwieldy, slow, heavy and pale as lead.
[Enter Nurse and Peter.]
O God, she comes! O honey nurse, what news?
Hast thou met with him? Send thy man away.

Nurse: Peter stay at the gate. *[Exit Peter.]*

Juliet: Now, good sweet nurse—O Lord, why lookest thou sad?
Though news be sad, yet tell them merrily;
If good, thou shamest the music of sweet news
By plating it to me with such a sour face.

Nurse: I am aweary, give me leave awhile.
Fie, how my bones ache. What a jaunt have I had!

Juliet: I would thou hadst my bones, and I thy news.
Nay, come, I pray thee speak. Good, good nurse, speak.

Nurse: Jesu, what haste! Can you not stay awhile?
Do you not see that I am out of breath?

> Even though the English may sound archaic to you, do the nurse's words sound realistic for someone of her age?

Juliet: How art thou out of breath when thou hast breath
To say to me that thou art out of breath?
The excuse that thou dost make in this delay
Is longer than the tale thou dost excuse.
Is thy news good or bad? Answer to that.
Say either, and I'll stay the circumstance.
Let me be satisfied, is't good or bad?

Nurse: Well, you have made a simple choice; you know
not to choose a man. Romeo? No, not he. Though
his face better than any man's, yet his leg exels all
men's; and for a hand and a foot, and a body, though
they not be talked on, yet they are past compare.
He is not the flower of courtesy, but, I'll warrant him, as
gentle as a lamb. Go thy ways, wench; serve God. What,
have you dined at home?

Juliet: No, no. But all this did I know before.
What says he of our marriage? What of that?

Nurse: Lord how my head aches! What a head have I!
It beats as it would fall in twenty pieces.
My back a t'other side—ah, my back, my back!
Beshrew your heart for sending me about
To catch my death with jaunting up and down.

Juliet: I' faith, I am sorry that thou art not well.
Sweet, sweet, sweet nurse, tell me, what says my love?

Nurse: Your love says, like an honest gentleman, and a
courteous, and a kind, and a handsome, and I warrant,
a virtuous—where is your mother?

Juliet: Where is my mother? Why, she is within.
Where should she be? How oddly thou repliest!
'Your love says, like an honest gentleman,
"Where is your mother?"'

Nurse: O God's Lady dear!
Are you so hot? Marry come up, I trow.
Is this the poultice for my aching bones?
Henceforward do your messages yourself.

Juliet: Here's such a coil! Come what says Romeo?

Nurse: Have you got to leave to go to shrift to-day?

Juliet: I have.

Nurse: Then hie you to friar Lawrence' cell;
There stays a husband to make you a wife.
Now comes the wanton blood upon your cheeks:
They'll be in scarlet straight at any news.
Hie you to church; I must another way,
To fetch a ladder, by the which
your love
Must climb a bird's nest soon
when it is dark.
I am the drudge, and toil in
your delight;
But you shall bear the burden
soon at night.
Go; I'll to dinner; hie you to
the cell.

Juliet: Hie to high fortune!
Honest nurse farewell.

> The plot would have advanced without the nurse's long delay in delivering Juliet her news from Romeo. What does Shakespeare gain by including this playful exchange?

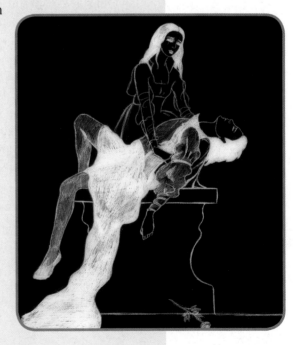

CHAPTER 7

・ Practice Your Skills

Analyzing Dramatic Elements

Write answers to the questions below about the scene from *Romeo and Juliet*.

1. What is the central conflict? Briefly describe it.

2. What is the setting? Describe it in a few sentences.

3. What stage direction might you add to this scene?

THEME, MOOD, AND TONE

Like short stories, plays express themes. Two important themes in Shakespeare's *Romeo and Juliet* are the power of love and the power of hate. Themes can be explicit or implicit. An **explicit theme** is one that is stated clearly in the play. When Juliet says "Love's heralds should be thoughts / which ten times faster glide than the sun's beams," she is expressing an explicit theme of the play: Young love is passionate and impatient. An **implicit theme,** in contrast, is not stated directly. Instead it is a message the viewer derives from the play's action. An implicit theme of *Romeo and Juliet* might be that ancient hatreds carried on too long create tragic outcomes.

You've learned that short stories convey **mood.** Plays convey mood also. The scene you just read from *Romeo and Juliet* swirls with Juliet's hope and excitement as well as the nurse's deadpan pessimism. Shakespeare's mastery is evident in the way he subtly foreshadows the events that will dash all of Juliet's plans and dreams.

Closely related to mood is tone. In drama, **tone** is the speaker's attitude toward his or her listener. The tone in the scene between Juliet and her nurse is playful and teasing, for the most part. Juliet seems unaware of her nurse's disapproval. Tone might also refer to the writer's attitude toward his or her characters, sympathetic or otherwise.

CHOOSING A CONFLICT OR PROBLEM

Like stories, plays are based on conflict. A conflict may be between two or more people, as when Juliet tries to get her nurse to hurry and tell her about Romeo. A conflict may also exist within a single person, as when Juliet talks to herself before the nurse returns. For a conflict to be interesting in a play, it must be seen and heard by the audience.

SKETCHING CHARACTERS

As in a story, the characters are usually the most important element of a play. In drama, the characters are brought to life by actors—people who use gestures, facial expressions, and tones of voice to capture the essence of a particular character in a unique way.

● **Practice Your Skills**

> ### *Sketching Characters*
>
> Who are the most interesting three people you know? Write a character sketch of each person you named. Write a paragraph describing the important facts and details about the person. Include enough detail so that an actor preparing to play the role of the character could learn a lot from your sketch.

DECIDING ON A SETTING

In a book or movie, the writer can create scenes that move from place to place. One scene might take place in an apartment and the next in a forest. Because of the difficulty in changing sets, most plays have only a few settings. It is the playwright's job to create an interesting, dramatic story that is enhanced by the setting. In the scene between the nurse and Juliet, the action takes place entirely in one room, probably Juliet's bedroom.

● **Practice Your Skills**

> ### *Visualizing Settings*
>
> Make a list of three or four places in your community that might make good settings for a play. For each location, state briefly your reason why it would make a good stage setting. Be sure your settings are specific enough to be recreated on a stage. For example, "school" is not a specific setting, because an entire school cannot be shown onstage at one time. "A dilapidated school room late at night" is specific enough.

WRITING DIALOGUE

The foundation of a play is its dialogue. It is the medium through which the playwright shows the plot development, expresses the characters' emotions, and creates conflict. When writing dialogue, choose words carefully to convey information about each character's culture, place in society, and personality. Just as in short stories, each character should have a distinct voice that is believable and natural.

Almost all of what the audience learns about each character comes from dialogue. We learn of Juliet's impatience when she says, ". . . from nine till twelve / Is three long hours; yet she is not come." We learn that the nurse is exasperated with Juliet when she responds, ". . . what haste! Can you not stay awhile?" The ability to express information and characterization at the same time makes play dialogue particularly rich in content.

WRITING STAGE DIRECTIONS

Playwrights usually supply stage directions for the reader (and the actor and director) about how the characters speak and move. Stage directions are usually found in *italic* print. Because the dialogue itself often conveys what the audience learns about the characters, most modern playwrights like to keep their stage directions brief. Shakespeare's stage directions tend to indicate when to enter or exit the stage or, as he jokingly wrote in his play *Pericles, Prince of Tyre,* "Exit, pursued by a bear." Some stage directions are necessary, however. They express meaningful actions, such as one character pushing another character. At the beginning of the play, there is usually a brief description of the set. When a new character appears, there is usually a brief physical description of the character, perhaps including how the character is dressed. **Props**—short for properties, the physical objects important to a scene—are also mentioned in stage directions.

● Practice Your Skills

Writing Dialogue and Stage Directions

Write a conversation between two strangers who get stuck together in an elevator. They are applicants competing for the same job: a computer trainee for a new Internet company in this building. One of them is claustrophobic, or afraid of confined spaces. Write at least five separate lines for each character. Then write at least two stage directions for each character. The stage directions should express action or emotion.

Using a Rubric for a Dramatic Scene or Play

Use the rubric below as a guide to revising your dramatic scene.

Dramatic Elements	**4** The plot, setting, characters, and dialogue are original and creative and express the writer's feelings.	**3** The plot, setting, characters, and dialogue are effective and express the writer's feelings.	**2** Most aspects of the plot, setting, characters, and dialogue are effective.	**1** Most aspects of the plot, setting, characters, and dialogue are ineffective.
Stage Directions	**4** The stage directions clearly indicate actions and states of mind and add depth.	**3** The stage directions indicate actions and states of mind.	**2** The stage directions indicate actions but do not go deeper.	**1** There are few if any stage directions.

PROJECT PREP *Another Genre* *From Story to Play*

Use the story you wrote about two people with different perspectives to write a scene with a similar theme. Ask your writing group to comment on your adaptation.

Writing a Poem

"I have never started a poem yet whose end I knew. Writing a poem is discovering," wrote Robert Frost. This section will give you practice in writing poems.

Poems can be serious, sad, or silly. Whatever you imagine can become a poem. The writer Lewis Carroll wrote the poem "Jabberwocky" as part of his fantasy novel, *Through the Looking Glass*. In the poem he coined, or made up, many of the words to achieve a humorous effect. Some of these words employ **onomatopoeia**—their sounds suggest their meaning—to create a whimsical, nonsensical mood. Read the poem aloud to savor its imaginative words and giggly tone.

Lewis Carroll enables his readers to come up with their own definitions of his nonsense words. In doing this he involves the reader intimately in his creation. When you read this poem, you are helping to create its meaning for yourself. What does the phrase *manxome foe* suggest to you? Since *foe* means "enemy," perhaps *manxome* means "fearful." What do you think?

Jabberwocky

'Twas brillig, and the slithy toves
    Did gyre and gimble in the wabe:
All mimsy were the borogoves,
    And the mome raths outgrabe.

"Beware the Jabberwock, my son!
    The jaws that bite, the claws that catch!
Beware the Jubjub bird, and shun
    The frumious Bandersnatch!"

He took his vorpal sword in hand:
    Long time the manxome foe he sought—
So rested he by the Tumtum tree,
    And stood awhile in thought.

And, as in uffish thought he stood,
    The Jabberwock, with eyes of flame,
Came whiffling through the tulgey wood,
    And burbled as it came!

One, two! One, two! And through and through
    The vorpal blade went snicker-snack!
He left it dead, and with its head
    He went galumphing back.

"And hast thou slain the Jabberwock?
    Come to my arms, my beamish boy!
O frabjous day! Callooh! Callay!"
    He chortled in his joy.

'Twas brillig, and the slithy toves
    Did gyre and gimble in the wabe:
All mimsy were the borogoves,
    And the mome raths outgrabe.

FINDING IDEAS FOR POEMS

Poetry depends on the thoughts and emotions of the writer. You can choose any subject about which you have strong feelings. For a humorous poem, your subject may be a joke that made you laugh so hard that you cried. It may be a hilarious comedy routine you recently saw performed. Or it may be a whimsical take on something serious, like "Jabberwocky." A good way to discover ideas that are already within you is to make a chart like the one below. You can further explore the examples by brainstorming, freewriting, clustering, and questioning with your writing group.

IDEA CHART	
Events	arguing with a friend; buying a new guitar; playing chess
Scenes	an empty classroom at night; a crowded store; a quiet park
Sensations	the sound of a subway train; the smell of varnished wood; the sight of rustling leaves

● **Practice Your Skills**

Finding Ideas for a Humorous Poem

Copy and complete the following word web. Add funny or unusual examples.

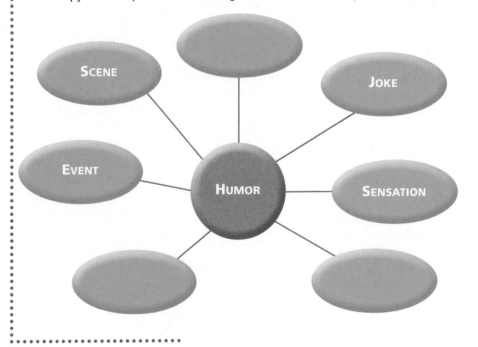

USING POETIC TECHNIQUES

The sound of language is part of poetry's essence. In fact, the full effect of a poem comes through only when it is read aloud. Not only can the sounds be beautiful, interesting, or strange, but they can make interesting connections among ideas in the poem and emphasize the poem's meaning. Poets also use sound devices for special effects and stirring the reader's emotions. In addition to onomatopoeia, here are some other sound devices you can use when you write a poem.

SOUND DEVICES	
Alliteration	Repetition of a consonant sound or sounds at the beginning of a series of words **B**aa, **b**aa, **b**lack sheep
Assonance	Repetition of a vowel sound within words H**o**ld the r**o**ll and st**o**ke the ch**o**ke.
Repetition	Repetition of an entire word or phrase One, two! One, two! And through and through
Consonance	Repetition of a consonant sound or sounds, used with different vowel sounds The **jaws** that bite, the **claws** that **c**atch!
Rhythm	Rise and fall of accented and unaccented syllables. "Jabberwocky" is a good example of rhythm and rhyme.
Rhyme	Repetition of accented syllables with the same vowel and consonant sounds 'Twas brillig, and the slithy toves Did gyre and gimble in the wabe: All mimsy were the borogoves, And the mome raths outgrabe.

Using Rhyme A rhymed poem usually has a pattern, or rhyme scheme, that can be shown by letters. Notice that the rhyme pattern for the poem below is **ABAB.** The first line rhymes with the third, and the second line rhymes with the last.

Sally, will you come out to **play?**	*a*
Yes, my dearest **friend.**	*b*
I'll play with you till the sky turns **gray**	*a*
And the day has reached its **end.**	*b*

You may also write poetry with other patterns, such as **AABB.** In this pattern, the first two lines rhyme and then the next two.

● **Practice Your Skills**

Developing Sound Devices

Write a series of statements on the subject of disagreements as follows. Your statements may be in the form of poetry or prose, but they must contain the listed sound devices.

1. a statement containing rhyme

2. a statement containing alliteration

3. a statement containing consonance

4. a statement using onomatopoeia

5. a statement containing assonance

Using Stanzas A stanza is a division of a poem separated by spacing. It is a group of lines standing together, apart from other such groups. Stanzas are defined according to the number of lines they contain: couplets (two lines), triplets (three lines), quatrains (four lines), and so on. Poetry containing specific patterns of rhyme and rhythm (meter) usually also contain a specific stanza pattern.

Writing Free Verse A **free-verse** poem is a poem without a regular pattern of rhyme or rhythm. Robert Frost said writing free verse was "like playing tennis with the net down." Repeated phrases and the rhythms of everyday speech are often employed. Free-verse poetry uses imagery to recreate a vivid scene or memory. In "Like Scales," the poet Julia Mishkin uses imagery to create a scene comparing nature (sheep in a field) to art (scales played on a piano).

Like Scales

The lamb in my neighbor's pasture
has caught her shaggy wool
on a fence and can't pull free.
All night we heard the frightened bleating,
5   low and intermittent. We were playing
a game about trivia made
specifically for my generation:
the babies of the post-war boom,
music lessons and ballet.
10 Luckily, it did not rain.
The stars wheeled overhead in that slow
design determined in another time.
What Persian astronomer-poet wrote
a celebrated collection of quatrains?
15 What does the name 'Zapruder' signify?

How many flamboyant musicians soared
before the age of thirty, plummeted
and died? And all the while
the gentle wind blowing blades
20 of grass in the field where the sheep graze.
When I was eight I was taken
to study piano in another town,
to a house between two meadows.
I fed the lamb small crusts
25 of bread. Sheep and Scarlatti!
Who tells them when it's time
to retire? Relentless, they move
toward the shed, one after another,
each evening. Has someone called them in?
30 Or do they just know, with a lucky affinity,
the day's end? And who
will free the lamb from her wiry bed?

● **Practice Your Skills**

Writing Free Verse Poems

Write a free verse poem, comparing and contrasting one person to another. After you have chosen a subject, jot down your answers to these questions.

1. What makes each of these people unique?

2. What main feelings do these people give you?

3. How would you recognize these people by sound? List two or three details.

4. How would you recognize these people by sight? List two or three details.

Then write your poem, using the details you have listed to help you come up with vivid images to compare and contrast the two people. To decide where your lines should end, read your poem aloud. Listen for places where the thought seems to break naturally. Create an ending for your poem that ties up the images and thoughts you have expressed.

GRAPHIC ELEMENTS

Poets also use graphic elements such as line length, capitalization, and punctuation to help them express their meaning. Look at the poem below, "First," by Douglas Florian. How does the placement of text and the use of space reflect and reinforce the poem's meaning?

> First things first,
> Last things last.
> Hours
>   pass
>   slowly.
> Years pass fast.

● Practice Your Skills

Using Graphic Elements

Review the poem you wrote in the previous activity. What graphic elements—line length, capitalization, or punctuation—can you use to emphasize the meaning and feeling of the poem? Make revisions and share your work with a partner for feedback.

FIGURATIVE LANGUAGE

Poets often try to express feelings and thoughts that are hard to put into words. For this reason, they often look to figures of speech to help them give the reader an idea of what they mean. **Figures of speech** are expressions that stray from their literal meaning in order to make an impact. Figures of speech are also called **figurative language.** The chart below shows some common figures of speech.

FIGURATIVE LANGUAGE	
Simile	comparison using the words *like* or *as* *The baby's eyes were as bright as spring sunshine.*
Metaphor	implied comparison that does not use *like* or *as* *The baby's eyes were bright spring sunshine.*
Imagery	use of visual details or details that appeal to other senses *The baby's eyes were bright spring sunshine; his skin the soft petal of a tulip.*
Personification	use of human qualities to describe something non-human *The sun smiled on the baby's sweet new life.*

Practice Your Skills

Developing Figurative Language for Poems

Add at least two figures of speech to your poem. Share the poem with your partner for feedback.

USING A POETRY RUBRIC

You can use the rubric below to evaluate your poetry or the poetry of others.

Poetic Techniques	**4** The rhyme scheme (if used) and sound devices create a strong effect and help express a meaningful idea.	**3** The rhyme scheme (if used) and sound devices create a strong effect and help express an idea.	**2** The rhyme scheme (if used) is inconsistent but sound devices help express meaning.	**1** The rhyme scheme (if used) is inconsistent and few if any sound devices are used.
Figurative Language	**4** The poem is enriched by a wide variety of memorable figurative language.	**3** The poem is enriched by a variety of figurative language.	**2** The poem uses figurative language once or twice.	**1** The poem uses no figurative language.
Graphic Elements	**4** The poem uses line length, capitalization, and punctuation creatively to help express the ideas precisely.	**3** The poem uses line length, capitalization, and punctuation to help express ideas.	**2** The poem uses line length, capitalization, and punctuation in predictable and uninspired ways.	**1** The poem's use of line length, capitalization, and punctuation seems unintentional.

PROJECT PREP *Prewriting* *From Story to Poem*

Carefully examine your original story looking for "poetry moments" and draft your poem. Decide what rhyme scheme, if any, you want it to have and make adjustments accordingly. Ask yourself where such poetic techniques as alliteration and repetition might enhance the meaning you are seeking to convey.

Writing Lab

Project Corner

Get Creative Video Game Manual

Create a video game based on the theme of differing perspectives that can cause a conflict, the theme you addressed in your short story. What would the setting be like? What is the conflict? How do players win? By what rules would players reach their goal? Write a user's manual to explain your video game.

Collaborate and Create Speak and Listen

With your classmates, **discuss the sorts of conflicts** that you and your friends have witnessed or been involved in. How many of these would you say were the result of different perspectives on an issue? How might you work to find ways to avoid these kinds of conflicts? What role might careful listening play in resolving these sorts of conflicts? (See pages 422–428 for more information on listening skills.)

Another Perspective

Rework It

Look at your story and try to **transform it into a completely different form** of expression. What if it were a graph or a chart? How could you translate it into a painting or a sculpture? Think of other ways your short story could be reborn.

In Spoken Communication   Apply and Assess
Dramatic Scene

1. You are on a committee that is organizing an orientation night for students who will be new at your school next year. You and some other students on the committee will write and perform scenes that represent aspects of life at your school. You want to show typical interactions in a classroom, the library, the cafeteria, the gym, and the hallway. *Write a lively scene* that shows an interaction in one of these settings. (You can find information on writing dramatic scenes on pages 174–180.)

In Everyday Life Poem About a Person

2. Your family reunion is fast approaching. You and your cousins have decided to create a book of poems about older members of your extended family. *Write a poem* about a grandparent, a great-aunt or uncle, or another family member. Vividly describe the person and an enjoyable experience you have had with him or her. Use poetic techniques, figurative language, and graphic elements to express your feelings and ideas. (You can find information on writing poetry on pages 181–187.)

Timed Writing ⏱ Celebrate with a Story

3. Your teacher is preparing to help your school celebrate President's Day and Martin Luther King Jr.'s birthday. You have chosen to write an original short story that honors the life and accomplishments of Abraham Lincoln, George Washington, or Martin Luther King Jr. Write a short story that fits the theme of this upcoming school event. An audience of students and teachers will read your story. Invent your own details and characters, but also use reference sources to find facts to include in your story. Base your story on a main conflict that will be resolved at the end. You have 30 minutes to write your story.

Before You Write Prewrite to develop important and vivid details of character and setting. Be sure the story has a beginning, middle, and end. Decide what conflict was at the center of your important moment and try to resolve this conflict by the end of the story. Also be sure to consider your purpose, occasion, and audience for the story.

After You Write Evaluate your work using the six-trait evaluation rubric on page 173.

CHAPTER **8**

Expository Writing

Expository writing presents information using facts and examples or explains by giving directions or listing steps in a process. For this reason it is also called **informative** or **explanatory** writing.

Here are some common examples of writing that explains or informs.

- **An online encyclopedia provides general facts and information** about Alaska.
- **You present a report on hermit crabs** to your science class.
- **A newspaper article features a profile** of a famous inventor.
- **A magazine illustrator draws a diagram** of a solar eclipse.
- **A family creates a genealogy tree** on their own Internet home page.
- **A user manual explains how to** set up a new online game.

Writing Project

How Does It Work? *Write an expository essay explaining how something works.*

Think Through Writing Explain how something with which you are familiar works. It could be a machine, such as a lawnmower; a scientific process, such as photosynthesis; a game, such as volleyball; a creative process, such as songwriting; or a constructive process, such as making a cheesecake. Explain it as though you are describing it to a person who is completely unfamiliar with the process you are describing.

Talk About It In your writing group, read the explanation you wrote and add to it as you think of new points to make. Try to be as specific as possible. How clearly could you follow one another's expository writing and speaking?

Read About It Read the following description of how hurricanes' wind speed increases. Think about the sorts of details that enable you to understand the processes being described.

Where a Hurricane Gets Its Force

Hurricanes are tropical creatures that begin to stir off the coast of Africa after the summer sun has heated the ocean to the temperature of balmy bathwater. This pool of warm water is essential to the formation of hurricanes, but not their only cause. An incipient disturbance will never mature into a hurricane unless the winds are favorable. That is why the climate cycle that produces El Niño and La Niña plays such a key role. El Niño favors weak easterlies and strong westerlies that shear the tops off swirling storm clouds. La Niña exerts an opposite influence, creating a bed of still air between two wind belts that invites hurricanes to form.

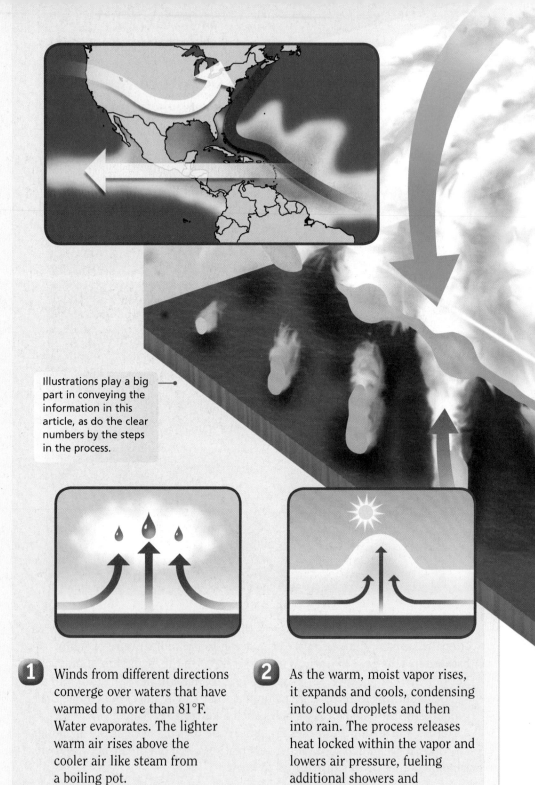

Illustrations play a big part in conveying the information in this article, as do the clear numbers by the steps in the process.

1 Winds from different directions converge over waters that have warmed to more than 81°F. Water evaporates. The lighter warm air rises above the cooler air like steam from a boiling pot.

2 As the warm, moist vapor rises, it expands and cools, condensing into cloud droplets and then into rain. The process releases heat locked within the vapor and lowers air pressure, fueling additional showers and thunderstorms.

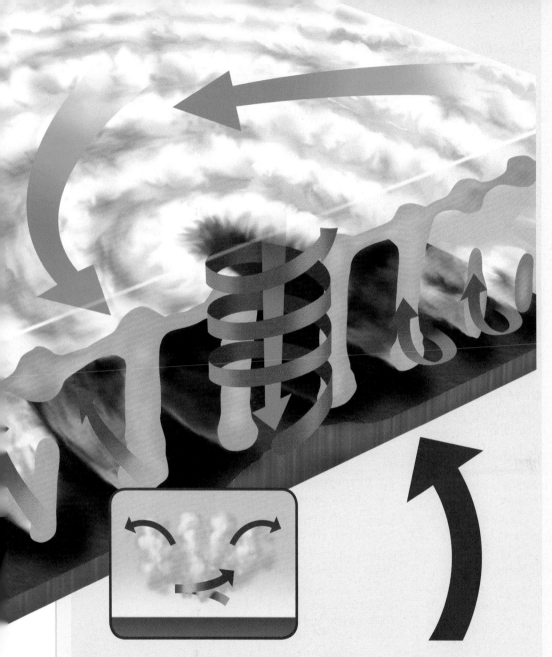

3 Picking up the direction of the earth's rotation, the winds in these thunderstorms circulate counterclockwise (clockwise in the Southern Hemisphere). Collectively they form a churning mass known as a tropical cyclone.

4 When the spiraling winds reach 74 m.p.h. the storm is called a hurricane. At its core is a chimney-like column of calm air (the eye) around which multiple thunderstorms swirl. The storms that form the eye wall are the most ferocious.

Respond in Writing Respond in writing to this description of hurricane wind speed. Are there any areas that you do not understand? What would the author need to do in order to present this information more clearly?

Develop Your Own Ideas Work with your classmates to develop ideas that you might use to write an expository essay about a process you know well.

Small Groups: In your small group, discuss each writer's topic. Make an organizer like the one below to help think of possible details for each author's explanation in each of the following categories.

Subject	Relevant Facts	Steps in the Process	Descriptive Details	Order Steps Are Presented

Whole Class: Make a master chart of all of the ideas generated by the small groups to see how different members of the class provided information for their readers about the process being explained.

Write About It You will next write an expository essay about a process you know well. Your may choose from any of the following possible topics, audiences, and forms.

Possible Topics	Possible Audiences	Possible Forms
• a machine, such as a car engine	• people familiar with the process you are describing	• an encyclopedia entry
• an organic process, such as growing tomatoes	• people unfamiliar with the process you are describing	• a magazine article
• a game, such as a video game	• people who want to learn how to do what you are describing	• a blog
• a creative process, such as playing piano	• people who need the information you are providing to counteract misinformation they've gotten from elsewhere	• a newspaper article
• a constructive process, such as building a deck		

Expository Writing Prewriting

The article you just read has many features of a good expository text. It **1)** explains a process; **2)** begins with a statement that makes the focus of the article clear; **3)** presents facts and examples in logical order and links ideas with transitions; **4)** uses illustrations to help explain the process; and **5)** uses reader-friendly formatting techniques, such as the numbers before each step in the process of how hurricances form. (See page 203 for more characteristics of a strong expository essay and pages 431–438 for more information on formatting user-friendly texts.) Follow the guidelines in this chapter to write your own clear expository texts.

① Getting the Subject Right

Ideas for expository essays can come from many different sources. Use the following techniques to think of possible subjects.

Strategies for Thinking of Expository Subjects

- Look through your journal, particularly your Learning Log and interest inventory, for ideas you could explain.
- Think about books, magazines, or newspaper articles you have read lately on subjects of special interest to you.
- Think about an interesting television show or movie you have watched recently.
- Think about a conversation you had recently that made you stop and think.
- Browse through the Media Center.
- Think about what interests you in your other classes.
- Talk to friends and family members and find out what they would like to know more about.
- Start freewriting and see what is on your mind.
- Use the clustering technique starting with the phrase *things I can explain.*

CONSIDERING YOUR AUDIENCE

Decide who your audience will be by using the following Audience Profile Chart.

Audience Profile Chart

- Who will read my work?
- What subjects would interest them?
- Which subject is the most suitable for my audience?

CHOOSING A SUBJECT

Now that you have several possible subjects and a good idea of who your readers will be, you can select the subject that seems most promising. You may find when you start working on that subject, however, that it was not as good an idea as you thought. In that case, you can always return to your prewriting ideas and try another subject. Use the following guidelines to choose a promising subject.

HERE'S HOW

Choosing an Expository Subject

- Choose a subject that interests you.
- Choose a subject that will interest your audience.
- Choose a subject you know enough about to explain accurately.

Now it's time to turn your subject into a thesis statement. As you develop your thesis statement, keep your readers' needs and interests in mind.

LIMITING AND FOCUSING A SUBJECT

Some subjects are too broad for an essay of several paragraphs. The subject of baseball, for example, could fill an entire book. Within this general subject, however, are several smaller subjects. These may include how to throw a curve ball or the meaning of the term *double play*. As part of planning your work, be sure to limit your subject so that it can be adequately covered in a brief essay.

Note how the broad, general subjects have been narrowed down to a manageable size.

GENERAL SUBJECT	MORE LIMITED	LIMITED SUBJECT
Nature	waterfalls	Niagara Falls
Hobbies	crafts	working with clay
Courses	science	using a microscope

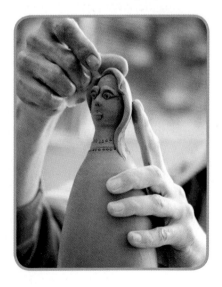

One good way to discover the smaller subject is to ask yourself questions about it. Among the many possible questions you can ask, try the ones on the next page.

Strategies for Limiting a Subject

- Who are some of the people associated with my subject?
- What are some specific examples of my subject?
- Where is my subject usually done or found?
- Why should people know about my subject?
- When was my subject first discovered?
- When did it become popular?

The final step in limiting a subject is to focus your thoughts by expressing the main idea in a sentence. This will become your working thesis statement.

Limited Subject	Niagara Falls
Question	What is unique about Niagara Falls?
Working Thesis Statement	Niagara Falls produces more energy than any other power plant in the state of New York.

PROJECT PREP *Prewriting* *Identifying a Topic*

Based on discussions you've had with your classmates, choose a topic for your expository writing. Select a topic appropriate for your audience, and use the strategies above to bring it into focus. Then develop your working thesis statement.

Think Critically

Analyzing

If you are writing an expository text to give directions or to explain a process, analyzing your subject will help you come up with the details you need. **Analyzing** means breaking something down into its parts to better understand it.

Suppose, for example, you are writing about how to release a bowling ball. You go bowling so often that releasing the ball is second nature to you. When you try to explain it clearly to someone else, however, you may need to analyze the action; or break it down into its parts, so the other person can understand it.

As you analyze the way you release the ball, you see that you are actually following several different steps. You take a series of steps. As you move, your arm straightens and swings the bowling ball back behind you. The opposing hand and arm follow through in a smooth motion as you release the ball. What seemed like one continuous motion was actually a series of smaller, intermediate steps that can be explained. Analyzing helps you recognize the smaller parts, or steps, within a whole so that you can explain them clearly to your reader.

Thinking Practice

Think of a physical motion that is second nature to you. It may be jumping into a double rope, doing a somersault, or simply skipping. Analyze the motion by breaking it down into its parts. Then team up with a partner and explain the steps so that your partner can easily understand them. After talking them through in detail, write them down, trying to keep them as clear and specific as possible.

② Gathering and Organizing Details

Now that you have a more focused, limited subject, you can begin listing the details that will help you explain that subject to readers. The kinds of details will depend on your main idea and your purpose for writing. If your purpose is to inform, you will probably use facts and examples. If your purpose is to explain or to give directions, your details will be the steps in a process.

LISTING DETAILS

The following main idea (limited subject) is one that calls for facts and examples. The writer's purpose is to explain.

Limited Subject	tar pits at Rancho la Brea
Focus	how prehistoric animals were trapped in pits
Fact	rainwater gathered on surface of tar pools and gave appearance of lake
Fact	animals came to drink and got caught in tar
Fact	their dead bodies attracted scavenging animals who also became trapped
Fact	tar helped preserve bones of animals
Examples	animals trapped include mammoths, saber-toothed tigers, and mastodons

To help you think of details, first make a list of questions that readers might have about your subject. Then jot down any facts or examples that will help you answer those questions. Your final list should include three to five details.

ARRANGING DETAILS IN LOGICAL ORDER

The final step in the prewriting stage is to arrange your list of supporting details in a logical order. A logical order is an arrangement that your readers will be able to follow clearly. The guidelines below will help you organize your brainstorming notes.

Strategies for Organizing Details

- Group related items together through classifying.
- If your purpose is to give information, arrange your details in the order of importance, interest, size, or degree.
- If your purpose is to give directions or to explain a process, arrange your details in the order in which they occur.

If your text calls for order of importance, interest, size, or degree, you may list your details in the **order of least to most** or **most to least.** In the following paragraph, the details are arranged in order of least to most.

MODEL: Order of Degree

Hungry Mammals

Different animals have different food requirements depending on their body weight, activity, and chemistry. — Topic Sentence
The relatively small chimpanzee, for example, eats an average of 4.5 pounds of food each day. The lion needs about 15 pounds of food, while the African elephant requires about 350 pounds. The record-holder for amount — Details in order of least to most
of food eaten daily is the blue whale. It eats about one ton of food each day. Despite this enormous amount, the whale actually consumes a smaller percentage of its body — Concluding Sentence
weight than does the chimpanzee.

If you are giving directions or explaining a process, your details should be arranged in the proper sequence, the order in which they are carried out. This type of order, called **sequential order,** is similar to chronological order. The following paragraph about mountain climbing uses sequential order.

MODEL: Sequential Order

Using Your Feet

The natural tendency of beginning climbers is to — Topic Sentence
look for handholds, but you must begin your climbing education by learning to look down for footholds. In the beginning tell yourself repeatedly, "Look down; look — Details in sequential order
down!" Once you have the habit of looking down, you must learn to see footholds. They may be very small or steeply sloping. The next step is to test the foothold by trying to stand on it. While you are learning, expect to slide off holds quite a bit. With more and more — Concluding Sentence
experience, you will learn to recognize footholds that you can stand on safely.

—Michael Loughman, *Learning to Rock Climb*

In essays that provide information, use **order of importance** or **size** with appropriate transitions. Arrange the details in the order of **least to most** or **most to least**. In essays that explain, use **sequential order** with transitions.

CHAPTER 8

PROJECT PREP *Prewriting* *Organization*

1. Use your prewriting work and the information on these pages to create an organizational plan for your essay. Create a formal or informal outline (see pages 318–319) or make a graphic organizer representing your organizational strategy.

2. Share your plan with your writing group. For each writer, discuss the order in which the information will be presented. Does it make sense? Can you suggest more effective ways of ordering information? Give each author suggestions on how to consider the arrangement of information so that readers can clearly follow the explanation.

The Power of Language ⚡

Colorful Verbs: In Living Color

Expository writing does not have to be dull and boring. Even an explanation of a simple process can be energized by colorful language. Newspaper and magazine writers, for example, use colorful language to transport readers right into the scene they are covering. Compare the two sentences below. The first, ho-hum sentence lacks colorful verbs. The second, which uses more precise and engaging verbs, has more drama and excitement.

> Still, the storm, going along the coast all the way to Massachusetts, brought punishing rains from Florida to Maine and caused widespread flooding.

> Still, the storm, skirting the coast all the way to Massachusetts, dumped punishing rains from Florida to Maine and triggered widespread flooding.

It is easy to see how colorful verbs bring clarity and definition to a word picture. The verbs *dumped* and *triggered* give a sense of the crushing weight and sudden harm brought by hurricanes. Colorful verbs can transform a rainstorm into a disaster.

Try It Yourself

Find three sentences you have written in which you have used "ordinary" verbs. Rewrite the sentences, substituting more colorful verbs. Then write three sentences on your project topic and use the most colorful verbs possible. Try to use those sentences in your essay. You can also look for more opportunities to use colorful verbs when you revise.

CHAPTER 8

Through prewriting you have explored your topic and examined what you know about it. You have also jotted down ideas and arranged them in a logical order. At this stage you are ready to write a first draft. The first draft need not be polished. It should, however, achieve the basic goals of an expository essay, summarized in the chart below.

QUALITIES OF A STRONG EXPOSITORY ESSAY

- It fulfills its purpose to present information or explain a process.
- It is appropriate for the audience and occasion.
- It states a thesis clearly and backs it up with ample supporting information and details, such as relevant, well-chosen facts, definitions, concrete details, quotations, and other information and examples.
- It has an engaging introduction, transitions connecting the body paragraphs to one another and clarifying the relationships among ideas and concepts, and a conclusion that follows from and supports the information or explanation presented.
- It may use reader-friendly formatting techniques such as bulleted or numbered lists and boldface heads.
- It may use graphics, such as charts and diagrams.
- It is free from errors in grammar, usage, and mechanics and follows all the Power Rules.

The following expository text presents information and is a model of good expository writing.

MODEL: Writing That Informs

From *The First Americans*
In the Beginning

Joy Hakim

Watch that band of people move across the plain. They look hungry and tired. The tribe is small, just twenty people in all, and only six are men of hunting age. But they are brave and their spears are sharp, so they will keep going. They follow the tracks of a mammoth.

Dramatic introduction with an easy-to-picture scene

If they kill the mammoth—a huge, woolly elephant—they will feast for much of the winter.

The trail of the great animal leads them where no people have gone before. It leads them onto a wide, grassy earth bridge that stretches between two continents. They have come from Asia. When they cross that bridge they will be on land that someday will be called America. The trail of the mammoth leads them from Asia to a new world.

Thesis Statement

They don't realize what a big step they are taking. They don't know they are making history. All they know is that they have lost the mammoth. He has outsmarted them. But it doesn't matter; the new land is rich in animals and fish and berries. They will stay.

Transitional Paragraph

All that happened a long time ago, when families lived in huts and caves and the bow and arrow hadn't even been invented. It was a time when ice blankets—called *glaciers*—covered much of the northern land. We call it the Ice Age. Some of the glaciers were more than a mile high. Nothing [humans have] built has been as tall.

Switch from scene to information

If you look at a map, you will find the Bering Sea between Asia and Alaska. That is where the earth bridge used to be. It was quite a bridge. Today we call it Beringia, and it is under water. Back in the Ice Age, Beringia was a thousand miles wide. It had no trees, but was full of lakes and the kind of wild plants that drew animals. Men and women followed the animals; they settled on Beringia and lived there for generations. Not all the people were big-game hunters. Some were seagoers. They fished and caught small animals and lived near the beach. We think they were very good sailors. They had boats covered with animal skins, and they killed whales and explored and settled the coastline. Gradually these people—the land rovers and the seagoers—took that big step onto the new continent.

Facts about Ice Age and arrival of humans in North America

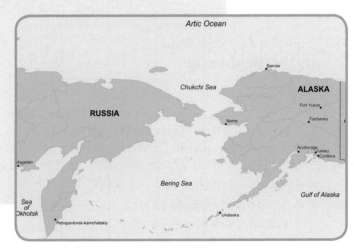

① Drafting an Effective Thesis Statement

A good way to begin drafting is to focus on your main idea—the point you want to make about your subject. During the prewriting stage, you expressed your main idea in a phrase. Now your task is to express that idea in a complete sentence. Your final thesis statement should be broad enough to cover all of the points that you plan to include in your essay. To make sure your thesis statement is appropriate, refer often to your prewriting notes.

If you had decided to write about students in Japan, your prewriting notes might look like the following.

Focused Subject	student attitudes in Japanese classrooms
Details	students are taught to respect those with knowledge and to treat them as teachers
	students are taught to listen carefully and to be humble when learning something
	students are eager to ask questions to increase their knowledge
	students believe that studying in a group can increase their knowledge

After reading over the notes, you might write the following topic sentence.

Initial Thesis Statement	Students in Japan are humble about learning.

This statement, however, is not broad enough to cover all the supporting points. It does not, for example, suggest anything about students working in groups. A revised, broader statement makes a better topic sentence.

Revised Thesis Statement	Students in Japan are encouraged to respect those with knowledge and to take advantage of all opportunities to learn.

PROJECT PREP *Drafting* *Thesis Statement*

Look over your prewriting work and list of supporting points and draft a thesis statement that is narrow enough to focus your essay but broad enough to cover your supporting points. Share your thesis statement with your writing group for feedback.

② Drafting the Essay Body

The body of an expository essay is made up of flowing, connected supporting sentences and paragraphs. Use your prewriting notes as you draft.

Tips for Drafting the Body

- Try to work fairly quickly. Do not worry about mistakes.
- Follow the order in which you placed your supporting details during prewriting.
- Every now and then, pause to read over what you have written. This process will help you keep track of the flow of your writing.
- When needed, add transitional words and phrases to help each sentence and paragraph lead smoothly into the next.

The following rough draft of an expository essay succeeded in getting all the ideas down in order. Transitions (highlighted) were added to improve the flow. However, the ideas are not developed adequately. In the next draft, the writer will expand this paragraph into several paragraphs, giving each main point a paragraph of its own.

MODEL: Expository Rough Draft

Students in Japan are encouraged to respect those with knowledge and to take advantage of all opportunities to learn. By far the most important attitude Japanese students bring to their learning is a respect for anyone with knowledge. That person is always regarded as the teacher. Related to this respect is the students' humble attitude toward learning. This attitude allows them to listen carefully in class and to ask questions eagerly to increase their knowledge. Finally, Japanese students are taught to respect what they can learn from classmates when working together in groups.

The thesis statement will be expanded into an introductory paragraph.

Each main point-- respect, humility, and group work— will be given its own paragraph.

PROJECT PREP Drafting Details and Support

Write your first draft. As you draft, plan to write at least one paragraph for your introduction, each main supporting point, and your conclusion. Use transitions to connect ideas within and between paragraphs so you achieve internal and external coherence.

3 Drafting the Conclusion

The conclusion brings your essay to a strong close. Without it, your essay may leave your readers hanging. To write a conclusion, first read over what you have written. Then write a conclusion that follows from and supports the information or explanation presented. Use one or more of the following strategies.

Strategies for Writing a Conclusion

- Restate the main idea in a fresh way.
- Refer back to an idea in the introduction.
- Summarize the paragraph, picking up key ideas or terms.
- Evaluate the details.
- Add an insight that shows new understanding of the main idea.

PROJECT PREP *Drafting* *Conclusion*

Draft your conclusion. Then in your writing group, ask for feedback on the effectiveness of the introduction and the development of ideas in the body of the essay. Is there enough elaboration and detail? Are there smooth transitions between paragraphs? Does the conclusion wrap up the essay effectively? Make notes of your partners' comments.

If you are like most writers, your first draft will not be the best you can do. In the revising stage of the writing process, you have a chance to improve your writing in a second or third draft. When revising, look at your draft as if you were the reader instead of the writer.

CHECKING FOR FOCUS AND COHERENCE

One way to improve your draft is to check it carefully for **focus**, or unity. An essay has focus when all of the paragraphs in the body relate directly to the main idea stated in the thesis. Paragraphs that stray from the main idea by including extraneous information or presenting information inconsistently cause readers to become confused and distracted.

Another way to improve a first draft is to make sure that it is coherent. In an essay with **coherence**, the ideas are presented in a logical order with clear transitions. While drafting you paid attention to presenting your ideas in a clear order and using transitions to help with the flow of your writing. As you revise check your writing to see if any idea got out of place, or if additional transitions could improve the flow even more.

● **Practice Your Skills**

Revising for Focus and Coherence

On separate paper, revise the following paragraph. Be sure that

• no ideas wander off the main point

• the ideas are presented in their most logical order

• transitions, if necessary, are added

A Blanket of Snow

Snow can actually help plants and animals keep warm in cold weather. The reason is that snow on the ground is warmer than the air above it. You can test this fact with a simple experiment. Take a reading of the temperature near the surface of a pile of snow. Borrow a thermometer from your parents. Read the temperature at ground level. You will see that it is warmer there than near the surface at the top of the pile. You could also take a temperature reading in the middle of the pile of snow if you want. The temperature there will be cooler than at ground level but warmer than at surface level. Because it stays warmer than the sometimes sub-zero air around it, snow can help keep plants and animals alive all through the winter months.

Use the checklist below to help you revise your writing.

 Evaluation Checklist for Revising

Checking Your Essay as a Whole

✓ Does the introduction set the tone, capture attention, and preview what is to follow? (page 96)

✓ Does the thesis statement make your main idea clear? (page 205)

✓ Is your main idea well developed, with well-chosen and relevant details, facts, and examples? (pages 205–206)

✓ Does your essay have focus, or unity? Does the topic sentence of each paragraph relate directly to the thesis statement? (page 208)

✓ If you give directions, do your supporting sentences provide the steps in the process? (pages 415–416)

✓ Are the paragraphs arranged in a logical order? (pages 199–200)

✓ Do transitions smoothly connect the paragraphs? (pages 203 and 206)

✓ Did you use techniques for achieving external coherence between paragraphs? (pages 206 and 208)

✓ Do you have a strong concluding paragraph? (page 207)

✓ Did you include a title? (page 99)

✓ Did you maintain a consistent tone throughout? (page 177)

Checking Your Paragraphs

✓ Does each paragraph have a topic sentence that is based on a fact? (pages 70–73)

✓ Does each paragraph use transitions to make it unified and achieve internal coherence? (pages 75–76)

✓ Are your details within each paragraph arranged in logical order? (page 93)

Checking Your Sentences and Words

✓ Did you use varied sentence types? (pages 53–59)

✓ Did you vary the length and beginnings of your sentences? (pages 53–59)

✓ Are your sentences clear and concise? (pages 60–63)

✓ Did you use precise language, domain-specific words when needed, and words that appeal to the senses? (pages 47–52)

✓ Did you establish and maintain a formal style? (see page 43)

✓ Did you include vivid images, figurative language, parallelism, and other rhetorical devices? (pages 45–51, 56, 78, and 186–187)

PROJECT PREP *Revising* *Second Draft*

Based on the feedback from your writing group, write a new draft of your essay. In addition to improving detail, organization, and paragraphing, pay attention to focus and coherence so that readers can follow your thinking.

When you are satisfied with the content of your essay, you can move on to editing, correcting mistakes in grammar, usage, mechanics, and spelling. Use proofreading symbols as a shorthand way of showing corrections.

The Language of Power *Sound-Alikes*

Power Rule: For sound-alikes and certain words that sound almost alike, choose the word with your intended meaning.

See It in Action The following examples illustrate the use of some common homophones.

its/it's At its core is a chimney-like column of calm air (the eye) around which multiple thunderstorms swirl. (*its* is a possessive pronoun meaning "belonging to it")

> Ana's coach reminded her that it's always a good idea to stretch after running. (*it's* means "it is")

where/were/wear Show me where it hurts. (*where* means "in what place")

> We were going to wear shorts, but it was too cold. (*were* is the past tense of "to be"; *wear* means "to have on the body")

bear/bare When he was hiking, Josh saw a bear and her cubs drinking from a stream. (*bear* is an animal)

> Norma couldn't bear the thought of living in an apartment with bare walls. (*bear* means "to tolerate"; *bare* means "plain" or "unadorned")

led/lead After her track meet, Ana said her legs felt like lead. (*lead* is a noun meaning "a heavy metal")

> Tony will lead the camp sing-along because everyone had so much fun when he led it last year. (*lead* is a verb meaning "to guide or direct"; *led* is the past tense of the verb *lead*)

Remember It Record this rule and the examples in the Power Rule section of your Personalized Editing Checklist.

Use It Read through your expository essay, checking to make sure you have chosen the correct homophones. Pay special attention to instances of *its* and *it's*.

You might want to read your paper three times, each time looking for a different kind of error. The Editing Checklist below can remind you how to focus your review.

Editing Checklist

✓ Did you read through your work to identify mistakes in grammar, spelling, or mechanics?

✓ Did you use the proofreading symbols on page 11 to edit your work?

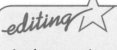

As always, review your writing and omit any words that you do not need. For practice in trimming away unnecessary words, edit the following sentence from a description about how a piano works.

> Then, the next step in the process follows, which is that the hammer strikes at and hits a string that is made of a metal.

PROJECT PREP *Editing and Publishing* *Reading and Sharing*

1. Exchange your new draft with a writing partner. Read each other's drafts, checking the spelling, punctuation, and usage closely.

2. Based on the feedback from your writing partner, prepare a final, polished version of your expository essay and publish it in the form you chose (see page 194) or through another appropriate medium. You might, for instance, identify a person who does not understand the process you have explained and give that person a copy. For example, if you wrote about how presidents are elected by the Electoral College, you might give the paper to someone who has just moved to the United States.

Use the following rubric to evaluate your own or another's expository text.

Ideas	4 The main idea is clear and focused and details convey information powerfully.	3 The main idea is clear and the text conveys information.	2 Some aspects of the topic are not clear and/or well developed.	1 Most aspects are not clear and/or well developed.
Organization	4 The organization is clear and easy to follow. Transitions provide coherence.	3 The organization is clear, but a few ideas seem out of place or disconnected.	2 Many ideas seem out of place and transitions are missing.	1 The organization is unclear and hard to follow.
Voice	4 The voice sounds natural and knowledgeable and is appropriate for the audience. The tone is consistent.	3 The voice sounds mostly natural and knowledgable and is right for the audience. The tone is consistent.	2 The voice sounds a bit unnatural and does not seem right for the audience. The tone seems to change in places.	1 The voice sounds mostly unnatural or is inappropriate for the audience. The tone is not appropriate or consistent.
Word Choice	4 Words are specific and figures of speech are used.	3 Words are vivid and specific.	2 Some words are overly general.	1 Most words are overly general.
Sentence Fluency	4 Varied sentences flow smoothly. Sentences vary in structure and length.	3 Most of the sentences are varied and smoothly flowing.	2 Some sentence patterns are not varied and some sentences are choppy.	1 Sentences are not varied and are choppy.
Conventions	4 Punctuation, usage, and spelling are correct and all Power Rules are followed.	3 There are only a few errors in punctuation, usage, and spelling and no Power Rule errors.	2 There are several errors in punctuation, usage, and spelling and no Power Rule errors.	1 There are many errors and at least one Power Rule error.

TIME OUT TO REFLECT

What parts of writing your expository text went smoothly? Why do you think they did? What parts were harder? Why? What have you learned that you can apply to the next time you write an expository text? Record your responses in your Learning Log.

In the Media

Create a "How-to" Multimedia Presentation

It can be a challenge to write to inform without being dull in your presentation. Since the advent of cable television, shows that cover cooking, home improvement, arts and crafts, and sewing have become very popular. One reason for this is that television producers have made these shows interesting and fun to watch. There are also more informational commercials (known as *infomercials*) on television. These are usually shorter shows that sell specific products—make-up, hair care, and exercise machines—using "ordinary" people to demonstrate the wide appeal and use of their products.

"How-to" presentations work well when they are clear and easy to follow. They can make complex tasks seem simple by showing how they are done, step by step. In addition, they might include helpful hints and other applications of the skills demonstrated. A show about making chocolate chip cookies might include shots of the cook, the audience, the dough, the oven, and tips for making other cookies.

Media Activity

Watch several how-to shows on television. Choose one and, if possible, record several episodes so that you can watch them several times. Take notes on ideas that you might use to create a "How-to" show of your own. Then work with a small group to create a multimedia presentation using text, graphics, images, and sound to explain how something works. You may base your presentation on the expository text you created earlier or choose a different subject. See **Electronic Publishing** (pages 431–445) for more information on creating multimedia presentations.

Writing Lab

Project Corner

Get Graphic
Change Genres

Explain your process using graphic images along with words. That is, **provide an illustrated explanation** of the process, either drawing the figures or borrowing them from another source.

Collaborate and Create Try It

Use directions written by a classmate explaining how to do some task. Try to **follow the directions** exactly as they are written. Note any directions that seem unclear or difficult, or that lead to results you think the writer did not intend.

Stage It Act It Out

In your writing group, **act out one piece of informational writing** using human characters for the aspects of the process. How could you represent a hurricane's increasing speed with students playing the parts of the process?

In the Workplace
Informative E-mail

1. You are an inventor and you have just delivered your newest invention to a prospective investor. The investor has sent you an e-mail because she does not know how to get your invention to work. She is not even sure what it is supposed to do. **Compose a reply e-mail** to the investor explaining how the gadget works and what it does. Give a step-by-step process for operating the invention. Be clear and exact in your explanation. (You can find information on writing e-mail messages on pages 451–455.)

In Academic Areas Informative Instructions

2. The local zoo has agreed to participate in a stuffed animal home-stay program with your district's elementary schools. The zoo will send a stuffed animal that represents a real animal in the zoo to spend a day in a classroom. The first animal to be placed is Tux the penguin. **Write an informative paragraph** for the students in the first classroom that will be receiving Tux's stuffed representative. In the paragraph include some general information about penguins and give instructions on how to care for them. Keep your audience and purpose in mind as you write. Make sure your paragraph is clear and progresses logically. Use transitions between ideas. (You can find information about writing paragraphs on pages 66–83.)

Timed Writing ⏲ Magazine Column

3. You write a monthly column for an online student magazine entitled "What I Know." Your editor allows you to write about any topic you know well. Your readers' favorite columns are the ones in which you focus on odd news stories, unusual animal behaviors, and other quirky topics. Write an informative magazine column about a subject you know well. Limit your subject to what can be covered in a short article. Keep the audience, purpose, and occasion in mind as you write and gear your voice and style toward them. Your article should contain an introduction, a body with supporting details, and a conclusion. Check your work for unity and coherence. You have 25 minutes to complete your work.

   Before You Write Consider the following questions: What is the subject? What is the occasion? Who is the audience? What is the purpose?

   After You Write Evaluate your work using the six-trait evaluation form on page 212.

Expository Writing Workshops

The workshops in this section of the chapter will help you write clear expository texts. During prewriting, be sure to consider the needs of your audience as you plan your explanations. During drafting put your thoughts in flowing sentences. Enliven your writing with a variety of rhetorical devices, such as similes, metaphors, and parallelism. (See pages 56, 78, and 186-187.) As you revise and edit your work, look for any weaknesses or errors in your writing and correct them. The result should be an explanation that is easy for your intended reader to follow.

1 Writing That Informs

When you are writing informatively, you can write from personal experience or outside your experience by using research.

PREWRITING

Think of a tradition your family follows for a holiday, birthday, or a family celebration. Make as many notes as you can about your family celebration: who is involved, how long this has been celebrated, when it is celebrated, special foods that are prepared, and other pertinent information. Meet with a partner and talk through the holiday, using your notes but also adding new ideas as they occur to you. Be as specific and detailed as you can.

DRAFTING

Use the details from your notes to draft an informative essay. Write an engaging introduction, and finish up with a strong conclusion.

REVISING BY CONFERENCING

Pair off with your partner. Have your partner read your essay aloud, and then read your partner's. Decide if any of the information presented is confusing.

Use your partner's comments and the **Evaluation Checklist for Revising** on page 209 to help you revise your essay. You do not have to incorporate all of your partner's comments.

EDITING

Check over your essay for errors, using the **Editing Checklist** on page 211.

PUBLISHING

Make a neat final copy. Consider the publishing suggestions on pages 32–33.

② Giving Directions

Any time you explain how to do something or get somewhere you are giving directions.

PREWRITING

How would you make an omelette? List all the steps, ingredients, and utensils needed to make an omelette.

DRAFTING

Use your list to draft an expository text giving directions on how to make an omelette.

REVISING BY CONFERENCING

Exchange your composition with a partner. Pantomime the directions as your partner reads them to you. Let your partner know if any parts of the directions are confusing.

Use your partner's comments and the **Evaluation Checklist for Revising** on page 209 to help you revise your directions. Incorporate only the comments on which you and your partner agree.

EDITING

Check over your text for errors, using the **Editing Checklist** on page 211.

PUBLISHING

Make a neat final copy, referring to the publishing suggestions on page 194.

③ Explaining Cause and Effect

Cause is why something happens and **effect** is the result. Start out by explaining the situation, then explain the cause for it, and its effects.

PREWRITING

Brainstorm these questions: What was the wisest choice you ever made? What factors led you to make this wise choice? What was the effect on you and on the people around you? Jot down some quick notes.

Meet with a partner to discuss your ideas. Try to express as clearly as possible the choice you made, what caused you to make the choice, and what the effect was. Ask for clarity if there is something your partner explains that you do not understand.

After you have discussed your ideas, decide how you will arrange them. Will you start with the effect and then explain the cause? Or will you start with the cause and then explain the effect? Sketch out an organizational strategy.

DRAFTING

Refer to your notes while drafting your cause-and-effect composition. Include an introduction, a well-developed body of supporting details, and a conclusion that provides a strong sense of closure.

REVISING BY CONFERENCING

Exchange your paper with a classmate. Ask your partner if the causes and effects are clear. Use your classmate's comments and the **Evaluation Checklist for Revising** to revise your composition.

EDITING

Check over your composition for errors, using the **Editing Checklist** on page 211.

PUBLISHING

Make a neat final copy using the suggested forms for publishing on page 194.

Comparing and Contrasting

A **compare-and-contrast** text examines the similarities and differences between two subjects.

This type of text will help you interpret, understand, and explain two related subjects or events (such as a kangaroo and a wallaby).

PREWRITING

If you are like most people, you like more than one type of music. Which are your two favorite types? Explore how they are similar and different. You might want to use a Venn diagram to help you see those similarities and differences.

After you have identified a number of similarities and differences, decide how you want to present them. You have two ways to organize your information in a compare-and-contrast text. One way is to write first about one subject (subject A) and then about the other subject (subject B). The second way is compare both subject A and subject B in terms of one similarity or difference. Then, you compare both of them in terms of another similarity or difference. Sketch out the plan you decide to use.

DRAFTING

Refer to your notes while drafting your comparison and contrast. Include an effective introduction, a well-developed body of supporting ideas, and a strong conclusion.

REVISING BY CONFERENCING

Exchange your paper with a classmate. Ask your partner if the similarities and differences are clear. Use your classmate's comments and the **Evaluation Checklist for Revising** to revise your composition.

EDITING AND PUBLISHING

Check over your composition for errors, using the **Editing Checklist** on page 211. Make a neat final copy using the suggested forms for publishing on page 194.

CHAPTER 9

Writing to Persuade

Persuasive writing states an opinion or claim and uses facts, examples, and reasons to convince readers. The kind of persuasive writing you will most often do in school is called **argumentative** writing.

Here are just a few examples of the ways in which persuasive writing is guiding important decisions in our lives.

- **You give a speech** telling your classmates why you are qualified to be class president.
- **Advertisers write television commercials** convincing people to buy their products.
- **A citizen writes a letter to a state representative** asking him to support a particular issue.
- **A doctor prepares a pamphlet for her patients** about living healthful lives.
- **Film critics write reviews of movies** convincing readers of their point of view.
- **Your state senator argues a bill** before Congress to promote early learning.

Writing Project *Persuasive*

Be Part of the Solution **Write an argumentative composition to influence others to be aware of an injustice in our society.**

Think Through Writing Think about something that you consider to be unfair in society. In what ways are people subjected to unfair conditions or denied something that they should have? Write about one situation that bothers you and that you would like to change.

Talk About It In your writing group, discuss the situations that bother you. Give your opinions about what is unfair about each issue. Also give your opinion about the best solutions to help address the problem.

Read About It In the following essay, Anna Quindlen shares her views on the plight of the homeless. What points is she trying to make about their circumstances?

From *Living Out Loud*
Homeless

Anna Quindlen

Her name was Ann, and we met in the Port Authority Bus Terminal several Januarys ago. I was doing a story on homeless people. She said I was wasting my time talking to her; she was just passing through, although she'd been passing through for more than two weeks. To prove to me that this was true, she rummaged through a tote bag and a manila envelope and finally unfolded a sheet of typing paper and brought out her photographs.

In the introduction, Quindlen draws readers in by focusing on one specific homeless person to personalize the subject.

They were not pictures of family, or friends, or even a dog or cat, its eyes brown-red in the flashbulb's light. They were pictures of a house. It was like a thousand houses in a hundred towns, not suburb, not city, but somewhere in between, with aluminum siding and a chain-link fence, a narrow driveway running up to a one-car garage and a patch of backyard. The house was yellow. I looked on the back for a date or a name, but neither was there. There was no need for discussion. I knew what she was trying to tell me, for it was something I had often felt. She was not adrift, alone, anonymous, although her bags and her raincoat with the grime shadowing its creases had made me believe she was. She had a house, or at least once upon a time

The very specific details of Ann's old house and her current grimy raincoat reach out to readers' emotions.

Project and Reading   221

she had had one. Inside were curtains, a couch, a stove, potholders. You are where you live. She was somebody.

I've never been very good at looking at the big picture, taking the global view, and I've always been a person with an overactive sense of place, the legacy of an Irish grandfather. So it is natural that the thing that seems most wrong with the world to me right now is that there are so many people with no homes. I'm not simply talking about shelter from the elements, or three square meals a day, or a mailing address to which the welfare people can send the check—although I know that all these are important for survival. I'm talking about a home, about precisely those kinds of feelings that have wound up in cross-stitch and French knots on samplers over the years.

Home is where the heart is. There's no place like it. I love my home with a ferocity totally out of proportion to its appearance or location. I love dumb things about it; the hot-water heater, the plastic rack you drain dishes in, the roof over my head, which occasionally leaks. And yet it is precisely those dumb things that make it what it is—a place of certainty, stability, predictability, privacy, for me and for my family. It is

> Quindlen draws a distinction here between basic needs and every person's deeper wants.

where I live. What more can you say about a place than that? That is everything.

Yet it is something that we have been edging away from gradually during my lifetime and the lifetimes of my parents and grandparents. There was a time when where you lived often was where you worked and where you grew the food you ate and even where you were buried. When that era passed, where you lived at least was where your parents had lived and where you would live with your children when you became enfeebled. Then suddenly, where you lived was where you lived for three years, until you could move on to something else and something else again.

And so we have come to something else again, to children who do not understand what it means to go to their rooms because they have never had a room, to men and women whose fantasy is a wall they can paint a color of their own choosing, to old people reduced to sitting on molded plastic chairs, their skin blue-white in the lights of a bus station, who pull pictures of houses out of their bags. Homes have stopped being homes. Now they are real estate.

People find it curious that those without homes would rather sleep sitting up on benches or huddled in doorways than go to shelters. Certainly some prefer to do so because they are emotionally ill, because they have been locked in before and they are damned if they will

be locked in again. Others are afraid of the violence and trouble they may find there. But some seem to want something that is not available at shelters, and they will not compromise, not for a cot, or oatmeal, or a shower with special soap that kills bugs. "One room," a woman with a baby who was sleeping on her sister's floor, once

Through concrete examples that everyone can relate to, Quindlen helps explain some of the abstract ideas of certainty, stability, and predicatability.

In this paragraph and the next, Quindlen implies her main idea: that the very nature of homes has been changing, from a stable center of family life to a temporary real estate arrangement.

Quindlen uses her belief that home means more than a place to meet basic needs to explain why some homeless people do not find comfort in shelters.

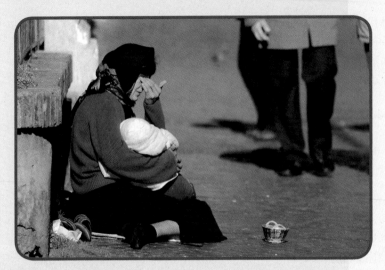

told me, "painted blue." That was the crux of it; not size or location, but pride of ownership. Painted blue.

This is a difficult problem, and some wise and compassionate people are working hard at it. But in the main I think we work around it, just as we walk around it when it is lying on the sidewalk or sitting in the bus terminal—the problem, that is. It has been customary to take people's pain and lessen our own participation in it by turning it into an issue, not a collection of human beings. We turn an adjective into a noun; the poor, not poor people; the homeless, not Ann or the man who lives in the box or the woman who sleeps on the subway grate.

Sometimes I think we would be better off if we forgot about the broad strokes and concentrated on the details. Here is a woman without a bureau. There is a man with no mirror, no wall to hang it on. They are not the home-less. They are people who have no homes. No drawer that holds the spoons. No window to look out upon the world. My God. That is everything.

> Quindlen argues that everyone should personalize homelessness in order to appreciate the depth of the problem.

Respond in Writing Respond to Anna Quindlen's essay on homeless people. What is she trying to persuade the reader to do? Has she changed your mind about anything or convinced you of something?

Develop Your Own Ideas Work with your classmates to develop ideas that you might use to write persuasively about an issue of unfairness in society today.

Small Groups: In your small group, discuss the writing you have done. Consider each argument based on the questions below.

- What specific issues did people write about?
- Into what general categories can you classify these issues?
- How has society helped to create the conditions that you consider to be unfair?
- In what way does this injustice affect those who are its victims?
- How does this situation affect you emotionally?
- What solutions do you recommend to change or relieve this injustice?

Whole Class: Make a master chart of all of the ideas generated by the small groups to see how different members of the class perceived inequity in society.

Write About It You will next write an essay in which you convince others that something in society is unfair. Your writing might concern any of the following possible topics, address any of the possible audiences, and take any of the possible forms.

Possible Topics	Possible Audiences	Possible Forms
• a law that places some people at a disadvantage • a set of attitudes that subject some people to unfair treatment • circumstances of a person's environment that place him or her at a disadvantage • circumstances related to a person's personal characteristics—such as race or gender—that place him or her at a disadvantage	• readers who have contributed to the problem • people who might be unaware that the problem exists • people who are personally affected by the problem • people who have the authority to help change the circumstances that lead to the problem • people who work for charitable foundations	• a letter • a blog • a newspaper essay • a speech to the government

Developing Your Skills of Persuasion

"In a republican nation, whose citizens are to be led by reason and persuasion and not by force, the art of reasoning becomes of first importance." So wrote Thomas Jefferson, and his words hold true to this day. When you seek to change an inequity in your society, a well-organized argumentative essay can be very convincing.

Of course, you will encounter opposition to your point of view, and you will probably stir some strong emotions. In order to meet counter-arguments you must be well-reasoned in your arguments. This chapter will help you develop your persuasive skills.

Structure

Like all essays, an argumentative essay has three main parts: an introduction, a body, and a conclusion. The chart below shows how to make each part fulfill its function.

Structuring an Argumentative Essay

- In the **introduction,** capture the audience's attention, present the issue, and introduce a claim in a thesis statement.
- In the **body of supporting paragraphs,** present reasons, facts, examples, and expert opinions to support your claims. Address counter-arguments, distinguishing your position from others. (See pages 231 and 234–235.)
- In the **conclusion,** present a summary or strong conclusive evidence—logically drawn from the arguments—that drives home the writer's opinion.

In a well-structured persuasive essay, each sentence must have a specific purpose and should flow logically from one to the next. As you read the essay below, notice how each sentence works toward persuading the reader.

MODEL: Persuasive Essay

Fire Drills at Home

Everyone has seen them: students crowded onto the school playground, coatless and shivering. Everyone also knows why they are there: a fire drill. The reason so many schools, teachers, and students go through the trouble of having fire drills is that the drills work, saving hundreds of lives a year. The question, then, is why don't more people have fire drills at home? Fire drills should be conducted in homes as well as in schools and other public buildings.

Strong image gets readers involved

Thesis Statement

First of all, having regular fire drills at home would allow all family members to practice what to do in an emergency. This practice would reduce panic during a fire and perhaps make the difference between escaping safely and being trapped. While it might be inconvenient, the value of a being prepared far outweighs the small inconvenience of a drill.

First Reason

Writer anticipates a concern and addresses it

Second, having home fire drills would set a good example in the neighborhood. Nearby families may be encouraged to have their own drills. The neighborhood may even want to have a community meeting and invite a representative from the fire department to talk about the best way to stay safe from fires.

Second Reason

Most important, having fire drills at home would probably lead people to be more safety-conscious so that fires would not get started in the first place. Most house fires begin in the kitchen. If family members learn and put into practice some basic safety precautions during cooking, accidental fires could be prevented. Having regular fire drills would be a steady reminder to take those precautions.

Most important reason saved for last

Yes, a household will be temporarily disrupted for a fire drill, just as classrooms are evacuated during the heart of a school day. However, house fires cause thousands of deaths and injuries each year. Even those lucky enough to escape unharmed often lose precious and irreplaceable belongings and memories. Isn't a fire drill that takes no more than a few minutes a few times a year worth enduring to prevent such losses?

Conclusion provides unity by referring back to the image in the introduction

Ending with a rhetorical question can leave your readers thinking seriously over your ideas.

CHAPTER 9

Transitions help stitch the essay together. *First of all, second,* and *most important* link the paragraphs and also show the relative importance of ideas.

PROJECT PREP   *Analyzing*   *Essay Structure*

1. In your writing group, discuss the structure of the model essay on fire drills. Design a graphic organizer that represents the structure of this essay.

2. Share your first rough writing with your group. Discuss what each writer needs to do to turn that beginning of an idea into a well-structured argumentative essay.

② Facts and Opinions

If you intend to change someone's mind, you must provide a convincing argument. Sticking to the facts is essential to building a strong case. Opinions have their place, but they cannot be used as proof. Learn to recognize opinions by watching for words such as *should, must, best,* and *worst.*

A **fact** is a statement that can be proved. An **opinion** is a belief or judgment that cannot be proved.

You can test whether a statement is factual in two ways. One way is to ask yourself whether you would be able to prove the statement through your own observation and experience.

Fact	There is a homeless shelter in our local church.
	(You could go to the church and see the shelter.)

The second way is to ask yourself whether you could prove it by consulting accepted authorities.

Fact	California has one of the largest homeless populations.
	(You cannot use your experience to test this statement, but you can verify it by consulting a recognized expert or an encyclopedia.)

Unlike facts, opinions cannot be proved. They are personal judgments, interpretations, preferences, and predictions that differ from person to person. Here are some examples.

Opinion	Homelessness is a **terrible problem in our society.**
	The **best** way to combat the problem is by creating jobs.

Here are some more words to watch for to spot opinions.

OPINION WORDS		
should	good, better, best	probably
ought	bad, worse, worst	might
can	beautiful	perhaps
may	terrible	maybe

In argumentative essays, the soundest opinions are those supported by factual evidence from credible sources, logical arguments, or both. These are called **claims**, statements asserted to be true.

Unsupportable Statement	Homelessness is the worst problem facing society. (No supporting facts could back up this judgment statement.)
Supportable Statement, or Claim	Building single-room occupancy dwellings is an effective answer to homelessness. (Data from the Department of Housing and Urban Development could provide evidence for the effectiveness of this plan.)

● Practice Your Skills

Recognizing Facts and Opinions

For each statement write *F* if it is a fact or *O* if it is an opinion.

1. Schools should allow students more say in which classes they take.

2. In July of 1985, musicians donated their talents to the Live Aid concert to raise money for hungry Africans.

3. Dolphins are beautiful creatures.

4. Dolphins use sonar to locate objects underwater.

5. Many companies in the United States now use recycled paper.

6. Everyone should use recycled paper.

7. The movie ratings should include more categories than the current four.

8. Old science fiction films, despite their clumsy special effects, are better than more recent ones.

9. Some guitars have six strings.

10. Six-stringed guitars have a twangier sound.

● Practice Your Skills

Revising a Paragraph with Facts

The following persuasive paragraph uses only opinions to support its position. Read the paragraph once. Then read it again along with the facts that follow on the next page. Use the pertinent facts to revise the paragraph.

A Throw-Away Culture

The people of the United States should learn to use things over and over instead of simply throwing them away. First of all, too much trash could harm the environment. Second, disposing of things so easily might lead to an overall throw-away attitude. Perhaps the reason that so many dogs and cats are put to sleep in animal shelters is that we have a throw-away attitude toward them too. Finally, throwing away so many things is expensive. Why not spend a little more money to buy a pen that could last a lifetime instead of buying many cheaper pens that you throw away after a month? This fairly new throw-away attitude has become the worst problem of our time.

Facts to use in revision:

- Plastics in disposable items remain in the environment for many years after the items have been thrown away.
- Americans throw out 3 to 5 pounds of garbage per day; this is more than half a ton of garbage per person each year.
- Each year 15 million dogs and cats are put to sleep in humane societies.
- Americans spend about $2 billion each year on disposable plastic and paper plates.
- Americans spend nearly $3 billion each year on disposable diapers.
- Other disposable items, such as pens, lighters, and razors, cost another $2 billion.

Writing Tip

Use **facts** and examples to convince readers. Do not use **opinions** to support your position.

PROJECT PREP **Prewriting** *Facts and Opinions*

Read your first rough draft (see page 225), looking for facts and opinions. Identify each supporting point in your writing as either opinion or fact. Underline the opinions in red ink. Underline facts, examples, or reasons in blue ink. If you have more red than blue, gather more facts, examples, and reasons from credible sources to back up your position and work them into your draft. (Refer to pages 288–289 for help in locating research sources.)

Think Critically

Developing Counter-Arguments

To form a strong argument, consider all possible objections to your position. Then think of a **counter-argument,** an answer to each objection. Suppose, for example, you are arguing that it is unfair of your community center to restrict from using the facilities anyone who is wearing a T-shirt showing a name or image associated with a rock band. How do your opponents feel about this?

Community Leaders' Opposition	How I Will Respond
Their views: The community center has the right and responsibility to set the rules.	Response: They serve the public and should be equally open to all points of view on the subject.
Their concerns: • Center serves a wide variety of youth and needs to be sure that kids are not exposed to bands or images that they or their parents find offensive. • The harm done by banning the T-shirts is less significant than the harm that could be done by allowing them and offending or disturbing others.	Answers: • The ban puts the needs of one group of youth over another, and that's not fair. • Band loyalty is a way young people have to express themselves and to deny that is censorship. Censorship is such a serious harm that the Bill of Rights includes an amendment protecting free speech.
Their counter-arguments: • Some young people have special sensitivities that entitle them to special treatment. • Students can wear whatever they want; they just can't use the community center if they choose to wear a band shirt.	Answers: • Either everyone is equal or everyone is not equal. Who decides who gets special treatment? • As a public facility, the center should be open to young people no matter what they wear.

Thinking Practice

Make a chart like the one above on your topic for an argumentative essay. Identify your readers' concerns and views, anticipate their counter-arguments, and be ready to respond to them. Discuss your chart with your writing group and give feedback to each author on improving the responses or identifying new opposing views.

③ Order of Importance and Transitions

A logical presentation of ideas helps you convince your readers. Placing the most important point at the end of a paragraph can give you a special advantage. For one thing, the last point tends to stick longer in a reader's mind. For another, placing your most persuasive point last gives your argument more impact.

TRANSITIONS FOR ORDER OF IMPORTANCE				
also	third	for example	more important	finally
first	besides	furthermore	most important	similarly
second	moreover	in addition	to begin with	in conclusion

The following paragraph was written to persuade readers that Jack London's book *The Call of the Wild* is more than just a story about a dog named Buck. Read the paragraph. Notice that the writer has arranged the supporting points from least to most important.

MODEL: Order of Importance

Lessons from the Wild

Although many people look at *The Call of the Wild* as a fast-moving adventure story about a dog, I think of it as something more. One reason I do is that it shows how it is possible to adapt to a new environment even when conditions are extremely bad. Buck changed his habits and a way of life in order to survive. Along with exciting action, I also saw how inhuman and uncivilized people can be, not only to dogs but also to each other. Men stole from one another, fought one another, and killed one another. The most important reason for considering this as more than just an ordinary action story is the lesson I learned from the way the story ended. Buck went off to become the leader of a pack of wolves because civilization in the Klondike was worse than life in the wild. More than just an adventure story, *The Call of the Wild* presents worthwhile lessons for us today.

Topic Sentence: Claim

Supporting Points: Order of least to most important

Concluding Sentence: Final appeal

PROJECT PREP *Prewriting* **Order and Transitions**

In your writing group, help each author think about how to order paragraphs logically. Then discuss the kinds of transitions that will help them order their points.

In the Media

Radio Advertising: Emotions and Audience

The basis of a strong argument is sound reasoning that relies on solid facts and that appeals to the reader's own sense of reason. However, many arguments include appeals to emotions as well. Anna Quindlen, for example, stirs emotions in her portrayal of Ann, the homeless woman.

Appeals to emotions require a clear understanding of audience; if you don't know your audience, you don't know what will stir their feelings. Advertising companies spend an enormous amount of time and money researching the age groups and income levels of their customers. Companies that create radio advertising also research the listening habits of the customers they want to attract. They have become clever about using music as a tie-in to a product and involving the emotions of listeners.

Music can instantly evoke a mood or a feeling. Hundreds of hip-hop, country, and rock-and-roll songs have been used to sell burgers, trucks, khaki pants, running shoes, and computers. An old rock-and-roll song may make someone in her fifties long for her youth. An advertiser selling a car to someone in that age group may use a rock-and-roll song together with a slogan that says "Age is a state of mind." The combination suggests that owning that car will make the buyer feel young.

Similarly, a hip-hop song evokes a feeling of "cool." If an advertiser has decided that the best potential market for the athletic shoes it is selling is young people, then a hip-hop song may just do the trick. Such an ad blends seamlessly into the music being played on the radio station that young people listen to all afternoon.

Media Activity

Rock-and-roll, hip-hop, and country radio stations all have specific audiences. To practice your persuasive writing skills, form three groups, one for each kind of station. Then write a radio ad selling a spatula to your target audience. What is the average age of your listeners? Are they male or female? Select a song that ties in to your product. Then think of a slogan that works with the song. Write a script, and, if possible, make a recording of your ad and play it for the class.

CHAPTER 9

1 Purpose, Subject, and Audience

In a persuasive essay, your purpose is to influence the opinions and the behavior of your readers—your audience. You want to persuade your audience to adopt your point of view and to take an action you might suggest. Your first step in carrying out this purpose is to develop a logical argument that supports your opinion.

Most of the success of a persuasive essay depends on careful planning during the prewriting stage. Choose a subject with care and take the time to prepare your argument thoroughly.

CHOOSING A SUBJECT

The subject you choose should be meaningful to you. The stronger your interest, the more convincing your persuasive essay will be. The subject you choose should also be somewhat controversial—one about which people tend to disagree. For instance, the treatment of the homeless in American society, the effectiveness of the welfare laws, and the care of American seashores are all issues about which people hold opposing points of view. Brainstorm for a list of issues about which you care and have strong opinions. Next narrow your choices by brainstorming, freewriting, or clustering on each of the issues you are considering. Then use the following guidelines to choose the best subject for your persuasive essay.

Guidelines for Choosing a Subject

- Choose a subject that is important to you.
- Choose a subject on which people hold very different opinions.
- Choose a subject that you can support with examples, reasons, and facts from your own experiences or from other reliable sources.
- Choose a subject for which there is an audience whose beliefs or behavior you would like to influence.

IDENTIFYING YOUR AUDIENCE'S COUNTER-ARGUMENTS

Sometimes when you write a persuasive essay, you may have to address an audience outside of the classroom. Learn as much as possible about that audience in advance in order to decide whether you can successfully persuade them or move them to action. Knowing your audience well also help you choose the best material to support your argument.

Questions for Analyzing the Position of Your Audience

- What views does my audience hold about my topic? How can I respond to those views?
- What concerns does my audience have about my topic? How can I answer these concerns persuasively?
- What counter-arguments might my audience support? How can I answer these?

● **Practice Your Skills**

Identifying Your Audience

Form a small group and identify five possible audiences for each of the following subjects.

Example	creating a new park in town
Audience	parents, children, day-care workers, landscape architects, senior citizens, gardeners, city council members

1. creating an arts initiative for the community
2. creating and supporting additional homeless shelters
3. establishing walking trails on local land

PROJECT PREP *Prewriting* *Reasoning*

In your writing group, discuss the audience each writer is intending to reach. Then discuss where that audience is likely to stand on the issue and how best to persuade that audience. Also help each author identify an appropriate voice for the persuasive purpose.

2 Establishing Your Thesis

Once you have chosen a subject and identified your audience, you are ready to develop your **thesis,** or the claim you will argue. In your thesis statement, avoid simply stating a fact or expressing a personal preference.

Fact	Throughout the world, well-tended parks can be found in many cities.
Preference	I think our city would benefit by having a beautiful park.
Thesis Statement (Claim)	While it may cost the citizens in the form of higher taxes, creating a park we all can enjoy will benefit our city.

Use the following guidelines to develop a thesis statement.

Guidelines for Developing a Thesis Statement

- Choose a debatable position—one that has at least two sides.
- State your claim simply and directly in one sentence.
- Give a supportable position or a recommendation for action.
- As you collect more information, continue to revise the thesis statement until it is clear-cut and defensible and covers all the evidence.

If your thesis is not debatable, supportable, and defensible, rethink your position or look for a more appropriate issue.

PROJECT PREP *Prewriting* *Thesis Statement*

Develop a debatable, supportable, and defensible thesis for your argumentative essay, taking all previous discussions and writing into account. Try to express your thesis statement in a complex sentence in which an opposing viewpoint is expressed in a subordinate clause and your thesis statement is expressed in an independent clause. (See page 237.) Get feedback from your writing group on your thesis.

The Power of Language ⚡

Clauses: Tip the Scale

Good persuasive writing includes consideration of other points of view. When you write your thesis statement, you can express opposing views in an independent clause (highlighted), followed by another independent clause expressing your viewpoint. This construction, however, puts your opponents' viewpoint on an equal footing with yours.

> **Two Independent Clauses**
>
> Most people are not homeless and do not need costly special services. Homelessness is an issue all people should work to alleviate.

A better way to express the same idea is to use a subordinate, or dependent, clause for the point of view you are disputing. This construction allows you to "tip the scale" in favor of your position. In the following example, the subordinate clause is highlighted.

> **One Subordinate, One Independent Clause**
>
> Although most people are not homeless and do not need costly special services, homelessness is an issue all people should work to alleviate.

By making this statement in a subordinate clause, you can acknowledge opposing views and *still* keep the focus on your viewpoint, expressed in the main clause.

Try It Yourself

Create a few sentences of your own in which you present your opponents' viewpoint in a subordinate clause and then your viewpoint in a main independent clause. Later, you can check your draft to see if there are any places you'd like to add a subordinate clause or create one from a main clause, as in the example.

Writing Tip

Place a comma after an introductory subordinate clause.

DRAFTING AN EFFECTIVE INTRODUCTION

An effective way to capture your audience's attention is to begin with a startling fact or a probing question. Give the reader a sense of how important the issue is by making sure that your claim is expressed clearly and forcefully. Experiment with emphasis by placing the thesis statement at different places to determine the most dramatic effect.

DRAFTING THE BODY

Devote at least one paragraph to each main point. Present your own supporting evidence and include the opposition's strongest counter-arguments. Ask and answer these three pairs of questions as you draft:

- What are the opposing views? How can I respond to them persuasively?
- What concerns does my audience have? How can I answer them persuasively?
- What counter-arguments might my audience have? How can I effectively and persuasively address those?

Remember to use transitional words (page 232) to guide the reader through your argument. Transitions create cohesion and also show the relationships among claims, counterclaims, reasons, and evidence.

DRAFTING THE CONCLUSION

Finally, draft a conclusion that follows from and supports the argument presented and makes a strong final appeal. If you want to persuade the readers to take some action, make a recommendation. Then add a title that is lively and challenging.

PROJECT PREP Drafting Following the Plan

Write a draft of your essay. Be aware of its structure and the purpose of each main part. Try taking a risk in your introduction by using a startling example or fact. Present your argument through solid reasoning and clear organization. Use transitions and language appropriate for your subject, occasion, and audience. Address opposing views thoroughly and respectfully. Wrap up your essay with a strong final appeal.

Persuasive Writing  Revising

Read your essay several times, each time addressing a different aspect of the writing.

 Evaluation Checklist for Revising

Checking Your Introduction

- ✓ Does the thesis statement present your claim effectively? (page 236)
- ✓ Will your introduction convince the readers that your topic is important? (page 238)

Checking Your Body Paragraphs

- ✓ Does each paragraph have a topic sentence? (pages 70–73)
- ✓ Have you supported your main points with logical reasoning and relevant evidence, using accurate, credible sources and demonstrating an understanding of the topic? (pages 228–230)
- ✓ Have you developed arguments and organized them clearly? (pages 234–236)
- ✓ Have you dealt with opposing views effectively? (pages 234–235)
- ✓ Have you used transitions to show relationships among claims, reasons, and evidence? (page 232)

Checking Your Conclusion

- ✓ Did you refer back to your thesis statement and/or make a recommendation? (page 238)
- ✓ Is your conclusion logically drawn from your arguments? (page 238)

Checking Your Words and Sentences

- ✓ Have you used subordinate clauses to express opposing views, keeping the focus on your position? (page 237)
- ✓ Have you used precise words as well as figures of speech to convey exactly what you mean? (pages 45–52)
- ✓ Have you established and maintained a formal style? (page 43)

PROJECT PREP *Revising* *Checking Organization and Logic*

Bring your draft to your writing group and take turns reading one another's drafts aloud. Focus on each author's body paragraphs. Help each author identify the main points of the argument and create a separate paragraph for each. Make suggestions for responding to counter-arguments. After the discussion, revise your draft based on feedback from your peers. Add, substitute, delete, and/or rearrange to make your paper as strong as it can be. As your teacher directs, submit your revised draft to him or her for review.

Carefully reread your revised draft for spelling, grammar, and usage. Put your writing aside for a time. Later, you will see mistakes that you missed.

The Language of Power *Possessive Nouns*

Power Rule: Use standard ways to make nouns possessive. (See pages 878–880.)

See It in Action To form the possessive of a singular noun, add an apostrophe and an *-s*. If a plural noun ends in *-s*, form the possessive by adding only an apostrophe. If a plural noun does not end in *s*, add an apostrophe and an *-s*. The examples below are from "Homeless."

> "One room," a woman with a baby who was sleeping on her sister's floor, once told me, "painted blue."
>
> It has been customary to take people's pain and lessen our own participation in it by turning it into an issue, not a collection of human beings.

Remember It Record this rule and examples in the Power Rule section of your Personalized Editing Checklist.

Use It Read through your short story and circle each possessive noun. Check each one to make sure you have formed the possessive correctly.

PROJECT PREP **Editing** *Checking Conventions*

Based on your teacher's feedback, revise your essay. Then edit your paper, referring to your Personalized Editing Checklist to avoid repeating errors you have made before. Asking a classmate or a family member to help you catch errors is a good strategy.

Ideas	4 The thesis statement clearly expresses a claim and is backed with facts and examples. Opposing views are addressed well.	3 The thesis statement expresses a claim. Facts and examples provide support. Opposing views are addressed.	2 The thesis statement is clear, but there is not enough support for it. Opposing views are not addressed well.	1 The thesis statement is missing or unclear, and there is little support. Opposing views are not addressed.
Organization	4 The organization is clear with frequent transitions.	3 A few ideas seem out of place or transitions are missing.	2 Many ideas seem out of place and transitions are missing.	1 The organization is unclear and hard to follow.
Voice	4 The voice sounds natural, engaging, and forceful.	3 The voice sounds natural and engaging.	2 The voice sounds mostly natural but is weak.	1 The voice sounds mostly unnatural and is weak.
Word Choice	4 Words are specific and powerful. Language is formal and respectful.	3 Words are specific and language is formal and respectful.	2 Some words are too general and/or emotional.	1 Most words are overly general.
Sentence Fluency	4 Varied sentences flow smoothly.	3 Most sentences are varied and flow smoothly.	2 Some sentences are varied but some are choppy.	1 Sentence structure is not varied or smooth.
Conventions	4 Punctuation, usage, and spelling are correct. The Power Rules are all followed.	3 Punctuation, usage, and spelling are mainly correct and Power Rules are all followed.	2 Some conventions are incorrect but all Power Rules are followed.	1 There are many errors and at least one failure to follow a Power Rule.

CHAPTER 9

PROJECT PREP *Editing* *Peer Evaluation*

In your writing group, evaluate one another's persuasive essay using the rubric above. Make any revisions that seem appropriate.

You have been considering your purpose, audience, and occasion throughout the process of writing your persuasive essay and have been making revisions accordingly. The medium in which you publish writing also has a bearing on the style and format of your work. Consider the requirements of each of the following types of publications.

CHARACTERISTICS OF ASSORTED PUBLISHING FORMATS	
Blog	• style is often more casual than printed text • may be written to invite interaction from readers in the form of comments to the blog • reader-friendly formatting techniques, such as bullet lists and a clear heading structure, assist in reading from the computer screen • graphics may be added to enhance the message • hyperlinks lead to related stories
Magazine article	• article's style and tone need to fit with the style and tone of the publication (For example, an article in a financial magazine would likely need to be somewhat formal.) • in some two-column magazines paragraphs tend to be short • graphics often accompany the article
E-mail notice	• e-mails need to be concise and to the point • the text is often "chunked" in manageable amounts for ease of reading • hyperlinks are often provided
Public announcement	• generally has very neutral and formal language • may include charts and other graphics

TIME OUT TO REFLECT After you publish your essay in the form you chose from page 225 or through another appropriate medium, reflect on what you have learned. If you have written a persuasive essay earlier in the year, how does it differ from the work you just completed? What did you do better in your most recent work? Is there anything you did better before? Record your reflections in your Learning Log.

Persuasive Presentations  Multimedia

At the beginning of the chapter you read an essay about people who are homeless. Consider how images, graphics, and sound might add to the persuasive power of Anna Quindlen's words. You can include visuals, sound, and text using presentation software to create a persuasive essay that will make a strong impression.

BUILDING A USER-FRIENDLY PRESENTATION

Presentation software is easy to use and can produce some powerful effects. However, make sure that the technology you use to communicate your position genuinely serves your purpose. Fancy techniques can sometimes detract from the message, so use good judgment when creating slides.

Here are some other points to keep in mind as you prepare an audience-friendly persuasive presentation.

Tips for Creating Effective Multimedia Presentations

Content
1. Keep it simple. Keep text to a minimum.
2. Include only the most important information.
3. Limit the number of bullet points per slide. Three or four should be the maximum.

Images and Video
4. Make sure the images and video support your key points.
5. Do not use graphics just as decoration.

Language
6. Limit the number of words you use.
7. Use parallel language. For example, if the first bullet point is a complete sentence, the second should be too.

Fonts
8. Heavy fonts are easier to read from a distance than light ones.
9. Keep the font size large enough to be seen easily at the back of the room.
10. Use only two font styles per presentation.

PROJECT PREP Publishing *Presentation*

Prepare a power presentation of your persuasive essay or of some key part of it. Begin by making a plan. Which points do you want to convey? What graphics, including videos, would help you support your thesis most effectively? What style would persuade your audience most powerfully? After you have a plan, use the software to create your presentation. Practice presenting it before you actually present it to the class.

Writing Lab

Project Corner

Speak and Listen
Group Discussion

Discuss with your classmates the inequities you have written about. **Express your opinions** on three main topics: 1) what kinds of people contribute to the problems, 2) what sorts of people are affected by them, and 3) what sorts of people help solve the problems. Are there any trends in the issues identified? What can teenagers do to help address the problems discussed?

Get Creative
Write a Poem

Choose some aspect of one of the problems addressed in your writing group to use as the basis for **writing a poem** that uses poetic techniques, figurative language, and graphic elements to express feelings and insights. (See pages 181–187 for information on writing poetry.) Present your poem to the rest of the class in the best way possible. After presenting your poem, ask a question to start a discussion on the feelings the poem evoked.

Collaborate and Create Make a Group Display

Use all of the issues identified in your class to **make a display** depicting what students in your class find to be injustices in society today and how they can be addressed. Be as creative as you can about ways to present your topics in the most visually appealing way possible. As a class, develop guidelines for creating the display and a rubric for assessing it. Also decide how to divide up the work so that everyone has a part in the activity. Set a timeline for completing the display.

In Academic Areas
Persuasive Report

1. As a health professional, you are worried about the amount of time young people spend wearing hats. You have noticed some ill effects of frequent hat wearing, including hair loss, difficulty seeing (when a brim is pulled low), and overheating of the brain. In your opinion this is scientific evidence and should not be taken lightly. You worked long and hard gathering data. Hats off to you! *Write a persuasive report* about your concerns to share with school principals nationwide. Persuade them to enact and enforce school rules against hats. Begin your report with a statement of your opinion, and support it with facts and examples. Arrange your points in a logical order. (You can find information on writing reports on pages 234–239.)

For Oral Communication Persuasive Speech

2. Your class has just nominated you to be Spring Festival chairperson. You will be in charge of the pie booth and get pies thrown at you all day. You don't think you deserve such an honor and know there is someone more worthy of the position. *Prepare a speech* to deliver to your classmates persuading them not to vote for you. Keep your audience and purpose in mind as you write your argument. Offer reasons, facts, and examples to convince them. Use transitions to connect ideas. (You can find information on preparing speeches on pages 417–421.)

Timed Writing 🕐 Persuasive Letter to the Editor

3. Your school has organized a half-time show for the big football game. At the end of the show, someone in a warthog costume covered with sparklers will march onto the field. The sparklers will be lit and the warthog will blaze for several seconds. The school's mascot is actually a panther, but the warthog costume was on sale. Even so, you do not feel this is a good use of the school's money. Write a persuasive letter to the editor of the school paper asking students to protest this frivolous waste of money. The letter should state your opinion and contain facts, examples, and reasons to support it. Think of possible objections to your opinion and address them. Use transitions to contrast your opinion to those objections. Write a strong concluding statement. You have 25 minutes to complete your work. (For help with budgeting time, see pages 374–375.)

Before You Write Consider the following questions: What is the subject? What is the occasion? Who is the audience? What is the purpose?

After You Write Evaluate your work using the six-trait rubric on page 241.

Persuasive Writing Workshops

The following essay-writing activities will give you practice in writing to persuade.

1 Supporting a Hypothesis with Facts

PREWRITING

Imagine that your science teacher has asked you to write a prediction based on current scientific knowledge. You have decided to write about athletes of the future. From your reading you have learned the following facts about athletes of today. Use these notes to form an opinion about athletes of the future. An opinion put forward to explain certain facts or to make a prediction is called a **hypothesis.**

- continue to break records
- use scientific studies to increase athletic ability
- use latest knowledge of nutrition to develop sound bodies
- use scientific training techniques

Once you have your hypothesis, freewrite and brainstorm ideas with a partner for a brief persuasive essay supporting it. Be sure to include arguments that defend your opinion against opposing ones. Remember to base your arguments on facts instead of opinions.

DRAFTING

Using your notes and the facts given, draft your persuasive essay. Use subordinate clauses to present opposing viewpoints without weakening your own stance. Make sure your points are presented in a logical order.

REVISING BY CONFERENCING

Reread your paper and revise it if necessary. Then exchange papers with a classmate. If the opinion in your partner's thesis statement differs from yours, are you convinced by the facts provided? If there is anything you do not understand, ask your partner to clarify. Tell your partner what you like about the essay and what could be improved. Make any changes you think would improve your composition.

EDITING

After you have revised your essay, edit it for errors in sentence structure, spelling, grammar, capitalization, and punctuation. Use the checklist on page 30 as a source for guidance. You may want to share your work with classmates or family members for additional feedback.

② Persuading with Reasons

PREWRITING

You just heard that your favorite television show may be canceled after this season. The network that carries the show has decided that the stars are overpaid and that the show has no social merit. You've decided to write a letter requesting that they keep the show. With a partner, express your opinions about the show and brainstorm a list of reasons why the network executives should keep the show on the air. Remember to address their particular concerns.

DRAFTING

Using your list of reasons, draft a letter requesting that the network decide in favor of keeping the show on the air. Use compelling reasons and wording. Be sure to use logical order and transitions as well as polite, reasonable language. You can acknowledge opposing viewpoints without taking away from your own reasoning.

REVISING BY CONFERENCING

When you are done drafting your letter, exchange papers with a classmate. Read your partner's letter carefully and give him or her suggestions for making it more persuasive. Tell your partner whether or not you agree with the support given to each reason. When your paper is returned, use your partner's suggestions and the **Evaluation Checklist for Revising** (see page 239) to revise your work.

EDITING

After revising your draft, check it for errors in grammar, punctuation, capitalization, and spelling. Use your Personalized Editing Checklist to avoid mistakes that you have made in other writing projects.

editing ☆

The following text uses emotionally charged words, which can weaken an argument. Revise the passage (you can use more than one sentence in the revision) in more reasonable language.

> Voting is an important part of being a citizen. If you are too apathetic to understand the grave responsibility of taking this right seriously, then you, my friend, are a hooligan.

PUBLISHING

Make a polished copy of your letter and give it to someone who might be interested in the television show. Ask the person to read it and give you feedback.

Writing About Literature

A **literary analysis** presents an interpretation of a work of literature and supports that interpretation with appropriate details and quotations from the work.

Works of literature include novels, plays, poems, and short stories. You have probably read many works of literature, and you may have shared your opinion in a book review. Following are a few examples of how people think, write, and speak about literature.

- **Book critics write about literature in their reviews** for print and for electronic media.

- **Publishers issue catalogs and other promotional materials** that convey information about their publications.

- **Educators speak about literature** for book groups and for students of literature.

- **Students select a play** to act in, direct, produce, and present to their community.

Writing Project — Interpretive Response

Literary Analysis *Write a response to a literary work that uses evidence from the work to support a thoughtful interpretation.*

Think Through Writing Think about a short story, novel, play, or poem that you like and write about why you like it. Explain what it is you like: the characters, the story, the theme, or whatever grabs you.

Talk About It In your writing group, discuss what you have written about. What kinds of stories or poems did people write about? What kinds of stories and poems do you and your group like? What do you like about them?

Read About It The following story by Cynthia Rylant tells a tale of two people whose paths cross at the wrong moments. Have you ever had an experience in which you wanted to meet someone, yet the right opportunity never came up? Think about what advantage telling the story through a third-person narrator might have.

Checkouts

Cynthia Rylant

Her parents had moved her to Cincinnati, to a large house with beveled[1] glass windows and several porches and the *history* her mother liked to emphasize. You'll love the house, they said. You'll be lonely at first, they admitted, but you're so nice you'll make friends fast. And as an impulse tore at her to lie on the floor, to hold to their ankles and tell them she felt she was dying, to offer anything, anything at all, so they might allow her to finish growing up in the town of her childhood, they firmed their mouths and spoke from their chests and they said, It's decided.

They moved her to Cincinnati, where for a month she spent the greater part of every day in a room full of beveled glass windows, sifting through photographs of the life she'd lived and left behind. But it is difficult work, suffering, and in its own way a kind of art, and finally she didn't have the energy for it anymore, so she emerged from the beautiful house and fell in love with a bag boy at the supermarket. Of course, this didn't happen all at once, just like that, but in the sequence of things that's exactly the way it happened.

She liked to grocery shop. She loved it the way some people love to drive long country roads, because doing it she could think and relax and wander. Her parents wrote up the list and handed it to her and off she went without complaint to perform what they regarded as a great sacrifice of her time and a sign that she was indeed a very nice girl. She had never told them how much she loved grocery shopping, only that she was "willing" to do it. She had an intuition which told her that her parents were not safe for sharing such strong, important facts about herself. Let them think they knew her.

Once inside the supermarket, her hands firmly around the handle of the cart, she would lapse into a kind of reverie[2] and wheel toward the produce. Like a Tibetan monk in solitary meditation, she calmed to a point of deep, deep happiness; this feeling came to her, reliably, if strangely, only in the supermarket.

---

1 **beveled:** Having two planes that meet at a sloping edge.
2 **reverie:** Daydream

Then one day the bag boy dropped her jar of mayonnaise and that is how she fell in love. He was nervous—first day on the job—and along had come this fascinating girl, standing in the checkout line with the unfocused stare one often sees in young children, her face turned enough away that he might take several full looks at her as he packed sturdy bags full of food and the goods of modern life. She interested him because her hair was red and thick, and in it she had placed a huge orange bow, nearly the size of a small hat. That was enough to distract him, and when finally it was her groceries he was packing, she looked at him and smiled and he could respond only by busting her jar of mayonnaise on the floor, shards of glass and oozing cream decorating the area around his feet.

She loved him at exactly that moment, and if he'd known this perhaps he wouldn't have fallen into the brown depression he fell into, which lasted the rest of his shift. He believed he must have looked the jackass in her eyes, and he envied the sureness of everyone around him: the cocky cashier at the register, the grim and harried store manager, the bland butcher, and the brazen bag boys who smoked in the warehouse on their breaks. He wanted a second chance. Another chance to be confident and say witty things to her as he threw tin cans into her bags, persuading her to allow him to help her to her car so he might learn just a little about her, check out the floor of the car for signs of hobbies or fetishes[3] and the bumpers for clues as to her beliefs and loyalties.

But he busted her jar of mayonnaise and nothing else worked out for the rest of the day.

Strange, how attractive clumsiness can be. She left the supermarket with stars in her eyes, for she had loved the way his long nervous fingers moved from the conveyor belt to the bags, how deftly (until the mayonnaise) they had picked up her items and placed them into her bags. She had loved the way the hair kept falling into his eyes as he leaned over to grab a box or a tin. And the tattered brown shoes he wore with no socks. And the left side of his collar turned in rather than out.

The bag boy seemed a wonderful contrast to the perfectly beautiful house she had been forced to accept as her home, to the *history* she hated, to the loneliness she had become used to, and she couldn't wait to come back for more of his awkwardness and dishevelment.

Incredibly, it was another four weeks before they saw each other again. As fate would have it, her visits to the supermarket never coincided with his schedule to bag. Each time she went to the store, her eyes scanned the checkouts at once, her heart in her mouth. And each hour he worked, the bag boy kept one eye on the door, watching for the red-haired girl with the big orange bow.

---

3 **fetishes:** An object of too much attention or reverence.

Yet in their disappointment these weeks there was a kind of ecstasy. It is reason enough to be alive, the hope you may see again some face which has meant something to you. The anticipation of meeting the bag boy eased the girl's painful transition into her new and jarring life in Cincinnati. It provided for her an anchor amid all that was impersonal and unfamiliar, and she spent less time on thoughts of what she had left behind as she concentrated on what might lie ahead. And for the boy, the long and often tedious hours at the supermarket which provided no challenge other than that of showing up the following workday . . . these hours became possibilities of mystery and romance for him as he watched the electric doors for the girl in the orange bow.

And when they finally did meet up again, neither offered a clue to the other that he, or she, had been the object of obsessive thought for weeks. She spotted him as soon as she came into the store, but she kept her eyes strictly in front of her as she pulled out a cart and wheeled it toward the produce. And he, too, knew the instant she came through the door—though the orange bow was gone, replaced by a small but bright yellow flower instead—and he never once turned his head in her direction but watched her from the corner of his vision as he tried to swallow back the fear in his throat.

It is odd how we sometimes deny ourselves the very pleasure we have longed for and which is finally within our reach. For some perverse reason she would not have been able to articulate, the girl did not bring her cart up to the bag boy's checkout when her shopping was done. And the bag boy let her leave the store, pretending not to notice her.

This is often the way of children, when they truly want a thing, to pretend they don't. And then they grow angry when no one tries harder to give them this thing they so casually rejected, and they soon find themselves in a rage simply because they cannot say yes when they mean yes. Humans are very complicated. (And perhaps cats, who have been known to react in the same way, though the resulting rage can only be guessed at.)

The girl hated herself for not checking out at the boy's line, and the boy hated himself for not catching her eye and saying hello, and they most sincerely hated each other without ever having exchanged even two minutes of conversation.

Eventually—in fact, within a week—a kind and intelligent boy who lived very near her beautiful house asked the girl to a movie and she gave up her fancy for the bag boy at the supermarket. And the bag boy himself grew so bored with his job that he made a desperate search for something better and ended up in a bookstore where scores of fascinating girls lingered like honeybees about a hive. Some months later the bag boy and the girl with the orange bow again crossed paths, standing in line with their dates at a movie theater, and, glancing toward the other, each smiled slightly, then looked away, as strangers on public buses often do, when one is moving off the bus and the other is moving on.

Respond in Writing Write freely to answer these questions: What does Rylant seem to be saying about missed opportunities? How does using the third-person point of view help Rylant tell her story?

Develop Your Own Ideas Work with your classmates to develop other ideas that might provide the basis for a literary analysis of this story.

Small Groups: In your small group, use an organizer like the one below to help you gather evidence to support your interpretation of Rylant's short story.

Overall Meaning (Theme): What is the major theme of this story?	
Literary Elements	Evidence from Story
What passage offers the best clues to the theme? Why?	
How does the setting affect the characters in the story?	
What do you learn about the characters' histories, personalities, and dreams?	
How does using a third-person narrator affect the story?	
What descriptive images does the author use?	
What motivates each character, and what consequences follow from his or her actions?	

Whole Class: Make a master chart of all of the ideas generated by the small groups to compare the insights made across the range of students in the class.

Write About It In this chapter you will write a literary analysis that considers important aspects of "Checkouts." Your analysis might be built on any of the following possibilities.

Possible Topics	Possible Audiences	Possible Forms
• an interpretation of a character's role in the story • an interpretation of theme • an interpretation of the narrator's role in the story • an interpretation of how the setting affects the theme	• English teachers • classmates • others who have read the story • the author	• an essay • a blog • a post to a Web-based discussion board • a letter

Structure of a Literary Analysis

When you write a response to a work of literature, you will most probably be writing an essay. Your analysis should include the features in the chart below.

STRUCTURE OF A LITERARY ANALYSIS	
Title	identifies which aspect of the work the writer will focus on
Introduction	names the author and the work; contains a thesis statement expressing an interpretation of some aspect of the work
Body	supports the thesis statement with details and direct quotations from the work. In some instances the body contains quotations from other respected sources, such as literary critics and biographers. It may also include the author's personal comments and letters.
Conclusion	summarizes, clarifies, or adds an insight to the thesis statement

Notice in the model below how the introduction lays the groundwork for the rest of the essay.

STUDENT MODEL: Introduction

In *My Sister's Keeper* by Jodi Picoult, the main character, Anna, is genetically enhanced to match her sister Kati's DNA. Kati has leukemia and her sister Anna is conceived so that her sister can live. For most of Anna's life she does not ask questions about why she is always giving bone marrow and blood to her older sister. When Anna starts thinking for herself, she hires an attorney and attempts to become "medically emancipated." This conflict sets up a major theme of the novel: where the family ends and the individual begins.

Cody Collins, Canton South High School, Canton, Ohio

PROJECT PREP *Evaluating* *Structure*

In your writing group, discuss how you might structure your literary analysis of "Checkouts" by Cynthia Rylant.

Responding to Literature

The American writer Ralph Waldo Emerson wrote: "'Tis the good reader that makes the good book." By that he probably meant that the reader helps create the meaning in a work of literature. Each reader uses his or her own past experiences to make sense of the writer's world.

Responding from Personal Experience

Reading literature is a creative process in which you, the reader, interact with the literature. Before writing a literary analysis, assess your response to what you have read. Your response is influenced by a number of factors.

Factors in a Reader's Response to Literature

- age, gender, and personality
- cultural or ethnic origins, attitudes, and customs
- personal opinions, beliefs, and values
- life experiences and general knowledge
- knowledge of literature and literary genres
- knowledge of the historical and social climate in which the work was written
- reading and language skills

Who you are, where you live, what you know, and what your interests are strongly affect your response to a story, poem, play, or novel. The more you identify with a work, the more you will probably enjoy reading it. Your responses to literature will not always be positive; sometimes a work will upset, annoy, or bore you. A negative response, however, is just as important as a positive one, and it also deserves to be explored.

Writer's Tip

Literary works mean different things to different readers. Responding from **personal experience** will help you discover what a literary work means to you.

All of the following techniques will help you respond to what you read. They will also help you make sense of those responses.

Personal Response Strategies

1. Freewrite answers to the following questions:

   a. When you approached this reading, did you have any expectations of the text? In other words, did you expect to be bored? To experience pleasure? To be stimulated? To have difficulty? Were your expectations met? How? Were you surprised? If so, explain why.

   b. Where in the poem, story, novel, or play do you see yourself? What character(s) do you identify with? Why? Do your feelings about the character or characters stay the same? Do they change? If so, when and why do they change?

   c. What characters remind you of other people you know? In what ways are they like those real people? In what ways are they different? How has your experience with those real people influenced your reactions to the characters in the work?

   d. If you were a character in the work, would you have behaved any differently? Why or why not? What actions or behaviors puzzle you?

   e. What experiences from your own life come to mind as you read this work? How are they similar to the events portrayed? How are they different? What feelings do you associate with the experiences? Are those feelings represented in the work?

   f. How does the work make you feel? Why?

2. Write a personal response statement explaining what the work means to you.

3. In small discussion groups, share your personal response statement and your various reactions to the questions above. Listen carefully to your classmates' reactions and, if appropriate, contrast them with your own. Be open to changing your responses if you find other points of view convincing. Afterward write freely about whether your ideas changed and why.

Listening Tip

Discussing literature can involve complex ideas and feelings. During class discussion, be sure to monitor your understanding by asking questions about anything you might not understand. Also repeat back what someone said if you want to be sure you caught the intended meaning.

● **Practice Your Skills**

Responding from Personal Experience

Read "Thank You, M'am" by Langston Hughes on pages 151–153. Then complete the following questions and activities.

1. What do you think about the boy in "Thank You, M'am"? Does he remind you of anyone you know? How would you describe him? What do you think about the woman in the story? Does she remind you of anyone you know?

2. When you were reading the story, did you predict the outcome? If not, why did you think the story would end differently?

3. Write about events in your life that came to mind when you read the story.

4. What else in your life came to mind as you read this story?

PROJECT PREP *Prewriting* *Personal Responding*

Review the short story "Checkouts" on pages 249–251. Then, using the Personal Response Strategies chart on page 255, freewrite a personal response to the story. Follow step 3 as well, meeting with your writing group.

② Responding from Literary Knowledge

In addition to responding from personal experience, good readers also use their previous reading experience to help them interpret a work of literature. When you respond in this way, you use your knowledge of literature (based on other stories or poems you have read) to identify and appreciate the literary elements in the work you are currently reading. In contrast to responding personally, you pay more attention to the work itself than to your personal reactions.

The chart below will help you understand the elements of fiction, poetry, and drama.

ELEMENTS OF LITERATURE	
FICTION	
Plot	the events that lead to a **conflict,** reach a **climax** (high point), and then finally end in a **resolution**
Setting	when and where the story takes place
Characters	the people in the story who advance the plot through their thoughts and actions
Dialogue	the conversations among characters that reveal their personalities, actions, and **motivations,** or reasons for behaving as they do
Mood	the atmosphere established in a work of art, such as pessimistic, romantic, realistic, or sorrowful
Tone	the writer's attitude toward her or his characters
Point of View	the "voice" telling the story—**first person** (*I*) or **third person** (*he* or *she*)
Theme	the main idea or message of the story
POETRY	
Persona	the person whose "voice" is saying the poem, revealing the character the poet is assuming
Meter	the pattern of stressed and unstressed syllables in each line
Rhyme Scheme	the pattern of rhymed sounds, usually at the ends of lines
Sound Devices	techniques for playing with sounds to create certain effects, such as **alliteration** and **onomatopoeia**
Poetic Techniques	**figurative language, similes** and **metaphors** (which create images by making comparisons)
Shape	the way a poem looks on the printed page, which may contribute to the underlying meaning of the poet's thoughts and feelings
Theme	the underlying meaning of the poem

The drama elements below show only features that differ from fiction and poetry.

DRAMA

Setting	the time and place of the action; lighting and stage sets, as described in the stage directions
Characters	the people who participate in the action of the play
Plot	the story of the play divided into acts and scenes and developed through the characters' words and actions
Theme	the meaning of a play, as revealed through the setting and the characters' words and actions

The following strategies will help you respond with your literary knowledge.

Literary Knowledge Strategies

Fiction and Drama

- Examine the plot (sequence of events) of the story.
- Identify the key events in the story and the meaning or significance of each one.
- Identify the major conflict in the story.
- Look closely at the main character. What is his or her motivation, or reason, for behaving as he or she does?
- Look closely at the setting. What are the most important details in the setting? What overall feeling do they convey?
- Express in your own words what you think the theme (message) of the story is. Use details from the story, including the title, to help explain the theme.

Poetry

- Identify the speaker in the poem.
- Describe the meter of the poem and explain how it adds to the feeling the poem conveys.
- Describe the rhyme scheme, if any, of the poem and explain how it contributes to the poem's overall effect.
- Identify any figures of speech and explain their purpose.

PROJECT PREP *Prewriting* *Responding from Literary Knowledge*

Freewrite a literary response to "Checkouts." Using the chart on page 257, identify the literary elements the author used to evoke your individual response. How did the plot, characters, setting, point of view, and tone influence how you responded to the story? Save your work for later use.

CHAPTER 10

① Choosing a Subject

You draw on your responses, personal and literary, to develop a subject for writing about literature. In some cases you will be assigned a subject for writing about literature. In other cases, however, you may be expected to choose your own subject. The questions below will help you think of subjects of personal interest.

Questions for Choosing a Subject

- What parts of the work do I find moving? Surprising? Disappointing? Why do they have an effect on me?
- What images or details made a strong impression on me? What do they contribute to the overall work?
- With which character do I identify most? Why?
- What makes the characters distinct from one another? What motivates each of them?

- What parts of the work puzzle me? What would I like to understand better?
- What does the work "say" to me? What message does it convey? What insight or understanding have I gained?

You will probably find the answers to some of these questions in the responses you have already made. Look through any written responses you have made to find aspects of the literary work that hold the most interest for you. It is also a good idea to reread the literary work to see if you have any fresh, new responses now that you have had a chance to become better acquainted with the work. One of your new insights, or one of the answers to the questions above, could become the subject for a composition about literature.

● Practice Your Skills

Choosing Subjects

Review "Thank You, M'am" on pages 151–153. For each of the following literary elements, think of a possible subject for writing about "Thank You, M'am."

Example   theme

Possible Answer   the importance of choice in everyday relationships

1. character   **2.** theme   **3.** tone   **4.** plot

② Limiting a Subject

If you have synthesized your personal and literary responses to a literary work, the chances are good that you have come up with an interesting subject that is suitably limited. A clearly focused, limited subject will keep your analysis from meandering aimlessly through a general discussion or simple summary of the literary work.

To test whether your subject is suitably limited, ask yourself whether you can express your subject in a phrase rather than a single word. If you can express your subject only in a single word, then ask yourself "What about [my subject] do I want to say?" until you can express your subject in a phrase.

Here is an example of how one student limited a subject about the setting of the story "Checkouts."

EXAMPLE: Limiting a Subject

Too General	the supermarket
Ask Yourself	What about the supermarket do I want to say?
Possible Answer	the importance of the supermarket
Suitably Limited	what the supermarket symbolizes to the girl

● Practice Your Skills

Limiting Subjects

Each of the following subjects is too broad for a brief composition about "Thank You, M'am." Write a suitably limited subject for each one.

Example	Mrs. Jones
Possible Answer	what Mrs. Jones stands for in the story

1. choice   **2.** learning a lesson
3. making mistakes   **4.** belief

PROJECT PREP *Prewriting* **Limiting a Subject**

Based on your personal and literary responses, develop a subject for an interpretive essay on "Checkouts." Take your limited subject to your writing group and ask for feedback. As you listen to your partners' ideas, be open to rethinking yours.

Think Critically

Synthesizing

When you are choosing a subject for a composition about literature, you use the skill of synthesizing. **Synthesizing** means bringing together. In your search for a meaningful subject, you bring together your personal and literary responses to a work of literature.

Suppose you have decided to write about "Thank You, Ma'm." You might make a chart like the one below to track your personal response to the story. Then look for a focus. In the chart below, the idea of learning lessons clearly intrigues the reader, who synthesizes personal response with a literary element.

PERSONAL RESPONSE	LITERARY ELEMENT
Everyone makes mistakes, and some mistakes are bigger than others. I like the way this story makes the point that important lessons can be learned from the mistakes you make—big or little. I know I've learned some! Mrs. Jones cares about teaching Roger what's right. My aunt talks to me the same way. She believes I'm a good kid, just like Mrs. Jones believes Roger is a good kid.	*Theme of "Thank You, Ma'm."* One theme of the story seems to be about learning lessons, and passing the learning on. Mrs. Jones tells Roger "I have done things, too, which I would not tell you, son—neither tell God, if he didn't already know." So she's learned lessons from those things and wants to help Roger learn, too. The title of the story even seems to support that theme. Roger thanks Mrs. Jones, probably not for the washing up or food, but for caring enough to teach a lesson.

Synthesis: Because I have had to learn lessons, I might see the theme of lesson-learning more readily than other readers, but there is evidence in the story that backs up that theme.

Thinking Practice

Now take another look at "Checkouts" on pages 249–251. Using the **Elements of Literature/Fiction** chart on page 257 and the skill of synthesizing, write a paragraph that combines your personal response to the short story with your literary response.

3 Developing a Thesis

Like other kinds of compositions, writing about literature develops one main idea, or **thesis.** Your clearly focused subject is just a step away from your thesis. In fact, your focused subject is like the subject of a sentence without the verb. To complete the "sentence," you need to pin down the exact statement you want to make about your subject. In the following example, notice how the thesis goes one step further and makes a complete statement about the subject.

EXAMPLE: Developing a Thesis

Focused, Limited Subject	how the story uses mother-son imagery
Thesis	In "Thank You, M'am," mother-son imagery is used to stress the importance of Roger's encounter with Mrs. Jones.

In the limited subject, there is not a complete statement about how the story uses mother-son imagery. In the thesis, the statement is completed with the addition of the phrase "to stress the importance of Roger's encounter with Mrs. Jones."

To develop your thesis, cast your focused, limited subject into the form of a complete sentence. Pin your subject down by saying something definite and concrete about it. Once again, you can ask yourself, "What *about* my subject?" until you have a statement that is expressed in a complete sentence.

Remember you can adjust and improve your thesis statement during drafting and revising. Even in its rough form, however, your thesis statement will help you develop the rest of your composition.

Writing Tip

After you have focused and limited your subject, express it in a complete sentence as a **thesis statement.**

PROJECT PREP Prewriting Thesis Statement

Review your focused, limited subject. If you are satisfied that you have clearly focused your subject, you are ready to proceed. To develop your working thesis statement, write your limited subject in the form of a sentence. Remember, you can change or adjust it as needed. Share your work with your writing group and give feedback to one another on the suitability of each writer's thesis statement.

4 Gathering Evidence

After clearly expressing your composition's thesis, you can move on to gathering evidence to support it. In most cases the evidence will be found in the literary work's dialogue, descriptions, and events, and in your interpretation of them.

When developing a list of supporting details for your analysis, skim the literary work from start to finish looking for any and all details that help support your thesis statement. For example, if you were writing about how mother-son imagery is used to stress the importance of Roger's encounter with Mrs. Jones in "Thank You, M'am," you would look for details that show how Roger's encounter with Mrs. Jones is an important one. You would also look for any references to mother-son imagery.

On separate sticky notes or note cards or on a computer, jot down each detail as you come across it, and put a page reference beside it so you can return easily to that spot if you need to read it again. You may also want to make a brief note to yourself about why you think the detail is important in supporting your thesis.

The note cards that follow show how a writer gathered evidence to support the thesis that mother-son imagery in "Thank You, M'am" is used to stress the importance of Roger's encounter with Mrs. Jones. Notice that the evidence is drawn from the story's narration as well as the dialogue.

MODEL: Gathering Evidence

Thesis: In "Thank You, M'am," by Langston Hughes, mother-son imagery is used to stress the importance of Roger's encounter with Mrs. Jones.

    After that the woman said, "Pick up my pocketbook, boy, and give it here." She still held him. But she bent down enough to permit him to stop and pick up her purse. Then she said, "Now ain't you ashamed of yourself?"

    Firmly gripped by his shirt front, the boy said, "Yes'm."

    The woman said, "You ought to be my son. I would teach you right from wrong. Least I can do right now is to wash your face. Are you hungry?"

    "No'm," said the being-dragged boy. "I just want you to turn me loose."

1. The woman said, "Pick up my pocketbook, boy, and give it here," and "Now ain't you ashamed of yourself?" (page 151) shows Mrs. Jones as strong disciplinarian set on teaching Roger a lesson, seems to be treating him as a disappointed mother would treat a son; Roger reacts by saying he is ashamed.

2. Mrs. Jones tells Roger plainly "You ought to be my son." says she would teach him right from wrong, and to wash his face; asks if he is hungry; declares he won't forget the fact that he chose to put himself in contact with her (page 152); actions and words show that she treats him

"Was I bothering *you* when I turned that corner?" asked the woman.

"No'm."

"But you put yourself in contact with *me*," said the woman. "If you think that that contact is not going to last awhile, you got another thought coming. When I get through with you, sir, you are going to remember Luella Bates Washington Jones."

"Eat some more, son," she said.

When they were finished eating she got up and said, "Now, here, take this ten dollars and buy yourself some blue suede shoes. And next time, do not make the mistake of latching onto my pocketbook *nor nobody else's*—because shoes come by devilish like that will burn your feet. I got to get my rest now. But I wish you would behave yourself, son, from here on in.

She led him down the hall to the front door and opened it. "Good night! Behave yourself, boy!" she said, looking out into the street.

The boy wanted to say something else other than, "Thank you, m'am," to Mrs. Luella Bates Washington Jones, but he couldn't do so as he turned at the barren stoop and looked back at the large woman in the door. He barely managed to say, "Thank you," before she shut the door. And he never saw her again.

---

as she would a misbehaving child with firmness but with compassion and concern for his well being; makes clear statement that this encounter will be one the boy will remember for a long time.

---

3. Mrs. Jones calls Roger "son" and "boy", she feeds him, gives him money to buy shoes, tells him to behave himself; Roger reacts by wanting to "say something else." (page 153)

Language and actions work to reinforce mother-son imagery; Mrs. Jones gives Roger food, money and more discipline. Roger reacts by feeling that he wants to say something—he is changed now and Mrs. Jones's large

---

body filling the doorframe indicates she has taken on a larger meaning in boy's eyes.

PROJECT PREP *Prewriting* *Gathering Evidence*

In your writing group, gather possible evidence that would support your thesis for your interpretation of "Checkouts." Use a graphic organizer like this one to track the details.

Detail	Significance of Detail

⑤ Organizing Details into an Outline

After you have collected as many supporting details as you can find, think about the best order to present them. The nature of your thesis will help determine the best order for your supporting details. For example, if your thesis involves comparison and contrast, you may begin by showing all the aspects that are alike, and then show all the aspects that are different. Or if your thesis involves analyzing a character's motivation, you may present your details in order of importance. (See page 232.) In some cases, you may even present the details in the order in which they appear in the story. This type of order, related to chronological order, would be useful to show how a character changes over time. (See page 166.) Order supporting details so that they support your thesis most effectively.

Once you have organized your details, write an outline to guide you as you draft or create a graphic organizer. An informal outline is a quick way to show the organizational plan of your composition. Below is an informal outline for a composition about "Thank You, M'am." The details are arranged in order of importance, as judged by the writer.

MODEL: Informal Outline

1. Introduction to include thesis statement: In "Thank You, M'am" mother-son imagery is used to describe the encounter between the characters.

2. Body

   1st detail: Mrs. Jones disciplines Roger, yet at same time tells him she will make sure he washes his face: Roger reacts by saying "Yes m'am" saying he is ashamed of his behavior 2nd detail: Mrs. Jones's own words ("you ought to be my son") 3rd detail: Mrs. Jones feeds Roger, calls him "son" and "boy," gives him money, tells him to "behave" 4th detail: Mrs Jones's own words "you are going to remember Luella Bates Washington Jones" 5th detail: Roger wants to say something other than thank you: encounter with Mrs. Jones has taken on larger meaning for him

3. Conclusion

PROJECT PREP   Prewriting   Outline

With your writing group, review your notes on "Checkout" and choose your supporting details. Use a graphic organizer to plan the analysis. For each body paragraph, focus on one point (a claim). Support the claim with evidence from the literature, and justify it with a warrant (a statement that explains how the evidence supports the claim).

Point	Claim	Evidence	Warrant
#1			

The Power of Language

Participial Phrases: Getting Into the Action

As you prepare to draft your literary analysis, consider ways you can use the power of language to make your writing pack the most punch. Participial phrases are versatile and expressive forms writers use to create action-packed imagery. A **participle** is a word that is formed from a verb but acts like an adjective by modifying a noun. Other words can join with a participle to form a **participial phrase.** Participial phrases are especially useful for creating a vivid sense that several things are happening at once. Consider the following sentence from "Checkouts."

> Some months later the bag boy and the girl with the orange bow again crossed paths, standing in line with their dates at a movie theater, and, glancing toward the other, each smiled slightly, then looked away, as strangers on public buses do, when one is moving off the bus and the other is moving on.

By using participial phrases, the author vividly relates—in a single sentence—the circumstances, the underlying emotions, and the delicate tension of this brief, final meeting. The following example shows how you can use participial phrases to combine simple sentences and highlight the relationship between ideas.

Two Sentences	The bag boy let her leave the store. He pretended not to notice her.
Combined	The bag boy let her leave the store, pretending not to notice her.

Try It Yourself

Write sentences modeled on the examples above. Try to write sentences on the topic you have chosen for your project and incorporate them into your draft if you can. During revision, you can add participial phrases to some sentences or combine two sentences by making one into a participial phrase.

Punctuation Tip

When you add "extra" details like this, making the writing more interesting, **separate the participial phrase** from the main part of the sentence **with a comma. If the participial phrase comes in the middle of the sentence,** enclose it in **two commas.**

With your informal outline as a guide, drafting your composition about literature is a matter of putting your ideas into flowing sentences. The following guidelines will help you draft the introduction, body, and conclusion of your composition.

Guidelines for Drafting a Literary Analysis

- In the introduction be sure to identify the title and the author of the work you are discussing.
- Use present-tense verbs throughout your essay.
- Include your thesis statement somewhere in the introduction. Refine it as needed and work it in as smoothly as possible.
- In the body of your essay, include your clearly organized supporting details, using transitions to show how one detail relates to another. Throughout your essay use direct quotations from the work if they strengthen the points you are trying to make. (Always enclose direct quotations in quotation marks.)
- In the conclusion draw together the details you have included to reinforce the main idea of your essay.
- Add a title that suggests the focus of your composition.

As you read the following model, notice how each part of the composition works to clarify or support the main idea. Your first draft will probably be less polished than this finished analysis. Just use this model to help you include all the necessary parts of your first draft.

MODEL: Composition About Literature

Mother-Son Imagery in "Thank You, M'am"

Title: Suggests focus of composition

In Langston Hughes's short story "Thank You, M'am," mother-son imagery is used throughout the story to stress the lasting importance of the encounter between the two main characters. When a young man named Roger attempts to steal a purse from a large woman named Luella Bates Washington Jones, not only does the "frail and willow-wild" Roger not get Mrs. Jones's purse, but she publicly disciplines him. Mrs. Jones quickly turns the dynamics of their relationship from victim and criminal to angry mother and regretful son—teaching Roger a lesson he will never forget.

Introduction: Identifies title, author, and thesis

From the moment Mrs. Jones and Roger encounter one another, Mrs. Jones is portrayed as a strong disciplinarian set on teaching a misbehaving child an important lesson. After Roger falls to the ground while trying to steal her purse, Mrs. Jones holds on to him, demanding, "Now ain't you ashamed of yourself?" She reacts to Roger as a disappointed mother would react to her own son: not only with firmness but also with compassion and concern for his well-being. And Roger reacts in kind, acknowledging that he is, in fact, ashamed of his behavior.

First Body Paragraph

As the story develops, other words and actions work to reinforce the mother-son imagery established in the story's opening scene. Even as Mrs. Jones lectures Roger, she tells him she has a "great mind to wash [his] face for [him]." Later, Mrs. Jones says to Roger directly, "You ought to be my son. I would teach you right from wrong." She takes Roger to her home, fixes him dinner, and asks that he comb his hair so he will look "presentable." After they eat Mrs. Jones gives Roger money so that he can buy a pair of shoes, and, calling him "son," admonishes him to "behave…from here on in."

Second Body Paragraph

The relationship between Mrs. Jones and Roger is, of course, surprising. Although these two people have just met under negative circumstances, an immediate, positive, nurturing relationship has formed. The importance of this relationship is established by the symbolic mother-son imagery. There is perhaps no relationship more important than the relationship between a parent and a child. Mrs. Jones tells Roger that his contact with her will "last awhile….When I get through with you, sir, you are going to remember Luella Bates Washington Jones." Roger's contact with Mrs. Jones is, in fact, relatively brief.

Third Body Paragraph

But when he sees Mrs. Jones's large body filling the doorframe in the last scene of the story, and feels that he *wants* to say something—something other than just "thank you"—it is clear that the impact will be permanent.

Conclusion: Reinforces thesis statement

PROJECT PREP *Drafting* *Literary Analysis*

Go over your notes and graphic organizers. With your writing group, discuss your plans for writing your analysis of "Checkouts." Invite comments from the group, and be open to using any of them that help support your thesis. Then draft your essay. When you are happy with your rough draft, submit it to your teacher for review, if appropriate.

Before revising your writing about literature, you may wish to share it with peers to see what they think is good about your writing and what they think could be improved. After receiving their comments, try to improve your composition to make it the best it can be. The following checklist will help you revise your writing about literature.

Evaluation Checklist for Revising

Checking Your Composition
✓ Do you have a strong introduction that identifies the author and work you will discuss? (pages 253 and 267)

✓ Does your introduction contain a clearly worded thesis statement? (pages 253 and 262)

✓ Does the body of your composition provide ample details and evidence from the work to support your thesis? (pages 253 and 267)

✓ Did you use quotes from the work to strengthen your points? (pages 263–264)

✓ Does your conclusion synthesize the details in the body of your composition and reinforce your thesis statement? (pages 253 and 267)

✓ Does your composition have unity and coherence? (pages 75–76)

✓ Did you add a title showing the focus of your composition? (pages 253 and 267)

Checking Your Paragraphs
✓ Does each paragraph have a topic sentence? (pages 70–74)

✓ Is each paragraph unified and coherent? (pages 75–76)

Checking Your Sentences and Words
✓ Are your sentences varied and concise? (pages 53–63)

✓ Did you use lively, specific words? (pages 45–52)

PROJECT PREP *Revising* Using a Checklist

Exchange the draft of your literary analysis with a partner. Comment on the strengths and weaknesses of your partner's paper. Consider your partner's comments as you use the preceding **Evaluation Checklist for Revising** to improve your draft. Also take into account any comments you have received from your teacher. Be sure your composition has an introductory paragraph in which you state and elaborate on your thesis statement; a series of body paragraphs in which you state claims and support them with evidence and incorporate quotations from the text; and a conclusion that explains how the evidence reinforces your overall thesis statement.

CHAPTER 10

Use the rubric below to evaluate a literary analysis.

Ideas	4 The thesis statement is clear. Evidence is solid. The analysis goes beyond mere summary.	3 The thesis statement is clear. Most evidence is solid. The analysis goes beyond mere summary.	2 The thesis statement could be clearer. Some evidence is solid, but there is too much simple summary.	1 The thesis statement is missing or unclear. There is little evidence, and the ideas rarely go beyond summary.
Organization	4 The organization is clear with abundant transitions.	3 A few ideas seem out of place or transitions are missing.	2 Many ideas seem out of place and transitions are missing.	1 The organization is unclear and hard to follow.
Voice	4 The voice sounds natural, engaging, and forceful.	3 The voice sounds natural and engaging.	2 The voice sounds mostly natural but is weak.	1 The voice sounds mostly unnatural and is weak.
Word Choice	4 Words are specific and powerful. Language is appropriate.	3 Words are specific and language is appropriate.	2 Some words are too general or are inappropriate.	1 Most words are overly general and inappropriate for the purpose and audience.
Sentence Fluency	4 Varied sentences flow smoothly.	3 Most sentences are varied and flow smoothly.	2 Some sentences are varied but some are choppy.	1 Sentences are not varied and are choppy.
Conventions	4 Punctuation, usage, and spelling are correct. Quotes are handled correctly. All Power Rules are followed.	3 Punctuation, usage, and spelling are mainly correct, and Power Rules are all followed.	2 Some punctuation, usage, and spelling are incorrect, but all Power Rules are followed.	1 There are many errors and at least one failure to follow a Power Rule.

PROJECT PREP Revising Using a Rubric

Evaluate your essay using this rubric and make any additional changes. Then ask a partner to evaluate your work using this rubric. Make further changes.

CHAPTER 10

When you are satisfied that your composition clearly conveys your interpretation of the work you have chosen to write about, you can move on to polishing it and presenting it to readers. The following checklist will help you edit your work. In the process of editing, use the proofreading marks on page 11.

 Editing Checklist

✓ Are your sentences free of errors in grammar and usage?
✓ Did you spell each word correctly?
✓ Did you capitalize and punctuate correctly?
✓ Did you use quotation marks around all direct quotations from the work?
✓ Did you check your Personalized Editing Checklist to make sure you have avoided errors you sometimes make?

editing ☆

While editing, read aloud what you've written before going on to the next part. Writers often catch obvious problems by going through each sentence and assessing how well the sentences build on one another. How would you edit the following statement if you came across it in your draft?

> The young boy and the old women strike an interesting balance. He is young, undisciplined, and needy. He has no social skills. She is the opposite.

CHAPTER 10

The Language of **Power** *Past Tense*

Power Rule: Use mainstream past tense forms of regular and irregular verbs. (See pages 674–682.)

See It in Action When you write about events that happened in the past, make sure you do not use a simple past tense when a past perfect is needed. For example, the sentence below, modified from "Checkout," uses unconventional verb forms.

> She loved him at exactly that moment, and if he'd knew this perhaps he wouldn't have fell into the brown depression he fell into, which lasted the rest of his shift.

Below is the correct version of the sentence that appears in the actual text.

> She loved him at exactly that moment, and if he'd known this perhaps he wouldn't have fallen into the brown depression he fell into, which lasted the rest of his shift.

Remember It Record this rule and example in the Power Rule section of your Personalized Editing Checklist.

Use It As you edit your paper, highlight the verbs. Make sure you have used a past-perfect form and not a simple past tense if one is needed.

PROJECT PREP *Editing* *Conventions*

Edit your revised draft for grammar errors. Try reading your draft aloud to hear sentences that sound incorrect. Also refer to your Personalized Editing Checklist to be sure you have avoided frequent errors and violations of the Power Rules. When you are satisfied with your changes and corrections, save your work, but do not yet prepare a final copy.

Writing a Literary Analysis

One of the most satisfying parts of the writing process is sharing your work with readers. When you have corrected all your errors, prepare a neat final copy of your literary analysis to present to readers. Some ways of publishing your composition about literature are listed below.

PROJECT PREP Publishing Connecting with Readers

1. For the chapter project, you were free to choose among three types of publications for your literary analysis: an essay (the most common medium for writing of this type); a blog or a Web-based discussion board (increasingly popular ways to share ideas about literature); and a letter (some people exchange letters or e-mails to share their understanding of literary works, much as people discuss works in a book group). In your writing group, discuss ways in which a blog and a letter would require different treatment from a writer. After the discussion with your writing group, make any changes that would be fitting for the medium you chose and make an effort to connect your literary analysis with one or more readers.

2. Entering your literary analysis in a competition is also a good way to share your work with others. For information on literary contests, write to the National Council of Teachers of English, 1111 Kenyon Road, Urbana, IL 61801. Be sure to follow standard manuscript form and follow any specific entry rules for the competition.

3. You may also want to publish a class anthology, or collection, of student compositions on literary works. Decide how to organize, illustrate, bind, and circulate your anthology.

With comments from your peers and teacher fresh in your mind, think back to responses to other essays you have written and considered publishing. Are your reviewers and teacher still making similar remarks? Record your findings, as well as strategies for improving, in the Learning Log section of your journal.

In the Media

Screenplay

In a book everything must be described. The setting, plot, and characters are all determined by words. In a movie, images, scenery, costumes, music, and actors can show in an instant something that in a book may have taken pages to describe. In a book the words on the page create images in your imagination. In a movie the images are created for you.

Media Activity

Reread the scene from "Checkouts" on pages 249–251 and write a paragraph telling how you would turn it into a screenplay. Remember there are many differences between these two forms. One offers a story in words alone, while the other uses visual aids, actors, music, and dialogue to tell the story. Writing a screenplay means taking out words that do not further the action of the story and including images that invoke the atmosphere on the page. Be sure to include information about the camera angles, sets, and props you want to include. Then change the scene into a script. Here is an example.

Jane *(a small, dark-haired woman, exotic)*: I don't know what happened to my purse. I have been in the store for an hour and I had it when I walked in. I realized just now that it is gone.

Police Officer *(Tall, imposing figure in full uniform, holding a pad of paper)*: Ma'am, I'll need to take down your name, address, and phone number. I know you are in shock, but we will find the perpetrator—don't you worry."

Share your paragraph with a partner. Take turns evaluating one another's ideas. Will your suggestions make a good film?

Writing about Literature Online

Talking about literature is such an enjoyable pastime that countless reading groups meet each week in the homes of members, sharing their views and questions about the chosen work of literature and usually sharing snacks and friendly conversation as well. With technology, though, reading groups no longer need living rooms; the Internet helps create virtual living rooms, and hundreds of reading communities discuss—actually write about—the books they are reading. Using message-board formats, participants can quote the text they are reading or comments other participants have made and further the discussion with their own view. Following is a post from a popular online reading group, BookTalk.org about the first chapter of Lewis Carroll's *Alice's Adventures in Wonderland,* in which Alice falls down the rabbit hole and begins her unusual adventures.

The first time she looks around the hall of doors, there's nothing there. The second time, she finds the glass table with the key that doesn't fit any doors. When she looks at the doors more closely, she finds the door that fits the key. What is the significance of her having to look twice? Is it the idea that we must look deeply to understand what we're seeing or is it that dreams change each time we look so we should keep looking until the dream gives us what we want? Or something else?

> Lewis Carroll wrote:
> 'Come, there's no use in crying like that!' said Alice to herself, rather sharply; 'I advise you to leave off this minute!' She generally gave herself very good advice, (though she very seldom followed it), and sometimes she scolded herself so severely as to bring tears into her eyes; and once she remembered trying to box her own ears for having cheated herself in a game of croquet she was playing against herself, for this curious child was very fond of pretending to be two people. 'But it's no use now,' thought poor Alice, 'to pretend to be two people! Why, there's hardly enough of me left to make ONE respectable person!'

I think this is a remarkable paragraph although I'm a little uncertain what to make of it. Is the writer being silly to play for humor, or is there a deeper point here?

Technology Tip

Use a search engine to identify online reading groups of interest to you. There are groups on a wide variety of book types, from Roman history to science fiction. When you find one you are interested in, follow the discussions for a while to decide if you want to participate.

Writing Lab

Project Corner

Speak and Listen Poetry Read Around

You have read short stories by Langston Hughes and Cynthia Rylant. Both writers have also written poems. Hughes, in fact, is best known as the "poet laureate" of the Harlem Renaissance. This was a time in the 1920s when the flowering of African-American arts in the Harlem neighborhood of New York became influential throughout the country and helped create an identity for African-American artists in all fields. Rylant's *Something Permanent,* in which she composed poems to accompany the famous depression-era photographs of Walker Evans, was named a Best Book for Young Adults in the American Library Association's 1995 awards. In the library or online, find a poem you especially like by either Rylant or Hughes. Practice reading it aloud. Then **share your poem in a "read around"** in which each student reads a poem and then leads a brief discussion of it. For the discussion, prepare a "starter" question that requires students to think about some key element of the poem. (See pages 416–421 for help with presentations and group discussions.)

Think Critically Predict

Write another ending to "Checkouts." What would happen to the characters had they actually talked? Be sure to base your sequel on the events of the original so that the characters are true to their original creation.

Get Technical Multimedia Presentation

With a partner, **put together a slide show presentation** using presentation software that explores some aspect of the Harlem Renaissance (see above). Some possible topics include:

- novelists
- playwrights
- visual artists
- musicians

For Oral Communication
Book Review E-mail

1. You really like to read, and your friends and classmates trust your evaluation of books and stories. Your friend Clara recently e-mailed you to ask your opinion on what book she should read for a book report at school. **Write an e-mail message** to Clara about the book you recommend. Begin your message with a topic sentence. Give a thorough literary analysis of the book, describing the theme, or message. Use details to support your points. (You can find information on writing e-mail messages on pages 451–453.)

In the Workplace Analytical Composition

2. You have just accepted a job as assistant editor at *Dandelion*, a journal devoted to creative expression among middle school students. The upcoming issue will feature poetry by famous writers as well as students. The editor of the journal has asked you to find a poem to reprint in *Dandelion* and to write an analysis of that poem. Find a poem and **write a composition** analyzing it. Discuss the subject, mood, and theme and speaker of the poem. Also analyze what images the words create and what feelings those images suggest. (You can find information on responding to poetry on pages 257–258.)

Timed Writing ⏱ Persuasive Essay

3. Your substitute English teacher is known for his controversial teaching ideas. Today he announced that from now on, students will only be required to watch movies. He has decided that works of literature are "lesser forms of instruction" because they are not as entertaining as movies. Although some of your classmates are excited by his proposed changes, you disagree with the teacher's theory. Write a composition for your school newspaper about why literature should be taught in eighth grade. Consider examples of literature that you think are just as entertaining, or more entertaining, than movies. Explain why certain poems, stories, novels, or plays have meaning for you. Use quotes from the work. You have 25 minutes to complete your work.

Before You Write Consider the following questions: What is the situation? What is the occasion? Who is the audience? What is the purpose?

After You Write Evaluate your work using the six–trait evaluation rubric on page 270.

Unit 3

Research and Report Writing

When you really want to know the answer to a question—how to throw a perfect curve ball, for example, or what other albums are available from a band you just heard—you track it down eagerly. Yet as soon as you have one answer, you find that there are now more questions to track down. Writing a research report on a topic of genuine interest to you can have the same pattern of questions, answers, more questions, more answers, and still more questions. Every time you think you have found your answer, a new door opens.

Every exit is an entry somewhere else.
—*Tom Stoppard*

Research: Planning and Gathering Information

Research reports are factual compositions that use information from books, magazines, the Internet, interviews, and other sources.

You can find—and supply—a storehouse of information in a research report. Reports are everywhere—in books, magazines, newspapers, and on the Internet. Below are a few examples of research reports.

- **Doctors release the results of a new study on exercise and health** and write a report to share their findings.

- **A filmmaker investigates how fast food restaurants market to teenagers.** The controversial documentary creates interest in promoting better nutrition in schools.

- **A sports writer spends a season with a college basketball team.** Afterward, she writes an article for an online magazine about the team.

- **Archaeologists uncover new information about an ancient legend** and write a paper to report on the discovery.

Writing Project — Research Report

The Legend of . . . Bigfoot, the Bermuda Triangle, Stonehenge, Pecos Bill, the Roswell UFO incident—all of these are fascinating legends. Prepare to write a report about a legend of your choosing.

Think Through Writing Write freely for five minutes about a legend that interests you.

Talk About It In your writing group, discuss the legends each student wrote about. Tell why the one you chose interests you.

Read About It Read Stephen Lyons' "Birth of a Legend." Do you think a Loch Ness Monster ever existed, or still exists? Why or why not?

MODEL: Research Report

Birth of a Legend

by Stephen Lyons

Many a man has been hanged on less evidence than there is for the Loch Ness Monster.

—G. K. Chesterton

> Starting with a strong quote raises interest and gives readers a context for what is to come.

When the Romans first came to northern Scotland in the first century A.D., they found the Highlands occupied by fierce, tattoo-covered tribes they called the Picts, or painted people. From the carved, standing stones still found in the region around Loch Ness, it is clear the Picts were fascinated by animals, and careful to render them with great fidelity. All the animals depicted on the Pictish stones are lifelike and easily recognizable—all but one. The exception is a strange beast with an elongated beak or muzzle, a head locket or spout, and flippers instead of feet. Described by some scholars as a swimming elephant, the Pictish beast is the earliest known evidence for an idea that has held sway in the Scottish Highlands for at least 1,500 years—that Loch Ness is home to a mysterious aquatic animal.

> The introduction captures attention and has readers wondering about the "swimming elephant" that goes back to ancient times.

In Scottish folklore, large animals have been associated with many bodies of water, from small streams to the largest lakes, often labeled Lock-na-Beistie on old maps. These water-horses, or water-kelpies, are said to have magical powers and malevolent intentions. According to one version of the legend, the water-horse lures small children into the water by offering them rides on its back. Once the children are aboard, their hands become stuck to the beast and they are dragged to a watery death, their livers washing ashore the following day.

> This and the following paragraph offer background on the mysterious beasts that live in lakes.

The earliest written reference linking such creatures to Loch Ness is in the biography of Saint Columba, the man credited with introducing Christianity to Scotland.

In A.D. 565, according to this account, Columba was on his way to visit a Pictish king when he stopped along the shore of Loch Ness. Seeing a large beast about to attack a man who was swimming in the lake, Columba raised his hand, invoking the name of God and commanding the monster to "go back with all speed." The beast complied, and the swimmer was saved.

When Nicholas Witchell, a future BBC correspondent, researched the history of the legend for his 1974 book *The Loch Ness Story,* he found about a dozen pre-20th-century references to large animals in Loch Ness, gradually shifting in character from these clearly mythical accounts to something more like eyewitness descriptions.

> The writer moves to present times to give a modern perspective on the legend.

But the modern legend of Loch Ness dates from 1933, when a new road was completed along the shore, offering the first clear views of the loch from the northern side. One April afternoon, a local couple was driving home along this road when they spotted "an enormous animal rolling and plunging on the surface." Their account was written up by a correspondent for *The Inverness Courier,* whose editor used the word "monster" to describe the animal. The Loch Ness Monster has been a media phenomenon ever since.

> The basic organizational strategy of this report is chronological order.

Public interest built gradually during the spring of 1933, then picked up sharply after a couple reported seeing one of the creatures on land, lumbering across the shore road. By October, several London newspapers had sent correspondents to Scotland, and radio programs were being interrupted to bring listeners the latest news from the loch. A British circus offered a reward of £20,000 for the capture of the beast. Hundreds of boy scouts and outdoorsmen arrived, some venturing out in small boats, others setting up deck chairs and waiting expectantly for the monster to appear.

The excitement over the monster reached a fever pitch in December, when *The London Daily Mail* hired an actor, film director, and big-game hunter named Marmaduke Wetherell to track down the beast. After only a few days at the loch, Wetherell reported finding the fresh footprints of a large, four-toed animal. He estimated it to be 20 feet long. With great fanfare, Wetherell made plaster casts of the footprints and, just before Christmas,

> The writer builds interest by reporting important "findings."

sent them off to the Natural History Museum in London for analysis. While the world waited for the museum zoologists to return from holiday, legions of monster hunters descended on Loch Ness, filling the local hotels. Inverness was floodlit for the occasion, and traffic jammed the shoreline roads in both directions.

The bubble burst in early January, when museum zoologists announced that the footprints were those of a hippopotamus. They had been made with a stuffed hippo foot—the base of an umbrella stand or ashtray. It wasn't clear whether Wetherell was the perpetrator of the hoax or its gullible victim. Either way, the incident tainted the image of the Loch Ness Monster and discouraged serious investigation of the phenomenon. For the next three decades, most scientists scornfully dismissed reports of strange animals in the loch. Those sightings that weren't outright hoaxes, they said, were the result of optical illusions caused by boat wakes, wind slicks, floating logs, otters, ducks, or swimming deer.

> The conclusion brings the reader back to scientific reality and wraps things up neatly.

Respond in Writing In your journal, respond to this article on the Loch Ness Monster. Did the article seem well researched? What evidence was given for the existence of the monster? What reasons were given for doubting its existence?

Develop Your Own Research Ideas Work with your classmates to brainstorm ideas for your research.

Small Groups: Discuss your responses to the article and your reasons for believing or doubting the existence of the Loch Ness Monster.

Whole Class: Share your answers with the class. As you listen to your classmates, take notes on a chart like the one on the next page. The completed chart will help you decide on a legend to research for this project.

Find Your Legend				
How did the legend begin?	What factual evidence exists?	What evidence suggests the legend may be untrue?	Why do people today believe the legend or not?	Do you believe the legend is true? Why or why not?

Write About It You will write a research report investigating the facts behind a legend of your choice. You can choose from the following possible topics, audiences, and forms.

Possible Topics	**Possible Audiences**	**Possible Forms**
• a legendary beast, such as the Abominable Snowman • a real person of legendary fame, such as Davy Crockett or Sam Houston • a legendary group of people, such as the Huns • a legendary event, such as the Battle at Thermopylae • a legendary place, such as the Lost City of Atlantis	• other teenagers • historians • the general public • a society dedicated to the legend • tour guides	• a written research report • a research report placed on a Web site • a research report captured on video • a research report recorded digitally

Planning a research report requires some detective work to find the library materials you need. *(See pages 298–310.)* The right supplies will help you keep track of your information as you collect it. These supplies include a folder with pockets, index cards, paper clips, and rubber bands.

1 Structure of a Report

The three main parts of a report are the **introduction,** the **body,** and the **conclusion.** In addition, a report ends with a page that lists your sources of information.

STRUCTURE OF A REPORT

Title	• suggests the topic of the report
Introduction	• captures the reader's attention
	• provides any background information that the reader may need to know
	• contains a sentence expressing the main idea of the report
Body	• supports the main idea stated in the introduction
	• follows the order of your outline
	• includes specific information from your sources
Conclusion	• brings the report to a close
	• summarizes the main idea
	• includes a comment that shows the importance of your subject
Sources Page	• lists your sources of information
	• appears at the end of the report

PROJECT PREP *Analyzing* *Report Structure*

In your writing group, analyze the report on the Loch Ness monster. Make a chart like the one below to record your analysis of each paragraph. Share your completed analysis with the rest of the class and compare notes. The first paragraph is done for you.

Paragraph #	Main Idea	Supporting Details	Purpose in Report
1	Oldest evidence of monster goes back 1500 years	Pictish carving of it; all other animal carvings are very accurate	Introduce topic and show legend's deep roots

CHAPTER 11

2 Choosing and Limiting a Subject

You can get ideas for subjects for a report by looking at books or magazines or surfing the Internet. Brainstorming is another good way to explore possible topics. (For more on brainstorming, see page 18.) You might also talk to someone who knows a lot about a subject that interests you. A good subject is one that truly interests you, requires research, and can be developed with the resources of your library.

Once you have chosen a major research topic or general subject, the next step is to limit it. Your subject should be limited enough to allow you to cover it thoroughly in a short report.

WAYS TO LIMIT A SUBJECT

1. **Divide the general subject into its smaller parts.**

Example	training guide dogs for the blind
Parts	basic obedience training; training for crossing streets; training for around the house

2. **Limit the subject to a certain time, place, or person.**

Example	training guide dogs for the blind
Place	how dogs are trained at San Rafael, California
Person	how Dorothy Eustis helped found the guide-dog program in the United States

● **Practice Your Skills**

Limiting Research Subjects

With a partner, decide whether each subject is suitable for a research report. Indicate your answer by writing personal experience or research after the proper number.

1. robots

2. popular spots in your neighborhood

3. the history of your neighborhood

4. efforts to protect the wildlife in the Everglades

5. your trip to the Everglades

6. differences among wide-bodied airplanes

7. clubs at your school

8. packing a picnic lunch

9. what causes thunder and lightning

10. how to keep safe in a thunderstorm

PROJECT PREP *Prewriting* *Subject Focus*

Look over your notes from the whole-class discussion. Choose a subject you would enjoy researching. Then limit your subject by dividing it into its smaller parts or limiting it to a certain time, place, or person. Get feedback on your limited subject from your writing group.

③ Developing Research Questions

After you have limited your subject, think about what you need to learn to write about the subject. A good way to plan your research is to jot down some questions that you want your report to answer. Writing these questions will help you look for answers in the most efficient and effective way. Suppose you had chosen the topic of sightings of UFOs. Your research questions might appear as follows:

MODEL: Research Questions

Major research question: How do scientists classify sightings of UFOs?

- What different kinds of sightings are there?
- What is a close encounter?
- How many kinds of close encounters are there?
- What do scientists think about UFO sightings?

After initial research, develop additional questions that may lead you down multiple paths of exploration so you gain a deep understanding of your topic.

PROJECT PREP *Prewriting* *Research Questions*

Use a modified KWL chart (**K**now, **W**ant to know, **L**earned) like the one below to generate a list of facts you already know and a list of questions you would like to answer through your research about the subject of your report.

What do I know about the subject?	What do I want to learn about the subject?	What have I learned about the subject?	What misconceptions have I uncovered?	What further questions are worth researching?

Then write a major research question that summarizes the specific questions and provides a focus for your research.

1 Finding and Previewing Sources

With your questions in mind you can write a plan for answering them. The strategies below will help you find the answers by gathering information from a wide variety of sources. Along the way you can write a research plan to keep your project on course.

Strategies for Gathering Information

- Begin by checking an encyclopedia in print or online. This will give you an overview of your subject. It may also contain a list of books and other references with more information.
- Use the online catalog to do a keyword search in the library or media center.
- Check your library's online databases or a news index such as *Facts on File* for magazine and newspaper articles on your subject.
- Use an Internet search engine to search for Web sites related to your topic. Remember, not all Web sites contain accurate and reliable information.
- Make a list of all your sources. For each **book or video** write the author, title, copyright year, publisher's name and location, and call number (if available). For each **periodical,** include the date (month, day, and year), the volume, the issue number, and the pages. For each **Web site,** include the exact address, the site author, and the date accessed. If you find the source through an online database include the name of the database along with the other information.
- Assign each source on your list a number that you can use to refer to that source in your notes.

Search Tip

When you are searching the Web, start with sites that have been reviewed by librarians. At the American Library Association's Web page *Great Web Sites for Kids* <http://www.ala.org/greatsites> you can search by subject or keywords. Results show which sites are best for middle school students.

Keeping careful track of the identifying information of your sources will save you much time and trouble when you have to prepare your finished report. The examples on the next page show how you can prepare source cards so they contain all the necessary information. Note that if you cannot find full information for a source, include just the information you have.

EXAMPLE: Source Card Information

Encyclopedia	"Unidentified Flying Object," Columbia Encyclopedia, 6th ed, 2 Mar. 2009 <www.bartleby.com/65>.
Book	UFO: The Definitive Guide to Unidentified Flying Objects and Related Phenomena by David Ritchie, New York, MJF Books, 1994, 001.942 RIT
Magazine	Omni Fall 1995, p 4. "A UFO foundation: Working together to find answers," by Gregory Benford, MAS Ultra – School Edition library database, 2 Mar. 2009
Web Sites	"CNN's Interview with Peter Sturrock (Transcript)" Aired June 29, 1998. 2 Mar. 2009 <http://www.ufoevidence.org/documents/doc541.htm>
	"The CUFOS Organization." The J. Allen Hynek Center for UFO Studies. ©1997–2007. 11 Mar. 2009 <http://www.cufos.org/org.html> (The last update to this Web site was 2007. The material was accessed on March 11, 2009.)

When researching a subject from the past, such as early UFO sightings, you may want to locate primary sources from that period, such as statements by alleged witnesses or scientists at that time. You might find such direct, firsthand information in magazines and newspapers of the era. Remember, you need to distinguish between direct statements and opinions or comments derived from those original statements. These resources, as well as books listed as out-of-print in an online resource, may be found in a library or media center collection on microfilm or in an online database that focuses on archived articles. (See page 310.)

Writing a Research Plan Preview the first sources you find to write a research plan. On the subject of UFOs, a plan might look like this.

Research Plan

After previewing the reference works and other sources I found, I have learned that there are a few key people involved in UFO research, especially J. Allen Hynek, and that the UFO subject is controversial.

Step 1 I will look for more information by and about J. Allen Hynek and the other key people. I'll do an author search in the library catalog and also do an Internet search on their names.

Step 2 I will look for different sides of the UFO controversy. I can check Web sites about UFOs, but I will be sure to include sites by reputable scientific organizations, such as NASA.

Step 3 I will evaluate my sources using the guidelines on pages 291 and 292. I will use the bibliographies of sources I find trustworthy to locate additional information.

Step 4 I will follow the **Guidelines for Smart Searching** on page 312 to conduct advanced searches in a variety of electronic sources, including databases, to track down accurate information.

Step 5 I will search until I can answer my research question, but I may change it as I learn more.

● Develop Research Skills

Creating Source Cards

Use the library or media center to find three sources for each subject below. At least one source should be a magazine. Create source cards like the ones shown to record your findings.

1. Information on Mars: Source Card

"Mars Express Probes Red Planet's Unusual Deposits" <u>NASA</u> 1 Nov. 2007. 3 April 2009 <<u>http://www.nasa.gov/mission_pages/mars/news/marsis-20071101.html</u>>

"Mars' dynamic, icy past," by Daniel Pendick, <u>Astronomy,</u> Sep. 2008, Vol 36 Issue 9, p. 18. <u>MAS Ultra – School Edition.</u> EBSCO, library database. 2 April 2009

2. creating Web pages
3. the goals of the Sierra Club
4. guide dogs for the blind
5. Old Faithful in Yellowstone Park

PROJECT PREP *Prewriting* **Gathering Information**

Use the **Strategies for Gathering Information** on page 288 to help you create a written plan for your research and to find the information you need for the topic you chose. Your sources should include at least one article from both a magazine and an encyclopedia. Check your source cards to be sure you have accurately recorded the necessary information. The call number or Internet address is especially important, since it will help you find your source again quickly if you need to refer to it many times. Save your source cards for future use.

2 Evaluating Sources

As you begin the research process, keep in mind that not all sources of information you discover will be equally useful to you. Before using a source, you need to evaluate it critically with some basic guidelines in mind. Regardless of your specific topic, all of your sources should be relevant, reliable, up-to-date, and unbiased.

EVALUATING PRINT SOURCES

Just because a particular print source is in your library catalog or database doesn't mean that it's appropriate for your project. You still need to decide if it's relevant to your subject and whether the information is up-to-date and appropriate to the kind of report you are writing. The following guidelines can help you evaluate print sources.

Guidelines for Evaluating Print Sources

- **Who's the authority?**
  Find out the author's background. A library catalog entry or online book reviews may give information about the education or experience that makes the author an expert. Magazine or newspaper articles often provide a brief summary of their author's credentials. Get recommendations from a teacher, librarian, or someone else who is knowledgeable about the topic.

- **Who's behind it?**
  See if the author is associated with a particular organization and whether that organization might be biased. Find out who published the book. If the publisher is unfamiliar, do an online search to find out more about it. A librarian can lead you to the best sources for particular types of information.

- **What's right for you?**
  Make sure the book or article is relevant to your limited subject. Some sources may be too general or too specific for what you are trying to accomplish. They may be written at a level that is either too simple or too complex for a student researcher.

- **Look inside.**
  Check the publication date to make sure the information is current. Read the book jacket or an inside page to find out about the author's background. Look at the table of contents and index to see whether your particular topic is covered in appropriate detail. Skim relevant sections to see if sources are given to back up the facts presented. Does the author support his or her opinions with solid evidence?

EVALUATING ONLINE SOURCES

When you check out a book from the library, a librarian or a committee of educators has already evaluated the book to make sure it's a reliable source of information. But remember, no one owns or regulates the Internet. Just because you read something online, doesn't mean it's true. How can you tell the difference? Here are a few guidelines on how to evaluate an online source.

Guidelines for Evaluating Online Sources

- **Play the name game.**
  First, find out who publishes the site. Does the URL end in ".com" (which means it's a commercial company)? If so, is it a reputable company? Or is It one you've never heard of that might just be trying to sell you something? An educational site in which the URL ends in ".edu," such as a college or university, might be a more reliable choice. A site sponsored by a well-known organization with a URL that ends in ".org," such as the American Red Cross <http://www.redcross.org>, would also probably be a reliable source.

- **Scope it out.**
  Click around the site and get a feel for what it's like. Is the design clean and appealing? Is it easy to get around the site and find information? Are the sections clearly labeled? Does the site accept advertising? If you think the site seems disorganized, or you just have a negative opinion of it, listen to your instincts and move on to another one.

- **Says who?**
  Suppose you find an article on the Web that seems chock-full of great information. The next question you need to ask yourself is, "Who is the author? Is the person recognized as an expert on the subject?" If you don't recognize the author's name, you can do a search on the Web, using the author's name as the keyword to get more information about him or her. In some cases, an article won't list any author at all. If you don't find an author's name, be cautious. A reliable site clearly identifies its authors and usually lists their professional background.

- **Is this old news?**
  If you are doing research on the pyramids, it's probably all right if the information wasn't posted yesterday. But if you're looking for information in quickly changing fields, such as science and politics, be sure to check the publication date before you accept the data as true.

- **Ask around.**
  Reliable Web sites frequently provide e-mail addresses or links to authors and organizations connected to the content on the site. Send off a quick e-mail to a few of these sources, tell them what you are writing, and ask them: "Is this material accurate?"

Perhaps the best way to find out if the information on any Web site or the information in any article (signed or unsigned) is accurate is to check it against another source—and the best source is your local library or media center.

You can learn more about using the Internet for research on pages 311–313.

PROJECT PREP   *Prewriting*   Using Sources

Go to the library and follow your research plan to gather information from a range of relevant sources, including print resources, the Internet, documentary or informative films, and other sources of information. Make sure that you corroborate each source, that is, find roughly the same information in more than one source. Find a minimum of five trustworthy sources that are relevant to your topic. Discuss with your writing partners the quality and reliability of each source that you consult.

After finding sources, check the table of contents and index for information you need. If you are using a magazine article, skim it. Then read the sections about your subject and take notes in your own words on note cards.

The following excerpt is from a book on UFOs. Read it, then study the sample note card and guidelines that follow it.

MODEL: Taking Notes from a Source

Of greatest interest to most students of the UFO phenomenon is the so-called close encounter, in which an observer witnesses UFO activity, or evidence of it, at a close range, perhaps less than 500 feet. Dr. J. Allen Hynek, one of the most celebrated students of UFOs, classified close encounters in three categories.

Close encounters of the first kind (CEI). Here a UFO is observed at close range but shows no apparent interaction with the observers or with its environment. The reported object may be spectacular and perform dramatic maneuvers, but it leaves no traces of its presence on the ground or elsewhere, and no contact with occupants of the object is reported.

Sample Note Card

Close encounters — topic

UFO: The Definitive Guide — source

—Close encounter (CE) is a sighting of a UFO at "less than 500 feet" of witness. — quotation

—in CEI, UFO does not affect environment

—object may look or act unusual — paraphrase

—no reports of contact with beings in the UFO

p. 66 — page number

Taking Notes

- Write the title of your source in the upper right-hand corner of your note card.
- Write a heading in the upper left-hand corner of your card to identify the part of the subject being discussed.
- Begin a new card whenever you start taking notes on a different part of your subject.
- Summarize main points in your own words.
- Record the page number from which your information is taken.
- Clip together all cards from the same source. Later you will sort them into categories.

● Develop Research Skills

Taking Notes

Using an index card, take notes on the following information from pages 20 and 21 of *Coral Reef Fishes* by Eswald Lieske and Robert Myers.

In many parts of the world there are underwater parks where marine life is protected. In the Caribbean and the Maldives, the economic prosperity of entire nations depends on their underwater parks and the tourists they attract. Underwater parks and marine conservation areas also benefit the fishermen by offering a refuge for heavily exploited species to grow and reproduce so that the species' continued presence outside conservation areas is ensured. The key to the future well-being of many of the world's fish resources is clear. The establishment of underwater parks is a necessity if the maximum and well-balanced benefits of food, recreation, education, and economic development of marine resources are to be realized.

Writing Tip

The goals of **note taking** for a research report are to summarize the main points in your own words and to record quotations that you might use in your report.

PARAPHRASE, DON'T PLAGIARIZE

If your sources are good, their authors will have taken time to think and write carefully about the subject. In fact, you are likely to come across a word, phrase, or short passage that is so well worded you would like to use it yourself. In those cases, write what you would like to use on your note card, and place quotation marks around it to remind you that the words belong to someone else. Presenting someone else's words as your own is **plagiarism,** a serious and unlawful action. When you are drafting your report, you can include the quoted material as long as you place it in quotation marks and credit the source. (See pages 327–330.) Otherwise, rewrite or paraphrase the material that interests you. When you **paraphrase,** you put something in your own words.

Original	The reported object may be spectacular and perform dramatic maneuvers, but it leaves no traces of its presence . . .
Quoted	In a CEI, the object "may be spectacular and perform dramatic maneuvers," but there will never be any evidence of its presence.
Paraphrased	The object in a CEI might do amazing things, but it disappears without leaving any evidence behind.

PROJECT PREP — Prewriting — Taking Notes

Based on your research question, begin to take notes on information to use in your research report. Use the most relevant and reliable sources you can find. Record the information on each card following the sample format shown on page 293. As you learn more about your topic, consider whether you need to revise the focus of your report.

Writing Lab

Project Corner

Speak and Listen
Rate Your Experience

Discuss your research experiences with finding valid sources of information on the Internet. Focus on the pros and cons of online research. Continue the discussion until you have identified at least five pros and five cons. (See pages 416–417 for information on taking part in group discussions.)

Collaborate and Create
Be a News Team

In a group of three or four, plan and **present a news story** about a modern-day legend. Plan who will present which part of the report. Make it as realistic and interesting as you can.

Chart It Reveal Your Sources

In your writing group, **make a chart** that shows the sources you have consulted for your research. Organize the chart according to categories, such as encyclopedias, books, documentary films, articles, and Web sites. Create your chart so that it rates the degree of reliability for each *type* of source and each *individual* source.

In Everyday Life
E-mail Report of Research

1. Your yearbook advisor wants you to find out what was popular this year among the students. The yearbook publishes photographs and descriptions of the fads and trends at your school annually. Observe students and take notes on what they are wearing and discussing. Survey some of your classmates about what they think is important and fashionable. Include background information from online sources. *Write an e-mail* to your advisor that describes how you researched five trends, fads, or ideas that are currently popular at your school.

In the Workplace Questions and Answers

2. You work for the quiz show *Beats Me!* and you need to write questions for the show every week. This week the host wants questions on the following subjects: Chinese cuisine, popular music of the 1980s, squirrels, and bicycles. *Write two questions* (one easy, one hard), along with their answers, for each of these subjects. Make sure that your questions are fair and clear and the answers are well researched. Consult reliable research sources to obtain your questions and answers.

Timed Writing ⏱ Memo to the Editor

3. You are a reporter for a consumer newsletter and you have been assigned a story on the worst deal of the year. Your editor wants you to investigate purchases that you, your friends, or your family have made that were disastrous. Your final report will warn people not to make a similar purchase. Write a memo to your editor describing the topic for your report. Include sources for the background information that will be the main topic of your report. You have 20 minutes to complete your work after you have identified the sources you will use.

Before You Write Consider the following questions: What is the subject, the audience, and the purpose?

After You Write Evaluate your work by reviewing your plan and checking that your sources are reliable as outlined on pages 291–292.

Research Companion

Libraries and media centers are storehouses of information. They are places where knowledge spanning centuries has been gathered. A library not only holds the answers to questions you already have, but also inspires you to ask new questions. In the past, when people thought about the library, they mostly thought of it as a place to find books. Today, however, most libraries operate as media centers where, in addition to books, you can find magazines, newspapers, and a wide range of reference materials in print, online, or in electronic formats.

Using the Library or Media Center

The library or media center is the best place to begin researching, whatever your topic may be. This storehouse of knowledge and information includes printed media, such as books, newspapers, magazines, encyclopedias, and other forms of writing, and an ever-increasing variety of electronic or online resources, such as downloadable electronic books, computer databases, and access to the Internet. Whenever you start a new research project, however, the most valuable resource may be the librarian or media specialist—the trained professional who can help you find the references that you need most.

FICTION

If you are researching a literary subject, you may need to use the section of the library devoted to literature. A book or story that is based on imaginary people and events is called **fiction.** Works of fiction are shelved in alphabetical order according to the author's last name. For special cases, most libraries follow the shelving rules listed below.

Guidelines for Finding Fiction

- Two-part names are alphabetized by the first part of the name.
  De Soto   **O'Connor**   **Van Buren**
- Names beginning with *Mc* or *St.* are alphabetized as if they began with *Mac* or *Saint.*
- Books by authors with the same last name are alphabetized first by last name, and then by first name.
- Books by the same author are alphabetized by the first important word in the title.

● Develop Research Skills

Arranging Fiction

List the novels in the order they should be placed on the shelf.

Words by Heart by Ouida Sebestyen

Powers by Ursula K. Le Guin

Athabasca by Alistair MacLean

Island of the Blue Dolphins by Scott O'Dell

Great Expectations by Charles Dickens

The Riddle-Master of Hed by Patricia McKillip

David Copperfield by Charles Dickens

A Formal Feeding by Zibby O'Neal

It's Crazy to Stay Chinese in Minnesota by Eleanor Wong Telemaque

Flowers for Algernon by Daniel Keyes

Grandpa and Frank by Janet Majerus

● Develop Research Skills

Solving Shelving Problems

List the following fiction authors in the order that their books would appear on the shelves.

Duane Decker	Paula Danziger
Adele De Leeuw	Rosamund Du Jardin
Lois Duncan	Daphne Du Maurier
Theodore DuBois	Dan D'Amelio
Paxton Davis	Alexandre Dumas

NONFICTION

In contrast to fiction, nonfiction books are about real people and events. Most libraries use the **Dewey decimal system** to arrange nonfiction books on shelves. This system was created more than 100 years ago by an American librarian named Melvil Dewey. In the Dewey decimal system, each book is assigned a number according to its subject. The following chart shows the ten categories in the Dewey decimal system.

DEWEY DECIMAL SYSTEM

000–099	General Works (reference books)
100–199	Philosophy
200–299	Religion
300–399	Social Science (law, education, economics)
400–499	Language
500–599	Science (mathematics, biology, chemistry)
600–699	Technology (medicine, inventions)
700–799	Fine Arts (painting, music, theater, sports)
800–899	Literature
900–999	History (biography, geography, travel)

Each of the ten main classes is broken up into smaller divisions. In the social science class, for example, the numbers 390–399 are reserved for books about customs and folklore. These smaller groups can be divided even further by using decimal points.

The number assigned to a book is the **call number.** The call number is written on the spine of the book. On the shelf, books are arranged in numerical order according to their call numbers.

BIOGRAPHIES AND AUTOBIOGRAPHIES

Biographies and autobiographies are usually shelved in a special section. Many libraries label each book with a *B* for biography or with the Dewey decimal number *920*. They are arranged in alphabetical order by the last name of the subject, not the author.

● **Develop Research Skills**

Using the Dewey Decimal System

Using the chart on this page, write the range of numbers and the general category for each of the following titles.

1. *Computer Games and Puzzles*
2. *The Life of Martin Luther King, Jr.*
3. *A Climber's Guide to Glacier National Park*
4. *The History of Jazz*
5. *The Philosophy of Gandhi*
6. *Algebra in Easy Steps*
7. *Religions of America*
8. *Geography of American Cities*
9. *The Poems of Robert Frost*
10. *Learning Basic Spanish*

Develop Research Skills

Solving Shelving Problems

Write the following Dewey decimal numbers and book titles in the order that the books would appear on the shelves.

1. 535.6   *Color—From Rainbows to Lasers*
2. 560.9   *Tales Told by Fossils*
3. 549.1   *Rocks, Gems, and Minerals*
4. 522.6   *Eavesdropping on Space*
5. 530.3   *Your World in Motion*
6. 550.9   *The Earth and Its Satellite*
7. 553.8   *The World of Diamonds*
8. 542.4   *Chemistry Magic!*
9. 523.5   *Mars, The Red Planet*
10. 551.4   *Exploring American Caves*

THE LIBRARY CATALOG

The **online catalog** is a computerized catalog that provides information on all the materials available in a library or media center. You use it by entering the title, author, or subject you are looking for. The computer will then display the results of your search. Some online catalogs can also tell if the material you are looking for is held by the library or media center you are in, whether it is currently available to check out, and what other libraries may have it. In some libraries, if a book is out on loan, you can even request that it be put on hold for you when it is returned.

ITEM INFORMATION ENTRY

The backyard astronomer's guide		Dickinson, Terence.	
Publisher:	Firefly Books,		
Pub date:	2008.		
Pages:	368 p. :		
ISBN:	9781554073443		
Item info:	1 copy available at Columbia Public Library.		
Holdings			
Columbia Public Library	Copies	Material	Location
522 DIC 3RD ED.	1	Book	Nonfiction

The online catalog record shown below provides more detailed information about the book than the item information entry above, which tells you where to find the book in the library.

ONLINE CATALOG RECORD

The backyard astronomer's guide	Dickinson, Terence.
Personal Author:	Dickinson, Terence.
Title:	The backyard astronomer's guide/Terence Dickinson & Alan Dyer.
Edition:	3rd ed., rev. & expanded
Publication info:	Richmond Hill, Ont. : Firefly Books, 2008.
Physical descrip:	368 p. : ill. ; 29 cm.
General Note:	"Revised and expanded."
Subject term:	Astronomy–Amateurs' manuals.
Added author:	Dyer, Alan, 1953-

To search the listings in an online catalog, you select a category—author, title, or subject—and enter the necessary commands. On some systems, you can also do a keyword search, just as you would on an Internet search engine. A keyword search can search the library's collections for both title and subject headings at the same time. If the book you are looking for is not listed or not available, the computer can tell you if it has been checked out and when it is due back. By using the Web to search other library databases, the media specialist can tell you if the book is available elsewhere.

Search Tip

When the library's online catalog displays the results of a search, instead of taking notes by hand, you can print out the information you need using the Print command. This will save you time and ensure that the information you are using to find a book is accurate.

Strategies for Finding Books

- Find out if the library has the book you want by looking it up on the online catalog.
- Read the screen to see if the book is likely to contain the information you need. Check the copyright date to see how current the information is.
- On a slip of paper, copy the call number, the title, and the name of the author for each book you want to find or print out the information.
- Use the call number to find each book. The first line of the call number tells which section of the library or media center to look in.

F or FIC	fiction section
B or 920	biography section
Dewey number	nonfiction section

- Then find each book on the shelves by looking for its call number, located on the spine.

CHAPTER 11

Using Reference Materials

Reference books, such as encyclopedias, dictionaries, atlases, and almanacs, are kept in a separate section of the library. Usually these books cannot be checked out. There are often study tables set up in this section so that you can use the books while you are in the library.

Now libraries and media centers are also often the best way to find the most reliable online reference sources. Most libraries subscribe to **online databases** that can be accessed through computers in the library. Often, anyone with a library card can use a computer at home to search the databases through the library's Web site. These databases provide a wealth of information that is not usually available for free just by searching on the Internet. Some databases are especially designed for students.

PERIODICALS—MAGAZINES AND NEWSPAPERS

Periodicals, including magazines and newspapers, are excellent sources for current information. You can usually search for periodical titles in the library's online catalog but you cannot search for individual articles. The library may keep copies for a few months of a daily newspaper and a few years of weekly or monthly magazines.

By subscribing to online databases, libraries now make it easy to find articles in a wide variety of magazines and newspapers. A librarian or media specialist can help you determine which databases are best for your research project. You can search in a database using keywords as you would with an Internet search engine. Database entries provide an abstract or short summary of the article so you can decide if it is useful to read the full text. Full text is available for many articles from the 1990s onward. These full text articles can be downloaded or printed. Many databases allow you to save your search results in folders for future reference.

You can learn more about searching with keywords on pages 311–312.

Following are some results from a search of an online database especially designed for students. The search used the keywords *electronic mail messages* and limited results to full text articles from the past year.

1. Find Your Perfect Pen Pal! *Girls' Life,* Feb/Mar2009, Vol. 15 Issue 4, p6–6, 2/3 p; Reading Level (Lexile): 1040; *(AN 36379418)*
   HTML Full Text

2. MURPHY, MEET OUR NEW DEPARTMENT. By: Copeland, Sue H. *Horse & Rider,* Jan2009, Vol. 48 Issue 1, p6–6, 1p; Reading Level (Lexile): 910; *(AN 35942647)*
   HTML Full Text PDF Full Text (577KB)

3. Ask the Experts. *PC Magazine,* Jan2009, Vol. 28 Issue 1, p78–79, 2p, 3 color; Reading Level (Lexile): 950; *(AN 35764052)*
   HTML Full Text PDF Full Text (910KB)

4. WE NEED TO CHAT! By: Blyth, Catherine. *Daily Mail,* 11/10/2008, p13, 1p; *(AN 35177891)*
   HTML Full Text

5. A SELECTION OF LETTERS FROM THE FRONT. By: Carroll, Andrew. *Military History,* Nov/Dec2008, Vol. 25 Issue 5, p36–42, 7p; Reading Level (Lexile): 1020; *(AN 35572164)*
   HTML Full Text PDF Full Text (3.1MB)

6. Adam Grosser's Arresting E-mail. *Business Week Online,* 10/13/2008, p9–9, 1p; Reading Level (Lexile): 1010; *(AN 34848150)*
   HTML Full Text

7. Facebook Blows It. By: Karlgaard, Rich. *Forbes,* 9/15/2008, Vol. 182 Issue 4, p31–31, 1/4p; Reading Level (Lexile): 1000; *(AN 34173046)*
   HTML Full Text

8. Now that summer's over, it's time for a homework assignment. By: Iezzi, Teressa. *Advertising Age,* 9/8/2008, Vol. 79 Issue 33, p18–18, 2/5p; Reading Level (Lexile): 1070; *(AN 34247573)*
   HTML Full Text

9. Why Chrome Won't Crash Windows. By: Beal, Andy. *Business Week Online,* 9/4/2008, p6–6, 1p; Reading Level (Lexile): 1100; *(AN 34252514)*
   HTML Full Text

10. YOU ARE WHAT YOU E-MAIL. By: Bachel, Beverly. *Career World,* Sep2008, Vol. 37 Issue 1, Special section p16–19, 4p; Reading Level (Lexile): 1090; *(AN 34474213)*
    HTML Full Text PDF Full Text (1.4MB)

● Develop Research Skills

Using Online Databases

Use the search results on page 305 to answer the following questions.

1. Which article has the most recent publication date?

2. What are the titles of two articles in *Business Week Online?*

3. Which article is about a social networking site?

4. What article would you read to find out how soldiers use e-mail?

5. What is the date of the publication of an article by Catherine Blyth?

6. What volume of *PC Magazine* contains an article by computer experts?

7. What is the title of the article of interest to people with horses?

8. Who is the author of the article "Why Chrome Won't Crash Windows"?

9. What are the titles of three magazine articles over one page in length?

10. Which of the articles has the lowest reading level?

ENCYCLOPEDIAS

Encyclopedias contain general information on a wide variety of subjects. The information is arranged in alphabetical order by subject. Guide letters on the spine help you find the right volume. Inside every volume are guide words at the top of each page to direct you to your subject. Most encyclopedias provide an index in a separate volume or at the end of the last volume. The index tells if your subject is discussed in more than one volume or if it is listed under another name.

Online encyclopedias are arranged in the same manner as printed encyclopedias—alphabetically—but there are no guide words, nor index. Instead, you enter the subject in a search box. The best online encyclopedias are the ones available through your library's databases. Beware of open-source encyclopedias that have unsigned articles that can be changed without being reviewed by an expert.

Print and Online	Through libraries and media centers:
	Compton's by Encyclopedia Britannica
	World Book Encyclopedia
	Encyclopedia Americana
	Grolier Multimedia Encyclopedia
Online	Reliable free encyclopedias:
	Columbia Encyclopedia http://www.bartleby.com/65/
	Encyclopedia.com http://www.encyclopedia.com

SPECIALIZED ENCYCLOPEDIAS

Specialized encyclopedias focus on one particular subject. They provide more information about a subject than general encyclopedias do. Specialized encyclopedias are also arranged in alphabetical order and just like general encyclopedias, they come in print and online versions. Following are some specialized encyclopedias.

Print
International Wildlife Encyclopedia

Encyclopedia of American Cars

World Sports Encyclopedia

Encyclopedia of American Facts and Dates

The McGraw-Hill Encyclopedia of Science and Technology

Complete Encyclopedia of Tropical Fish

Online
Encyclopedia Smithsonian
http://www.si.edu/Encyclopedia_SI/default.htm

A collection of almost 50 different encyclopedias
http://www.encyclopedia.com

GENERAL BIOGRAPHICAL REFERENCES

Biographical references are works that give information about the lives of famous people, past and present. Some provide only a paragraph of facts, such as birth date, education, family, occupation, and awards. Others contain long articles about each person in the volume. Your library may also have an online biographical database. Following are some well-known biographical references.

Print
Current Biography

Who's Who in America

Merriam-Webster's Biographical Dictionary

Dictionary of American Biography

American Men and Women of Science

Online
Biography http://www.biography.com

● **Develop Research Skills**

Using General Biographical References

Using a biographical reference book or database, match the famous American cartoonists in the first column with the comic strip character they created in the second column.

1. C. C. Beck   *Captain America*
2. Jim Davis   *Peanuts*
3. Al Capp   *Little Orphan Annie*
4. Jack Kirby   *Captain Marvel*
5. Alex Raymond   *Dennis the Menace*
6. Harold Gray   *Popeye*
7. Hank Ketcham   *Doonesbury*
8. Charles Schultz   *L'il Abner*
9. Elzie C. Segar   *Flash Gordon*
10. Gary Trudeau   *Garfield*

ATLASES

Atlases are collections of maps. They usually include many different kinds of maps, some showing climate, some showing population density. In addition, many atlases include charts with facts about mountains, deserts, rivers, oceans, and natural resources. The table of contents and the index of each atlas directs you to the information you need. Following are some popular atlases.

Print   *The Times Atlas of the World*

         Hammond Odyssey World Atlas

         Rand McNally International World Atlas

         Goode's World Atlas

         The National Geographic Atlas of the World

Online   *National Atlas of the United States*
         http://www-atlas.usgs.gov/

ALMANACS AND YEARBOOKS

Almanacs and *yearbooks* are published once a year. For this reason they contain much up-to-date information. They cover a wide variety of subjects, such as famous people, unusual achievements, the economy, politics, countries, and sports. Following are some of the most popular almanacs and yearbooks.

Print	*Information Please Almanac*
	World Almanac and Book of Facts
	Guinness Book of World Records
Online	*The Old Farmer's Almanac* http://www.almanac.com
	Infoplease http://www.infoplease.com/

SPECIALIZED DICTIONARIES

Specialized dictionaries contain entries about one specific subject. Some, for example, are limited to sciences. Others may be limited to geography. One kind of dictionary, called a thesaurus, includes only synonyms. The following list shows the variety of specialized dictionaries.

Print	*Roget's 21ˢᵗ Century Thesaurus in Dictionary Form*
	Merriam-Webster Dictionary of Synonyms and Antonyms
	American Heritage Student Science Dictionary
	Dictionary of American History
Online	English and foreign language dictionaries http://dictionary.reference.com/
	Roget's Thesaurus http://thesaurus.reference.com/

● Develop Research Skills

Using Specialized Reference Materials

Following is a list of library resources. Number a piece of paper from 1 to 10. Then write the best source for answering each question.

specialized encyclopedia   atlas   biographical reference

almanac   specialized dictionary

1. In what part of Alaska is the capital located?

2. When and where was actor-comedian Bill Cosby born?

3. What does the term *fielder's choice* mean in baseball?

4. What is a harvest moon?

5. What does the term *staccato* mean in music?

6. What river flows through the Grand Canyon?

7. What policy for naming hurricanes was adopted in 1979?

8. For what sport is Michelle Kwan known?

9. What are the chief crops grown in Indiana?

10. What does the term *Manifest Destiny* mean in American history?

● **Develop Research Skills**

Finding Facts in Reference Materials

Use the library's reference materials to find the answers to the ten questions listed above.

VERTICAL FILES

The **vertical file** is a collection of leaflets, catalogs, pamphlets, newspaper clippings, and brochures kept in filing cabinets. Inside the file drawers, items are arranged in folders in alphabetical order according to subject.

MICROFORMS

To save space, many libraries store older issues of some magazines and newspapers in **microform:** either **microfilm** (a reel of film) or **microfiche** (a sheet of film). You can view these types of film by using a special projection machine. Check with a librarian to see if there are indexes such as the *Readers' Guide to Periodical Literature* or newspaper indexes to help you locate articles on specific topics.

RECORDED MATERIALS

Most libraries have a section where the recorded materials are kept. These usually include CDs and DVDs, and perhaps audiotapes, records, videos, and CD-ROMs. You will find these materials indexed in the online catalog. Some of the recorded materials may be borrowed and others can only be used in the library. Many libraries and media centers have listening, viewing, and computer rooms where these types of materials can be used.

TIME OUT TO
REFLECT

You have seen that some information in a library or media center is in print form, while other information is in electronic form. Each format has its own advantages. What advantages did you find in using the Internet to gather information instead of going to print or bound materials? Were there any advantages to looking in books instead of going online? In what situations would each form of information be most useful? Record your reflections in your journal.

Using the Internet for Research

The Information Superhighway could be the best research partner you've ever had. It's fast, vast, and always available. But like any other highway, if you don't know your way around, it can also be confusing. It takes time to learn how to navigate the Net and zero in on the information you need. The best thing to do is practice early and often. Don't wait until the night before your paper is due to learn how to do research on the Internet!

GETTING STARTED

Just as there are several different ways to get to your home or school, there are many different ways to arrive at the information you're looking for on the Internet.

Internet Public Library Perhaps the best place to start your search for reliable information on the Web is to go to the Internet Public Library site, recently renamed ipl2 <http://www.ipl.org/>. This virtual reference library provides links to Web sites that have been reviewed and recommended by librarians. The home page is organized with links to sections much like those at your local library or media center. There are even special sections for kids and teens. Clicking on the links that relate to your topic will take you to a list of suggested resources.

Search Bar Another good first step is your browser's search bar. Type a word or short phrase that describes what you're searching for. Then select the search tool you wish to use. You can usually customize your browser by adding the search tools you use most often to the drop-down menu. Some of these tools, sometimes referred to as **search engines,** include:

AltaVista—http://www.altavista.com/   Google—http://www.google.com/

Ask—http://www.ask.com/   Lycos—http://www.lycos.com/

Bing—http://www.bing.com/   Yahoo!—http://www.yahoo.com/

Dogpile—http://www.dogpile.com/

Search services usually list broad categories of subjects, plus they may offer other features, such as "Random Links," "Top 25 Sites," and options for customizing. Each one also has a search field. Type in a **keyword,** a word or short phrase that describes your area of interest. Then click Search or press the Enter key on your keyboard. Seconds later a list of Web sites known as "hits" will be displayed, all containing the word you specified in the search field. Scroll through the list and click the page you wish to view.

So far this sounds simple, doesn't it? The tricky part about doing a search on the Internet is that a single keyword may yield a hundred or more sites. Plus, you may find many topics you don't need. For example, suppose you are writing a science paper about the planet Saturn. If you type the word *Saturn* into the search field, you'll turn up some articles about the planet, but you'll also get articles about NASA's Saturn rockets and Saturn, the automobile company.

SEARCH SMART

Listed below are a few pointers on how to narrow your search, save time, and search *smart* on the Net. Not all search strategies work with all search engines.

Guidelines for Smart Searching

- The keyword or words that you enter have a lot to do with the accuracy of your search. Focus your search by adding the word "and" or the + sign followed by another descriptive word. For example, try "Saturn" again, but this time, add "Saturn + space." Adding a third word, "Saturn + space + rings" will narrow the field even more.

- On the other hand, you can limit unwanted results by specifying information that you do *not* want the search engine to find. If you type "dolphins not football," you will get Web sites about the animal that lives in the ocean rather than the football team that uses Miami as its home base.

- Specify geographical areas using the word "near" between keywords as in "islands near Florida." This lets you focus on specific regions.

- To broaden your search, add the word "or" between keywords. For example, "sailboats or catamarans."

- Help the search engine recognize familiar phrases by putting words that go together in quotes such as "Tom and Jerry" or "bacon and eggs."

- Sometimes the site you come up with is in the ballpark of what you are searching for, but it is not exactly what you need. Skim the text quickly anyway. It may give you ideas for more accurate keywords. There might also be links listed to other sites that are just the right resource you need.

- Try out different search engines. Each service uses slightly different methods of searching, so you may get different results using the same keywords.

- Check the spelling of the keywords you are using. A misspelled word can send a search engine in the wrong direction. Also, be careful how you use capital letters. By typing the word *Gold,* some search services will only bring up articles that include the word with a capital *G.*

SAVING A SITE FOR LATER

You may want to keep a list handy of favorite Web sites or sites you are currently using in a project. This will save you time because you can just click on the name of the site in your list and return to that page without having to retype the URL.

Different browsers have different names for this feature. For example, AOL's Netscape™ calls it **My Links,** Mozilla's Firefox™ calls it a **bookmark,** while Microsoft's Internet Explorer™ calls it **favorites.**

INTERNET + MEDIA CENTER = INFORMATION POWERHOUSE

Although the Internet is a limitless treasure chest of information, remember that it's not cataloged. It can be tricky to locate the information you need, and sometimes that information is not reliable. The library is a well-organized storehouse of knowledge, but it has more limited resources. If you use the Internet *and* your local media center, you've got everything you need to create well-researched articles, reports, and papers.

Using the Internet and Media Center

Use the Internet to

- get great ideas for topics to write about
- gather information about your topic from companies, colleges and universities, and professional organizations
- connect with recognized experts in your field of interest
- connect with other people who are interested in the same subject and who can put you in touch with other sources

Use the Media Center to

- find reliable sources of information either in print or online
- get background information on your topic
- cross-check the accuracy and credibility of online information and authors

CHAPTER 12

Research: Synthesizing, Organizing, and Presenting

When you are working on a craft, you need to plan your project and gather your materials before putting the pieces together. In the previous chapter you have done the same thing for your research report. You have

- chosen and limited a subject;
- posed a major research question;
- written a research plan;
- used your library and media center to find sources;
- evaluated those sources; and
- taken notes.

The activities in this chapter will take you through the rest of the process of preparing a research report.

Writing Project *Research Report*

The Legend of . . . *Complete your research report that investigates myths and legends.*

Review In the previous chapter you gathered and organized information for your research report, using your major research question as the focus for your inquiry and refining that question. You have taken notes from sources to record information to use when answering your research question and have converted both graphic and written material from your sources to written notes for your report. You may have used a word processing program to take notes as you accumulated new information. In this chapter you will learn how to take the information you have gathered and use it to write the research report itself.

Writing a Research Report Synthesizing

To prevent your report from being a mere collection of facts, you need to synthesize what you have learned to develop your own insights. To **synthesize** means to merge together information from different sources and your own experience and understanding. The following diagram shows the steps you can take to synthesize information.

SYNTHESIZING INFORMATION FROM DIFFERENT SOURCES

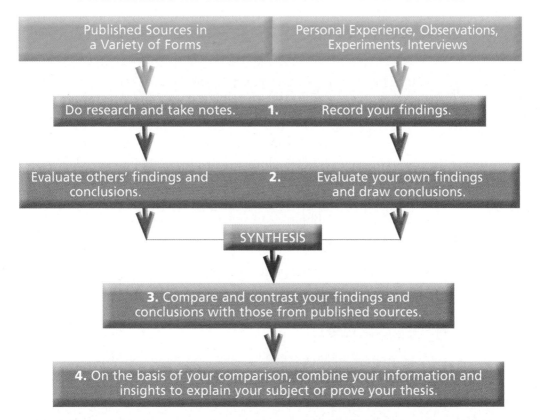

Published Sources in a Variety of Forms		Personal Experience, Observations, Experiments, Interviews
Do research and take notes.	**1.**	Record your findings.
Evaluate others' findings and conclusions.	**2.**	Evaluate your own findings and draw conclusions.

SYNTHESIS

3. Compare and contrast your findings and conclusions with those from published sources.

4. On the basis of your comparison, combine your information and insights to explain your subject or prove your thesis.

PROJECT PREP *Prewriting* *Synthesis*

Review your research question and all the notes you took as you conducted research. Follow the steps in the diagram above to synthesize the information, beginning with step 2. Write a brief paragraph evaluating the findings and conclusions of others. Write a second brief paragraph evaluating your own views on the subject. Then complete steps 3 and 4. Write a few sentences explaining how you combined the various sources of information to build the understanding you now have.

1 Organizing Your Notes

As you take notes, you will start to see how ideas are related. Ideas that seem to relate to a similar theme can be grouped together into a single category. Building a system of categories helps you see the bigger picture of the information you gathered. Categorizing is the first step in organizing your notes into an outline.

First, use the headings on your note cards to organize your information into categories. Once you have determined your categories, you can easily sort through your notes and clip together all the cards that belong in each category.

This is also a good time to review your major research question. See if the information you have gathered answers the question. Ask yourself if you want to narrow or broaden the question and the topic of your report. Consider whether you need to do additional research.

The writer of the research report on UFO sightings sorted the notes into the following categories.

Category 1   Distant sightings

Category 2   Close encounters with UFOs

Category 3   Close encounters with alien creatures

> **Writing Tip**
>
> Group your notes into three to five main categories that are broad enough to include all your information.

PROJECT PREP *Prewriting* *Organization of Information*

Sort the information for your report by looking for three to five broad categories. Look for big ideas that cover all the important themes of your notes to serve as the broad categories. Review your major research question and see if you need to make it broader or more narrow. Save your notes for later use.

Think Critically

Summarizing

When you take notes before you synthesize, you use the skill of **summarizing.** When you summarize, you record the writer's most important points in your own words, leaving out unnecessary details.

Thinking Practice

Read the paragraph below. Then summarize it by completing the activities below.

The Human Ear

The human ear consists of three parts—the external ear, the middle ear, and the internal ear—each of which performs different functions. The external ear receives sound waves traveling through the air and directs them toward the middle ear. The middle ear concentrates sound waves and conducts them to the internal ear. The internal ear converts sound vibrations to nervous impulses that are then carried by the acoustic nerve to the brain. Only when nerve impulses reach the brain do we hear sound.

—Joan Elma Rahn, *Ears, Hearing, and Balance*

1. Look up any unfamiliar words and define them in your own words.
2. Write the main idea of this paragraph in your own words.
3. Write three or more sentences summarizing the rest of the paragraph.

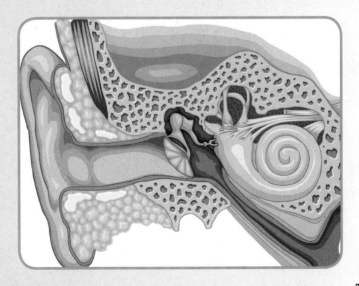

② Outlining

Once your notes are categorized, you can begin to outline your report.

HERE'S HOW

Preparing an Outline

- Use the headings on your note cards to group the cards into a few categories. Save the cards that do not fit into any category for possible use in the introduction or conclusion.
- Make a list of your categories. Then, using Roman numerals (I, II, III, etc.), arrange your categories in a logical order. (page 199)
- Use the categories as the main topics in your outline.
- Using your note cards, list subtopics under each main topic. (Use capital letters for subtopics.)

The categories on UFO sightings can be arranged logically in order of degree. In arranging these categories, the writer followed the order that experts used to classify UFO sightings.

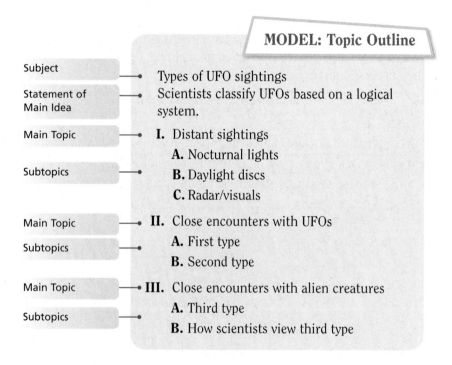

MODEL: Topic Outline

Subject	Types of UFO sightings
Statement of Main Idea	Scientists classify UFOs based on a logical system.
Main Topic	**I.** Distant sightings
	A. Nocturnal lights
Subtopics	**B.** Daylight discs
	C. Radar/visuals
Main Topic	**II.** Close encounters with UFOs
Subtopics	**A.** First type
	B. Second type
Main Topic	**III.** Close encounters with alien creatures
Subtopics	**A.** Third type
	B. How scientists view third type

After you have finished your outline, use the following guidelines to check its form.

Outline Form

- Include a title and a statement of the main idea.
- Use a Roman numeral and a period for each main topic.
- Use a capital letter and a period for each subtopic.
- Always include at least two subtopics under each main topic.
- Indent as shown in the above model.
- Capitalize the first word of each entry.

You can also make an informal outline or use some other graphic organizer to get your thoughts straight. Maybe you find something like the following easier for you to use in planning and organizing your report.

Writing Tip

Use your note-card categories as the main topics of an outline. Then use your notes to add subtopics to the outline.

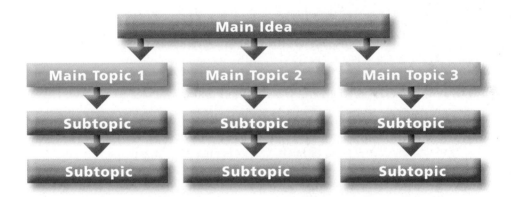

PROJECT PREP *Prewriting* *Outline*

Use your note cards—which contain summaries from your readings—to develop the outline for your report. Now that you have assembled the information you will use, create an outline that reflects your purposes. Discuss with your writing group whether or not you need to revise your outline before finalizing it. When you have settled on a final form of the outline, you can begin drafting your report.

The Power of Language ⚡

Adverbial Clauses: Scene Setters

Since the elementary grades, you have been using adverbial clauses, not only in speech but in writing. You create such clauses by putting a subordinating word like *when, if, because, until, while, since,* or *although* in front of a sentence. (See pages 632–634.) In the following sentences from "Birth of a Legend," scene-setting phrases indicate time or place and explain how something was done.

Creating a Subordinate Clause

Independent Clause	The Romans first came to northern Scotland in the first century A.D.
Subordinate Clause	When the Romans first came to northern Scotland in the first century A.D. (Subordinating word added. Subordinate clauses cannot stand alone.)
Subordinate Clause plus Independent Clause	When the Romans first came to northern Scotland in the first century A.D., they found the Highlands occupied by fierce, tattoo-covered tribes . . . . (Subordinating clause now serves as a scene setter for the independent clause.)

Use adverbial clauses when you want to subordinate one idea to another. Here is another example from "Birth of a Legend."

> But the modern legend of Loch Ness dates from 1933, when a new road was completed along the shore, . . .

Try It Yourself

Write two sentences with adverbial clauses on the topic of your project. If possible, use these sentences in your draft. Otherwise, during revision, see if there are places in your writing where subordinating one sentence to another would have a strong effect and help set the scene.

Punctuation Tip

When subordinate clauses **begin a sentence,** they should be **followed by a comma.** Usually a comma is not used if the subordinate clause comes at the end.

CHAPTER 12

After outlining your report, you are ready to write the first draft. Your first draft should include all three parts of the report—the introduction, body, and conclusion. (See page 285.)

1 Drafting the Introduction

Think about your readers as you write the introduction. Remember that they have not done the research you have just completed. They will not even know what your report is about until they begin reading. Use the following guidelines to write a strong introduction.

Writing an Introduction

A strong introduction

- captures the reader's attention
- provides any needed background information
- contains a sentence stating the main idea

The following introduction shows how all three items in the preceding chart can be smoothly worked into the opening paragraph of a report on the subject of UFO sightings.

MODEL: Introduction of a Report

Have you ever noticed something unusual in the night sky? If so, you are not alone. Thousands of people have reported seeing unidentified flying objects (UFOs) over the years. One expert, J. Allen Hynek, developed a way to classify the thousands of sightings that are regularly reported to the authorities. He based his system on the distance between the UFO and the witness.

Strong Introduction

Main Idea

---

1. Based on the information you have assembled, write a draft of the introduction to your research report. Use your major research question to draft a thesis statement that will guide your paper. Let's say, for instance, that your major research question is, "According to legend, at the Battle of Thermopylae a small Spartan force (300 soldiers plus a few thousand conscripts from other city-states) battled an enormous Persian army (according to legend, up to 1,000,000 soldiers) before being defeated. What does historical evidence say about who fought this battle?"

2. You could rephrase this question as the following thesis statement: "According to legend, at the Battle of Thermopylae a small Spartan force (300 soldiers plus a few thousand conscripts from other city-states) battled an enormous Persian army (according to legend, up to 1,000,000 soldiers) before being defeated, yet the real facts are difficult to ascertain. However, evidence does point to reliability of the account of Herodotus."

3. When you have completed your introductory paragraph, meet with your writing group and read one another's introductions. Help one another formulate a clear thesis statement and develop It briefly so that the introduction clearly sets up the report that will follow.

② Drafting the Body

In the body of your report you will present the evidence to explain your topic by accurately synthesizing ideas from several sources. You will summarize or paraphrase what you have learned, draw conclusions about your findings in a systematic way, and give relevant reasons to support them. Follow the order of your outline and write a variety of complete sentences and well-developed paragraphs. Use transitions to guide your readers from idea to idea. (Refer to pages 122 and 140.) Compare the following body of a report to the outline on page 318.

Also notice how the writer smoothly included quotes and paraphrases. Sources are cited in parentheses. This method of citing sources is called **parenthetical citation.** A parenthetical citation briefly identifies the source and page number of information.

MODEL: Body of a Report

The first main category of UFOs in Hynek's system may be called distant sightings. Any sighting in which the witness is more than five hundred feet away from the UFO falls into this group. Within this group there are three main types of sightings. One is the "nocturnal light," which is any light seen in the night sky that cannot be explained. A second is the "daylight disc." This group includes unidentified objects of any shape seen during the daytime. The last type of distant sighting is the "radar/visual." These UFOs are seen by a witness and recorded on radar at the same time (O'Neill 12).

> From Roman Numeral I in Outline

The second main group of UFO sightings includes those that occur within five hundred feet of a witness. These are called close encounters. This group is also divided into three smaller groups. A "close encounter of the first kind" is a sighting in which the witness sees a UFO but feels no effects from it. No trace of the UFO is left after this kind of close encounter. A "close encounter of the second kind," however, does involve evidence. The evidence may include scorch marks on grass, footprints, odors, headaches, or electrical disturbances (Ritchie 66).

> From Roman Numeral II

All UFO sightings are controversial. None is more so than the last type of close encounter, the "close encounter of the third kind." In this kind of sighting, a witness reports seeing occupants in the UFO. Sometimes the occupants are short; sometimes they are human size. Some people claim to have been taken aboard a spacecraft (Ritchie 66). Many scientists pay no attention to these reports because people's stories seem so strange (Benford).

> From Roman Numeral III

editing ★

A good report includes only the necessary information. Practice trimming away unnecessary words and information from the following passage of a report about investigations of the night sky.

It is certainly possible that nothing will come of our elaborate celestial preparations. We hope, however, that we have the ability to influence the outcome of various astronomical investigations. Therefore, it is extremely necessary that we push forward on this pressing issue.

PROJECT PREP   Drafting   Body

1. Use your outline and notes to draft the body of your report. Summarize your findings and present the evidence that explains your topic in an organized way. Your outline should help you decide in what order you should present your information, what the topic of each paragraph should be, and what information and facts should be included to support that topic. Make sure the information is consistent throughout the report. Give reasons for your conclusions. Add a parenthetical citation each time you include a quotation or an idea that is not your own. Simply identify the source and page number in parentheses, as in the model. As long as you know which source you mean, you can rewrite each citation in the proper form, if necessary, when you revise your draft.

2. When you have drafted the body paragraphs, in which you specifically address the facts you have gathered, bring your draft to your writing group. Help one another evaluate the extent to which each paragraph is dedicated to a clear and specific topic that helps you answer your research questions.

③ Drafting the Conclusion

A strong conclusion provides a wrap-up of the details in the body of a report. Use the following guidelines whenever you write a conclusion to a report.

Writing a Conclusion

- Restate your main idea in new words.
- Include a comment that shows the importance of your subject.
- Round out the report by referring to an idea in the introduction without repeating it exactly.
- Avoid simply repeating the ideas in the body.
- Avoid adding a completely new idea.
- Avoid such phrases as "Now you have seen . . ." or "I have just told you . . ."

The following conclusion to the report on UFO sightings reinforces the main idea and shows its importance.

MODEL: Conclusion of a Report

Many distant UFO sightings can eventually be explained as weather balloons, comets, or meteors ("Unidentified Flying Object"). Some sightings turn out to be hoaxes (O'Neill 17). Close encounters are more difficult to explain. Because the witness is closer, there is less chance of making a mistake about the object. Some scientists say that all close encounters are just things that the witnesses imagined. Others would like to see more investigation of close encounters that have physical evidence (Sturrock). Hynek established an institute to study UFOs and this group still collects data on the different types of sightings ("CUFOS Organization"). Perhaps someday scientists will find a way to explain this mystery.

PROJECT PREP Drafting Conclusion

Using the guidelines and the model, write a strong conclusion for your report. Bring it to your writing group, and help one another evaluate the conclusion. Does it clearly give an answer to the major research question? Has each writer given relevant reasons for conclusions? Are you persuaded that each writer's topic has been understood? Help each author produce a conclusion that answers the major research question and settles, if possible, any confusion regarding fact and fiction in the topic.

④ Including Visuals

Many reports can be enhanced with the use of visuals. Visuals can include illustrations, photos, graphs, and charts. In the case of a report that is to be published on a Web page, movie clips may also be included. If you are using a word processing program to prepare your report, and you have a scanner, you can scan the images directly into your document. With some programs, you can also enter data and the program will prepare a graph or table of your choosing.

The most important thing to remember when deciding whether to include a visual in your report is that it must clarify or extend the meaning of your text. In other words, all visuals must be relevant to your topic and be included for a reason. Visuals can help deepen your reader's understanding if used and placed properly.

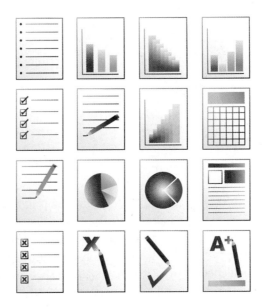

WRITING A TITLE

Once you have finished your first draft, give your report an interesting title. Your title should catch your reader's interest.

> **PROJECT PREP** *Drafting* *Visuals and Title*
>
> Read your report to a friend or family members. Have them help you think of interesting visuals that might make your text clearer or add to its meaning. Then give your report a title that alerts readers to the subject of your report. Save your draft for later use.

5 Citing Sources

When you write a report, you sometimes use other people's research to help you make your own point. If you paraphrase or quote the ideas of another person, you must include a note called a **citation** that gives credit to the original source.

Laws protect authors, illustrators, photographers, and publishers whose materials have been copyrighted. Using another person's words, pictures, or ideas without giving proper credit is called **plagiarism,** a serious offense. Whenever you use source materials, therefore, you must give credit to the authors—even if you only paraphrase. You have already taken steps to avoid plagiarism by taking notes in your own words and by recording the author, the page number, and the exact words of any quotation you plan to use. The easiest method of citing sources is parenthetical citations.

PARENTHETICAL CITATIONS

Parenthetical citations are brief notes in parentheses right after the words or ideas you have borrowed. They give the reader enough information to identify the source in a list of works cited at the end of your report. Refer to the following examples to help you use parenthetical citations correctly.

MODERN LANGUAGE ASSOCIATION (MLA) STYLE GUIDELINES	
Book or Article by One Author	Give author's last name and page number(s): (Scott 66).
Book or Article by Two or More Authors	Give all of the authors' names and page number(s): (Sheehan and O'Meara 55).
Article; Author Unnamed	Give a shortened form of the title of the article (unless title is already short) and page number(s), unless the article is a single page: ("Signs of Life on Mars?").
Article in a Reference Work; Author Unnamed	Give title (full or shortened). No page number is necessary if the article is a single page from an encyclopedia arranged alphabetically: ("Mars").
Online Article; Author Named	Give author's last name; include a page or paragraph number only if the online source includes them; do not use page references from a print version of the article: (Taylor).
Online Article or Web Page; Author Unnamed	Give title of article (full or shortened) or Web page, as used on the works-cited page: ("Mars Express Probes").

Parenthetical citations should be as close as possible to the words or ideas being credited. Place them at the end of a phrase, clause, or sentence so that you will not interrupt the flow of the sentence. If you have used information from the exact same source in several sentences in a row, you may place the citation at the end of the last sentence. See examples in the model report on page 325.

WORKS-CITED PAGE

A **works-cited page** is a list of sources at the end of your report included regardless of the style of citation you use in the body of the report. The works-cited page lists complete information about each source you have used to write your paper. The sources are listed alphabetically by the author's last name or by the title if there is no author listed. The model shows the works-cited page for the report on UFO sightings. The list gives the details for the sources in the parenthetical citations. (See pages 327–330.)

> **MODEL: Works-Cited Page**

Works Cited

Benford, Gregory. "A UFO Foundation: Working Together to Find Answers." *Omni* Fall 1995: 4. *MAS Ultra – School Edition*. Web. 2 Mar. 2009.

"The CUFOS Organization." *CUFOS*. J. Allen Hynek Center for UFO Studies, 2007. Web. 11 Mar. 2009.

O'Neill, Terry. Introduction. *UFOs: Fact or Fiction*. Ed. O'Neill. Farmington Hills: Greenhaven, 2003. 1–21. Print.

Ritchie, David. *UFO: The Definitive Guide to Unidentified Flying Objects and Related Phenomena*. New York: MJF, 1994. Print.

Sturrock, Peter. Interview by Natalie Allen. CNN, 29 June 1998. *UFO Evidence*. Web. 2 Mar. 2009. Transcript.

"Unidentified Flying Object." *The Columbia Encyclopedia*. 6th ed. 2007. *Bartleby.com*. Web. 2 Mar. 2009.

Page numbers are usually given for articles but not for books in works cited. In each example note the order of information, the indentation, and the punctuation. When citing online sources, always give the date you accessed the site. Use the following examples for help in compiling a works-cited page.

MLA GUIDE TO WORKS-CITED PAGE

General Reference Works	Squyres, Steven W. "Mars." *World Book Encyclopedia.* 2009 ed. Print.
Books by One Author	Scott, Elaine. *Mars and the Search for Life.* New York: Clarion, 2008. Print.
Books by Two or More Authors	Sheehan, William, and Stephen James O'Meara. *Mars: The Lure of the Red Planet.* Amherst: Prometheus, 2001. Print.
Articles in Magazines	Pendick, Daniel. "Methane Reveals Red Planet's Active Innards." *Astronomy* Apr. 2009: 20. Print.
Articles; Author Unnamed	"Signs of Life On Mars?" *Current Science* 17 Apr. 2009: 12. Print.
Articles in Newspapers	Chang, Kenneth. "Mars Rover Doing Well After Memory Glitch." *New York Times* 30 Jan. 2009: A1. Print.
Articles from Online Databases	Pendick, Daniel. "Mars' Dynamic, Icy Past." *Astronomy* Sept. 2008:18. *MAS Ultra – School Edition.* Web. 2 Apr. 2009.
Articles from Web Sites	Taylor, Michael Ray. "10 Years Later, Life-on-Mars Debate Still On." *Chron.com.* Houston Chronicle, 5 Aug. 2006. Web. 3 Apr. 2009.

These entries follow the style recommended in the *MLA Handbook for Writers of Research Papers* (7th ed.). Notice that the citation includes the medium for each source—print or Web. The MLA no longer recommends including URLs for most online sources because they change so frequently. If your teacher asks you to include a URL, enclose it in angle brackets as the last entry in the citation.

Example with URL   Taylor, Michael Ray. "10 Years Later, Life-on-Mars Debate Still On." *Chron.com.* Houston Chronicle, 5 Aug. 2006. Web. 3 Apr. 2009. <http://www.chron.com/disp/story.mpl/space/4096212.html>.

Sometimes your teacher may ask you to include a works-consulted page—often called a **bibliography**—on which you include all the works you consulted but did not necessarily cite in your research report. A works-consulted page or bibliography uses the same form as the works-cited page.

PROJECT PREP *Drafting* *Parenthetical Citations, Works-Cited Page*

Review what you have learned about citing sources correctly. Then, reread the first draft of your report and write the parenthetical citations in the proper form. Place the citations so they do not disrupt the flow of the sentence. Finally, prepare a works-cited page to add at the end of your report. If you have a source that does not fit one of the categories described above, refer to the *MLA Handbook for Writers of Research Papers* for information on how to cite the source correctly. Save your completed draft for revising.

In the Media

Documentary

Sometimes a documentary might be the most meaningful format in which to present a research report. A documentary is a research report on film. It uses images, narration, interviews, and sound to tell a story about different subjects. Unlike a newspaper or TV news report, a documentary does not have space constraints. As a result, documentaries are able to cover their subjects more in depth. A documentary can be about a wide variety of subjects—women's baseball leagues, insects, civil-rights leaders, a particular town—anything that has an interesting story. It can be expository or persuasive.

Like other journalistic media forms, documentaries may seem at first like they are objective presentations of the truth. In fact they are just as biased as any other type of media. They reflect the values and biases of the individuals who make them. Camera angles, editing, lighting—all of these factors affect how the story gets told. Michael Moore, a documentary filmmaker, brought this issue into national discussion when he released his 1989 documentary *Roger & Me,* about his attempt to speak to the head of General Motors. Critics complained that Moore was obviously biased in his presentation of the story. Supporters argued that documentaries are always biased and that at least it was easy to tell what Moore's perspective was. He has since made more documentaries on such subjects as the war in Iraq and the health care system.

Media Activity

Start by watching at least two documentaries to get a feel for how they are structured. Then pick a topic for which a documentary might be the most meaningful format, and write a brief paragraph explaining why. Then write an outline for it that states the topic, what the issues are, and how you plan on presenting them. Think about whom you would need to interview, as well as what images, graphics, and sounds you could use to support your story.

When you have finished, trade outlines with a classmate to give one another feedback. If you have access to video equipment, use the information on pages 431–445 to produce your own short documentary.

Writing a Research Report   Revising

A report should flow smoothly and be easy to follow. Before revising, set your report aside for a while. Later, see whether your project looks the way you want it to look. Ask yourself whether you have achieved the purpose that you had in mind. Consider whether you have kept a consistent focus on your intended audience. How well have you achieved the form that you chose for your project? Imagine you are a reader seeing it for the first time. Then use the checklist below to help improve your first draft.

✓ Evaluation Checklist for Revising

Checking Your Report

- ✓ Does your introduction contain a sentence expressing the thesis of the report? (pages 321–322)
- ✓ Does the body of your report support the thesis with specific evidence and examples and answer your major research question? (pages 323–324)
- ✓ Did you give relevant reasons for your conclusions? (page 325)
- ✓ Did you use your own words? (pages 295 and 327)
- ✓ Did you use transitions? (pages 122 and 140)
- ✓ Does your report have unity and coherence? (pages 75–76)
- ✓ Does your report fulfill its purpose and suit your chosen audience? (page 284)
- ✓ Does your conclusion add a strong ending? (page 325)
- ✓ Does your report have a title? (page 326)
- ✓ Does your report have citations and a works-cited page? (pages 327–330)

Checking Your Paragraphs

- ✓ Does each paragraph in the body have a topic sentence? (pages 69–70)
- ✓ Is each paragraph unified and coherent? (pages 75–76)

Checking Your Sentences

- ✓ Are your sentences varied? (pages 53–59)
- ✓ Are your sentences concise? (pages 60–62)
- ✓ Did you use specific, vivid words and figurative language? (pages 45–52, 56, and 186–187)

PROJECT PREP Revising *Using Feedback*

Based on the feedback from your writing group, and on the checklist above, write a new draft of your research report. Then exchange work with a member of your writing group and give each other suggestions for further revision. Listen to all suggestions and revise your work as you feel necessary. Save your work for further revising and for editing.

One of the final stages in writing a research report is to edit your work for proper grammar, mechanics, spelling, and usage.

The Language of Power *Fragments*

Power Rule: Use sentence fragments only the way professional writers do, after the sentence they refer to and usually to emphasize a point. Fix all sentence fragments that occur before the sentence they refer to and ones that occur in the middle of a sentence. (See page 656.)

See It in Action In the first draft, the writer of the report on UFOs wrote:

> UFO sightings are often controversial. Because they cannot be explained by ordinary evidence.

The highlighted sentence begins with a subordinating conjunction, making it into a subordinate clause that cannot stand alone. While professional writers occasionally use shorter "sentences" of this nature for emphasis, usually such fragments are best connected to the sentence that comes before. So during editing, the writer removed the period and capital letter and joined the two clauses.

> UFO sightings are often controversial because they cannot be explained by ordinary evidence.

Remember It Record this rule in the Power Rule section of your Personalized Editing Checklist.

Use It Check your research report to make sure you have not used sentence fragments ineffectively. Watch especially for fragments that go with the sentence that follows them or for fragments that contain an *-ing* form of a verb.

PROJECT PREP **Editing** *Checking for Conventions*

Check your work for grammar, usage, mechanics, and spelling. As you edit your research report, refer to your Personalized Editing Checklist. When you are finished, use the rubric on the following page to measure the strength of each of the six traits in your writing.

Using a Six-Trait Rubric — Research Reports

Ideas	4 The text conveys a thesis statement and has abundant supporting details drawn from reliable sources.	3 The text conveys a thesis statement and has ample details from suitable sources.	2 The text conveys a thesis statement and has some supporting details from acceptable sources.	1 There is no thesis statement and the text fails to offer support from research.
Organization	4 In each paragraph and the essay as a whole, the organization is clear with abundant transitions.	3 In some paragraphs a few ideas seem out of place or transitions are missing.	2 Many ideas seem out of place and transitions are missing.	1 The organization is unclear and hard to follow.
Voice	4 The voice sounds engaging and is appropriate for purpose and audience.	3 The voice sounds natural and is appropriate for purpose and audience.	2 The voice sounds mostly unnatural with some exceptions.	1 The voice sounds mostly unnatural.
Word Choice	4 Words are specific. All terms are explained or defined.	3 Words are specific and some terms are explained or defined.	2 Some words are overly general and some technical terms are not explained.	1 Most words are overly general.
Sentence Fluency	4 Varied sentences flow smoothly.	3 Most sentences are varied and flow smoothly.	2 Some sentences are varied but some are choppy.	1 Sentences are not varied and are choppy.
Conventions	4 Punctuation, usage, and spelling are correct. The Power Rules are all followed.	3 Punctuation, usage, and spelling are mainly correct and Power Rules are all followed.	2 Some punctuation, usage, and spelling are incorrect but all Power Rules are followed.	1 There are many errors and at least one failure to follow a Power Rule.

PROJECT PREP Evaluating Peer Evaluation

Read your paper once more and make all necessary changes. Exchange papers with a writing partner for one final critique. Use the feedback to prepare a final, polished version of your report.

Writing a Research Report  Publishing

An important part of report writing is publishing—the purpose of writing in this form is to present information. During the process of writing a research report, the writer learns about his or her subject in order to pass the information on to an interested reader. When deciding how to publish a research report, keep in mind the subject and who might benefit from reading about it.

PUBLISHING OPTIONS FOR RESEARCH REPORTS

A written report	Requirements: clear, well organized writing with smooth transitions presented in a neat, error-free copy with citations handled appropriately; illustrations may help explain some of the ideas; reader-friendly formatting techniques such as bullet points and headings can help convey information
A multimedia presentation	Requirements: unified blend of print, sound, video, and/or other media that uses the best features of each medium to make the points clear; the print portion as well as the presentation as a whole should not include unnecessary details or information
An oral report	Requirements: Clear writing that will be easy for a listener to understand without re-readings; visual aids as needed; delivery that uses voice, gesture, and a range of speaker strategies to convey information clearly
An investigative newspaper report	Requirements: A "lead" that gets readers involved in the report right away; short paragraphs to look good in newspaper columns

PROJECT PREP Publishing *Adjusting for Format*

Present a final copy of your research report to an interested reader. Choose a format that will be meaningful to your audience. With your teacher's permission, you and your classmates might display your reports on a table in your school library or media center.

TIME OUT TO
REFLECT

In what ways have your research and report-writing skills improved after going through this process? Find a report that you wrote earlier in the year. Is it different from the one you just wrote? How? What did you do differently in this recent report? What report-writing skills would you like to improve upon? Record your thoughts in your Learning Log.

Writing Lab

Project Corner

Speak and **L**isten
Discuss and Present

With your classmates, **discuss how legends come into being** and how facts get exaggerated over time. If you hear a story that sounds hard to believe, how can you verify it to get the true story? What examples are there in modern society of facts getting exaggerated to create a legendary reputation for a person, place, thing, or event? Then use presentation software to share the findings from your research. Show this presentation to your classmates and get feedback on how you might improve your presentations on future occasions.

Communicate **A**cross **C**ultures Translate

If you are learning another language or if you speak another language at home, **translate your report** into that language. Have a speaker of that language evaluate your translation for accuracy and fluency.

Collaborate and **C**reate A Modern Legend

With your writing group, **create a modern legend** based on a real person. What would you need to exaggerate in order to make the person's deeds legendary? What events could you fabricate to add to the legend?

Experiment Try a Different Form

Review the suggested project forms on page 284. Think about how your project would be different if it were in one of the forms you didn't use or another that comes to mind. Choose a part of your project and **rewrite it in that new form.** What changes would you need to make? Write a brief paragraph explaining those changes.

In Everyday Life
Report on the Latest Trends

1. Return to the research you did in Chapter 11 about fads and trends at your school (see page 297). *Prepare a brief report* for your classmates about what you have learned. Make sure your report contains a thesis statement that you support with evidence drawn from your research. Draw conclusions about what fads or trends seem to be most popular and give reasons for your conclusions. Decide which format would be most meaningful for your report, and publish it in that format. You may, for example, share your report in a written or oral form with your classmates or you may post it on your blog.

In the Workplace Quiz Show Report

2. Your boss at the quiz show *Beats Me!* is thinking about doing a whole show with a single theme. The theme would be based on one of the subjects you researched earlier (see page 297). *Write a brief report* on the subject that is most interesting to you. Build on your earlier research and notes by conducting some additional research. Organize your ideas in a logical way and summarize what you learned. Conclude your report by giving reasons why you think this subject would make an interesting theme for a quiz show.

Timed Writing 🕐 Consumer Report

3. Return to the research plan you developed in Chapter 11 about disastrous purchases (see page 297).

   Complete the report for the consumer newsletter by focusing on one purchase. As a story in a newsletter your report should be informative and fun to read, and it should warn people not to make a similar purchase. Use the sources you found earlier to gather information.

   Begin your report with a thesis statement that identifies the subject of your story and the main points that you want to make about it. Your report should include evidence that supports your point, and it should be organized to ensure coherence and logical progression. You have 30 minutes to complete your work.

   Before You Write Consider the following questions: What is the subject? What is the occasion? Who is the audience? What is the purpose?

   After You Write Evaluate your work using the six-trait rubric on page 334.

Guide to 21st Century

School and Workplace Skills

The single most important factor in determining America's success in the 21st century will be maintaining our ability to be an innovative and creative society.

—Congressman Ron Kind

Technology cannot shape the present, or even the future, of humankind without the creative collaboration of people from all parts of the world. Thinking critically and creatively, communicating clearly, collaborating, and using technology wisely: these are the skills needed for success in the 21st century.

Critical Thinking and Problem Solving for Academic Success

21ST CENTURY

Essential Skills

Every day in school, you are asked to use your **critical thinking** and **problem-solving skills**. In Part I of this guide, you will learn how to apply these skills in order to succeed academically.

1 Critical Thinking

USING REASONING

The word *reasoning* refers to the process of making inferences, making judgments, or drawing conclusions. In your social studies class, for example, you use reasoning to determine the causes of a rebellion. Using sound reasoning is essential for every task you perform in school. Always check for errors in your reasoning. Make sure that your reasoning is logical and is based on facts, examples, or other types of support. When you start with a general concept or theory and support it with specifics or apply it to specifics, you are using the **deductive** method. When you start with specifics and build to a general point, you are using the **inductive** method. (See page 94.)

ANALYZING OUTCOMES

In your academic subjects, you often examine cause-and-effect relationships. In your social studies class, you may explore how events and other factors led to the passing of a law. In your science class, you may study the interaction between chemicals or the parts of a system, such as an ecosystem. Understanding these relationships and interactions is essential for analyzing outcomes, or results. It will help you gain insight into how systems and processes work.

EVALUATING AND DRAWING CONCLUSIONS

Thinking critically means much more than simply understanding information. You need to analyze and evaluate evidence, claims, and different points of view. You need to make inferences and interpret information. You should also make connections and synthesize information. Then you should draw conclusions. Critical thinking also involves reflecting on your learning in order to evaluate your skills and methods. Learning how to evaluate information effectively and draw logical conclusions will help you make sound judgments and decisions in school and in your daily life. You can develop specific critical thinking skills through activities on pages 56, 73, 94, 115, 137, 158, 198, 231, 261, and 317.

② Developing Solutions

SOLVING PROBLEMS

To solve problems, you should use sound reasoning, analyze outcomes, and evaluate and draw conclusions. In other words, you should use your critical thinking skills. For example, when you encounter a problem on a test, first look for connections between it and other problems you have solved in the past. Next decide if the solution should follow certain conventions or patterns. Remember to use logical reasoning and then draw conclusions to determine the correct solution. When you have to solve complex problems, ask questions. Then synthesize and evaluate information and different viewpoints to produce strong, creative solutions. Developing and applying your problem-solving skills in school will prepare you for resolving problems in other areas of your life.

A. Learning Study Skills

Apply Critical Thinking Skills

Every day in school, you need to use your critical thinking skills in order to think actively about what you read and hear. Critical thinking involves asking questions, making connections, analyzing, and interpreting. Critical thinkers also evaluate and draw conclusions. When you analyze the point of view used in a story or evaluate the evidence in an argument, you are using your critical thinking skills.

Thinking critically also involves reflecting on your learning. Evaluating the methods you use to study and prepare for assignments and tests will help you identify your strengths. It will also help you determine how you can learn more effectively.

In this section, you will develop your study skills. Improving these skills will help you become a better critical thinker and help you succeed in school.

Developing Effective Study Skills

Adopting good study habits will help you complete your daily classroom assignments. Improve your study habits by using the following strategies.

Strategies for Effective Studying

- Choose an area that is well lighted and quiet.
- Equip your study area with everything you need for reading and writing. You can easily access a dictionary and thesaurus online, but you may want to have print versions of these resources on hand.
- Keep an assignment book for recording due dates.
- Allow plenty of time to complete your work. Begin your assignments early.
- Adjust your reading rate to suit your purpose.

Adjusting Reading Rate to Purpose

Your **reading rate** is the speed at which you read. Depending on your purpose in reading, you may choose to read certain materials quickly or slowly, using the techniques of scanning, skimming, or close reading.

For example, if your purpose is to get a quick impression of the contents of a newspaper, you should scan the headlines. If you want to identify the main ideas of an article, you should skim it. On the other hand, if your purpose is to learn new facts or understand details, you should read the article closely.

Whether you are reading a newspaper, an article in a periodical, or a textbook, you can read with greater effectiveness and efficiency if you adjust your reading rate to suit your purpose for reading.

SCANNING

Scanning is reading to get a general impression and to prepare for learning about a subject. To scan, you should read the title, headings, subheadings, picture captions, words and phrases in boldface or italics, and any focus questions. Using this method, you can quickly determine what the material is about and what questions to keep in mind. Scanning is also a way to familiarize yourself with everything a book has to offer. Scan the table of contents, appendix, glossary, and index of a book before reading.

SKIMMING

After scanning a chapter, a section, or an article, you should quickly read—or skim—the introduction, the topic sentence of each paragraph, and the conclusion. **Skimming** is reading quickly to identify the purpose, thesis, main ideas, and supporting details of a selection.

CLOSE READING

Most of your assignments for school will require close reading, which is an essential step for critical thinking. You use **close reading** for locating specific information, following the logic of an argument, or comprehending the meaning or significance of information. After scanning a selection or chapter, read it more slowly, word for word, to understand the text's meaning fully. You can then apply your critical thinking skills to analyze and interpret information and ideas. Be sure to evaluate points and draw conclusions so that you can make judgments and decisions. Pose questions based on your close reading to help you solve problems.

READING A TEXTBOOK—SQ3R

When you read a textbook, you should combine the techniques of scanning, skimming, and close reading by using the **SQ3R study strategy.** This method helps you understand and remember what you read. The *S* in *SQ3R* stands for *Survey,* the *Q* for *Question,* and the *3R* for *Read, Recite,* and *Review.*

THE SQ3R STUDY STRATEGY	
Survey	First get a general idea of what the selection is about by scanning the title, headings, subheadings, and words that are set off in a different type or color. Also look at maps, tables, charts, and other illustrations. Then read the introduction and conclusion or summary.
Question	Decide what questions you should be able to answer after reading the selection. You can do this by turning the headings and subheadings into questions or by looking at any study questions in the book.
Read	Now read the selection. As you read, try to answer your questions. In addition, find the main idea in each section and look for important information that is not included in your questions. After reading, review the important points in the selection and take notes. *(See pages 293–295.)*
Recite	Answer each question in your own words by reciting or writing the answers.
Review	Answer the questions again without looking at your notes or at the selection. Continue reviewing until you answer each question correctly.

● **Practice Your Skills**

Choosing a Reading Strategy

List all the reading you have to do in the next week in order to complete assignments and prepare for tests. Choose one of these tasks and select two of the four reading strategies—scanning, skimming, close reading, and the SQ3R study strategy. Then complete the task twice, using a different strategy each time. When you are done, write a paragraph comparing and contrasting the two strategies you used. What were the benefits or drawbacks of each strategy? What did you learn from this activity about choosing a reading strategy?

② Taking Notes

Taking notes when reading a textbook or listening to a lecture will help you identify and remember important points. It will also prepare you to engage in critical thinking. Once you identify and record key information, you can make connections, evaluate points, and draw conclusions. Three methods for taking notes are the informal outline, the graphic organizer, and the summary.

In an **informal outline,** you use words and phrases to record main ideas and significant details. Notes in this form are helpful in studying for an objective test because they emphasize specific facts.

In a **graphic organizer,** words and phrases are arranged in a visual pattern to indicate the relationships between main ideas and supporting details. This is an excellent tool for studying information for an objective test, for preparing an open-ended assessment, or for writing an essay. The visual organizer allows you instantly to see important information and the relationships among ideas.

In a **summary** you use sentences to express important ideas in your own words. A summary should not simply restate the ideas presented in the textbook or lecture. Instead, a good summary should express relationships among ideas and state conclusions. For this reason, summarizing is useful for preparing for an essay test.

In the following passage, the essential information for understanding the work of Leonardo da Vinci is underlined. Following the passage are examples of notes in the form of an informal outline, a graphic organizer, and a summary.

MODEL: Essential Information

Leonardo da Vinci, an Italian man of the Renaissance, is believed to be one of the greatest artists of all time. He was also, however, a genius in many other areas of study. Because his notebooks survived, we know that he laid out plans for hundreds of inventions and machines. Among them are designs for a flying machine, a helicopter, a parachute, a movable bridge, artillery, an alarm clock, and revolving stages. He was fascinated by anatomy and produced the first accurate drawings of the human body. However, he is probably most famous for his paintings, such as *The Last Supper*. His work inspired many other artists—among them another giant of the Renaissance, Michelangelo.

Informal
Outline

Leonardo da Vinci

1. Great Italian artist and scientist during the Renaissance
2. Sketched plans for hundreds of inventions and machines: flying machine, helicopter, parachute, movable bridge, artillery, alarm clock, revolving stages
3. Created the first accurate drawings of the human body
4. Most famous for his paintings
5. Inspired other artists, such as Michelangelo

Graphic
Organizer

Leonardo da Vinci

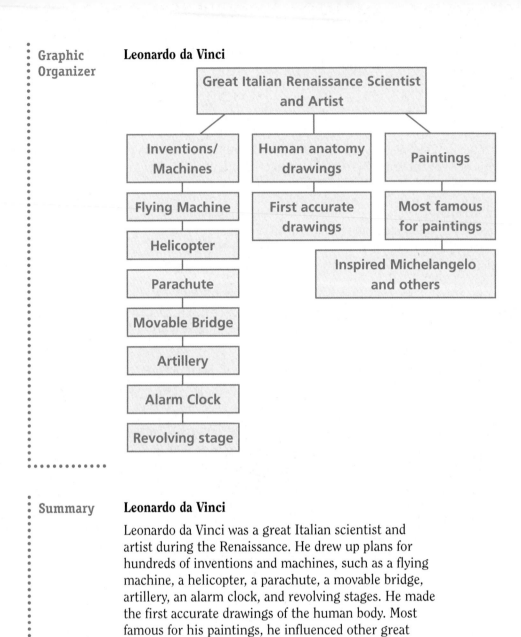

Summary

Leonardo da Vinci

Leonardo da Vinci was a great Italian scientist and artist during the Renaissance. He drew up plans for hundreds of inventions and machines, such as a flying machine, a helicopter, a parachute, a movable bridge, artillery, an alarm clock, and revolving stages. He made the first accurate drawings of the human body. Most famous for his paintings, he influenced other great artists like Michelangelo.

Whichever note-taking method you use, the following strategies will help you make your notes clear and well organized.

Strategies for Taking Notes

- Label your notes with the title and page numbers of the chapter or the topic and date of the lecture.
- Record only the main ideas and important details.
- Use the title, headings, subheadings, and words in special type to help you select the most important information.
- Use your own words; do not copy word for word.
- Use as few words as possible.

● **Practice Your Skills**

Taking Notes

With a partner, list your reading assignments for the next week. Then discuss which method of note taking—an informal outline, a graphic organizer, or a summary—you would use for each assignment. Explain each choice.

③ Preparing Subject-Area Assignments

The strategies you have learned for reading and taking notes can be applied to assignments in any subject area. Mathematics and science textbooks often list rules, formulas, or models that you can apply to solve problems. In history courses, pay special attention to interpreting maps, charts, graphs, time lines, documents, and statistical data. Use your critical thinking skills to analyze outcomes and understand how systems work. Analyze and connect the information presented in different formats and draw conclusions based on this information.

Tips for Preparing Subject-Area Assignments

- Carefully read and follow directions.
- Adjust your reading rate to suit your purpose.
- In reading your textbook, use the SQ3R method. (See page 344.)
- Take notes on your reading. Organize your notebook by keeping notes on the same topic together.
- For review, keep a separate list of vocabulary, key terms and concepts, or rules and equations.
- Keep a list of questions you think of as you read, listen, or review. Seek answers promptly.
- Participate in study groups, following the principles of cooperative learning.
- Leave ample time to study for tests. Anticipate and answer the questions you think will be asked.

B. Taking Standardized Tests

Applying Your Critical Thinking and Problem-Solving Skills

To succeed on standardized tests, you should become familiar with the kinds of questions you will be asked. Learning test-taking strategies will help you become a better test taker as well.

Applying your critical thinking skills is also essential for success. Standardized test questions, such as analogies, require you to use reasoning to determine the correct answer. Other types of test items, such as reading comprehension questions, ask you to analyze, infer, interpret, make connections, and draw conclusions.

For all types of test questions, you need to use your problem-solving skills. You must determine what a question is asking and how you should arrive at the correct answer. You should decide if a particular question is a familiar type. If it is, decide if the answer should match certain conventions or patterns.

Learning to apply your critical thinking and problem-solving skills effectively will help you not only when taking tests but also when completing your daily classroom assignments. Using these skills effectively will help you in all aspects of your daily life as well.

In this section, you will develop your skills in taking standardized tests. Improving these skills will help you do your best on classroom, school-wide, or statewide assessments.

Strategies for Taking Standardized Tests

A standardized test measures your academic progress, skills, and achievement in such a way that the results can be compared with those of other students who have taken the same test. Standardized tests that assess your verbal skills, or your ability to use language, include vocabulary tests, analogy tests, sentence-completion tests, reading comprehension tests, and tests of standard written English.

The best way to do well on standardized tests is to work consistently on your school subjects throughout the year, to read widely, and to learn test-taking strategies.

Strategies for Taking Standardized Tests

- Relax. Although you can expect to be a little nervous, concentrate on doing the best you can.
- Read the test directions carefully. Answer the sample questions to be sure you understand what the test requires.
- Preview the whole test; skim it to get an overview of the kinds of questions on the test.
- Plan your time carefully. Note how much time is allotted for each part of the test.
- Answer first the questions you find easiest. Skip hard questions, coming back to them later if you have time.
- Read all choices before you choose an answer. If you are not sure of the answer, try to eliminate choices that are obviously wrong. Educated guessing often helps.
- If you have time, check your answers. Be sure you have correctly marked your answer sheet.

1 Vocabulary Tests

One kind of vocabulary test asks you to find **antonyms**—words that mean the opposite of other words. For instance, in the following test item, you must find the antonym for *complex* among the five choices.

COMPLEX:

(A) mysterious   (B) complicated   (C) simple

(D) fancy   (E) harmless

(The answer is (C) because *simple* means the opposite of *complex*. (B) is incorrect because *complicated* is a synonym for *complex*. In (A), (D), and (E), the words do not mean the opposite of *complex*.)

Test items about **synonyms** have the same format as antonym items. However, instead of choosing the answer that means the opposite of a given word, you choose the word that has the same meaning.

WANDER:

(A) tempt   (B) ask   (C) hide

(D) stray   (E) rush

(The answer is (D) because *stray* has the same meaning as *wander*.)

Always consider every choice carefully. You can often infer the meaning of a word by using a prefix, a root, or a suffix as a clue.

● Practice Your Skills

Recognizing Antonyms

Write the letter of the word that is most nearly opposite in meaning to the word in capital letters.

1. STURDY:
- (A) strong
- (B) unhealthy
- (C) weak
- (D) faithful
- (E) upright

2. SPECIFIC:
- (A) qualified
- (B) general
- (C) difficult
- (D) trained
- (E) precise

3. NOTABLE:
- (A) princely
- (B) special
- (C) unimportant
- (D) official
- (E) smart

4. BENEFICIAL:
- (A) friendly
- (B) dishonest
- (C) expensive
- (D) reliable
- (E) harmful

5. INCOMPETENT:
- (A) disloyal
- (B capable
- (C) unbroken
- (D) significant
- (E) unstable

● Practice Your Skills

Recognizing Synonyms

Write the letter of the word that is most nearly similar in meaning to the word in capital letters.

6. ORNAMENTAL:
- (A) bright
- (B) ugly
- (C) useful
- (D) decorative
- (E) extra

7. VARIETY:
- (A) store
- (B) value
- (C) amusement
- (D) assortment
- (E) collection

8. FREQUENTLY:
- (A) often
- (B) rarely
- (C) seldom
- (D) never
- (E) sometimes

9. RADIANT:

    (A) enjoyable   (B) clever   (C) dull

    (D) glowing   (E) warm

10. COMMOTION:

    (A) calmness   (B swiftness   (C) sympathy

    (D) boredom   (E) disturbance

2 Analogies

Analogy questions test your skill at figuring out relationships between words. To complete an analogy, you need to use reasoning. Your first step is to decide how the given words—the first pair of words, usually in capital letters—are related to each other. The next step is to decide which other pair has the same kind of relationship as the given pair.

The single colon in an analogy question stands for the words *is to,* and the double colon stands for the word *as.*

STALE : FRESH :: old : new

The above example reads, "Stale is to fresh as old is to new." That is, *stale* has the same relationship to *fresh* as *old* has to *new*. *Stale* is the opposite of *fresh,* just as *old* is the opposite of *new*. Explaining an analogy to yourself in one sentence can help you to figure out the answer. In the following example, you might say to yourself, "A pecan is a type of nut."

PECAN : NUT ::

(A) mouse : hamster   (B) allergy : rash   (C) jazz : music

(D) artist : easel   (E) flower : rose

(The answer, *(C) jazz : music,* expresses the same item-to-category relationship.)

Keep in mind that the word order in an analogy is very important. If the given pair of words in the analogy expresses a part-to-whole order, for example, the words in the correct answer should also appear in part-to-whole order.

Some analogies are written in sentence form.

Rapid is to *slow* as *raw* is to ▢.

(A) bitter   (B) cooked   (C) hard

(D) quick   (E) cold

(The first two italicized words are antonyms. Therefore, the correct answer is *(B) cooked,* the opposite of *raw.*)

Knowing some of the common types of analogies, like those in the following chart, will help you figure out word relationships. In the first step for completing an analogy, determining whether the relationship between the words is one of the familiar, conventional types will make it easier to select the correct answer.

COMMON TYPES OF ANALOGIES

Analogy	Example
word : synonym	accomplish : achieve
word : antonym	combine : separate
part : whole	keypad : cell phone
cause : effect	chemicals : pollution
worker : tool	surgeon : scalpel
worker : product	architect : plan
item : purpose	microscope : magnify
item : category	spoon : utensil

● Practice Your Skills

Recognizing Analogies

Write the letter of the word pair that has the same relationship as the word pair in capital letters.

1. ADD : SUBTRACT ::

    (A) possess : have   (B) fly : soar

    (C) arrive : leave   (D) laugh : smile

    (E) shock : surprise

2. NEVER : ALWAYS ::

    (A) gradually : steeply   (B) powerfully : strongly

    (C) bravely : boldly   (D) kindly : politely

    (E) often : frequently

21ST CENTURY

3. HOUR : DAY ::

    (A) second : minute   (B) clock : hand

    (C) week : schedule   (D) watch : time

    (E) day : sun

4. CONDUCTOR : BATON ::

    (A) building : wire   (B) key : locksmith

    (C) saw : board   (D) pipe : plumber

    (E) farmer : tractor

5. TIGHTEN : LOOSEN ::

    (A) distrust : doubt   (B) empty : fill

    (C) employ : hire   (D) hold : grasp

    (E) joy : happy

● **Practice Your Skills**

Completing Analogies

Complete the analogy by writing the letter of the word that best completes the sentence.

6. *Refrigerator* is to *food* as *wallet* is to ▨ .

    (A) money   (B) cold   (C) pocket

    (D) handbag   (E) purse

7. *Elbow* is to *arm* as *knee* is to ▨ .

    (A) leg   (B) bend   (C) ankle

    (D) wrist   (E) foot

8. *Look* is to *see* as *listen* is to ▨ .

    (A) say   (B) silent   (C) hear

    (D) notice   (E) noise

9. *Jeans* is to *tuxedo* as *cabin* is to ▨ .

    (A) wood   (B) material   (C) palace

    (D) small   (E) dormitory

10. *Smooth* is to *satin* as *rough* is to ▨ .

    (A) velvet   (B) tan   (C) difficult

    (D) sandpaper   (E) cotton

3 Sentence-Completion Tests

Sentence-completion tests measure your ability to comprehend what you read and to use context correctly. Each item consists of a sentence with one or more words missing. First read the entire sentence. Then read the answer choices. Use logical reasoning to select the answer that completes the sentence in a way that makes the most sense. Read the following item, and then find the word that most appropriately completes the sentence.

Dr. Sawyer's mechanical assistant, Robbie, represents the ideal use of ▒.

(A) friendship   (B) automation

(C) gasoline   (D) nurses

(E) hospitals

(The answer is *(B) automation.* The clue *mechanical assistant* tells you that Robbie is a robot created to help the doctor, which is an effective use of automation.)

Some sentence-completion questions have two blanks in the same sentence, with each answer choice including two words. Find the correct answer in this example.

While all the other members of the jury thought the man was ▒, a single ▒ voted "not guilty."

(A) friendly . . . witness   (B) guilty . . . juror

(C) mean . . . officer   (D) innocent . . . defense lawyer

(E) nice . . . judge

(The answer is *(B) guilty . . . juror.* The other choices do not fit the context. A juror sits on a jury, and since the single juror found the man not guilty, the other members must have believed he was guilty.)

Completing Sentences

Write the letter of the word that best completes each of the following sentences.

1. Kathleen is reading the ▦ of Thomas Edison because she is interested in his life as well as in his inventions.
   (A) encyclopedia   (B) scientific papers
   (C) calculations   (D) biography
   (E) paperback

2. Be sure to save your ▦; it will show when you bought your sweater and how much you paid for it.
   (A) receipt   (B) bag
   (C) tag   (D) wish list
   (E) wallet

3. James was nicknamed "Stretch" because he was so lean and ▦.
   (A) hunched   (B) serious
   (C) short   (D) clumsy
   (E) tall

4. "I can't ▦ the outcome of the game," the coach said, "but I can tell you that our players are ready to put up a good fight."
   (A) decide   (B) overcome
   (C) predict   (D) dream
   (E) wish

5. Superman didn't even ▦ when the boulder fell on him; but he just stood there instead, hands on hips, unmoved.
   (A) celebrate   (B) think
   (C) talk   (D) crawl
   (E) flinch

Completing Sentences with Two Blanks

Write the letter of the words that best complete each of the following sentences.

6. After ▨ accidents, a new school law was passed that ▨ skateboards on school grounds.

(A) five . . . encourages (B) some . . . requires
(C) several . . . prohibits (D) numerous . . . permits
(E) many . . . allows

7. In areas of high ▨, such as the Rocky Mountains, the air is thin and breathing is ▨.

(A) rainfall . . . shallow (B) elevation . . . difficult
(C) scenery . . . easy (D) sea level . . . humid
(E) trees . . . delightful

8. When you fill out the order form, ▨ the size and color of the T-shirt you want so your order can be filled ▨.

(A) name . . . slowly (B) reduce . . . incorrectly
(C) contrast . . . mysteriously (D) compare . . . quickly
(E) specify . . . accurately

9. Stuck in the middle of nowhere, the ▨ passengers wondered if the ▨ train would ever move again.

(A) anxious . . . stationary (B) cheerful . . . heavy
(C) thrilled . . . loaded (D) worried . . . rotating
(E) hungry . . . gliding

10. *Carnaval,* a large ▨ in Brazil, is famous for its showy samba dances and its costumes of many ▨ colors.

(A) ceremony . . . brown (B) boat . . . dull
(C) celebration . . . brilliant (D) parade . . . white
(E) funeral . . . feathered

4 Reading Comprehension Tests

Reading comprehension tests assess your ability to understand and to analyze written passages. The information you need to answer the test questions may be either directly stated or implied in the passage. You must use your critical thinking skills to make inferences as you read, to analyze and interpret the passage, and to draw conclusions in order to answer the questions. The following strategies will help you answer questions on reading comprehension tests.

Strategies for Reading Comprehension Questions

- Begin by skimming the questions that follow the passage so you know what to focus on as you read.
- Read the passage carefully. Notice the main ideas, organization, style, and key words.
- Study all possible answers. Avoid choosing one answer the moment you think it is a reasonable choice.
- Use only the information in the passage when you answer the questions. Do not rely on your own knowledge or ideas on this kind of test.

Most reading comprehension questions will focus on one or more of the following characteristics of a written passage.

- **Main Idea** At least one question will usually focus on the central idea of the passage. Remember that the main idea of a passage covers all sections of the passage—not just one section or paragraph.

- **Supporting Details** Questions about supporting details test your ability to identify the statements in the passage that back up the main idea.

- **Implied Meanings** In some passages not all information is directly stated. Some questions ask you to infer or interpret in order to answer questions about points that the author has merely implied.

- **Purpose and Tone** Questions on purpose and tone require that you interpret or analyze the author's purpose for writing and his or her attitude toward the subject.

Reading for Comprehension

Read the following passage and write the letter of the correct answer to each question that follows it.

Nelson Mandela, a leader in the African National Congress, dared to resist apartheid. The apartheid system divided South Africa's people into groups based on race—white South Africans and black South Africans. The apartheid laws said that each group must live, learn, work, and play separately. As a result of apartheid, white South Africans had the best land, jobs, schools, and opportunities. Apartheid made discrimination the law.

Nonwhite people fought the laws, using violence when necessary. Armed troops of the white government broke up the rallies, killed protesters, and imprisoned anti-apartheid leaders.

Nelson Mandela was sentenced to life in prison, and even from there, he inspired his South African followers. For ten thousand days—until 1990—he remained in prison. He became a symbol for the hardship his people endured.

1. The best title for this passage is
(A) The History of South Africa.
(B) Nelson Mandela's Jail Sentence.
(C) Nelson Mandela's Struggle Against Apartheid.
(D) Discrimination and the Law.
(E) Prisons in South Africa.

2. The purpose of paragraph 1 is
(A) to explain the system of apartheid.
(B) to give biographical information about Mandela.
(C) to argue against apartheid.
(D) to tell about the African National Congress.
(E) to explain why Mandela was imprisoned.

3. The passage indicates that the nonwhite people
(A) cooperated with the government.
(B) lived separately, but attended the same schools as whites.
(C) discriminated against whites.
(D) spent considerable time in prison.
(E) resisted the government with violence when necessary.

21ST CENTURY

4. This passage would most likely appear in

(A) a front-page newspaper article.

(B) a book on the important people of our times.

(C) a book on the history of the United States.

(D) a textbook on the history of African art.

(E) the conclusion of a book entitled *Separate but Equal.*

5. The main purpose of paragraph 3 is

(A) to show the importance of prison.

(B) to explain prison sentences in South Africa.

(C) to protest against life sentences.

(D) to explain the effects of Mandela's life on others.

(E) to set up the central conflict between the two races in South Africa.

THE DOUBLE PASSAGE

You may be asked to read a pair of passages, called the double passage. Then you will be asked questions about each passage individually and about the relationship between the two passages. The two passages may present similar or opposing views, or they may complement each other in various ways. A brief introduction preceding the passages may help you anticipate the relationship between them. Questions about double passages require you to use your critical thinking skills in order to make connections and synthesize information.

All of the questions follow the second passage. The first few questions relate to Passage 1, the next few questions relate to Passage 2, and the final questions relate to both passages. You may find it helpful to read Passage 1 first and then immediately answer the questions related only to it. Then read Passage 2 and answer the remaining questions.

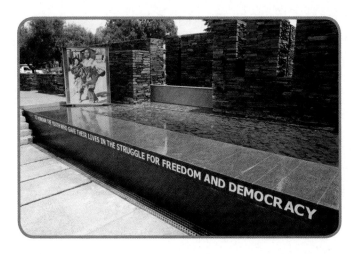

Reading for Double-Passage Comprehension

The following passages are about the battles between Native Americans and the white settlers. The first passage is the recollection of the 1876 Battle of the Little Big Horn by Wooden Leg, a Northern Cheyenne. The second is an 1877 surrender speech by Chief Joseph of the Nez Percé tribe. Read each passage, and answer the questions that follow.

Passage 1

In my sleep I dreamed that a great crowd of people were making lots of noise. Something in the noise startled me. I found myself wide awake, sitting up and listening. My brother too awakened, and we both jumped to our feet. A great commotion was going on among the camps. We heard shooting. We hurried out from the trees so we might see as well as hear.

The shooting was somewhere at the upper part of the camp circles. It looked as if all of the Indians there were running away toward the hills to the westward or down toward the village. Women were screaming and men were letting out war cries. Through it all we could hear old men calling: "Soldiers are here! Young men, go out and fight them."

Passage 2

I am tired of fighting. Our chiefs are killed. Looking Glass is dead. Toohoolhoolzote is dead. The old men are all dead.

It is the young men who say yes and no. He who led on the young men is dead. It is cold and we have no blankets. The little children are freezing to death.

My people, some of them, have run away to the hills, and have no blankets, no food; no one knows where they are—perhaps freezing to death.

I want to have time to look for my children and see how many I can find. Maybe I shall find them among the dead.

Hear me, my chiefs. I am tired; my heart is sick and sad.

From where the sun now stands I will fight no more forever.

1. According to the author of Passage 1, which of the following best explains the reason the young men were called to fight?

(A) A crowd of people were having a celebration on their property.

(B) Their fellow Native Americans were being attacked.

(C) Women carrying babies were running.

(D) The tribe elders had given up their duties.

(E) They were startled by loud noise.

2. The purpose of Passage 1 is to
   (A) argue for the Cheyenne tribe's victory at Little Big Horn.
   (B) recount all the events of the Battle of Little Big Horn.
   (C) describe the relationship between the Native Americans and the white settlers.
   (D) show the importance of fighting back.
   (E) tell the story of Wooden Leg's experience of this day.

3. Which of the following best describes the purpose of Chief Joseph's speech in Passage 2?
   (A) to argue for equality
   (B) to demonstrate the harshness of the environment
   (C) to explain the reasons for his surrender
   (D) to show how tired he is
   (E) to encourage other tribes to keep fighting

4. The details in Passage 2 show Chief Joseph's
   (A) gaiety.
   (B) sorrow.
   (C) forcefulness.
   (D) relief.
   (E) energy.

5. Which of the following attitudes is expressed by both authors?
   (A) The white men who fought the Native Americans caused turmoil.
   (B) The white man and the Native American can live happily in peace.
   (C) Fighting is the best way to defend yourself against invaders.
   (D) Surrender saves women and children.
   (E) Native Americans were more violent than the white settlers.

⑤ Tests of Standard Written English

Objective tests of standard written English assess your knowledge of the language skills used for writing. They contain sentences with underlined words, phrases, and punctuation. The underlined parts contain errors in grammar, usage, mechanics, vocabulary, or spelling. These tests ask you to use your problem-solving skills to find the error in each sentence or to identify the best way to revise a sentence or passage.

ERROR RECOGNITION

The most familiar way to test students' knowledge of grammar, usage, capitalization, punctuation, word choice, and spelling is by asking them to find errors in sentences. A typical test item of this kind is a sentence with five underlined choices. Four of the choices suggest possible errors in the sentence. The fifth choice states that there is no error. Read the following sentence and identify the error, if there is one.

> The <u>people</u> of <u>Haiti</u> won their <u>Independence</u> from <u>France</u> in 1804.
>   A   B   C   D
>
> <u>No error</u>
> E
>
> (The answer is *C*. The word *independence* should not be capitalized.)

The following list identifies some of the errors you should look for on a test of standard written English.

- lack of agreement between subject and verb
- lack of agreement between pronoun and antecedent
- incorrect spelling or use of a word
- missing, misplaced, or unnecessary punctuation
- missing or unnecessary capitalization
- misused or misplaced italics or quotation marks

Sometimes you will find a sentence that contains no error. Be careful, however, before you choose *E (No error)* as the answer. It is easy to overlook a mistake, since common errors are the kind generally included on this type of test.

Remember that the parts of a sentence that are not underlined are presumed to be correct. You can use clues in the correct parts of the sentence to help you search for errors in the underlined parts.

● Practice Your Skills

Recognizing Errors in Writing

Write the letter of the underlined word or punctuation mark that is incorrect. If the sentence contains no error, write *E*.

> **(1)** In the <u>year</u> 1919, the <u>native</u> people of India<u>,</u> longed for their
>   A   B   C
> independence. **(2)** After nearly two and a half centuries of <u>British</u> rule, they
>   A
> were ready to fight<u>,</u> and live as free people in <u>their</u> own land. **(3)** A small,
>   B   C
> quiet man named <u>Mohandas</u> <u>Gandhi</u> spoke out for <u>Freedom</u>. **(4)** "There is a
>   A   B   C

better way," he said, "Than choosing violence or terrorism." **(5)** He taught
     A   B   C   A

his fellow Indians the principles of peaceful, passive protest! **(6)** "I know,"
          B   C   D

he said, "non-violence is a weapon for the brave and the courageous. **(7)** It
        A   B   C

takes patience to let angry people, attack you and not attack them in return.
     A   B   C   D

(8) How difficult it is to follow this grand law of love," he said, "but are not
                   A   B

all great, and good things difficult to do?" **(9)** The world began to notice
    C   D   A

and be impressed by this man's courage and principles. **(10)** He was called
 B   C   D

Mahatma, or "Great Soul," by the millions who followed and love him.
      A   B   C D

SENTENCE-CORRECTION QUESTIONS

Sentence-correction questions assess your ability to recognize appropriate phrasing. Instead of locating an error in a sentence, you must use your problem-solving skills to select the most appropriate and effective way to write the sentence.

In this kind of question, a part of the sentence is underlined. The sentence is then followed by five different ways of writing the underlined part. The first way shown, *(A),* simply repeats the original underlined portion. The other four choices present alternative ways of writing the underlined part. The choices may differ in grammar, usage, capitalization, punctuation, or word choice. Consider all answer choices carefully. If there is an error in the original underlined portion, make sure the answer you choose solves the problem. Be sure that the answer you select does not introduce a new error and does not change the meaning of the original sentence.

Look at the following example.

The statue *Venus of Milo* is displayed in a french museum.

    (A) *Venus of Milo* is displayed in a french museum.

    (B) *Venus of Milo,* is displayed in a french museum.

    (C) *Venus of Milo* is displayed in a French museum.

    (D) *Venus of Milo* is displayed, in a french museum.

    (E) *Venus of Milo* is displayed in a French Museum.

(The answer is *(C).* The word *French* is a proper adjective and should be capitalized. *(E)* is incorrect because the word *museum* is a common noun and should not be capitalized.)

Correcting Sentences

Write the letter of the most appropriate way of phrasing the underlined part of each sentence.

1. Modern paper is made from <u>wood containing acids that release, and decay slowly.</u>

(A) wood containing acids that release, and decay slowly.

(B) wood containing acids that release and decay slowly.

(C) wood, containing Acids that release and decay slowly.

(D) wood containing acids that release, and decay, slowly.

(E) wood containing acids that release and decay, slowly.

2. The ancient Egyptians made paper from <u>tree bark and some of it still exists.</u>

(A) tree bark and some of it still exists.

(B) tree bark, and some of it, still exists.

(C) Tree Bark, and some of it still exists.

(D) Tree Bark and some of it still exists.

(E) tree bark, and some of it still exists.

3. The <u>Chinese first wrote on silk but then</u> someone invented paper.

(A) Chinese first wrote on silk but then

(B) chinese, first wrote on silk but then

(C) Chinese, first wrote on silk, but then

(D) chinese first wrote on silk but then

(E) Chinese first wrote on silk, but then

4. The Chinese paper was made of <u>bark and rags, that was mixed and placed</u> over a frame.

(A) bark and rags, that was mixed and placed

(B) bark and rags that were mixed and placed

(C) bark and rags, that are mixed and placed

(D) bark and rags that were mixed, and placed

(E) bark, and rags, that are mixed and placed

5. Eventually a <u>paper mill opened in Spain and the art of paper making</u> spread.

(A) paper mill opened in Spain and the art of paper making

(B) paper mill opened in spain and the art of paper-making

(C) paper mill opened in Spain, and the art of papermaking

(D) Paper Mill opened in Spain and the art of paper making

(E) paper mill opened, in Spain, and the art of paper-making

REVISION-IN-CONTEXT

Another type of multiple-choice question that appears on some standardized tests is called revision-in-context. These questions are based on a short passage and assess your reading comprehension skills, your writing skills, and your understanding of the conventions of standard written English. The questions following the passage ask you to choose the best revision of a sentence, a group of sentences, or the essay as a whole. To select the correct answer, use your critical thinking skills to evaluate the relative merits of each choice. You may also be asked to identify the writer's intention. To do so, you will need to analyze the passage carefully to determine the writer's purpose.

Practice Your Skills

Correcting Sentences

Carefully read the following passage about the book *Uncle Tom's Cabin* by Harriet Beecher Stowe. Write the letter of the correct answer to the questions that follow.

> **(1)** The novel *Uncle Tom's Cabin* by Harriet Beecher Stowe made many people in the 1850s very uncomfortable. **(2)** It told the story of the lives of slaves in the South. **(3)** Many of the slaves were shown in a positive way, and the white slave owners were shown in a negative way. **(4)** Stowe wanted to tell the people of the United States, in both the North and the South, that slavery was wrong. **(5)** Stowe's father was a minister. **(6)** This gave her the idea to use religion for her argument by making some of the slaves full of Christian goodness and faith. **(7)** The black characters were shown with a lot of sympathy, and the book really made a big difference in the way people saw slavery at that time. **(8)** When Abraham Lincoln met Mrs. Stowe, he said to her, "So, you're the little woman who wrote the book that started this great war!" **(9)** Whether she started the war or not, she did a good job of persuading people against slavery.

1. Sentence 1 can best be described as
   (A) a supporting detail.
   (B) an analysis.
   (C) a topic sentence.
   (D) a summary.
   (E) an example.

2. Which of the following is the best revision of sentence 3?
   (A) Slaves were shown in a positive way. White slave owners were shown in a negative way.
   (B) Many slaves were shown in a positive way, while the white slave owners were shown in a negative way.

(C) A lot of the slaves were shown in a positive way, and the white slave owners were shown in a negative way.

(D) Consequently, many of the slaves were shown in a positive way, and instead, the white slave owners were shown in a negative way.

(E) The slaves were positive, but the slave owners were negative.

3. What is the writer's intention in sentence 4?

(A) to restate the opening sentence

(B) to interest the reader in the novel

(C) to state Stowe's purpose for writing the novel

(D) to summarize the plot of the novel

(E) to offer evidence for sentence 3

4. Which of the following is the best revision of sentence 7?

(A) The black characters were shown with a lot of sympathy, and the book made a big difference in the way people saw slavery at that time.

(B) The black characters were really shown sympathetically, and the book made a difference in the way people saw slavery at the time.

(C) The black characters were really nice. Stowe's book made a lot of difference in the way people saw slavery at the time.

(D) Because the black characters are really nice, the book made people see slavery really differently.

(E) Because the black characters were shown sympathetically, the book changed the way people saw slavery at the time.

5. What is the purpose of sentence 9?

(A) to criticize Stowe's achievements

(B) to contradict Abraham Lincoln's statement

(C) to object to slavery

(D) to present a conclusion about Stowe's novel

(E) to compare life and fiction

C. Taking Essay Tests

Applying Critical Thinking Skills

Essay tests are designed to assess both your understanding of important ideas and your critical thinking skills. You will be expected to analyze, connect, and evaluate information and draw conclusions. You may be asked to examine cause-and-effect relationships and to analyze outcomes. Some questions may address problems and solutions. Regardless of the type of question you are asked, your essay should show sound reasoning. You must be able to organize your thoughts quickly and to express them logically and clearly.

In this section, you will develop your skills in taking essay tests. Your critical thinking skills are essential in performing well on these tests.

1 Kinds of Essay Questions

Always begin an essay test by reading the instructions for all the questions. Then, as you reread the instructions for your first question, look for key words.

NARRATIVE, DESCRIPTIVE, AND PERSUASIVE PROMPTS

Following are some sample essay prompts and strategies for responding to them.

Narrative Writing Prompt

Think of a time when you worked hard to achieve a goal and succeeded. Tell what happened to make you want to achieve this goal and how you went about it.

Analyze the Question The key words in this question are "tell what happened." That is your cue that you will be relating a story.

Sketch Out the Key Parts You may want to make a chart like the following to be sure that you include all the necessary parts. Refer to the question for the headings in the chart.

STORY PLANNING SKETCH

Why you decided to set the goal	
How you went about it	
Stumbling blocks along the way	
How you finally achieved the goal	

Use What You Know About Narrative Writing Think of other narratives you have written and remember their key features: an attention-getting beginning that introduces a conflict, a plot that unfolds chronologically and often includes dialogue, a resolution to the conflict. Draft accordingly.

Save Time to Revise and Edit Read over your essay and look for any spots where adding, deleting, rearranging, or substituting would improve your essay. Edit it for correct conventions. Pay special attention to punctuation with dialogue.

Descriptive Writing Prompt

What holiday do you like the best? Choose your favorite and think about the day itself and how your family celebrates it. Write a well-organized detailed description of that holiday using words that appeal to the senses.

Analyze the Question The key words in this question are "detailed description." The directions to use "words that appeal to the senses" is another important item. It sets up the expectation that you will include vivid sights, sounds, smells, tastes, and feelings.

Sketch Out the Key Parts You may want to make a chart like the following to be sure that you include all the necessary parts. Refer to the wording of the question to determine the headings in the chart.

DESCRIPTION PLANNING SKETCH

Identification of holiday	
Vivid sights	
Vivid sounds	
Vivid smells, tastes, and feelings	

Use What You Know About Descriptive Writing Call to mind the key features of descriptive writing: a main idea that represents an overall attitude toward the subject; sensory details that support that overall feeling; a conclusion that reinforces the main impression. Draft accordingly.

Save Time to Revise and Edit Read over your essay and look for any spots where adding, deleting, rearranging, or substituting would improve your essay. Edit it for correct conventions.

21ST CENTURY

Persuasive Writing Prompt

A student in your math class proposed that the class should be able to earn free time by completing all the day's work with a B or better. Your math teacher has invited all members of your class to try to convince her this is a good idea. Write a letter to your math teacher to convince her this is a good idea.

Analyze the Question The key words in this question are "to convince." Those words tell you that you will be writing a persuasive text to convince people to do or believe something.

Sketch Out the Key Parts You may want to make a chart like the following to be sure that you include all the necessary parts. Refer to the question for the headings in the chart.

PERSUASIVE PLANNING SKETCH	
What you are trying to persuade about	
Reason #1	
Reason #2	
Reason #3	
Why your opinion will lead to the best possible benefits	

Use What You Know About Persuasive Writing Call to mind the key features of persuasive writing: a main idea that expresses an opinion; facts, examples, reasons, and other supporting details arranged in logical order, often order of importance; a look at why other opinions are not as sound; a conclusion that reinforces your opinion.

Save Time to Revise and Edit Read over your essay and look for any spots where adding, deleting, rearranging, or substituting would improve your essay. Edit it for correct conventions.

EXPOSITORY WRITING PROMPTS

Probably most of the essay tests you will take will ask you to address an expository writing prompt. Look for the key words in each of the following kinds of expository essay questions.

KINDS OF ESSAY QUESTIONS

Analyze	Separate into parts and examine each part.
Compare	Point out similarities.
Contrast	Point out differences.
Define	Clarify meaning.
Discuss	Examine in detail.
Evaluate	Give your opinion.
Explain	Tell how, what, or why.
Illustrate	Give examples.
Summarize	Briefly review main points.
Trace	Show development or progress.

As you read the instructions, jot down everything that is required in your answer, or circle key words and underline key phrases in the instructions, as in the following example.

Compare and contrast the types of Indian writing systems and their purposes. Include specific details to support or illustrate each point.

● **Practice Your Skills**

Interpreting Essay Test Items

Write the key direction word in each item. Then write one sentence explaining what the prompt asks you to do.

Example   Explain how a seed becomes a flower.

Possible Answer   *Explain*—Tell how a seed develops into a flower and what is necessary for this to occur.

1. In your own words, define *electromagnetic field*.

2. Briefly summarize one of the articles in *National Geographic*.

3. Evaluate one of Edgar Allan Poe's short stories.

4. In a five paragraph essay, contrast space technology in 1969 with today's technology.

5. Discuss the reasons for or against a movie rating system.

② Writing an Effective Essay Answer

The steps in writing a well-constructed essay are the same for an essay test as they are for a written assignment. The only difference is that in a test situation you have a strict time limit for writing. As a result, you need to plan how much time you will spend writing each answer and how much time you will devote to each step in the writing process. As a rule of thumb, for every five minutes of writing, allow two minutes for planning and organizing and one minute for revising and editing.

PREWRITING

Begin planning your essay by brainstorming for main ideas and supporting details. Then decide how you will organize your ideas. For example, you may decide to arrange your ideas in the order of importance, interest, or degree. To help you organize your answer, create a simple informal outline or a graphic organizer. Your outline or graphic organizer will help you present your ideas in a logical order, cover all your main points, and avoid omitting important details.

Informal
Outline

Indian Writing Systems

  1. Mayan glyphs used as a calendar
  2. Aztec pictographs used to keep records
  3. Inca quipu knots used to count crops and
      population

Graphic
Organizer

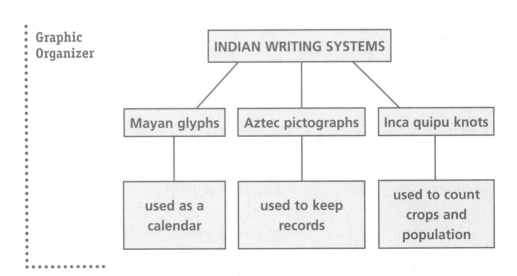

INDIAN WRITING SYSTEMS		
Mayan glyphs	Aztec pictographs	Inca quipu knots
used as a calendar	used to keep records	used to count crops and population

Your next step is to write a thesis statement that expresses your main idea and covers all of your supporting ideas. Often you can write a suitable thesis statement by rewording the test question.

Essay Prompt	Compare and contrast the types of Indian writing systems and their purposes. Include specific details to support or illustrate each point.

Thesis Statement	There were many types of Indian writing systems that served various purposes.

DRAFTING

As you write your essay answer, keep the following strategies in mind.

Strategies for Writing an Essay Answer

- Write an introduction that includes the thesis statement.
- Follow the order of your outline. Write one paragraph for each main point, beginning with a topic sentence.
- Be specific. Back up each main point by using supporting details, such as facts and examples.
- Use transitions to connect your ideas and examples.
- End with a strong concluding statement that summarizes your main ideas or brings your essay to a close.
- Write clearly and legibly because you will not have time to copy your work.

In the United States today, we use a Roman alphabet to write our ideas and keep records. Of course, we have computers today, but we have had paper for writing for a very long time. Before the arrival of the Europeans, Indians had different systems for writing. There were many types of Indian writing systems that served various purposes. The most highly developed systems came from the Maya, the Aztec, and the Inca.

Thesis Statement

Mayan writing contained symbols called glyphs, which were carved in stone and on bark paper. They used these glyphs to create a calendar that is considered by some to be more accurate than those of the ancient Egyptians, Greeks, or Romans.

Aztec writing was made up of pictures called pictographs. These pictographs were used mainly to keep records. Even the Spanish explorers learned to read Aztec writing.

The Inca had a system of tying knots on a string called a *quipu*. The quipu used the decimal system, much as we do. The knots at the end stood for 1, those farther up counted for 10, and those still higher up stood for 100. Crop records and population information were recorded by this method.

These systems had their own complex rules that the people of each group learned to use. Records of all types have always been important to society. How we keep records will change in the future as technology and our needs change.

Concluding Statement

21ST CENTURY

REVISING

Leave time to revise and edit your essay answer. To keep your paper as neat as possible, mark any corrections or revisions clearly, and write additional material in the margins. As you revise, consider the following questions.

Checklist for Revising an Essay Answer

✓ Did you follow the instructions completely?
✓ Did you interpret the question accurately?
✓ Did you begin with a thesis statement?
✓ Did you include facts, examples, or other supporting details?

✓ Did you organize your ideas and examples logically in paragraphs, according to your informal outline or graphic organizer?

✓ Did you use transitions to connect ideas and examples?

✓ Did you end with a strong concluding statement that summarizes your main ideas or brings your essay to a close?

EDITING

After you have made revisions, quickly read your essay to check for mistakes in spelling, usage, or punctuation. As you edit, check your work for accuracy in the following areas.

✓ Check your work for:

✓ agreement between subjects and verbs (pages 741–742)

✓ forms of comparative and superlative adjectives and adverbs (pages 764–770)

✓ capitalization of proper nouns and proper adjectives (pages 801–811)

✓ use of commas (pages 827–846)

✓ use of apostrophes (pages 878–886)

✓ division of words at the end of a line (pages 896–897)

❸ Timed Writing

You will be tested on your ability to organize and express your thoughts in a limited time. Your teacher may ask you to write a twenty-minute, two-hundred-word essay that will then be judged on how well you covered the topic and organized your essay. To complete such an assignment, consider organizing your time as follows:

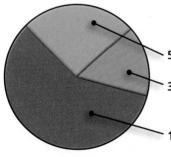

5 minutes: Brainstorm and organize ideas.

3 minutes: Revise your work and edit it for mistakes.

12 minutes: Write a draft.

Strategies for Timed Tests

- Listen carefully to instructions. Find out if you may write notes or an outline on your paper or in the examination book.
- Find out if you should erase mistakes or cross them out by neatly drawing a line through them.
- Plan your time, keeping in mind your time limit.

The more you practice writing under time constraints, the better prepared you will be for tests. You will find timed writing prompts on all of the following pages.

Practice Your Skills

Completing a Timed Writing Assignment

Give yourself twenty minutes to write an essay on the following topic.

In one school district, many parents and teachers were concerned about the kinds of television shows students were watching and the amount of time they spent in front of the TV. Although these adults thought that watching TV could have benefits, they believed that students' television-watching habits were having negative effects on their attitudes and grades. How would you solve this problem? Explain how your solution(s) would ensure that television had a positive impact on students.

Begin by creating an informal outline or a graphic organizer and writing a thesis statement. As you draft your essay, follow the **Strategies for Writing an Essay Answer** on page 372. Be sure to revise and edit your essay.

Communication and Collaboration

Essential Skills

In Part II of this guide, you will learn effective communication and collaboration skills. These skills are essential for success in the diverse world of the 21st century.

1 Communication

THE PURPOSE OF COMMUNICATION

In all areas of your life, you communicate for a variety of purposes—to inform, instruct, motivate, and persuade, for example. In school, you might give a speech to motivate your teammates before a championship game. You might persuade your principal to let you start a new club. In the future, you might work as a camp counselor and give instructions and directions to campers. You might send an invitation to inform people about a fundraising event for a charity. Having a clear purpose is essential for communicating your ideas successfully in both speech and writing.

EXPRESSING IDEAS EFFECTIVELY

In school and in your future career, you will use a variety of forms of communication, such as e-mail, a speech, or a letter. You will communicate in a variety of contexts, such as a school assembly or a group discussion. No matter what the form or context is, your goal is to express your thoughts and ideas as effectively as possible. Use words precisely and correctly and state your ideas in a specific, concise manner. Suit your tone to your purpose and audience. Provide valid support for your ideas and present information in a logical order. In a speech or presentation, use facial expressions, gestures, and other forms of nonverbal communication to help convey your message.

USING MEDIA AND TECHNOLOGY EFFECTIVELY

On a daily basis, you can use many forms of media and technology to help you communicate. You can e-mail, text message, or Twitter a friend, and complete business forms online. To prepare a speech, you can look up words in an online dictionary and research your subject on the Internet. You can use software to create a power presentation. To use media and technology effectively, you should make sure they suit the purpose and context of your communication.

LISTENING EFFECTIVELY

To listen effectively, you need to do much more than simply understand what words mean. Your goal is to gain knowledge and to identify the speaker's purpose, values, and attitudes. Skillful listeners also evaluate the speaker's message, views, and intentions. Listening effectively means listening actively so that you can understand, appreciate, evaluate, and remember what you have heard.

COMMUNICATING IN A DIVERSE WORLD

You probably attend school with people from diverse social and cultural backgrounds whose lifestyle, religion, and first language may be different from your own. To communicate effectively in school and in your future job, listen actively in order to understand different traditions, values, and perspectives. Be sure to respect these differences when you express your thoughts and ideas.

2 Collaboration

ACHIEVING A COMMON GOAL

In school and in the workplace, you often collaborate with others on diverse teams. To be an effective team member, you need to be open-minded and flexible. Make sure that all team members have an equal opportunity to be heard, and respect and value differences. Remember to maintain a positive attitude and to put the group's needs before your own. Help the group resolve conflicting opinions and work toward a compromise in order to achieve its goal. By sharing responsibility, team members will collaborate successfully.

A. Vocabulary

Apply Communication Skills

What do forceful writers and speakers and expert readers and listeners all have in common? They have a large vocabulary at their command.

Having a large vocabulary will help you to write and speak well. You will be able to choose words that best express your ideas and suit your purpose, audience, and the context. Developing your vocabulary will also help you to read and listen effectively. You will be able to understand the precise meanings of words so that you can comprehend an author's or a speaker's ideas and intentions.

This section will discuss the origins of the English language. You will also learn ways to figure out the meanings of unfamiliar words and to expand your vocabulary. The more words you know and use correctly, the more successful you will be. You will become a more effective communicator and a more skillful reader and listener—in and out of school.

The Growth of the English Language

Just like people, languages are born and then develop. Many factors can influence the development of a language. Immigration, technology, and popular culture are some of the factors that have greatly influenced the English language. To better understand the vocabulary you use, you need to understand where English comes from and how the language has changed.

① Origins and Borrowed Words

The English language and all other languages come from a single language that was spoken thousands of years ago. At some point in history, a form of English branched off as a separate language. The growth of English through time is divided into three major stages: Old English, Middle English, and Modern English. If you were to hear Old or Middle English spoken, they would probably sound like foreign languages and not at all like the English you speak today. This is because English has developed over the centuries. Words have been added, and spellings, meanings, and pronunciations have changed. In fact, English is still in the process of developing today.

The following examples show how some words have changed over time.

Old English	Modern English
moder	mother
faeder	father
weorold	world
eage	eye
buttorfleoge	butterfly

WORDS FROM OTHER LANGUAGES

Although there are many different sources for new words, over half of the words in the English language have been borrowed from other languages. Many words come from Greek and Latin, while others have been adopted from a wide variety of languages and cultures. The following chart shows the sources of some English words.

WORDS FROM OTHER LANGUAGES			
Arabic	algebra	candy	magazine
Dutch	buoy	landscape	skipper
French	cartoon	dentist	liberty
Greek	astronaut	comedy	ocean
Irish	bog	leprechaun	shamrock
Italian	balcony	spaghetti	violin
Latin	colony	missile	script
Scottish	clan	glen	slogan
Spanish	breeze	mustang	poncho

WORDS WITH UNUSUAL ORIGINS

Borrowing words from other languages is only one way English grows. New words come into the language in a variety of other ways. Some words, called **compound words**, are formed by combining two words.

poundcake   fingerprint   flashlight   houseboat

Some words are a blend of two words.

Blends	fry + sizzle = frizzle
	squirm + wiggle = squiggle

Some words are shortened forms of longer words.

Shortened Forms	ad	advertisement
	lunch	luncheon

Some words imitate sounds.

Sounds	plunk	strum	yap

Some names of people and places have also become words.

Names	**Cheddar:** Cheddar cheese was named for this village in England where the cheese was first made.
	Anders Celsius: The Celsius scale was named for the Swedish astronomer who invented it.
	Gabriel Daniel Fahrenheit: The Fahrenheit scale was named for the German physicist who invented it.

Some words are acronyms. **Acronyms** are words that are formed from the first letters or syllables of other words.

Acronyms	**loran:** long-range navigation
	SAT: Scholastic Aptitude Test
	sonar: sound navigation and ranging

Finding Unusual Origins

Tell how each of the following words came into the English language by writing *compound, blend, shortened form, sound, name,* or *acronym*. Use a dictionary (see pages 383–390) and the examples on page 380 to help you.

1. crunch

2. ACT

3. gym

4. watt

5. birdseed

6. OPEC

7. motorcycle

8. downtown

9. moonbeam

10. phone

21ST CENTURY

② Spelling and Pronunciation

The spelling and pronunciation of many English words have changed over the centuries. These changes in pronunciation can sometimes account for what might seem like the odd spelling of words. For example, the silent *k* in many modern English words is left over from the time when words, such as *knee* and *knight,* used to be pronounced with hard *c* or strong *k* sounds at the beginnings of the words. Gradually, the pronunciation of the words changed, but the spelling stayed the same, reflecting the words' history.

③ Meaning

The meanings of words have also changed over the years. In recent times, for example, the need for a vocabulary to describe computer-related concepts and ideas has prompted the addition of new definitions to old words. The word *mouse* used to refer mainly to "a small rodent." Now it also means "a device that moves a cursor on a computer screen." The word *computer* also has a past. Before it came to mean "an electronic machine," it had meant "a person who computes."

④ Compound Words

Compound words are made by combining two words into one. For example, *pine* plus *apple* becomes *pineapple. Down* plus *stairs* makes the word *downstairs.* Many new words have been added to English in this way.

Making Compound Words

Write five compound words. For each compound, use one word from list A and one from list B. Use each word only once.

List A	moon	rail	sea	life	pan
List B	guard	shore	cake	light	road

● Practice Your Skills

Writing with Compound Words

With a partner, write a paragraph that uses at least 10 compound words. You can include the words from the previous activity if you wish.

⑤ Academic Language

Each subject you study has its own vocabulary. The vocabulary of content areas you study in school is called **academic language.** In math you use academic language when you talk about *subtraction, semicircles,* or *triangles.* In science you use academic language when you talk about *acceleration, omnivores, equilibrium, centigrade,* or *quadriceps.* In social studies you use academic language when you talk about *federalism, republic,* or *exports.* Many academic terms come from Latin. (See pages 379 and 385.) This book is filled with the academic language of English language arts. *Topic sentence, chronological order, revising, prepositional phrase,* and even the term *academic language* itself are examples of the academic language of English.

● Practice Your Skills

Writing with Content-Area Vocabulary of English

The glossary at the back of this book includes all the terms that are important to know in 8th grade language arts. With a partner, choose 10 words from the glossary that you could use in a brief composition. Then collaborate in writing a composition that uses those words. If you find that some just don't fit, replace them with others from the glossary that do.

21ST CENTURY

● **Practice Your Skills**

Writing with Content-Area Vocabulary of Science

Skim through the glossary of your science textbook. With a partner, choose 10 words from the glossary that you could use in a brief composition. Then collaborate in writing a composition that uses those words. If you find that some just don't fit, replace them with others from the glossary that do.

Developing Your Dictionary Skills

Whenever you need to confirm the definition, spelling, pronunciation, or part of speech of a word, you should look up the word in a dictionary. You can use a dictionary to research the origin of a word as well. Some dictionaries also provide synonyms (words with similar meanings). Dictionaries come in book form, but you can access many dictionaries online. Learning how to use a print or an online dictionary will help you to communicate effectively.

Word Location

Most dictionaries are organized similarly. Dictionaries are structured so that you can find information quickly and easily.

ALPHABETICAL ORDER

The words in a dictionary are listed in alphabetical order. A dictionary includes many different kinds of entries. A two-word or a hyphenated compound word is alphabetized as if there were no space or hyphen between each part of the word. An abbreviation is alphabetized letter by letter, not by the word it stands for.

Notice the strict letter-by-letter alphabetical order in the following list.

Single Word	valentine
Two-Word Compound	vanishing point
Prefix	vice-
Phrase	vice versa
Abbreviation	VP

Guide Words

Guide words are the words printed in **boldface** type at the top of each page of a print dictionary. They show you the first and last words defined on that page. The guide words *Pittsburgh/place,* for example, show you that *pity* and *placate* are listed on that page. The words *planet* and *platform,* however, would appear on later pages.

● **Practice Your Skills**

Alphabetizing Different Kinds of Entries

Make two columns on a piece of paper. Alphabetize each set of words. Write the first alphabetized list of words in the first column, and the second alphabetized list of words in the second column.

1. jackpot janitor Japanese jack-o'-lantern
javelin January jam session Jack Frost
Jan. jackknife

2. nickname New Jersey numero uno no-show
NYC non- news conference Nobel Prize
NJ nitty-gritty

2 Information in an Entry

The dictionary presents a wealth of information about each word. All of the information for each word is called the **entry.** Key parts of the entry are the entry word, pronunciation, definitions, and word origin. The following entry for the word *catalog* shows these four main parts. In this section, you will learn about these four parts as well as other information that may be included in an entry.

pronunciation

entry word — **cat•a•log** or **cat•a•logue** (kăt' l-ôg', -ŏg') *n.* **1a.** A list or itemized display, as of titles, course offerings, or articles for exhibition or sale, usually including descriptive information or illustrations. **b.** A publication, such as a book or pamphlet, containing such a list or display: *a catalog of fall fashions; a seed catalog.* **2.** A list or enumeration: *"the long catalogue of his concerns: unemployment, housing, race, drugs, the decay of the inner city, the environment and family life"* (Anthony Holden). **3.** A card catalog. *v.* **–loged, –log•ing, –logs** or **–logued, –logu•ing, –logues** *–tr.* **1.** To make an itemized list of: *catalog a record collection.* **2a.** To list or include in a catalog. **b.** To classify (a book or publication, for example) according to a categorical system. *–intr.* **1.** To make a catalog. **2.** To be listed in a catalog: *an item that catalogs for 200 dollars.* [Middle English *cathaloge,* list, register, from Old French *catalogue,* from Late Latin *catalogus,* from Greek *katalogos,* from *katalegein,* to list : *kata–,* down, off; see CATA– + *legein,* to count; see **leg–** in Appendix I.] **–cat' a•log' er, cat' a•logu' er** *n.*

definitions —

word origin —

The American Heritage Dictionary of the English Language,
Fourth Edition, © 2006, Houghton Mifflin Company.

THE ENTRY WORD

A quick glance at the entry word will give you three pieces of useful information. The entry word shows you (1) how to spell the word, (2) whether the word should be capitalized, and (3) where the word should be divided into syllables.

Spelling

The entry word shows how to spell a word correctly. Some words have more than one correct spelling. The most common spelling, called the **preferred spelling,** is given first. The second spelling is called the **variant spelling.** Always use the preferred spelling of a word in your writing. In the model dictionary entry for *catalog* shown above, *catalog* is the preferred spelling and *catalogue* is the variant spelling.

A dictionary also shows how to spell the plurals of nouns, the principal parts of verbs, and the comparative and superlative degrees of adjectives and adverbs. Usually these words or parts are given only if the spelling or forms are irregular.

Principal Parts	ac•quit (ə-kwĭt') tr.v. –quit•ted, –quit•ting, –quits
Noun Plural	ox (ŏks) n., pl. ox•en (ŏk' sən)
Adjective Forms	sil•ly (sĭl' ē) adj. –li•er, –li•est

Words formed by adding a suffix to the entry word are often shown at the end of the entry. These related forms are called **derived words**. For example, in the model entry for *catalog* on page 385, the derived word *cataloger* and the **variant spelling** *cataloguer* are listed.

● Practice Your Skills

Correcting Spelling Errors

The following words are misspelled. Write the correct spelling for each word. Use a dictionary to check your spelling.

1. patrioticly
2. sopranoes
3. qualifyed
4. friendlyest
5. prefered

6. thiner
7. whinnyed
8. choosen
9. growed
10. shelfs

Capitalization

If a word should be capitalized, the entry word will be printed with a capital letter. If a word is capitalized only when it is used in certain ways, the word will be shown with a capital letter near the appropriate definition.

Syllables

Sometimes when you write, you need to divide a word at the end of a line. The entry word shows you how a word is divided into syllables. Remember that you cannot break a word in the middle of a syllable.

dis•hon•or	loy•al•ty	twen•ti•eth

21ST CENTURY

RELATED FORMS OF THE WORD

Entries in the dictionary also give the plurals of nouns, the principal parts of verbs, and the comparative and superlative forms of adjectives and adverbs. Usually these words or parts are listed only if the spelling or forms are irregular.

Principal Parts	com•mute (kə-myo͞ot') *v.* –mut•ed, –mut•ing, –mutes
Noun Plural	mouse (mous) *n., pl.* mice (mīs)
Adjective Forms	rust•y (rŭs'tē) *adj.* –i•er, –i•est

Sometimes words are made by adding a suffix to the entry word. These related forms are shown at the end of the entry and are called **derived words.** For example, at the end of the entry for *noisy* in a dictionary, you will find *noisily* and *noisiness* listed.

● Practice Your Skills

Checking Spelling

Write each word with the ending given in parentheses. Use a dictionary to check your spelling.

Example	drive (ing)
Answer	driving

1.	chief (s)	**6.**	degree (ed)
2.	envelop (ed)	**7.**	chimney (s)
3.	lazy (er)	**8.**	dredge (ing)
4.	shelf (s)	**9.**	happy (est)
5.	big (er)	**10.**	lug (ed)

● Practice Your Skills

Checking Spelling Online

Use an online source such as dictionary.com to check the spelling of each of the following words. If the word is spelled correctly, write C. If it is spelled incorrectly, write the correct spelling.

1. begger

2. deferred

3. hopeing

4. receive

5. knowledge

PRONUNCIATION

A **phonetic spelling** appears in parentheses after each entry word, as in the model entry for *catalog* on page 385. The phonetic spelling shows how to pronounce the word correctly.

A complete pronunciation key at the beginning of a print dictionary explains all the letters and symbols used in the phonetic spellings. In addition, most dictionaries provide a shortened form of the key on every other page for easy reference.

In the phonetic spellings of words, there may be marks over some vowels. These marks are called **diacritical marks.** They show the different sounds a vowel can make. For example, in the phonetic spelling of *catalog* in the model entry, the diacritical mark over the *a* tells you that the letter should be pronounced as a short *a*. Use the key to find out how to pronounce a vowel with a diacritical mark.

Accent Marks An accent mark (') in a phonetic spelling tells you which syllable should be pronounced with the most stress.

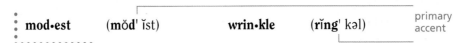

mod·est   (mŏd' ĭst)   **wrin·kle**   (rĭng' kəl)   primary accent

Some words have two accent marks. The darker one, called the **primary accent**, tells you which syllable receives more stress. The lighter one, called the **secondary accent**, tells you which syllable receives slightly less stress.

ex·plo·ra·tion (ĕk′splə-rā' shən)

primary accent

secondary accent

● Practice Your Skills

Practicing Pronunciation

Some of the following words might be new to you. Look them up in a dictionary to learn their meaning and pronunciation. Then, in pairs, take turns pronouncing them to practice. Keep practicing until you have the pronunciation just right.

1. artificial
2. intimidate
3. eligible
4. jeopardize
5. intermittent
6. benefactor
7. mandatory
8. deterrent
9. illuminate
10. propaganda

DEFINITIONS

Many words have more than one definition. The model entry for *catalog* on page 385 gives nine definitions. To find the definition that fits a particular context, be sure to read all of the definitions carefully. Then decide which meaning makes sense in the sentence. Sometimes dictionaries include example sentences or phrases, as in the model for *catalog*. Read these examples carefully as well because they show how the words are used.

Parts of Speech To indicate what part of speech a word is, most dictionaries use the following abbreviations.

n.	noun	*pron.*	pronoun
v.	verb	*prep.*	preposition
adj.	adjective	*conj.*	conjunction
adv.	adverb	*interj.*	interjection

Many words may be used as more than one part of speech. In such cases, as in the entry for *catalog* on page 385, two or more abbreviations will appear in one entry. Be sure that you first find the right part of speech in an entry when you search for the definition of a word. Then read all the definitions for that part of speech in order to find the appropriate definition.

Synonyms Words that have similar meanings are called **synonyms.** At the end of some entries, dictionaries list synonyms and explain how the meanings of the synonyms differ from that of the entry word. These lists can come in handy when you are writing or preparing a speech. You can use the lists to find the most appropriate words to express your meaning and intention.

● **Practice Your Skills**

Identifying Different Uses of a Word

Look up the word *cast* in a dictionary. Write the correct part of speech and the correct definition for *cast* as it is used in each sentence.

1. On Tuesday I will <u>cast</u> my vote for Debbie.

2. During an eclipse the moon takes on a copper <u>cast</u>.

3. Rhonda has to wear the <u>cast</u> on her arm for six weeks.

4. The teacher <u>cast</u> her eyes on the whispering students.

5. We <u>cast</u> our lines into the trout-filled lake.

6. On my trip to the museum, I admired a small bronze <u>cast</u> of a horse.

7. Steven Spielberg <u>casts</u> many young people in his films.

8. Reindeer <u>cast</u> their antlers yearly and grow new ones.

9. Bruce and Eddie <u>cast</u> the rope across the stream.

10. The <u>cast</u> of the play received a standing ovation.

WORD ORIGINS

As you learned in the beginning of this chapter on pages 379–381, words have entered the English language in many different ways. The dictionary provides information about the history, or origin, of words. This information is usually in brackets and may appear at the beginning or the end of an entry. For example, the model entry for *catalog* on page 385 tells you that the word comes from the Greek word *katalegein,* meaning "to list." In the front or back of a print dictionary, you can find an explanation of the symbols and abbreviations used to tell about word origins.

NEW COLLEGE EDITION

THE AMERIC...

Expanding Your Vocabulary

If you come across a word that is new to you, what do you do? For example, suppose you came across this sentence.

Mario was indecisive and had a hard time choosing which pair of sneakers to buy.

Perhaps you already know that *indecisive* means "not able to decide" or "tending to change one's mind frequently." However, it is more likely that the word is unfamiliar to you. One way to learn its meaning is to look it up in a dictionary. In this chapter you will learn several other ways to unlock the meaning of an unfamiliar word and to expand your vocabulary.

Context Clues

One of the ways you can learn the meaning of a word is through context clues. The **context** of a word is the sentence, the surrounding words, or the situation in which the word occurs.

In the sentence above about Mario, the words "had a hard time choosing which pair of sneakers to buy" act as a context clue. They help you figure out that *indecisive* means "not able to decide."

The following examples show three common types of context clues.

Definition	Objects in space that emit strong radio signals are **quasars.**
Example	**Fossil fuels,** such as coal, oil, and natural gas, are nonrenewable resources.
Synonym	Much of our knowledge about Norse explorers comes from **sagas.** These long stories were recited and passed from one generation to the next.

In the first item above, the word *quasars* is defined in the sentence. The whole point of the sentence is to tell what the word means. In the second item, coal, oil, and natural gas help the reader understand what fossil fuels are by giving examples. In the third item, the context clue *long stories* comes in the next sentence. It is a synonym (a word that means nearly the same thing as another word) for *sagas.*

● Practice Your Skills

Using Paragraph Context Clues

Write each underlined word and its meaning. Use the context of the paragraph to help you define the words. Then check your answers in a dictionary.

The explorers found themselves in a <u>barren</u> land, with no signs of life anywhere. The hot desert sun <u>parched</u> the earth. Water was nowhere to be found. Suddenly they heard the frightening rattle of a snake. The snake was so well <u>camouflaged</u> that the men could not see it against the rocks, stumps, and sand. They fled quickly to safety, hoping that the snake would not <u>pursue</u> them. During the long, hot weeks of exploration, snakes were only one kind of <u>hazard</u> these newcomers would have to face. Once they <u>misjudged</u> the difficulty of the trail. Although they hiked only a few miles that day, they were overcome by <u>fatigue.</u> On another day an explorer began to <u>falter.</u> He stumbled as he walked, having been <u>deprived</u> of food for too long. Soon the tired travelers began to <u>yearn</u> for the cool shade and the safety of their homes far away.

● Practice Your Skills

Practicing Pronunciation

Use a print or online dictionary to look up the pronunciation of the words in the previous activity. Then in pairs, take turns pronouncing them to practice. Keep practicing until you have the pronunciation just right.

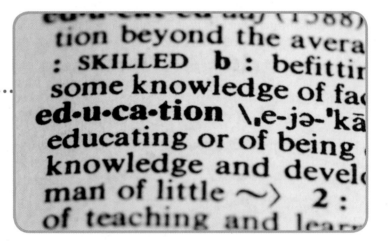

2 Base Words, Prefixes, and Suffixes

BASE WORDS

In addition to using context clues, you can unlock the meanings of unfamiliar words by breaking words down into their parts. For example, you might come across the word *rename.* You probably recognize one part of this word, *name.* This part is called the base word. A **base word** is a complete word that can stand alone. Other word parts can be added to a base word to make new words. The base words in the following examples are in boldface type.

| Base Words | mis**read** | de**bug** | re**appoint**ment | **value**less |

PREFIXES

The part of a word that comes before the base word is called a **prefix.** A prefix can be one syllable or more than one. In *rename,* the prefix *re-* means "again," so *rename* means "name again." The following chart defines some common prefixes.

Prefix	Meaning	Example
bi-	two	bi + weekly = biweekly
co-	together, joint or jointly	co + author = coauthor
de-	out of, remove from	de + plane = deplane
il-	not	il + legal = illegal
in-	not	in + secure = insecure
mis-	bad, badly, wrong, wrongly	mis + place = misplace
pre-	before	pre + historic = prehistoric
re-	again	re + gain = regain

● Practice Your Skills

Practicing Pronunciation

In a dictionary, find the pronunciation of the words on the right end of each row in the chart above. Then in pairs, practice pronouncing each one.

Combining Prefixes and Base Words

For each item, write the prefix that has the same meaning as the underlined word. Then write the complete word that is defined after the equal sign.

> Example   <u>before</u> + view = to see beforehand
>
> Answer   pre-, preview

1. <u>together</u> + operate = work together
2. <u>remove</u> + fog = to clear away the fog
3. <u>not</u> + logical = lacking in clear thinking
4. <u>before</u> + determine = to decide beforehand
5. <u>wrongly</u> + behave = to behave wrongly
6. <u>two</u> + annual = happening twice a year
7. <u>again</u> + organize = to set up a new order
8. <u>not</u> + appropriate = not appropriate
9. <u>remove</u> + forest = to clear away trees
10. <u>not</u> + legible = not readable

SUFFIXES

The part of a word that comes after the base word is called a **suffix.** Suffixes, like prefixes, can change the meanings of words and can have one or more syllables. Unlike prefixes, however, many suffixes can change a word from one part of speech to another. In the following chart, notice how suffixes can change a word's part of speech.

Suffix	Meaning	Example
-ance, -ence	state of	exist + ence
-ist	one who does or makes something	art + ist
-ment	state of	arrange + ment
-ness	state of	well + ness
-en	make, become	bright + en
-ize	make, cause to be	public + ize
-able, -ible	capable of	drink + able
-less	without	pain + less
-ly	in a certain way	quiet + ly

Using Suffixes to Form Words

Write each base word twice, each time adding a different suffix. Then write the part of speech of each new word. Use the list of suffixes on page 394 to help you.

Example	light
Possible Answers	lighten—verb, lightly—adverb

1. accept		**6.** rough	
2. vocal		**7.** plain	
3. firm		**8.** mean	
4. weak		**9.** motor	
5. manage		**10.** rapid	

③ Synonyms

When you write or speak, you want to express your meaning exactly. English is so rich in words that you can often choose among many words with similar meanings to find just the right one. A word that has nearly the same meaning as another word is called a **synonym.**

Although synonyms have similar meanings, they often convey slightly different shades of meaning. In the following sentences, for example, the word *padded* paints a more precise picture than *walked* does.

The wolf **walked** through the deep forest.

The wolf **padded** through the deep forest.

You can use a dictionary to find synonyms. (See page 389.) You can also use a thesaurus. (See page 309.)

● **Practice Your Skills**

Choosing the Better Word

Write the synonym in parentheses that fits the meaning of each sentence. Use a dictionary for help.

Example   Everyone in the room admired Stephen's (persistence, stubbornness).

Answer   persistence

1. What (disguise, camouflage) are you going to wear to Jenna's party?
2. By exercising, Kitty was able to (lessen, reduce) her weight by 12 pounds.
3. What shall we do with the (leftover, surplus) mashed potatoes?
4. While we are on vacation, our next-door neighbor will (nourish, feed) the fish.
5. Bill went home to (change, modify) his clothes before going out to play softball.
6. Here is a great joke that everyone in the audience is sure to (scoff, laugh) at!
7. When the glass hit the floor, it shattered into hundreds of tiny (fractions, fragments).
8. Michael's older brother got a ticket for (outdoing, exceeding) the speed limit.

④ Antonyms

An **antonym** is a word that means the opposite of another word. Dictionaries may list antonyms for some words. The following pairs of words are antonyms.

Antonyms	abundant—scarce	ban—allow
	precise—inexact	exterior—interior
	temporary—permanent	meek—bold

Antonyms show a contrast between extremes. Often, however, there are words in between the two extremes that show a smaller degree of contrast. For example, the words *warm, cool,* and *chilly* fall between the extremes of *hot* and *cold.* Knowing the whole range of words you can use to express an idea will help you choose exactly the right word when you write.

Recognizing Antonyms

Write the letter of the answer choice that is most nearly opposite in meaning to the word in capital letters. Then check your answers in a dictionary.

1. ELABORATE (A) fancy (B) complicated (C) untruthful (D) simple
(E) long

2. ANXIETY (A) fearfulness (B) eagerness (C) satisfaction (D) shyness
(E) calmness

3. DEPRIVE (A) give (B) cry (C) take (D) withhold (E) punish

4. PACIFY (A) soothe (B) relax (C) upset (D) hinder (E) touch

5. MYSTIFY (A) evaporate (B) clarify (C) confuse (D) decrease (E) startle

21ST CENTURY

B. Letters and Forms

Apply 21st Century Communication Skills

In the 21st century, people are communicating and sharing information much more than they have in the past. To communicate effectively, always have a clear purpose in mind and use technology wisely.

Real-World Communication

1 Communicating for a Purpose

In your personal life and in the business world, you communicate and share information for a variety of purposes: to inform, instruct, motivate, or persuade, for example. You might write a friendly letter, filled with words of encouragement, to motivate a good friend who lacks confidence. You might send a letter of regret, a type of social letter, to inform a friend that you can't attend her party. In a letter of complaint, a type of business letter, you might persuade a company to correct a billing error. When you complete a business form, your purpose is to inform a company or an organization by providing specific facts and details.

Whether you are writing a letter or filling out a form, you should always keep your purpose in mind. Your goal is to write in a clear, concise manner because you want your readers to know exactly what you mean.

❷ Using Technology to Communicate

In the 21st century, you have many ways to communicate. You can text or "tweet" a friend, e-mail a request, or post a complaint online. With all these options, electronic communication—particularly e-mail—has replaced letter writing to a great extent. However, writing a letter can be more effective or appropriate than sending an e-mail depending on your purpose, the context, and the impact you want to make. Use these guidelines to determine whether to send a letter or an e-mail.

Send a letter in the following circumstances:

- You want to express sincere, serious emotions, such as get-well wishes or thanks for a favor or a gift.
- You want to show that you have put thought and care into communicating.
- You want to introduce yourself formally or make an impact on your audience by using impressive stationery, for example.
- You are including private, confidential information. Keep in mind that e-mail is not a private form of communication, and you should never include confidential information in an e-mail. A recipient can forward an e-mail to others without your knowledge, and companies can read their employees' e-mails. Also, hackers can break into e-mail systems and steal information.
- You need to have formal documentation of your communication, or you are sending authentic documents.

Send an e-mail in the following circumstances:

- You want to communicate quickly with someone.
- You want to send a message, perhaps with accompanying documents, to several people at once.
- You have been instructed by a business or an organization to communicate via e-mail.

The Purpose and Format of Letters

Letters fall into two general categories: personal letters and business letters. In each category, letters can serve many different purposes. Regardless of your purpose, your goal when you write a letter is to convey ideas, opinions, and information in an effective way.

For each category of letters, there is a correct format to use, which is demonstrated in this chapter. Following the appropriate conventions will help you to communicate clearly and create a positive impression.

① Writing Personal Letters

You probably text a friend when you want to send a brief, quick message. You may use e-mail for fast, but more extended communication. However, if you want to express your feelings or provide a personal touch, or if the occasion is formal, you should write a personal letter. Friendly letters and social letters are two types of personal letters. When you write a friendly or a social letter, make sure you convey your ideas, opinions, and feelings precisely. Include whatever important information is necessary to make your message clear and complete. Be sure to provide a sense of closure to your letter.

FRIENDLY LETTERS

A **friendly letter** is an informal letter that you write to a friend or a relative. In your letter, you might convey your ideas and opinions, describe your feelings, or include important information. Although friendly letters are casual in style, they still follow certain conventions. All friendly letters have five main parts: the heading, salutation, body, closing, and signature. A friendly e-mail, like a letter, should contain a proper salutation and closing.

The parts of a friendly letter are explained in the following chart.

PARTS OF A FRIENDLY LETTER	
Heading	The heading includes your full mailing address with your ZIP code. Use the two-letter abbreviation for your state. Always include the date after your address. Follow the rules for capitalizing proper nouns and using commas in an address.
Salutation	The salutation is your greeting. Always capitalize the first word and all proper nouns. Use a comma after the salutation. Dear Aunt Sally,　　　Dear Grandpa,
Body	The body is the main part of the letter. It includes your conversational message. Remember to indent the first line of each paragraph.
Closing	End your letter with a brief personal closing followed by a comma. Capitalize the first word only. Your nephew,　　　With love,
Signature	Sign your name below the closing.

The following model shows the correct format for a friendly letter.

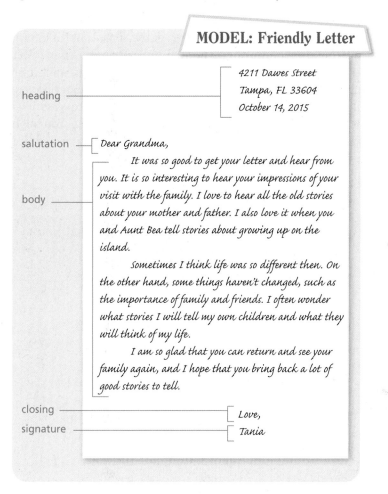

MODEL: Friendly Letter

heading

4211 Dawes Street
Tampa, FL 33604
October 14, 2015

salutation

Dear Grandma,

body

It was so good to get your letter and hear from you. It is so interesting to hear your impressions of your visit with the family. I love to hear all the old stories about your mother and father. I also love it when you and Aunt Bea tell stories about growing up on the island.

Sometimes I think life was so different then. On the other hand, some things haven't changed, such as the importance of family and friends. I often wonder what stories I will tell my own children and what they will think of my life.

I am so glad that you can return and see your family again, and I hope that you bring back a lot of good stories to tell.

closing

Love,

signature

Tania

The envelope for a friendly letter may be handwritten. It should contain the same information as that on the envelope for a business letter. (See page 409.) Be sure both your address and the receiver's address are clear and complete.

● Practice Your Skills

Writing a Friendly Letter

Write an informal letter to a friend that reflects your opinion about something that you have done recently. For example, you might tell about a movie you have seen or a trip to a place such as a museum. Ask questions to encourage a response. Demonstrate a sense of closure by ending your letter with a statement about your friendship. Be sure to follow the conventions of a friendly letter. Send your letter, and remember to reply in a timely fashion when you receive a response.

INFORMATIONAL LETTERS

Sometimes you might want to convey interesting ideas or important information in a letter. These **informational letters** have many of the same traits of informational or expository writing, though they are often informal and can use the friendly letter format. For example, you might have a great new idea for a video game and want to share it with your cousin, who programs video games for a living. As you describe your game to him, you would use the same techniques you would use in an expository text: clear organization, lots of supporting ideas, and a natural sounding voice. You might also have occasion to send important information in a letter. Once again, you would need to take the same care in your letter as you would in an expository text.

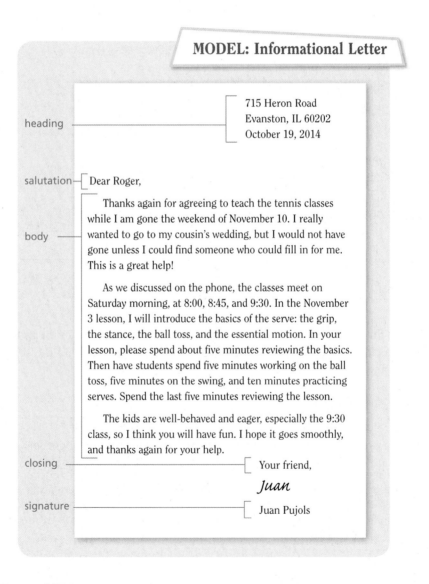

MODEL: Informational Letter

heading

715 Heron Road
Evanston, IL 60202
October 19, 2014

salutation — Dear Roger,

body —

Thanks again for agreeing to teach the tennis classes while I am gone the weekend of November 10. I really wanted to go to my cousin's wedding, but I would not have gone unless I could find someone who could fill in for me. This is a great help!

As we discussed on the phone, the classes meet on Saturday morning, at 8:00, 8:45, and 9:30. In the November 3 lesson, I will introduce the basics of the serve: the grip, the stance, the ball toss, and the essential motion. In your lesson, please spend about five minutes reviewing the basics. Then have students spend five minutes working on the ball toss, five minutes on the swing, and ten minutes practicing serves. Spend the last five minutes reviewing the lesson.

The kids are well-behaved and eager, especially the 9:30 class, so I think you will have fun. I hope it goes smoothly, and thanks again for your help.

closing ————————— Your friend,

Juan

signature ————————— Juan Pujols

● **Practice Your Skills**

Writing an Informational Letter

Imagine that you have asked a friend to take your place in doing some job while you are out of town. Write a letter conveying the information in a well-organized and complete way. Then exchange letters with a partner. Ask your partner if he or she would be able to follow the directions based on the information in your letter. After you and your partner have shared feedback, revise your letter as necessary.

● **Practice Your Skills**

Writing a Letter to Share Ideas

Think of a change you would like to make in your school. Write a letter explaining your idea to a friend or relative who goes to another school. Use the conventions of a friendly letter and provide a meaningful closure.

SOCIAL LETTERS

Social letters have a specific purpose. They are sent, for example, to thank someone for a gift or a favor, to invite someone to an event, or to inform someone that you cannot accept an invitation. Social letters have a more formal tone than friendly letters, but they follow the same conventions.

Get-Well Letters A get-well letter is short and to the point. Such letters let people know that you are wishing for their fast recovery. Keep the tone sensitive but upbeat.

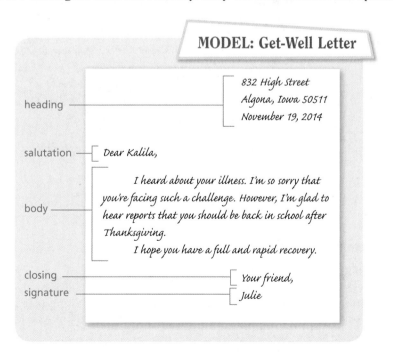

MODEL: Get-Well Letter

heading
832 High Street
Algona, Iowa 50511
November 19, 2014

salutation
Dear Kalila,

body
I heard about your illness. I'm so sorry that you're facing such a challenge. However, I'm glad to hear reports that you should be back in school after Thanksgiving.
I hope you have a full and rapid recovery.

closing
Your friend,

signature
Julie

● **Practice Your Skills**

Writing a Get-Well Letter

Imagine that you have just learned that your cousin had to be hospitalized with a bad case of the flu. Write a get-well letter. Then exchange letters with a partner. Check that your partner followed the appropriate conventions and used an appropriate tone. After you and your partner have shared feedback, revise your letter as necessary.

Thank-You Letters A thank-you letter expresses your gratitude or appreciation. The following model shows the correct format for a thank-you letter.

MODEL: Thank-You Letter

> 711 Country Mile Drive
> Houston, TX 7701
> November 26, 2015
>
> Dear Uncle Pete,
>
> Thank you very much for the subscription to the online encyclopedia. It is fantastic! I have already used it to do some research for a school report on one-celled animals. It is great to be able to do my research right from my computer at home instead of having to go to the library. I know I will use the encyclopedia often in the future.
>
> Thanks again for the perfect gift. I am looking forward to seeing you over the holidays.
>
> Your favorite nephew,
> Tony

● **Practice Your Skills**

Writing a Thank-You Letter

Imagine that you have just received a gift from a friend who lives in another country. Write a thank-you note to your friend expressing your appreciation for the gift. Be sure to use the correct format for a thank-you letter.

Invitations An **invitation** informs someone about an event you would like him or her to attend. It includes the time and place and any other important information your guests need to know. This information might tell how to get to the event or how to dress (formally or informally). Sometimes invitations tell the receivers whether they may bring a guest or whether they are expected to bring food or a gift.

MODEL: Invitation

> 46 Alexis Lane
> Santa Clara, CA 95050
> December 1, 2015
>
> Dear Janine,
>
>   I know it has been a while since we spoke, so I hope you are doing well. Our family has been busy, but I want to let you know that you are invited to my holiday party on Friday, December 22, at 8:00 p.m. at the above address. The dress code will be informal but festive. Please feel free to bring a friend. R.S.V.P.
>
>   Sincerely,
>   Wanda Reckhaus

● **Practice Your Skills**

Writing an Invitation

You are giving a New Year's Eve party. Where will it be held? What time should the guests arrive? What other information might your guests need to know? Draft the invitation to your party, using the appropriate conventions. Then read your letter carefully to make sure you haven't omitted any important information. Make any necessary revisions.

Letters of Regret A **letter of regret** informs someone that you will be unable to attend an event to which you have been invited. In it, you explain why you will be unable to attend, and you express your regret. Invitations that say "RSVP" (an abbreviation for "please reply") often require a written response. (See the model of an invitation on page 405.) You should always respond to an invitation in a timely fashion so that the person planning the event knows how many people he or she can expect.

MODEL: Letter of Regret

22 Salamander Drive
Albuquerque, NM 87111
January 5, 2015

Dear Elsie,

I am so sorry that I will be unable to attend your potluck dinner party next week. My grandfather has taken ill in Cincinnati, and my whole family is going there to be with him. Thank you for thinking of me, and I hope you have a nice party. I'll talk to you when I get back.

Sincerely,
Lucas Martinez

● **Practice Your Skills**

Writing a Letter of Regret

Imagine that a friend has asked you and a few others to go to a movie for her birthday. Decide what movie the group is going to see. Then write a letter of regret explaining why you cannot go. Be sure to follow the appropriate conventions.

② Writing Business Letters

A **business letter** is a formal letter that calls for some action on the part of the receiver. Letters of request, order letters, and letters of complaint are three types of business letters. The most effective business letters state their purpose and convey ideas simply and directly. They are concise; they include important information and leave out unnecessary details.

Business letters have six main parts, one more part than friendly letters. This part is called the inside address. The inside address contains the name and address of the person to whom you are writing.

There are many formats or styles for business letters. In the **modified block style,** the heading, closing, and signature are on the right. The inside address, salutation, and body all start at the left margin. A blank line is left between each paragraph in the body of the letter, and the first line of each paragraph is indented. The models of business letters in this chapter use the modified block style.

Tips for Writing Business Letters

- Use white stationery, preferably 8½ by 11 inches.
- Leave one-inch margins on all sides.
- Be sure to keep an electronic copy or a hard copy of every business letter you send.

The parts of a business letter are explained in the following chart.

PARTS OF A BUSINESS LETTER

Heading	The heading of a business letter is the same as that of a friendly letter. Include your full address followed by the date. Follow the rules for capitalizing proper nouns and using commas in an address.
Inside Address	Start the inside address two to four lines below the heading. Write the name of the person who will receive the letter if you know it. Use *Mr.*, *Ms.*, *Mrs.*, or *Dr.* before the name. If the person has a title, such as Executive Director, write it on the next line. Then write the receiver's address. Follow the rules for capitalizing and punctuating addresses.
Salutation	Start the salutation two lines below the inside address. Use a colon after the salutation. If you do not know the person's name, use *Sir or Madam*. Dear Mrs. Walters: Dear Sir or Madam:
Body	Two lines below the salutation, begin the body of the letter. Skip a line between paragraphs, and indent the first line of each new paragraph.
Closing	Use a formal closing. Start the closing two lines below the body. Line up the closing with the left-hand edge of the heading. Capitalize the first word only, and use a comma at the end of the closing. Sincerely, Yours truly, Sincerely yours, Very truly yours,
Signature	In a business letter, your name appears twice. First type or print your name four lines below the closing. Then sign your name in the space between the closing and your typed or printed name. Do not use *Mr.* or *Ms.* to refer to yourself.

The following model shows the correct format for a business letter.

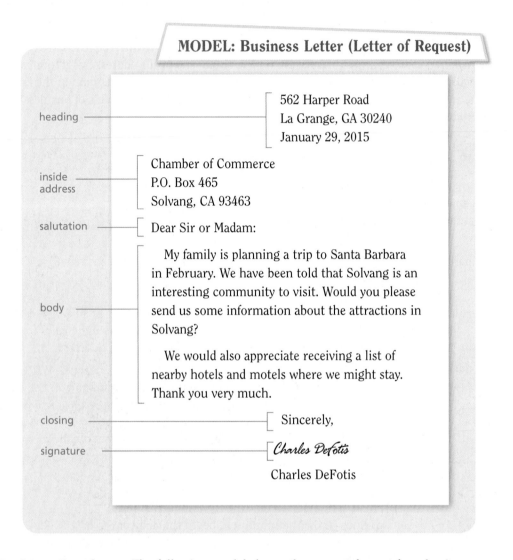

MODEL: Business Letter (Letter of Request)

heading
562 Harper Road
La Grange, GA 30240
January 29, 2015

inside address
Chamber of Commerce
P.O. Box 465
Solvang, CA 93463

salutation
Dear Sir or Madam:

body
My family is planning a trip to Santa Barbara in February. We have been told that Solvang is an interesting community to visit. Would you please send us some information about the attractions in Solvang?

We would also appreciate receiving a list of nearby hotels and motels where we might stay. Thank you very much.

closing
Sincerely,

signature
Charles DeFotis

Charles DeFotis

Business Envelopes The following model shows the correct format for a business envelope. If you use a word-processing program to type the letter, you should also type the envelope. If you handwrite the letter, you can handwrite the envelope neatly. Place your name and address in the upper left-hand corner. The receiver's address, which is the same as the inside address in a business letter, is centered on the envelope.

Use a business-sized envelope that matches the stationery on which you wrote your letter. Fold the letter in thirds, and place it in the envelope so that the receiver will take it out right-side up.

Charles DeFotis
562 Harper Road
La Grange, GA 30240 — sender's address

Chamber of Commerce
P.O. Box 465
Solvang, CA 93463 — receiver's address

BUSINESS E-MAILS

A business letter sent via e-mail should be just as formal as a letter sent by mail. Follow these guidelines when sending a business e-mail.

Guidelines for Writing a Business E-mail

- Include a formal salutation and closing. Format the body of the letter correctly.
- Use proper grammar and punctuation.
- Check your spelling. (Some e-mail programs have their own spell-check function. Use it!)
- Double-check the person's e-mail address to be sure you have typed it correctly.
- In the subject line of the e-mail, remember to specify the topic you are writing about.

LETTERS OF REQUEST

Requesting information is one common purpose of a business letter. When requesting information, be specific about the information you need. Include appropriate facts and details, but be sure to exclude extraneous information. Remember to state your request politely and express your thanks in order to give closure to your letter. (For a model of a letter of request, see page 408.)

Practice Your Skills

Writing a Letter of Request

Write a letter to a major zoo in the United States to request information about the animals' living quarters. Your goal is to find out to what extent the zoo tries to recreate the animals' natural surroundings. Also request any free materials the zoo might have. Remember to specify the kind of information you wish to receive. Express your thanks in order to give closure to your letter. Be sure to follow the conventions of a business letter.

ORDER LETTERS

You can also use a business letter to order merchandise from catalogs and advertisements. Because your reader needs specific information to fill your order accurately, you should include important information about the merchandise such as the description, size, order number, price, and the quantity of the items you want. If you enclose payment for your purchase, your letter should state the amount you have enclosed. Check your arithmetic to be sure you have included the proper amount.

MODEL: Order Letter

4333 West Silvestre Avenue
Bluff Dale, TX 76433
May 10, 2015

Hollywood Heaven
643 Baker Road
Detroit, MI 48222

Dear Sir or Madam:

Please send me the following items from your 2015 spring catalog:

1 poster (36 x 24) of Darth Vader and Luke Skywalker from *Star Wars*
Order # 45-H-112 $9.95
1 *Wizard of Oz* T-shirt, blue, size small
Order #41-T-33588 $14.95

TOTAL $24.90

I have enclosed a check for $27.40 to cover the cost of the merchandise, plus $2.50 for shipping and handling.

Sincerely,

Raphaela Gomez
Raphaela Gomez

Writing an Order Letter

Use the following information to write an order letter. In your letter, state your purpose clearly. Include all the appropriate information your reader needs to fill your order. Be sure this information is well organized. Remember to follow the conventions of a business letter.

Address	Order Department, Sports City, 1789 Juneway Place, Scranton, PA 18510
Order	1 baseball jacket, blue, size medium, Order #880-3G, $22.00; 1 medium-weight Home Run King baseball bat, Order #670-2E, $8.00; $3.75 for shipping and handling

LETTERS OF COMPLAINT

When you write a **letter of complaint,** you should state the problem politely and provide complete information about it. Then tell how you think the problem might be corrected. For example, if you receive an item that does not work properly, you should state what the item is, why it doesn't work properly, and what you expect the company to do about the problem. Remember to use a professional, courteous tone, no matter how angry you might be.

● **Practice Your Skills**

Registering a Complaint

Imagine that you and a friend went to see a new hit movie. Unfortunately, the movie theater was having technical difficulties, which ruined your experience of watching the film. Write an e-mail to the movie theater in which you register a complaint. Include a description of the problem and suggest what the theater should do to retain you as a loyal patron. Review your e-mail to make sure that you haven't left out any important information. Remember to use a professional, polite tone and to follow the conventions of a business e-mail.

Completing Business Forms

You will need to fill out business forms for a variety of reasons. For example, you might subscribe to a magazine or apply for a student discount pass. Today, you can often complete forms online. However, there are still many occasions when you will be asked to fill out a paper form. The following guidelines will help you complete a paper form.

Completing Business Forms

- Read all of the directions carefully before you begin to fill out the form.
- If the form is long or complex, you may want to write the answers on a separate sheet of paper first. Then copy the answers onto the form in ink.
- Check both sides of the form to make sure you do not miss any questions written on the back.
- Do not leave blanks. If a question does not apply to you, write *N/A* (not applicable) in the space provided.
- Always use blue or black pen.
- Be sure to print neatly and clearly.
- Remember to sign the form if needed.
- Read over the form when you are finished to be sure your answers are accurate and complete.

Most banks offer different kinds of savings accounts to suit the various needs of their customers. The following models are samples of forms that can be obtained and filled out at your local bank.

The following model is an example of a form you would complete in order to open a savings account at a bank.

Savings Bank Application Form

Tri-Town Savings Bank

Type of Account: *Savings*

Customer's Name: *Karen Kelly*

Home Address (Street): *16 River Drive*

(City): *Hanover*   (State): *NH*   (Zip): *03755*

Phone: *603-646-1212*   Date of Birth: *4/24/01*

Social Security: *184-46-4380*

Initial Deposit: *$100.00*   Branch: *Hanover*

Signature: *Karen Kelly*   Date: *2/18/15*

When you want to put money into your savings account, you fill out a deposit slip, like the following sample form.

Deposit Slip

Tri-Town Savings Bank   Date _3/17/15_

Karen Kelly
NAME ON ACCOUNT (PLEASE PRINT)

ACCOUNT NUMBER

| 8 | 8 | 5 | – | 9 | 3 | 3 |

CASH	50	00
CHECKS	43	00
(LIST SEPARATELY)	25	50
TOTAL	118	50

Practice Your Skills

Completing a Business Form

Think of an organization you would like to join, such as a community center or a local museum, a magazine you would like to subscribe to, or a contest you would like to enter. Write a letter to request a form, pick one up from a local organization, or print a form from the organization's website. Then, following the guidelines in **Completing Business Forms** on page 412, fill out the form. Exchange forms with a partner. Check that your partner filled out the form completely.

C. Directions and Speeches

Apply 21st Century Communication and Collaboration Skills

To communicate effectively, two things have to happen: A speaker must send a clear message, and a listener must hear and understand it.

In the diverse world of the 21st century, you will communicate with people from various social and cultural backgrounds. When you give a speech, the members of your audience may have diverse views and beliefs. You may listen to a speaker who has a perspective very different from your own. You may collaborate in a group discussion with classmates from a variety of backgrounds. In all these cases, you should respect the varied opinions and values of others. Doing so will enrich your understanding and help you communicate and collaborate effectively.

You can practice and improve your speaking, listening, and collaborating skills just like any other skills. This section will help you sharpen these skills, which are important for school and all other areas of your life.

Developing Your Informal Speaking Skills

In the lyrics to one of his most famous songs, "The Sound of Silence," Paul Simon says, "People talking without speaking, people hearing without listening. . . ." Even when you are speaking informally, it is important to be clear and exact. Otherwise, although you may be "talking," you will not be communicating.

Informal speaking is a form of speech that is suitable for everyday use or for casual occasions. Although **informal speeches** are short and require little or no advance preparation, remember to keep your purpose in mind as you speak. Take the time to organize your thoughts and use precise language in order to communicate effectively.

It is also necessary, as Paul Simon wrote, to *listen* and not just *hear*. Listening skills will be discussed later in the chapter. However, keep in mind the importance of listening effectively as you learn to develop your informal speaking skills.

 **Giving Directions**

Giving directions is an important type of informal speech. Clear directions show organized thinking. They are also easy to follow. Compare the following two sets of directions to the football stadium.

Unclear	Follow this road for a while until you come to a light. Then go west. The stadium should be near there.
Clear	To get to the football stadium, continue on Maple Street until you come to the second traffic light. That is Spring Street. You will see a gas station on the near corner and a medical building on the far corner. Turn left on Spring Street and go half a mile. The stadium will be on your right.

The second set of directions would be clearer to a listener because it includes a specific distance, street names, and landmarks. The first set of directions does not provide clear, precise information.

The following strategies will help you give clear, concise directions.

 Guidelines for Giving Directions

- Use words like *right, left,* or *straight* rather than *north, south, east,* or *west.*
- Use the names of streets or highway numbers if you know them.
- Mention landmarks whenever possible.
- Include the approximate number of blocks or miles if you know this information.
- If possible, draw a map.
- Do not give directions for a difficult shortcut.
- If you are unsure of the correct directions, do not guess. Help the other person find someone else to ask for information.
- Speak clearly and slowly.
- Look directly at the other person as you give him or her directions.
- Pay attention to the other person's facial expressions and body language. They may indicate that he or she does not understand your directions.
- Repeat the directions or have the other person repeat the directions to you.

● **Practice Your Skills**

Improving Directions

Rewrite the following directions to make them more specific. Use the guidelines above and your imagination to help you include necessary details. After you have rewritten the directions, draw a map to accompany them.

I think the aquarium is near the river. To get there, go north for several miles. You will come to a railroad crossing. Before the crossing take a right. Soon you will see a big building. Take another right and you should come to the river in a little while. Down the road a bit, you will see the aquarium.

● **Practice Your Skills**

Giving Directions

Write directions for traveling from your home to your school. Include as many specific details as possible. Then read your directions aloud to a partner. Ask your partner to suggest ways to improve your directions.

② Participating in Group Discussions

In a **group discussion,** you collaborate with others. You share ideas and information and exchange opinions in order to accomplish a goal. Your goal might be to solve a problem or to reach a decision. By developing your group discussion skills, you will learn to state your ideas effectively and to listen carefully to others' ideas. You will also learn to collaborate respectfully with others. Keep the following guidelines in mind the next time you are in a group discussion—at home or at school.

Guidelines for Participating in Group Discussions

- Come to the discussions prepared.
- Draw on your preparation by referring to evidence on the topic as you support your ideas and opinions with facts or examples.
- Listen carefully to what others have to say, and follow up with questions to elaborate.
- Keep an open mind, and appreciate diverse perspectives.
- Respond respectfully to others' views. If you disagree with someone's point, do it politely and explain why you disagree. Be open, though, to revising your views based on what others say.
- Ask questions if you do not understand information or another person's views.
- Keep in mind that everyone in the group should have an equal opportunity to speak.
- Be flexible and try to help your group accomplish its goal, whether that involves drawing a conclusion or reaching a decision or consensus.

● **Practice Your Skills**

Participating in a Group Discussion

Form a group with three or four classmates, and hold a group discussion. Discuss the differences between elementary school and middle school. Your goal is to choose three differences that you think are essential for students to know before they enter middle school. Be sure to follow the Guidelines for Participating in Group Discussions. Present your choices to the rest of the class. Tell why your group chose these three differences.

Developing Your Formal Speaking Skills

A formal speech is different from an informal speech in two basic ways. A **formal speech** is prepared in advance and is usually longer than an informal speech. A formal speech may be anything from a science or book report, presented in front of a class, to a guided tour of a school. You will have many opportunities in school and in your future career to deliver speeches. Learning to express your ideas well and to use media and technology effectively will help you deliver a successful speech.

Preparing Your Speech

The preparation of a formal speech is similar to the preparation of a written report. (See pages 285–287.) The main difference is that you will practice your speech and deliver it orally rather than presenting your ideas in writing.

CHOOSING AND LIMITING A SUBJECT

To choose a subject for your speech, first make a list of topics that you know something about. Then choose one that will interest both you and your audience. For example, if you were speaking to parents who wanted to learn about your school, you might inform them about your school's athletic programs. However, if you were speaking to your basketball teammates, this subject would not interest them. Instead, you might talk about your opponents in the upcoming championship game.

After deciding on a subject, you need to consider the amount of time you have to deliver your speech. If you have only ten minutes, you will need to limit your subject and talk about just one aspect or part of it. For example, you could limit the subject of the athletic programs your school offers by talking about just gym classes and not about after-school sports activities.

Practice Your Skills

Choosing and Limiting a Subject

Limit each subject so that it is suitable for a ten-minute speech.

Example	trees
Possible Answer	the giant redwoods in California

1. vacations
2. China
3. inventions

4. the Great Lakes
5. the solar system
6. baseball

UNDERSTANDING YOUR PURPOSE

The purpose of your speech determines the points you make and the way you present your information. Most speeches have one of the following three purposes: to inform, to persuade, or to entertain. The purpose of a speech may also be to motivate or to instruct.

PURPOSES OF SPEECHES	
Purpose	Examples
to inform	• to explain the effect of the moon on ocean tides • to explain the structure of icebergs
to persuade	• to encourage students to do volunteer work • to convince the school administration to sponsor a school newspaper
to entertain	• to tell about the first time you made Thanksgiving dinner for your family and forgot to cook the turkey • to tell about the first and only time you tried to ski

Practice Your Skills

Determining a Purpose for a Speech

Label the purpose of each speech *to inform, to persuade,* or *to entertain.*

1. to explain a solar eclipse
2. to tell about a picnic involving 25 people and a rainstorm
3. to trace the history of the National Football League
4. to encourage your school to plan more field trips
5. to explain how Sacajawea helped Lewis and Clark explore the West

Practice Your Skills

Choosing a Subject and a Purpose for Your Speech

You will be presenting a ten-minute speech to your class. The topic is "Someone Who Changed the World." Brainstorm or freewrite to choose a subject that suits your audience and the length of your speech. Then select a purpose for your speech. Write down your subject and purpose, and save your work for later use.

GATHERING AND ORGANIZING YOUR INFORMATION

The next steps in preparing your speech are to gather and organize information. These steps are similar to those you follow when writing a report. (See pages 288–295.) You should also collect audiovisual aids. Follow these guidelines to complete these steps.

Gathering Information

- List what you already know about your subject.
- Gather more information from books and magazines in the library or from Internet sources. You could also interview someone who is knowledgeable about the subject.
- Find interesting examples and quotations to include.
- Take notes on the information you find. Writing information on index cards will make it easy to organize your notes as you prepare your outline. Use a new card for each new idea. Be sure to note the source for your information in case you need to find it again.

Collecting Audiovisual Aids

- Decide whether any audiovisual aids, such as maps, pictures, slides, CDs, or DVDs will add to the impact of your speech. Audiovisual aids should be used to add to points or to help make points clear. They should never be distracting to your audience.
- Make sure that any audiovisual aids you choose suit the purpose and context of your speech.
- Plan how and when you will use the aids in your speech.
- Gather or create the audiovisual aids you will use.

Organizing Information

- Make an outline of your speech. Unlike an outline for a report, an outline for a speech should include your introduction and your conclusion.
- The introduction of your speech should capture the attention of your audience. It should also include the main idea of your speech.
- The body of your speech should include your supporting points. Arrange your points in a logical order. Think of the transitions you will use to connect your ideas when you speak.
- The conclusion of your speech should summarize your main idea.

● **Practice Your Skills**

Gathering Information with Note Cards

Use index cards to take notes on the following paragraph from www.altculture.com. A sample card has been filled out for you.

> <u>Superpremium, socially conscious ice cream.</u> Founded in 1978 by Ben (Bennett R.) Cohen (b. 1950) and Jerry Greenfield (b. 1951), who started their empire in a vacant Vermont gas station with a $12,000 investment and the resolution to stay in business one year. Their first franchise opened in 1981, with distribution outside Vermont beginning in 1983. After going public in 1984, Ben & Jerry's Homemade Inc. sales grew to an annual revenue, in 1994, of some $150 million worth of Wavy Gravy, Maple Walnut, White Russian, and numerous other flavors in grocery stores, delis, and its approximately 100 "scoop shops." It thus equals Häagen-Dazs in superpremium ice cream market share.

Source: www.altculture.com
—Started by Ben Cohen and Jerry Greenfield
—began in vacant gas station in Vermont—1978
—$12,000 initial investment

● **Practice Your Skills**

Gathering and Organizing Information for Your Speech

Look back at the subject and purpose you chose for your speech. Write what you know about your subject on note cards. Next, find information for at least four more note cards by using Internet or library resources. Then organize your cards, and write an outline of your speech. Prepare any audiovisual aids you will use.

② Practicing Your Speech

Practicing your speech aloud is a necessary step for delivering a successful speech. Each time you practice your speech, you will feel more confident. As a result, you are less likely to be nervous when you deliver your speech in front of an audience. Use the following guidelines as you practice your speech.

Guidelines for Practicing Your Speech

- Read your outline several times until you are familiar with all the information and feel comfortable presenting your points.
- Practice in front of a long mirror so that you will be aware of your facial expressions and gestures, such as biting your lips or clenching your hands.
- Practice looking around the room as you talk. Good eye contact is important.
- Practice using your audiovisual aids.
- Time the length of your speech. If it is too long, decide what information you can omit. If it is too short, you should find more information.
- Practice over a period of several days.

After practicing your speech several times, try delivering it before family members or friends. Ask for suggestions for improving your speech. If possible, make an audio or a video recording of your speech, and review your delivery.

Practice Your Skills

Practice Your Speech

Practice your speech alone several times. Then, with a partner, take turns practicing your speeches in front of each other. Share your feedback with each other. Use your partner's comments to improve your speech, and then practice your revised speech.

3 Delivering Your Speech

If you have followed the guidelines for preparing and practicing your speech, you will be ready to deliver it. Follow these guidelines to deliver an effective speech.

Guidelines for Delivering Your Speech

- Be well prepared and have all the materials you need, such as your outline and audiovisual aids or equipment.
- Wait until your audience is quiet and settled.
- Take a deep breath and begin.
- Stand with your weight evenly divided between both feet. Avoid swaying back and forth.
- Look directly at the people in your audience, not over their heads. Try to make eye contact.
- Speak slowly, clearly, and loudly enough to be heard.
- Use gestures and facial expressions to emphasize your main points.
- Make sure that everyone in your audience can see your audiovisual aids, such as charts and power presentation slides.

● **Practice Your Skills**

Delivering Your Speech

Present the speech you have practiced before a group of classmates. Then, in your journal, list what you think you did well and what you would like to improve in your next speech. You may want to use the **Oral Presentation** Evaluation Form on page 428 to assess your speech or to provide feedback to your classmates about their speeches.

Developing Your Listening Skills

Listening is more than just hearing words. It involves understanding and appreciating a speech or presentation. It also requires the use of critical thinking skills to evaluate what another person has said. This section will help you develop your listening skills.

Guidelines for Listening to an Oral Presentation

During the Presentation:
- Pay attention.
- Do not interrupt or make noise.
- Listen to understand, appreciate, and evaluate.
- Notice how the speaker may use pauses to make points.
- Observe how gestures, voice, and facial expressions add to the message.
- Listen for changes in volume, tone, and pitch used to emphasize important ideas.

After the Presentation:
- If possible, ask the speaker to explain anything you did not understand.
- If the speaker is available, thank him or her for the presentation.

❶ Listening to Enjoy and Appreciate

One of the most important aspects of listening is enjoying and appreciating a presentation. You will remember more about a presentation you enjoyed than about one that does not interest you. Paying attention and listening carefully will help you enjoy a speech. You will also better appreciate what the speaker is trying to say and accomplish.

● **Practice Your Skills**

Listening to Enjoy and Appreciate

With a partner, take turns reading the following poem aloud. While you are listening to your partner read, try to enjoy and appreciate the poem. Close your eyes if that helps you focus as you listen. When you have each heard the poem, answer the questions that follow it.

The Dream Keeper

Bring me all of your dreams,
You dreamers,
Bring me all of your
Heart melodies
That I may wrap them
In a blue-cloth
Away from the too-rough fingers
Of the world.

—Langston Hughes

- Did you enjoy the poem? Why or why not?
- Were there any words you didn't understand? If so, look them up in a dictionary. Then listen to the poem again. Did that change your enjoyment?
- Even if you did not enjoy the poem, did you appreciate what the poet was trying to convey? Why or why not?

2 Listening for Information and Taking Notes

When you listen to gain information, focus your attention on the main idea and supporting ideas of the speech. You should also determine the speaker's purpose, whether it is to inform, instruct, motivate, or persuade.

LISTENING FOR THE MAIN IDEA AND PURPOSE

In a well-planned speech, the main idea, along with the speaker's purpose, will be in the introduction. Often the speaker will state both directly in a single sentence. For example, if you heard the sentence *Lightning can strike twice, and here's how to protect yourself from being struck even once,* you would know that the speech is about how lightning strikes. You would also know that the speaker's purpose is to inform you about how to stay safe in a storm.

Be alert during the introduction because the speaker does not always state the main idea and purpose directly. Instead, the speaker may convey the main idea and purpose through a question, a quotation, or a personal example.

LISTENING FOR SUPPORTING IDEAS

Once you have identified a speaker's main idea and purpose, listen for his or her major supporting ideas. Be alert for clues such as *There are three reasons that . . . or I will explain the four main causes of. . . .* Such phrases often introduce major supporting ideas. A speaker may also introduce major supporting ideas with transitional expressions such as *first, second, third, moreover, most important,* or *finally.*

Developing Your Listening Skills   **423**

Listen, as well, for supporting details that the speaker offers to clarify or drive home ideas. These supporting details often take the form of facts and examples, such as statistics, quotations from experts, and anecdotes. In some cases a speaker will alert you to an important supporting detail by introducing it with a phrase such as *for example, studies show that,* or *according to one expert.*

Keep in mind that not all details are important. As you listen to the speech, focus on major supporting ideas and details that help you understand and evaluate the speaker's main idea. If any points are unclear and the speaker is available after the presentation, ask questions to clarify the points.

TAKING NOTES WHILE LISTENING

Taking notes on speeches helps you to listen carefully. To take notes, you need to listen for important points and then organize the information clearly. Use the following guidelines to help you take notes.

> **HERE'S HOW** **Guidelines for Taking Notes on Speeches**
>
> • Write the main idea presented in the introduction of the speech.
> • Write the main topics, using Roman numerals (I, II, III) in an outline form.
> • Under each main topic, write the subtopics, or supporting ideas, using capital letters (A, B, C). Listen for clues to the supporting ideas, such as "There are three main reasons that. . . ." or "I will explain the four main causes of. . . ."
> • At the end of the outline, write a restatement of the main idea. This is the summary.

When you take notes, do not write down everything. If you do, you probably will miss important points. Write only the information that is necessary for remembering the most important points accurately. Your notes will then help you remember the other details.

The following notes in outline form are based on a ten-minute speech about the development of gymnastics.

MODEL: Notes in Outline Form

Gymnastics, a sport in which physical feats are performed in an artistic manner, has a long history.   •——— Main Idea

I. Began in ancient Greece   •——— Main Topic
  A. Greeks had gymnasiums with fields for throwing discuses and javelins   •——— Subtopic
  B. Romans adopted Greek ideas; added them to their military training

II. Died out between A.D. 392 and the 1700s
  A. Revived in Germany by Frederick Jahn
  B. He added side bar with pommels, horizontal bars, parallel bars, balance beams, jumping standards

III. Brought to the U.S. in the 1800s by immigrants
  A. Americans participated in first international competition in 1881
  B. Four Americans won first gold medals in gymnastics in USA in 1904 Olympics

Gymnastics started in ancient Greece but died out for many centuries until it was revived in the 1700s. Americans did not become involved in gymnastics until the 1880s. They have participated in international competition since then.   •——— Summary Statement

● Practice Your Skills

Listening for Information and Taking Notes

With a partner, choose a news program to watch on TV or to listen to on the radio. You can also listen to a podcast. Working separately, take notes on the information you hear. Then you and your partner should compare notes. Did you leave out any important ideas? Did you include any unnecessary details?

③ Listening Critically

When you listen, your goal is not only to understand but also to evaluate what the speaker is saying. To listen critically, you need to listen very carefully and pay close attention to the speaker's choice of words.

HERE'S HOW Guidelines for Listening Critically

- Identify the speaker's purpose and intentions. Is the speaker trying to persuade you to do or buy something, for example?
- Think about the values and attitudes expressed by the speaker. What principles or qualities are important, according to the speaker? How does the speaker feel about the topic?
- Consider how the speaker's purpose, values, and attitudes affect the way he or she talks about the topic.
- Delineate a speaker's argument and specific claims, evaluating the soundness of the reasoning and relevance and sufficiency of the evidence. Take note of irrelevant evidence if it is introduced.

Be on the lookout for the following types of techniques and statements that may be used to mislead or influence you.

To learn more about the techniques of persuasion, see Writing to Persuade, pages 220–247.

FACT AND OPINION

A **fact** is a statement that can be proved. An **opinion** is a personal feeling or judgment. Because opinions are often stated as facts, you must listen carefully to tell them apart.

Fact	Dogs belong to the canine family.
Opinion	Dogs are people's best friends.

● Practice Your Skills

Understanding Fact and Opinion

Label each statement *fact* or *opinion*.

1. All books by Mark Twain are interesting.

2. Halloween is always the last day of October.

3. Tiger gasoline is the best gasoline to buy.

4. My sister is three years younger than I am.

5. *Rumble Fish* was written by S. E. Hinton.

BANDWAGON

Commercials and advertisements sometimes include a bandwagon statement. A **bandwagon** statement leads you to believe that everyone is using a certain product. In other words, everyone is "jumping on the bandwagon." A bandwagon statement can be misleading because it suggests that if you do not jump on the bandwagon, you will be different from everyone else.

> **Bandwagon Statement** Don't be left out. Join the healthy generation and take Peak-of-Health vitamins.

TESTIMONIAL

In a **testimonial** a famous person encourages you to buy a product. Such a statement can be misleading if the person's fame has nothing to do with judging the product.

> **Testimonial Statement** Hi! I'm baseball star Bob Mose. Bran Buds gives me the energy I need to hit the ball out of the park!

LOADED WORDS

Another type of statement that may mislead or influence you is one that contains loaded words. **Loaded words** are ones that are carefully chosen to appeal to your hopes or fears rather than to reason or logic. In the following advertisement, the word *embarrassment* was chosen to stir up the listener's emotions.

> **Loaded Word** When standing close to that special person, avoid embarrassment by using Why Worry Antiperspirant.

● Practice Your Skills

Evaluating for Misleading Information

Label each statement *bandwagon, testimonial,* or *loaded words.*

1. All beautiful people wear Glow cosmetics.

2. A hardworking basketball player like me, Dan Dunk, needs Hi-Jumps on his feet to win the game.

3. Eliminate unsightly blemishes with Freshface.

4. True pet lovers feed their cats Kaviar Katmeal.

4 Listening to Evaluate

Through self-assessment, your classmates' feedback, and assessing the speeches of others, you can improve your speaking and listening skills and help your classmates to improve theirs. The following form can help you to assess a speech.

ORAL PRESENTATION EVALUATION FORM

Subject: _____

Speaker: _____ **Date:** _____

Content

Was the subject appropriate for the audience?

Was the subject appropriate for the length of the speech?

Was the purpose clear? Was it appropriate for the audience?

Was the main idea clear?

Did all the ideas clearly relate to the subject?

What was the speaker's point of view?

Were the speaker's reasoning and use of evidence sound?

Was any irrelevant evidence introduced?

Organization

Was the introduction clear and interesting?

Did the introduction include the main idea?

Did the ideas in the body of the speech follow a logical order?

Were transitions used between ideas?

Did the conclusion summarize the main idea?

Presentation

Was the speaker well prepared?

Did the speaker use an outline well?

Did the speaker talk loudly and clearly enough?

Did the speaker pace the delivery well?

Did the speaker make eye contact with the audience?

Did the speaker use an appropriate pitch and tone of voice?

Did the speaker use gestures and pauses effectively?

If the speaker used audiovisual aids, were they effective?

Comments: _____

_____

Media and Technology

Part I	Critical Thinking and Problem Solving for Academic Success
Part II	Communication and Collaboration
Part III	Media and Technology

Essential Skills

You already understand the importance of literacy, or the ability to read and write. In the 21st century, literacy—meaning "knowledge of a particular subject or field"—in the areas of information, media, and technology is also essential. Part III of this guide will help you develop literacy in these three areas. This knowledge will help you succeed in school and in your future jobs.

1 Information Literacy

Today, a tremendous amount of information is available at your fingertips. To acquire information literacy, you must know how to access, manage, evaluate, and use this wealth of information. Learning advanced search strategies will help you locate information efficiently and effectively from a range of relevant print and electronic sources. Evaluating the reliability and validity of sources will help you assess their usefulness. Then you can synthesize information in order to draw conclusions or to solve a problem creatively. Understanding the difference between paraphrasing and plagiarism and knowing how to record bibliographic information will ensure that you use information in an ethical, legal manner. Part III of this guide will help you build your information literacy skills by showing you how to use the Internet to access information.

You can learn more about information literacy on pages 298–313.

2 Media Literacy

Media messages serve a variety of purposes. They can have a powerful influence on your opinions, values, beliefs, and actions. Part III of this guide will help you develop your media literacy skills by showing you how to use both print and nonprint media to communicate your message. You will learn how to use these media to create effective messages that suit your audience and purpose. You will also learn about the types of tools available for creating media products.

You can learn more about media literacy on pages 46, 80, 104, 142, 169, 213, 233, 274, and 331.

3 Technology Literacy

In the 21st century, knowing how to use technology to research, evaluate, and communicate information is essential. You must also know how to use different forms of technology, such as computers and audio and video recorders, to integrate information and create products. Part III of this guide will show you how to use technology effectively to access information and to publish and present your ideas in different media.

You can learn more about technology literacy on pages 243 and 436–443.

A. Electronic Publishing

Apply Media and Technology Literacy

Everything you may ever have to say or write requires some medium through which you express it and share it with others. The ability to use available media and technology to their fullest potential will enable you to communicate your ideas effectively and to a widespread audience. For now, most academic and workplace communication still depends on print technology. By using that to its full capability, you will prepare yourself for the inevitable improvements and upgrades that will be a feature of communication in the future.

In this section, you will develop your skills in using available technology in your communication.

Digital Publishing

The computer is a powerful tool that gives you the ability to create everything from newsletters to multimedia reports. Many software programs deliver word-processing and graphic arts capabilities that once belonged only to professional printers and designers. Armed with the knowledge of how to operate your software, you simply need to add some sound research and a healthy helping of creativity to create an exciting paper.

WORD PROCESSING

Using a standard word-processing program, such as Microsoft Word™, makes all aspects of the writing process easier. Use a word-processing program to:

- create an outline;
- save multiple versions of your work;
- revise your manuscript;
- proof your spelling, grammar, and punctuation;
- produce a polished final draft document.

USING A SPELL CHECKER

You can use your computer to help you catch spelling errors. One way is to set your Preferences for a wavy red line to appear under words that are misspelled as you type. You can also set your Preferences to correct spelling errors automatically.

A second way to check your spelling is to choose Spelling and Grammar from the Tools menu. Select the text you want to check and let the spell checker run through it looking for errors. While a spell checker can find many errors, it cannot tell you if a correctly spelled word is used correctly. For example, you might have written *The books were over their*. The spell checker will not identify an error here, even though the correct word is *there*, not *their*.

FASCINATING FONTS

Once your written material is revised and proofed, you can experiment with type as a way to enhance the content of your written message and present it in a reader-friendly format. Different styles of type are called **fonts** or **typefaces**. Most word-processing programs feature more than 30 different choices. You'll find them listed in the Format menu under Font.

Or they may be located on the toolbar at the top left of your screen.

Most fonts fall into one of two categories: **serif** typefaces or **sans serif** typefaces. A serif is a small curve or line added to the end of some of the letter strokes. A typeface that includes these small added curves is called a serif typeface. A font without them is referred to as sans serif, or in other words, without serifs.

> Times New Roman is a serif typeface.
>
> Arial is a sans serif typeface.

In general, sans serif fonts have a sharp look and are better for shorter pieces of writing, such as headings and titles. Serif typefaces work well for body copy.

Each typeface, whether serif or sans serif, has a personality of its own and makes a different impression on the reader. Specialized fonts, like the examples in the second paragraph on the next page, are great for unique projects (posters, invitations, and personal correspondence) but less appropriate for writing assignments for school or business.

Since most school writing is considered formal, good font choices include Times New Roman, Arial, Helvetica, or Bookman Antiqua. These type styles are fairly plain. They allow the reader to focus on the meaning of your words instead of being distracted by the way they appear on the page.

With so many fonts to choose from, you may be tempted to include a dozen or so in your document. Be careful! Text printed in multiple fonts can be EXTREMELY confusing to read. Remember that the whole idea of using different typefaces is to enhance and clarify your message, not muddle it!

A SIZABLE CHOICE

Another way to add emphasis to your writing and make it reader-friendly is to adjust the size of the type. Type size is measured in points. One inch is equal to 72 points. Therefore, 72-point type would have letters that measure one inch high. To change the point size of your type, open the Format menu and click Font.

Or use the small number box on the toolbar at the top left side of your screen.

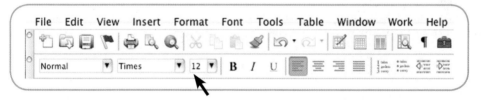

For most school and business writing projects, 10 or 12 points is the best size of type for the main body copy of your text. However, it's very effective to increase the type size for titles, headings, and subheadings to highlight how your information is organized. Another way to add emphasis is to apply a style to the type, such as **bold,** *italics,* or underline. Styles are also found in the Format menu under Font.

Or look for them—abbreviated as **B** for bold, *I* for italics, and U for underline—in the top center section of the toolbar on your screen.

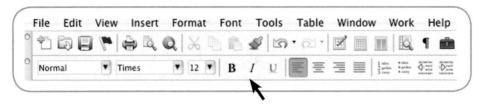

If you have access to a color printer, you may want to consider using colored type to set your heading apart from the rest of the body copy. Red, blue, or other dark colors work best. Avoid yellow or other light shades that might fade out and be difficult to read.

Use different type sizes, styles, and colors sparingly and consistently throughout your work. In other words, all the body copy should be in one style of type. All the headings should be in another, and so on. Doing so will give your work a unified, polished appearance.

TEXT FEATURES

Text features such as **bulleted lists** and **numbered lists** are useful ways to organize information and give it a reader-friendly format. If you create pages of text in which information isn't broken up in any way, your readers may lose focus or have trouble identifying your main points. Instead, use bulleted or numbered lists to highlight important information and present it clearly and simply. To create these lists, open the Format menu and click on Bullets and Numbering. You can also click on the numbered or bulleted list on the toolbar at the top right of your screen.

A sidebar is another useful text feature for presenting information. A **sidebar** is a section of text that is placed alongside the main copy. Often the text in a sidebar appears in a box. Use sidebars to present additional, interesting information that relates to your main topic but doesn't belong in the body of your report or paper.

LAYOUT HELP FROM YOUR COMPUTER

One way to organize the information in your document is to use one of the preset page layouts provided by your word-processing program. All you have to do is write your document using capital letters for main headings and uppercase and lowercase letters for subheadings. Set the headings apart from the body copy by hitting the "return" key. Then open the Format menu and click the Autoformat heading. Your copy will probably look like the illustration on the next page.

You can probably use this automatic, preset format for most of the writing you do in school. You'll also find other options available in the File menu under Page Setup.

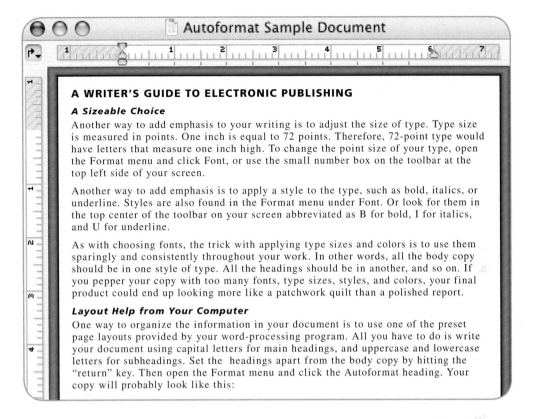

A WRITER'S GUIDE TO ELECTRONIC PUBLISHING

A Sizeable Choice

Another way to add emphasis to your writing is to adjust the size of type. Type size is measured in points. One inch is equal to 72 points. Therefore, 72-point type would have letters that measure one inch high. To change the point size of your type, open the Format menu and click Font, or use the small number box on the toolbar at the top left side of your screen.

Another way to add emphasis is to apply a style to the type, such as bold, italics, or underline. Styles are also found in the Format menu under Font. Or look for them in the top center of the toolbar on your screen abbreviated as B for bold, I for italics, and U for underline.

As with choosing fonts, the trick with applying type sizes and colors is to use them sparingly and consistently throughout your work. In other words, all the body copy should be in one style of type. All the headings should be in another, and so on. If you pepper your copy with too many fonts, type sizes, styles, and colors, your final product could end up looking more like a patchwork quilt than a polished report.

Layout Help from Your Computer

One way to organize the information in your document is to use one of the preset page layouts provided by your word-processing program. All you have to do is write your document using capital letters for main headings, and uppercase and lowercase letters for subheadings. Set the headings apart from the body copy by hitting the "return" key. Then open the Format menu and click the Autoformat heading. Your copy will probably look like this:

Here you can change the margins and add headers, footers, and page numbers. Headers and footers are descriptive titles that automatically appear at the top or bottom of each page without your having to retype them each time. For example, you may wish to add the title of your project and the date as a header or footer to each page.

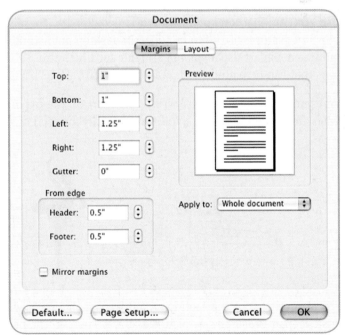

To insert a header or a footer, go to View and click on Header and Footer. Note that page numbers may also be inserted by way of the Insert option on your menu bar.

Header

Project Title Here ¶

Date Here ¶

LET'S GET GRAPHIC

The old saying "A picture is worth a thousand words" is particularly true when it comes to spicing up papers and reports. Publishing and presentation software programs such as Macromedia FreeHand™ and Microsoft PowerPoint™ give you the ability to include photographs, illustrations, and charts in your work that can express your ideas more clearly and succinctly than words alone.

The key to using graphics effectively is to make sure each one conveys a message of importance. Don't use them just for decoration. Be sure they add something meaningful, or you'll actually detract from your written message.

Drawings Many paint and draw programs allow you to create an illustration or **import** (bring in from another program) one into your document. Drawings can help illustrate concepts that are difficult to describe, such as mechanical parts or procedures. Cartoons can also add a nice touch. If you use them sparingly, they can lighten up an otherwise dry, technical report.

Clip Art Another kind of drawing is called clip art. These simple, black-and-white or color line pictures are often included in desktop publishing or word-processing programs. Pre-drawn clip art usually is not suitable for illustrations, but it does work well as graphic icons that can help guide your reader through various parts of a long report.

For example, suppose you are writing a report on the top arts programs in the United States. You might choose the following clip art for each of the sections:

When you introduce the section of your report that deals with music, you might use the music icon at the large size pictured above. Then, in the headings of all the following sections that deal with music, you might use a smaller version of the icon that looks like this:

Music Trends

Using clip art as icons in this manner lets your readers know at a glance which part of the report they are reading.

Charts and Graphs One of the best ways to communicate information about numbers and statistics is by using charts and graphs. Programs such as Microsoft PowerPoint® allow you to create bar graphs, pie charts, and line graphs that can communicate fractions, figures, and comparative measurements much more powerfully than written descriptions.

Photographs With the widespread availability of digital cameras and scanners, adding photos to your project is an easy and effective way to enhance your content. Using a digital camera or a scanner, you can load photos directly into your computer. Another option is to shoot photographs with a regular camera, but when you have them developed, specify that they be returned to you as "pictures on disc," which you can open on your computer screen. Photographic images are stored as bits of data in an electronic file. Once you have the photos in your computer, you can use a graphics program to manipulate the images in a variety of ways and create amazing visual effects. You can crop elements out of the photo, add special filters and colors, combine elements of two different pictures into one—the possibilities are endless.

After you have inserted the edited photo into your document, be careful when you print out your final draft. Standard printers often don't reproduce photographs well. You may want to take your document on disc to a professional printing company and have it printed out on a high-resolution printer to make sure you get the best quality.

Captions and Titles While it's true that a single photo can say a great deal, some pictures still need a little explanation in order to have the strongest impact on your reader. Whenever you include an illustration or photograph in a document, also include a simple caption or title for each image.

Add captions in a slightly smaller type size than the body copy and preferably in a sans serif typeface. Use the caption to add information that isn't immediately apparent in the photo. If there are people in the picture, tell readers who they are. If the photo features an odd-looking structure, explain what it is. Be smart with your captions. Don't tell readers the obvious. Give them a reason to read your caption.

Stand-Alone Graphics Occasionally you may include well-known graphics or logos in a report. These graphics convey powerful messages on their own and don't require captions. Examples of these logos or symbols include:

Nonprint Media—Audio and Video

The world we live in is becoming increasingly more multimedia-savvy. Many businesses rely extensively on multimedia presentations to market their products or convey messages to consumers and employees. Exciting opportunities exist for people who can produce clear, concise messages in audio and visual formats.

PRE-PRODUCTION—PUT IT ON PAPER FIRST

Although the final presentation of your subject material may be an audio recording or a video, your project needs to begin on paper first. When you write down your ideas, you do four things:

- Organize your thoughts.
- Narrow your focus.
- Isolate the main messages.
- Identify possible production problems.

Resist the urge to grab an audio recorder or camera and run off to record your project. That's a sure-fire way to create an unorganized mess. Take the time to plan your production.

Concept Outline The first task in the writing process is a short, one-page document that describes the basic idea of the project. Ideally this should be three paragraphs—one paragraph each describing the beginning, the middle, and the end. Do not go forward until you have clearly identified these three important parts of your project.

Brief Next write one to two pages that describe in detail the point of your project: how it will be used, who the intended audience is, what the purpose is, and what you hope to achieve with the presentation. Do you want your audience to be informed about something? Motivated to do something? Emotionally moved in some way?

Treatment The next phase of the writing process fleshes out the ideas you expressed in your outline and brief. The treatment is several pages long. It contains descriptions of the characters, dialogue, and settings and describes the presentation scene by scene. Include in your treatment descriptions of the mood and the tone of your piece. If your project is a video, set the stage by describing the overall look and feel of the production.

Script   Once you've completed the first three steps, you are ready to go to script. Everything that is mentioned in the script will wind up in the audio recording or on the screen. Conversely, anything that is left out of the script will likely be overlooked and omitted from the final production. So write this document carefully.

For an audio recording, the script contains all narration, dialogue, music, and sound effects. For a video, it contains all of these elements plus descriptions of the characters, any sets, props, or costumes, plus all camera shots and movements, special visual effects, and onscreen titles or graphic elements. In short the audio script encompasses everything that is heard, and the video script covers everything that is seen and heard.

Storyboard   Last, for video productions, it's also helpful to create storyboards—simple frame-by-frame sketches with explanatory notes jotted underneath—that paint a visual picture of what the video will look like from start to finish.

Pre-production Tasks   The final stages of pre-production include assembling all the elements you will need before you begin producing your audio recording or video. Here's a general checklist.

✔ Pre-Production Checklist

Audio Tasks

- ✓ Arrange for audio recording equipment
- ✓ Cast narrator/actors
- ✓ Find music (secure permission)
- ✓ Arrange for sound effects
- ✓ Set up recording schedule
- ✓ Coordinate all cast and crew
- ✓ Arrange for transportation if needed
- ✓ Rehearse all voice talent

Video Tasks

- ✓ Arrange for video equipment (including lighting and sound recording equipment)
- ✓ Cast narrator/host/actors
- ✓ Find music (secure permission)
- ✓ Arrange for sound/visual effects
- ✓ Set up shooting schedule
- ✓ Coordinate all cast and crew
- ✓ Arrange for transportation if needed
- ✓ Set up shooting locations (secure permission)
- ✓ Arrange for costumes, props, sets
- ✓ Arrange for make-up if needed
- ✓ Rehearse all on-camera talent

Video Production Schedule Tucked into the list of pre-production tasks is "Set up recording/shooting schedule." For a video, this means much more than just deciding what day and time you will begin shooting.

During the video production phase of your project, the idea is to shoot everything that your script calls for in the final production. Often the most efficient way to do this is what is called "out-of-sequence" filming. This means that, rather than shooting scenes sequentially (that is, in the order that they appear in the script), you shoot them in the order that is most convenient. Later you will edit them together in the correct order in post-production.

For example, your video might begin and end in the main character's office. Rather than shoot the first office scene, then move the cast and crew to the next location, then later at the end of the day return to the office, it might be easier to shoot both office scenes back-to-back. This will save a great deal of time and effort involved in moving people, lights, and props back and forth.

Lighting may be a factor in the order in which you shoot your scenes. For example, scenes 3, 4, and 7 may take place in the daytime, and scenes 1, 2, 5, and 6 may take place at night.

To accommodate all of these factors, you will need to plan your shooting schedule carefully. The difference between a smooth shoot day and chaos is a well thought-out shooting schedule.

Last, for video or audio recording, it's also a good idea to assemble your team for a pre-production meeting before you begin. This is your chance to read through the script together, go over time schedules, review responsibilities of each person involved, and answer any questions or discuss potential problems before you begin the production process.

PRODUCTION

At last, it's production time! There are a number of different formats you can use for audio and video recording. Talk to the AV expert in your school or check with the media center for help in selecting the best format to use. Get tips, as well, for how to use the audio or video equipment to achieve the best results and produce a polished, professional project.

Next, if you are producing a video, think carefully about how you will shoot it. Consider the kinds of camera shots, camera moves, and special effects you will use.

Camera Shots To hold the interest of your audience, use a variety of camera shots and angles. Check your local library or media center for good books on camera techniques that describe when and how to use various shots—from long shots to close-ups, from low angles to overhead shots. As a rule, every time you change camera shots, change your angle slightly as well. This way, when the shots are edited together, you can avoid accidentally putting two nearly identical shots side-by-side, which creates an unnerving jarring motion called a "jump cut."

Do some research on framing techniques as well to make sure you frame your subjects properly and avoid cutting people's heads off on the screen.

Camera Moves Learn about ways to move the camera in order to keep your audience interested. Three common, but effective camera moves are panning, tracking, and zooming. **Panning** means moving the camera smoothly from one side of the scene to another. Panning works well in an establishing shot to help orient your audience to the setting where the action takes place.

Tracking means moving the camera from one place to another in a smooth action as well, but in tracking, the camera parallels the action, such as moving alongside a character as he or she walks down the street. It's called tracking because in professional filmmaking, the camera and the operator are rolled forward or backward on a small set of train tracks alongside the actor or actress.

Zooming means moving the camera forward or back, but zooming actually involves moving the lens, rather than the camera. By touching the zoom button, you can focus in on a small detail that you would like to emphasize, or you can pull back to reveal something in the background.

The important factor in any kind of camera move is to keep the action fluid and, in most cases, slow and steady. Also, use camera movement sparingly. You want to keep your audience eager and interested, not dizzy and sick!

Cuts Another good way to keep your presentation moving is to use frequent cuts. While the actual cuts will be done during post-production, you need to plan for them in production. Professional filmmakers use the word *coverage* for making sure they have ample choices for shots. You can create coverage for your production by planning shots such as those on the following pages.

Here are three kinds of video shots:

establishing shot — This shot sets up where the action of the story will take place. For example, if your story takes place inside an operating room, you might begin with an establishing shot of the outside of the hospital.

reaction shot — It's a good idea to get shots of all on-camera talent even if one person does not have any dialogue but is listening to, or reacting to, another character. This gives you the chance to break away from the character who is speaking to show how his or her words are affecting other people in the scene.

cutaway shot — The cutaway shot is a shot of something that is not included in the original scene, but is somehow related to it. Cutaways are used to connect two subjects. For example, the first shot may be of a person falling off a boat. The second shot could be a cutaway of a shark swimming deep below the water.

Special Effects If you are adventurous, you may want to try some simple special effects. For instance, dry ice can create smoke effects. You can also have your actors freeze; then stop the camera, remove an object from the set, and restart the camera. This technique will make objects seem to disappear as if by magic. Other effects can be achieved by using false backdrops, colored lights, and filters.

Technology Tip

You may already have video editing tools on your computer or your school's computer. Many Apple® computers and Windows™-based PCs come equipped with free video editing software. These programs are simple to use and can produce very effective videos or slide shows that are coordinated with music and narration and that feature interesting transitional elements like fades and dissolves. (See next page.) These programs also allow you to edit your video in a way that makes for easy uploading to video file-sharing sites. There are also free video editing tools online. Check out the computer you use most often to see what video tools it may have on it, and follow a tutorial to learn how to use the tool.

POST-PRODUCTION—THE MAGIC OF EDITING

Once all of your video recording is complete, it's time to create the final cut—that is, your choice of the shots you wish to keep and the shots you wish to discard. Be choosy and select the footage with only the best composition, lighting, focus, and performances to tell your story.

There are three basic editing techniques:

in-camera editing	In this process you edit as you shoot. In other words, you need to shoot all your scenes in the correct sequence and in the proper length that you want them to appear. This is the most difficult editing process because it leaves no margin for error.
insert editing	In insert editing you transfer all your footage to a new video. Then you record over any scenes that you don't want with scenes that you do want in the final version.
assemble editing	This process involves electronically copying your shots from the original source in your camera onto a new blank source, called the edited master, in the order that you want the shots to appear. This method provides the most creative control.

Consider including effects such as a dissolve from one shot to another instead of an abrupt cut. A *dissolve* is the soft fading of one shot into another. Dissolves are useful when you wish to give the impression that time has passed between two scenes. A long, slow dissolve that comes up from black into a shot, or from a shot down to black, is called a *fade* and is used to open or close a show.

In addition to assembling the program, post-production is the time to add titles to the opening of your program and credits to the end of the show. Computer programs, such as Adobe Premiere™, can help you do this. Some cameras are also equipped to generate titles. If you don't have any electronic means to produce titles, you can always mount your camera on a high tripod and focus it downward on well-lit pages of text and graphics placed on the floor. Then edit the text frames into the program.

Post-production is also the time to add voiceover narration and music. Voiceovers and background music should be recorded separately and then edited into the program on a separate sound track once the entire show is edited together. Video editing programs for your computer, such as Adobe® Premiere®, allow you to mix music and voices with your edited video.

After post-production editing, your video production is ready to present to your audience or upload to a video file-sharing site.

Publishing on the Web

You can become a part of the Web community by building and publishing a Web site of your own. In fact, you may already have a Web presence with your account on a social network such as Facebook®, which provides a medium for publishing your thoughts and linking to the sites of those you have designated as your "friends." Maybe you have even created your own social network through Ning or communicated with other members of your school on Twitter. Many businesses now have a presence in one or more social networks, appreciating the opportunity to interact wtih customers and collaborators.

Traditional Web sites, however, are still the main medium through which most organizations and businesses communicate. Web sites have universal access; the ability to use photos, illustrations, audio, and video; unlimited branching capabilities; and the ability to link with related content.

If you are going to create a Web site, take advantage of all of these features. Your goal should be to make your site interesting enough that visitors will want to stay, explore, and come back to your site again—and that takes thought and planning.

PLANNING YOUR SITE

First you need to capture your thoughts and ideas on paper before you publish anything. Start with a one-page summary that states the purpose of your Web site and the audience you hope to attract. Describe in a paragraph the look and feel you think your site will need in order to accomplish this purpose and hold your audience's attention.

Make a list of the content you plan to include in your Web site. Don't forget to consider any graphics, animation, video, or sound you may want to include.

Next go on a Web field trip. Ask your friends and teachers for the URLs of their favorite Web sites. (URL stands for Universal Resource Locator.) Visit these sites, and ask yourself, "Do I like this site? Why or why not?" Determine which sites are visually appealing to you and why. Which sites are easy to navigate and why? Chances are the sites you like best will have clean, easy-to-read layouts, be well written, contain visually stimulating graphic elements, and have intuitive **interfaces** that make it simple to find your way around.

One sure drawback in any Web site is long, uninterrupted blocks of text. Decide how to break up long passages of information into manageable sections. Will there be separate sections for editorial content? News? Humor? Feedback? Which sections will be updated periodically and how often?

Make a few rough sketches for your site. How do you envision the home page of your site? What will the icons and buttons look like? Then give careful thought to how the pages will connect to each other, starting with the home page. Your plan for connecting the pages is called a **site map**.

Because the Web is an interactive medium, navigation is critical. Decide how users will get from one page to another. Will you put in a navigation bar across the top of the page or down the side? Will there be a top or home page at the beginning of each section?

Once you have planned the content, organized your material into sections, and designed your navigation system, you are ready to begin creating Web pages.

PUTTING IT ALL TOGETHER

Writing for the Web is different from writing for print. The Web is a fast medium. Keep your messages succinct and to the point. Use short, punchy sentences. Break up your copy with clever subheads. Try not to exceed 500 to 600 words in any single article on any one page.

In order to turn text into Web pages, you need to translate the text into a special language that Web browsers can read. This language code is called HTML—HyperText Markup Language. There are three methods available:

- You can use the Save As Web Page feature in the File menu of most word-processing programs.

- You can import your text into a Web-building software program and add the code yourself if you know how.

- You can easily find free sofware programs online that will do the work for you. Web-building software programs are referred to as WYSIWYG (pronounced "Wiz-E-Wig"), which stands for "What You See Is What You Get."

Web-building software also allows you to create links to other Web pages using a simple process called **drag and drop**. Be sure to read the directions that come with your software package for complete instructions.

BLOGS

Blogs (short for weblogs) are a type of Web page. In many ways, they are like online diaries or journals, where "bloggers" post the latest events of their lives and their thoughts and feelings on a wide range of subjects. Some blogs have other purposes, such as to promote community among speakers of certain languages or to influence politics. Among the most popular blogs are those devoted to celebrity news and to animal photos with funny captions. The most popular blog software is free and easy enough to use so that anyone with Web space can build one.

B. Using the Internet

Apply Information and Technology Literacy

The "age of information" dawned in the last half of the 20th century. Success in the 21st century requires the ability to access, evaluate, and wisely use the abundance of information made available by advances in technology. Developing an understanding of the changing technologies and skill in putting them to work for your purposes are key competencies for the rest of your schooling and for your adult life ahead.

In this section, you will develop your skills for understanding and making the most of what the Internet has to offer.

How Does the Internet Work?

The Internet is made up of thousands of networks all linked together around the globe. Each network consists of a group of computers that are connected to one another to exchange information. If one of these computers or networks fails, the information simply bypasses the disabled system and takes another route through a different network. This rerouting is why the Internet is so valuable to agencies such as the U.S. Department of Defense.

No one "owns" the Internet, nor is it managed in a central place. No agency regulates or censors the information on the Internet. Anyone can publish information on the Internet as he or she wishes.

In fact, the Internet offers such a vast wealth of information and experiences that sometimes it is described as the Information Superhighway. So how do you "get on" this highway? It's easy. Once you have a computer, a modem, and a telephone or cable line, all you need is a connection to the Internet.

THE CYBERSPACE CONNECTION

A company called an Internet Service Provider (ISP) connects your computer to the Internet. Examples of ISPs that provide direct access are Microsoft

Network, Earthlink, Comcast, and AT&T. You can also get on the Internet indirectly through companies such as America Online (AOL).

ISPs charge a flat monthly fee for their service. Unlike the telephone company, once you pay the monthly ISP fee, there are no long-distance charges for sending or receiving information on the Internet—no matter where your information is coming from, or going to, around the world.

ALPHABET SOUP—MAKING SENSE OF ALL THOSE LETTERS

Like physical highways, the Information Superhighway has road signs that help you find your way around. Each specific group of information on the World Wide Web is called a **Web site** and has its own unique address. Think of it as a separate street address of a house in your neighborhood. This address is called the URL, which stands for Uniform Resource Locator. It's a kind of shorthand for where the information is located on the Web.

Here's a typical URL: **http://www.perfectionlearning.com.**

All addresses, or URLs, for the World Wide Web begin with **http://.** This stands for HyperText Transfer Protocol and is a programming description of how the information is exchanged.

The next three letters—**www**—let you know you are on the World Wide Web. The next part of the URL—**perfectionlearning**—is the name of the site you want to visit. The last three letters, in this case **com**, indicate that this Web site is sponsored by a **com**mercial company. Here are other common endings of URLs you will find:

- "org" is short for **org**anization, as in http://www.ipl.org, which is the URL of the Web site for the Internet Public Library, ipl²: Information You Can Trust.
- "edu" stands for **edu**cation, as in the Web address for the Virtual Reference Desk, http://thorplus.lib.purdue.edu/reference/index.html, featuring online telephone books, dictionaries, and other reference guides.
- "gov" represents **gov**ernment-sponsored Web sites, such as http://www.whitehouse.gov, the Web site for the White House in Washington, D.C.

To get to a Web site, you use an interface called a **browser**. Two popular browsers are Microsoft Internet Explorer® and Mozilla Firefox®. A browser is like a blank form where you fill in the information you are looking for. If you know the URL of the Web site you want to explore, all you have to do is type it in the field marked Location, click Enter on your keyboard, and wait for the information to be delivered to your computer screen.

BASIC INTERNET TERMINOLOGY

Here are some of the most frequently used words you will hear associated with the Internet.

address	The unique code given to information on the Internet. This may also refer to an e-mail address.
bookmark	A tool that lets you store your favorite URL addresses, allowing you one-click access to your favorite Web pages without retyping the URL each time.
browser	Application software that supplies a graphical interactive interface for searching, finding, viewing, and managing information on the Internet.
chat	Real-time conferencing over the Internet.
cookies	A general mechanism that some Web sites use both to store and to retrieve information on the visitor's hard drive. Users have the option to refuse or accept cookies.
cyberspace	The collective realm of computer-aided communication.
download	The transfer of programs or data stored on a remote computer, usually from a server, to a storage device on your personal computer.
e-mail	Electronic mail that can be sent all over the world from one computer to another.
FAQs	The abbreviation for Frequently Asked Questions. This is usually a great resource to get information when visiting a new Web site.
flaming	Using mean or abusive language in cyberspace. Flaming is considered to be in extremely poor taste and may be reported to your ISP.
FTP	The abbreviation for File Transfer Protocol. A method of transferring files to and from a computer connected to the Internet.
home page	The start-up page of a Web site.

HTML	The abbreviation for HyperText Markup Language—a "tag" language used to create most Web pages, which your browser interprets to display those pages. Often the last set of letters found at the end of a Web address.
http	The abbreviation for HyperText Transfer Protocol. This is how documents are transferred from the Web site or server to the browsers of individual personal computers.
ISP	The abbreviation for Internet Service Provider—a company that, for a fee, connects a user's computer to the Internet.
keyword	A simplified term that serves as subject reference when doing a search.
link	Short for hyperlink. A link is a connection between one piece of information and another.
network	A system of interconnected computers.
online	To "be online" means to be connected to the Internet via a live modem connection.
plug-in	Free application that can be downloaded off the Internet to enhance your browser's capabilities.
podcast	An audio or video file on the Internet that is available for downloading to a personal media device.
real time	Information received and processed (or displayed) as it happens.
RSS	A format for distributing content to people or Web sites. It stands for "Really Simple Syndication." With an RSS "feed," users can get updates from sites of interest without having to go to the sites for the information.
search engine	A computer program that locates documents based on keywords that the user enters.
server	A provider of resources, such as a file server.
site	A specific place on the Internet, usually a set of pages on the World Wide Web.
social network	An online community of people who share interests and activities, usually based on the Web.

spam	Electronic junk mail.
surf	A casual reference to browsing on the Internet. To "surf the Web" means to spend time discovering and exploring new Web sites.
upload	The transfer of programs or data from a storage device on your personal computer to another remote computer.
URL	The abbreviation for Uniform Resource Locator. This is the address for an Internet resource, such as a World Wide Web page. Each Web page has its own unique URL.
Web 2.0	The so-called second generation of the World Wide Web, which promotes programming that encourages interaction and collaboration.
Web site	A page of information or a collection of pages that is being electronically published from one of the computers in the World Wide Web.
Wiki	Technology that holds together a number of user-generated web pages focused on a theme, project, or collaboration. Wikipedia is the most famous example. The word *wiki* means "quick" in Hawaiian.
WWW	The abbreviation for the World Wide Web. A network of computers within the Internet capable of delivering multimedia content (images, audio, video, and animation) as well as text over communication lines into personal computers all over the globe.

Communicating on the Internet

E-mail, mailing lists, and newsgroups are all great ways of exchanging information with other people on the Internet. Here's how to use these useful forms of communication, step-by-step.

① Using E-mail

Any writer who has ever used e-mail in his or her work will agree that sending and receiving electronic messages is one of the most useful ways of gathering information and contacts for writing projects.

Once you open your e-mail program, click on the command that says Compose Mail or New Message. This will open a new blank e-mail similar to the one pictured below. Next, fill in the blanks.

Type the person's e-mail address here. There is no central listing of e-mail addresses. If you don't have the person's address, the easiest way to get it is to call and ask the person for it. You can address an e-mail to one or several people, depending on the number of addresses you type in this space.

Cc stands for courtesy copy. If you type additional e-mail addresses in this area, you can send a copy of the message to other people.

Bcc stands for blind courtesy copy. By typing one or more e-mail addresses here, you can send a copy of the message to others without the original recipient knowing that other people have received the same message. Not all e-mail programs have this feature.

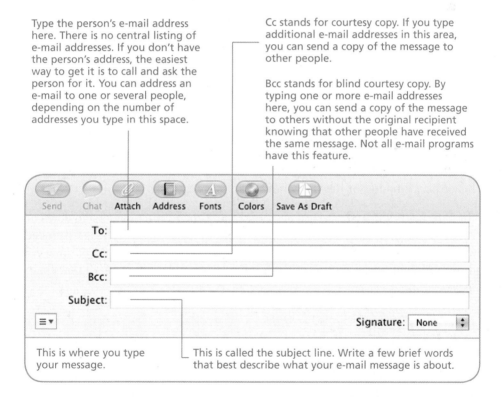

This is where you type your message.

This is called the subject line. Write a few brief words that best describe what your e-mail message is about.

SAY IT WITH STYLE

Like regular letters, e-mail can assume different tones and styles, depending on to whom you are writing. Usually informal e-mails and instant messages (IMs) to close friends are light, brief, and to the point. In the case of more formal e-mails, such as a request for information from an expert or a museum, keep the following guidelines in mind.

Guidelines for Writing E-mails

- Make sure your message is clear and concise.
- Use proper grammar and punctuation.
- Check your spelling. (Some e-mail programs have their own spell-check function—use it!)
- Double-check the person's e-mail address to be sure you've typed it correctly.

ATTACH A LITTLE SOMETHING EXTRA

When you send e-mail, you can also send other information along with your message. These are called **attachments**. Depending on your e-mail program's capabilities, you can attach documents, photos, illustrations—even sound and video files. Click Attach, and then find and double-click on the document or file on your computer that you wish to send.

After you have composed your message and added any attachments you want to include, click the Send button. Your message arrives in the other person's mailbox seconds later, regardless of whether that person lives right next door or on the other side of the world.

FOLLOW UP

Just because you have sent a message, you shouldn't automatically assume that the other person has received it. Internet Service Providers (ISPs) keep all messages that are sent until the recipient requests them. The person you sent your e-mail to might be away from his or her computer or may not check messages regularly.

Also, the Internet is still an imperfect science. From time to time, servers go down or other "hiccups" in electronic transmissions can occur, leaving your message stranded somewhere in cyberspace. If you don't get a reply in a reasonable amount of time, either resend your original e-mail message or call the person and let him or her know that your message is waiting.

YOU'VE GOT MAIL

When someone sends you an e-mail message, you have several options:

Reply Click Reply, and you can automatically send back a new message without having to retype the person's e-mail address. (Be sure you keep a copy of the sender's e-mail address in your Address Book for future use.)

Forward Suppose you receive a message that you would like to share with someone else. Click Forward, and you can send a copy of the message, plus include a few of your own comments, to another person.

Print In some instances, you may need to have a paper copy of the e-mail message. For example, if someone e-mails you directions to a party, click Print to take a hard copy of the instructions with you.

Store Do you want to keep a message to refer to later? Some e-mail programs allow you to create folders to organize stored messages.

Delete You can discard a message you no longer need just by clicking Delete. It's a good idea to throw messages away regularly to keep them from accumulating in your mailbox.

❷ Other Online Communication

Another way to communicate online is Internet Relay Chat (IRC), or "chat rooms" for short. Chat rooms focus on a large variety of topics, so it's possible you'll be able to find a chat room where people are discussing the subject you are writing about.

"Chat" is similar to talking on the telephone except, instead of speaking, the people in the chat room type their responses back and forth to each other. As soon as you type your comment, it immediately appears on the computer screen of every person involved in the "conversation." There are also more advanced forms of chat available on the Net, such as video chat and voice chat.

One-to-one chatting, or instant messaging, is probably something you do frequently. With instant messaging, you need to "accept" as a buddy or contact each person you will communicate with.

In contrast, anyone in a chat room can talk to you, and the anonymous nature of a chat room can make people less inhibited than they might otherwise be in person. If you sense that one of the participants in your chat room is responding inappropriately, ask your parents or teacher to step in, or simply sign off.

Join the Group

Mailing lists and newsgroups are larger discussion forums that can help you get even more information about a specific subject.

Mailing Lists To find a directory of available mailing lists, enter "mailing list directory" in a search engine. If you find a mailing list that interests you and wish to subscribe to it, just send a message to the administrative address. You will start to receive messages from the mailing list within a few days.

Remember, mailing lists use e-mail to communicate, so be sure to check your e-mail often because once you subscribe to a list, it's possible to receive dozens of messages in a matter of days.

Another good idea is to read the messages in your new mailing list for a week or so before submitting a message of your own. This will give you a good idea of what has already been discussed so you can be considerate about resubmitting old information.

You can reply to a message any time you wish. However, it doesn't do anyone any good to respond by saying "Yes, I agree." Get in the habit of replying to messages only when you have something important to add. Also, be sure to repeat the original question in your reply so that people understand which message you are responding to.

Be sure that you really want to belong to a mailing list before you subscribe. Unwanted e-mail can be a nuisance. Fortunately, if you change your mind, you can always unsubscribe to mailing lists at any time.

Newsgroups To join a newsgroup, check with your ISP. Service providers frequently list available topics under the heading "Newsgroups." Newsgroups are named with two or more words separated by a period. For example, there is a newsgroup named rec.sport.baseball. college. The first three letters—"rec"—defines the main subject, in this case recreation. Each word that follows—sport, baseball, and college—narrows the scope of the subject to an increasingly more specific area of interest.

As with mailing lists, you can always unsubscribe to newsgroups at any time.

As in any social setting, there are a few guidelines to follow when you are talking to people online—via e-mail, in a chat room, or in a newsgroup. This conduct is called **netiquette**. Netiquette requires that you refrain from harsh or insulting language and from writing in all uppercase letters, which can feel like shouting. It requires you to respect other people's privacy, ideas, and work. Don't forward a message or attach documents written by someone else without first asking the author's permission. Don't send spam, unwanted messages for the purpose of selling something.

Online Collaboration and Web 2.0

The Web is always changing. One big change from its earliest days is the ease with which people can collaborate online. For example, your writing group could use Google Docs (http://docs.google.com) to work together on writing projects: to share drafts, to edit your peers' work, and to set schedules and guidelines. Through Google Docs, everyone who is invited to do so can have access to documents and edit them online.

Another useful tool for collaboration is the **wiki**, a platform for creating linked pages on a common theme or for a common project. Wikipedia is the best known example. You can start your own free wiki at wiki.com and explore how you can use it in your learning.

Cyberbullying

More than half of teenagers recently surveyed reported that they have been the victim of online bullying, also called cyberbullying, or known someone who has been. **Cyberbullying** is the use of such technology as the Internet and cell phones to deliberately hurt or embarrass someone. Cyberbullies often assume fake identities to trick people. They also knowingly spread lies and often post pictures of someone without his or her permission. Cyberbullies can trick their victims into revealing personal information which is then abused.

Victims react in different ways. Some take such reasonable measures as blocking an offending user or refusing to read comments that might be hurtful and deleting them as soon as they arrive. Some seek help from adults, who sometimes help the victim report the problem to the appropriate authorities. Other teens have a more negative and painful reaction. They might withdraw from their usual pastimes and suffer from problems with self-esteem. Or they might get caught up in the negative swirl and try to bully back.

The National Crime Prevention Council (NCPC) makes these suggestions to teens to stop cyberbullying.

- Refuse to pass along cyberbullying messages.
- Tell friends to stop cyberbullying.
- Block communication with cyberbullies.
- Report cyberbullying to a trusted adult.

The NCPC developed a slogan to summarize what to do: "Delete cyberbullying. Don't write it. Don't forward it."

Unit 4

Grammar

Suppose you came across three puzzle pieces, each with a word written on it. One piece has *saw*; one has *him*; and the third has *I*. You would have little doubt how to put those pieces together to form a sentence everyone would understand. The reason that *I saw him* is the only order that makes sense is because of the common grammar you share with others who speak English. Each word plays a distinctive role in communicating a message. Grammar explains how those pieces fit together.

No one should ever have to read a sentence twice because of the way it is put together. — *Wilson Follett*

The Sentence

How can you use sentences to paint powerful images and to tell interesting stories?

The Sentence: Pretest 1

The following draft paragraph is hard to read because it contains several sentence errors. Revise the paragraph so that it reads more smoothly. The first error has been corrected as an example.

> Frida Kahlo was born in 1907 in Mexico in 1925, she was in a bus accident. Her spine and many other bones were broken. Her injuries caused her extreme pain. For the rest of her life. Kahlo was often alone as she recovered from the accident. This is why she often painted her own portrait. She used personal elements, Such as her pets, to show a side of herself. She chose other elements to set the mood, such as neutral tones to show strength and the ability to survive difficult circumstances.

The Sentence: Pretest 2

Directions

Write the letter of the term that identifies the underlined words in each sentence.

1. The largest salt-water lake is the Caspian Sea.

2. The South Pole and the North Pole are both icy.

3. Land and ice form the South Pole.

4. The North Pole is not land but is floating ice.

5. From out of Egypt flows the Nile River.

6. The tallest mountain in the world.

7. Mauna Loa in Hawaii is known as the biggest active volcano.

8. Hot deserts cover parts of northern Africa but yield to lush forests further south.

9. Look at this map of the Ganges River in India.

10. The Ganges River possesses the widest delta of all rivers.

1. **A** simple subject
   B simple predicate
   C complete subject
   D complete predicate

2. **A** compound subject
   B compound verb
   C verb phrase
   D inverted order

3. **A** complete subject
   B verb phrase
   C compound verb
   D complete predicate

4. **A** complete subject
   B simple subject
   C compound subject
   D complete predicate

5. **A** simple subject
   B inverted order
   C complete predicate
   D natural order

6. **A** sentence fragment
   B complete subject
   C simple subject
   D inverted order

7. **A** complete predicate
   B verb phrase
   C compound subject
   D compound verb

8. **A** complete predicate
   B inverted order
   C verb phrase
   D compound verb

9. **A** sentence fragment
   B complete subject
   C imperative sentence
   D complete predicate

10. **A** simple subject
    B simple predicate
    C verb phrase
    D inverted order

Before you even knew what a sentence was, you were talking in sentences. As you listened to conversations, you learned to organize your words into a variety of sentences, too. You learned how to ask for things and how to tell about things. With practice you mastered the ability to communicate your complete thoughts to other people.

13 A   **A sentence is a group of words that expresses a complete thought.**

> I ate a pizza for lunch today.
>
> I had carrots and ranch dressing for a snack.
>
> Jessie gave me a glass of lemonade.

The preceding examples are sentences. Because these sentences express a complete thought, they will all be easily understood by anyone who hears them. Once in a while, of course, everyone includes an incomplete thought or two in writing or conversation.

13 A.1   A group of words that expresses an incomplete thought is called a **sentence fragment.**

Because a fragment is only a part of a sentence, some of the meaning of the sentence is lost, and listeners can misunderstand what is being said. The following groups of words are sentence fragments.

> Regina had.
>
> Not quite enough.
>
> Brownies.

To form a complete sentence, you need to add the missing information.

> Regina had soup and salad.
>
> She said that it was not quite enough.
>
> Tomorrow she will bring brownies.

Listen to the informal conversations that take place at school and at home. You will notice that people use sentence fragments all the time. Indeed, it would seem odd if they didn't use fragments. On the other hand, when people speak or write formally, they use complete sentences to make their meaning clear.

Informal	Great pizza!
Formal	I think pizza is a delicious and healthful food.

Revise a short story or play you have worked on recently. Include sentence fragments to make the dialogue sound authentic. Be sure to avoid fragments in your formal writing, however.

You can learn more about sentence fragments on pages 656–661.

● Practice Your Skills

Recognizing Sentences

Label each group of words *S* if it is a sentence or *F* if it is a sentence fragment.

1. Eating a healthful breakfast.

2. Green vegetables include broccoli, string beans, peas, and lettuce.

3. Nutrients are necessary for your body.

4. Your body grows.

5. Amount of energy.

6. Try to eat a balanced diet.

7. Foods belong in five basic food groups.

8. Milk, yogurt, and cheese.

9. You should not eat a lot of sweets.

10. Good snack foods.

● *Connect to Writing:* Revising

Completing Sentences

Add information to create sentences out of four of the sentence fragments above. Be sure to begin each sentence with a capital letter and to end it with a punctuation mark.

13 B   The **subject** of a sentence names the person, place, thing, or idea that the sentence is about.

➤ Complete Subjects

In the exercise on the preceding page, some subjects—such as *green vegetables*—have more than one word. These subjects are **complete subjects.**

13 B.1   A **complete subject** includes all words used to identify the person, place, thing, or idea that the sentence is about.

To find a complete subject, ask yourself either, *Who or what is doing something?* or *About whom or what is some statement being made?*

> ┌──complete subject──┐
> **The birds in our backyard** fly from tree to tree.
> (*The birds in our backyard* is the complete subject.)

> ┌──complete subject──┐
> **The birds' nest in the yard** is filled with baby birds.
> (*The birds' nest in the yard* is the complete subject.)

➤ Simple Subjects

Within each complete subject, there is one main word that clearly answers either *Who or what is doing something?* or *About whom or what is some statement being made?* This main word is called the **simple subject.**

13 B.2   A **simple subject** is the main word in the complete subject.

In these examples, the complete subject is in bold type; the simple subject is underlined.

> **The <u>author</u> of my favorite book** talked at the conference.
> (Who or what is doing something? The simple subject is *author*.)
> **The first <u>speaker</u>** wrote many nonfiction books.
> (Who or what is doing something? The simple subject is *speaker*.)
> **<u>Grant's Used Bookstore</u> on Brooks Road** is closed on holidays. (*Grant's Used Bookstore* is the simple subject. All three words are considered the name of one place.)

A complete subject and a simple subject can be the same.

> **Katharine** writes in her journal every day.
>
> **Everyone** read the assignment about whales.

Throughout the rest of this book, the simple subject will be called *the subject*.

● Practice Your Skills

Finding Complete and Simple Subjects

Write each complete subject. Then underline each simple subject.

1. People have been writing for a long time.
2. Writers found different useful surfaces to write on.
3. The ancient Egyptians made paper from reeds.
4. The fresh, flat reeds were pressed together.
5. Colonial Americans used parchment for important records.
6. The parchment for the Bill of Rights was made from linen fibers.
7. Modern paper is made from wood pulp.
8. Each new decade of science brings new and improved materials.
9. Computers are very important today.
10. Many writers rely heavily on the computer.

● *Connect to Writing:* Drafting

Writing Complete Sentences

Add a complete subject to each sentence.

1. _____ is going to the library after school.
2. _____ is across the street from the grocery store.
3. _____ has a supply of magazines and newspapers.
4. _____ can be used for a research project.
5. _____ hook up to the Internet.

● *Connect to Writing:* Book Review

Using Complete and Simple Subjects

Write a review of a favorite book. In your review, praise the book and recommend it to your classmates. Remember to briefly describe the main character, the setting, and the plot. Consider using the book title as the complete subject of your first sentence.

13 C   The **predicate** tells something about the subject.

➤ Complete Predicates

To express a complete thought, a sentence must have a subject and a predicate.

13 C.1   A **complete predicate** includes all the words that tell what the subject is doing or tell something about the subject.

To find a complete predicate, first find the subject. Then ask yourself, *What is the subject doing?* or *What is being said about the subject?*

┌complete predicate┐
Dinosaurs **roamed the earth.** (The subject is *dinosaurs*. What did the dinosaurs do? *Roamed the earth* is the complete predicate.)

┌────────────complete predicate────────────┐
Mario **visited the dinosaur exhibit at the museum.** (The subject is *Mario*. What is being said about Mario? *Visited the dinosaur exhibit at the museum* is the complete predicate.)

➤ Simple Predicates

13 C.2   A **simple predicate,** also called a **verb,** is the main word or phrase in the complete predicate.

Within each complete predicate, there is one main word or phrase that tells something about the subject or tells what the subject is doing. This main word or phrase is called the **simple predicate,** or **verb.**

Verbs that tell what a subject is doing are **action verbs.** Action verbs can show physical action, mental action, or ownership. In the following examples, the complete predicates are in **bold** type, and the simple predicates, or verbs, are underlined twice.

My brother **takes terrific photographs.** (What is the main word in the complete predicate? What does the subject do? The simple predicate is *takes*.)

Marisa **dreamed about the photography contest.** (What is the main word in the complete predicate? What did the subject do? The simple predicate is *dreamed*.)

Some verbs do not show action. These verbs tell something about a subject. The following common verb forms are used to make a statement about a subject.

COMMON VERBS THAT MAKE STATEMENTS

| am | is | are | was | were |

The film **is on the table.**

His camera lens **was a gift from his grandmother.**

Just as a complete and simple subject can be the same, so can a complete predicate and a simple predicate.

The camera **broke.**

The lens **froze.**

You can learn about subject and verb agreement in Chapter 25.

When You Speak and Write

When you speak or write, use verbs that will make your ideas exciting and interesting. If possible, use action verbs rather than verbs that make a statement. Notice the difference among the verbs in the following sentences.

The flash of the camera **is** bright. (verb that makes statement)

The flash of the camera **blinded** me. (action verb)

The flash of the camera **startled** me. (action verb)

The verbs *blinded* and *startled* paint a much clearer picture than the verb *is*.

Select a piece of writing from your portfolio. Underline the verbs in three of the paragraphs. Revise two sentences that have verbs that make statements by replacing them with action verbs.

● Practice Your Skills

Finding Complete Predicates and Verbs

Write each complete predicate. Then underline each verb.

1. Your eyes have features like those of a camera.
2. The iris is a kind of shutter.
3. An automatic light meter controls the shutter.
4. The shutter opens wide in darkness.
5. It becomes very small in bright light.
6. The lens serves as a color filter.
7. The lens filters certain colors.
8. An eye changes its focus from near to far.
9. The cornea serves as a cover for the eye.
10. The eyelids and tears clean the cornea.

● *Connect to Writing:* Revising

Using Vivid Verbs

Rewrite the following sentences, replacing each verb with a more vivid verb.

1. At the gallery I saw photographs by Ansel Adams.
2. His photographs show images in black and white.
3. His photographs show the power found in stillness.
4. He created a new procedure for photographers.
5. Adams mixed technology, nature, and spirit.
6. He used filtration for dramatic contrasts in his photographs.

● *Connect to Writing:* Prewriting

Using Vivid Verbs

The fifth graders at a neighborhood school are holding a dance contest. You and several of your classmates have been asked to judge the contest. Write a description of the best dance for the other judges. Use vivid verbs in your description.

 # Verb Phrases

13 C.3   A **verb phrase** includes the main verb plus any helping, or auxiliary, verbs.

Helping Verbs

Sometimes a verb needs the help of other verbs, which are called **helping verbs,** or **auxiliary verbs.** Here is a list of common helping verbs.

COMMON HELPING VERBS	
Be	am, is, are, was, were, be, being, been
Have	has, have, had
Do	do, does, did
Others	may, might, must, can, could, shall, should, will, would

The verb phrases in the following examples are underlined twice. The helping verbs are in bold type.

> The artist **is** painting the colorful landscape today.
>
> The artist **will be** sketching pictures of the hills.

You can learn about subject and verb agreement with verb phrases on pages 741–742.

● **Practice Your Skills**

Finding Verb Phrases

Write each verb phrase.

1. Artists are sharing their thoughts and feelings about their subjects.
2. An artist could be drawing an imaginary scene.
3. Some artists have planned one painting for several years.
4. These artists will read a history of a place.
5. A few ambitious painters will live in the place.
6. New sculptors should begin with a good teacher.
7. They will learn the techniques of the masters.
8. Teachers may ask their students questions about their subject.
9. New artists will learn about line, color, and space.
10. Any good teacher will demand hard work.

Interrupted Verb Phrases

A verb phrase is often interrupted by one or more words. The verb phrases in the following examples are in **bold** type.

We **should** never **have crossed** that desert.

Some vegetables **will** not **grow** well in the desert.

To find the verb phrase in a question, turn the question around to make a statement.

Have people **discovered** oil and natural gas beneath some deserts?

(People *have discovered* oil and natural gas beneath some deserts.)

Throughout the rest of this book, a verb phrase will be called a verb.

When You Write

Not and its contraction *n't* are never part of a verb phrase.

That camel **did** not **stop** at the oasis.

That camel **did**n't **stop** at the oasis.

When you are writing formally, avoid using the contraction *n't*. You can use it in speaking or in informal writing, however.

You can learn more about contractions on pages 743 and 883–884.

● Practice Your Skills

Finding Verb Phrases

Write each verb phrase.

1. Camels are often used for desert travel.

2. Camels can travel for days with little food or water.

3. The hump on a camel's back is used for fat storage.

4. Arabian camels will often eat thorny plants.

5. They can carry heavy supplies.

6. A camel might live 40 years.

7. Camels have traveled up to 25 miles in one day.

8. They will hardly ever act obstinate.

9. Have you ever ridden a camel?

10. Nomads didn't build permanent homes in the desert.

11. Early people could not live in deserts for very long.

12. Some Indians had settled in the Sonoran Desert.

13. They were soon learning techniques for good crops.

14. These Indians would sometimes dig canals with sticks and poles.

15. The canals would carry water to the settlements.

● *Connect to Writing:* **Narrative Paragraph**

Using Verbs

Imagine that you have just returned from a trip through a desert.

1) Write a list of verbs that will tell your friends about your experiences. The verbs should tell them what you did.

2) Use your list of verbs to write a paragraph for your friends about your trip. Describe your experiences in the order they happened. Brainstorm answers to the following questions before writing your first draft.

• Which desert did you visit? Where is it?

• What did you do first? What was your impression of this experience?

• What did you do second? Why was this experience important?

• What was the most amazing feature of the desert? Why?

3) When you have finished, underline the verbs.

CHAPTER 13

☑ *Check Point:* **Mixed Practice**

Write the subject and verb in each sentence.

1. Insects have great strength.

2. An ant, for example, moved a stone fifty-two times its own weight.

3. A beetle carried something on its back 850 times its own weight.

4. A person with similar strength could do great things.

5. Such an individual could probably pull a 14,000-pound trailer truck.

6. Scientists haven't overlooked the other unusual feats of insects either.

7. A mosquito can carry something twice as heavy as itself.

8. Some insects can fly hundreds of miles nonstop.

9. Butterflies in large swarms have flown from the United States to the island of Bermuda.

10. Sailors have also seen insects far out at sea.

The subject of a sentence is not always in the same place. Sometimes it comes before the verb and sometimes it comes after the verb. Sometimes the subject does not appear in the sentence. In this case the subject is understood.

Natural Order and Inverted Order

13 D   A sentence is in **natural order** when the subject comes before the verb. When the verb or part of the verb phrase comes before the subject, the sentence is in **inverted order.**

In the examples of natural order below, each subject is underlined once, and each verb is underlined twice.

> The Civil War lasted from 1861 until 1865.
>
> This war caused many deaths.

To find the subject in a sentence in inverted order, turn the sentence around to its natural order.

> **Inverted Order**   From deep in the forest appeared the soldiers.
>
> **Natural Order**   The soldiers appeared from deep in the forest.
>
> **Inverted Order**   Out of the dark night roared the thunder of a cannon.
>
> **Natural Order**   The thunder of a cannon roared out of the dark night.

Questions are usually written in inverted order. To find the subject easily in a question, change the question into a statement.

> **Question**   Did differences arise between the North and the South?
>
> **Statement**   Differences did arise between the North and the South.
>
> **Question**   Was the North a place of large cities?
>
> **Statement**   The North was a place of large cities.

CHAPTER 13

Sentences beginning with **there** or **here** followed by *is, are, was, were,* or another form of the verb *be* are also in inverted order. To find the subject easily in such a sentence, turn it around to its natural order.

Inverted Order	Here is an artifact from the Civil War.
Natural Order	An artifact from the Civil War is here.
Inverted Order	There is a Civil War museum in Gettysburg, Pennsylvania.
Natural Order	A Civil War museum is in Gettysburg, Pennsylvania. (Sometimes *there* must be dropped for the sentence to make sense.)

You can learn about subject and verb agreement with inverted order on pages 746–748.

● **Practice Your Skills**

Finding Subjects and Verbs

Write the subject and verb in each sentence.

1. For what reasons was the Civil War important?

2. There are economic, political, social, and emotional reasons.

3. Here is an explanation of the conflict.

4. From the fighting came great devastation to the South's agriculture.

5. Did many people in the South survive starvation?

6. In the North were the winners with a strong industrial economy.

7. To the South moved some Northerners after the end of the war.

8. How did the free African Americans feel?

9. For all Americans there was the powerful federal government.

10. After four years of conflict came a time of reconstruction.

● *Connect to Writing:* **Persuasive Paragraph**

Varying the Positions of Subjects

The year is 1861, and Abraham Lincoln is president of the United States. You are a Northern industrialist. You want to convince a Southern plantation owner that slavery should no longer be allowed. Write a paragraph that expresses your belief. Try to persuade the Southern plantation owner to agree with you. In your argument be sure to vary the position of the subjects of your sentences to keep the owner's interest.

Varying Sentence Beginnings

Add interest to the following paragraph by changing five sentences into inverted order.

> Seven states had left the United States of America by March 1861. They formed the Confederate States of America. The Confederate soldiers used cannons on Fort Sumter. President Abraham Lincoln declared war. He called up troops to save the United States. Four more states in the South joined the Confederacy. Many leaders on both sides thought the South could win the war. These leaders saw divisions in the country. Four slave states did not leave the union. Their citizens were divided during the Civil War. Both sides incorrectly predicted a short war.

➤ Understood Subjects

13 D.1   When the subject of a sentence is not stated, the subject is an **understood *you.***

The subject *you* is not stated in a command or a request.

Command   (**you**) Wait for me in the library.

Request   (**you**) Please check out that book for me.

● Practice Your Skills

Finding Subjects and Verbs

Write the subject and verb in each sentence. If the subject is an understood *you*, write *you* in parentheses.

1. Get ready for the modern public library.

2. Please follow me on a tour.

3. The public library offers a variety of adventures.

4. May I first display the nonprint media?

5. Look at the videotapes, DVD, and microfilm.

6. Please click on the computer's database.

7. Do the icons identify clearly the library's holdings?

8. Take a right turn for the books and magazines.

9. Please enjoy the fun of listening and viewing.

10. Look for biographies behind the nonfiction section.

Using the Understood You

Rewrite the following instructions using the understood *you.*

> First, you should decide on a research subject. Then, you look at the title of the book. You find the year of publication on the back of the title page. Next, you should read the table of contents. You can note the length of the chapters on your subject. You might also look at the list of the book's topics in the index. Then you can often read about the author. Last, you can make a decision about the usefulness of the book.

✔ *Check Point:* Mixed Practice

Write the subject and verb in each sentence. If the subject is an understood *you,* write *you* in parentheses.

1. Have you ever given a speech?

2. Try it sometime.

3. There are many opportunities for speeches.

4. Do not think of the experience as difficult or scary.

5. To many speakers it is a thrill.

6. Prepare your information.

7. Practice your delivery.

8. At the end of the speech is a sense of accomplishment.

9. There is a speaker somewhere inside you.

10. Will you make a speech next week?

Power Your Writing: Let It Flow

Good writing flows smoothly sentence to sentence; it has **fluency.** Read "The Fixed" by Annie Dillard on pages 85–86. Notice how the sentences move fluidly from one description to the next. Dillard varies the patterns of her sentences by structuring them differently. Revise a piece of writing you completed recently by following the hints below.

- Use sentences of various lengths and types.
- Repeat important words from one sentence to the next.
- Don't begin every sentence with the subject.

Sometimes sentences contain more than one subject and/or more than one predicate.

➤ Compound Subjects and Predicates

13 E A **compound subject** is two or more subjects in one sentence that have the same verb and are joined by a conjunction. A **compound predicate** is two or more verbs that have the same subject and are joined by a conjunction.

In the following examples, each subject is underlined once and each verb is underlined twice. Compound subjects can have two, three, or even more subjects.

One Subject	Sacajawea joined the expedition.
Compound Subject	Lewis **and** Clark explored the West.
Compound Subject	Sacajawea, Lewis, **and** Clark traded horses with the Shoshone.

A pair of conjunctions such as *either/or, neither/nor,* or *both/and* may also join the parts of a compound subject.

Either Lewis **or** Clark had brought supplies.

You can learn about subject and verb agreement with compound subjects on pages 749–750.

When You Write

Writers often combine two short sentences that have the same verb. The new sentence will have a compound subject. Combining sentences makes writing flow smoothly.

Separate	**Lewis** traveled into new territory. **Clark** traveled into new territory.
Combined	**Lewis** and **Clark** traveled into new territory.

Review a piece of writing you completed recently. Combine short sentences that have the same verb, creating a sentence with a compound subject.

CHAPTER 13

Finding Compound Subjects

Write each compound subject. Remember that the conjunction is not part of a compound subject.

1. Meriwether Lewis and William Clark led an expedition.

2. President Jefferson and Congress sponsored the trip in 1804.

3. Science, profit, and politics motivated the planners.

4. Neither Lewis nor Clark would go alone across the country.

5. New places and dangers challenged them.

Connect to Writing: Revising

Writing Sentences with Compound Subjects

Combine each pair of sentences into one sentence with a compound subject. Use *and* or *or* to connect your subjects.

1. Meriwether Lewis had served in the army. William Clark also was in the military.

2. Plants were studied. Animals were studied.

3. The Missouri River was explored. The Yellowstone River was explored, too.

4. The Rocky Mountains were crossed. The Cascade Range was crossed.

5. The Mandan people helped the expedition. The Shoshone also helped.

In the examples below, each subject is underlined once, and each verb in the predicate is underlined twice.

One Verb   The <u>rabbit</u> <u>ate</u> the food.

Compound Verb   The <u>rabbit</u> <u>ate</u> the food **and** <u>hopped</u> away.

A sentence can include both a compound subject and a compound verb.

The <u>rabbit</u> **and** the <u>squirrel</u> <u>scampered</u> away **and** <u>searched</u> for food.

Writers often combine two short sentences that have the same subject to make their writing smoother. The following sentences were combined with a compound verb.

Separate	The squirrel **looked** around cautiously. The squirrel quickly **scurried** up the tree.
Combined	The squirrel **looked** around cautiously and quickly **scurried** up the tree.

Review a piece of writing you completed recently. Combine short sentences that have the same subject, creating a sentence with a compound verb.

● **Practice Your Skills**

Finding Compound Verbs

Write each verb. Remember that a conjunction is not part of a compound verb.

1. A school science project requires careful observation but prohibits dangerous experiments.
2. One eighth grader chose her pet, focused on nutrition, and wrote a hypothesis.
3. Nailah watched and collected data on her pet rabbit Brad.
4. For three weeks she carefully measured and recorded Brad's food.
5. The baby rabbit ate quickly and did not see Nailah.

● *Connect to Writing:* **Revising**

Writing Sentences with Compound Predicates

Combine each pair of sentences into one sentence with a compound verb. Use *and, or,* or *but* to connect verbs.

1. Scientists perform their own experiments. Scientists observe the results.
2. They set up controls for their experiments. They test their hypotheses.
3. Scientists take notes. They write down their observations.
4. Some scientists mix chemicals in test tubes. They store chemicals in test tubes also.
5. Archaeologists dig gently. They look for artifacts.

Kinds of Sentences · Lesson 6

A sentence can make a statement, ask a question, give a command, or express strong feeling. The punctuation mark at the end is determined by the purpose of that sentence.

13 F There are four different kinds of sentences: **declarative, interrogative, imperative,** and **exclamatory.**

13 F.1 A **declarative sentence** makes a statement or expresses an opinion and ends with a period.

> One, three, and seven are prime numbers. (statement)
>
> Geometry is harder than algebra. (opinion)

13 F.2 An **interrogative sentence** asks a question and ends with a question mark.

> How is math important to your life?

13 F.3 An **imperative sentence** makes a request or gives a command and ends with either a period or an exclamation point.

> Answer problems 1–4 on page 63 of your mathematics book. (mild request)
>
> Don't forget to study! (strong command)

13 F.4 An **exclamatory sentence** expresses strong feelings and ends with an exclamation point.

> What an interesting problem that is!

Classifying Sentences

Write each sentence. Label each one using the following abbreviations. Then write the correct punctuation mark.

1. Sometimes you have to use indirect measurement to calculate distances
2. Do you know how to use indirect measurement
3. Suppose a six-foot fence casts an eight-foot shadow
4. You know that a telephone pole casts a twenty-five-foot shadow
5. About how high is the telephone pole
6. Don't shake your head at me
7. How simple the procedure is to a mathematician
8. The shadows of the post and the pole are proportional
9. Use cross products of the proportions to approximate the corresponding height of the telephone pole
10. The telephone pole is approximately nineteen feet, six inches high

● *Connect to Writing:* Editing

Punctuating Sentences

Dialogue in a story or play reveals the thoughts and feelings of the characters. To increase the interest of the reader or audience, dialogue should have different types of sentences. The sentences should be punctuated correctly to show how the dialogue is to be read or heard. Rewrite the following dialogue adapted from Mark Twain, using the correct end mark for each sentence.

HASTINGS: Henry, how would you like to go to London

HENRY: Thank you, no

HASTINGS: Listen to me I'm thinking of taking a month's option on the Gould and Curry Extension for the locators

HENRY: And—

HASTINGS: They want one million dollars for it

Diagraming Subjects and Verbs

A **sentence diagram** is a picture made up of lines and words. It can help you identify and analyze all the parts of a sentence.

Subjects and Verbs A baseline is a horizontal line that is the foundation of all sentence diagrams. A straight, vertical line separates the subject (or subjects) on the left from the verb (or verbs) on the right. Capital letters are included in the diagram, but punctuation is not. In the second example, notice that the whole verb phrase is written on the baseline.

People work.

People	work

Roy has been sleeping.

Roy	has been sleeping

Questions A question is diagramed as if it were a statement.

Has Dale arrived? (Dale has arrived.)

Dale	has arrived

Understood Subjects When the subject of a sentence is an understood *you,* as in a command or a request, place *you* in parentheses in the subject position.

Watch.

(you)	Watch

CHAPTER 13

Compound Subjects and Verbs Place the parts of a compound subject or a compound verb on parallel horizontal lines. Then put the conjunction connecting each part on a broken line between them. In the first example, notice that the two conjunctions are written on either side of the broken line.

Both girls and boys attended.

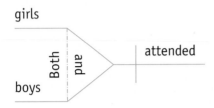

Karen and Bart dived or swam.

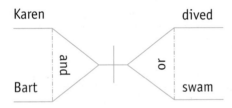

● Practice Your Skills

Diagraming Subjects and Verbs

Diagram the following sentences or copy them. If your teacher tells you to copy them, draw one line under each subject and two lines under each verb. If the subject is an understood *you*, write *you* in parentheses.

1. Cats are sleeping.

2. Be quiet!

3. Both young and old are resting.

4. Are you watching?

5. Cats wake and leave.

6. Josh and I are following and watching.

7. Josh, listen.

8. They are purring.

9. Do cats bite?

10. They might come and stay.

Assess Your Learning

Finding Subjects and Verbs

Write the subject and verb in each sentence. Label each **S** for subject or **V** for verb.

1. Warm air and moisture rise into the sky.
2. At a certain height, the warm air cools.
3. At the cooler temperatures, the air can't hold all its moisture.
4. The extra moisture then changes into small drops of water or bits of ice.
5. From those droplets clouds will develop.
6. About 100,000,000 droplets form one large raindrop.
7. Cirrus, stratus, and cumulus are the names of the three main types of clouds.
8. Clouds are always changing their shapes.
9. Weather forecasters can look at clouds and learn much about the day's weather.
10. Do you see any clouds in the sky today?

Finding Subjects, Verbs, and Understood *You*

Write the subjects and verbs in the following sentences. Label each **S** for subject or **V** for verb. If the subject is an understood *you*, write *you* in parentheses.

1. Stand beside Barbara for the picture.
2. Amanda does not have a paper route anymore.
3. Sing more softly.
4. At the aquarium one porpoise blows a horn and leaps through a hoop.
5. From behind the door jumped a clown.
6. Wade has never ridden on a subway.
7. Look for the clues in the mystery.
8. On the top of the tent lay the compass.
9. Mozart and Beethoven were famous composers.
10. Should the dogs go out now?

■ Writing Sentences

Write sentences that follow the directions below. (The sentences may come in any order.) Write about one of the following topics or a topic of your choice: a race you have seen or a race you have participated in.

1. Write a declarative sentence.

2. Write an interrogative sentence.

3. Write an imperative sentence.

4. Write an exclamatory sentence.

5. Write a sentence in which the subject *you* is understood.

Underline each subject once and each verb twice. Remember to add capital letters and end punctuation.

The Sentence: Posttest

Directions

Write the letter of the term that correctly identifies the underlined word or words in each sentence.

(1) <u>Throughout the art museum were hung priceless paintings.</u> (2) <u>Edvard Munch's most well-known painting</u> is *The Scream*. (3) The famous painter Paul Gauguin <u>worked as a stockbroker</u>. (4) Van Gogh <u>was born</u> in 1853 in the Netherlands. (5) In public buildings <u>Diego Rivera</u> painted a series of murals. (6) Salvador Dali <u>studied</u> and <u>painted</u> in Madrid and Paris. (7) <u>Rossetti</u> and <u>Alighieri</u> share the same first name: Dante. (8) <u>Dante Gabriel Rossetti</u> was an English painter and poet. (9) The famous poem *The Inferno* <u>was written</u> by Dante Alighieri. (10) <u>Where was Pablo Picasso born?</u>

1. **A** simple subject
   B inverted order
   C complete subject
   D sentence fragment

2. **A** compound subject
   B complete subject
   C verb phrase
   D inverted order

3. **A** complete subject
   B verb phrase
   C compound verb
   D complete predicate

4. **A** complete subject
   B compound subject
   C verb phrase
   D complete predicate

5. **A** simple subject
   B inverted order
   C complete predicate
   D compound subject

6. **A** compound verb
   B complete predicate
   C simple verb
   D inverted order

7. **A** simple subject
   B verb phrase
   C compound subject
   D compound verb

8. **A** verb phrase
   B inverted order
   C compound subject
   D simple subject

9. **A** imperative sentence
   B complete predicate
   C verb phrase
   D simple verb

10. **A** declarative sentence
    B sentence fragment
    C interrogative sentence
    D simple subject

Writer's Corner

Snapshot

13 A A **sentence** is a group of words that expresses a complete thought. (pages 460–461)

13 B The **subject** names the person, place, thing, or idea the sentence is about. (pages 462–463)

13 C The **predicate** tells something about the subject. (pages 464–469)

13 D A sentence is in **natural order** when the subject comes before the verb. When the verb or part of the verb phrase comes before the subject, the sentence is in **inverted order.** (pages 470–472)

13 E A **compound subject** is two or more subjects in one sentence that have the same verb and are joined by a conjunction. A **compound predicate** is two or more verbs that have the same subject and are joined by a conjunction. (page 474–476)

13 F There are four different kinds of sentences: **declarative, interrogative, imperative,** and **exclamatory.** (pages 477–478)

Power Rules

Be sure sentences have **subject-verb agreement.** (pages 736–740)

Before Editing	**After Editing**
We goes to the store every Saturday.	*We go* to the store every Saturday.

Join **run-on sentences** with a conjunction and/or proper punctuation or separate them into complete sentences. (pages 662–664)

Before Editing	**After Editing**
I cleaned my room, I surprised Mom.	I cleaned my room, *and* I surprised Mom.
We went to a movie, we enjoyed it.	We went to a movie. *We* enjoyed it.

Add words to **sentence fragments** to create sentences. (pages 460–461)

Before Editing	**After Editing**
A long day at school. We were tired.	*After* a long day at school, *we* were tired.

Editing Checklist

Use this checklist when editing your writing.

✓ Am I sure that all my sentences are complete? (See pages 460–461.)
✓ Do all my subjects and verbs match in every sentence? (See pages 736–740.)
✓ Did I vary my sentence order? (See pages 470–472.)
✓ Did I join compound subjects and compound predicates with the appropriate conjunctions? (See pages 474–476.)
✓ Did I use different types of sentences? (See pages 477–478.)

Use the Power

Discuss with a classmate what you have learned about sentence structure in this chapter. Summarize the most important points, including the four kinds of sentences and how to correct sentence fragments.

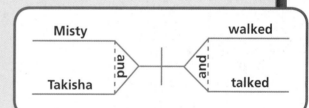

Study the diagram. It shows the correct way to diagram this sentence:

Misty and Takisha walked and talked.

Now diagram this nonsense sentence.

Todo and Miso dalmped and dremessed.

Create two nonsense or imaginative sentences for your partner to diagram. Go over each other's diagrams and share them with your teacher and classmates.

Nouns and Pronouns

How can you use nouns and pronouns to create lively and precise prose?

Nouns and Pronouns: Pretest 1

The following draft paragraph about dream catchers is hard to read because it contains unnecessary repetition. Revise the paragraph so that it reads more smoothly. One correction has been made as an example.

    In American Indian legend, dream catchers like ~~them~~ _those_ above were used to catch good dreams. The dream catcher lets good dreams slip through the outer holes and slide down the soft feathers. Them bad dreams pass through the hole in the center. Some of the dream catchers are made of colorful materials. That hanging from the line use the colors of earth and nature. Dream catchers are popular in the american southwest. Dream catchers are often decorated with feathers and beads. Some people hang dream catchers above children's beds to protect children from nightmares.

Nouns and Pronouns: Pretest 2

Directions

Read the passage and choose the word or words that correctly complete each sentence. Write the letter of the correct answer.

___(1)___ is a short history of denim jeans. ___(2)___ are also called blue jeans or dungarees. In the mid-1800s in the ___(3)___, the first jeans were designed for a ___(4)___ of workers. The jeans were constructed as durable work clothes, and ___(5)___ had reinforced seams. ___(6)___ were reinforced with copper rivets at points of stress. My research tells ___(7)___ that as time went on, other workers across the country bought ___(8)___ blue jeans. Eventually, people in other countries started wearing ___(9)___ as well. Nowadays, both men and women stock ___(10)___ closets with jeans.

1. A This
   B Them
   C These
   D Those

2. A Them
   B We
   C They
   D That

3. A united states
   B united States
   C United states
   D United States

4. A fleet
   B batch
   C crew
   D herd

5. A we
   B he
   C it
   D they

6. A Each
   B Any
   C Most
   D Everything

7. A me
   B her
   C him
   D them

8. A himself
   B themselves
   C herself
   D itself

9. A them
   B they
   C that
   D you

10. A my
    B our
    C their
    D your

Nouns Lesson 1

There are thousands of words in English, but there are only eight **parts of speech.**
A word's part of speech is determined by the job it does in a sentence. The same word
may be used as a noun in one sentence and as an adjective in another sentence.

THE EIGHT PARTS OF SPEECH

noun (names)	**adverb** (describes, limits)
pronoun (replaces noun)	**preposition** (relates)
verb (states action or being)	**conjunction** (connects)
adjective (describes, limits)	**interjection** (expresses strong feelings)

Suppose you were in another country and could not speak the language. The words that
you would want to know first are those that name people, places, things, or ideas. These
words are called **nouns.** The most frequently used part of speech is the noun.

14 A   A **noun** is a word that names a person, a place, a thing, or an idea.

NOUNS

People	girl, men, scientist, Dr. Taylor, meteorologist
Places	buildings, cities, Dallas, Atlantic Ocean
Things	rain, wind, trees, cotton, clouds, devices
Ideas and Qualities	love, friendship, kindness, thoughtfulness courage, patriotism, faith, ideals, ambition

14 A.1   **Concrete nouns** refer to things that can be seen or touched. **Abstract
nouns** refer to ideas or concepts that cannot be seen or touched.

CONCRETE AND ABSTRACT NOUNS

Concrete Nouns	cotton, city, rain, flower, tractor, table
Abstract Nouns	faith, courage, reason, friendship, happiness

You can learn about forming plurals of nouns on pages 918–919.

When you speak or write, using specific nouns can add interest to your ideas. Notice the difference between the nouns in the following sentences.

General Nouns	The **animals** hid in their den during the **storm.**
Specific Nouns	The **foxes** hid in their den during the **hurricane.**
General Nouns	The **family** lost its crop of **vegetables.**
Specific Nouns	The **Jensen family** lost its crop of **potatoes.**

● **Practice Your Skills**

Finding Nouns

Write each noun. There are 31 nouns.

1. A hurricane begins over the ocean in hot regions of the world.
2. Strong winds whirl.
3. The sky becomes dark with clouds, and rain begins to fall.
4. A hurricane can blow down trees on the land.
5. These storms usually begin in June and end in late November.
6. Scientists called meteorologists predict the path of these storms.
7. An enormous amount of energy is used by a hurricane.
8. People may need faith and courage during a hurricane.
9. Cities in the path of a hurricane are given specific information.
10. Many different scientific devices forecast these destructive storms.

● *Connect to Writing:* **Revising**

Using Specific Nouns

Rewrite each sentence, replacing the underlined general nouns with more specific nouns.

1. You should stock up on supplies before a hurricane.
2. The man showed courage during the storm.
3. Our neighbors went to the shelter at a school.
4. A new car was crushed by a tree.
5. The police had to close the street because power lines were down.

Compound and Collective Nouns

14 A.2 Some nouns are made up of more than one word. These kinds of nouns are called **compound nouns.**

Compound nouns may be written as a single word (*baseball*), two words (*home run*), or with a hyphen (*T-shirt*). Use a dictionary to check the spelling of a compound noun.

COMPOUND NOUNS	
One Word	football, dugout, sideline
Two Words	first base, Super Bowl, jump ball
Hyphenated Words	good-bye, runner-up, warm-up

14 A.3 **Collective nouns** name a group of people, animals, or things.

COMMON COLLECTIVE NOUNS			
band	congregation	flock	orchestra
class	crew	group	swarm
committee	crowd	herd	team
colony	family	league	tribe

● **Practice Your Skills**

Identifying Compound and Collective Nouns

Make two columns. Label one column *Compound Nouns* and the other column *Collective Nouns.* List compound and collective nouns in the appropriate column.

1. The first lady threw the first pitch.

2. The baseball landed next to the pitcher.

3. The crowd cheered.

4. Not a seat could be found at the ballpark.

5. The first batter hit the ball to the shortstop.

6. He was a new player in this league.

7. The team tried to help him feel better.

8. They wanted to boost his self-esteem.

9. The next batter hit a home run.

10. The ball narrowly missed the foul line.

Writing Compound Nouns

Write correctly the compound noun or nouns in each sentence. If a compound noun is correct, write **C**. Use a dictionary to check your answers.

1. The band from the high school played at halftime.

2. The stadium was packed with well wishers.

3. A reporter covered the game for a newspaper.

4. The quarter back took the field.

5. Our family waited for the kickoff.

➤ Common and Proper Nouns

14 A.4   A **common noun** names any person, place, or thing. A **proper noun** names a particular person, place, or thing.

Proper nouns begin with a capital letter.

COMMON NOUNS	PROPER NOUNS
girl	Amy Clark
country	United States
book	*Hatchet*

As you can see from the chart, some proper nouns may be more than one word. Even though *United States* is two words, it is still the name of only one place.

You can learn more about capitalizing proper nouns in Chapter 27 on pages 801–808.

CHAPTER 14

Distinguishing Between Common and Proper Nouns

Write each noun and label it **C** for common or **P** for proper.

1. Daniel Bernoulli was a scientist.
2. Bernoulli was born in Switzerland.
3. His main interests were water and air.
4. During his lifetime, he published Bernoulli's Principle.
5. This scientific principle helped Orville Wright and Wilbur Wright.
6. The Wright brothers used the principle to fly at Kitty Hawk.
7. As air blows faster across a wing, the wing lifts.
8. The velocity or speed of the air is generated by the engine.
9. The first flight of 120 feet in North Carolina was powered by a twelve-horsepower engine.
10. The Wright brothers completed 105 flights.
11. They created the Wright Company to build airplanes.
12. As a result of Bernoulli's Principle, two Americans became famous.

Write each noun. (A date is a noun.)

1. In 1981, an experiment gave hope to the future of wildlife along Currant Creek in Wyoming.
2. The cattle had eaten all the grass and shrubs.
3. The creek was a muddy hole.
4. The answer was to build dams to form ponds.
5. The townspeople found two scientists with an idea.
6. They brought beavers to Currant Creek.
7. Because there were no trees left, men hauled in logs.
8. The busy beavers built several dams.
9. Soon grass and trees began to sprout.
10. Other states now use these hardworking animals.

● *Connect to Writing:* **Autobiography**

Using Nouns

You have been asked to write a brief autobiography for publication in a local newspaper. The newspaper editor has asked you to include the following information:

- full name
- place and date of birth
- your favorite book
- your school's name
- your favorite movie
- name of a person you admire

Write a brief paragraph about yourself for the newspaper, using both common and proper nouns. When you have finished, underline all the nouns that you used. Be sure to correctly capitalize proper nouns.

Now that you can recognize nouns, you can learn to identify pronouns.

14 B   **A pronoun is a word that takes the place of one or more nouns.**

Look at each pair of sentences below. Notice how pronouns save the second sentence of each pair from being repetitious.

> When Franklin Roosevelt was president, Franklin Roosevelt started many programs.
>
> When Franklin Roosevelt was president, **he** started many programs.
>
> Meg bought Roosevelt's biography, and Meg read the biography.
>
> Meg bought Roosevelt's biography, and **she** read **it.**

Pronoun Antecedents

In the preceding examples, the pronouns *he, she,* and *it* take the place of nouns.

14 B.1   **The word or group of words that a pronoun replaces, or refers to, is called its antecedent.**

An antecedent usually comes before the pronoun. It may be in the same sentence as the pronoun or in another sentence. In the following examples, arrows point from the pronouns to their antecedents.

> Roosevelt created many **programs. They** helped people.
> (The antecedent is in the preceding sentence.)
>
> **Eleanor Roosevelt** told **her** husband about the sick children.
> (The antecedent is in the same sentence.)

A pronoun can have more than one antecedent.

> The **president** and **first lady** visited **their** family.

Sometimes more than one pronoun can refer to the same antecedent.

> **Franklin Roosevelt** took **his** secretary with **him.**

Finding Pronouns and Antecedents

Write each pronoun. Beside each pronoun, write its antecedent.

1. Franklin Roosevelt began his first term as president in 1933.

2. Roosevelt had been struck with polio in 1921, and he was confined to a wheelchair.

3. The campaign trail presented its challenges.

4. The president told the American people the only thing to fear was fear itself.

5. Eleanor Roosevelt also addressed the people and their problems.

6. The voters were worried about their money and their futures.

7. Roosevelt and the citizens were tired of the Depression and its problems.

8. Fifteen proposals were sent to Congress, and it soon passed them.

9. The New Deal did not end the Depression, but it did lessen the financial hardships of many Americans.

10. The New Deal was designed to make people feel better, and it did.

Personal Pronouns

14 B.2   Of all the different kinds of pronouns, **personal pronouns** are used most often. There are first-person, second-person, and third-person pronouns.

The following is a list of the singular and plural forms for each person.

PERSONAL PRONOUNS		
	Singular	Plural
First Person (speaker)	I, me, my, mine	we, us, our, ours
Second Person (person spoken to)	you, your, yours	you, your, yours
Third Person (person or thing spoken about)	he, him, his, she, her, hers, it, its	they, them, their, theirs

The following sentences show the ways in which personal pronouns are used.

First-Person Pronouns	**I** must remember to take **my** book report with **me** to school tomorrow.
	We haven't seen **our** grades yet.
Second-Person Pronouns	**You** shouldn't try to read the book without **your** glasses.
	You may sit next to each other and share **your** notes.
Third-Person Pronouns	**He** told **her** that the book was **his**.
	They have taken **their** computer with **them** on **their** vacation.

Reflexive and Intensive Pronouns

14 B.3 You can add *–self* or *–selves* to some personal pronouns. These pronouns, called **reflexive** and **intensive pronouns,** are used to refer to or to emphasize a noun or another pronoun.

REFLEXIVE AND INTENSIVE PRONOUNS	
Singular	myself, yourself, himself, herself, itself
Plural	ourselves, yourselves, themselves

Robert kept telling **himself** that he would finish the book of short stories.

(The reflexive pronoun *himself* refers to *Robert*.)

We committed **ourselves** to a successful book fair.

(The reflexive pronoun *ourselves* refers to *We*.)

The students **themselves** came up with the idea for a book fair.

(The intensive pronoun *themselves* emphasizes who came up with the idea. Intensive pronouns often come immediately after the antecedent.)

Never use intensive or reflexive pronouns by themselves. They must always have an antecedent. Also, never use *hisself* or *theirselves*.

Finding Personal Pronouns

Write the personal, reflexive, and intensive pronouns in the following sentences.

1. I went to the book fair with my English class during third period.

2. Mr. Jenkins himself helped us pick out some books for our book reports.

3. He suggested that we choose books for young adults by well-known authors.

4. Christopher chose *The Outsiders* by S. E. Hinton for his report.

5. Did you know that S. E. Hinton is a woman?

6. She wrote *The Outsiders* in 1967, but it is still popular with middle-school students today.

7. Maya looked for a Walter Dean Myers book for herself because he is her favorite author.

8. She found several of them in a special display of works by African American authors.

9. They were next to some copies of *M. C. Higgins, the Great* by Virginia Hamilton.

10. Were you able to locate any novels by Anne McCaffrey for your report on science fiction?

Connect to Writing: Revising

Using Personal Pronouns

Rewrite the following short biography, using personal pronouns to replace the overused common and proper nouns.

> Jules Verne was born in 1828, in Nantes, France. Jules Verne was a French writer. Jules Verne studied law but eventually Jules Verne began writing. Verne soon discovered that Verne had an ability to write about imaginary journeys and other fantasies having to do with science. Verne's writing became known as science fiction. Science fiction was a new kind of writing. Jules Verne wrote many stories. One story Verne wrote was *Twenty Thousand Leagues Under the Sea. Twenty Thousand Leagues Under the Sea* was made into a movie. The first movie version came out in 1916. Other films were released in 1954 and 1993. Jules Verne mixed humor, adventure, and scientific discovery in a book called *Around the World in Eighty Days. Around the World in Eighty Days* also became a movie.

Indefinite Pronouns

14 B.4   An **Indefinite pronoun** usually does not have a definite antecedent. Instead, indefinite pronouns usually refer to unnamed people or things.

COMMON INDEFINITE PRONOUNS		
all	either	none
another	everybody	no one
any	everyone	nothing
anybody	everything	one
anyone	few	several
anything	many	some
both	most	someone
each	neither	something

Did **anyone** notice **something** strange about the problem?

Can **anybody** take **all** of these calculators to the desk?

No one knew **anything** about the math problem.

You can learn about indefinite pronouns being used as adjectives on pages 724–726.

● **Practice Your Skills**

Finding Indefinite Pronouns

Write each indefinite pronoun.

1. Does anyone know about ratios and percents?

2. Nothing makes sense in the assignment.

3. Each seems to have the same idea.

4. Someone told me that ratios and percents are fractions.

5. No one, however, explained how fractions compare with whole numbers.

6. Everybody has had experience comparing a number such as 10 with 100.

7. Some claim to use ratios and percents every day.

8. Will anybody help clear up the confusion?

9. Several knew that 10 is one-tenth of 100.

10. One suggested that 10 is 10 percent of 100.

➤ Demonstrative and Interrogative Pronouns

14 B.5 **Demonstrative pronouns** do what their name suggests. They demonstrate, or point out, people or things.

DEMONSTRATIVE PRONOUNS			
this	that	these	those

This is a beautiful house.

That was a great idea!

These are the bedrooms.

Lee already saw **those.**

This and *these* point to people or things that are near. *That* and *those* point to people or things that are farther away.

14 B.6 **Interrogative pronouns** are used to ask questions.

INTERROGATIVE PRONOUNS				
what	which	who	whom	whose

What did you want?

Which did he choose?

Who will figure out the cost of lumber?

Whom did you choose to survey the property?

Whose are those work boots?

● *Connect to Speaking and Writing:* Interview

Using Interrogative Pronouns

Choose someone you admire in your school, family, or neighborhood. Make a list of questions to ask this person about his or her life, work, interests, or achievements. Be sure to use a variety of interrogative pronouns in your questions.

Interview the person you selected, using the questions you have already listed. Then write what you have learned about him or her in a short paragraph for the school newspaper. Be sure to use a variety of pronouns.

● Practice Your Skills

Finding Pronouns

Write each demonstrative and interrogative pronoun. Label each one **D** for demonstrative or **I** for interrogative.

1. What is the charitable organization building homes for families?
2. Who communicates between the project and the headquarters of Habitat for Humanity?
3. These are homes for families willing to do the work.
4. Who works on the new homes besides the future owners?
5. Which are the best resources for the personnel in the volunteer pool?
6. These could include retirees, crafts persons, or students.
7. Who is the former American president with Habitat for Humanity?
8. That is Jimmy Carter.
9. Who wants to call and volunteer?
10. This could be a great challenge!

✅ *Check Point:* Mixed Practice

Write each pronoun. Label each one *personal, reflexive, intensive, indefinite, demonstrative,* or *interrogative.*

1. What makes the dog special to Americans?
2. The canine is singled out from all of the 4,236 other animals as our "best friend."
3. Some may not agree, but dogs are important canines.
4. They are descended from wolves.
5. Despite their differences in size and shape, all are members of the same species.
6. You can see genetic differences for yourself, but they themselves are small.
7. Mature dogs—and wolves—can have puppies once they are mature adults.
8. It is a fact of science.
9. The next time you look into your dog's big eyes, think about the wolf.
10. That is something I will do.

Assess Your Learning

Finding Nouns

Write each noun. (A date is a noun.) You will find 26 nouns.

The first American woman to become an astronomer was Maria Mitchell. She was born in Nantucket, an island off the coast of Massachusetts. For many years, even though she was working as a teacher, she spent much time studying the stars and galaxies with her father in their observatory. In 1847, she sighted a new comet. Later she received a great honor. A committee decided to give her name to the comet she had found. Eventually she became a professor at Vassar College. Maria Mitchell wrote about her own work and encouraged many students to study astronomy.

Finding Personal Pronouns and Antecedents

Write each personal pronoun. Then beside each one, write its antecedent.

1. The pet store owner said to the customer, "I have a most unusual dog in my store."

2. "Would you be interested?" the owner asked the customer.

3. The owner pointed to a little brown dog near them.

4. The owner looked at the customer and continued, "You will like this dog!"

5. "It costs only ten dollars," the owner added.

6. The dog heard the conversation and cried out, "Buy me!"

7. The dog pleaded to the customer, "I can cook and clean your house."

8. Because the customer was so surprised to hear the dog talk, he asked the owner, "Why are you selling this dog?"

9. The customer added, "I have never heard a dog talk before!"

10. "Because," said the owner, "I can't stand a bragger!"

CHAPTER 14

■ Writing Sentences

Write sentences that follow the directions below. (The sentences may come in any order.) Write about one of the following topics or a topic of your own choice: a favorite family activity or something enjoyable you do with a friend.

Write a sentence that . . .

1. includes a noun that names a person, a place, or a thing.
2. includes a noun that names an idea.
3. includes a common noun and a proper noun.
4. includes a collective noun.
5. includes a compound noun.
6. includes a personal pronoun and its antecedent.
7. includes a reflexive or intensive pronoun.
8. includes one or two indefinite pronouns.
9. includes a demonstrative pronoun.
10. includes an interrogative pronoun.

When you are finished, put an *N* over each noun and a *P* over each pronoun.

Nouns and Pronouns: Posttest

Directions

Read the passage and decide which kind of noun or pronoun the underlined word in each sentence is. Write the letter of the correct answer.

(1) Katya joined our school's teen court this semester. (2) She will meet after school with other members of the court. (3) First, they list the cases for the day on the chalkboard. (4) They will listen to the disputes and complaints of students. (5) The group will decide on a course of action for each situation. (6) This may be a recommendation for disciplinary action if the student is guilty. (7) We all know, however, that someone may be unjustly accused. (8) For these people, the teen court will prove their innocence. (9) The teen court has shown itself to be fair. (10) Who wants to volunteer for court next semester?

1. **A** common noun
   B collective noun
   C proper noun
   D compound noun

2. **A** indefinite pronoun
   B reflexive pronoun
   C personal pronoun
   D antecedent

3. **A** compound noun
   B collective noun
   C proper noun
   D abstract noun

4. **A** proper noun
   B abstract noun
   C pronoun
   D common noun

5. **A** collective noun
   B pronoun
   C proper noun
   D reflexive pronoun

6. **A** reflexive pronoun
   B demonstrative pronoun
   C indefinite pronoun
   D interrogative pronoun

7. **A** indefinite pronoun
   B demonstrative pronoun
   C reflexive pronoun
   D intensive pronoun

8. **A** pronoun
   B collective noun
   C concrete noun
   D abstract noun

9. **A** demonstrative pronoun
   B reflexive pronoun
   C indefinite pronoun
   D personal pronoun

10. **A** demonstrative pronoun
    B personal pronoun
    C interrogative pronoun
    D intensive pronoun

Writer's Corner

Snapshot

14 A A **noun** names a person, a place, a thing, or an idea. (pages 488–493)

14 B A **pronoun** takes the place of one or more nouns. (pages 494–500)

Power Rules

Check that **nouns showing possession have the correct punctuation.** To make a singular noun possessive, add *'s*. To make most plural nouns possessive, add an apostrophe only. (pages 878–879)

Before Editing	After Editing
That baseball glove is Jimmys.	That baseball glove is *Jimmy's*.
The houses roofs all need repair	The *houses'* roofs all need repair.

Use pronouns in place of some nouns to make sentences more interesting. (pages 494–497)

Before Editing	After Editing
Jaden read a book, and Jaden enjoyed it.	*Jaden* read a book, and *he* enjoyed it.
I live in Austin. Austin is a great city.	I live in Austin. *It* is a great city.

The **pronouns** you use must **match the nouns** they replace. (page 494)

Before Editing	After Editing
We ate fresh berries. It was delicious.	We ate fresh berries. *They were* delicious.
The contest is between Fatima and Al.	The contest is between Fatima and *him*.

Editing Checklist

Use this checklist when editing your writing.

✓ Did I make sure that all compound and collective nouns are spelled correctly? (See pages 490–491.)

✓ Did I make sure that the proper nouns in my sentences are capitalized? (See pages 491–493.)

✓ Did I vary my use of nouns and pronouns? (See pages 488–500.)

✓ Did I use reflexive and intensive pronouns correctly, and did they agree with their antecedents? (See pages 496–497.)

Use the Power

In conversation, a speaker can clarify confusing language. The speaker is right there and can answer questions if a listener gets confused. Notice how Joseph asks Kay to clarify a pronoun she uses.

> **"Kay, would you teach me how to play the piano?"**
>
> **"Sure, Joseph. In return, will you teach me how to play the guitar?"**
>
> **"That sounds like a deal."**
>
> **"Before we start," Kay said, "we will need to tune it."**
>
> **"Tune what," asked Joseph, "the guitar or the piano?"**
>
> **"Well, both," she said, "now that you bring it up."**

A writer cannot accompany his or her piece of writing with answers to a reader's questions. The writer must take care to make his or her writing clear.

Review a piece of writing you have completed recently. Underline all pronouns once and all antecedents twice. Revise sentences or paragraphs in which pronoun antecedents are missing or unclear.

Verbs

How can you make your writing sing by adding just the right verbs?

Verbs: Pretest 1

The following draft paragraph about the figurine above is hard to read because it contains several agreement errors and some vague verbs. Revise the paragraph by correcting the errors and replacing the vague verbs. One verb has been corrected as an example.

       Humans from nearly every era and culture has̶ *have* dug clay from the earth and shaped it into dwellings, pottery, and figures. Often, these objects is all that is left of a vanished culture. Archaeologists uncovered this clay figure and many others like it near Veracruz, Mexico. Historians hasn't agreed on the purpose and meaning of the mysterious "smiling" figures. The sculptures seem to show a celebration involving song, rhythmic instruments, and dance. Some historians believe the figures represent a god of dance, music, and joy. Others disagree. They believe the figures was used in rituals involving intoxication and sacrifice.

Verbs: Pretest 2

Directions

Decide which words are linked by the underlined verb in each sentence. Write the letter of the correct answer.

Go ahead and call me a fashionista, but hats are my passion. **(1)** For example, my five charming berets <u>are</u> all flat, round, and woolen. **(2)** My eight baseball caps <u>have been</u> popular on and off the field for years. **(3)** When the weather is threatening, my sou'wester <u>can be</u> life-saving headgear. **(4)** My treasured gentleman's silk top hat <u>must have been</u> expensive when it was new. **(5)** My two pith helmets <u>were</u> once a necessity in the baking sun of the tropics. **(6)** This felt fedora <u>will be</u> perfect for any costume party. **(7)** This antique tiara <u>seems</u> very delicate. **(8)** The most beautiful tiara I own <u>is</u> a jeweled one. **(9)** The tiara <u>was</u> a headdress of the ancient Persians. **(10)** Today's tiara <u>is</u> often a simple circle of flowers.

1. **A** berets, woolen
   B charming, berets
   C berets, flat, round, woolen
   D five, charming

2. **A** caps, field
   B baseball, popular
   C caps, popular
   D baseball, caps

3. **A** weather, life-saving
   B sou'wester, headgear
   C headgear, life-saving
   D threatening, headgear

4. **A** silk, expensive
   B top, expensive
   C gentleman's, expensive
   D top hat, expensive

5. **A** two, once
   B helmets, necessity
   C helmets, sun
   D My, tropics

6. **A** fedora, party
   B This, fedora
   C This, perfect
   D fedora, perfect

7. **A** tiara, delicate
   B tiara, antique
   C antique, delicate
   D This, tiara

8. **A** tiara, beautiful
   B tiara, one
   C beautiful, jeweled
   D tiara, jeweled

9. **A** tiara, Persians
   B tiara, headdress
   C tiara, a
   D The, Persians

10. **A** Today's, flowers
    B tiara, a
    C tiara, circle
    D tiara, simple

Without a verb, a group of words is not a sentence. When writing, remember that you must include a subject and a predicate. Without a verb, your predicate is incomplete.

15 A   **A verb is a word used to express an action or a state of being. An action verb tells what action a subject is performing.**

To find an action verb, first find the subject of the sentence. Then ask yourself, *What is the subject doing?* Some action verbs show physical action.

> **Physical Action**
>
> The band **played.** (The subject is *band*. What did the band do? *Played* is the action verb.)
>
> They **marched** across the field. (The subject is *They*. What did they do? *Marched* is the action verb.)

Some action verbs show mental action. Others show ownership or possession.

> **Mental Action**
>
> I **forgot** the dancer's name.
>
> I **know** the steps to that dance.
>
> **Ownership**
>
> Jeffrey **has** two paintings.
>
> They **belong** to him.

When You Write

Use verbs to create vivid pictures for your audience. When you choose your verbs carefully, you help paint a picture for your audience.

> **Less vivid**   The car's tires **made noise** as it **sped** around the track.
>
> **More vivid**   The car's tires **squealed** as it **zoomed** around the track.

Revise a composition or piece of creative writing you completed recently by changing dull overused verbs to more vivid verbs.

CHAPTER 15

● Practice Your Skills

Finding Action Verbs

Write each action verb.

1. Musicians, dancers, and artists create beautiful artwork for other people.
2. A dancer performs with his or her body.
3. An artist paints with his or her hands.
4. A musician plays an instrument.
5. These performers rarely forget their goal of entertainment.
6. Musicians and dancers practice every day.
7. Artists strive for perfection.
8. They often display their works in art shows.
9. These artists express themselves creatively in their respective crafts.
10. They believe in their art and in themselves.

● Practice Your Skills

Finding Action Verbs

Write each action verb.

1. Once a year we attend a festival.
2. Glorious music reaches our ears.
3. Sometimes we listen to the lively music.
4. Flavorful scents lead to foods of many nations.
5. I taste these wonderful dishes.
6. The food melts in my mouth.
7. Next I count the number of craft booths.
8. Artists display jewelry, pottery, and paintings.
9. I search for the perfect item.
10. I enjoy this super event!

● *Connect to Writing:* Prewriting

Using Specific Verbs

Imagine that you have just returned from an exciting event and you want to tell a classmate about it. Make a list of action verbs that show what you experienced at this event. Then list some activities and things you did while there. Match the action verbs to each activity.

Action verbs can be transitive or intransitive.

15 B **Transitive verbs** express action directly toward a person or a thing.
Intransitive verbs express action that is not directed at a person or a thing.

To decide whether an action verb is transitive or intransitive, say the subject and verb. Then ask the question *What?* or *Whom?* A word that answers either question is called an **object.** An action verb that has an object is transitive. An action verb that does not have an object is intransitive.

Transitive	Marie **dropped** a beaker in the laboratory. (Marie dropped what? *Beaker* is the object. Therefore, *dropped* is a transitive verb.)
	Marie **told** us about her first day at work. (Marie told whom? *Us* is the object. Therefore, *told* is a transitive verb.)
Intransitive	She **works** at a chemical company. (She works what? She works whom? Because there is no object, *works* is an intransitive verb.)

A few verbs can be transitive in one sentence and intransitive in another sentence.

Transitive	The scientist **wrote** an experiment.
	(The scientist wrote what? *Experiment* is the object.)
Intransitive	The scientist **wrote** slowly.
	(The scientist wrote what or whom? There is no object.)

You can learn more about objects on pages 563–567.

● **Practice Your Skills**

Understanding Transitive and Intransitive Verbs

Write the verb in each sentence. Label the verb *T* for transitive or *I* for intransitive.

1. Many companies use organic compounds.

2. They make CDs, athletic shoes, and videotapes with organic compounds.

3. An organic compound usually comes from a carbon-based compound.

CHAPTER 15

4. In fact, more than 90 percent of all compounds include carbon-based, organic elements.

5. As early as 1830, scientists made artificial organic compounds in their laboratories.

6. Now artificial organic compounds number in the millions.

7. Scientists discover more and more organic compounds.

8. Companies create new products all the time.

9. Their research progresses slowly sometimes.

10. New products require a great deal of testing.

Power Your Writing: Getting into the Action

A **participle** is a word formed from a verb. It acts like an adjective by modifying a noun or pronoun. A participle can be turned into a **participial phrase** by joining it with other words. Participial phrases are useful for creating a vivid sense that several things are happening at once. Consider the following sentence from "Checkouts" by Cynthia Rylant.

> Some months later the bag boy and the girl with the orange bow again crossed paths, **standing** in line with their dates at a movie theater, and, **glancing** toward the other, each smiled slightly, then looked away, as strangers on public buses do, when one is moving off the bus and the other is moving on.

By using participial phrases, the author vividly relates—in a single sentence—the circumstances, the underlying emotions, and the delicate tension of this brief, final meeting. The example below shows how you can use a participial phrase to combine a simple sentence and highlight the relationship between ideas.

Two Sentences	The bag boy let her leave the store. He pretended not to notice her.
Combined	The bag boy let her leave the store, **pretending** not to notice her.

Review a composition you have completed recently. Look for places you can combine two sentences with a participial phrase.

15 C A **helping verb,** or **auxiliary verb,** is a verb that is combined with a main verb to form a **verb phrase.**

The following is a list of common helping verbs.

COMMON HELPING VERBS	
be	am, is, are, was, were, be, being, been
have	has, have, had
do	do, does, did
others	may, might, must, can, could, shall, should, will, would

15 C.1 A **verb phrase** is made up of a main verb and one or more helping verbs.

A verb phrase may have one or more helping verbs.

> Those insects **are** distributing pollen.
>
> Those bees **have been** gathering honey.

One or more words may interrupt a verb phrase. *Not* and its contraction *n't,* for example, often interrupt verb phrases.

> New species of winged insects **have** suddenly appeared.
>
> He **should**n't proceed without assistance.

To find the verb phrase in a question, turn the question into a statement.

> **Question** **Have** you seen the ants' tunnels?
>
> **Statement** You **have** seen the ants' tunnels.

● **Practice Your Skills**

Finding Verb Phrases

Write each verb phrase. Remember that a verb phrase may be interrupted by one or more words.

1. Have you ever counted the number of different bugs in a field at one time?

2. This would not have been an easy task.

3. Scientists have identified about five million different species of insects.

4. From one batch of eggs, some insects can produce two thousand offspring.

5. Ants have built some incredible underground cities with areas for specific activities.

6. Some ants will kidnap the workers from another colony of ants.

7. Do you know today's temperature?

8. You can count the chirps of a single cricket for fourteen seconds.

9. Then you should add forty to the number of cricket chirps.

10. You will then have a nearly accurate Fahrenheit temperature.

✔ Check Point: Mixed Practice

Write the verb or verb phrase in each sentence.

1. Runners have always called the marathon the great competitive sport.

2. Today many people across the country are racing in the triathlon.

3. This race includes a 2.4-mile swim, a 112-mile bicycle race, and a 26-mile run.

4. The competitors do swim the 2.4 miles in the choppy waters of the ocean.

5. According to records, the triathlon started in Hawaii in 1978.

6. Only twelve athletes competed in that first triathlon.

7. This competition was first called the Iron Man Triathlon.

8. Over the years more and more women were joining the competition.

9. Within three years the triathlon had become a major event in the United States.

10. More than four thousand people from across the world started in the race that year.

CHAPTER 15

● *Connect to Writing:* Observation Report

Using Verbs

Imagine that you are a social scientist interested in the family. Choose a public location such as an amusement park, a sporting event, or a fast-food restaurant. Observe the behavior of parents and their children. Write a brief report for parents that summarizes public "family behavior." Use verb phrases to describe the behaviors. Underline the verb phrases.

➤ Using Linking Verbs

15 D   A **linking verb** links the subject with another word in the sentence. The other word either renames or describes the subject.

Verbs that do not show action are called state-of-being verbs. These verbs make statements about a subject. State-of-being verbs are often used as linking verbs. This means that they join the subject to another word in the sentence.

> Christopher's favorite class **is** chemistry. (*Is* links *class* with *chemistry*. *Chemistry* renames the subject.)
>
> The temperatures in the lab **have been** very low. (*Have been* links *temperatures* with *low*. *Low* describes the temperatures—*the low temperatures*.)

The verbs in this list of common linking verbs are forms of the verb *be*.

COMMON LINKING VERBS				
be	shall be	should be	have been	should have been
is	will be	would be	has been	may have been
am	can be	may be	had been	might have been
are	could be	might be	will have been	must have been
was				
were				

When You Write

Professional writers choose strong and direct action verbs to keep readers interested. Notice the difference between the verbs in these sentences. Which sentence sounds more interesting? Why?

The scientist **is** in the laboratory.

The scientist **struggles** in the laboratory.

● **Practice Your Skills**

Finding Linking Verbs

Write each linking verb. Then write the words that the verb links.

1. The sun is the star closest to Earth.

2. The sun must be a medium-sized star.

3. It should be a distance of ninety-three million miles away from Earth.

4. Earth is our home.

5. Earth's rotation around the sun must be the cause of day and night.

6. In 365 days it will be another year.

7. Without the sun, Earth would be a dark and cold place.

8. The sun is Earth's source of light and heat.

9. The sun has been the subject of many Native American dances.

10. Many early cultures were believers in the sun's importance in their lives.

➤ Additional Linking Verbs

Forms of the verb *be* are not the only words that can be used as linking verbs. Additional linking verbs are listed in the box below.

ADDITIONAL LINKING VERBS			
appear	grow	seem	stay
become	look	smell	taste
feel	remain	sound	turn

Any of the verbs in the box can link a subject with a word that either renames or describes the subject.

That painter **became** the new teacher. (*Teacher* renames the subject *painter*.)

Yesterday the future **felt** very bright. (*Bright* describes the subject—*the bright future*.)

Like other verbs, these linking verbs can also have helping verbs.

The art teacher **is becoming** hoarse.

That painting **does look** beautiful.

Finding Linking Verbs

Write each linking verb. Then write the words that each verb links.

(1) Grant Wood's *Parson Weems's Fable* has become a famous and somewhat perplexing painting. (2) After over 70 years, the painting still remains a mystery. (3) In many ways the scene appears familiar. (4) Yet at the same time it seems somewhat odd. (5) Could that figure in the foreground be Parson Weems? (6) The small figure behind him looks familiar, like a tiny George Washington. (7) The house and lawn feel too perfect. (8) The cherry trees appear exactly the same shape. (9) George's father seems unaware of George's actions. (10) George himself looks unconcerned.

➤ Linking Verb or Action Verb?

Some linking verbs you just studied can also be used as action verbs. When you come across one of these verbs, ask yourself this question: *What is the verb doing in the sentence?* If the verb links a subject to a word that renames or describes it, it is a linking verb. If the verb is used to show action, it is an action verb.

Linking Verb	The man in that picture **looked** happy. (*Looked* links *happy* and *man. Happy* describes the subject *man.* The sentence is about the *happy man.*)
Action Verb	For days the girl **looked** desperately for that calendar. (*Looked* shows action. It tells what the girl did. Also, there is no word in the sentence that renames or describes the subject.)

● Practice Your Skills

Distinguishing Between Linking Verbs and Action Verbs

Write each verb. Then label each one *linking* or *action.*

(1) The twenty-first century feels the same as the last century. (2) We turned the page on our calendar. (3) Neither our experiences nor our feelings suddenly became different. (4) Our lives remain the same. (5) The outside air smells clean and fresh. (6) The food still tastes delicious. (7) We stay in the same neighborhood. (8) No one suddenly grew anxious. (9) Everything appears normal. (10) Did you feel the change from one century to another?

Assess Your Learning

Finding Action and Linking Verbs

Write each verb or verb phrase. Then label each one *action* or *linking.*

1. The grocer weighed the cheese.
2. The waves were pounding against the shore.
3. The battery in our car is dead.
4. Over the weekend the ocean remained rough.
5. The heart of a normal adult will beat about 38 million times each year.
6. Once again the computer was correct.
7. More than three hundred United States citizens have appeared on the stamps of other countries.
8. Sodium in salt can contribute to high blood pressure.
9. The roses near the house smell fragrant.
10. Benjamin Franklin was the founder of the first public library in the United States.

Finding the Verb

Write each verb or verb phrase. Then label each one *action* or *linking.*

The morning of August 24, A.D. 79, was normal in Pompeii, a beautiful little city in Italy. Everyone was talking about that evening's sports contests. Mount Vesuvius, a nearby volcano, seemed peaceful. For 1,500 years the volcano had been inactive. Then around noon it suddenly erupted. Hot rock and ash fell like rain from the sky. Huge clouds of ash, smoke, and poisonous gases grew dark and thick. People could not see the sun anymore. After eight days the volcano finally became quiet. Pompeii, however, had disappeared under twenty feet of ash and rock.

▩ Writing Sentences

Write sentences that follow the directions below. (The sentences may come in any order.) Write about one of the following topics or a topic of your own choice: a pet or a wild animal. You could also write about an animal you would like to be and why.

Write a sentence that . . .

    1. includes an action verb.

    2. includes a linking verb.

    3. includes a verb phrase.

    4. includes an interrupted verb phrase.

    5. includes *taste* as an action verb.

    6. includes *taste* as a linking verb.

    7. includes *look* as an action verb.

    8. includes *look* as a linking verb.

    9. includes *appear* as an action verb.

    10. includes *appear* as a linking verb.

When you finish, underline each verb or verb phrase.

Verbs: Posttest

Directions

Decide which word receives the action of the underlined verb in each sentence. Write the letter of the correct answer. If the verb is intransitive, write **D**.

(1) <u>Do</u> not <u>use</u> those rusty nails. (2) I <u>have been designing</u> this entertainment stand for weeks. (3) The paint <u>should dry</u> for at least three hours. (4) The lumber store downtown <u>is having</u> a sale on cedar planks. (5) I <u>will go</u> to the lumber store for you this afternoon. (6) In shop class we <u>are</u> now <u>building</u> a cedar chest. (7) I <u>will</u> also <u>put</u> a durable lock on mine. (8) Marcos <u>stayed</u> in the shop room for several hours after school. (9) Mr. Mandell <u>told</u> us about the various projects. (10) I <u>could hear</u> the jigsaw from across the room.

1. **A** those
   B rusty
   C nails
   D intransitive verb

2. **A** stand
   B entertainment
   C weeks
   D intransitive verb

3. **A** dry
   B hours
   C three
   D intransitive verb

4. **A** downtown
   B sale
   C planks
   D intransitive verb

5. **A** store
   B afternoon
   C lumber
   D intransitive verb

6. **A** chest
   B class
   C cedar
   D intransitive verb

7. **A** also
   B lock
   C mine
   D intransitive verb

8. **A** room
   B hours
   C school
   D intransitive verb

9. **A** various
   B projects
   C us
   D intransitive verb

10. **A** across
    B jigsaw
    C room
    D intransitive verb

Writer's Corner

Snapshot

15 A A **verb** is a word used to express an action or a state of being. An **action verb** tells what action a subject is performing. (pages 508–509)

15 B **Transitive verbs** express action directly toward a person or a thing. **Intransitive verbs** express action that is not directed at a person or a thing. (pages 510–511)

15 C A **helping verb**, or **auxiliary verb**, is a verb that is combined with a main verb to form a **verb phrase**. (pages 512–513)

15 D A **linking verb** links the subject with another word in the sentence. (pages 514–516)

Power Rules

Use the proper form of **helping verbs with negatives** such as *not* and *n't*. (page 512)

Before Editing	After Editing
Before Editing	**After Editing**
She didn't be able to finish the book in time.	She *won't* be able to finish the book in time.
I ain't a fan of baseball.	*I'm not* a fan of baseball.

Check that you have **subject-verb agreement** when using the verb *have*. (pages 736–738)

Before Editing	After Editing
Before Editing	**After Editing**
Mary have a lot of homework.	Mary *has* a lot of homework.
They has two dogs.	They *have* two dogs.

Editing Checklist

Use this checklist when editing your writing.

✓ Did I make sure that all my sentences contain at least one verb?
  (See pages 508–509.)
✓ Did I make sure that if my verb is transitive, the object is clear?
  (See pages 510–511.)
✓ Did I make sure that I used the correct form of each helping verb
  in my sentences? (See pages 512–513.)
✓ Did I use the correct linking verbs in my sentences? (See pages 514–516.)

Use the Power

Like links in a chain, linking verbs connect a subject with another word in
the sentence.

Noun (Subject)	Linking Verb	Other Word
wheelbarrow	is	broken
chickens	seem	confused
poem	appears	simple

An action verb is like colorful ink, a small drop of which can change the
appearance of an entire glass of water. Consider the example below. Notice
how a single strong action verb carries the descriptive power of four words
that say the same thing.

Weak Verb and Phrase   The girl **thought a long time** about the poem.

Strong Action Verb   The girl **pondered** the poem.

Revise a recent composition by replacing weak verbs and wordy descriptions
with more colorful and descriptive action verbs.

Adjectives and Adverbs

How can you add interest and detail to your writing with adjectives and adverbs?

Adjectives and Adverbs: Pretest 1

The following draft paragraph about the Henry Moore sculpture shown above is hard to read because it contains vague, repetitive, and incorrect adjectives and adverbs. Revise the paragraph so that it reads more smoothly. The first sentence has been edited as an example.

> British artist Henry Moore created the ~~brown~~ *bronze* sculpture "Family Group" for the grounds of a english school. It is one of his first really good works in bronze. The familiar yet somewhat abstract figures interlock nice. As the parents' arms flow together, they form a fluid "knot" with the child. Moore shows in this sculpture that he believes very very much in the beauty and dignity of the human form.

Adjectives and Adverbs: Pretest 2

Directions

Write the letter of the term that correctly identifies the underlined word in each sentence.

(1) Natalie has organized a <u>maid</u> service. **(2)** Natalie is <u>very</u> efficient at cleaning. **(3)** She knows the proper way to clean a <u>Persian</u> rug. **(4)** She can turn <u>grimy</u>, moldy bathroom tiles into sparkling clean tiles within minutes. **(5)** Whether a table is made of <u>cherry</u> wood or metal, Natalie knows which cleaner to use. **(6)** Natalie does all her work on <u>Saturdays</u>. **(7)** Her dad drops her off at the client's house and picks her up <u>later</u>. **(8)** With her earnings Natalie buys the <u>best</u> cleaning supplies. **(9)** She has <u>some</u> money left over for the week. **(10)** In addition, she deposits <u>some</u> into her account.

1. **A** adjective
   B noun
   C proper adjective
   D adverb

2. **A** adjective
   B noun
   C proper adjective
   D adverb

3. **A** article
   B noun
   C proper adjective
   D adverb

4. **A** adjective
   B noun
   C proper adjective
   D adverb

5. **A** adjective
   B noun
   C proper adjective
   D adverb

6. **A** proper adjective
   B article
   C proper noun
   D adverb

7. **A** adjective
   B noun
   C proper adjective
   D adverb

8. **A** adjective
   B noun
   C proper adjective
   D adverb

9. **A** adjective
   B noun
   C pronoun
   D adverb

10. **A** adjective
    B noun
    C pronoun
    D adverb

Imagine what writing would be like if the only parts of speech were nouns and verbs. It would be dull and lifeless! Fortunately, there are words that can change or add meaning to other words. These words are called modifiers. **Modifiers** describe other words. They add color and exactness to a sentence. One kind of modifier is an adjective.

16 A   An **adjective** is a kind of modifier. It modifies a noun or a pronoun.

➤ Using Adjectives

An adjective answers the question *What kind? Which one? How many?* or *How much?* about nouns and some pronouns. In the following examples, an arrow points to the noun or pronoun each adjective modifies.

What Kind?	The **rough** seas upset the **rich** passengers.
Which One?	**These** ships are better than **that** one.
How Many?	**Few** people liked the **two** ships.
How Much?	A **little** space would be a **great** relief.

When You Speak and Write

When you speak or write, use adjectives to change the mood of a sentence. Note the difference the adjectives make in the following sentences.

It was a **cold** and **snowy** night.

It was a **moonlit** and **silvery** night.

It was a **dark** and **dreary** night.

It was a **starry** and **cloudless** night.

Select a piece of writing from your portfolio. Underline the adjectives. Experiment with changing the mood of a passage by replacing some of the adjectives.

Finding Adjectives

Write each adjective except *the* and *a*. Beside each, write the word it modifies.

(1) A channel runs through several islands off the coast of New Zealand. **(2)** The narrow and risky route is a shortcut for ships. **(3)** On a stormy morning in 1871, the *Brindle* approached the channel. **(4)** Suddenly a young porpoise jumped up in front of the ship. **(5)** The friendly porpoise swam near the ship. **(6)** It then led the ship safely through the deep waters. **(7)** For years the brave porpoise led ships through the channel—except for one ship, the *Penguin*. **(8)** In 1903, a passenger on the *Penguin* shot the defenseless porpoise. **(9)** The porpoise survived, but it never again guided the *Penguin* through the dangerous channel. **(10)** In 1909, the *Penguin* sank in the channel with many casualties.

● *Connect to Writing:* **Revising**

Using Specific Adjectives

Rewrite each sentence, filling in the blank with a specific adjective. The words in parentheses tell what kind of adjective to use.

1. ___ groups of animals that make the ocean their home are dolphins, porpoises, and beluga whales. (How many?)

2. Dolphins, porpoises and ___ whales are actually related to each other. (What kind?)

3. These animals will go to ___ lengths to help other dolphins that are wounded. (How much?)

4. The beluga whale lives in the ___ waters near the North Pole. (What kind?)

5. ___ whales are also called white whales. (What kind?)

➤ **Different Positions of Adjectives**

Usually an adjective comes right before the noun or the pronoun it modifies. Sometimes, though, an adjective can follow the word it modifies or come after a linking verb.

Before a Noun	The **brave, adventurous** explorer led an expedition through the jungle.
After a Noun	The explorer, **brave** and **adventurous,** led an expedition through the jungle.
After a Linking Verb	The explorer was **brave** and **adventurous.**

A writer often uses a variety of specific adjectives that will appeal to the reader's five senses.

See	**Gray** smoke billowed from the chimney.
Touch	The **warm** embers indicated recent campers.
Taste	Jo found an orange that was **sweet** and **juicy.**
Smell	A **tangy citrus** scent filled the room.
Hear	**Gruff** sounds of wolves reached us.

Review a short story or poem you have completed recently. Underline the adjectives. Add at least three adjectives that appeal to different senses.

PUNCTUATION WITH TWO ADJECTIVES

Sometimes you will write two adjectives together before or after the noun they describe. If those two adjectives are not connected by *and* or *or,* you might want to put a comma between them. To decide if a comma belongs or not, read the adjectives with the word *and* between them.

- If the adjectives read well, use a comma to replace the *and.*
- If the adjectives do not read well with the word *and* between them, do not add a comma.

Comma Needed	The journey began on a humid, hot day.
	(*A humid and hot day* reads well.)
Comma Not Needed	They saw **several incredible** lands.
	(*Several and incredible lands* does not read well.)

Usually no comma is needed after a number or after an adjective that refers to size, shape, or age. For example, no commas are needed in the following sentence.

Six large ships had **big outdoor decks.**

You can learn more about commas between adjectives on pages 829–830.

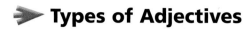

Types of Adjectives

Two special types of adjectives are **articles** and **proper adjectives.**

Articles

16 A.1 *A, an,* and *the* form a special group of adjectives called **articles.**

Be careful when selecting between the articles *a* and *an*. Use *a* before words that begin with a consonant sound. Use *an* before words that begin with a vowel sound.

I picked up **a** microphone and made **an** announcement.

● Practice Your Skills

Finding Adjectives

Write each adjective. (Do not write articles.) Beside each, write the word it modifies.

(1) In 1519, Ferdinand Magellan, a courageous mariner, led five ships from Spain. **(2)** Magellan sailed across the broad Atlantic. **(3)** He took the southern route along the eastern coast of South America. **(4)** His sailors, restless and weary, soon rebelled against the long and dangerous journey. **(5)** One ship left and returned to familiar waters. **(6)** With four ships in 1520, Magellan found the narrow, dangerous passage to the Pacific. **(7)** The sea captain expected to reach Asia in a few weeks, but the voyage lasted four months. **(8)** The crew, hungry and desperate, ate wooden sawdust and leather riggings. **(9)** Magellan never finished the tragic journey. **(10)** He was killed in a brutal war in the Philippines.

● *Connect to Writing:* **Prewriting**

Linking Specific Adjectives with Nouns

Imagine that you are going on a journey to another town, state, or country—or even just to the mall or a friend's house. Make a list of five nouns that name the places along the way to your destination. Then make a list of adjectives that describe the places on your noun list. Try to include at least two adjectives for each noun. Be sure to make the adjectives as specific as possible.

Proper Adjectives

16 A.2   A **proper adjective** is a modifier based on a proper noun.

France is a proper noun because it is the name of a particular place. Similarly, the adjective *French* is a **proper adjective.** Proper adjectives begin with capital letters.

PROPER NOUNS AND ADJECTIVES	
Proper Nouns	Europe, America
Proper Adjectives	European explorer, American trade

● Practice Your Skills

Finding Proper Adjectives

Write each proper adjective. Beside each one, write the word it modifies.

1. In 1497, John Cabot established the first British claim in North America.
2. The first permanent European settlement in the United States was in St. Augustine.
3. In the early 1600s, English and Dutch colonists began settling North America.
4. New York City was founded in 1612 when Dutch ships arrived on the Hudson River.
5. Swedish colonists settled Delaware and southern New Jersey.
6. Farms in South Carolina were in the style of Spanish plantations.
7. One of the first crops exported from the American colonies was cranberries.
8. The Spanish government expanded its holdings in North America.
9. La Salle claimed the Mississippi River valley for the French people.
10. Fur trade with Native American tribes was crucial to the Europeans.

● *Connect to Writing:* Editing

Capitalizing Proper Adjectives

Rewrite the sentences, capitalizing each proper adjective.

1. Near 1630, english Puritans settled in New England.
2. The center of each puritan village was a meetinghouse.
3. Were there any scottish people on the *Mayflower?*
4. The architecture and windmills throughout colonial New York were a result of dutch influence.
5. King Philip's War was caused by disagreements over native american land.

Adjective or Noun?

A word's part of speech depends on how it is used in a sentence. *Street* and *water*, for example, can be either nouns or adjectives.

Noun	The narrow **street** was crowded.
Adjective	**Street** cleaners are working near our apartment building.
Noun	**Water** is important to our lives.
Adjective	A **water** plant is near my home.

● **Practice Your Skills**

Distinguishing Between Adjectives and Nouns

Write *adjective* or *noun* to identify each underlined word.

(1) A <u>water</u> technician looks for contamination. **(2)** The technician collects and tests <u>water</u>. **(3)** Water from a city <u>well</u> and local lakes is tested. **(4)** In the laboratory the <u>well</u> water is examined carefully. **(5)** Workers may add a <u>chemical</u> to the water supply. **(6)** Technicians treat water with <u>chemical</u> additives. **(7)** These technicians take courses in chemistry, mathematics, and <u>biology</u>. **(8)** The <u>biology</u> courses cover everything from basic cells to zoology. **(9)** A <u>future</u> technician should also have mechanical skills. **(10)** A technician's job in the <u>future</u> will include maintenance duties and repairing water pumps.

 Adjective or Pronoun?

A word can be a pronoun in one sentence and an adjective in another sentence. For example, *this* is a pronoun if it stands alone and takes the place of a noun. *This* is an adjective if it modifies a noun or a pronoun.

Adjective	**This** number is a prime number. (*This* modifies *number*.)
Pronoun	**This** is a prime number. (*This* replaces the noun *number*.)
Adjective	**Which** problem did you solve? (*Which* modifies *problem*.)
Pronoun	**Which** did you solve? (*Which* replaces the noun *problem*.)

The following pronouns can be used as adjectives in a sentence.

WORDS USED AS PRONOUNS OR ADJECTIVES				
Demonstrative	**Interrogative**		**Indefinite**	
this	what	all	either	neither
these	which	another	few	other
that	whose	any	many	several
those		both	more	some
		each	most	

The possessive pronouns *my, your, his, her, its, our,* and *their* are sometimes called **pronominal adjectives** because they answer the adjective question *Which one?* Throughout this book, however, these words will be considered pronouns.

● **Practice Your Skills**

Distinguishing Between Adjectives and Pronouns

Label each underlined word as an *adjective* or a *pronoun.*

1. <u>What</u> rule is used for dividing rational numbers?

2. <u>That</u> is the inverse operation for multiplying rational numbers.

3. <u>What</u> did you say?

4. <u>That</u> mathematical operation is very simple.

5. In fact, <u>several</u> numbers can be multiplied or divided.

6. Because rational numbers can be used together, we include <u>several</u> in our homework.

7. However, too <u>many</u> numbers confuse some students.

8. <u>Many</u> confuse the operations and the inverses.

9. <u>Which</u> group do you belong to—the comfortable or the confused?

10. I don't know <u>which</u>.

Write each adjective. Beside each one, write the word it modifies.

> **(1)** Which animal is the oddest creature on Earth? **(2)** The answer is easy. **(3)** It is the Australian platypus. **(4)** The platypus is a primitive animal. **(5)** Unlike most kinds of mammals, the platypus lays eggs. **(6)** The eggs have a tough, leathery covering. **(7)** Baby platypuses are blind and helpless. **(8)** The feet of the platypus are unusual. **(9)** They have webs for swimming, but they also have hard claws for digging. **(10)** The back legs of male platypuses have daggers of bone. **(11)** The daggers, narrow and hollow, are like the fangs of a rattlesnake. **(12)** The platypus can shoot a deadly poison through the daggers. **(13)** A jab from one of these daggers can instantly kill an enemy. **(14)** A platypus pokes around in river mud with a broad bill.

Power Your Writing: Adjectives

By using vivid adjectives, a writer can paint a verbal masterpiece. A single descriptive word can sometimes speak volumes about a character, a place, a mood, or an event. In the following excerpt from *Rascal,* note how Sterling North uses adjectives to intensify the action.

> But we couldn't have been more surprised when a **furious** mother raccoon exploded from her lair screaming her rage and dismay. Wowser nearly fell over backward to avoid the **flying** claws and **slashing little** teeth. A moment later the **big** raccoon had racked her way up a **slender** oak tree.

Compare the vague sentences below with the vivid sentences from *Rascal*. Notice how the adjectives help you visualize the characters and the action.

Vague	He turned and looked at the racoon. (The reader cannot relate to how Wowser is feeling.)
Vivid	After being challenged, badgered, and insulted, he eventually would turn his **worried** face and **great sad** eyes upon his tormentor. (The reader can relate to Wowser's anxiety and sadness—human qualities.)
Vague	Wowser was a dog. (What kind of dog?)
Vivid	Wowser was an **affectionate,** perpetually **hungry** Saint Bernard.

Revise a piece of fiction you have worked on recently by replacing vague passages with more descriptive sentences.

16 B An **adverb** is a word that modifies a verb, an adjective, or another adverb.

Using Adverbs

Just as nouns and pronouns have adjective modifiers, verbs, adjectives, and adverbs also have modifiers. These modifiers are called adverbs. **Adverbs** make the meaning of verbs, adjectives, and other adverbs more precise.

Many adverbs end in –*ly*.

> Hold the rope **tightly** as you lower the bucket **slowly.**

The common adverbs in the following list do not end in –*ly*.

COMMON ADVERBS			
again	far	never	soon
almost	fast	next	still
already	hard	not (n't)	then
also	here	now	there
always	just	often	too
down	late	quite	very
even	more	rather	well
ever	near	so	yet

Adverbs That Modify Verbs

Most adverbs modify verbs. To find these adverbs, ask yourself *Where? When? How?* or *To what extent?* about each verb. A word that answers one of these questions is an adverb. When it modifies a verb, an adverb can usually be placed anywhere in the sentence.

Where?   Last spring everyone gathered **outside** to watch the race.

When?   **Sometimes** we race in the fall.

How?   She ran **quickly.**

To What Extent?   The sun **completely** disappeared.

More than one adverb can modify the same verb.

Ray **never** ran **fast.**

When there are helping verbs in addition to the main verb, an adverb modifies the entire verb phrase.

You should accept a compliment **graciously.**

An adverb sometimes interrupts a verb phrase in a statement or a question.

Statement   I have **always** enjoyed running.

Question   Did**n't** she know her competitors?

● **Practice Your Skills**

Finding Adverbs

Write each adverb and the word or words it modifies.

(1) Toni Cade Bambara's *Raymond's Run* always gives readers food for thought. **(2)** The girl in the story, Squeaky, truly fears nothing. **(3)** She loudly tells everyone about her racing wins. **(4)** She works hard for her goals. **(5)** The story is even told from Squeaky's point of view. **(6)** Squeaky does often seem bossy. **(7)** The kids in the neighborhood do not believe her. **(8)** The same kid has always won this race. **(9)** Squeaky fiercely protects her disabled brother Raymond. **(10)** When Squeaky races, Raymond also prepares himself for the race. **(11)** Even though he is not an official runner, he races. **(12)** Squeaky proudly watches Raymond's commitment and achievements. **(13)** She suddenly decides something important. **(14)** Squeaky will now become Raymond's coach.

● *Connect to Writing:* **Revising**

Using Adverbs

Revise the following sentences by adding adverbs. Use adverbs that make each sentence's meaning more precise. After you have revised each sentence, underline the adverb.

1. A tree limb fell and blocked the path of the runner.

2. She recovered her strength and determination.

3. Her opponent was gaining and looked as if she might win.

4. The girl wanted to win the race.

5. Who would cross the finish line?

➤ Adverbs That Modify Adjectives and Other Adverbs

The majority of adverbs modify verbs. Occasionally an adverb, such as *quite, rather, so, somewhat,* or *very,* modifies an adjective or another adverb. Such adverbs—called **intensifying adverbs**—usually come immediately before the words they modify.

Modifying an Adjective	Inventors are **very** creative. (*Creative* is an adjective. *Very* is an adverb that modifies *creative*. It tells how creative inventors are.)
Modifying an Adverb	The inventor worked **especially** fast. (*Fast* is an adverb. *Especially* is an adverb that modifies *fast*. It tells how fast the inventor worked.)

You can learn more about using adjectives and adverbs in Chapter 26.

When you speak or write, you convey your ideas better when you use specific modifiers. Try to avoid repeating adverbs or using vague adjectives in your writing or speech. The following sentences repeat the same adverb and use vague adjectives.

Vague	Pedro is a **very very good** inventor.
	Megan is **really** a **very sweet** person.

Spoken or written, the following sentences are more effective because the modifiers are more specific and less repetitive.

Specific	Pedro is a **creative** and **extremely intelligent** inventor.
	Megan is a **generous** person.

Revise a piece of writing you have completed recently by replacing vague adjectives and repetitive adverbs with more specific modifiers.

● **Practice Your Skills**

Finding Adverbs

Write each adverb and the word or words it modifies.

(1) Inventors are definitely curious about the way things work. **(2)** They are almost always creating with their imaginations. **(3)** Inventors must work especially hard at solving problems. **(4)** Their inventions are often amazing. **(5)** One quite important invention was Clarence Birdseye's quick-freeze food. **(6)** He identified a very important need and found a surprisingly effective solution. **(7)** Inventors have been known to take things already useful and turn them into unusually important products. **(8)** Many have also found incredibly simple solutions to highly complex problems. **(9)** Who do you think would be overwhelmingly voted the most influential inventor of the twentieth century? **(10)** Technology and science have quite dramatically advanced because of new inventions.

Connect to Writing: Descriptive Paragraph

Using Adverbs

Imagine you are watching a family harvesting vegetables on their farm. Write a paragraph that describes the scene. Describe how the family members move in the rows. Describe the sharpness of their tools and how they fill and move their baskets. Compare or contrast the speed of the harvesting done by an older family member and a child. Use adverbs to emphasize your ideas.

Check Point: Mixed Practice

Write each adverb and the word or words it modifies.

1. The Beatles have a very strong fan base.
2. Older listeners quite naturally listen to the music of their youth.
3. Younger fans have also noticed the "Fab Four."
4. The Beatles will very likely have the best-selling recordings in the extremely long history of music.
5. The early albums recently have been digitally remastered perfectly to CDs.
6. In fact, songs such as "Michelle" and "Yesterday" are especially clear compared to the records of the 1960s.
7. The Beatles are now accepted by a large audience.
8. Their music is commonly heard in commercials on television.
9. This new popularity must surely please older adults.
10. They can easily share their music with their teenagers.

Check Point: Mixed Practice

Write each adjective and adverb. (Do not write articles.) Beside each, write the word or words that the adjective or adverb modifies.

1. Humans communicate in various ways.
2. Words and actions are the main means of human communication.
3. Music has always been a universal method of communication.
4. People very often send messages through songs.
5. Some people also express their ideas and feelings through body movements.
6. Others communicate more through their facial expressions.
7. Communication is especially important in groups.
8. People must be extremely careful of other people's feelings.
9. Good communication skills are developed gradually.
10. People should be good speakers and excellent listeners.

➤ Diagraming Adjectives and Adverbs

Adjectives and adverbs are both diagramed on a slanted line below the words they modify.

The eager crowd is arriving.

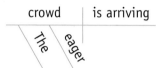

Everyone looks excited.

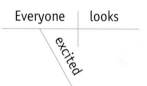

Ushers, helpful and efficient, mingle.

People are noisily talking.

The band concert starts soon.

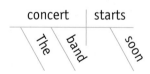

CHAPTER 16

Adverbs That Modify Adjectives or Other Adverbs An adverb that modifies an adjective or another adverb is also connected to the word it modifies. It is written on a line parallel to the word it modifies.

A very costly error occurred quite recently.

Too often these obviously careless mistakes happen.

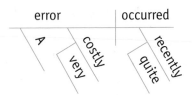

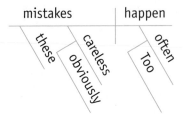

● **Practice Your Skills**

Diagraming Adjectives and Adverbs

Diagram the following sentences or copy them. If you copy them, draw one line under each subject and two lines under each verb. Then label each modifier *adjective* or *adverb*.

1. Many birds fly here.
2. Three large birdfeeders are always filled.
3. Many different birds land hurriedly.
4. They walk back and forth.
5. Their little mouths open widely.
6. Suddenly the dog barks loudly.
7. They fly away very quickly.
8. The very curious dog looks around.
9. It goes away again.
10. Quite soon the hungry birds will return.

Assess Your Learning

Finding Adjectives and Adverbs

Make two columns on your paper. Label the first column *Adjectives* and the second column *Adverbs.* Then in the proper column, write each adjective and adverb.

1. In 1883, a volcano on Krakatoa erupted suddenly.

2. This eruption was the most violent explosion of modern times.

3. Volcanic ash soared fifty miles into the atmosphere.

4. The ash constantly circled the earth.

5. The dark cloud of ash severely blocked the sun.

6. In fact, the normal amount of heat could not reach the earth during the whole next year.

7. Weather patterns changed throughout the world.

8. The northern states were unusually cold in 1884.

9. That year was "the year without a summer."

10. After forty years the island of Krakatoa finally became green again.

Identifying Adjectives and Adverbs

Write each adjective and adverb. Then beside each one, write the word or words each one modifies.

1. Words and actions are the main means of human communication.

2. Animals also have various methods of communication.

3. Very often the songs of birds convey messages.

4. Some animals communicate with body movements.

5. Communication is especially important in groups.

CHAPTER 16

Distinguishing Among Different Parts of Speech

Write each underlined word. Then label each one *noun, pronoun,* or *adjective.*

1. Which airplane hangar is off limits to the public?

2. I have math after lunch.

3. What book did this come from?

4. Party decorations were hung across the barn door.

5. Several desserts were on the lunch menu.

6. What is the answer to the second math problem?

7. I need a new picture frame for this photograph.

8. Which would you prefer to fly, a glider or a jet?

9. Several of my friends have been invited to the party.

10. Did you paint the picture of the barn?

Writing Sentences

Write sentences that follow the directions below. (The sentences may come in any order.) Write about this topic or one of your own choice: a memorable dream you have had.

Write a sentence that . . .

1. includes two adjectives before a noun.

2. includes an adjective after a linking verb.

3. includes two adjectives after a noun.

4. includes a proper adjective.

5. includes an article.

6. includes *that* as an adjective.

7. includes *that* as a pronoun.

8. includes an adverb at the beginning of a sentence.

9. includes an adverb in the middle of a sentence.

10. includes an adverb at the end of a sentence.

Adjectives and Adverbs: Posttest

Directions

Read the passage and decide which word or words are modified by the underlined word or words. Write the letter of the correct answer.

The carnivorous boa constrictor lives in South America. All boas, no matter what kind they are, are **(1)** <u>usually</u> called *boa constrictors* by people who don't know that there are about **(2)** <u>sixty</u> different species of boas. **(3)** <u>Primarily,</u> boas live in trees. The rubber boa, however, is a **(4)** <u>burrowing</u> species, and the **(5)** <u>western</u> United States is its home. The length of adult boas varies from eight inches to over **(6)** <u>fifteen</u> feet long. **(7)** <u>Most</u> species of boa give birth to live young, not eggs. Boas live **(8)** <u>mainly</u> in warm areas of North and South America. A **(9)** <u>hungry</u> boa captures rats and birds by biting them. Then the boa **(10)** <u>powerfully</u> squeezes its prey until the prey can't breathe.

1. A *boa constrictors*
   B are called
   C boas
   D people

2. A different
   B boa
   C of
   D species

3. A live
   B boas
   C trees
   D species

4. A species
   B rubber boa
   C is
   D however

5. A home
   B its
   C is
   D United States

6. A long
   B length
   C feet
   D boas

7. A boa
   B birth
   C species
   D live

8. A warm
   B live
   C areas
   D North and South America

9. A A
   B them
   C captures
   D boa

10. A squeezes
    B boa
    C until
    D can't breathe

Writer's Corner

Snapshot

16 A An **adjective** is a kind of modifier. It modifies a noun or a pronoun. (pages 524–531)

16 B An **adverb** is a word that modifies a verb, an adjective, or another adverb. (pages 532–536)

Power Rules

Some adverbs have negative meanings. **Avoid double negatives**—using negative words with such adverbs. (page 773)

Before Editing

It *won't hardly* matter if we work hard.

The shirt *won't barely* fit him anymore.

After Editing

It *will hardly* matter if we work hard.

The shirt *will barely* fit him anymore.

Editing Checklist ✔

Use this checklist when editing your writing.

✓ Did I use adjectives to make my writing more detailed and lively?
(See pages 524–527 and 535.)

✓ Did I use the correct article to modify each noun? (See page 527.)

✓ Did I make sure that all proper adjectives are capitalized? (See page 528.)

✓ Did I use adverbs to make my writing more interesting? (See pages 532–536.)

Use the Power ⚡

The table below lists four nouns and four verbs. Look at each noun. Then come up with a list of adjectives you might use to describe the look, feel, smell, taste, or sound of each noun. Create a similar list of adverbs you might use to modify each verb. A few words have been added to the two lists as examples.

NOUNS				VERBS			
car	friend	bell	cake	talk	run	laugh	act
red				*loudly*			
fast				*quickly*			

Review a composition you have completed recently, looking for adjectives and adverbs. Add detail and color by replacing repetitive and vague modifiers with more lively adjectives and adverbs.

Other Parts of Speech and Review

How can you create fluency in your writing by using prepositions and conjunctions to join ideas and sentences?

Other Parts of Speech and Review: Pretest 1

The following draft paragraph about the artistic movement known as abstract expressionism is hard to read because it contains unnecessary repetition and other errors. Revise the paragraph so that it reads more smoothly. One of the errors has been corrected as an example.

The painting above is an example of *abstract expressionism*, a painting style that began in New York in the 1940s. Jackson Pollock was one of the early American pioneers of ~~abstract expressionism~~ *this* style. Jackson Pollock invented a method of painting he called the "drip" technique in which he filled the canvas with drips and splashes of paint. He used hardened brushes, sticks, and even basting syringes to fling, drip, splash, or squirting paint at the canvas. Jackson Pollock stopped trying to show a figure or recognizable objects on his paintings. He was more interested in the paint itself. He also stopped using the upright easel! Instead, he placed large unframed canvases on the floor and walking all around the painting! He said that it made him feel closer at the painting, to be *in* the painting.

Other Parts of Speech and Review: Pretest 2

Directions

Write the letter of the term that correctly identifies the underlined word in each sentence.

(1) At the circus you <u>always</u> hear the calliope. (2) A calliope has a <u>keyboard</u> like one on a piano. (3) The keyboard is attached to <u>steam</u> whistles. (4) The calliope appeared in 1855 <u>and</u> was a hit. (5) <u>It</u> was first used for entertainment on riverboats. (6) <u>After</u> twenty years steamboats no longer used it. (7) Soon it found a home under the <u>circus</u> tent. (8) Even today the calliope <u>remains</u> the instrument commonly used by circuses and carnivals. (9) <u>Yippee!</u> We are going to the circus on Saturday. (10) Perhaps <u>I</u> will see a calliope up close.

1. **A** preposition
   B verb
   C adverb
   D adjective

2. **A** noun
   B adjective
   C pronoun
   D adverb

3. **A** verb
   B adjective
   C adverb
   D noun

4. **A** interjection
   B preposition
   C adverb
   D conjunction

5. **A** noun
   B interjection
   C verb
   D pronoun

6. **A** interjection
   B preposition
   C conjunction
   D adverb

7. **A** adjective
   B noun
   C adverb
   D preposition

8. **A** verb
   B adjective
   C adverb
   D preposition

9. **A** conjunction
   B preposition
   C verb
   D interjection

10. **A** noun
    B pronoun
    C verb
    D interjection

When someone gives you directions, a preposition such as *beside, on,* or *under* could make all the difference in finding what you are looking for.

> Look for Kate's painting **beside** the desk.
>
> Look for Kate's painting **on** the desk.
>
> Look for Kate's painting **under** the desk.

17 A **A preposition** is a word that shows the relationship between a noun or pronoun and another word in a sentence.

Prepositions are used to convey location, time, or direction. They also provide details. Notice that some prepositions can be more than one word.

COMMON PREPOSITIONS

about	because of	during	of	toward
above	before	except	off	under
according to	behind	for	on	underneath
across	below	from	out of	until
after	beneath	in	over	up
against	beside	in front of	past	upon
along	between	inside	since	up to
among	beyond	into	through	with
around	by	like	throughout	within
at	down	near	to	without

● **Practice Your Skills**

Supplying Prepositions

Complete each sentence. Fill in the blank with a preposition that makes sense.

(1) To make a batik, use muslin, acrylic paint, paintbrushes, and white tempera paint ___ an applicator bottle. **(2)** Plan a design ___ the month of your birthday or another event. **(3)** Place a piece of muslin ___ a table. **(4)** Put newspapers ___ the muslin ___ the table's protection. **(5)** ___ the white tempera paint, draw a design ___ the muslin.

Prepositional Phrases

A preposition is usually part of a group of words called a **prepositional phrase.**

17 A.1 A **prepositional phrase** is a group of words made up of a preposition, its object, and any words that modify the object.

Prepositional Phrases	Did you speak **with the baseball players?**
	(*Players* is the object of the preposition *with*.)
	Within a few months, the season will be finished.
	(*Months* is the object of the preposition *within*.)
	The players **on the team** will be friends.
	(*Team* is the object of the preposition *on*.)

A prepositional phrase can have more than one object. Such a phrase has a **compound object of a preposition.**

Compound Object of a Preposition	Boxes **of uniforms, bats, and balls** filled the dugout.

A sentence can have more than one prepositional phrase.

Before the game they rode **to the ball field.**

During the game some players go **into a frenzy around the dugout.**

● **Practice Your Skills**

Finding Prepositional Phrases

Write each prepositional phrase. Underline the preposition and circle its object.

(**1**) Baseball was originally played without any special equipment. (**2**) It was probably based on the English game of rounders. (**3**) In the early days, bases were tall stakes. (**4**) Many players ran into the stakes and were hurt. (**5**) Later the stakes were replaced with rocks. (**6**) Unfortunately, the rocks were also dangerous to the baseball players. (**7**) Eventually sandbags were placed at each base. (**8**) Early baseball bats were adapted from sticks. (**9**) In 1861, there was no limit for the length of a bat. (**10**) The diameter of a bat was restricted to 2½ inches. (**11**) Baseballs in terrible condition were used. (**12**) For many years baseball was played without gloves. (**13**) The first baseball glove was developed by Charles Waite. (**14**) It was like an ordinary winter glove.

Adding Prepositional Phrases

Complete each sentence. Fill in the blank with a prepositional phrase that completes the meaning of the sentence.

(1) The baseball player came ___. **(2)** He spoke ___. **(3)** The baseball player held the attention ___. **(4)** The students crowded around their guest ___. **(5)** The athlete shook hands ___. **(6)** He wrote his name ___.

➤ Preposition or Adverb?

Some words can be a preposition in one sentence and an adverb in another sentence. *Around,* for example, is a preposition when it is part of a prepositional phrase. *Around* is an adverb, however, when it stands alone and is not part of a prepositional phrase.

Preposition The student moved the cursor **around** the computer screen.

(*Around the computer screen* is a prepositional phrase.)

Adverb Alana moved the cursor **around.**

(*Around* is an adverb that tells where Alana moved the cursor.)

● **Practice Your Skills**

Distinguishing Between Prepositions and Adverbs

For each underlined word, write *P* for preposition or *A* for adverb.

(1) Some students had never used the help program <u>before</u>. **(2)** <u>Before</u> the first day of school, they had only used the computer to play games. **(3)** When they first are offered the "Help" option, they zip <u>past</u>. **(4)** They have gone <u>past</u> that key many times. **(5)** Through blank pages, error messages, and odd warning sounds, they stumble <u>along</u>. **(6)** Many hope that a teacher will stop <u>by</u>. **(7)** Others wait for their friends to come <u>by</u> to help them.

✔ *Check Point:* **Mixed Practice**

Write each prepositional phrase.

(1) Fireflies live in warm areas throughout the world. **(2)** During the daytime many fireflies eat plant pollen. **(3)** Fireflies lay their eggs on the ground. **(4)** Newly hatched fireflies burrow underneath the ground or hide within old stumps. **(5)** The red-and-green lights from one kind of firefly resemble traffic signals. **(6)** Scientists have recently learned much about firefly light. **(7)** The firefly's light comes from light organs on the underside of the abdomen. **(8)** The light of fireflies is not hot. **(9)** This cool light is produced by chemical reactions inside the insect. **(10)** The firefly's light stops after a final chemical reaction.

A connecting word is called a **conjunction.** There are three kinds of conjunctions: **coordinating, correlative,** and **subordinating.** An **interjection** is a word that expresses emotion.

17 B A **conjunction** is a word that connects words or groups of words. An **interjection** is a word that expresses strong feelings.

Conjunctions

17 B.1 A **coordinating conjunction** is a single connecting word.

The conjunctions in the following list are used to connect single words or groups of words.

COORDINATING CONJUNCTIONS			
and	but	or	yet

Connecting Words	*Jack London* **and** *Jamie Gilson* are good writers. (connects nouns)
	Have you ever heard of *him* **or** *her?* (connects pronouns)
	They *read* **and** *reviewed* their books. (connects verbs)
	Her book was *long* **but** *funny.* (connects adjectives)
	He wrote *slowly* **yet** *urgently.* (connects adverbs)
Connecting Groups of Words	She looked *on the chair* **and** *under the chair.* (connects prepositional phrases)
	He *began the story* **but** *did not finish it.* (connects complete predicates)
	He should finish the story, **or** *it will be ruined.* (connects sentences)

17 B.2   **Correlative conjunctions** are pairs of conjunctions.

Correlative conjunctions are word pairs that connect words or groups of words.

CORRELATIVE CONJUNCTIONS		
both/and	either/or	neither/nor

Connecting Words	**Both** *Lois Duncan* **and** *Gary Paulsen* are writers. (connects nouns)
	That book is **neither** *good* **nor** *interesting.* (connects adjectives)
Connecting Groups of Words	The book is **either** *in the car* **or** *on the shelf.* (connects prepositional phrases)
	Either *we will read it now,* **or** *we will wait for the next semester.* (connects sentences)

When You Write

Be sure the words or groups of words you connect with a conjunction are parallel in structure. Otherwise your writing can be confusing.

Not Parallel	Sam likes to help by cooking and serves the meals.
Parallel	Sam likes to help by **cooking** and **serving** the meals.

The third kind of conjunction is a subordinating conjunction. You can learn about subordinating conjunctions on pages 633–634.

➤ Interjections

Words that show strong emotion, such as *ugh, whew,* and *wow,* are interjections.

17 B.3   An **interjection** is a word that expresses strong feelings.

An interjection usually comes at the beginning of a sentence. It is followed by an exclamation point or a comma.

Ouch! That snack is hot.

Oh, I just remembered the dishes in the oven!

COMMON INTERJECTIONS					
aha	no	oops	ugh	wow	yikes
goodness	oh	ouch	well	yes	yippee

When You Write

Avoid overusing interjections. They lose their emphasis when you use too many of them. Try to save them for truly strong emotions so they will have a greater impact on your reader.

● **Practice Your Skills**

Finding Conjunctions and Interjections

Write and label each conjunction as *conj.* and each interjection as *inter.*

(1) Wow! Have you ever read Jack London's story "To Build a Fire"? (2) It is a chilling story of a man and a dog in the Yukon. (3) Oh, the Yukon offers amazing adventures! (4) Neither the man nor the dog is prepared for what happens next. (5) The temperature is 75°F below zero, but the inexperienced man does not know how cold it is. (6) First the man gets his feet wet, and then he is slow to get a fire going. (7) Ouch, the frostbite starts with sharp pain! (8) As he goes numb, both the inexperienced man and the loyal dog know they are in trouble. (9) Hurrah! A match finally sparks, the fire blazes, and they seem to be saved. (10) Alas, neither the man nor the dog will ever leave the cold Yukon.

● *Connect to Writing:* **Book Review**

Using Conjunctions and Interjections

Write a book review of your favorite book for a teen TV station. Be sure to summarize the book and to tell important events. You can discuss characters and story problems. Be sure to describe the events as they happened and to use conjunctions and interjections to keep your audience interested.

17 C The **part of speech** of a word is how the word is used in a sentence.

A word does not take on a part of speech until it is used in a sentence. Suppose, for example, that someone asked you what part of speech the word *play* is. Before answering, you would have to determine how *play* is used in a particular sentence because *play* can be used as three different parts of speech.

Noun	I saw a **play.**
Verb	She can **play** that sport well.
Adjective	The toddler rode in her little **play** car.

To find a word's part of speech, ask yourself, *What is the word doing in this sentence?*

Noun Is the word naming a person, place, thing, or idea?

Riley saw two different **events** in the swimming **competition.**

He has **faith** in the **Olympic Committee.**

Where is the **Olympic Stadium?**

Pronoun Is the word taking the place of a noun?

This is **his** present to **you.**

The medal is **hers.**

Verb Is the word showing action? Does it link the subject with another word in the sentence?

The athlete **has competed** in the event.

He **studied** his opponent's serve.

The tennis ball **was** very light.

Adjective Is the word modifying a noun or a pronoun? Does it answer the question *What kind? Which one? How many?* or *How much?*

The **college** coach seems **friendly.**

Almost everyone saw the **two** events.

Adverb	Is the word modifying a verb, an adjective, or another adverb? Does it answer the question *How? When? Where?* or *To what extent?*

The **very** young girl ran **extremely** fast.

The archer won a gold medal **immediately.**

Preposition	Is the word showing a relationship between a noun or a pronoun and another word in the sentence? Is it a part of a phrase?

***Before** the race,* she asked advice ***from** the Olympic Committee.*

Conjunction	Is the word connecting words or groups of words?

Bring your camera **and** some film.

Track is her favorite sport, **but** she is developing an interest in swimming.

Interjection	Is the word expressing strong feeling?

Wow! Those runners are quick.

Ouch! Did you see the jumper hit the bar?

● **Practice Your Skills**

Determining Parts of Speech

Write each underlined word. Beside each one, write its part of speech: *noun, pronoun, verb, adjective, adverb, preposition, conjunction,* or *interjection.*

(1) Wilma Rudolph was born <u>on</u> June 23, 1940, in St. Bethlehem, <u>Tennessee</u>. **(2)** At age four, she <u>suffered</u> attacks <u>of</u> double pneumonia and scarlet fever. **(3)** After these illnesses she <u>totally</u> lost the use of her <u>left</u> leg. **(4)** For the next seven years, she could <u>not</u> walk <u>without</u> braces on her legs. **(5)** With enormous <u>determination</u> she <u>painfully</u> exercised every day. **(6)** Wilma Rudolph even <u>played</u> basketball in her <u>backyard</u>. **(7)** <u>Incredible!</u> By high school she was a very healthy champion athlete. **(8)** During this time she broke records in <u>both</u> track <u>and</u> basketball. **(9)** In college <u>she</u> set world records as a sprinter and then set her eyes on the <u>Olympics</u>. **(10)** In 1956, Rudolph was <u>a</u> member <u>of</u> the American Olympic 400-meter relay team. **(11)** Each member of <u>the</u> team <u>received</u> a bronze medal. **(12)** In 1960, this courageous athlete became the first <u>American</u> woman to win <u>three</u> gold medals in track and field.

Practice Your Skills

Identifying Words as Different Parts of Speech

Write each underlined word. Then write how each word is used, using the following abbreviations.

noun = *n.*   verb = *v.*   adjective = *adj.*

1. Can you <u>name</u> the greatest athlete of the twentieth century?
2. His <u>name</u> is respected by people around the world.
3. According to *Sports Illustrated,* the answer to this <u>name</u> game is Muhammad Ali.
4. My dad plays the game of <u>golf</u>.
5. He <u>golfs</u> in many tournaments.
6. Do you know the brand of his <u>golf</u> clubs?
7. Tara Lipinsky is <u>skating</u> professionally now.
8. She won a gold medal in figure <u>skating</u>.
9. Her <u>skating</u> days are far from over.
10. Which sport do you <u>watch</u>?

Connect to Writing: Problem and Solution

Using the Parts of Speech

Every day people overcome problems to succeed at something. Think about a problem you have overcome or helped someone overcome. Then write several paragraphs telling about the problem and how it was solved. Pay careful attention to your word choice. Try to use as many parts of speech as you can.

Assess Your Learning

Finding Prepositions, Conjunctions, Interjections, and Prepositional Phrases

Write each sentence. Above the sentence, label each preposition **prep.**, each conjunction **conj.**, and each interjection **interj.** Then underline each prepositional phrase.

Example   Together Sam and Joey ran around the track.

                                        conj.   prep.
Answer   Together Sam and Joey ran <u>around the track</u>.

1. The lawyers for the trial spoke slowly but precisely.
2. After the rain the air seemed cooler, and the grass looked greener.
3. Yikes! Did you see that worm crawl up my toe and leg?
4. Either sleet or snow is expected today.
5. The black walnut grows widely over the eastern half of the United States.
6. Congratulations! Both your son and daughter have won.
7. The surefooted horse walked along the steep mountain trail without any difficulty.
8. In spite of their curiosity, neither Sam nor Earl has been inside the old mine or shack.
9. Gosh! Amanda walked onto the stage and immediately forgot her lines.
10. At that moment a huge dog dashed into our yard.

Identifying Parts of Speech

Write each underlined word. Then, beside each one, write its part of speech: **noun, pronoun, verb, adjective, adverb, preposition, conjunction,** or **interjection.**

1. David <u>and</u> <u>Dora</u> dawdled <u>dreamily</u> down the deck.
2. The <u>brisk</u> <u>breeze</u> blighted the bright <u>blossoms</u>.
3. <u>Several</u> sheep were sheared <u>swiftly</u> <u>with</u> sharp scissors.
4. The humble hermit hummed <u>happily</u> on <u>his</u> hickory <u>harmonica</u>.
5. The butler <u>bought</u> the butter, <u>but</u> he found <u>it</u> bitter.

6. Ugh! I saw a slippery slug hug a beetle bug.

7. Shellfish shells seldom sell.

8. Double-bubble gum bubbles beautifully.

9. Wealthy Wanda wears Swiss wristwatches.

10. Sunshine shines softly on scenic seashores.

Writing Sentences

Write sentences that follow the directions below. Then label the use of each italicized word in the sentence.

1. Use *apple* as a noun and an adjective.

2. Use *turn* as a noun and a verb.

3. Use *both* as a pronoun and an adjective.

4. Use *in* as an adverb and a preposition.

5. Use *toy* as a noun and an adjective.

6. Use *each* as a pronoun and an adjective.

7. Use *down* as an adverb and a preposition.

8. Use *plant* as a noun, a verb, and an adjective.

9. Use *well* as a noun, an adverb, and an interjection.

10. Use *light* as a noun, a verb, and an adjective.

Other Parts of Speech and Review: Posttest

Directions

Write the letter of the term that correctly identifies the underlined word or words in each sentence.

    (1) A protractor plots <u>and</u> measures angles. (2) The instrument with two pointed <u>arms</u> is a compass. (3) The compass <u>is used</u> for drawing circles or arcs. (4) A straightedge is the tool to use for drawing <u>straight</u> lines. (5) A ruler makes a handy <u>straightedge</u>. (6) <u>With</u> the ruler you can also measure lengths and widths. (7) For great lengths or distances, a tape measure is <u>also</u> useful. (8) A yardstick is the measuring instrument preferred by <u>many</u>. (9) We must <u>not</u> forget the calculator either. (10) In addition, most people also <u>like</u> a good eraser.

1. A pronoun
   B adverb
   C conjunction
   D adjective

2. A noun
   B pronoun
   C preposition
   D adjective

3. A adverb
   B interjection
   C verb
   D conjunction

4. A verb
   B adverb
   C noun
   D adjective

5. A preposition
   B noun
   C verb
   D conjunction

6. A interjection
   B noun
   C adjective
   D preposition

7. A adverb
   B adjective
   C preposition
   D noun

8. A preposition
   B adjective
   C pronoun
   D adverb

9. A preposition
   B conjunction
   C adjective
   D adverb

10. A preposition
   B verb
   C adjective
   D adverb

Writer's Corner

Snapshot

17 A A **preposition** is a word that shows the relationship between a noun or a pronoun and another word in a sentence. A **prepositional phrase** is a group of words made up of a preposition, its object, and any words that modify the object. (pages 546–548)

17 B A **conjunction** connects words or groups of words. An **interjection** is a word that expresses strong feelings. (pages 549–551)

17 C The **part of speech** of a word is determined by its usage. There are eight parts of speech: **nouns, verbs, adjectives, adverbs, pronouns, prepositions, conjunctions,** and **interjections.** (pages 552–554)

Power Rules

Be sure that you use the correct pronoun as an **object of a preposition.** (pages 714–715)

Before Editing	After Editing
Give the book to Randy and he.	Give the book to Randy and *him*.
This is a secret to be kept between you and I.	This is a secret to be kept between you and *me*.

Be sure that you join **run-on sentences** with a conjunction and/or proper punctuation. (pages 549–550 and 663–664)

Before Editing	After Editing
We went to the park, we played fetch with the dog.	We went to the park; we played fetch with the dog.
They saw the movie, they didn't like it.	They saw the movie, *but* they didn't like it.

Editing Checklist

Use this checklist when editing your writing.

✓ Did I make sure that I chose the preposition that makes the most sense? (See pages 546–548.)

✓ Did I make sure that my prepositional phrases are complete? (See pages 547–548.)

✓ Did I choose the most appropriate conjunctions to connect words and groups of words? (See pages 549–550.)

✓ Did I use an exclamation point or comma after an interjection? (See pages 550–551.)

✓ Did I vary my use of the parts of speech? Did I use the parts of speech correctly? (See pages 552–554.)

Use the Power

Prepositional phrases are often used to add location information to a sentence. Compare these two sentences.

Ricardo thought he saw a snake.

Ricardo thought he saw a snake **in the shed.**

Select a piece from your portfolio and highlight the prepositional phrases. If there are no prepositional phrases, add some! Experiment by placing the prepositional phrases in different places in your sentences.

CHAPTER 18

Complements

How can you use complements, or completers, to focus your writing?

Complements: Pretest 1

The following draft paragraph is hard to read because it contains short choppy sentences and missing complements. Revise the paragraph so that it reads more smoothly. Two sentences have been combined as an example.

> Horace Pippin was the grandson of slaves and domestic workers who lived in New York. He started ~~drawing~~ at a young age. ~~He liked drawing then.~~ After losing the use of his right hand in World War I, he began painting. Painting helped overcome bouts of depression. In 1937, an art collector noticed paintings in the window of a repair shop. Soon after, the Museum of Modern Art in New York City made an offer to exhibit the paintings. This offer was to Pippin. This opportunity launched his career as a folk artist. Painting from memory and imagination, Pippin created boldly colored landscapes, still lifes, and scenes from the war. He also painted scenes of everyday activities in the lives of African Americans. *Domino Players* shows a family at home, which is Pippin's own.

Complements: Pretest 2

Directions

Write the letter of the term that correctly identifies the underlined word in each sentence.

(1) Have you ever thrown a <u>snowball</u>? (2) One snowball is several thousand <u>snowflakes</u>. (3) Since 1940, scientists have studied <u>snowflakes</u>. (4) They have offered the <u>public</u> interesting information about snowflakes. (5) Each snowflake is <u>unique</u>. (6) Snowflakes generally have eight <u>sides</u>. (7) Their patterns, however, are always <u>different</u>. (8) Scientists often give these different <u>patterns</u> names. (9) The smallest flakes are extremely <u>tiny</u>. (10) Snowflakes are probably the most beautiful <u>forms</u> in nature.

1. **A** direct object
   B indirect object
   C predicate nominative
   D predicate adjective

2. **A** direct object
   B indirect object
   C predicate nominative
   D predicate adjective

3. **A** direct object
   B indirect object
   C predicate nominative
   D predicate adjective

4. **A** direct object
   B indirect object
   C predicate nominative
   D predicate adjective

5. **A** direct object
   B indirect object
   C predicate nominative
   D predicate adjective

6. **A** direct object
   B indirect object
   C predicate nominative
   D predicate adjective

7. **A** direct object
   B indirect object
   C predicate nominative
   D predicate adjective

8. **A** direct object
   B indirect object
   C predicate nominative
   D predicate adjective

9. **A** direct object
   B indirect object
   C predicate nominative
   D predicate adjective

10. **A** direct object
    B indirect object
    C predicate nominative
    D predicate adjective

18 A   A **complement** is a word that completes the meaning of a simple subject/verb sentence.

You know that every sentence has a subject and a verb.

> Laura found.   Paulo seems.

The groups of words above have a subject and a verb, but each one needs another word to complete its meaning. This additional word is called a complement, or completer.

> Laura found her **painting.**
>
> Paulo seems **inspired.**

There are four main kinds of complements. **Direct objects** and **indirect objects** always follow action verbs. **Predicate nominatives** and **predicate adjectives** always follow linking verbs and are called **subject complements.**

Direct Object	Maria drew a **cartoon.**
Indirect Object	Maria gave **me** the cartoon.
Predicate Nominative	Her drawing is my favorite **cartoon.**
Predicate Adjective	Maria's cartoon is **humorous.**

Direct Objects Lesson 2

A **direct object** is always a noun or a pronoun that follows an action verb.

18 B   A **direct object** is a noun or pronoun that receives the action of an action verb.

To find a direct object, first find the subject and the action verb in a sentence. Then ask yourself *Whom?* or *What?* after the verb. The answer to either question will be a direct object. In the following examples, the subjects are underlined once, and the verbs are underlined twice.

Direct Objects

Mark will exhibit two **paintings.**

(Mark will exhibit what? *Paintings* is the direct object.)

Carrie invited **them** to the museum.

(Carrie invited whom? *Them* is the direct object.)

To find the direct object in a question, change the question into a statement.

Question   Did you view the exhibit?

Statement   You did view the **exhibit.**

(You did view what? *Exhibit* is the direct object.)

18 B.1   A **compound direct object** consists of two or more direct objects following the same verb.

Compound Direct Object

Uncle Luke sells **paintings** and **sculptures.**

(Uncle Luke sells what? The compound direct object is *paintings* and *sculptures.*)

You can learn about action verbs and transitive verbs on pages 508–511.

● **Practice Your Skills**

Finding Direct Objects

Write the action verb in each sentence. Then beside it, write the direct object. Some sentences may have a compound direct object.

(1) As a young person, Marc Chagall loved Russia. **(2)** The future painter studied the landscape, the buildings, and the people. **(3)** He saw beauty in all these things. **(4)** One day he drew a wonderful portrait of a man. **(5)** Chagall drew more and more pictures. **(6)** The young Russian had found his career. **(7)** Later, he studied art in Paris. **(8)** In Paris, Chagall joined the Cubism art movement. **(9)** He used bright colors and fantasy in his paintings. **(10)** He met his future wife in Russia. **(11)** The couple made their home in Paris. **(12)** Chagall's art contained many poetic images. **(13)** He decorated the ceiling of the Paris Opera. **(14)** Later, he designed many stained-glass windows. **(15)** With bright colors and vivid images, he expressed his optimistic nature.

● **Practice Your Skills**

Adding Direct Objects to Sentences

The following sentences are a set of directions for making a rubbing of a textured object using a piece of paper and a pencil. Write each sentence, filling each blank with one or more direct objects.

1. Have you ever made a ▢ of interesting textures?
2. You should gather ▢ .
3. You should find ▢ with unusual and interesting textures.
4. First, you lay ▢ over your object.
5. Second, you rub the ▢ with a colored pencil or pastel.
6. Finally, you choose the ▢ for your picture.

Indirect Objects

Like a direct object, an **indirect object** is a noun or pronoun that follows an action verb. To have an indirect object, a sentence must have a direct object.

> **18 C** An **indirect object** is a noun or pronoun that answers the questions *To whom?* or *For whom?* or *To what?* or *For what?* after an action verb.

To find an indirect object, first find the direct object. Then ask yourself, *To whom? For whom? To what?* or *For what?* about the direct object. The answer to any of these questions will be an indirect object. An indirect object always comes before a direct object.

Indirect Objects

⌐i.o.⌐ ⌐d.o.⌐
The guest speaker showed the **senators** the video.
(*Video* is the direct object. The guest speaker showed the video to whom? *Senators* is the indirect object.)

⌐i.o.⌐ ⌐d.o.⌐
The guide gave **everyone** a sample.
(*Sample* is the direct object. The guide gave a sample to whom? *Everyone* is the indirect object.)

> **18 C.1** A **compound indirect object** consists of two or more indirect objects that follow the same verb.

Compound Indirect Object

⌐i.o.⌐ ⌐i.o.⌐ ⌐d.o.⌐
I bought **Mandy** and **them** souvenirs.
(I bought souvenirs for whom? The compound indirect object is *Mandy* and *them*.)

⌐i.o.⌐ ⌐i.o.⌐ ⌐d.o.⌐
They showed **Jack** and **Tim** the souvenirs.
(They showed the souvenirs to whom? The compound indirect object is *Jack* and *Tim*.)

CHAPTER 18

When You Speak and Write

You can say and write more in fewer words by combining related sentences through the use of direct and indirect objects. Notice how the twelve words in the first two sentences below can be combined to make one sentence of seven words.

> I bought a gift of apples. I gave the apples to Mary.
>
> I bought Mary a gift of apples.

Review a piece of writing you have completed recently. Look for pairs of related sentences you can combine by using direct and indirect objects.

● **Practice Your Skills**

Finding Indirect Objects

Write each indirect object.

(1) Fate has dealt Max Cleland an unusual life. (2) His parents promised the young boy from Georgia a college education. (3) At college, the United States Army granted the sophomore a commission in the Reserve Officer Training Corps. (4) In 1964, the Army gave the college graduate a commission in Vietnam. (5) A grenade during combat assigned Max a new role as a physically challenged veteran. (6) Life in a wheelchair handed the amputee new opportunities. (7) The people of Georgia gave the former political science major a job as a state legislator. (8) A few years later, President Carter sent the official an invitation to direct the U.S. Veterans Administration. (9) From 1997 until 2003, voters in his home state gave Cleland the honor of serving in the U.S. Senate. (10) This remarkable man gives other people inspiration.

● **Practice Your Skills**

Finding Compound Indirect Objects

Write each compound indirect object.

(1) American expansion in the 1800s gave Alaska, Panama, and Hawaii economic growth. (2) Building the Panama Canal supplied Europe, the United States, and the rest of the world quicker travel routes. (3) The purchase of Alaska from Russia provided American citizens and investors oil, gold, and copper resources. (4) In the early 1800s, Hawaii offered Americans and others economic opportunities. (5) Key location and rich soil brought Hawaii and the rest of the Pacific region opportunities for trade. (6) The Pacific region handed the United States and other countries strategic ports. (7) The Hawaiians sold planters and businesses their land. (8) These beautiful islands give their people and businesses sugar cane and pineapples.

Write the object or objects in each sentence. Label the direct objects *d.o.* and the indirect objects *i.o.*

1. The teacher gave everyone a food guide from the health book.

2. Did you find Jesse and me a cookbook?

3. We are planning nutritious meals.

4. We made them a fruit salad with fruit from the garden.

5. I made the family eggs and toast for breakfast.

6. Jesse gave Luis a glass of milk.

7. Will you lend me your recipe for that salad?

8. Mom showed Jesse and me the ingredients for the recipe.

9. Add this cucumber and tomato.

10. We brought our teacher some delicious salad for her lunch.

● *Connect to Writing:* **Business Letter**

Using Indirect Objects

Imagine that you have just returned from a trip to Hawaii. Write a thank-you letter to a Hawaiian business from which you purchased something. Express your appreciation for either good service or a great product. Before writing, ask yourself the following questions to help choose your topic.

• What product might I purchase only in Hawaii?

• What would be special about a trip to Hawaii?

• Would I most appreciate a sailing, fishing, or dining experience on this island?

Keep the letter short by using action verbs, direct objects, and indirect objects.

A **predicate nominative** is a noun or a pronoun that follows a linking verb. A predicate nominative is also called a **subject complement** because it identifies, renames, or explains the subject of a sentence.

> **18 D** A **predicate nominative** is a noun or a pronoun that follows a linking verb and identifies, renames, or explains the subject.

To identify a predicate nominative, you will need to be able to recognize a linking verb. Refresh your learning by studying the chart below.

COMMON LINKING VERBS	
Be Verbs	is, am, are, was, were, be, being, been, shall be, will be, can be, should be, would be, may be, might be, has been, have been, had been
Others	appear, become, feel, grow, look, remain, seem, sound, stay, taste, turn

You can learn more about linking verbs on pages 514–516.

To find a predicate nominative, first find the subject and the linking verb. Then find the noun or the pronoun that identifies, renames, or explains the subject. This word will be a predicate nominative.

Predicate Nominative

He was the **actor** of the year.
(*Actor* renames the subject *he*.)

That is my favorite **movie.**
(*Movie* renames the subject *that*.)

Was that **they** in the movie?
(Change a question into a statement. *That was they in the movie. They* renames the subject *that*.)

Might she be a famous **actress?**
(Change a question into a statement. *She might be a famous actress. Actress* renames the subject *she*.)

18 D.1 A **compound predicate nominative** consists of two or more predicate nominatives following the same verb.

Two early <u>actresses</u> of television <u><u>were</u></u> **Lucille Ball** and **Imogene Coca.**

(*Lucille Ball* and *Imogene Coca* both rename the subject *actresses*.)

● **Practice Your Skills**

Finding Predicate Nominatives

Write each predicate nominative.

1. Television is the electronic transmission of images and sound.
2. An important period in television history was the early part of the 1950s.
3. During that period, former radio listeners became an audience of television viewers.
4. A television set became the new technology for most homes.
5. All through the 1970s, television remained the main form of home entertainment.
6. Was TV the final chapter of the home entertainment industry?
7. During the 1980s, video games were the new technological wonder.
8. A game system became a standard technology in many homes.
9. Today, handheld devices are the technological wonders.
10. Is technology a permanent part of home entertainment?

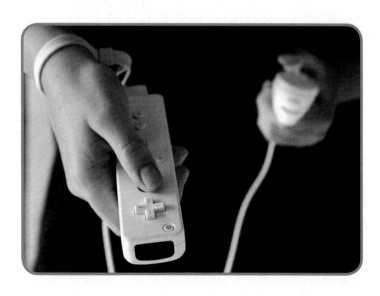

Practice Your Skills

Supplying Predicate Nominatives

Write a predicate nominative that completes each sentence. Beside each predicate nominative, write the word it renames. (If you use a pronoun as a predicate nominative, use only *I, you, he, she, it, we,* or *they.*)

1. One of the most popular television shows today is ▇ .

2. Members of my family who like the show are ▇ and ▇ .

3. Two reasons for its popularity are its ▇ and its ▇ .

4. Its appeal to young people is its ▇ .

5. My favorite character on the show always has been ▇ .

6. Was that ▇ who was a guest star last week?

Connect to Writing: Revising

Replacing Predicate Nominatives

Revise each sentence, replacing the underlined predicate nominative with a proper or common noun.

1. The owner of the local TV station is <u>she</u>.

2. The stars of the early morning news show are <u>she</u> and <u>he</u>.

3. Who are <u>they</u> in the studio?

4. "It is <u>I</u>," said Gary Rogers.

5. The executive producer of daytime programming is <u>he</u>.

Connect to Writing: Poetry

Using Predicate Nominatives

Write a poem of at least eight lines and have each line begin with the phrase "I am." Use predicate nominatives to complete each line. You might include your various roles in your family, at school, and in your community. You also may name the things that you do, such as "I am a baseball player." Use adjectives to modify your predicate nominatives to create individual images and sounds in your poem.

A **predicate adjective** is a subject complement that follows a linking verb and that modifies, or describes, the subject of the sentence.

18 E   **A predicate adjective** is an adjective that follows a linking verb and modifies the subject.

To find a predicate adjective, find the subject and the linking verb. Then find an adjective that follows the verb and describes the subject. This word will be the predicate adjective.

Predicate Adjectives

That silent <u>movie</u> <u>seems</u> unusually **comical.**

(*Comical* describes the subject—the *comical movie.*)

Is that <u>movie</u> too **long?**

(Change a question into a statement. *That movie is too long. Long* describes the subject—the *long movie.*)

18 E.1   A **compound predicate adjective** consists of two or more predicate adjectives that follow the same verb.

Compound Predicate Adjective

The <u>theater</u> <u>was</u> **clean** and **comfortable.** (Both *clean* and *comfortable* describe the subject *theater.*)

● **Practice Your Skills**

Finding Predicate Adjectives

Write each predicate adjective. (Some sentences may have a compound predicate adjective.)

1. Surprisingly, the costumes in the movie are colorful.
2. The dancer is amazingly graceful.
3. The eyes of the singer appeared especially beautiful and kind.
4. The music is soft but fast.
5. The actor sounded confident during his interview with the director.
6. Those questions seemed easy to him.
7. Some songs from the movie are incredibly rhythmical.
8. Over the past year, the actress has become quite popular.
9. Was that movie very good?
10. The characters seemed unusually fascinating and realistic.

● **Practice Your Skills**

Supplying Predicate Adjectives

Write a predicate adjective that completes each sentence.

1. Today English class became ▢ .

2. The poetry assignment seemed ▢ .

3. I wrote in my journal that the assigned poem is ▢ and ▢ .

4. All during class, the other students were ▢ and ▢ .

5. The classroom atmosphere felt ▢ .

6. The teacher looked rather ▢ when she read the poem aloud.

✔ *Check Point:* **Mixed Practice**

Write the complement or complements in each sentence. Then label each one, using the following abbreviations.

predicate adjective = *p.a.*   indirect object = *i.o*

predicate nominative = *p.n.*   direct object = *d.o.*

(1) The amusement park had its start in France during the eighteenth century. (2) Originally it was a place only for relaxation. (3) Park directors soon gave these parks games and rides. (4) Around 1860, Coney Island became the biggest attraction in New York City. (5) It was fun for people of all ages. (6) Coney Island developed three parks within its borders. (7) Steeplechase Park was the most popular of those three. (8) Other cities were anxious for amusement parks of their own. (9) Soon cities across the country built new parks. (10) The introduction of the theme park gave directors of parks new ideas.

● *Connect to Writing:* **Movie Review**

Using Predicate Adjectives

Write a movie review of your favorite movie for the school newspaper. State your opinion of the movie. Try to use vivid and specific predicate adjectives in your sentences to make your opinion clear to the reader. When you have finished your review, underline the predicate adjectives you used.

➤ Using Sentence Patterns

Good writers not only select the correct words, but also place them in the right order or in the right pattern. Following are examples of five basic sentence patterns.

PATTERN 1: S-V (subject–verb)

   S   V
Dogs bark.
      S   V
Many dogs bark at strangers.

PATTERN 2: S-V-O (subject–verb–direct object)

    S   V   O
Students enjoy sports.
      S   V   O
Most students at my school really enjoy team sports.

PATTERN 3: S-V-I-O (subject–verb–indirect object–direct object)

   S   V   I   O
Friends give us fruit.
      S   V   I   O
Several friends often give us fruit from their trees.

PATTERN 4: S-V-N (subject–verb–predicate nominative)

    S   V   N
My collection is stamps.
       S   V   N
My biggest collection is stamps from foreign lands.

PATTERN 5: S-V-A (subject–verb–predicate adjective)

    S   V   A
Customers were restless.
      S   V   A
The customers in the restaurant were very restless.

To find the pattern of a sentence, drop the adjectives, adverbs, and prepositional phrases.

S   V   N

~~The~~ Pentagon is ~~the largest office~~ building ~~in the world~~.

● **Practice Your Skills**

Identifying Sentence Patterns

Write the sentence pattern of each sentence. Use the abbreviations beside each pattern on page 573.

1. The copper weather vane on the roof creaks.
2. Students in the school annually hold an art exhibit.
3. The waterfall near our camp sounded quite pleasant.
4. My grandfather proudly showed the dinner guests his bowling trophies.
5. The fireworks at the Fourth of July celebration brightly lit the dark sky.
6. The old bed in the attic feels very lumpy.
7. My next-door neighbor just became a reporter.
8. The wind howled like a wolf last night.
9. The autumn leaves suddenly turned very colorful.
10. My little sister bought her best friend two goldfish.

● **Practice Your Skills**

Expanding Sentences

Each of the following sentences follows a different sentence pattern. Expand each sentence by adding adjectives, adverbs, and/or prepositional phrases.

1. (S-V) Airplanes landed.
2. (S-V-O) Hikers found paths.
3. (S-V-I-O) Children told visitors stories.
4. (S-V-N) The winner was a friend.
5. (S-V-A) Weather is uncertain.

Diagraming Complements

The **sentence base** includes a subject, a verb, and sometimes a complement. Complements are diagramed on the baseline or are attached to it.

Direct Objects A direct object is placed on the baseline after the verb. The direct object and the verb are separated by a vertical line that stops at the baseline.

I have already read that book.

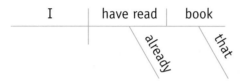

Compound Direct Objects Place the parts of a compound direct object on parallel horizontal lines. Then put the conjunction connecting each part on a broken vertical line between them.

Jonathan repaired the fence and gate.

Indirect Objects An indirect object is diagramed on a horizontal line that is connected to the verb by a slanted line.

Give me a chance.

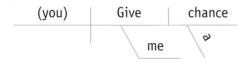

Subject Complements A predicate nominative or a predicate adjective is placed on the baseline after the verb. These subject complements are separated from the verb by a slanted line that points back toward the subject.

Alaska is the largest state.

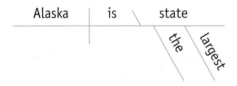

The morning air was quite damp.

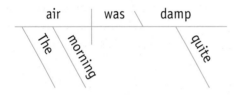

➤ Subject Complements

Diagram the following sentences or copy them. If you copy them, draw one line under each subject and two lines under each verb. Label each complement using these abbreviations.

d.o. = direct object	*p.n.* = predicate nominative
i.o. = indirect object	*p.a.* = predicate adjective

1. My soft sculpture won first prize.

2. Dad gave me some new stamps.

3. A doll collection is a good hobby.

4. I have made a tool chest and a plant stand.

5. Your paintings look very real.

6. Will you show Ben and me your coin collection?

7. Haven't you given him your old bottle caps?

8. Some old books are dusty and smelly.

9. Play us another song.

10. My favorite hobbies are the drums and art.

Assess Your Learning

Finding Direct and Indirect Objects

Write each complement. Then label each one *d.o.* for direct object or *i.o.* for indirect object. (Some sentences have a compound complement.)

1. Pitcher plants trap insects in their hollow leaves.

2. Each Mother's Day Ann serves her mother breakfast.

3. Ayako feeds her turtle special food.

4. Will you do a favor for me?

5. Before dinner, show Bruce and him the new calf.

6. On his birthday José gave a card and a present to Rosa.

7. Orchids take their food and water from the air.

8. Brian likes most fresh vegetables.

9. Our neighbors gave us a fan during the heat wave.

10. Wish me luck.

Finding Subject Complements

Write each complement. Then label each one *p.n.* for predicate nominative or *p.a.* for predicate adjective. (Some sentences have a compound complement.)

1. The state flower of Alaska is the forget-me-not.

2. Chinese food is certainly tasty and nutritious.

3. Your fingerprints are different from everyone else's.

4. Did Mark become an officer in the Honor Society?

5. The harpies of Greek mythology were hideous monsters.

6. The new band members are she and Carlos.

7. The action in a hockey game is fast and furious.

8. That must have been Shaniqua on the telephone.

9. In the moonlight the swamp looked ghostly.

10. The winds of Antarctica are constant and violent.

Identifying Complements

Write each complement. Then label each one **d.o.** for direct object, **i.o.** for indirect object, **p.n.** for predicate nominative, or **p.a.** for predicate adjective.

1. Yesterday my family bought a computer.

2. The computer is a basic, no-frills model.

3. We are, however, happy about our high-tech purchase.

4. Today we sent an Internet provider our application.

5. Now we can send e-mails to all our friends.

6. Sharing the computer is a challenge.

7. Everyone is eager for an hour or two at the keyboard.

8. My brother actually offered me ten dollars for my turn!

Writing Sentences

Write five sentences that follow the directions below. (The sentences may come in any order.) Write about the following topic or about a topic of your own choice: the funniest present you ever gave or received.

Write a sentence that . . .

1. includes a direct object.

2. includes an indirect object and a direct object.

3. includes a predicate nominative.

4. includes a predicate adjective.

5. includes a compound direct object.

When you have finished, underline and label each complement.

Complements: Posttest

Directions

Write the letter of the term that correctly identifies the underlined word in each sentence.

(1) The cello is a stringed musical <u>instrument</u> of the violin family. (2) I like the deep, rich <u>voice</u> of the cello. (3) The sound of the cello is a beautiful <u>bass</u>. (4) Compared to the violin, the cello is quite <u>large</u>. (5) Someone told <u>me</u> the measurements of the cello. (6) The entire instrument is about forty-seven <u>inches</u> in length. (7) Nowadays, cellos have four <u>strings</u>. (8) The first cellos were a <u>product</u> of the sixteenth century. (9) Crafters often gave these early <u>cellos</u> five strings. (10) Cellos were <u>popular</u> in ensembles.

1. **A** direct object
   B indirect object
   C predicate nominative
   D predicate adjective

2. **A** direct object
   B indirect object
   C predicate nominative
   D predicate adjective

3. **A** direct object
   B indirect object
   C predicate nominative
   D predicate adjective

4. **A** direct object
   B indirect object
   C predicate nominative
   D predicate adjective

5. **A** direct object
   B indirect object
   C predicate nominative
   D predicate adjective

6. **A** direct object
   B indirect object
   C predicate nominative
   D predicate adjective

7. **A** direct object
   B indirect object
   C predicate nominative
   D predicate adjective

8. **A** direct object
   B indirect object
   C predicate nominative
   D predicate adjective

9. **A** direct object
   B indirect object
   C predicate nominative
   D predicate adjective

10. **A** direct object
    B indirect object
    C predicate nominative
    D predicate adjective

Writer's Corner

Snapshot

18 A A **complement** is a word that completes the meaning of a simple subject/verb sentence. (page 562)

18 B A **direct object** is a noun or pronoun that answers the question *Whom?* or *What?* after an action verb. (pages 563–564)

18 C An **indirect object** is a noun or pronoun that answers the questions *To whom?* or *For whom?* or *To what?* or *For what?* after an action verb. (pages 565–567)

18 D A **predicate nominative** is a noun or a pronoun that follows a linking verb and identifies, renames, or explains the subject. (pages 568–570)

18 E A **predicate adjective** is an adjective that follows a linking verb and modifies the subject. (pages 571–572)

Power Rules

Use **subject forms of pronouns** in subject position. Use the **object form** when a pronoun is a direct object, an indirect object, or the object of a preposition. (pages 712–716)

Before Editing	**After Editing**
Bill and *me* are in the fall play.	Bill and *I* are in the fall play.
I made a snack for Shelby and *he*.	I made a snack for Shelby and *him*.

Check for **fragments** and correct them by combining them with a related sentence. (pages 549–550 and 656–661)

Before Editing	**After Editing**
Chocolate is delicious. *Hard to stop eating.*	Chocolate is delicious *and* hard to stop eating.
For Valentine's Day my dad bought my mom some roses. *And some chocolate.*	For Valentine's Day my dad bought my mom some roses *and* some chocolate.

Editing Checklist

Use this checklist when editing your writing.

✓ Did I make sure that all the subject/verb pairs in my sentences have the necessary complements? (See page 562.)

✓ Did I make sure that the questions *Whom?* and *What?* in my sentences are answered with direct objects? (See pages 563–564.)

✓ Did I make sure that the questions *To whom?* and *To what?* in my sentences are answered with indirect objects? (See pages 565–567.)

✓ Do the predicate nominatives in my sentences help to explain the subject? (See pages 568–570.)

✓ Do the predicate adjectives in my sentences modify the subject? (See pages 571–572.)

Use the Power

Complements help you add variety and detail to your sentences. Without them the English language would be a rather poor vehicle for communicating ideas. Consider these sentences.

The Venus' flytrap is. It traps and consumes.

Complements allow you to complete the ideas.

The Venus' flytrap is **a plant.** It traps and consumes **insects.**

By modifying complements you can add a great deal of detail.

The Venus' flytrap is **an unusual carnivorous plant.** It traps and consumes **insects with its snap-like traps.**

Review a composition you completed recently. Underline and identify complements in five sentences. Can you provide more detail by modifying the complements?

CHAPTER 19

Phrases

How can you use phrases to add variety and detail to your writing?

Phrases: Pretest 1

The draft paragraph below is hard to read because it contains several phrase errors, such as misplaced modifiers and punctuation problems. Revise the paragraph so that it reads more smoothly. The first sentence has been edited as an example.

Pablo Picasso␣a twentieth-century artist␣often expressed strong emotions through his paintings. For clues to its meaning, he created scenes that would compel viewers to study the work. Picasso painted *The Tragedy* (shown above) during his Blue Period (1901–1904). In this period he used shades of blue to paint images of beggars and lonely people. The Blue Period, was followed by his Rose Period (1905–1906). In shades of pink, he painted images of circus performers. These paintings, continued to reflect a sense of isolation in warm colors.

Phrases: Pretest 2

Directions

Write the letter of the term that correctly identifies the underlined word or words in each sentence.

(1) The cassowary, <u>a large bird</u>, does not fly. (2) Cassowaries live <u>in the rain forests</u> of Australia and Malaysia. (3) The largest living birds, <u>ostriches</u>, are found in Africa. (4) Ostriches lay their eggs <u>in holes</u> in the sand. (5) The height <u>of an ostrich</u> can be eight feet. (6) Another flightless bird, <u>the large, brownish rhea</u>, lives in Africa. (7) The speed of a running rhea can surpass that <u>of a horse</u>. (8) The five-foot rhea feeds <u>on plants and insects</u>. (9) The emu is a fourth type <u>of flightless bird</u>. (10) Their large greenish eggs are hatched <u>by the male</u>.

1. **A** adjectival phrase
   B adverbial phrase
   C appositive
   D appositive phrase

2. **A** adjectival phrase
   B adverbial phrase
   C appositive
   D appositive phrase

3. **A** adjective
   B adverbial phrase
   C appositive
   D appositive phrase

4. **A** adjectival phrase
   B adverbial phrase
   C appositive
   D appositive phrase

5. **A** adjectival phrase
   B adverbial phrase
   C appositive
   D appositive phrase

6. **A** adjectival phrase
   B adverbial phrase
   C appositive
   D appositive phrase

7. **A** adjectival phrase
   B adverbial phrase
   C appositive
   D appositive phrase

8. **A** adjectival phrase
   B adverbial phrase
   C appositive
   D appositive phrase

9. **A** adjectival phrase
   B adverbial phrase
   C appositive
   D appositive phrase

10. **A** adjectival phrase
    B adverbial phrase
    C appositive
    D appositive phrase

Prepositional Phrases Lesson 1

A **phrase** is a group of words that acts like a single part of speech. A phrase does not have a subject or a verb. One kind of phrase is a prepositional phrase.

19 A A **prepositional phrase** is a group of words that begins with a preposition, ends with a noun or a pronoun, and is used as an adjective or an adverb.

Prepositional phrases are used to convey location, time, direction, and to provide details.

Location	Place the bird guide **in the backpack.**
Time	We will start our first bird walk **in the morning.**
Direction	The plan is to walk **toward the lake.**
Details	The woman **with the binoculars** is our guide.

The following is a list of common prepositions.

COMMON PREPOSITIONS

about	below	inside	to
above	beneath	into	towards
according to	beside	like	under
across	between	near	underneath
after	beyond	of	until
against	by	off	up
along	down	on	upon
among	during	out of	up to
around	except	over	with
at	for	past	within
because of	from	since	without
before	in	through	
behind	in front of	throughout	

You can learn more about prepositions on pages 546–548.

Finding Prepositional Phrases

Write each prepositional phrase in the following paragraph.

(1) A most unusual hotel is located in Africa. (2) The hotel is not built on the ground. (3) Instead, it is forty feet above the ground in the branches of a giant tree. (4) Underneath the tree is a large salt deposit. (5) During the evening the animals from the jungle come to the salt deposit for a lick. (6) The guests at the hotel sit on the screened porch above the salt deposit. (7) From their easy chairs, in comfort and safety, they can watch the wild animals.

Adjectival Phrases

An adjectival phrase is a prepositional phrase that is used like a single adjective.

| Single Adjective | *"Fiddler on the Roof"* is a **long** CD. |
| Adjectival Phrase | *"Fiddler on the Roof"* is a CD **with fourteen songs.** |

19 A.1 An **adjectival phrase** is a prepositional phrase that is used to modify a noun or a pronoun.

An adjectival phrase answers the question *Which one?* or *What kind?* just as a single adjective does.

Which One?	The cassette **on the right** is hers.
	I like the songs **on that CD.**
What Kind?	Dad prefers music **from the disco era.**
	Mom has a car **without a CD player.**

A sentence can have more than one adjectival phrase.

That kind **of song** is for parents **with young children.**

Friends **from the community** came to the benefit **for the school band.**

Sometimes an adjectival phrase may modify a noun or a pronoun in another phrase.

The show **about music of the past** was fascinating.

The section **on swing music across the ages** was cool.

When You Write

Watch for places where you can combine short sentences with an adjectival phrase.

Two Sentences	Leo buys a lunch. Lunch is pizza and milk.
Combined	Leo buys a lunch **of pizza and milk.**
Two Sentences	Jana emptied her purse. Her purse was full of coins.
Combined	Jana emptied her purse **of its coins.**

● **Practice Your Skills**

Finding Adjectival Phrases

Write each adjectival phrase.

(1) Louis Armstrong was a native of New Orleans. (2) He has been called the king of jazz trumpet players. (3) He joined the famous jazz band of Kid Ory. (4) However, this player of the trumpet preferred small bands. (5) A typical Armstrong recording is a mixture of voice and trumpet. (6) Armstrong's influence on jazz was enormous. (7) He played a variety of melodic variations. (8) Once he played a series of 250 high C notes in a row! (9) Some of his popular records include duets with Bessie Smith. (10) People outside jazz know Armstrong's "Hello, Dolly" and "Mack the Knife."

● **Practice Your Skills**

Finding Adjectival Phrases

Write each adjectival phrase. Then write the word it modifies.

1. One musical by Richard Rodgers and Oscar Hammerstein is *Carousel.*

2. A carousel ride begins this story about two people and their friends.

3. The person in front of the carousel attracts Julie's attention.

4. Billy makes a sound like a loud microphone.

5. Julie rides the white horse on the carousel.

6. A carousel is another name for a merry-go-round.

7. Billy loves Julie with the curly hair.

8. Billy's death in a fight is sad.

9. The Starkeeper in heaven sends Billy back home.

10. Billy must do something of value.

● *Connect to Writing:* **Revising**

Combining Sentences Using Adjectival Phrases

Combine each group of sentences into one sentence by using an adjectival phrase.

1. Julie has brown hair. Her hair has curls.

2. She has an accent. The accent is from New England.

3. She wears the same clothes. She wears laced shoes and a frilly dress.

4. Julie is a happy person. She always has a smile on her face.

➤ Misplaced Adjectival Phrases

An adjectival phrase should be as close as possible to the word it describes. When a phrase is too far away from the word it describes, it is called a **misplaced modifier.** Misplaced modifiers can confuse the meaning of a sentence or make it sound silly.

Misplaced Modifiers	The children laughed at Zany Mr. Science **in the audience.** (The sentence seems to be saying that Zany Mr. Science is in the audience.)
	In the glass jar, Tom studied the squirming bugs. (Tom seems to be in the glass jar.)
	In the dish, the bugs ate the food. (The reader might think the bugs are in the dish.)

To correct a misplaced modifier, place the adjectival phrase as close as possible to the word it describes.

Correct Modifiers	The children **in the audience** laughed at Zany Mr. Science. (Now the children, not Zany Mr. Science, are in the audience.)
	Tom studied the squirming bugs **in the glass jar.** (Now the bugs, not Tom, are in the glass jar.)
	The bugs ate the food **in the dish.** (Now the food, not the bugs, is in the dish.)

Identifying Misplaced Modifiers

If a sentence contains a misplaced modifier, write *I* for incorrect. If a sentence is correct as written, write **C.**

1. In the nature preserve, the class visited the animals.

2. The science teacher taught a lesson about the different species.

3. She explained the procedure of the trip.

4. Maps were handed out to the students of the woods.

5. With a skinny tail Matt saw a small gray mouse.

6. Glenda fed peanuts to the squirrels from a jar.

7. A skunk had a broad white stripe on the path.

8. With huge wings Jen saw an American eagle.

9. Take that lunch basket to Mr. Reynolds with the wooden handles.

10. We quickly ate our lunch of sandwiches and juice.

● *Connect to Writing:* **Revising**

Correcting Misplaced Adjectival Phrases

Rewrite the incorrect sentences from the preceding exercise, placing each adjectival phrase closer to the word it modifies.

● *Connect to Writing:* **Character Sketch**

Using Adjectival Phrases

Write a short, colorful description of a character for a young adult novel. Bring the character to life by describing physical and personal details of the person. The model for your character could be a friend, a neighbor, or a relative. To help make the character interesting, use adjectival phrases.

Adverbial Phrases

An **adverbial phrase** is a prepositional phrase that is used like a single adverb.

> **Single Adverb**   The artist spoke **softly.**
>
> **Adverbial phrase**   The artist spoke **in a whisper.**

19 A.2   An **adverbial phrase** is a prepositional phrase that is used mainly to modify a verb.

An adverbial phrase usually answers the question *Where? When?* or *How?* just as a single adverb does. Occasionally, an adverbial phrase answers the question *Why?*

> **Where?**   The artists moved **to the valley.**
>
> **When?**   **On Monday** the artist began his clay pot.
>
> **How?**   The artist worked **on a precise schedule.**
>
> **Why?**   He bought tools **for his new project.**

When an adverbial phrase is placed with a verb phrase, it modifies the entire verb phrase.

> **For one hour** the clay has been fired slowly.

Two adverbial phrases can modify the same verb. Also notice that adverbial phrases may appear anywhere in a sentence.

> **Before Friday** I must bring clay **to the artist.**
>
> The artist waited **for clay for five days.**

An adjectival phrase may also modify the object of the preposition of an adverbial phrase.

> The artist dropped her new pot **into a puddle of water.**

If a short adverbial phrase begins a sentence, usually no comma is needed. However, a comma should be placed after an introductory adverbial phrase of four or more words, after two or more introductory phrases, or after a phrase that ends in a date.

No Comma	**During the exhibit** you can see clay pots.
Comma	**During the pottery exhibit,** you can see clay pots.
Comma	**During the pottery exhibit at the museum,** you can see clay pots.
Comma	**During 1999,** the museum had an exhibit of clay pots.

● Practice Your Skills

Finding Adverbial Phrases

Write each adverbial phrase. Beside each one, write the word or words it modifies.

1. Early settlers worked with clay.

2. They created their work without machinery.

3. In the bright sunshine, they began their work.

4. First they dumped raw clay onto a work surface.

5. In the beginning, the clay was shaped with the hands and fingers.

6. They turned and pressed the clay for a long time.

7. Artists made shapes with tools and with coils.

8. The potters fired their creations in an oven.

9. On occasion, the artists decorated their creations.

10. Shards have been found during archaeological digs.

● *Connect to Writing:* Editing

Writing Sentences: Punctuating Adverbial Phrases

Rewrite each sentence, correctly punctuating the adverbial phrases. If a sentence is correct, write **C.**

1. At the start of the 1950s the United States enjoyed much prosperity.

2. During that decade Americans put World War II behind them.

3. Through government support many men and women were going to college.

4. Like the economy families were booming.

5. With an increase in wages Americans bought more.

6. With the savings from technological advances companies were making more money.

7. According to economic experts the United States turned into a country of consumers.

8. By 1955 computers were being used in many large institutions.

9. In fifteen years income jumped 46 percent.

10. By the end of the decade some people had color TVs.

✓ Check Point: Mixed Practice

Write each prepositional phrase. Then label each one *adj.* for adjectival or *adv.* for adverbial.

1. For family fun you can go on a treasure hunt in the United States.

2. Can you mine samples of gemstones in America?

3. At North Carolina's "gem mining" businesses, you might choose a bucket of dirt from a specific gemstone mine.

4. Then you search for the stone of your preference.

5. You shovel your dirt into a wooden flume and water rushes through it.

6. You recognize flashes of colors.

7. Some stones might not look promising in rock form.

8. Cutting will unveil the color and beauty of the stones.

9. A dark brown stone might actually be cut into a ruby.

10. Many families have searched for samples of garnets, sapphires, emeralds, and topazes.

11. There are also geological rewards for digging in shale.

12. Families are digging for fossils in different locations.

13. A trip to Wyoming could yield souvenirs of fossils of prehistoric plants or creatures.

14. The layers of rock in this state have revealed everything from palms to alligators.

● *Connect to Writing:* E-mail

Using Adverbial Phrases

Write an e-mail to a friend about where you would like to go on your next school vacation. Describe your plans. For variety in your sentences, begin at least two sentences with an adverbial phrase. Use commas as needed.

To add description to a sentence, a noun or pronoun is added immediately after another noun or pronoun. These identifying words are called **appositives.**

> We talked about our common interest, **poetry.**
>
> (*Poetry* explains what the common interest is.)
>
> We student poets, **Ryan and I,** left early.

19 B An **appositive** is a noun or a pronoun that identifies or explains another noun or pronoun in the sentence.

When an appositive has modifiers, it is called an **appositive phrase.** A prepositional phrase may also be a part of an appositive phrase, as in the third example below.

> Mr. Lewis, **the poetry club sponsor,** works hard.
>
> Take this memo to Ms. Burns, **a poetry teacher.**
>
> Haddam Middle School, **the school near the bus station,** is the location for the poetry contest.

Power Your Writing: Who or What?

You can strengthen your descriptions by adding appositives and appositive phrases. The following sentence from *The Fixed* describes the appearance of a moth emerging from a cocoon. Notice that the appositive phrase is set off by a comma.

Appositive Phrase	It emerged at last, a sodden crumple.

In the example below from *Rascal,* the appositive phrase provides details about a character in a story. Notice that the phrase is set off with two commas.

Appositive Phrase	Pat Delaney, a saloonkeeper who lived a couple of blocks up the street, said that Saint Bernards drool for the best of all possible reasons.

Revisit a composition you have completed recently. Add at least two appositive phrases to strengthen your descriptions.

If the information in an appositive or appositive phrase is essential to the meaning of a sentence, no commas are needed. The information is essential if it identifies a person, place, or thing.

Essential   The poem **"Mother to Son"** was written by Langston Hughes.
(If **"Mother to Son"** were dropped, the sentence would not be clear. The appositive is essential and no commas are needed.)

A comma is needed before and after an appositive or an appositive phrase if the information is not essential to the meaning of the sentence. If the sentence is clear without the appositive, then the appositive is usually not essential.

Not Essential   "Mother to Son," **a poem by Langston Hughes,** is one of my teacher's favorite poems.
(The sentence is still clear without the appositive phrase. A comma is needed before and after the appositive phrase.)

You can learn more about using commas with appositives on pages 841–843.

● **Practice Your Skills**

Finding Appositives and Appositive Phrases

Write each appositive or appositive phrase.

(1) Jazz in the 1920s inspired people such as Langston Hughes, an African American poet. **(2)** Writers and artists gathered in Harlem, a section of New York City. **(3)** The group in Harlem became a movement of African American culture, the Harlem Renaissance. **(4)** The Harlem Renaissance, a time of growth and achievement for African American writers, remains important today. **(5)** Two poets, Countee Cullen and Claude McKay, wrote of their experiences before coming to Harlem. **(6)** Langston Hughes, a poet, novelist, and playwright, published his first collection of poems in 1926. **(7)** This collection, *The Weary Blues,* would be followed by many other works. **(8)** Like Walt Whitman, his favorite poet, Hughes wrote about America. **(9)** Many readers also know the excellent writing of Zora Neale Hurston, a famous novelist from Florida. **(10)** Arna Bontemps, poet and novelist, was the historian of the Harlem Renaissance.

● *Connect to Writing:* **Editing**

Punctuating Appositives and Appositive Phrases

Rewrite each sentence, correctly punctuating the appositive or appositive phrase. If a sentence is correct, write **C**.

1. Georges Bizet the composer was born in Paris.

2. His reputation is based on the opera *Carmen*.

3. Bizet a child star studied music at an early age.

4. At nineteen he won the Paris Conservatory's big prize the Prix de Rome.

5. Bizet a student of piano preferred composing.

6. He became a hardworking composer in Rome the capital of Italy.

✔ *Check Point:* **Mixed Practice**

Write the prepositional and appositive phrases. Write *P* for preposition and *A* for appositive.

(1) What do you know about the most powerful men in our history, the former presidents of the United States? **(2)** George Washington, the father of our country, reportedly had wooden false teeth. **(3)** The second president, John Quincy Adams, felt more comfortable working with ideas rather than with people. **(4)** Thomas Jefferson, the successor to Adams, was inaugurated in everyday street clothes. **(5)** General Andrew Jackson was defeated by John Quincy Adams, the son of the second president, in 1824. **(6)** Jackson, a self-made man and a war hero, won the 1828 election by a landslide. **(7)** The political party of President James K. Polk, the Democrats, pushed him into war with Mexico in 1846. **(8)** Abraham Lincoln defeated opponents Stephen A. Douglas, John Breckinridge, and John Bell. **(9)** Lincoln won a clear majority of the electoral votes, 180 out of 303. **(10)** When Lincoln was assassinated in 1865, Vice President Andrew Johnson, a former Democratic senator from Tennessee, became the President.

● *Connect to Writing:* **Friendly Letter**

Using Appositives and Appositive Phrases

A close friend of yours is going with you to spend the weekend at your grandmother's house. Your grandmother has never met your friend. Write a letter to your grandmother. Describe your friend. Use appositives and appositive phrases to provide specific details. Use commas with the appositives as necessary.

CHAPTER 19

Diagraming Phrases

In a diagram, prepositional phrases are connected to the words they modify.

Adjectival Phrases An adjectival phrase is connected to the word it modifies. The preposition is placed on a connecting slanted line. The object of the preposition is placed on a horizontal line that is attached to the slanted line.

Your recipe for chicken is delicious.

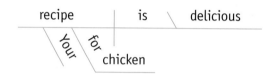

Sometimes an adjectival phrase modifies the object of a preposition of another phrase.

Juanita waited by the swings in the park.

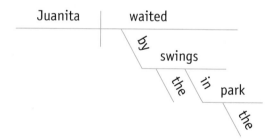

Adverbial Phrases An adverbial phrase is connected to the verb it modifies.

During the night we heard some strange noises.

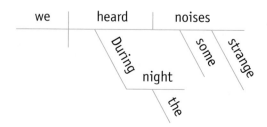

Appositives and Appositive Phrases An appositive or an appositive phrase is diagramed in parentheses next to the word it identifies or explains.

I chose Wendy, my best friend at school.

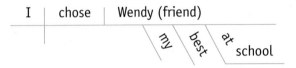

Jamul, the soloist in the musical, performed flawlessly.

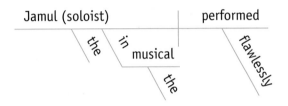

● **Practice Your Skills**

  Diagraming Phrases

  Diagram the following sentences, or copy them. If you copy them, draw one line under each subject and two lines under each verb. Put parentheses around each phrase and label it *adjectival, adverbial,* or *appositive.*

  1. Each of the infielders made one error.

  2. She put the package by the back door.

  3. This book about boats is informative.

  4. I groomed my dog, a friendly collie, with a special brush.

  5. Simon, my oldest cousin, sings in a band.

Assess Your Learning

Finding Phrases

Write each prepositional phrase and each appositive phrase. Then label each one *adj.* for adjectival, *adv.* for adverbial, or *app.* for appositive.

1. The rain beat against our windows.
2. The water below the cliff is deep and icy.
3. During the first inning, Curt made a home run.
4. With great speed Stephanie walked nervously past the old house.
5. In the cave we searched for unusual crystals.
6. The decision will affect many areas within the city.
7. Leon found Hissy, his pet snake, in the kitchen.
8. The Choy family has moved into the new house with a two-car garage.
9. This tree, a large oak, expels approximately seven gallons of water through its leaves in one day.
10. I painted the walls blue, my favorite of all colors.
11. Mrs. Gellar, the woman with all the cats, adopted a new kitten.
12. The reports in this basket have not been graded yet.
13. The table in the southwest corner of the lunchroom is my favorite table.
14. Mr. Richard Moon, the new language arts teacher, seems interesting.
15. This container of sandwiches should be taken to the party.

Identifying Phrases

Write each phrase. Then write the word the phrase modifies or describes.

1. A private company started the Pony Express, a mail delivery system, in 1860.
2. The company established a network of relay stations that were ten or fifteen miles apart.
3. Pony Express riders carried United States mail by horseback between California and Missouri.
4. At each station a rider transferred mail to a fresh horse.
5. Each of the riders rode three horses.

6. Then a new rider at the next station took over.

7. The usual time for delivery, eight days, was not speedy.

8. The cost of the service was very high.

9. The Pony Express lasted for only eighteen months.

10. The completion of a faster delivery method, the first transcontinental telegraph line, abruptly ended the service.

▄ Using Phrases

Write five sentences that follow the directions below. (The sentences may come in any order.) Write about one of the following topics or a topic of your own choice: how you earn money or how you would like to earn money.

Write a sentence that . . .

1. includes an adjectival phrase.

2. includes an adverbial phrase.

3. includes an introductory adverbial phrase.

4. includes an appositive.

5. includes an appositive phrase.

When you have finished, underline and label each phrase. Then check for the correct punctuation of each sentence.

Directions

Write the letter of the word or words that the underlined phrase modifies or describes.

The scientist Jane Goodall was born **(1)** <u>in London</u> in 1934. In her twenties she began her life's work, **(2)** <u>the study of animals</u>. She booked passage to Africa and began assisting an anthropologist, **(3)** <u>the now-famous Louis Leakey</u>. She later established a field camp **(4)** <u>in the Gombe Stream Game Reserve</u>. Goodall's subject of study, **(5)** <u>chimpanzees</u>, became the focus of her life's work. **(6)** <u>During her years there</u>, she made numerous significant observations **(7)** <u>about the behavior</u> **(8)** <u>of chimpanzees</u>. They make sounds that are like language. They hunt, and they engage **(9)** <u>in warfare</u>. Interestingly, chimpanzees also experience awe **(10)** <u>at natural wonders</u> like waterfalls.

1. A Jane Goodall
   B was born
   C 1934
   D scientist

2. A life's
   B work
   C began
   D twenties

3. A assisting
   B Africa
   C passage
   D anthropologist

4. A established
   B She
   C camp
   D field

5. A subject
   B Goodall's
   C became
   D focus

6. A she
   B there
   C made
   D observations

7. A significant
   B observations
   C chimpanzees
   D made

8. A behavior
   B observations
   C made
   D about

9. A hunt
   B make
   C engage
   D they

10. A experience
   B chimpanzees
   C Interestingly
   D awe

Writer's Corner

Snapshot

19 A A **phrase** is a group of words that acts like a single part of speech. It does not have a subject or a verb. An **adjectival phrase** is a prepositional phrase that is used like a single adjective; an **adverbial phrase** is a prepositional phrase that is used like a single adverb. (pages 584–591)

19 B An **appositive** is a noun or a pronoun that identifies or explains another noun or pronoun in the sentence. When an appositive has modifiers, it is called an **appositive phrase**. (pages 592–594)

Power Rules

Be sure that your sentences are complete and not **sentence fragments.** (pages 656–661)

Before Editing	**After Editing**
The girl with red hair.	*Sally is* the girl with red hair.
Working all evening on his homework.	*He was* working all evening on his homework.

Check that the pronouns used in **prepositional phrases** are in the objective case. (pages 714–716)

Before Editing	**After Editing**
We went to the movies with Mary and *she*.	We went to the movies with Mary and *her*.
She gave the newspapers to Randy and *he*.	She gave the newspapers to Randy and *him*.

Editing Checklist

Use this checklist when editing your writing.

✓ Did I use phrases within my sentences? (See pages 584–594.)
✓ Did I make sure that prepositional phrases end with a noun or pronoun?
 (See pages 584–587.)
✓ Did I use modifiers in the correct place and avoid misplaced modifiers?
 (See pages 587–588.)
✓ Did I make use of appositives? (See pages 592–594.)

Use the Power

A phrase can be placed at the beginning, in the middle, and at the end of a sentence. This freedom can lead to **misplaced modifiers.** Try your hand at placing phrases in the right location. Look at the sentence and phrase pairs below. Decide where the phrase should go in each sentence. Then circle the word or words in the sentence that the phrase is modifying.

Sentence	Phrase
The dog chewed.	on a bone
The people watch the football game.	in the stands
The children put on a play for the community.	from the school
The Butlers had to pack their suitcases.	before they left on their trip
Gerry studied the monkeys.	with the black and white tails

Appositives are one of the best tools in the writer's toolbox. They provide a quick and easy way to add detail in a piece of writing. Revise a composition you completed recently by adding appositives and appositive phrases.

Verbals and Verbal Phrases

How can you add details and a sense of action to your writing with verbals and verbal phrases?

Verbals and Verbal Phrases: Pretest 1

The following draft paragraph about the cave painting shown above is hard to read because it contains several errors. Revise the paragraph so that it reads correctly. One of the errors has been corrected as an example.

> This painting is one of over a hundred prehistoric paintings in the Chauvet Cave in southeastern France was discovered in 1994 by three cave explorers. The painting includes four horses- three rhinoceroses, a bison, and an aurochs- an ancestor of today's domestic cattle. Carefully date the painting, scientists have discovered it is more than 30,000 years old. At that time, people were nomadic and lived mainly by hunt and gather food.

Verbals and Verbal Phrases: Pretest 2

Directions

Write the letter of the term that correctly identifies the underlined word or words in each sentence.

1. Our plans include <u>crossing the Rio Grande</u>.
2. I have learned <u>to find many rivers on maps</u>.
3. The Mississippi River flows from Minnesota <u>to the Gulf of Mexico</u>.
4. <u>Stretching for 210 miles</u>, the Thames is in England.
5. The Congo, <u>known also as the Zaire</u>, is very long.

1. A prepositional phrase
   B gerund phrase
   C participial phrase
   D infinitive phrase

2. A prepositional phrase
   B gerund phrase
   C participial phrase
   D infinitive phrase

3. A prepositional phrase
   B gerund phrase
   C participial phrase
   D infinitive phrase

4. A prepositional phrase
   B gerund phrase
   C participial phrase
   D infinitive phrase

5. A prepositional phrase
   B nonessential phrase
   C essential phrase
   D infinitive phrase

A **verbal** looks like a verb. In fact, it is a verb form, but it serves as another part of speech—such as an adjective or a noun.

The following examples show the verbals *waiting* and *broken*. *Waiting* is a form of the verb *wait*; *broken* is a form of the verb *break*. In these sentences they serve as adjectives, not verbs. Verbals that act like adjectives are called participles.

> She helped the **waiting** customer.
>
> The workers threw away the **broken** boxes.

There are three kinds of verbals: **participles, gerunds,** and **infinitives.** Often these verbals are linked with related words to form **verbal phrases.** Because all verbals are verb forms, they can add energy and liveliness to your writing.

20 A A **participle** is a verb form that is used as an adjective.

The two forms of a participle are **present participles** and **past participles.** Present participles always end in *–ing*. Past participles usually end in *–ed* or *–d*. Some, however, have irregular endings, such as *–n, –t,* or *–en*.

VERB	PRESENT PARTICIPLE	PAST PARTICIPLE
look	looking	looked
fade	fading	faded
talk	talking	talked
tear	tearing	torn
send	sending	sent

> **Present Participle** Everyone enjoys the **challenging** work.
>
> **Past Participles** The mathematician's **framed** diploma was a **prized** possession.

Like an adjective, a participle modifies a noun or a pronoun. Also like an adjective, it answers the question *Which one?* or *What kind?*

CHAPTER 20

Which One?	The **humming** computer filled the air with sound.
	The **crowded** table is filled with reports.
What Kind?	The **interesting** problem will be solved quickly.
	The **ruined** shipment must be replaced.

● Practice Your Skills

Recognizing Participles

Write each participle.

1. A New York City trucking company makes regular shipments to Boston, Hartford, Portland, and Albany.
2. The company's pressing problem is to find the best and safest routes.
3. The puzzled manager knows the driving distances between each pair of cities.
4. The manager interviews each experienced driver.
5. A young woman steps forward with a sharpened pencil.
6. The smiling driver asks for an atlas, some paper, and a ruler.
7. Let's make a map that shows the connected cities.
8. First, draw a point on the page for each of the designated cities.
9. Then draw lines between the scattered dots.
10. We can add together the lengths of the edges and find the solution to the confusing problem.

● Practice Your Skills

Finding the Words Participles Describe

Write each participle. Then write the word or words it modifies.

1. My math teacher made an amazing statement.
2. Geometry is a needed skill for people of all ages.
3. Children play with building blocks.
4. The differing shapes teach them about the world.
5. Julie stacked many varied wood blocks as a child.
6. Experienced architects and builders combine shapes in their structures.
7. Cooks use a variety of different shapes in their baked goods.
8. Scientists study the shapes of living things.
9. Her moving words inspired me.
10. Dedicated teachers can make geometry fun.

⇒ Participle or Verb?

A participle is formed from a verb, but it cannot be used alone as a verb. To act as a verb, a participle needs a helping verb before it.

Participle	Everyone clapped for the **prancing** horses.
Verb	The horses **were prancing** across the ring.
Participle	The **banging** door was very noisy.
Verb	The door **was banging** all day.

● **Practice Your Skills**

Distinguishing Between Participles and Verbs

Write each underlined word. Then label each one as either *P* for participle or *V* for verb.

1. The <u>writing</u> teacher made an assignment.

2. The class members are <u>writing</u> furiously.

3. The whole class is <u>working</u> on the same story.

4. One student writes about a <u>working</u> actress.

5. At first, the actress likes the long <u>auditioning</u> sessions.

6. She is <u>auditioning</u> with hundreds of other actors.

7. Is her confidence <u>suffering</u> as the acting parts go to others?

8. She did not deliver a <u>suffering</u> performance.

9. Someday, she will not be <u>standing</u> in line for parts.

10. She will win <u>standing</u> ovations.

⇒ Participial Phrases

Because a participle is a verb form, it has some of the features of a verb. It can have one or more complements. In addition, it can be modified by an adverb or an adverbial phrase. A participle and any modifiers or complements form a participial phrase.

20 A.1   A **participial phrase** is a participle with its modifiers and complements—all working together as an adjective.

Participle with an Adverb	The **very daring** explorers headed to the Americas.
Participle with a Prepositional Phrase	Early settlers, **hoping for new lives,** soon followed.
Participle with a Complement	**Risking life and limb,** they left their homeland.

PUNCTUATION WITH PARTICIPIAL PHRASES

A participial phrase that comes at the beginning of a sentence is always followed by a comma.

Listening carefully, the colonists learned from the native people.

Participial phrases in the middle or at the end of a sentence may or may not need commas. If the information in the phrase is **essential** to the meaning of the sentence, no commas are needed.

If the information in a participial phrase is **not essential** to the sentence, commas must separate it from the rest of the sentence. A participial phrase is not essential if it can be removed without changing the basic information in the sentence.

Essential	The crops **growing in that field** must be harvested. (Commas are not needed because the participial phrase is needed to identify which crops must be harvested.)
Nonessential	The corn, **growing ever taller,** will probably be sweet. (Commas are needed because the participial phrase could be removed from the sentence without changing the main information: *The corn will probably be sweet.*)

To learn more about essential and nonessential phrases, see pages 843–846.

Connect to Writing: Historical Narrative

Using Participial Phrases

Use each of the participial phrases below to write a sentence about what you think may have happened to the Roanoke colonists. Then write a story about what you think happened to the Roanoke colonists. Use your participial phrases to add vivid images to the story. Underline the participial phrases you use.

searching for food   hidden from sight   locked in a steel-like grip

seeking a clue   running swiftly

● Practice Your Skills

Finding Participial Phrases

Write each participial phrase. Then underline the participle.

1. Remembering the thirteen colonies, most people think of the English as the early settlers of North America.
2. In the 1500s, Spanish conquistadors, searching for treasure, began the exploration of North America.
3. Finding gold and silver, the Spanish settled in the Americas even earlier than the English.
4. The city of St. Augustine, located on Florida's Atlantic coast, was a certain success.
5. Founded in 1564, St. Augustine became the oldest Spanish settlement of the United States.
6. The settlement, surrounded by a wooden fence, was a safe place for early settlers.
7. Later, the settlement had many streets lined with houses and stores.
8. Giving up its claim to Florida, Spain turned St. Augustine over to the English.
9. Refusing the English ways, many residents kept their Spanish customs.
10. Today many visitors searching for information about the past tour St. Augustine.

Recognizing Participial Phrases as Modifiers

Write each participial phrase. Then write the word it modifies.

1. Have you been to Roanoke Island, located off the coast of North Carolina?
2. In 1587, a band of English colonists, led by John White, settled there.
3. The 117 colonists, including 17 women and 9 children, faced difficult winters.
4. John White's daughter gave birth to a baby girl named Virginia Dare.
5. Seeking supplies and more colonists, John White sailed to England.
6. Delayed for three years, the Englishman found the island empty on his return.
7. The only clue was the word *Croatoan* carved on a gatepost.
8. White set out for that island, located about one hundred miles to the south.
9. Sweeping into the area, a bad storm kept White on Roanoke Island instead.
10. Roanoke Island, deserted by the colonists, never offered further clues about their disappearance.

Power Your Writing: Getting into the Action

Participles are especially useful in your writing for creating a vivid sense that several things are happening at once. Read the following sentence from "Checkouts" (pages 249–251) and note the effect of the participial phrases on the sense of action.

> Some months later the bag boy and the girl with the orange bow again crossed paths, standing in line with their dates at a movie theater, and, glancing toward the other, each smiled slightly, then looked away, as strangers on public buses do, when one is moving off the bus and the other is moving on.

With participial phrases, the author conveys in a single sentence the circumstances, the emotions, and the tension of this chance encounter.

Review a piece of descriptive writing you have completed recently. Add details and description through the use of well-placed participial phrases.

Misplaced Participial Phrases

In the last chapter, you learned that an adjectival phrase placed too far from the word it modifies is called a **misplaced modifier.** Since a participial phrase acts like an adjective, it also becomes a misplaced modifier if it is placed too far from the word it describes.

The travel agent called the people **looking for a hotel in Williamsburg.**

(A reader might think that in this sentence the people are looking for a hotel.)

Looking for a hotel in Williamsburg, the travel agent called the people.

(In this sentence the travel agent, not the people, is looking for a hotel.)

The above examples have different meanings, but both make sense. Some misplaced modifiers, however, result in misunderstanding or even silliness—such as the following example.

Misplaced Modifier	**Hanging on the wall of the old house in Williamsburg,** Ben saw a beautiful painting.
	(This sentence suggests that Ben, not the painting, was hanging on the wall.)

To correct a misplaced modifier, first decide what the intended meaning of the sentence is. Then find the word that should be modified. Place the phrase near that word.

Correct Modifier	Ben saw a beautiful painting **hanging on the wall of the old house in Williamsburg.**
	(Now the participial phrase is close to the word it is describing.)

● Practice Your Skills

Identifying Misplaced Participial Phrases

Write each participial phrase. Beside each phrase, write **C** if it is placed correctly or **I** if it is placed incorrectly.

1. Many people enjoy the sights walking around Williamsburg, Virginia.
2. Dating back to the 1770s, the tourists are seeking a glimpse of the past.
3. Inhabitants of the old town reenact eighteenth-century life wearing authentic costumes.
4. Made with logs and mortar, amateur historians can visit a variety of homes and shops.

5. They can smell bread baking in old ovens.

6. Working ancient looms by hand, the visitors can see colonial women.

7. Made of cotton, the old-style dresses are not as colorful as today's fashions.

8. Unpaved with asphalt, people go up and down the streets.

9. Lacking electricity and large windows, the homes are like caves.

10. The visitors appreciate their cool hotel rooms exhausted after a day in Williamsburg.

Connect to Writing: Revising

Correcting Misplaced Participial Phrases

Rewrite the incorrect sentences from the preceding exercise so that the misplaced participial phrases are placed correctly.

Gerunds and Gerund Phrases Lesson 2

Another verbal is a gerund. Like a present participle, a gerund also ends in *-ing*. However, unlike a participle, a **gerund** is used as a noun, not as an adjective.

20 B A **gerund** is a verb form that is used as a noun.

A gerund is used in the same ways a noun is used.

Subject	**Hiking** is great exercise.
	(*Hiking* tells what the sentence is about.)
Direct Object	The campers enjoy **hiking.**
	(What do the campers enjoy? *Hiking* is the direct object.)
Indirect Object	My grandparents give **hiking** all their attention.
	(They give what? *Attention* is the direct object. They give attention to what? *Hiking* is the indirect object.)
Object of a Preposition	The hardest part of **hiking** is a steep, rocky trail.
	(*Hiking* is the object of the preposition *of.*)
Predicate Nominative	My brother's favorite activity is **hiking.**
	(*Hiking* renames the subject *activity.*)
Appositive	Terry has a new hobby, **hiking.**
	(*Hiking* identifies the hobby.)

● Practice Your Skills

Finding Gerunds

Write each gerund.

1. Exercising makes many people feel younger.

2. Directing is Matthew's passion.

3. The twins' favorite sport is bicycling.

4. Swimming provides hours of enjoyment.

5. More than anything else, Alicia loves dancing.

6. The thrill of skiing is fun for Amanda and Jim.

7. Traveling has always been a favorite activity for the Martinez family.

8. My favorite pastime, skating, is not difficult.

9. Racing is a wonderful sport for participants and observers.

10. The gymnast gives practicing his top priority.

Gerund or Participle?

Because a gerund and a participle both end in *-ing,* it is easy to confuse them. Remember that a gerund is used as a noun, and a participle is used as an adjective.

Gerund   Jessica's **writing** is quite good.

(*Writing* is used as a noun, the subject of the sentence.)

Participle   The **writing** lessons were fantastic.

(*Writing* is an adjective that tells what kind of lessons.)

● **Practice Your Skills**

Distinguishing Between Gerunds and Participles

Write each underlined verbal. Label each one as either a *participle* or a *gerund.*

1. Today's <u>reading</u> assignment was fun.
2. The <u>reading</u> is "The Zodiacs" by Jay Neugeborn.
3. The main character wants a <u>winning</u> baseball team.
4. <u>Winning</u> is the main objective, so he recruits a star pitcher.
5. The <u>pitching</u> star is promised newspaper coverage and new uniforms.
6. The Zodiacs' <u>pitching</u> is excellent, but the hitting is average.
7. George's high <u>batting</u> average wins many games for the team.
8. The Zodiacs' luck runs out, however, when George's <u>batting</u> and pitching go haywire.
9. There is a <u>running</u> joke about George's temper.
10. George's <u>running</u> has improved.

Gerund Phrases

A gerund is often combined with modifiers and complements to form a **gerund phrase**.

20 B.1   A **gerund phrase** is a gerund with its modifiers and complements—all working together as a noun.

The examples on the following page show how a gerund phrase can be made up of several different groups of words.

Gerund with an Adjective	Jon's **colorful painting** won him many awards.
Gerund with an Adverb	**Painting expressively** creates superb results.
Gerund with a Prepositional Phrase	I always enjoy **painting on the beach.**
Gerund with a Complement	**Painting natural scenes** relaxes me.

● **Practice Your Skills**

Finding Gerund Phrases

Write each gerund phrase.

1. Learning about art is important.

2. Some artists enjoy interpreting the world around them.

3. Their understanding of colors is complex.

4. Artists see hues of both warm and cool coloring.

5. Landscape painting requires colors for atmosphere.

6. For example, cool and subtle colors may make for sad or peaceful viewing.

7. Choosing warm colors may attract viewers.

8. Using cool colors relaxes me.

9. Choosing the best colors for a subject is only one of the artist's skills.

10. Painting rapidly may provide only an impression of a subject.

● **Practice Your Skills**

Completing Gerund Phrases

Write a gerund that can complete the gerund phrase in each sentence. Then use the following abbreviations to identify the other words in each gerund phrase.

adjective = *adj.*   adverb = *adv.*
prepositional phrase = *p.p.*   complement = *c.*

1. ___ the styles of famous artists sometimes helps young painters.

2. Thousands of art students remember ___ to the city's art museum.

3. ___ pieces of art requires a great deal of attention.

4. ___ through an exhibit is not advisable.

5. ___ a long visit to an art gallery is a good idea.

The third kind of verbal is the infinitive. **Infinitives** are usually used as nouns, but can also be used as adjectives or adverbs.

> **20 C** An **infinitive** is a verb form that can be used as a noun, an adjective, or an adverb. The word *to* usually comes before an infinitive.

Noun
To wait was the only choice during the gasoline shortage.
(*To wait* is the subject. It tells what the sentence is about.)

Jordan plans **to wait.**
(Jordan plans what? *To wait* is the direct object.)

Adjective
The best time **to wait** was in the morning. (*To wait* describes *time.*)

Do you have a good reason **to wait?** (*To wait* modifies *reason.*)

Adverb
Jordan drove to the back of the line **to wait.** (*To wait* modifies *drove;* it tells why Jordan drove to the back of the line.)

We always went to the gas station **to wait.** (*To wait* tells why we went.)

CHAPTER 20

● Practice Your Skills

Finding Infinitives

Write each infinitive.

1. In the 1970s, the gasoline shortage showed Americans the need to conserve.
2. Gas stations began to close.
3. Owners had little gasoline to sell.
4. This forced the price of gas to increase.
5. The number of cars on the road began to decrease.
6. People lined up at the pumps for hours to fill up.
7. Most Americans had big cars then, but they learned to conserve.
8. To drive was important for workers.
9. Oil prices were allowed to jump.
10. A new way of life was about to begin.

Infinitive or Prepositional Phrase?

Sometimes infinitives are confused with prepositional phrases that begin with *to*. Remember that an infinitive is the word *to* plus a verb form. A prepositional phrase is the word *to* plus a noun or pronoun.

Infinitive	That CD is fun **to play.**
	(The phrase ends with a verb form, *play*.)
Prepositional Phrase	Please bring the CD **to class.**
	(The phrase ends with a noun, *class*.)

● **Practice Your Skills**

Distinguishing Between Infinitive and Prepositional Phrases

Write each underlined phrase. Then label it *I* for infinitive or *P* for prepositional phrase.

1. From the age of four, Ludwig van Beethoven used many hours each day <u>to practice</u>.
2. He went <u>to lessons</u> every day of the week except Sunday.
3. At age eleven he was encouraged <u>to compose</u>.
4. He was sent to the royal court <u>to play</u>.
5. At the royal court, Bach's music became known <u>to him</u>.
6. In 1792, Beethoven was sent <u>to Vienna</u>.
7. The plan was for him <u>to study</u>.
8. After Mozart died, Beethoven went <u>to Haydn</u> for lessons.
9. Student and teacher started <u>to argue</u>.
10. Beethoven was forced <u>to stop</u> his lessons.

 Infinitive Phrases

Like the other verbals, an infinitive can be combined with modifiers or complements to form an infinitive phrase.

20 C.1   An **infinitive phrase** is an infinitive with its modifiers and complements—all working together as a noun, an adjective, or an adverb.

An infinitive phrase can be made up of several different combinations of words as shown in the examples on the next page.

CHAPTER 20

Infinitive with an Adverb	She told us **to read thoughtfully.**
Infinitive with a Prepositional Phrase	We plan **to read around the clock.**
Infinitive with a Complement	Don't hesitate **to open the book.**

When You Write

When you list three or more verbals or verbal phrases in a series, use the same form, or *parallel structures*, for each of the items. This is called *parallelism*.

Not Parallel	When she enters high school, Alyssa plans to study painting, drawing, and how to make prints.
Parallel	When she enters high school, Alyssa plans to study painting, drawing, and printmaking.

● Practice Your Skills

Finding Infinitive Phrases

Write each infinitive phrase.

1. Many writers use infinitives to write their most famous lines.
2. The main character in Shakespeare's *Hamlet* says, "To be, or not to be; that is the question."
3. After reading a quotation from Alexander Pope's "An Essay on Criticism," I decided to read the entire essay.
4. Read the whole work to understand the meaning.
5. Be sure to give credit to the author.
6. I want to find the whole quotation for "ignorance is bliss."
7. You need to check Grey's works for this quotation.
8. To recite a quotation accurately is important.
9. Not all quotations are made to impress people.
10. On his return to Ohio, Senator John Sherman said, "I have come home to look after my fences."

Adding Infinitives

Write each sentence, adding an infinitive that makes sense.

1. When were you taken ___ your first play?

2. I'm trying ___ the year.

3. In New York, I had a chance ___ the world of theater.

4. ___ a show on Broadway is a rare treat.

5. Alex is ready ___ to his first play.

● *Connect to Writing:* **Giving Directions**

Using Infinitives and Infinitive Phrases

Write a short comic or dramatic scene to share with your class. The scene should have lots of action but no dialogue. Write stage directions for the actors as they silently act out the scene. Use infinitives and infinitive phrases.

✔ *Check Point:* **Mixed Practice**

Write each underlined phrase. Then label each one a *participial phrase,* a *gerund phrase,* or an *infinitive phrase.*

1. Sofonisba Anguissola was to become a famous artist in Spain.

2. Born in the sixteenth century in Italy, she broke new ground.

3. Back then, studying school subjects was usually not a part of a young girl's life.

4. The young woman went against the tradition of only boys studying art.

5. Back then, many people thought girls were meant to sew and to be good wives.

6. Like the boys, she learned to draw portraits.

7. Joining the boys in their classes, Anguissola studied many subjects.

8. Her father was impressed by a portrait drawn by her.

9. The king of Spain asked her to become a painter in his court.

10. She agreed to travel from Italy to Spain.

11. Wanting a portrait of themselves, people came to the new court artist.

12. She liked most to paint children.

13. Offering a record of history, Anguissola's art shows how people lived hundreds of years ago.

14. Nothing stopped her from becoming an artist.

Diagraming Verbals and Verbal Phrases

Before diagraming a sentence with a verbal in it, you will have to determine how the verbal is used.

Participial Phrases A participial phrase is diagramed under the word it modifies. It is written in a curve. If the participial phrase has a complement it is diagramed after the participle. A vertical line separates the complement from the participle. A single participle is diagramed exactly the same way as the participle *making* is diagramed below, except that it has no complement or modifiers. The single participles *running* and *untied* are diagramed in the second example below.

Everyone watched the robin **making its nest.**

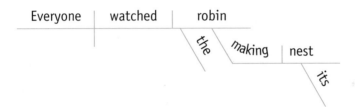

The **running** toddler tripped on his **untied** shoelaces.

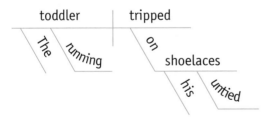

CHAPTER 20

Gerund Phrases Because a gerund phrase is used as a noun, it can be diagramed in any noun position. The first gerund in the example below is used as a subject. Notice that the complement *popcorn* and the prepositional phrase *in a movie theater* are part of the gerund phrase. The second gerund phrase is used as an object of the preposition *of*. A single gerund is diagramed exactly the same way the gerunds *eating* and *enjoying* are diagramed below, except that they have no complements or modifiers. The single gerund *dancing* is diagramed in the second sentence below.

Eating popcorn in a movie theater is an important part of **enjoying the movie.**

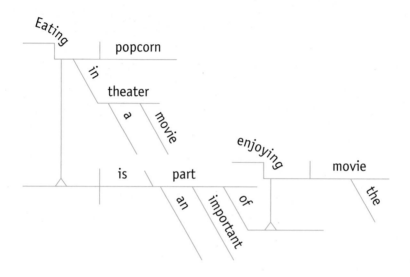

Dancing is a particularly good form of exercise.

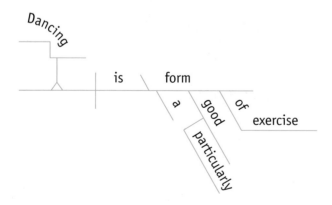

Infinitive Phrases Because an infinitive phrase may be used as an adjective, an adverb, or a noun, it is diagramed in several ways. The infinitive phrase in the first example below is used as a direct object. The infinitive phrase in the second example is used as an adjective. Single infinitives are diagramed exactly the same way *to identify* and *to use* are diagramed below, except that they have no complements or modifiers. The single infinitives *to study* and *to learn* are diagramed in the third example.

For a new badge I need **to identify ten constellations.**

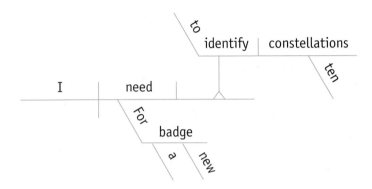

This is the best pencil **to use for the test.**

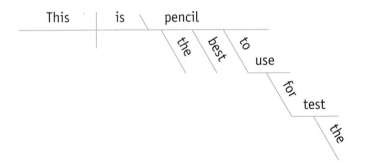

To study might be the only way **to learn.**

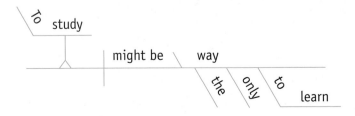

Diagraming Verbal Phrases

Diagram the following sentences or copy them. If you copy them, draw one line under each subject and two lines under each verb. Then put parentheses around each verbal phrase and label each one *part.* for participial, *ger.* for gerund, or *inf.* for infinitive.

1. The student delivering the speech is the class president.
2. Giving a speech can be difficult for some people.
3. They may speak too quietly to be heard.
4. I need to practice my speech for science class.
5. The best time to prepare for the presentation is this afternoon.
6. Practicing a speech aloud is helpful.
7. Turning on my stopwatch, I timed my speech.
8. I needed to shorten my speech.
9. Shortening a speech is sometimes harder than writing the material.
10. My speech, shortened to exactly ten minutes, is now complete.

CHAPTER 20

Assess Your Learning

Finding Participial Phrases and Infinitive Phrases

Write each participial phrase and infinitive phrase. Label each phrase *part.* for participial phrase or *inf.* for infinitive phrase.

1. The matador, facing the bull, waved his red cape to challenge it.
2. Rising since noon, the temperature is now 98 degrees.
3. These mittens, knit by my aunt, are now too small to wear comfortably.
4. Using a telescope, Galileo could see the rings around Saturn.
5. Sitting up, Ginger began to beg for a dog biscuit.
6. The first steam locomotive to be built in the United States was the *Tom Thumb,* built in 1830.
7. We had a wonderful campsite overlooking the lake.
8. Drumming on the telephone pole, the woodpecker dug a hole for its nest.
9. The sun's rays, focused through glass, can start a fire.
10. The spaniel, barking ferociously, raced through the tall grass to catch the rabbit.
11. The child carrying the Easter basket is my niece.
12. The gifts to wrap for the Christmas party are on the table.
13. Drawn in black ink, the sketch showed a teddy bear wearing overalls.
14. The Valentine cards to distribute to my friends are in my backpack.

Finding Gerund Phrases and Infinitive Phrases

Write each gerund phrase and infinitive phrase. Label each phrase *ger.* for gerund phrase or *inf.* for infinitive phrase.

1. I have found a new hobby, bird watching.
2. To do this, sitting quietly near some trees is the first step.
3. The hardest part is waiting patiently to catch glimpses of the birds.
4. Seeing a bright red cardinal up close is worth the wait.
5. I give watching the cardinal my complete attention.

6. I love listening to the various chirps of birds.
7. Besides looking through binoculars, I often perform another activity, recording birdsongs.
8. I attract songbirds by putting birdseed nearby.
9. To record their beauty, perhaps I will sketch them.
10. Studying birds' habits and songs is an enjoyable hobby to practice regularly.

Using Verbal Phrases

Write five sentences that follow the directions below.

1. Include the participial phrase *singing at the top of his lungs* at the beginning of a sentence.
2. Include the participial phrase *won by the girls' basketball team* in a sentence.
3. Include the gerund phrase *falling asleep at night* at the beginning of a sentence.
4. Include the infinitive phrase *to prevent the flu* at the beginning of a sentence.
5. Include the infinitive phrase *to see a rodeo* in a sentence.

   When you have finished, underline and label each phrase. Then check for correct punctuation of each sentence.

Verbals and Verbal Phrases: Posttest

Directions

Write the letter of the term that correctly identifies the underlined word or words in each sentence.

1. <u>Watching a program on television</u>, I became intrigued by carnivorous fish.
2. Fascinated, I remained <u>to watch the show in its entirety</u>.
3. <u>Eating flesh with razor-sharp teeth</u> is how piranhas survive.
4. Piranhas, <u>traveling in groups</u>, usually prey on other fish.
5. I went <u>to the library</u> to find out more about them.

1. **A** prepositional phrase
   B gerund phrase
   C participial phrase
   D infinitive phrase

2. **A** prepositional phrase
   B gerund phrase
   C participial phrase
   D infinitive phrase

3. **A** prepositional phrase
   B gerund phrase
   C participial phrase
   D infinitive phrase

4. **A** prepositional phrase
   B nonessential phrase
   C essential phrase
   D infinitive phrase

5. **A** prepositional phrase
   B gerund phrase
   C participial phrase
   D infinitive phrase

Writer's Corner

Snapshot

A **verbal** is a verb form that acts like another part of speech—such as an adjective or a noun. (pages 604–618)

20 A A **participle** is a verb form that is used as an adjective. A **participial phrase** is a participle with its modifiers and complements—all working together as an adjective. (pages 604–611)

20 B A **gerund** is a verb form that is used as a noun. A **gerund phrase** is a gerund with its modifiers and complements—all working together as a noun. (pages 612–614)

20 C An **infinitive** is a verb form that can be used as a noun, an adjective, or an adverb. The word *to* usually comes before an infinitive. (pages 615–618)

Power Rules

Be sure that all verbals and verbal phrases in your writing are part of complete sentences.

Before Editing	**After Editing**
Hoping to find the lost artifacts. The scientists had traveled to South America.	*Hoping to find the lost artifacts, the* scientists traveled to South America.
She asked Sara. To pick up some things for dinner.	She asked Sara *to* pick up some things for dinner.

Editing Checklist

Use this checklist when editing your writing.

✓ Did I use verbals to make my sentences more clear and intersting? (See pages 604–618.)

✓ Did I use commas correctly to set off participial phrases? (See page 607.)

✓ Did I make sure that modifiers are in the correct place to avoid misplaced modifiers? (See pages 610–611.)

✓ Did I make sure that all gerunds are used as nouns? (See pages 612–614.)

✓ Did I use complete infinitive phrases? (See pages 616–618.)

Use the Power

To activate the power of verbals in your own writing, try one or more of these steps.

Begin with a simple sentence.

The dog hears its master.

Add one or more participial phrases.

The dog, **wagging its tail wildly,** hears its master.

Add a gerund phrase.

The dog, wagging its tail wildly, hears **its master's whistling.**

Add an infinitive phrase.

Hearing its master's whistling, the dog, wagging its tail wildly, decides **to greet her.**

Clauses

How can you use clauses to connect related ideas and to add interest to your writing?

Clauses: Pretest 1

The following first draft about the artist M. C. Escher is hard to read because there are several clause fragments. How would you revise the paragraph so that it reads correctly? The first error has been corrected as an example.

> M. C. Escher was the youngest child in a family with three boys. The son of a civil engineer, Escher studied literature and architecture before becoming a graphic artist. His artworks have become increasingly popular over the years. Because they combine humor and precision to create optical illusions and unexpected perspectives. Escher is most famous for his *tessellations.* Which are patterns of shapes that fit together with no space in between. He used people, places, and objects he encountered as inspiration for his prints.

Clauses: Pretest 2

Directions

Write the letter of the term that correctly identifies the underlined word or words in each sentence of the following paragraph.

Unusual Inventions

(1) <u>Because chickens peck at each other</u>, someone invented chicken glasses. (2) The glasses, <u>which extend to the back of a chicken's neck</u>, protect its eyes. (3) <u>How you wake up</u> was the inspiration for another invention. (4) <u>A clock has blocks</u> that hang over your head. (5) <u>When the alarm rings</u>, the blocks fall on you. (6) <u>You will want the following invention</u>. (7) <u>It's a hat that is attached to a parachute</u>. (8) It comes with padded shoes <u>that soften the landing</u>. (9) A twirling spaghetti fork's handle <u>that you can move with your thumb</u> has a small wheel. (10) <u>The fork spins around, and it rolls up the spaghetti</u>.

1. **A** independent clause
   B adverbial clause
   C complex sentence
   D adjectival clause

2. **A** adverbial clause
   B noun clause
   C independent clause
   D adjectival clause

3. **A** noun clause
   B adjectival clause
   C misplaced modifier
   D simple sentence

4. **A** independent clause
   B noun clause
   C adverbial clause
   D adjectival clause

5. **A** misplaced modifier
   B adjectival clause
   C adverbial clause
   D independent clause

6. **A** simple sentence
   B complex sentence
   C subordinate clause
   D compound sentence

7. **A** compound sentence
   B simple sentence
   C subordinate clause
   D complex sentence

8. **A** noun clause
   B adverbial clause
   C misplaced modifier
   D adjectival clause

9. **A** noun clause
   B misplaced modifier
   C simple sentence
   D adverbial clause

10. **A** simple sentence
    B subordinate clause
    C compound sentence
    D complex sentence

In this chapter you will learn about three kinds of sentences: simple, compound, and complex. Before you can fully understand the different kinds of sentences, you must learn about groups of words called **clauses.**

21 A   **A clause is a group of words that has a subject and a verb.**

Both a clause and a phrase are made up of a group of words, but only a clause has a subject and a verb. Notice that the clause in the second example below has a subject (underlined once) and a verb (underlined twice).

> **Phrase**   We will play **after halftime.**
>
> **Clause**   We will play **after halftime is over.**

There are two kinds of clauses: independent and dependent clauses. The first we will study is the **independent,** or **main, clause.**

21 A.1   An **independent (main) clause** can stand alone as a sentence because it expresses a complete thought.

When an independent clause stands by itself, it is called a **sentence.** It only becomes an independent clause when it appears in a sentence with another clause. In the following example, the clauses are joined with a comma and a conjunction.

> Alicia hit the ball, **and** the crowd cheered.

Both of these clauses can stand alone as single sentences. This means that the two clauses are independent clauses.

> Alicia hit the ball. The crowd cheered.

The second kind of clause is called a **subordinate clause,** or **dependent clause.** It has the name *dependent* because it depends on another clause to give it meaning. It cannot stand alone as a sentence.

21 A.2   A **subordinate (dependent) clause** cannot stand alone as a sentence because it does not express a complete thought.

Look at the following examples. Neither of the subordinate clauses expresses a complete thought—even though each has a subject and a verb.

```
   ┌──subordinate clause──┐ ┌── independent clause ──┐
   After the game ended, the players left the field.
   ┌── independent clause ──┐ ┌────── subordinate clause ──────┐
   They enjoyed the game that they watched last night.
```

● **Practice Your Skills**

Distinguishing Between Clauses

Write each underlined clause. Then label it *independent* or *subordinate*.

1. Panels that the ancient Greeks carved show players using crooked sticks to hit a small object.
2. Field hockey was played in Europe during the Middle Ages, but the game was once outlawed in England.
3. Field hockey interfered with archery training, which was the basis of the national defense.
4. Even though field hockey was played worldwide after 1850, it did not become popular in the United States.
5. Although it became part of the Olympics in 1908, field hockey was not organized in the United States until the 1920s.
6. Henry Greer arranged matches between teams that were made up of men from New York.
7. While it is not certain, the first men's field hockey match in the United States probably occurred in 1928.
8. Because the U.S. Olympic Committee wanted an American team, it organized the men's hockey teams.

● **Practice Your Skills**

Identifying Subordinate Clauses

Write the subordinate clause from each sentence.

1. Field hockey is a sport that is usually played on grass or artificial turf.
2. Each team consists of eleven players who run strategic plays across the field.
3. The striker starts the game when he or she initiates a pass-back play.
4. After the striker hits the ball, it cannot immediately cross the center line.
5. Before the ball is sent across the center line, it must be touched by another player.

Like phrases, subordinate clauses can be used in several different ways.

21 B   **Subordinate clauses** can be used as adverbs, adjectives, and nouns.

Adverbial Clauses

A subordinate clause can be used the same way a single adverb or an adverbial phrase is used. Such a clause is called an adverbial clause.

Single Adverb	Let's meet **here.**
Adverbial Phrase	Let's meet **at the music history museum.**
Adverbial Clause	Let's meet **where we met last time.**

21 B.1   An **adverbial clause** is a subordinate clause that is used mainly to modify a verb.

An adverbial clause answers the adverb question *How? When? Where? Under what conditions?* or *Why?* Notice in each of the following examples that an adverbial clause modifies the whole verb phrase.

How?	Adam described the old instruments **as if he had seen them all before.**
When?	**When he saw the old harpsichord,** his mouth dropped open.
Where?	We will go **wherever the next concert is.**
Under What Conditions	**If you have never seen a wooden flute,** go to the winds room immediately.
Why?	We missed the first performance of the lute **because Anthony's watch had stopped.**

CHAPTER 21

Subordinating Conjunctions

An adverbial clause begins with a **subordinating conjunction.** A few of the subordinating conjunctions listed in the following box—such as *after, as, before,* and *until*—can also be used as prepositions. Remember that these words are subordinating conjunctions only if they are followed by a group of words with a subject and a verb.

COMMON SUBORDINATING CONJUNCTIONS				
after	as long as	even though	than	whenever
although	as soon as	if	though	where
as	as though	in order that	unless	wherever
as far as	because	since	until	while
as if	before	so that	when	

> ***As soon as* the conductor arrives,** the concert will begin.
>
> Bring your binoculars ***so that* you can see the musicians.**
>
> The musicians prepare ***before* the concert begins.**
>
> They arrange their music ***so that* it is easy to read.**

PUNCTUATION WITH ADVERBIAL CLAUSES

Always place a comma after a dependent adverbial clause that comes at the beginning of a sentence.

> **Since the conductor has arrived,** the concert can begin.

● Practice Your Skills

Supplying Subordinate Conjunctions

Complete each sentence by filling in the blank with a subordinating conjunction that makes the sentence's meaning clear.

1. Cristofori invented the piano around 1700 _____ he worked for the Medici family in Florence, Italy.

2. _____ the piano is a popular instrument, more solo compositions have been written for it than any other instrument.

3. _____ it is so versatile, the piano is well liked by people of all ages.

4. The piano can make a wide variety of sounds _____ it is just one instrument.

5. _____ most pianos have eighty-eight keys, not all keyboards have that many.

● **Practice Your Skills**

Finding Adverbial Clauses

Write each adverbial clause. Then identify the verb that each clause modifies.

1. Most people move to America because they are seeking a better way of life.
2. Before 1865, most immigrants came from Europe after the conditions in their native countries became difficult.
3. Families immigrated because their governments treated them unfairly.
4. As soon as the Civil War ended, the flood of newcomers grew.
5. Even though many still immigrated from western Europe, a larger number from eastern and southern Europe sought the American Dream.
6. Immigration reached its peak before World War I started.
7. As though they had all heard the same stories, people from Mexico, China, and Japan joined the immigration.
8. Because many immigrants did not speak English, they did not blend easily into American society.
9. Long-time citizens considered the newcomers different because their cultures were unfamiliar.
10. The immigrants clustered together so that they would feel safe.

● *Connect to Writing:* **Editing**

Punctuating Adverbial Clauses

Rewrite the following sentences, adding commas where needed. If a sentence is correct, write **C**.

1. Because she feels guilty about Myra a classmate tells the story "Day of the Butterfly."
2. Until her illness keeps her from class Myra is treated differently from the others.
3. Because Myra is sick she does not come to school one day.
4. The class visits the hospital while Myra is a patient.
5. When Myra does not return to school the narrator wishes she had been kinder to the immigrant girl.

Adjectival Clauses

You may recall that a single adjective or an adjectival phrase is used to modify a noun or a pronoun. A subordinate clause can be used in the same way. Such a clause is called an adjectival clause.

Single Adjective	The 1950s was a **great** decade.
Adjectival Phrase	The 1950s was a decade **beyond our expectations.**
Adjectival Clause	The 1950s was a decade **that we will never forget.**

21 B.2   An **adjectival clause** is a subordinate clause that is used to modify a noun or a pronoun.

An adjectival clause answers the adjective question *Which one?* or *What kind?* Usually an adjectival clause modifies the noun or pronoun directly in front of it.

Which One?	Ken's home, **which is blue and white,** is new.
What Kind?	Cathy likes houses **that are close to the schools.**

Relative Pronouns

Most adjectival clauses begin with a relative pronoun. A **relative pronoun** relates an adjectival clause to the noun or the pronoun the clause modifies.

RELATIVE PRONOUNS				
who	whom	whose	which	that

I just met Cindy, **who lives in the yellow house in our neighborhood.**

Barbara, **whose house is in that development,** hopes to make many friends.

Sometimes a relative pronoun simply begins an adjectival clause. At other times, it is the subject of an adjectival clause.

I haven't seen a house **that I like.**

I haven't seen a house **that is like yours.**

PUNCTUATION WITH ADJECTIVAL CLAUSES

No punctuation is used with an adjectival clause that contains information that is essential to identify a person, place, or thing in the sentence.

Essential   A vaccine **that will prevent the disease** was discovered in the laboratory.

A comma or commas should set off an adjectival clause that is nonessential. A clause is nonessential if it can be removed from the sentence without changing the basic meaning of the sentence. A clause is usually nonessential if it modifies a proper noun.

Nonessential   The scientist, **who works in the laboratory,** found the cure.

The relative pronoun *that* is used in an essential clause, and *which* is usually used in a nonessential clause.

● Practice Your Skills

Finding Adjectival Clauses

Write each adjectival clause. Then underline the relative pronoun.

1. The 1950s was the decade that established the United States as a world leader.
2. The men and women who played a role in World War II wanted to have families.
3. The American population, which was 150 million, boomed to more than 179 million.
4. The children of the families, who are now called Baby Boomers, fueled the economy.
5. Changes came to a country that enjoyed prosperity.

6. Polio, which had struck many children, became less of a threat.

7. Dr. Jonas Salk, who developed a polio vaccine, saved many children from the disease.

8. William Levitt developed Levittown, which was the first suburban development.

9. Much attention focused on the automobile, which became a necessity.

10. There were few homes that did not have a TV.

● Practice Your Skills

Identifying the Words Adjectival Clauses Describe

Write each adjectival clause. Then write the word that each clause modifies.

1. Some artists paint thousands of tiny dots that form images.

2. Georges Seurat, who painted in the late 1800s, used dots of different colors.

3. He studied art in museums where he learned about painters and their techniques.

4. First, Seurat made drawings that were in black and white.

5. He then turned to a new approach that used light and color.

6. He also stopped using lines, which give a boxed-in feeling.

7. His paintings were often on large canvases that took years to cover.

8. They portrayed people who were having fun outdoors.

9. People who were at home in the city were frequent subjects.

10. His most famous painting is *A Sunday on la Grande Jatte—1884,* which shows a day in the park.

● *Connect to Writing:* Editing

Punctuating Adjectival Clauses

Write the following sentences, adding commas where needed. If a sentence needs no commas, write **C** for correct.

1. My grandfather fought in World War II which was fought in Europe, Asia, and Africa.

2. My grandmother who worked in a factory has vivid memories.

3. She remembers the families who raised their own gardens.

4. The garden that grew next door was very large.

5. These gardens which were called Victory Gardens gave citizens plenty of food.

Misplaced Adjectival Clauses

Place an adjectival clause as near as possible to the word it modifies. A clause that is too far away from the word it modifies is called a **misplaced modifier.**

Misplaced   Mandy sold the flowers, **who runs the garden shop.**

Correct   Mandy, **who runs the garden shop,** sold the flowers.

Practice Your Skills

Recognizing Misplaced Adjectival Clauses

Write *C* if an adjectival clause is placed correctly or *I* if an adjectival clause is placed incorrectly.

1. "Science is everywhere," Mrs. Lee told me, who is a true scientist.
2. My father, who is a chemist, agrees with this idea of Mrs. Lee.
3. Looking up at the stars is an example of science that glow in the dark.
4. Energy has always interested me, which makes machinery work.
5. The car that goes up a ramp in a parking garage illustrates motion.
6. My mother uses chemistry to make cookies, who is a wonderful baker.
7. The light from the sun, which shines brightly, reaches the flowers.
8. The magnet entertained my brother that hung on the refrigerator.
9. My youngest sister that spins around loves her new wind-up toy.
10. "Where is the bee?" said my friend that is buzzing in my ear.

Connect to Writing: Revising

Correcting Sentences with Misplaced Adjectival Clauses

Rewrite the incorrect sentences from the preceding exercise, placing the adjectival clauses correctly. Use commas where needed.

Noun Clauses

A subordinate clause can be used like a single noun. Such a clause is called a **noun clause.**

Single Noun   Show us the **poem.**

Noun Clause   Show us **what you read.**

21 B.3   A **noun clause** is a subordinate clause that is used like a noun.

A noun clause can be used in the same ways that a noun can be used.

Subject	**Whatever poem you choose** is fine with me.
	(*Whatever poem you choose* is what the sentence is about.)
Direct Object	We'll read **whatever poem is your favorite.**
	(We'll read what? *Whatever poem is your favorite* is the direct object.)
Indirect Object	Give **whoever reads first** your attention.
	(The direct object is *attention*. Give attention to whom? *Whoever reads first* becomes the indirect object.)
Object of a Preposition	Matt was confused by **what the poem implied.**
	(*What the poem implied* is the object of the preposition *by*.)
Predicate Nominative	That poem is **what I expected.**
	(*What I expected* renames the subject, *poem*.)

All the words in the box below can begin a noun clause.

COMMON INTRODUCTORY WORDS FOR NOUN CLAUSES		
how	when	whoever
if	where	whom
that	whether	whomever
what	which	whose
whatever	who	why

Remember that the words *who, whom, whose, which,* and *that* may also begin adjectival clauses. Do not rely on the introductory words alone to identify a noun clause. Instead, decide how the subordinate clause is used in a sentence.

Noun Clause	I believe **that she will win the poetry contest.**
	(The clause is used as a direct object—I believe what?)
Adjectival Clause	The fact **that she will win the poetry contest** is widely known.
	(The clause is used to describe the noun *fact*—which fact?)

● Practice Your Skills

Finding Noun Clauses

Write each noun clause.

1. Who wrote America's best-known poetry is an easy question.
2. Americans are often interested in what Robert Frost wrote.
3. Frost's poems state that human life is a struggle with nature and society.
4. He never forgot that his life was full of disappointment.
5. His family life was what is described as tragic.
6. He gave whatever he was writing his full attention.
7. Whoever reads "The Road Not Taken" must think.
8. His poems are about what we think during day-to-day events.
9. For Frost, life is what pleases and worries us.
10. The award-winning poet was not swayed by what other poets wrote.

● Practice Your Skills

Identifying the Use of Noun Clauses

Write each noun clause. Then label each one using the following abbreviations.

subject = *s.*   object of a preposition = *o.p.*
direct object = *d.o.*   predicate nominative = *p.n.*
indirect object = *i.o.*

1. Why someone writes poetry is a personal matter.
2. Give whoever writes poetry high praise.
3. Poetry requires that you think like an artist.
4. The approach to your subject determines how well your poem will turn out.
5. Whatever subject you choose must be well thought out.
6. When you write poetry can also be important.
7. The value of a poem is also measured by what the reader gets from it.
8. Whoever attempts to skim a poem is missing out.
9. The speaker of your poem is whomever you wish.
10. In a narrative poem, a poet must relate whatever historical event is being told.

Write each subordinate clause. Label each one as an *adverbial clause,* an *adjectival clause,* or a *noun clause.*

1. Many swimmers have crossed the English Channel, which is just over twenty miles wide at its narrowest point.
2. Whoever accomplishes the feat is admired.
3. In 1961, Antonio Abertondo attempted something that no one else had ever done before.
4. Abertondo, who was forty-two years old, swam across the channel and back without a stop.
5. When he arrived at Dover Beach, he was covered with grease for protection against the cold water.
6. He swam steadily for the next eighteen hours and fifty minutes until he reached the coast of France.
7. Abertondo was not stopped by what the cold sea had to offer.
8. When he reached the English coast, he had been swimming for forty-three hours and fifteen minutes.
9. The last mile, which had taken him two hours, had been the hardest.
10. Abertondo showed that he was a determined man.

CHAPTER 21

The ability to recognize independent and subordinate clauses will help you understand sentence structure.

21 C There are three kinds of sentences: **simple, compound,** and **complex.**

In the example sentences that follow, subjects are underlined once and verbs are underlined twice.

➤ Simple and Compound Sentences

21 C.1 A **simple sentence** contains one independent clause.

> Terry caught several fish in the mountain stream.
>
> We cooked the fish over our campfire.
>
> The cat pounced on the leftover fish.

A compound sentence is made up of two or more sentences. The sentences are usually joined by the conjunction *and, but, or,* or *yet.*

21 C.2 A **compound sentence** consists of two or more independent clauses.

Each independent clause in a compound sentence can stand alone as a separate sentence.

> ┌── independent clause ──┐   ┌─independent clause─┐
> Kim has the tackle box, and Michael has the net.
> ┌independent clause┐   ┌── independent clause ──┐
> Kim held the net, and Michael reeled in the fish.
> ┌── independent clause ──┐   ┌─ independent clause ─┐
> The fishing party is ready, but the guide is not here.

● Practice Your Skills

Recognizing Simple and Compound Sentences

Label each sentence *simple* or *compound.*

1. Dogs cannot tell the difference between the colors red and green.

2. Moths usually fly at night, and butterflies fly during the day.

3. A lobster may easily grow a lost claw.

4. The brown pelican dives for fish, but the white pelican scoops fish from the water's surface.
5. The earthworm has no lungs.
6. The fastest land animal is the cheetah.
7. The walrus is a marine animal like a seal.
8. Many insects have feelers and wings, but spiders do not have either.
9. A grain of sand in the shell of an oyster may eventually become a pearl.
10. The animal brain is smaller, and it usually cannot reason.

Compound Sentence or Compound Verb?

Sometimes a simple sentence that has a compound verb is mistaken for a compound sentence. Notice the difference in the following sentences.

Compound Sentence   The sailor untied the lines, and the ship moved away from the dock.

Compound Verb   The sailor untied the lines and jumped onto the ship.

PUNCTUATION WITH COMPOUND SENTENCES

There are several ways to connect the independent clauses in a compound sentence. One way is to join them with a comma and a coordinating conjunction.

We left the dock at 6:30, **but** Ian did not arrive until 7:00.

You can also join the independent clauses with a semicolon and no conjunction.

The fish were biting; everyone on the boat was catching a big fish with each cast.

Practice Your Skills

Distinguishing Between Simple and Compound Sentences

Label each sentence *simple* or *compound*.

1. In 1606, the Virginia Company of London requested and received a settlement charter for North America.
2. The company acted quickly, and more than 140 settlers left England.
3. The settlers had dreams of finding gold and setting up trade.
4. In 1607, three ships entered Chesapeake Bay and sailed up the river.

5. Nearly one hundred people settled on a peninsula, and nature quickly tested them.

6. Only a few of the Jamestown colonists dug wells and cleared land for their spring gardens.

7. The rest searched for gold and hoped for wealth.

8. Disease and hunger devastated the colonists, and fewer than thirty-eight greeted the supply ships.

9. Captain John Smith took control and organized the survivors.

10. Jamestown survived another year, but the recovery was short-lived.

● *Connect to Writing:* **Editing**

Punctuating Compound Sentences

Rewrite each compound sentence, making sure that commas, conjunctions, and semicolons are used properly. If a sentence is punctuated correctly, write **C.**

1. Hunters and gatherers roamed the earth in early times and no one settled in any one place.

2. Most people settled as farmers but not all did.

3. The land of the Greeks became overcrowded, and some Greeks formed colonies overseas.

4. Early on Rome was a monarchy but later on it became a republic.

5. The Roman Empire declined; Germanic tribes took over the western half of the former empire.

➤ Complex Sentences

If you can recognize independent and subordinate clauses, you can also recognize complex sentences.

21 C.3   A **complex sentence** consists of one independent clause and one or more subordinate clauses.

┌──────adverbial clause──────┐ ┌──────── independent clause ────────┐
Since we have extra time, we can drive around the islands.

┌──────── independent clause ────────┐┌──adjectival clause──┐
I have already driven on the new road that opened last week.

When You Write

When you write, think about your audience as you choose the kinds of sentences you use. Paragraphs composed of many simple sentences are appropriate for young children. Compound and complex sentences are more appropriate for older readers. Notice the difference in the following sentences.

> The electric car was new. **We** did not have to recharge the battery.
>
> The electric car was new, **and** we did not have to recharge the battery.
>
> **Because** the electric car was new, we did not have to recharge the battery.

Select a piece of writing from your portfolio. Are the sentence types appropriate for the intended audience? If not, revise two or three paragraphs so that they suit the intended audience.

● Practice Your Skills

Distinguishing Among Simple, Compound, and Complex Sentences

Label each sentence *simple*, *compound*, or *complex*.

1. The first steam-driven cars were unpopular because they were noisy and dirtied the air.
2. Early postal trucks were made so that a mule could be substituted for a failed engine.
3. Postal trucks have steering wheels on the right side.
4. An electric car gets its power from a battery, but the battery must be recharged.
5. Electric cars are inexpensive to run and help protect our air.
6. Electric cars were popular in the 1890s and 1900s, but cars with gasoline engines soon replaced them.
7. Although people had hired vehicles for thousands of years, the word *taxicab* was not used until the 1800s.
8. Now in many large cities people cannot get around and cannot conduct their daily lives without taxicabs.
9. The longest bicycle, which was built for thirty-five people, was made in Denmark in 1976.
10. The bicycle weighed more than a ton, and it was seventy-two feet long.
11. All the riders had to work together and must have had enormous confidence in the person at the handlebars.
12. Some astronauts who went to the moon traveled in a lunar rover.

Label each sentence *simple,* *compound,* or *complex.*

1. Charles Willson Peale never saw a painting until he was a grown man.

2. He was a saddle maker by trade and lived in Annapolis, Maryland.

3. One day Peale went to Norfolk for supplies and saw paintings for the first time.

4. He did not like any of the paintings; they did not look realistic.

5. When he returned home, he took up painting with a great deal of energy and talent.

6. He took lessons in Boston and even went to London for more lessons.

7. After he had made some money from his paintings, he became a full-time painter.

8. Peale loved painting, but his enjoyment was not enough for him.

9. He taught his skills to his seventeen children and all his relatives and created a family of artists.

10. Charles Willson Peale became the famous patriot artist who painted George Washington's portrait.

George Washington by Charles Wilson Peale

Connect to Writing: **Drafting**

Writing Complex Sentences

Find out more about what life was like for a member of your family when he or she was a young person. Then write five complex sentences about his or her early life. Be sure to punctuate your sentences correctly.

➤ Diagraming Sentences

All simple sentences have one baseline. Diagrams for compound and complex sentences, however, have two or more baselines. Each clause has its own baseline.

Compound Sentences These sentences are diagramed the way two simple sentences are. The baselines of the separate sentences, however, are joined by a broken line on which the conjunction is placed. The broken line connects the verbs.

Dad enjoys movies, but Mom prefers the theater.

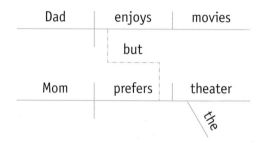

Complex Sentences In a complex sentence, an adverbial clause is diagramed beneath the independent clause. The subordinating conjunction belongs on a broken line that connects the verb in the adverbial clause to the word the clause modifies.

After I watch the movie, I am going to bed.

An adjectival clause is also diagramed beneath the independent clause. The relative pronoun is connected by a broken line to the noun or the pronoun the clause modifies.

The dancer who is best is my friend.

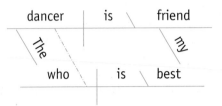

A noun clause is diagramed on a pedestal in the same place a single noun with the same function would be placed. The noun clause in the following diagram is the subject.

Whoever wrote the screenplay was brilliant.

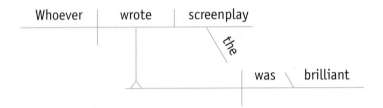

● **Practice Your Skills**

Diagraming Sentences

Diagram the following sentences or copy them. If you copy them, draw one line under each subject and two lines under each verb. Put parentheses around each subordinate clause. Then label each subordinate clause *adv.* for adverb, *adj.* for adjective, or *n.* for *noun.*

1. A snail has no legs, but it does have a foot.

2. Rao will collect tickets, and Diane will usher.

3. Before the rain started, I closed the car windows.

4. Why the cabin burned is a mystery.

5. Mrs. O'Reilly, who just moved here, will teach the new computer course.

Assess Your Learning

■ Finding and Identifying Subordinate Clauses

Write each subordinate clause. Then next to each one, label it **adv.** for adverb, **adj.** for adjective, or **n.** for **noun.**

1. As soon as the bell rings, I will go to the cafeteria and eat lunch.
2. Grandmother will give you whatever you want for your fourteenth birthday.
3. We must find the people whose car is blocking ours.
4. Phina can't eat now because she has a swim meet in less than an hour.
5. I laughed at how comical John's costume looked.
6. I know Mr. Myers, whom you mentioned in your note.
7. When my dog doesn't recognize a visitor, she barks and growls menacingly.
8. Whoever owns that beagle won three blue ribbons in last night's show.
9. Don't put the glass where it will get broken.
10. The first baseball game that was a tie occurred in 1854.
11. Because Terry was early, he got the best seat in the house.
12. Measure the cloth before you cut it.
13. The flan that Marisela made is delicious!
14. After the fax arrived, Ms. Styles took it to the principal.
15. Whatever made these marks in the dirt was quite heavy.

■ Identifying Kinds of Sentences

Label each sentence **simple, compound,** or **complex.**

1. If the ice on the south polar cap melted, the water would cover the Statue of Liberty up to her nose.
2. The waves crashed, and the sandpipers ran toward them.
3. Al climbed over the stone wall that bordered the farm.
4. The sphinx moth curls up its tongue and uses it as a pillow.
5. The center lost the ball, and five players fell on it.

CHAPTER 21

6. We left early for the train station but had a flat tire.

7. A fly can walk upside down on a ceiling because it has special pads on each of its six feet.

8. Although the weather was bad, we kept playing.

9. Eskimos buy refrigerators so that food won't freeze.

10. A spider spins a web of silk that it makes inside its body.

▩ Using Sentence Structure

Write sentences that follow the directions below. (The sentences may come in any order.) Write about one of the following topics or a topic of your choice: your idea of an ideal place to live or the best things about where you live now.

1. Write a simple sentence.

2. Write a complex sentence with an introductory adverbial clause.

3. Write a complex sentence with an adjectival clause.

4. Write a compound sentence.

5. Write a complex sentence with a noun clause.

When you have finished, label each sentence *simple, compound,* or *complex.* Then check the punctuation of each one.

Clauses: Posttest

Directions

Write the letter of the term that correctly identifies the underlined words in each sentence.

(1) <u>Whoever gazes at the moon</u> tends to be romantic. (2) The constellations <u>that I recognize</u> include the Big Dipper, the Little Dipper, and Orion. (3) <u>Do not look directly at the sun or an eclipse.</u> (4) I spotted the comet <u>as soon as it appeared.</u> (5) <u>If you use a telescope, you can see many more details of the moon's surface.</u> (6) <u>When we studied asteroids</u>, I made a three-dimensional model of an asteroid belt. (7) The moving model of the solar system is in the closet <u>that I made as a child.</u> (8) <u>Whoever could name the planets in order from the sun</u> received bonus points on the test. (9) <u>I peered through the fog, but I could not see any stars tonight.</u> (10) The students <u>who enjoy astronomy</u> may sign up for an extra-credit assignment.

1. **A** independent clause
   B adverbial clause
   C noun clause
   D adjectival clause

2. **A** adverbial clause
   B noun clause
   C independent clause
   D adjectival clause

3. **A** simple sentence
   B complex sentence
   C subordinate clause
   D compound sentence

4. **A** independent clause
   B noun clause
   C adverbial clause
   D adjectival clause

5. **A** misplaced modifier
   B subordinate clause
   C compound sentence
   D complex sentence

6. **A** independent clause
   B adverbial clause
   C noun clause
   D adjectival clause

7. **A** misplaced modifier
   B simple sentence
   C noun clause
   D adverbial clause

8. **A** noun clause
   B adverbial clause
   C misplaced modifier
   D adjectival clause

9. **A** noun clause
   B compound sentence
   C simple sentence
   D complex sentence

10. **A** noun clause
    B adverbial clause
    C misplaced modifier
    D adjectival clause

Snapshot

21 A A **clause** is a group of words that has a subject and a verb. An **independent clause** can stand alone as a sentence. A **subordinate clause** cannot stand alone as a sentence. (pages 630–631)

21 B **Subordinate clauses** can be used as adverbs, adjectives, and nouns. An **adverbial clause** is a subordinate clause that is used mainly to modify a verb. An **adjectival clause** is a subordinate clause used to modify a noun or a pronoun. A **noun clause** is a subordinate clause that is used like a noun. (pages 632–641)

21 C There are three main types of sentences: **simple** (containing one independent clause), **compound** (containing two or more independent clauses), and **complex** (containing one independent clause and one or more subordinate clauses). (pages 642–646)

Power Rules

Fix sentence fragments by revising words and/or correcting punctuation to make complete sentences.

Before Editing	**After Editing**
After the tornado. The whole town had to be rebuilt.	After the tornado, *the* whole town had to be rebuilt.
He did not finish his dinner. Because he did not like spinach.	He did not finish his dinner *because* he did not like spinach.

Editing Checklist

Use this checklist when editing your writing.

✓ Did I make sure that all my main clauses express a complete thought? (See page 630.)

✓ Did I make sure that my subordinate clauses are not standing alone? (See pages 630–631.)

✓ Did I vary my use of clauses and include adverb, adjective, and noun clauses? (See pages 632–641.)

✓ Did I vary my use of simple, compound, and complex sentences to make my writing more interesting? (See pages 642–646.)

Use the Power

Using different types of sentences—simple, compound, and complex— helps create a pleasing and smooth rhythm in the reader's mind. To help you remember the different kinds of sentences, you can think of an independent clause as a horse and a dependent clause as a cart that can't move on its own.

	The horse cantered through the woods. (simple sentence, one independent clause)
	The first horse cantered, but the second horse wanted to stop and eat the grass. (compound sentence, two independent clauses)
	While the cart trailed behind, the horse kept up a steady pace. (complex sentence, one dependent and one independent clause)

Sentence Fragments and Run-ons

How can you clarify your meaning and add sentence variety by fixing unintended sentence fragments and run-ons?

Sentence Fragments and Run-ons: Pretest 1

The following draft paragraph about the artist Eadweard Muybridge is hard to read because it contains sentence fragments and run-ons. Revise the paragraph so that it reads more smoothly. The first sentence fragment has been corrected as an example.

> During the 1860s and 1870s, Englishman Eadweard Muybridge (1830–1904) was recognized for his photographs of the Yosemite wilderness in the United States. In 1872, Leland Stanford hired Muybridge. To settle a bet. He wanted to prove that as a horse gallops, all four of its hooves are simultaneously off the ground. During each stride. To prove this, Muybridge produced a sequential series of photographs using several cameras, he set them up along the race track. Each with a tripwire for the horse to set off as it ran by. At the time, the 1870s, this was a radically innovative way to study movement. In 1879, Muybridge invented the zoopraxiscope it was a machine that reproduced the motion of the galloping horse. Using the photographs Muybridge's machine was the forerunner of cinematography.

Sentence Fragments and Run-ons: Pretest 2

Directions

Read the passage. Write the letter of the best way to write each underlined section. If the underlined section contains no error, write **D**.

Hurricanes

(1) Develops into a hurricane only when conditions are perfect. (2) To grow, hurricanes need warm waters, high humidity, and high winds. Hurricanes can last up to (3) two or three weeks but they weaken if they travel over cold water or land. Hurricanes take place only in the Atlantic and Eastern Pacific. In (4) the Northern Pacific and Philippines. Such storms are called typhoons. (5) In the Southern Pacific, they are called cyclones.

1. **A** A storm develops into a hurricane. Only when
   B A storm develops into a hurricane only when
   C Develops into a hurricane, only when
   D No error

2. **A** To grow. Hurricanes need
   B To grow. Hurricanes needing
   C To grow into hurricanes need
   D No error

3. **A** two or three weeks, but they weaken
   B two or three weeks. But they weaken
   C two or three weeks they weaken
   D No error

4. **A** In the Northern Pacific and Philippines are such storms
   B In the Northern Pacific and Philippines having such storms
   C In the Northern Pacific and Philippines, such storms
   D No error

5. **A** In the Southern Pacific. They are called cyclones.
   B They are called cyclones, which is in the Southern Pacific.
   C They are called, cyclones, in the Southern Pacific.
   D No error

You have learned that to express a complete thought, a sentence must have a subject and a verb. An incomplete sentence is called a sentence fragment.

22 A **A sentence fragment is a group of words that does not express a complete thought.**

In the example sentences that follow, subjects are underlined once and verbs are underlined twice.

> **No Subject** Wrote an editorial about the traffic problem.
> (Who wrote an editorial?)
>
> **Sentence** Bob wrote an editorial about the traffic problem.
>
> **No Verb** The new members of the city council.
> (What did they do?)
>
> **Sentence** The new members of the city council sponsored a seminar.

When you edit your writing, always check specifically for any missing subjects or missing verbs.

● Practice Your Skills

Distinguishing Between Sentences and Fragments

Label each group of words as a *sentence* or a *sentence fragment.*

1. The newspaper prints national and local news articles.
2. Every city with a large population.
3. Most readers prefer delivery in the morning.
4. Many people read the sports page first.
5. Many people like to read the comics.
6. Contain informative articles about houses.
7. The comics used to be printed in black-and-white.
8. Represents a terrific bargain for the cost.

● *Connect to Writing:* Revising

Correcting Sentence Fragments

Revise the sentence fragments from the preceding exercise to make complete sentences.

CHAPTER 22

A complete sentence must have a subject and a verb. Because a phrase does not have either a subject or a verb, it can never stand alone as a sentence. When phrases are written alone, they result in **phrase fragments**.

22 B   **A phrase fragment** is a group of words that is incorrectly punctuated as a sentence but is missing a subject and a verb.

The following examples of phrase fragments are in bold type. Notice that the fragments are capitalized and punctuated as if they were sentences.

Prepositional Phrase	Every morning I deliver the newspaper. **Onto the Johnsons' front porch.**
Appositive Phrase	Every payday I will collect from Mr. Johnson. **The oldest customer on my paper route.**
Participial Phrase	**Sitting on his front porch.** He reads the newspaper.
Infinitive Phrase	**To please Mr. Johnson.** I will deliver the newspaper on time.

CHAPTER 22

Practice Your Skills

Distinguishing Between Sentences and Fragments

Label each group of words as a *sentence* or a *phrase fragment*.

1. Comics are fun to read.

2. To make people laugh.

3. Of a scene or a complete scene in the strip.

4. With exaggerated features and in common clothes.

5. A strip about families or animals will appeal to all ages.

6. From a group of soldiers to talking pets.

7. Many feelings besides humor.

8. Ranging from poking fun to social satire.

9. Charles Schulz was a comic-strip artist.

10. Creator of the comic strip called *Peanuts*.

Ways to Correct Phrase Fragments

Always look for phrase fragments when you edit your writing. If you find any, you can correct them by adding a subject and a verb to make the phrase into a separate sentence or by attaching the phrase to a related group of words that has a subject and a verb.

The following examples show ways to correct the phrase fragments on the preceding page.

the phrase fragments on the preceding page.

Corrected Prepositional Phrase Fragments	Every morning I deliver the newspaper. **It flies onto the Johnsons' front porch.** (subject and verb added)
	Every morning I deliver the newspaper **onto the Johnsons' front porch.** (attached to a sentence)
Corrected Appositive Phrase Fragments	Every payday I will collect from Mr. Johnson. **He is the oldest customer on my paper route.** (subject and verb added)
	Every payday I will collect from Mr. Johnson, **the oldest customer on my paper route.** (attached to a sentence)
Corrected Participial Phrase Fragments	**He is sitting on his front porch.** He reads the newspaper. (subject and verb added)
	Sitting on his front porch, he reads the newspaper. (attached to a sentence)
Corrected Infinitive Phrase Fragment	**To please Mr. Johnson,** I will deliver the newspaper on time. (attached to a sentence)

Practice Your Skills

Distinguishing Between Sentences and Fragments

Label each group of words as a *sentence* or a *phrase fragment*.

1. In the charter colonies of Connecticut and Rhode Island of the 1760s.
2. The colonists from these places elected their own representatives.
3. From Great Britain an appointed governor.
4. Elected representatives passed their own legislation.
5. The colonies of Maryland, Delaware, and Pennsylvania.

6. Depending on the authority of the delegated officials.
7. The people elected only the lower representatives.
8. To live in the royal colonies of Georgia, Massachusetts, New Hampshire, New Jersey, North Carolina, and Virginia.
9. Ruled directly by Great Britain all of the royal colonies.
10. With little or no say in their own government.

● *Connect to Writing:* **Editing**

Combining Sentences and Phrase Fragments

Add each phrase fragment to the first sentence to form a complete sentence.

1. The Dutch first settled New Netherland. A name later changed to New York.
2. The British captured New Netherland in 1684. Adding it to their royal colonies.
3. The Swedish lost control of Delaware. Lost to the Duke of York.
4. William Penn purchased Delaware from England. The founder of Pennsylvania.
5. English law obligated colonists. To remain loyal to their king.

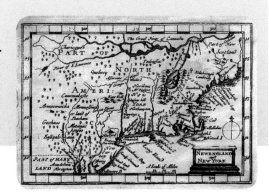

● *Connect to Writing:* **Revising**

Correcting Phrase Fragments

Rewrite each phrase fragment to make a complete sentence.

1. By the people and for the people.
2. The community.
3. With the same rights for everyone.
4. Depending on other people for leadership.
5. To enjoy the benefits of democracy.
6. Voting for personal rights.

Clause Fragments Lesson 3

A subordinate clause often looks very much like a complete sentence because it has a subject and a verb. When it stands alone, however, it becomes a clause fragment because it does not express a complete thought.

> **22 C** A **clause fragment** is a subordinate clause that is incorrectly written as a sentence.

The following examples in **bold** type are clause fragments. Notice that they are punctuated and capitalized as if they were complete sentences. The subjects are underlined once; the verbs are underlined twice.

Adverbial Clause Fragments	**When I design a product.** I list the materials necessary to make it.
	Products are tested. **So that safety and longevity can be guaranteed.**
Adjectival Clause Fragments	Stella is the engineer. **Who is in charge of testing.**
	Is this the design for the seats? **That uses a great deal of plastic?**

● Practice Your Skills

Distinguishing Between Sentences and Fragments

Label each group of words *S* for sentence or *CF* for clause fragment.

1. Telephones last a long time and are durable.

2. When you pick up the telephone.

3. Notice the materials it is made of.

4. Because most of its parts are made of plastic.

5. Plastic is a modern material.

6. Plastic is a synthetic polymer-based material.

7. That can be easily molded into various shapes.

8. After they are manufactured from organic compounds.

9. If you notice ordinary things in your life.

10. That are made of synthetic polyethylene.

11. Check the tags on furniture.

12. When you are at department stores.

13. Don't be surprised to see different plastics listed.

Ways to Correct Clause Fragments

You can correct clause fragments in one of two ways. You can make the subordinate clause into an independent clause, or you can attach a clause fragment to a related sentence next to it.

Corrected Adverbial Clause Fragments	**When I design a product,** I list the materials necessary to make it. (attached to a sentence) Products are tested. **Safety and longevity can be guaranteed.** (made into an independent clause)
Corrected Adjectival Clause Fragments	Stella is the engineer **who is in charge of testing.** (attached to a sentence) Is this the design for the seats **that uses a great deal of plastic?** (attached to a sentence)

● Practice Your Skills

Distinguishing Between Sentences and Fragments

Label each group of words as a *sentence* or a *clause fragment*.

1. Before the Spanish explorers wandered throughout Florida.
2. A civilized, well-governed society inhabited the peninsula.
3. The Seminoles were some of the earliest inhabitants of Florida.
4. Who settled in many areas and farmed the fertile land.
5. The Seminoles left burial mounds and other artifacts.
6. Which suggest the existence of some form of government.
7. The Native Americans had a loose confederation of tribes.
8. In which different tribes were constantly trying to control each other.
9. Rules were made to keep the confederation working.
10. That gave power to the chief of each tribe.

● *Connect to Writing:* Revising

Correcting Clause Fragments

Rewrite the clause fragments from the preceding exercise to make complete sentences. Remember that you can attach a clause fragment to another sentence.

A common mistake some writers make when they are writing too fast is to combine several thoughts and write them as one sentence. The result is a **run-on sentence**.

22 D   **A run-on sentence is two or more sentences that are written together and are separated by a comma or no mark of punctuation at all.**

Run-on sentences are usually written in either of two ways.

With a Comma	The concert is beginning, it will be over by lunchtime. (This error is commonly called a comma splice.)
With No Punctuation	Danny conducted the orchestra the musicians played very hard.

● Practice Your Skills

Distinguishing Between Sentences and Run-on Sentences

Label each group of words **S** for **sentence** or **RO** for **run-on sentence**.

1. Conductors direct an orchestra, chorus, or opera production.
2. Conductors usually specialize in orchestral or choral conducting, each specialization shares many common elements.
3. They have a difficult job many jobs are rolled into one title.
4. They must study and memorize many thousands of measures of music.
5. While conducting, they turn from the sheet music, they must be free to look at the orchestra or the chorus.
6. Conductors must rehearse with the performers they also have to find new music to perform.
7. They must be able to conduct a group and to know about each instrument.
8. Conductors give advice they give orders.
9. They must be in excellent physical condition, they work like athletes.
10. Orchestra conductors often use a baton choral conductors usually depend on their hands.

Ways to Correct Run-on Sentences

There are three ways to correct a run-on sentence. You can turn it into two separate sentences, a single compound sentence, or a single complex sentence.

Run-on Sentences

The <u>movie</u> <u>is beginning</u>, <u>it</u> <u>will be</u> over by three o'clock.

The <u>aliens</u> <u>roamed</u> outer space the <u>creatures</u> <u>searched</u> for food.

Separate Sentences

The <u>movie</u> <u>is beginning</u>. <u>It</u> <u>will be</u> over by three o'clock.

The <u>aliens</u> <u>roamed</u> outer space. The <u>creatures</u> <u>searched</u> for food.

Compound Sentences

The <u>movie</u> <u>is beginning</u>; <u>it</u> <u>will be</u> over by three o'clock.
(The two independent clauses are joined by a semicolon.)

The <u>movie</u> <u>is beginning</u>, but <u>it</u> <u>will be</u> over by three o'clock.
(The two independent clauses are joined by a comma and the coordinating conjunction *but*.)

Complex Sentences

Because the <u>movie</u> <u>is beginning</u>, <u>it</u> <u>will be</u> over by three o'clock.
(The first independent clause is made into a subordinate clause with the addition of the subordinating conjunction *because*. The subordinate clause is joined to the independent clause with a comma.)

As the <u>aliens</u> <u>roamed</u> outer space, the <u>creatures</u> <u>searched</u> for food.
(The first independent clause is made into a subordinate clause with the addition of the subordinating conjunction *as*. The subordinate clause is joined to the independent clause with a comma.)

CHAPTER 22

When You Write

Fiction writers sometimes include run-on sentences to create a sense of constant movement or meandering in their writing. Formal academic writing should never contain run-on sentences.

● **Practice Your Skills**

Distinguishing Between Sentences and Run-on Sentences

Label each group of words **S** for sentence or **RO** for run-on sentence.

1. Science fiction has been a popular form of literature for many years, many readers enjoy this special form of fantasy.

2. Science fiction allows writers to offer adventures in the future.

3. The stories may tell of adventures on other planets they may narrate stories of time travel or space travel.

4. Its setting in the future separates science fiction from historical fiction.

5. Science fiction focuses on the future, historical fiction looks to the past.

6. Usually a successful writer of science fiction knows a good deal of science, the crafty writer often takes science to an extreme.

7. Of course, with the rapid advance in technology and science, this special type of literature has grown in the last fifty years.

8. Some popular science fiction writers include Ray Bradbury, Kurt Vonnegut, and Isaac Asimov there are hundreds of other well-known writers.

9. This type of writing comes in many forms, it is also very close to folklore.

10. Have you read any science fiction, who is your favorite writer?

Connect to Writing: Revising

Correcting Run-on Sentences

Rewrite the run-on sentences from the exercise above to make correct sentences.

Check Point: Mixed Practice

Label each group of words *S* for sentence, *F* for fragment, or *RO* for run-on sentence.

1. John Milton is a famous British author of the seventeenth century.

2. Milton wrote poetry, pamphlets, and drama he was blind for half of his life.

3. Before he left school and became a professional writer.

4. All of his writing mixed religion and politics.

5. He wrote several long works his most famous work is *Paradise Lost*.

6. Based on the Bible, the very long poem tells the story of the Garden of Eden.

7. Having more than ten thousand lines and recited by the blind poet to his daughters for revision.

8. "Lycidas" was written to commemorate a person who had drowned.

9. A writer of booklets on education and literature who had many enemies and few friends.

10. Blindness is a challenge that some people believe is impossible to overcome, John Milton's life proves just the opposite.

Assess Your Learning

Correcting Sentence Fragments

Correct each sentence fragment. Add punctuation marks where needed.

1. Beginning in the nineteenth century. Ice hockey was first played in eastern Canada.
2. We found a battered trunk. In the old red barn.
3. Before you go to bed. Please lock the front door.
4. Dad was in the yard. When the phone rang.
5. We could see the horses. Jumping over the fence.
6. Swimming for hours. We enjoyed our day at the beach.
7. I lost my purse. But found the car keys on the lawn.
8. The score was tied. Between Weston and Newton High.
9. In the museum. We saw our first mummy.
10. Six-day bicycle races were a fad. In the early 1900s.

Correcting Run-on Sentences

Correct each run-on sentence. Add capital letters, conjunctions, and punctuation marks where needed.

1. Duluth is about 2,000 miles from the Atlantic, its harbor is reached through the St. Lawrence Seaway.
2. I always buy mysteries I love to read them.
3. The Winter Olympics were held in Japan in 1972, it was the first time the games had been held in Asia.
4. The American Revolution began in 1775 it ended in 1783.
5. Most of the snakes in the United States are harmless, many of them benefit farmers.
6. I eat a healthful diet I eat salads, fish, and vegetables.
7. Alexander Hamilton's picture is on the ten-dollar bill, Andrew Jackson's is on the twenty.
8. Bill lifts weights, he trains every day.

9. The first Academy Awards® ceremony was held in 1927, only 250 people attended.

10. Martin takes Latin he studies an hour a night.

Correcting Sentence Errors

Rewrite the following paragraph, correcting each sentence fragment and run-on sentence. Add capital letters, conjunctions, and punctuation marks where needed.

(1) You may have a microwave oven in your home. **(2)** But did you know that microwaves also carry television programs through space? **(3)** When you call overseas. **(4)** The call may be transmitted to a satellite by microwave. **(5)** You may have seen towers with unusual satellite dishes these are microwave towers. **(6)** Ships and airplanes may use microwaves. **(7)** To detect objects around them. **(8)** A radar dish on the ground beams microwaves they strike an object and bounce back.

Writing Sentences

Write five sentences that follow the directions below. Beware of sentence fragments and run-ons. Write about an important invention or about a topic of your choice.

1. Write a sentence that contains only a subject and a verb.

2. Write a sentence that consists of a simple sentence with an attached phrase.

3. Write a sentence that consists of a simple sentence with an attached clause.

4. Write a sentence containing the word *and* that is not a run-on sentence.

5. Write a sentence containing the word *but* that is not a run-on sentence.

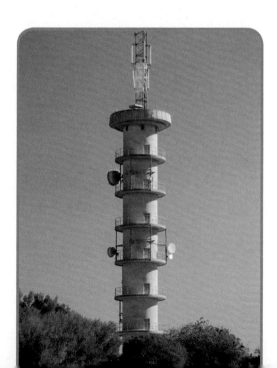

Sentence Fragments and Run-ons: Posttest

Directions

Read the passage. Write the letter of the best way to write each underlined section. If the underlined section needs no change, write **D.**

Norway

Because Norway has little farmland, fishing is important there. Norway is **(1)** so mountainous. That the land is hard to cultivate. People raise dairy cattle, and timber is an important product. The Lapps of the North **(2)** raise reindeer. For their milk and meat. Long ocean **(3)** inlets they are called fjords slice Norway's western coast. **(4)** When farmland is available. It tends to be at the heads of fjords. For the most part, however, the people of Norway live in cities. **(5)** Oslo is the capital, and Bergen and Trondheim are two more big cities.

1. **A** so mountainous, that the land
   B so mountainous that the land
   C so mountainous, the land
   D No error

2. **A** raise reindeer for their milk
   B raise reindeer and for their milk
   C raise reindeer. Mainly for their milk
   D No error

3. **A** inlets. They are called *fjords* slice
   B inlets called *fjords* slicing
   C inlets called *fjords* slice
   D No error

4. **A** When farmland is available. Tending to be
   B When farmland is available, it tends to be
   C Farmland is available, it tends to be
   D No error

5. **A** Oslo is the capital, Bergen and Trondheim are two more big cities.
   B Oslo is the capital. And Bergen and Trondheim are two more big cities.
   C Oslo, the capital, Bergen, and Trondheim, are two more big cities.
   D No error

Writer's Corner

Snapshot

22 A   A **sentence fragment** is a group of words that does not express a complete thought. (page 656)

22 B   A **phrase fragment** is a group of words that is incorrectly punctuated as a sentence but is missing a subject and a verb. (pages 657–659)

22 C   A **clause fragment** is a subordinate clause that is incorrectly written as a sentence. (pages 660–661)

22 D   A **run-on sentence** is two or more sentences that are written together and are separated by a comma or no mark of punctuation at all. (pages 662–664)

Power Rules

Fix **run-on sentences** by joining them with a conjunction and/or proper punctuation. (pages 663–664)

Before Editing	After Editing
Walt opened a restaurant, it was successful.	Walt opened a restaurant, *and* it was successful.
Every day I walk to school it is a long way.	Every day I walk to school. *It* is a long way.

Be sure your sentences are complete. Add any necessary words to **sentence fragments** to make complete sentences.

Before Editing	After Editing
David threw the ball. Caught it.	David threw the ball. *Mary* caught it.
The students in room 109. They had a bake sale.	The students in room 109 had a bake sale.

Editing Checklist

Use this checklist when editing your writing.

✓ Did I make sure that all my sentences have a subject and a verb? (See page 656.)

✓ Did I make sure that my sentences are complete and have correct punctuation? (See page 656.)

✓ Did I make sure my sentences express a complete thought and are not clause fragments or phrase fragments? (See pages 657–661.)

✓ Did I divide run-on sentences into two or more complete sentences or use a semicolon? (See pages 663–664.)

Use the Power

There are several ways to correct fragments and run-ons. The chart below shows some of the ways.

Fragment	Corrected Fragment
In the variety show.	**Krista and her friends auditioned for a part** in the variety show.
After they finished their dance routine.	**They felt optimistic** after they finished their dance routine.

Run-on	Corrected Run-on
The rehearsals were every day after school, the effort was worth it.	The rehearsals were every day after school, **but** the effort was worth it.
	Although the rehearsals were every day after school, the effort was worth it.

Review a composition you have worked on recently. Correct any fragments or run-ons you find.

Unit 5

Usage

Children learn how to cross the street by doing it many times with the grownups who care for them. They also learn how to talk from doing it many times with the adults and older children around them. The language patterns children learn make up their English *usage*. Sometimes the usage learned at home is the same as conventional English usage, and sometimes it is different. Conventional usage—the pattern of English usage you will find in this unit—is good for everyone to learn, since it is used in school and in many workplaces.

English usage is sometimes more than mere taste, judgement, and education—Sometimes it's sheer luck, like getting across the street.
—*E. B. White*

Using Verbs

How can understanding how to use verbs help you improve your writing?

Using Verbs: Pretest 1

The first draft below contains several errors in the use of verbs. The first error is corrected. How would you revise the rest of the draft so that all the verbs are used correctly?

Pieter Bruegel the Elder (1525–1569) is ~~is~~ *was* a Flemish artist. Today, both he and his son Pieter Bruegel the Younger is known for their vibrant work. The Elder paints lively peasants at work and play. He will also be an engraver, illustrator, and printer. His elaborate landscapes, appreciated for their originality and craftsmanship, reveal a love of nature. Both painters will document their times. Their work are often satirical or allegorical and show the paradoxes and ironies of the human condition. Both painters work in the 1550s in what is now Belgium. Both Bruegels, father and son, gave audiences today a clear and fascinating picture of everyday activities from five hundred years ago.

Using Verbs: Pretest 2

Directions

Read the passage and choose the word or group of words that belongs in each underlined space. Write the letter of the correct answer.

Oliver Wendell Holmes is the name of two famous Americans. The first Holmes, Oliver Wendell Holmes, Senior, __(1)__ in 1809. He __(2)__ up in a wealthy and cultured New England home. In his youth, Holmes __(3)__ his first poem, "Old Ironsides." Holmes __(4)__ medicine, but his fame __(5)__ as a man of letters—a poet and speaker. His poem "The Chambered Nautilus" __(6)__ by students for generations. After he __(7)__ at Harvard for some years, Oliver Wendell Holmes, Junior, __(8)__ to the Supreme Court in 1902. He __(9)__ as "The Great Dissenter" because of his eloquent dissents on many cases. His writings __(10)__ a series of lectures widely read today by law students.

1. **A** was born
   B born
   C is borning
   D borned

2. **A** grow
   B growed
   C grew
   D has grown

3. **A** publish
   B published
   C was published
   D had been published

4. **A** is practicing
   B has practiced
   C practice
   D practiced

5. **A** was achieved
   B achieved
   C is achieving
   D has achieved

6. **A** has read
   B is read
   C has been read
   D reads

7. **A** having taught
   B will have taught
   C had taught
   D teaches

8. **A** appoints
   B was appointed
   C appointed
   D is appointing

9. **A** knew
   B known
   C had known
   D was known

10. **A** were included
    B are including
    C include
    D will include

A verb not only shows action or tells something about its subject. It also tells when something happened.

Present Action	Every day I **eat** a sandwich.
Past Action	Yesterday I **ate** a sandwich.
Future Action	Tomorrow I **will eat** a sandwich.

Different forms of a verb can express different times. These are called the **tense of a verb.** From the four main forms of a verb, called the principal parts, all the different tenses of a verb are developed.

23 A The **principal parts** of a verb are the **present,** the **present participle,** the **past,** and the **past participle.**

Following are the principal parts of the verb *cook*. Notice that the present participle and the past participle must each have a helping verb when they are used as verbs.

Present	I **cook** one night a week.
Present Participle	I *am* **cooking** tonight.
Past	I **cooked** last week.
Past Participle	I *have* **cooked** two times this month.

You can find a list of helping verbs on pages 512 and 741.

➤ Regular Verbs

Most verbs form their past and past participle just like the verb *cook*—by adding *-ed* or *-d* to the present. These verbs are called regular verbs.

23 A.1 A **regular verb** forms its past and past participle by adding *-ed* or *-d* to the present.

The principal parts of the verbs *wish, jump, wonder,* and *agree* are listed on the next page. Notice that the present participle is formed by adding *-ing* to the present form. Also, as the rule says, the past and past participle are formed by adding *-ed* or *-d* to the present.

CHAPTER 23

Present	Present Participle	Past	Past Participle
wish	(is) wishing	wished	(have) wished
jump	(is) jumping	jumped	(have) jumped
wonder	(is) wondering	wondered	(have) wondered
agree	(is) agreeing	agreed	(have) agreed

When you add *-ing* or *-ed* to verbs such as *taste, skip, cry,* and *picnic,* the spelling changes. If you are unsure of the spelling of a verb form, check the dictionary.

Present	Present Participle	Past	Past Participle
taste	(is) tasting	tasted	(have) tasted
skip	(is) skipping	skipped	(have) skipped
cry	(is) crying	cried	(have) cried
picnic	(is) picnicking	picnicked	(have) picnicked

When the present participle or past participle is used as a main verb, it is always joined with a helping verb.

I *am* waiting.   I *have* watched.

He *is* waiting.   She *has* watched.

They *are* waiting.   They *had* watched.

● **Practice Your Skills**

Writing the Principal Parts of Regular Verbs

Make four columns on your paper. Label them **present, present participle, past,** and **past participle.** Then write the four principal parts of each of the following regular verbs. Use **is** with the present participle and **have** with the past participle. Check a dictionary if you are unsure of the spelling of a verb form.

1. talk   **7.** play

2. jump   **8.** share

3. drop   **9.** move

4. suppose   **10.** stop

5. ask   **11.** knock

6. use   **12.** gaze

Writing Sentences with Regular Verbs

Write the principal parts of the regular verbs *start, row,* and *wrap.* Then write a sentence using each of the principal parts of these verbs.

● *Connect to Writing and Speaking:* **Note**

Using Verb Forms

You need to send your pet to the veterinarian. You cannot go with your pet, so you decide to write a note to the vet. A useful note should give information about your pet's history, especially its health history. (If you don't have a pet, imagine that you do.) Use some of the following verbs as you write your note. Read your note aloud to a partner.

- Past form of *see*
- Past participle of *grow*
- Present participle of *begin*
- Past participle of *begin*
- Present participle of *eat*
- Past participle of *do*

 Irregular Verbs

A few verbs, called irregular verbs, form their past and past participle differently from regular verbs.

23 A.2　An **irregular verb** does not form its past and past participle by adding *-ed* or *-d* to the present.

Remember that the word *is* is not part of the present participle and the word *have* is not part of the past participle. They have been added to the lists of irregular verbs on this and the following page to remind you that all present participles and past participles must have a form of one of these helping verbs when they are used as verbs in sentences.

Group 1　These irregular verbs have the same form for the present, the past, and the past participle.

GROUP 1			
Present	**Present Participle**	**Past**	**Past Participle**
burst	(is) bursting	burst	(have) burst
cost	(is) costing	cost	(have) cost
hit	(is) hitting	hit	(have) hit
put	(is) putting	put	(have) put
let	(is) letting	let	(have) let

CHAPTER 23

Group 2 These irregular verbs have the same form for the past and the past participle.

GROUP 2			
Present	**Present Participle**	**Past**	**Past Participle**
bring	(is) bringing	brought	(have) brought
buy	(is) buying	bought	(have) bought
catch	(is) catching	caught	(have) caught
make	(is) making	made	(have) made
say	(is) saying	said	(have) said
leave	(is) leaving	left	(have) left
lose	(is) losing	lost	(have) lost
teach	(is) teaching	taught	(have) taught

● **Practice Your Skills**

Recognizing the Correct Verb Form

Label each underlined verb form *past* or *past participle.* Remember that a helping verb is used with a past participle.

1. All the newscasters <u>said</u> to expect a storm.

2. The last two storms <u>caught</u> us by surprise.

3. We have <u>lost</u> our electricity during the last three storms.

4. The worst storm <u>hit</u> last January.

5. Our experiences have <u>taught</u> us important lessons.

6. One storm <u>left</u> us without power for three days.

7. We have just <u>put</u> new batteries in our flashlights.

8. Laura has <u>brought</u> in some firewood.

9. Last time we <u>made</u> a fire to keep us warm.

10. We have <u>bought</u> extra canned food.

● *Connect to Speaking and Listening:* **Reading a Dialogue**

Correcting Improperly Used Verbs

Read the following dialogue aloud with a partner. As you read, correct any verb errors you find.

Marisol: Has the rain let up yet?

Anna: No, it has still coming down. Have you brung your umbrella?

Marisol: No, I lose it last week.

Anna: That's the third umbrella your mother has buyed for you! Where were you when yesterday's storm hitted?

Marisol: The storm catched me by surprise. I putted a bag over my head.

Anna: I'll bet the rain make you very wet, anyway. I hope this teached you to be more careful with your umbrellas.

Marisol: My mother sayed the same thing to me.

Group 3 These irregular verbs form the past participle by adding *-n* to the past tense.

GROUP 3			
Present	**Present Participle**	**Past**	**Past Participle**
break	(is) breaking	broke	(have) broken
choose	(is) choosing	chose	(have) chosen
freeze	(is) freezing	froze	(have) frozen
speak	(is) speaking	spoke	(have) spoken
steal	(is) stealing	stole	(have) stolen

CHAPTER 23

Group 4 These irregular verbs form the past participle by adding *-n* to the present.

GROUP 4			
Present	**Present Participle**	**Past**	**Past Participle**
blow	(is) blowing	blew	(have) blown
draw	(is) drawing	drew	(have) drawn
drive	(is) driving	drove	(have) driven
give	(is) giving	gave	(have) given
grow	(is) growing	grew	(have) grown
know	(is) knowing	knew	(have) known
rise	(is) rising	rose	(have) risen
see	(is) seeing	saw	(have) seen
take	(is) taking	took	(have) taken
throw	(is) throwing	threw	(have) thrown

● **Practice Your Skills**

Determining the Correct Verb Form

Write the correct verb form for each sentence.

1. This snowstorm has (took, taken) us off guard.

2. The strong winds have (grew, grown) fiercer since yesterday morning.

3. The weather station just (gave, given) tomorrow's forecast.

4. It has (drew, drawn) a gloomy picture of the blizzard's devastation.

5. Winter has (stole, stolen) up on us this year.

6. I have never (knew, known) it to snow in October.

7. I nearly (froze, frozen) this morning!

8. A chilly wind has (blew, blown) all day.

9. I (saw, seen) very few people outdoors.

10. No one (drove, driven) on the icy streets.

Practice Your Skills

Using the Correct Verb Form

Write the correct past or past participle of each verb in parentheses.

1. We have not (see) such a storm in ten years.

2. The plaza fountain has (freeze) solid.

3. The snow has (drive) most people off the streets.

4. It has (throw) the whole town into confusion.

5. The snowdrifts have (rise) higher than the tops of the cars.

Connect to Writing: Editing

Correcting Improperly Used Verbs

Write the following sentences, replacing any incorrect verb with the correct verb form. If a sentence is correct, write **C**.

1. The lake has froze over enough for skating.

2. Many families have took their children there.

3. They knew the ice was safe.

4. A few people have driven snowmobiles across the lake.

5. I even seen a Shetland pony with bells and a small sleigh.

Connect to Speaking: Delivering a Weather Report

Correcting Improperly Used Verbs

Read the following weather report aloud to a classmate, correcting verb errors.

(1) We're giving bad news and good news this afternoon. (2) Yesterday's storm blown so hard that most of Rockridge lost its electrical power. (3) Low temperatures froze water lines across the city. (4) Many pipes broken last night. (5) Wise drivers have give up and are staying off the icy roads. (6) However, we've saw some signs that our bad weather is ending. (7) The temperature has rose ten degrees today. (8) The sunshine is shown through.

Group 5 These irregular verbs form the past and past participle by changing a vowel. In these verbs the *i* in the present changes to an *a* in the past and to a *u* in the past participle.

GROUP 5			
Present	**Present Participle**	**Past**	**Past Participle**
begin	(is) beginning	began	(have) begun
drink	(is) drinking	drank	(have) drunk
ring	(is) ringing	rang	(have) rung
sing	(is) singing	sang	(have) sung
sink	(is) sinking	sank	(have) sunk
swim	(is) swimming	swam	(have) swum

Group 6 These irregular verbs form the past and past participle in other ways.

GROUP 6			
Present	**Present Participle**	**Past**	**Past Participle**
come	(is) coming	came	(have) come
do	(is) doing	did	(have) done
eat	(is) eating	ate	(have) eaten
fall	(is) falling	fell	(have) fallen
go	(is) going	went	(have) gone
ride	(is) riding	rode	(have) ridden
run	(is) running	ran	(have) run
wear	(is) wearing	wore	(have) worn
write	(is) writing	wrote	(have) written

● **Practice Your Skills**

Determining the Correct Verb Form

Write the correct verb form for each sentence.

1. All day the cattle (ate, eaten) the long grass beside the river.

2. They (drank, drunk) from the river too.

3. Paco (rode, ridden) to the river.

4. He (sang, sung) out loudly, "Get along there!"

5. When he shouted, the anxious herd (ran, run) into the river.

6. Now most have (swam, swum) safely across.

7. However, one calf (sank, sunk) into the mud.

8. It has (fell, fallen) and cannot get to its feet.

9. Paco has (went, gone) to pull the calf up the bank.

10. His long day has (wore, worn) him out.

● **Practice Your Skills**

Using the Correct Verb Form

Write the correct past or past participle of each verb in parentheses.

1. Tom has (write) a letter to his brother.

2. We (begin) the cattle drive last month.

3. We have (come) two hundred miles since then.

4. I have (wear) out the seat of my pants!

5. I have (eat) too many cold suppers.

6. Two of our cowhands (fall) sick recently.

● **Practice Your Skills**

Finding the Principal Parts of Verbs in a Dictionary

Look up each of the following irregular verbs in a dictionary. Then write the principal parts of each.

1. shrink	**5.** pay	**9.** fight	**13.** forget
2. fly	**6.** bleed	**10.** shake	**14.** stick
3. wake	**7.** show	**11.** hide	
4. beat	**8.** hurt	**12.** build	

✔ *Check Point:* **Mixed Practice**

Write the correct past or past participle of each verb in parentheses.

1. Our community's older citizens have (see) big changes in the last fifty years.

2. Once the Clearwater River (run) through a valley of farmland and forests.

3. People (swim) and fished there in the summer.

4. Then the city engineers (build) a dam.

5. This (come) about because we needed more power.

6. We got a modern power station, but we (lose) a fourth of our farmland.

23 B   The verbs *bring* and *take*, *learn* and *teach*, and *leave* and *let* are often confused.

➤ *Bring* and *Take*

Bring indicates motion toward the speaker. *Take* indicates motion away from the speaker.

Present	Present Participle	Past	Past Participle
bring	(is) bringing	brought	(have) brought
take	(is) taking	took	(have) taken

Bring	She **brings** us the newspaper every morning.
	She **is bringing** us the newspaper now.
	She **brought** us the newspaper yesterday at 6:00 a.m.
	She **has brought** us the newspaper for two years now.
Take	**Take** this newspaper to the Smith family.
	Ryan **is taking** the newspaper to the Smith family today.
	His brother **took** the newspaper to the Smith family yesterday.
	Sometimes I **have taken** the newspaper to the Smith family.

● Practice Your Skills

Using the Correct Verb

Read the following sentences aloud to practice using the correct verb form.

1. The teacher brought in some giant sunflowers for us to paint.
2. Please bring me the jar of yellow paint.
3. If you are going past Maria, take her this new jar of paint.
4. Maria dropped the paint jar as she took it from me.
5. Kim is bringing some rags to wipe up the paint.
6. Lila has taken away the broken glass.
7. Justin has brought us more yellow paint.
8. Matthew took my small brush and gave me his wide one.
9. Jessie brought her painting here and left it.
10. Laura is taking her painting to our teacher.

CHAPTER 23

Using the Correct Verb

Write the correct verb for each sentence.

1. Have all of you (brought, taken) your artwork to share with us today?

2. Angela is (bringing, taking) me a bracelet.

3. Please (bring, take) your statue to the display table over there.

4. Deanna (brings, takes) a picture from Bill's hand.

5. Devon (brought, took) her painting to the bulletin board at the back of the room.

6. The twins (brought, took) in a mosaic to show us.

7. Sam is (bringing, taking) his sculpture to the art show downtown.

8. Emily often (brings, takes) me collages of seashells.

9. Please (bring, take) your mobile here.

10. Did someone (bring, take) the pastel chalk drawing from the table?

Learn and *Teach*

Learn means "to gain knowledge." *Teach* means "to instruct" or to "show how."

Present	Present Participle	Past	Past Participle
learn	(is) learning	learned	(have) learned
teach	(is) teaching	taught	(have) taught

Learn   He **learns** best in the morning.

He **is learning** all the irregular verbs.

He **learned** two groups of verbs yesterday.

He **has learned** half of the verbs already.

Teach   **Teach** me the new song.

She **is teaching** me several new songs.

She **taught** me one song yesterday.

She **has taught** me two songs already.

● Practice Your Skills

Using the Correct Verb

Read these sentences aloud to practice using the correct verb form. Be prepared to explain why each verb is correct.

1. Mr. Klein <u>teaches</u> us art two days a week.
2. We <u>learn</u> to use a new technique each month.
3. Last week we <u>learned</u> how to model clay figures.
4. This week Mr. Klein <u>is teaching</u> us to apply glazes.
5. This morning he <u>taught</u> us how glazes change after they are fired.
6. I <u>learned</u> that pale glazes turn brilliant colors in the kiln.
7. I <u>am</u> also <u>learning</u> from my friend Sara.
8. Sara and her mother <u>teach</u> art classes after school.
9. She <u>has taught</u> me a lot about mixing colors.
10. Through practice I <u>have learned</u> how to make a rich turquoise.

● **Practice Your Skills**

Using the Correct Verb

Write the correct verb for each sentence.

1. My research for art class is (learning, teaching) me a lot about Pueblo pottery.
2. I (learned, taught) that a Hopi artist, Nampeyo, was a modern pioneer in her field.
3. She (learned, taught) her three daughters about her work.
4. Each generation has (learned, taught) from the previous generation.
5. Many generations of potters have (learned, taught) their skills to their daughters and sons.
6. Even today expert potters (learn, teach) their apprentices about pots.
7. Some potters (learn, teach) to use old methods.
8. I am (learning, teaching) about pottery styles.
9. I (learned, taught) myself how to tell them apart.
10. I (learned, taught) that San Juan Pueblo is known for red-on-tan pottery.

 # Leave and *Let*

Leave means "to depart" or "to go away." *Let* means "to allow" or "to permit."

Present	Present Participle	Past	Past Participle
leave	(is) leaving	left	(have) left
let	(is) letting	let	(have) let

Leave   **Leave** now before the storm.

She **is leaving** here in five minutes.

She **left** an hour ago.

She **has** never **left** this early before.

Let   **Let** the dog inside.

He **is letting** the dog inside now.

He **let** the dog inside last week.

He **has let** the dog inside several times today.

● **Practice Your Skills**

Using the Correct Verb

Read these sentences aloud to practice using the correct verb form. Be prepared to explain why each verb is correct.

1. The city <u>is letting</u> us use the fairgrounds for our art exhibit again.
2. They <u>have left</u> us more room than last year.
3. The art teachers <u>have let</u> us choose our favorite artwork.
4. I <u>let</u> my friend Roberto hang his oil paintings with mine.
5. We always <u>let</u> a committee arrange the hall.
6. I worked on the exhibit so late that I <u>left</u> at 6:00 p.m.
7. I <u>have</u> usually <u>left</u> around 3:00 p.m.
8. I <u>am leaving</u> for the fairgrounds now.
9. We <u>are</u> not <u>letting</u> anyone in until 9:00 a.m.
10. We <u>are leaving</u> the art on display through Sunday.

● **Practice Your Skills**

Using the Correct Verb

Write the correct verb for each sentence.

1. We have always (left, let) our teachers plan the show.
2. We are (leaving, letting) parents come on Friday for a preview.
3. I (left, let) a note about the show on the kitchen table for my parents.
4. Did you (leave, let) your parents know the time?
5. My parents have just (left, let) the house.
6. Mr. Klein is (leaving, letting) the sixth graders hand out the catalogs.
7. I hope your parents aren't (leaving, letting) yet.
8. Don't (leave, let) until you've seen Elena's sculpture of the fox.
9. The crowd will (leave, let) you through.
10. Who (left, let) that sculpture on the table?

● *Connect to Writing:* **Catalog**

Using Problem Verbs

You are helping to write a catalog for the summer recreation program in your community. Many popular classes are being offered. Think of three possible classes and write descriptions of these activities. In your descriptions use at least one form of each of the six problem verbs *bring/take, learn/teach,* and *leave/let.*

✔ *Check Point:* **Mixed Practice**

Write the correct verb for each sentence.

1. The ranger is (learning, teaching) us about the seashore.
2. The ranger says, "(Bring, Take) me that broken shell."
3. The broken shell was (left, let) on the rocks by a gull.
4. Gulls have (learned, taught) to break open shells.
5. A big wave washed over some kelp and (brought, took) it back out to sea.
6. The ranger will not (leave, let) us touch any tide pool creatures.
7. A small fish is (bringing, taking) its prey into the green seaweed.
8. A tern has (left, let) a trail of footprints across the wet sand.
9. I stood still to (leave, let) a crab scuttle quietly across the rocks.
10. The ranger (learned, taught) us to respect the life of the shore.

Every verb has six tenses: the present, past, future, present perfect, past perfect, and future perfect.

23 C   The time expressed by a verb is called the **tense** of a verb.

In the following examples, the six tenses of *walk* are used to express action at different times.

Present	Every day I **walk** five miles.
Past	I **walked** five miles yesterday.
Future	I **will walk** again tomorrow.
Present Perfect	For two years I **have walked** each morning.
Past Perfect	I **had not walked** much before that.
Future Perfect	I **will have walked** eight hundred miles by May.

Uses of the Tenses

The examples of the different tenses of *walk* show that verbs in the English language have six tenses. All of these tenses can be formed from the principal parts of verbs—with the helping verbs *have, has, had, will,* and *shall.*

Present tense is used to express an action that is going on now. To form the present tense, use the present form (the first principal part of the verb) or add *-s* or *-es* to the present form.

Present Tense	I **paint** pictures.
	Michele **gives** tours.

Past tense expresses an action that already took place or was completed in the past. To form the past tense of a regular verb, add *-ed* or *-d* to the present form.

To form the past tense of an irregular verb, check a dictionary for the past form or look for it on pages 676–687.

Past Tense	I **painted** a picture last night.
	Michele **gave** a tour yesterday.

Future tense is used to express an action that will take place in the future. To form the future tense, use the helping verb *will* or *shall* with the present form.

> **Future Tense**   **Shall** I **paint** another picture tomorrow?
>
> Michele **will give** a tour at noon on Tuesday.

You can learn more about the correct use of shall *and* will *on page 788.*

Present perfect tense expresses an action that was completed at some indefinite time in the past. It also expresses an action that started in the past and is still ongoing. To form the present perfect tense, add *has* or *have* to the past participle.

> **Present Perfect Tense**   I **have painted** portraits of my family members.
>
> Michele **has given** tours for a long time.

Past perfect tense expresses an action that took place before some other action. To form the past perfect tense, add *had* to the past participle.

> **Past Perfect Tense**   I **had painted** landscapes before I painted portraits.
>
> Michele took a break after she **had given** the tour.

Future perfect tense expresses an action that will take place before another future action or time. To form the future perfect tense, add *shall have* or *will have* to the past participle.

> **Future Perfect Tense**   I **will have painted** three new pictures by the end of the month.
>
> Michele **will have given** hundreds of tours before her job ends.

When You Write

When writing about yourself, in a résumé for example, use tenses correctly so that the reader does not misunderstand when an event occurred.

Incorrect	I will have refined my unique portrait style.
Correct	Before 2012 ends, I will have refined my unique portrait style.

Look over a recent personal narrative and be sure you have used the correct tenses in describing what you have done in the past and plan to do in the future.

Verb Conjugation

A **conjugation** gives the singular and plural forms of a verb in its six tenses. Below is a conjugation of the irregular verb *give,* whose principal parts are *give, giving, gave, given.*

CONJUGATION OF THE VERB *GIVE*

Present

Singular	Plural
I give	we give
you give	you give
he, she, it gives	they give

Past

Singular	Plural
I gave	we gave
you gave	you gave
he, she, it gave	they gave

Future

Singular	Plural
I shall/will give	we shall/will give
you will give	you will give
he, she, it will give	they will give

Present Perfect

Singular	Plural
I have given	we have given
you have given	you have given
he, she, it has given	they have given

Past Perfect

Singular	Plural
I had given	we had given
you had given	you had given
he, she, it had given	they had given

Future Perfect

Singular	Plural
I will/shall have given	we will/shall have given
you will have given	you will have given
he, she, it will have given	they will have given

The present participle is used to conjugate only the progressive tenses of verbs. Those verbs are covered on pages 695–696.

CHAPTER 23

Identifying Verb Tenses

Write the tense of each underlined verb.

1. Hidden Cave <u>lies</u> within a hillside in the Nevada desert.

2. Ancient people <u>had stored</u> their valuables in it more than 3,500 years ago.

3. Four boys <u>rediscovered</u> its entrance in 1927.

4. "We <u>will use</u> this as a hideout," the boys decided.

5. Years later an archaeologist heard that a miner <u>had found</u> old "junk" in a cave.

6. In 1940, S. M. and Georgetta Wheeler first <u>excavated</u> the cave.

7. Three generations of archaeologists <u>have looked</u> for artifacts in the cave.

● **Practice Your Skills**

Understanding Verb Tenses

Write the correct verb tense in parentheses for each sentence.

1. The excavation (had ended, have ended), and then the cave was opened to the public.

2. Archaeologists (has provided, provided) many artifacts for the museum.

3. Today the Churchill County Museum (offers, offered) free tours of the cave.

4. The museum (has trained, will have trained) volunteers as tour guides.

5. Tours (are given, will give) on two Saturdays each month.

When You Speak and Write

In addition to tense, a verb also has **mood**. Mood indicates the way an idea is expressed.

Indicative (to make a statement) The flowers **bloomed**

Interrogative (to ask a question). **Did** the flowers **bloom**?

Imperative (to give a command) **Water** the flowers!

Subjunctive (to express ideas contrary to fact or to express a proposal, demand, or request after the word *that*) Tara suggested that the flowers **be watered** every other day.

Conditional (to express ideas about something that has not yet happened or that can happen only under certain conditions) **If** you stop watering them, the flowers **will die**.

In the subjunctive mood, present tense, third-person singular verbs do not have the final *–s* or *–es* ending. The verb *be* in the subjunctive mood is *be* in the present tense and *were* in the past tense. Avoid shifts in mood when you write.

Connect to Writing: **Drafting**

Using Verb Tenses

Write six sentences, using the tense of the verb indicated for each below.

1. Present tense of *learn*
2. Past tense of *go*
3. Future tense of *bring*
4. Present perfect tense of *ride*
5. Past perfect tense of *sing*
6. Future perfect tense of *write*

➤ Shifts in Tense

When you read a story, you quickly learn when it took place by noting the tense of the verbs. When you write, you pass on that same information to your readers. If you suddenly shift tenses, you probably will confuse your readers.

23 C.1   Avoid unnecessary shifts in tense within a sentence or within related sentences.

A shift in tense can occur within a sentence itself or within related sentences.

Inconsistent	*past* After I **laid** the blanket on the beach, *present* the sun **goes** behind a cloud.
Consistent	*present* After I **lay** my blanket on the beach, the *present* sun **goes** behind a cloud.
Consistent	*past* After I **laid** my blanket on the beach, *past* the sun **went** behind a cloud.
Inconsistent	*present* *future* I **wear** sun block and I **will not** suffer a burn.
Consistent	*future* *future* I **will wear** sun block and I **will not** suffer a burn.
Consistent	*present* *present* I **wear** sun block and I **do not** burn.

Identifying Shifts in Verb Tense

Write **S** if a sentence contains a shift in verb tense. If a sentence is correct, write **C**.

1. Jupiter orbits the Sun far beyond our planet, and Europa circled Jupiter.

2. The astronomer Galileo discovered Europa in 1610 when he trained his homemade telescope on Jupiter.

3. He saw three bright stars near this planet and takes note of their positions.

4. It astonished him when they will appear in new positions the next night.

5. He rightly concluded that these were moons, not stars.

6. Today we have stronger telescopes, but we cannot see Europa clearly through telescopes.

7. In the 1980s, the staff at the Jet Propulsion Laboratory developed a spacecraft that they name *Galileo*.

8. When NASA launched the *Galileo* spacecraft toward Jupiter in 1989, it carries the Hubble space telescope.

9. A space telescope maintains a radio link to Earth and transmitted images and data back to scientists.

10. The *Galileo* sent back images that will continue to teach us facts about Europa.

● *Connect to Writing:* Description

Using the Tenses

Imagine that you are standing on the top of a mountain. You are looking over a vast landscape, and you can see birds flying high and horses in the valley below. Write a journal entry describing what you see, hear, feel, and smell as you survey the scene.

Describe the events in the order they happen. When you have finished your description, underline six verbs that you used.

Progressive Verb Tenses

Each verb has a **progressive tense.** These tenses are used to express continuing or ongoing action. The progressive tenses add a special meaning to verbs that the regular tenses do not. Notice the differences in meaning in the following examples.

Present	She **runs.**
	(*Runs* shows that she can or does run.)
Present Progressive	She **is running.**
	(*Is running* shows that she is running right now.)

The use of progressive tenses of verbs often brings a sense of excitement because something is happening right now. That is why sports announcers and radio commentators often use the progressive tense when they describe something happening in the present.

To form the progressive, add a form of the verb *be* to the present participle. Notice in the following examples that all of the progressive forms end in *-ing.*

Present Progressive	I am giving.
Past Progressive	I was giving.
Future Progressive	I will (shall) be giving.
Present Perfect Progressive	I have been giving.
Past Perfect Progressive	I had been giving.
Future Perfect Progressive	I will (shall) have been giving.

● **Practice Your Skills**

Identifying Progressive Verb Tenses

Write each verb phrase.

1. Lila has been enjoying gymnastics for years.

2. She was taking classes before her fourth birthday.

3. In June, she will have been performing on the bars for six years.

4. She has been improving in the last two years.

5. Until last year, she had been practicing at the gym.

6. Now she is taking lessons with a private coach.

7. She has been competing locally.

8. I was watching her yesterday.

9. Next month she will be going to a competition in Dallas.

10. Her family is supporting her dream.

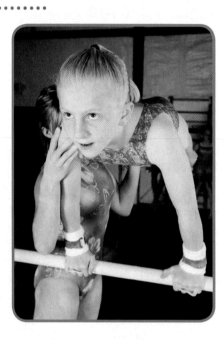

● *Connect to Writing:* **Drafting**

Using Progressive Verb Tenses

Write five sentences using the indicated progressive tense of each verb given below.

1. Past progressive of *watch*

2. Future progressive of *wear*

3. Present perfect progressive of *read*

4. Past perfect progressive of *wonder*

5. Future perfect progressive of *study*

● *Connect to Writing:* **Observation Log**

Using Progressive Verbs

Look around the classroom and observe what is going on right now. Take notes about what you see. Then write an entry for a classroom observation log, explaining what you see and hear. Use progressive forms of verbs. When you have finished, compare your entry with a classmate's, and then bind all the entries together for a classroom observation log.

In addition to tense, a verb is in active voice or passive voice. Writers can use either the active voice or the passive voice to tell about an action.

23 D The **active voice** indicates that the subject is performing the action. The **passive voice** indicates that the action of the verb is being performed upon the subject.

Active Voice	Mr. Takamoto **placed** the round stones in the garden.
Passive Voice	The round stones **were placed** in the garden by Mr. Takamoto.
Active Voice	The wind **rattles** the tall stalks of bamboo.
Passive Voice	The tall stalks of bamboo **are rattled** by the wind.

A verb in the passive voice consists of a form of the verb *be* plus a past participle. The forms of *be* used for the passive voice are *is, are, was, were, has been, have been,* and *had been.* Study the following examples.

Active Voice	The wind **blew** over the small pine on the hill. (*The wind* is performing the action.)
Passive Voice	The small pine on the hill **was blown** over by the wind. (The pine is receiving the action of the verb. *Was* is a form of the verb *be*, and *blown* is the past participle of *blow*.)

➤ Use of Active Voice and Passive Voice

Avoid the passive voice in your writing. Passive voice verbs are often weak and wordy. When you write, use the active voice as much as possible. The active voice is more forceful and adds life to your writing. There will be times when the passive voice is appropriate, however, as when the doer of the action is unknown or not the focus of the sentence.

Passive Voice	Irises *were planted* beside the stream.

CHAPTER 23

● **Practice Your Skills**

Recognizing Active Voice and Passive Voice

Write the verb in each sentence and label it *active* or *passive.*

1. The art of gardens is honored by the Japanese.
2. In Japan most householders with land maintain a garden.
3. The distinct features of Japanese gardens were developed centuries ago.
4. Tidy flower beds and straight paths give gardens an unnatural look.
5. Japanese gardens are known for their natural settings.
6. Few brightly colored flowers grow in these gardens.
7. Mostly evergreens are planted there.
8. Many gardens contain ponds or waterfalls.
9. The visitor is soothed by the sound of water.

● *Connect to Speaking and Writing:* **Vocabulary Comprehension**

Discuss the terms *active voice* and *passive voice* with a partner. Brainstorm ways to remember what the terms mean and how to use them in your writing. Write two sentences, each of which uses both active and passive voice. Read your sentences aloud.

● *Connect to Writing:* **Revising**

Changing Verbs to Active Voice

Rewrite each sentence, changing the underlined verb from **passive voice** to **active voice.**

1. This year's county fair gardening competition was entered by my family.
2. A Japanese-style garden was created by us.
3. The plan was drawn by my sister.
4. The plants were arranged by my mother and me.
5. We were given second prize by the judges.

● *Check Point:* **Mixed Practice**

Rewrite each sentence, correcting any incorrect verb forms or shifts in tense.

1. Artist Murakami Kagaku was born in 1888 and dies in 1939.
2. He led a new movement in Japanese-style art for modern painters.
3. He blends Western art techniques with traditional Japanese techniques.
4. By the time he was fourteen, he is winning prizes for his work in color.
5. Later he becomes more interested in landscapes in ink.

Assess Your Learning

▪ Using the Correct Verb Form

Write the correct verb form for each sentence.

1. On our trip to Florida, we (saw, seen) several models of cities of the world at a theme park.

2. Luis (threw, throwed) the ball to home plate.

3. I had never (swam, swum) in salt water before today.

4. Mom (knowed, knew) Dad in high school.

5. Have you ever (rode, ridden) in a helicopter?

6. Mom always (brang, brought) the mail in every afternoon.

7. During the last three days, I (teached, taught) my sister how to ride a bike.

8. Several students have (wrote, written) poems for the school's fiftieth anniversary.

9. Have you (chose, chosen) a name for your dog yet?

10. I have already (ate, eaten) lunch.

▪ Using the Correct Verb Form

Find and correct each verb form that is incorrectly used in the following sentences. If a sentence is correct, write **C.**

1. The sun finally come out in the afternoon.

2. You should have seen the large audience at our play.

3. These vines have growed three feet in one week.

4. Hurricane-force winds have sank several boats at the town marina.

5. Who drunk all the milk?

6. I should have took a book with me to the doctor's office.

7. That basketball player has stole the ball from the opposing team several times.

8. Yesterday we begun math class with a surprise quiz.

9. Have you gave a donation to that charity?

10. The stock market has fallen six points since yesterday.

CHAPTER 23

■ Identifying Verb Voice

Write each verb and label it *active* or *passive.*

1. After the play the curtain was slowly lowered.

2. Dr. Jonas Salk discovered the polio vaccine.

3. Air-conditioning was invented in 1902 by Willis H. Carrier.

4. Darrell painted the garage last summer.

5. Neil Armstrong made his walk on the moon in 1969.

6. In right-handed people, motor control is ruled by the left half of the brain.

7. Cindy auditioned for the school play.

8. Altitude is measured by an altimeter.

9. The beaver's dam was constructed in one evening.

10. Reds, greens, and blues form the picture in color television.

■ Using Verbs Correctly

Write five sentences that follow the directions below.

Write a sentence that . . .

1. includes the past tense of *write.*

2. includes the future tense of *rise.*

3. includes the past perfect tense of *speak.*

4. includes any forms of the verbs *bring* and *take.*

5. includes any forms of the verbs *learn* and *teach.*

Using Verbs: Posttest

Directions

Read the passage and choose the word or group of words that belongs in each underlined space. Write the letter of the correct answer.

Golda Meir __(1)__ as Israel's first and only female prime minister. She __(2)__ Goldie Mabovitch in Russia in 1898. She __(3)__ briefly in the United States. Then, in 1921, she __(4)__ to Palestine. Within a short time, she __(5)__ the labor movement. She __(6)__ as minister of labor in 1949. Later, she __(7)__ as minister of foreign affairs.

Meir __(8)__ prime minister in 1969. Although she __(9)__ after the 1973 Arab-Israeli War, she __(10)__ for her dedication to the goal of peace in the Middle East.

1. **A** knew
   B is known
   C having been known
   D knowing

2. **A** born
   B has been born
   C was born
   D is borning

3. **A** teached
   B taught
   C has taught
   D is teaching

4. **A** moved
   B moving
   C moves
   D has been moved

5. **A** is joining
   B joins
   C has been joined
   D had joined

6. **A** chose
   B choosed
   C was chosen
   D is choosing

7. **A** was served
   B serving
   C has served
   D served

8. **A** was elected
   B elected
   C had elected
   D is electing

9. **A** criticized
   B was criticizing
   C was criticized
   D will have been criticized

10. **A** remembers
    B will be remembered
    C has remembered
    D will remember

Writer's Corner

Snapshot

23 A   The **principal parts** of a verb are the **present,** the **present participle,** the **past,** and the **past participle.** (pages 674–675)

23 B   The verbs **bring** and **take, learn** and **teach,** and **leave** and **let** are often confused. (pages 683–688)

23 C   The time expressed by a verb is called the **tense** of a verb. (pages 689–696)

23 D   The **active voice** indicates that the subject is performing the action. The **passive voice** indicates that the action of the verb is being performed upon the subject. (pages 697–698)

Power Rules

Use the correct **verb tense** to show time. (pages 689–696)

Before Editing	**After Editing**
Next week I *go* on a tour.	Next week I *will go* on a tour.
Last year they *will paint* their house.	Last year they *painted* their house.

Use the correct form of the verb to show **recurring action.** (pages 695–696)

Before Editing	**After Editing**
Every year she *brought* a pie for Thanksgiving.	Every year she *brings* a pie for Thanksgiving.
They *took* a family trip every summer.	They *take* a family trip every summer.

Use a consistent **verb tense** except when a change is truly necessary. (pages 689–696)

Before Editing	**After Editing**
When she *is* walking the dog, she *found* her lost key.	When she *was* walking the dog, she *found* her lost key.
The baby *takes* a toy and *threw* it.	The baby *took* a toy and *threw* it.

Editing Checklist

Use this checklist when editing your writing.

✓ Did I make sure that I used the proper tense of each verb? (See pages 689–696.)

✓ Did I make sure to spell all regular and irregular verbs correctly? (See pages 674–682.)

✓ Did I use the correct tense to express time? (See pages 689–696.)

✓ Did I make sure that most of my sentences are in the active voice, rather than the passive voice? (See pages 697–698.)

Use the Power

Use this chart to help you choose the correct forms of verbs.

	Past	Present	Future
Simple	past tense form He *walked*.	base form He *walks*.	*will* + base form He *will* walk.
Progressive	*was* or *were* + present participle He *was* walking.	*am*, *is*, or *are* + present participle He *is* walking.	*will be* + present participle He *will be* walking.
Perfect	*had* + past participle He *had* walked.	*has* or *have* + past participle He *has* walked.	*will have* + past participle He *will have* walked.
Perfect progressive	*had been* + present participle He *had been* walking.	*has* or *have been* + present participle He *has been* walking.	*will have been* + present participle He *will have been* walking.

Write a paragraph about your favorite sports team. Use vivid verbs and apt descriptions, and try to use the active voice.

Using Pronouns

How can you use pronouns to make your writing flow smoothly?

Using Pronouns: Pretest 1

The first draft below contains several errors in the use of pronouns. The first error has been corrected. How would you revise the sentences to correct the remaining errors?

This colorful painting from 1924 shows a typical family at leisure. Henri Matisse, one *his* of the most significant artists of the twentieth century, often used color to express ~~their~~ impressions or feelings. Both the warm red colors and the repeated shapes contribute to the feeling of unity in this family scene.

As a young man in France, Matisse abandoned the study of law to devote himself to art. Him and his fellow artists experimented with using color in a very spontaneous way. Them sought to emphasize purity of line, decorative pattern, and color in a visual plane. Discovering that he could make certain colors glow and vibrate against one another, Matisse continued to experiment with color and light, stripping his paintings to they're bare essentials. He was an artist for who strong colors were essential in creating striking effects.

Disabled by arthritis in the last years of his life, Matisse continued creating art through collage. Its artworks include sculpture, printmaking, stained glass, and drawing.

Using Pronouns: Pretest 2

Directions

Read the passage and choose the pronoun that belongs in each underlined space. Write the letter of the correct answer.

My cousins moved to Seattle, Washington, and last year I visited __(1)__ there for the first time. The skyline amazed __(2)__. __(3)__ is dominated by the Space Needle, a tall tower left over from the World's Fair in 1962. __(4)__ rotating restaurant is wonderful.

Seattle lies on Puget Sound, and __(5)__ there seems to love the water. Lake Washington runs along the east of the city. The most famous resident there may be Bill Gates, __(6)__ has a house near the water. My cousins took me out on __(7)__ powerboat, and __(8)__ passed many fabulous lakeshore homes.

I liked the market downtown. Fish vendors wrap fish for tourists, to __(9)__ they then toss the neatly packaged salmon. One man tossed a gigantic fish to my cousins and __(10)__. Luckily, we caught it!

1. **A** her
   B them
   C it
   D they

2. **A** me
   B I
   C my
   D mine

3. **A** He
   B They
   C We
   D It

4. **A** It
   B Her
   C Its
   D It's

5. **A** both
   B many
   C several
   D everybody

6. **A** its
   B whom
   C who
   D her

7. **A** their
   B theirs
   C they
   D its

8. **A** us
   B we
   C he
   D him

9. **A** who
   B whose
   C him
   D whom

10. **A** me
    B I
    C we
    D he

Personal pronouns have different forms, called **cases**, depending on whether they are subjects, objects, or possessives in a sentence.

She helped **him.**

Rob helped **his** aunt.

24 A   **Case** is the form of a noun or pronoun that indicates its use in a sentence.

In English, there are three cases: the **nominative case,** the **objective case,** and the **possessive case.** The nominative case is also called the **subjective case**.

NOMINATIVE CASE
(used for subjects and predicate nominatives)

	Singular	Plural
First Person	I	we
Second Person	you	you
Third Person	he, she, it	they

OBJECTIVE CASE
(used for direct objects, indirect objects, and objects of prepositions)

	Singular	Plural
First Person	me	us
Second Person	you	you
Third Person	him, her, it	them

POSSESSIVE CASE
(used to show ownership or possession)

	Singular	Plural
First Person	my, mine	our, ours
Second Person	your, yours	your, yours
Third Person	his, her, hers, its	their, theirs

CHAPTER 24

Practice Your Skills

Recognizing Personal Pronouns

Write the personal pronoun or pronouns in each sentence. Label each pronoun *nominative, objective,* or *possessive.*

1. Our family went to the amusement park and beach.

2. My mother bought ride tickets for Melissa, Matt, and me.

3. She and my father went to relax on the beach.

4. Melissa asked us to go on the roller coaster with her.

5. Matt said that he always gets sick on the roller coaster.

6. He saw some friends on the Ferris wheel and waved at them.

7. They and Matt rode on the spaceship ride.

8. I got a glimpse of their faces as they whirled around.

9. Later we all went on the water slide.

10. It is a favorite ride of mine!

➤ The Nominative Case

The personal pronouns in the following box are in the nominative case.

NOMINATIVE CASE		
	Singular	Plural
First Person	I	we
Second Person	you	you
Third Person	he, she, it	they

Pronouns in the nominative case are used in two ways.

24 A.1   The **nominative case** is used for subjects and predicate nominatives.

Subject   **She** rescued the dog.

Predicate   The man in the blue suit is **he.**
Nominative

You can learn more about personal pronouns on pages 495–496 and 723–727.

Pronouns Used as Subjects

A subject names the person, place, or thing the sentence is about. Because the pronouns in the sentences below are used as subjects, the nominative case is used.

Subjects   **I** decorated my room.

Do **they** live in that apartment?

(Turn a question into a statement: *They do live in that apartment.* Then it is easy to see that *they* is the subject.)

When a sentence has only one subject, choosing the correct pronoun is usually not a problem. If a sentence has a compound subject, however, it is easy to make a mistake.

Compound   Mom and (I, me) painted the fence.
Subject

To find the correct pronoun, say the sentence as if each pronoun stood alone.

Correct   **I** painted the fence.

Incorrect   **Me** painted the fence.

By separating the choices, you can see and hear which pronoun is correct. The nominative case *I* is the correct form to use.

Correct   Mom and **I** painted the fence.

You can learn more about finding the subject of a sentence on pages 462–463.

● **Practice Your Skills**

Using Pronouns as Subjects

Read each sentence aloud, trying each pronoun separately. Then read the sentence aloud again, choosing the correct pronoun.

1. Her friends and (she, her) are in the band.

2. Ben's brother and (he, him) play trumpets.

3. (They, Them) and French horns are brass instruments.

4. After a year Rosa and (I, me) were pretty good clarinet players.

5. After playing clarinets, (he, him) and Efrain switched to oboes.

6. Can Tyler or (I, me) play the tuba?

7. Weren't the boys and (she, her) at the last rehearsal?

8. Beatrice and (we, us) heard them last Saturday.

9. Can't you and (he, him) come to the next concert?

10. Vanessa and (they, them) sound terrific.

● **Practice Your Skills**

Using Pronouns as Subjects

Complete each sentence by writing an appropriate pronoun. Do not use **you** or **it**.

1. His family and ___ went to the band concert.

2. The musicians and ___ were outdoors in the plaza.

3. Weren't Rachel's sister and ___ playing in the band?

4. Why don't you and ___ spread our blankets over there?

5. Are your parents and ___ music lovers?

6. After a while, the tuba player and ___ showed up.

Pronouns Used as Predicate Nominatives

A **predicate nominative** is a word that follows a linking verb—such as *is, were,* or *has been*—and identifies or renames the subject. A pronoun used as a predicate nominative is in the nominative case.

Predicate Nominatives	The best dancer is **he.**
	Are the two in costumes **they?**
	(Turn a question into a statement: *The two in costumes are they.* Then it is easy to see that *they* renames the subject.)

Check for the correct case of a pronoun in a compound predicate nominative by turning the sentence around to make the predicate nominative the subject. Then say each pronoun separately to learn which is correct.

Predicate Nominative	The musicians will be Brett and (she, her).
Statement	Brett and (she, her) will be the musicians.
Correct	**She** will be a musician.
Incorrect	**Her** will be a musician.
Correct	The musicians will be Brett and **she.**

Sometimes sentences with pronouns used as predicate nominatives *sound* wrong even though they are technically correct. When you write, you can avoid these awkward-sounding sentences by reversing them. Turn the predicate nominatives into the subjects.

Awkward	The best dancer is **he.**
Better	**He** is the best dancer.
Awkward	The two in costumes are **they.**
Better	**They** are the two in costumes.
Awkward	The musicians will be Brett and **she.**
Better	**She** and Brett will be the musicians.

When You Write and Speak

Expressions like *It's me* or *That's her* are acceptable in informal speech. When you speak or write formally, however, the required expressions are *It is I* and *That is she* because *I* and *she* are predicate nominatives.

Look at a recent essay. Be sure you have used predicate nominatives correctly.

You can learn more about predicate nominatives on pages 568–570.

● **Practice Your Skills**

Using Pronouns as Predicate Nominatives

Turn each sentence around to make the predicate nominative the subject. Read each sentence aloud, trying each pronoun separately. Then write each sentence, choosing the correct pronoun.

1. The stars of the movie are Nate and (she, her).

2. I'm sure that the actor who played the role of Nekka was (he, him).

3. The giant slug is (she, her) or Michael Yee.

4. The grossest characters were (him, he) and the Vaxons.

5. The biggest fans of science-fiction movies are Brittany and (I, me).

6. The renters of the latest movie are the twins' parents and (they, them).

7. The happiest moviegoers were Brian and (I, me).

8. Is the producer of this movie (she, her) or Jeff Ogawa?

9. The lucky winner of this year's Oscar might be (they, them).

10. The best actors of our own generation could be you and (I, me).

Practice Your Skills

Using Pronouns as Predicate Nominatives

Write the correct pronoun for each sentence.

1. The masters of the universe will definitely be (we, us).

2. The saboteurs of the Juno mission were Nekko and (they, them).

3. The crew members who saw the explosions were the Jermiz and (I, me).

4. The Vaxons' foes have always been the Jermiz and (we, us).

5. Aren't their most cunning leaders (her, she) and the Pandit of Dreewald?

6. Is it (they, them) who are the allies of the slugs?

7. Should the ambassador to Nekka be the Captain or (she, her)?

8. The Peacekeepers are (we, us) and the other inhabitants of Galaxy Four.

9. That is (they, them) on our radar screen.

Practice Your Skills

Supplying Pronouns in the Nominative Case

Complete each sentence by writing an appropriate pronoun. Do not use **you** or **it**.

1. The first ones in the movie theater will be José and ___.

2. That is ___ at the head of the line.

3. The movie's biggest fans are ___.

4. Where's Tanya? Daniel and ___ promised to be here on time.

5. My two oldest friends are Tanya and ___.

Connect to Writing: Editing

Correcting Nominative Case Errors

If an underlined pronoun is in the wrong case, write it correctly. If it is in the correct case, write **C**.

1. José or <u>him</u> will save us seats.

2. Are Brady and <u>her</u> sitting over there?

3. Julia and <u>them</u> are waving at us.

4. The ones with the best seats in the theater are the Green family and <u>us</u>.

5. Scott and <u>they</u> can't see the screen very well.

Connect to Speaking and Listening: Cross-Curricular Learning

Drama in the Nominative Case

Define the term *predicate nominative* for a partner. Then take turns thinking up and miming sentences such as "You and I have big feet" or "The best ping-pong players are he and she." As one of you acts out the sentence, the partner must say the sentence correctly out loud.

 ✅ *Check Point:* **Mixed Practice**

Complete each sentence by writing an appropriate pronoun. Do not use *you* or *it*.

 1. The Blues and ___ were loyal to different emperors.
 2. The Blues' allies were the Greens and ___.
 3. Neither Angelus nor ___ would join the Blues.
 4. ___ talked our cousin out of joining the rebels.
 5. When the Blues rioted, Justinian's advisors and ___ wanted to flee.
 6. Theodora's supporters and ___ would rather die than flee.

The Objective Case

The following personal pronouns are in the objective case.

OBJECTIVE CASE		
	Singular	Plural
First Person	me	us
Second Person	you	you
Third Person	him, her, it	them

24 A.2 The **objective case** is used for direct objects, indirect objects, and objects of prepositions.

> **Direct Object**   The Web site interested **us.**
>
> **Indirect Object**   Mom gave **us** directions to the site.
>
> **Object of a Preposition** She always shares interesting sites with **us.**

Pronouns Used as Direct and Indirect Objects

A **direct object** follows an action verb and answers the question *Whom?* or *What?*

> **Direct Object**   The Walkers invited **us.**
> (Invited whom? *Us* is the direct object.)
>
> Did you see **them?** (Turn a question into a statement: *You did see them.* You did see whom? *Them* is the direct object.)

CHAPTER 24

An **indirect object** comes before a direct object and answers the question *To or for whom?* or *To or for what?*

Indirect Object	Ms. Green gave **us** the assignment. *(i.o.)* *(d.o.)* (Ms. Green gave what? *Assignment* is the direct object. She gave the assignment to whom? *Us* is the indirect object.) Did you give **her** the tickets? *(i.o.)* *(d.o.)* (Turn a question into a statement: *You did give her the tickets.* You did give what? *Tickets* is the direct object. You did give the tickets to whom? *Her* is the indirect object.)

Check for the correct case of a compound object in the same way you check for the correct case of a compound subject. Say the nominative and objective case pronouns separately.

Direct Object	Did Miguel thank Chris and (he, him)?
Incorrect	Miguel did thank **he.**
Correct	Miguel did thank **him.**
Correct	Did Miguel thank Chris and **him?**
Indirect Object	Mom handed Kim and (I, me) a gift.
Incorrect	Mom handed **I** a gift.
Correct	Mom handed **me** a gift.
Correct	Mom handed Kim and **me** a gift.

You can learn more about direct objects and indirect objects on pages 563–567.

● *Connect to Writing:* **Dialogue**

Using the Objective Case

You are making a movie for teenagers about two space explorers who crash on an inhabited planet. Someone who speaks the explorers' language takes them to the planet's leaders. Write dialogue for a scene in which the explorers and the leaders meet. Use at least three personal pronouns in the objective case. Use at least two pronouns as indirect objects.

Using Pronouns as Direct and Indirect Objects

Read each sentence aloud, trying each pronoun separately. Then read the sentence aloud again, choosing the correct pronoun.

1. My mother showed Sarah and (I, me) our new brothers.

2. The doctors had given Dad and (she, her) some sad news about Sam.

3. Because of an unusual condition, Sam's legs would never support (he, him).

4. The news from the doctors shocked my family and (I, me) at first.

5. His inability to use his legs did give him and (we, us) problems sometimes.

6. My parents took my brothers, sister, and (I, me) to the mountains.

7. My mother's father had taught her two sisters and (she, her) the sport of skiing.

8. Sam was very excited because our parents bought (he, him) a special toboggan.

9. First, Mom showed Sam and (we, us) the basics of skiing.

10. Then Dad showed (he, him) the principles of sit-skiing.

11. In no time at all, we joined the other skiers and (they, them) at the top of the hill.

12. Dad told Mom and (we, us) about Sam's skill on the slopes.

13. I didn't remind (he, him) about the need to shift his weight.

14. Because of his skill, Sam made Sarah and (I, me) a little jealous.

➤ Pronouns Used as Objects of Prepositions

A **prepositional phrase** begins with a preposition, such as *with, to, by,* or *for.* A prepositional phrase ends with the object of a preposition. A pronoun used as an object of a preposition is in the objective case.

Objects of Prepositions	Did David talk to **her**?
	(*To her* is the prepositional phrase.)
	Nicole wrote a report about **them**.
	(*About them* is the prepositional phrase.)

You can find a list of prepositions on pages 546 and 584.

When You Write

The preposition *between* can be confusing. When trying to sound correct, people sometimes use nominative case and say *between you and I.* However, all pronouns used as objects of prepositions must be in the objective case.

Incorrect	The argument was *between* **she** and **I.**
Correct	The argument was *between* **her** and **me.**

Look at a recent composition, and check to be sure you have used the nominative case pronouns correctly—particularly after the word *between.*

● **Practice Your Skills**

Using Pronouns as Objects of Prepositions

Read the following sentences aloud to practice saying the underlined pronouns and hearing them used correctly.

1. Grandma showed some old photos to Alex and <u>me</u>.

2. We looked at our grandpa and <u>her</u> when they were teenagers.

3. We laughed together at their friends and <u>them</u>.

4. Their clothes seem really weird to our friends and <u>us</u> today.

5. The skirts on her friends and <u>her</u> looked like beach umbrellas.

6. They wore several petticoats under <u>them</u>.

7. She pointed out the plaid shirts on Grandpa and <u>them</u>.

8. We hunted for Grandma and <u>him</u> in their graduation picture.

9. We finally saw Grandpa between his friend Howie and <u>her</u>.

10. They gave their college sweaters to Nancy and <u>me</u> for a costume party.

● **Practice Your Skills**

Using Pronouns as Objects of Prepositions

Write the correct pronoun for each sentence.

1. We talked to Grandpa and (she, her) about their parties.

2. No party in the neighborhood could start without Nancy and (I, me).

3. Grandpa remarked to (we, us) that the boys usually brought food.

4. Grandma did not agree with (he, him) about that fact.

5. One summer our parents gave a tape player to my sister and (I, me).

6. My uncle bought new tapes for my cousin and (we, us).

7. We would dance to (they, them) every afternoon after school.

8. Everyone danced to the fast songs except Howie and (he, him).

Supplying Pronouns in the Objective Case

Complete each sentence by writing an appropriate pronoun. Do not use *you* or *it*.

1. Baby-sitting was a good job during the summer for my sister and ___.
2. Mrs. Spencer had called the two of ___.
3. She has four children and needed a trustworthy sitter for ___.
4. The Spencers told our parents and ___ the date and time.
5. We had the telephone numbers of their friends and ___.
6. "Put Bradley's toy elephant in bed with ___," said his mother.

● *Connect to Writing:* **Drafting**

Writing Sentences with Pronouns

Write five sentences following the instructions below.

1. Include *Dad and me* as a compound direct object in a statement.
2. Include *Sarah and us* as a compound direct object in a question.
3. Include *Zack or him* as a compound indirect object in a statement.
4. Include *the team members and them* as a compound indirect object in a question.
5. Include *Alison and her* as a compound object of a preposition.

● *Connect to Writing:* **Editing**

Using Pronouns in the Objective Case

Rewrite the following paragraph, correcting only those pronouns that are in the wrong case.

(1) The children played happily with Linda and I until nine o'clock. (2) Then Linda told Bradley and they that it was bedtime. (3) First her and I took Bunnie and Bonnie into the bathroom. (4) They brushed their teeth. (5) Then I read Bradley a story. (6) He sat between his little sister Becky and I. (7) Linda asked for help, and I left they for a minute. (8) When I came back, Bradley had gone into the kitchen with Becky. (9) He had found some crayons and was using they on his and Becky's arms. (10) I took the crayons away from Becky and he. (11) Bunnie got out of bed and sat in the sooty fireplace. (12) "If the Spencers ask we again," I said, "you and me are unavailable."

Complete each sentence by writing an appropriate pronoun. Do not use *you* or *it.*

1. Mom took Jordan and ___ to the mall.

2. Can anyone see a parking space for ___?

3. I waited for Jordan and ___ at the top of the escalator.

4. ___ spotted Eric's dad and Eric in the sportswear department.

5. We know their whole family and ___ from Little League games.

6. Eric's brother hangs around with my friend Adam and ___.

➤ The Possessive Case

The following personal pronouns are in the possessive case.

POSSESSIVE CASE		
	Singular	**Plural**
First Person	my, mine	our, ours
Second Person	your, yours	your, yours
Third Person	his, her, hers, its	their, theirs

24 A.3 The **possessive case** is used to show ownership or possession.

Possessive pronouns can be divided into two groups: (1) those that are used like adjectives to modify nouns and (2) those that are used alone.

USES OF POSSESSIVE PRONOUNS	
Used Like Adjectives	my, your, his, her, its, our, their
Used Alone	mine, yours, his, hers, its, ours, theirs

Pronouns used as adjectives are sometimes called pronominal adjectives.

My hat is here, but **yours** is over there.

Her sweater is yellow, and **mine** is green.

Apostrophes are used with possessive nouns, but they are never used with possessive forms of personal pronouns.

Possessive Noun	Is this **Jessica's** coat?
Possessive Pronoun	Is this coat **hers?** (not *her's*)

You can learn about apostrophes with possessive nouns on pages 878–880.

● Practice Your Skills

Using Possessive Pronouns

Read each sentence aloud, trying each pronoun separately. Then read the sentence aloud again, choosing the correct pronoun.

1. I am writing (my, mine) report on an animal's use of tools.

2. What are you writing (your, yours) on?

3. Lin's report is on gorillas, and so is (my, mine).

4. Miguel is doing (him, his) on animal communication.

5. Kevin and Mali are planning (their, theirs) presentations together.

6. Leah has offered us (her, hers) book on African apes.

7. Can Anna, Rick, and I pool (our, ours) source materials?

8. Kayla's report is done, but Wes and I need two more days for (our, ours).

9. Have Pedro and Matt finished (their, theirs) yet?

10. This book is losing (it, its) cover.

● Practice Your Skills

Using Possessive Pronouns

Write the correct pronoun for each sentence.

1. Are you ready with (your, yours) presentation?

2. I rehearsed (my, mine) until midnight.

3. Juan and Matt are showing slides of (his, their) camping trip.

4. Sita and I have made maps for (our, ours).

5. Julia has written out (her, hers) notes on large file cards.

6. The twins found much of (theirs, their) material on the Internet.

7. I dried (my, mine) model outside, and the neighbor's dog stepped on it.

8. The dog left (it, its) muddy footprints all along one side.

9. Susannah, it will be (our, ours) turn in a few more minutes.

10. My throat is dry. How about (your, yours)?

● *Connect to Writing:* **Editing**

Correcting Possessive Pronouns

Write each underlined pronoun. If it is correct, write **C**. If it is incorrect, write it correctly.

1. I studied Paki the gorilla and <u>her</u> baby.
2. We had left the two of them alone in <u>theirs</u> cage.
3. For some reason Paki was neglecting that baby of <u>her</u>.
4. Eventually we separated Kishina and <u>hers</u> mother.
5. We put Kishina in <u>our</u> nursery for human contact.

 Possessive Pronoun or Contraction?

Sometimes some contractions are confused with personal pronouns because they sound alike.

POSSESSIVE PRONOUNS AND CONTRACTIONS	
Possessive Pronouns	its, your, their, theirs
Contractions	it's (it is), you're (you are), they're (they are), there's (there is)

The best way to separate these words in your mind is to say the two words that a contraction stands for.

Possessive Pronoun or Contraction?	Is (you're, your) coat here?
Incorrect	Is **you are** coat here?
Correct	Is **your** coat here?

You can learn more about contractions on pages 883–884.

The Cases of Personal Pronouns • Lesson 1   **719**

When You Write

When you speak, some contractions and possessive pronouns sound the same. When you write, you have to know which one to use. A frequent mistake is writing *it's* for *its*. No possessive pronoun has an apostrophe. When you aren't sure whether to write *it's* or *its*, mentally substitute the word *his*. If *his* makes sense, then write *its*.

> The dog knocked over **its** dish.
>
> The dog knocked over **his** dish.

Read over a recent essay looking for the words *its* or *it's*. Be sure each is used correctly.

Practice Your Skills

Using Possessive Pronouns and Contractions

Read the following sentences aloud. Identify each word as a ***possessive pronoun*** or a ***contraction.*** If you aren't sure, test the word in one of the ways you have learned about.

1. Which boat in the harbor is yours?
2. It's the one with the bold red stripe.
3. When is your boat leaving?
4. Aren't you afraid you're going to be late?
5. No, there's still an hour before it's time to go.
6. Look, there's Zach! Where are your sisters?
7. They're buying their tickets for the boat ride.
8. Didn't you bring your camera?
9. No, I lost its case, so I plan to use theirs.
10. You're going to have a great time on your tour.

Practice Your Skills

Distinguishing Between Possessive Pronouns and Contractions

Write the correct word in parentheses for each sentence.

1. There's the island of Crete on (your, you're) left.
2. (Theirs, There's) the place where the Minoans lived.
3. (Their, They're) cities and palaces fell into ruins.
4. (Your, You're) going to tour the palace of Knossos.
5. (Its, It's) been partially excavated.

Pronoun Problem: *Who* or *Whom?*

24 B   *Who* and *whom* are **interrogative pronouns.** They are used to ask questions.

In Chapter 14 you learned about interrogative pronouns. When using the pronouns *who* and *whom* to ask questions, people sometimes confuse them. *Who* is in the **nominative case** and can be the subject.

> **Subject**   **Who** decorated the classroom for the party?

Whom is in the **objective case** and can be used as a direct object or as an object of a preposition.

> **Direct**   **Whom** did you see during the school trip?
> **Object**   (Turn a question into a statement. *You did see whom during the school trip. Whom* is the direct object.)
>
> **Object of a**   From **whom** did you receive those magazines?
> **Preposition**   (*From whom* is a prepositional phrase.)

Whose can also be used as an interrogative pronoun. It always shows possession.

> **Whose** is this backpack on the floor?
> (*Whose* refers to *backpack.*)
> Looking at all the backpacks, we didn't know **whose** were **whose!**
> (*Whose* is used as a subject and then as a predicate nominative.)

You can learn more about interrogative pronouns on pages 499–500.

When You Write

When do you use *who* and when do you use *whom?* To remember when to use these pronouns, get together with a classmate and help one another memorize the lines below:

> Who is the subject?
> To whom is the action directed?

Together, make up more hints to help you remember grammar rules in this chapter.

● **Practice Your Skills**

Using Who and Whom Correctly

Complete each sentence, using the interrogative pronouns **who, whom,** and **whose** correctly.

1. ___ needs a ride to the game?

2. To ___ did you give the game schedule?

3. ___ will be shortstop in this game?

4. ___ is the coach considering as catcher?

5. This glove belongs to ___?

6. ___ is that bat?

● *Connect to Writing:* **Editing**

Correcting Sentences with Interrogative Pronouns

Rewrite each sentence, correcting the interrogative pronoun. If the pronoun is correct, write **C.**

1. Who did the coach send into the batting box first?

2. Whom came up to bat with the bases loaded in the final inning?

3. For who were the fans cheering?

4. Whose fly ball did Jeff catch?

5. Whom tagged out Katie?

● *Connect to Reading, Speaking, and Writing:* **Science Report**

Using Pronouns

With a partner, read several essays on a recent scientific study, such as new information on the incidence of brain damage in football players or current research on language acquisition in infants. Discuss how you will use this information to write a short report on the subject. Together, draft, write, and proofread the report. Create an introduction that draws in your reader and a conclusion that sums up your ideas. Use at least two nominative, objective, possessive, and interrogative pronouns in your report.

The word or group of words that a pronoun refers to or replaces is called the pronoun's **antecedent.** In the following sentences, *Maria* is the antecedent of *her,* and *Waltons* is the antecedent of *they.*

Pronouns and Antecedents

Maria raised **her** hand and volunteered.

The **Waltons** are our neighbors. **They** are planning a garage sale.

Because a pronoun and its antecedent both refer to the same person, place, or thing, they must be in agreement.

24 C   A pronoun must agree in **number** and **gender** with its **antecedent.**

Number is the term used to indicate whether a noun or pronoun is singular (one) or plural (more than one). A pronoun must be singular if its antecedent is singular. It must be plural if its antecedent is plural.

Singular   **Luis** is preparing **his** presentation for the meeting.

Plural   The **teachers** have turned in **their** grades for the semester.

The personal pronouns *you, your,* and *yours* can be either singular or plural.

Gender tells whether a noun or a personal pronoun is masculine, feminine, or neuter. A personal pronoun must also agree with its antecedent in gender. The chart below lists personal pronouns according to their gender.

GENDER OF PERSONAL PRONOUNS	
Masculine	he, him, his
Feminine	she, her, hers
Neuter	it, its

Things and places are neuter in gender. Unless animals are given proper names, they are usually also considered neuter.

CHAPTER 24

Masculine	Brian forgot **his** sneakers.
Feminine	Amy gave **her** cat a bath.
Neuter	Wash the **car** and wax **it**.

The plural pronouns *them* and *their* have no gender. They can have masculine, feminine, or neuter antecedents. Their antecedents may also be combinations of masculine and feminine.

The three **women** presented **their** report to the board.

The **men** and **women** on the board compared **their** notes.

● Practice Your Skills

Making Pronouns and Their Antecedents Agree

Complete each sentence by writing an appropriate pronoun.

1. We cut or arrange ____ hair in the styles of our culture.

2. Native Americans wore ____ hair in various ways.

3. Most of them wore ____ hair long.

4. Sometimes a man's braids had fur woven into ____.

5. The feathers in the hair of a man showed ____ status as a warrior.

6. Some men wore ____ hair long and loose.

➤ Indefinite Pronouns as Antecedents

An indefinite pronoun does not refer to any person or thing in particular. It can be the antecedent of a personal pronoun. Some indefinite pronouns are singular, and others are plural. Still other indefinite pronouns may be either singular or plural.

When one of the following indefinite pronouns is the antecedent of a personal pronoun, the personal pronoun must be singular.

SINGULAR INDEFINITE PRONOUNS					
anybody	each	everybody	neither	no one	somebody
anyone	either	everyone	nobody	one	someone

Singular   One of the boys can't open **his** locker.

Someone in the girls' chorus forgot **her** music.

Sometimes the gender of a singular indefinite pronoun is not indicated in the sentence. Standard English solves this problem by using *his or her.*

Everyone must finish **his or her** homework.

Although sentences like the previous one are correct, some may sound awkward. You can often eliminate awkwardness by rewriting a sentence in the plural form.

All **students** must finish **their** homework.

When one of the following indefinite pronouns is the antecedent of a personal pronoun, the personal pronoun is plural.

PLURAL INDEFINITE PRONOUNS			
both	few	many	several

Plural   Several of the women offered **their** help.

Both of my brothers lost **their** keys.

When one of the following indefinite pronouns is the antecedent of a personal pronoun, that pronoun can be either singular or plural.

SINGULAR OR PLURAL INDEFINITE PRONOUNS				
all	any	most	none	some

A personal pronoun used with one of these indefinite antecedents agrees in number and gender with the object of the preposition that follows it. See the examples on the following page.

Singular	All of the **art** was returned to **its** owner.
Plural	**Some** of the **players** wore **their** uniforms.

● **Practice Your Skills**

Making Personal Pronouns Agree with Indefinite Pronouns

Complete each sentence by writing an appropriate pronoun.

1. Everyone contributed ____ ideas for the mural.

2. Several of the students submitted ____ designs.

3. Many asked ____ families for donations of supplies.

4. Some of the merchants let us paint on ____ walls.

5. No one wore ____ good clothes to the work party.

6. Will anyone bring ____ camera tomorrow?

● *Connect to Writing:* **Drafting**

Writing Sentences to Eliminate Awkward Constructions

Find sentences in the preceding exercise that you completed with **his** or **her**. Rewrite these sentences in the plural form.

● *Connect to Writing:* **Friendly Letter**

Using Personal Pronouns and Antecedents

Think of a photograph that has been taken of you. Write a letter to a relative describing the day the picture was taken. Tell how you felt about having your picture taken and what the photographer did to prepare you for the photograph. Use at least five personal pronouns and make sure that they agree with their antecedents.

➤ Unclear or Missing Antecedents

The meaning of your writing and speaking can become confusing if the pronouns you have used do not have clear antecedents.

24 C.1   Every personal pronoun should clearly refer to a specific antecedent.

Unclear	**I** missed the concert because **you** couldn't get tickets.
	(Who is the *you* in this sentence?)
Clear	**I** missed the concert because **I** couldn't get tickets.
Missing	My brother is a musician, but I know nothing about **it.**
	(What does *it* refer to? The antecedent is missing.)
Clear	My brother is a musician, but I know nothing about **music.**

● Practice Your Skills

Correcting Unclear or Missing Antecedents

Write **I** for each antecedent that is unclear or missing and **C** for each antecedent that is used correctly.

1. We can't go to the aquarium Monday because you need reservations.

2. Many people have Monday off, so the aquarium will be busier than usual.

3. When Julia and Amy set the date, she promised to buy the tickets.

4. Paul bought tickets for Mark when he was in Monterey.

5. I could take the bus, but you must have the exact change.

6. The aquarium schedule can be obtained by contacting it at 555–1029.

7. I read a newspaper article about the jellyfish, and I am looking forward to it.

8. The aquarium staff recently finished the new display of marshland birds. All of them are from our own area.

9. Ashley's parents are marine biologists, so she knows a lot about it.

10. When a seal looks into my eyes, it probably asks itself what kind of creature I am.

● *Connect to Writing:* Revising

Correcting Sentences with Unclear or Missing Antecedents

Rewrite the incorrect sentences from the preceding exercise, making the antecedents clear.

● *Connect to Writing:* **Family Description**

Using Pronouns

If you were to write a description of your family relaxing, what written images would you include? How would you tie those images together? Write a one-page description of your family doing something together that they enjoy. What is each person doing? Use as many pronouns as you can, and write your description in the first person, using *I*. Include your feelings about the scene you are describing.

✔ *Check Point:* **Mixed Practice**

Write the correct pronoun for each sentence.

(1) (Who, Whom) knows why women's shirts often button differently from men's? **(2)** We can find the answer to (our, your) question in the thirteenth century. **(3)** In those days, everyone had lots of buttons on (their, her or his) clothes. **(4)** A woman's dress might have scores of buttons on (her, it). **(5)** For many men and women, (your, their) right hand was the more skillful one. **(6)** A man dressed himself, so (his, their) coat overlapped from left to right. **(7)** A rich woman, on the other hand, had maids to dress (her, them). **(8)** Right-handed maids did (her, their) work more easily when garments overlapped right to left. **(9)** (Who, Whom) is dressed by maids today? **(10)** Few of the manufacturers design (its, their) shirts for today's women.

Assess Your Learning

Using Pronouns Correctly

Write the correct word in parentheses.

1. Althea and (she, her) are equal partners in the delivery service.

2. During the Boston Tea Party, some of the ships in the harbor lost (its, their) cargo.

3. Should the tickets be sent to you or (he, him)?

4. (Who, Whom) did you just introduce to Ryan?

5. Was that (he, him) on the subway?

6. Give Daniel or (she, her) the money from the car wash.

7. The director chose David and (she, her) for the leads.

8. (They're, Their) work on the project was excellent.

9. Either of the women will give (her, their) report.

10. The volleyball game will be played between our relatives and (they, them).

Correcting Pronoun Errors

Write each sentence and correct any error in the use of pronouns. If a sentence is correct, write **C**.

1. The final decision must be made by Ellen and he.

2. Who did you choose for the lead in the play?

3. Clara and him will be school monitors this term.

4. Isn't that she by the side of the pool?

5. Tell Ana and they about the play.

6. Mr. Brown and his wife have sold there farm.

7. Ruth gave Lily and she matching sweaters.

8. To whom am I speaking?

9. With Roscoe and he as my helpers, we cleaned the house.

10. You must sign you're name on this line.

Making Pronouns Agree with Antecedents

Write the pronoun that correctly completes each sentence.

1. Both of the girls must give   speeches today.
2. Amanda has gone to the movies with   friends.
3. Mr. and Mrs. Ruiz are away on   vacation.
4. One of the female plaintiffs will plead   own case.
5. All of the beach has white sand covering   .
6. The pony ran quickly to   mother.
7. Most of the apples have worms in   .
8. Lloyd couldn't find   hockey stick anywhere.
9. Several of the chorus members will sing   own songs.
10. Everyone on the boys' relay team has   racing time.

Using Pronouns Correctly

Write ten sentences that follow the directions below.

Write a sentence that . . .

1. includes *Bill and I* as subjects.
2. includes *him and her* as direct objects.
3. includes the prepositional phrase *between you and me*.
4. includes the words *your* and *you're*.
5. includes the words *their* and *they're*.
6. includes *who*.
7. includes *whom*.
8. includes *nobody* as the subject.
9. includes *some of the bread* as the subject.
10. includes *some of the papers* as the subject.

Using Pronouns: Posttest

Directions

Read the passage and choose the pronoun that belongs in each underlined space. Write the letter of the correct answer.

When Sirimavo Bandaranaike's husband was assassinated in 1959, __(1)__ took over as Sri Lanka's prime minister. That made __(2)__ the first female prime minister the world had ever seen. The position was __(3)__ for five years and then for seven more years in the 1970s. In 1994, __(4)__ succeeded __(5)__ own daughter as prime minister when the younger woman became president.

__(6)__ of the people in Sri Lanka are Sinhalese, __(7)__ are Buddhist by tradition. A smaller percentage are Tamil, of Hindu background.

Civil wars have torn apart this small nation, __(8)__ is a bloody and violent history. First Tamil guerrillas attack government forces, and then the government forces push __(9)__ back. This back-and-forth fighting has gone on as long as __(10)__ remembers.

1. A he
 B she
 C it
 D her

2. A she
 B he
 C her
 D it

3. A her's
 B hers
 C it's
 D our

4. A she
 B her
 C it
 D we

5. A hers
 B she
 C her
 D his

6. A One
 B Most
 C Neither
 D Each

7. A whose
 B who's
 C whom
 D who

8. A whom
 B whose
 C who
 D who's

9. A him
 B it
 C they
 D them

10. A anyone
 B several
 C many
 D they

Writer's Corner

Snapshot

24 A **Case** is the form of a noun or pronoun that indicates its use in a sentence. There are three cases: **nominative, objective,** and **possessive.** (page 706)

24 B *Who* and *whom* are **interrogative pronouns.** They are used to ask questions. (pages 721–722)

24 C A **pronoun** must agree in number and gender with its **antecedent.** (pages 723–728)

Power Rules

Check that you use **subject pronouns** in the subject's place. (pages 708–709)

Before Editing	**After Editing**
Me and *him* like baseball.	*He* and *I* like baseball.

Check that you use **object pronouns** in the object's place. (pages 712–717)

Before Editing	**After Editing**
Give the papers to Maria and *he*.	Give the papers to Maria and *him*.
This trophy is for *she*.	This trophy is for *her*.

Some words have sound like other words. Be sure you use the correct word in your sentence. (pages 719–720)

Before Editing	**After Editing**
Their two of my closest friends.	*They're* two of my closest friends.
Feed the guinea pig *it's* food.	Feed the guinea pig *its* food.

Editing Checklist

Use this checklist when editing your writing.

✓ Did I make sure that I used the nominative case for subjects and predicate nominatives? (See pages 706–707.)

✓ Did I make sure that I used the objective case for direct objects, indirect objectives, and objects of prepositions? (See pages 706 and 712.)

✓ Did I use the correct possessive pronouns and spell them correctly? (See pages 706 and 717–720.)

✓ Did I use the correct interrogative pronouns in my questions? (See pages 721–722.)

✓ Did I make sure that my pronouns agree in number and gender with their antecedents? (See pages 723–728.)

Use the Power

It is possible to use too many pronouns. It is also possible to use too few. Find a comfortable place between these two extremes.

Too Many Pronouns (What is going on?)	She told her that they were going to go there around noon. Then he called up and they decided they would try to get there before them, but then they changed their plans. No wonder they didn't see them that day.
Too Few Pronouns (Still not sure what is going on.)	Maria told Sue that Maria and Sue were going to go to the movies around noon. Then Sam called and said that Sam and Matt would meet Maria and Sue at the movies. Then Maria and Sue decided to try to get there before Sam and Matt. Then Maria and Sue changed their plans. Matt and Sam didn't see Maria and Sue that day.
Between the Two Extremes (at least someone got to see the movie!)	Maria and Sue decided to go to the movies around noon. Then Sam called and said that he and Matt would meet them there. For some reason, Maria and Sue changed their plans. Matt and Sam decided that they would see the movie anyway.

Subject and Verb Agreement

How can you make your subjects and verbs work together so that your ideas are clear?

Subject and Verb Agreement: Pretest 1

The following first draft contains several errors in subject-verb agreement. The first error has been corrected. How would you revise the draft so that subjects and verbs agree?

In the early 1900s, with many British men fighting in WWI, the female artist of England came into ~~their~~ *her* own. Vanessa Bell, now considered a major contributor to British portrait drawing and landscape painting in the 20th century, works for years to receive recognition. Bell and her sister, the writer Virginia Woolf, was important members of the Bloomsbury Group, a collection of artists and philosophers who was eager to break with tradition. Bell's painting above show a view from a window at her home. The window and objects seems to invite the viewer to share in the calm beauty of the day. Bell died in 1961 at the age of 81.

Subject and Verb Agreement: Pretest 2

Directions

Write the letter of the best way to write the underlined word. If an underlined part contains no error, write **D.**

A grouse, a quail, or a pheasant **(1)** <u>are</u> a close relative of the turkey. There **(2)** <u>was</u> turkeys in Mexico long ago. Turkeys in the United States today **(3)** <u>come</u> from these Mexican birds. The feathers of a male bird **(4)** <u>is</u> greenish brown. Each of the males **(5)** <u>have</u> a flock of females. The flock **(6)** <u>wanders</u> in the woods during the day. At night males and females **(7)** <u>roost</u> in trees. Neither a female nor a young male **(8)** <u>gobble</u>. Adult males with bristly beards **(9)** <u>make</u> that sound. **(10)** <u>Hasn't</u> you heard gobbling in the woods?

1. **A** is
   B were
   C are being
   D No error

2. **A** is
   B were
   C was being
   D No error

3. **A** comes
   B coming
   C is coming
   D No error

4. **A** is being
   B am
   C are
   D No error

5. **A** are having
   B have had
   C has
   D No error

6. **A** wandering
   B wander
   C were wandering
   D No error

7. **A** roosts
   B is roosted
   C was roosting
   D No error

8. **A** were gobbling
   B are gobbling
   C gobbles
   D No error

9. **A** makes
   B is making
   C has made
   D No error

10. **A** Haven't
    B Isn't
    C Has
    D No error

Subject and Verb Agreement: Pretest **735**

You would never wear two shoes that did not match. Just like your pair of shoes, subjects and verbs must match. The subject and verb in *A dog barks* and *Dogs bark* go together. The subject and verb in *Dogs barks* do not go together. Subjects and verbs match when there is **agreement** between them.

25 A   **A verb must agree with its subject in number.**

 ## Number

As you may recall, **number** is the term used to indicate whether a word is *singular*—meaning "one"—or *plural*—meaning "more than one." Nouns, pronouns, and verbs all have number.

 ## The Number of Nouns and Pronouns

The plural of most nouns is formed by adding *-s* or *-es* to the singular form. A few nouns, however, form their plurals in other ways. A dictionary always lists irregular plurals.

NOUNS			
Singular	monkey	church	mouse
Plural	monkey**s**	church**es**	m**ice**

Pronouns also have number. For example, *I, he, she,* and *it* are singular, and *we* and *they* are plural. *You* can be singular or plural.

● **Practice Your Skills**

Determining the Number of Nouns and Pronouns

Label each word *singular* or *plural.*

1. we	**7.** day	**13.** star
2. boxes	**8.** cities	**14.** teacher
3. it	**9.** he	**15.** she
4. birds	**10.** calves	**16.** sweater
5. men	**11.** feet	**17.** they
6. teeth	**12.** colors	**18.** elevator

CHAPTER 25

The Number of Verbs

Most present-tense verbs ending in *-s* or *-es* are singular. Plural forms in the present tense do not end in *-s* or *-es*.

	Singular		**Plural**
A bird {	sleep**s**. eat**s**. fli**es**.	Birds {	sleep. eat. fly.

Be, have, and *do* have special singular and plural forms in the present tense. *Be* also has special forms in the past tense. This chart shows the special forms of *be, have,* and *do.*

FORMS OF *BE, HAVE,* AND *DO*		
	Singular	**Plural**
be	is (present) was (past)	are (present) were (past)
have	has	have
do	does	do

In the following examples, each subject is underlined once and each verb is underlined twice.

Singular   The bird is a robin.

A robin has a red breast.

The robin was in a tree.

Plural   The birds are robins.

Robins have red breasts.

The robins were in a tree.

Determining the Number of Verbs

Write each verb and label it *singular* or *plural.*

1. falcons travel

2. a cheetah speeds

3. pigeons fly

4. cheetahs race

5. it is

6. snails were

7. eagles soar

8. a robin appears

9. we observe

10. we care

11. an ostrich runs

12. I arrive

➤ Singular and Plural Subjects

Since nouns, pronouns, and verbs all have number, the number of a verb must agree with the number of its noun or pronoun subject.

25 A.1 A singular subject takes a singular verb. A plural subject takes a plural verb.

To make a verb agree with its subject, ask yourself two questions: *What is the subject?* and *Is the subject singular or plural?* Then choose the correct verb form.

When You Write

Keeping in mind the rules you just studied will help you remember how to make subjects and verbs agree. Even the most experienced speakers and writers sometimes get confused. One question that you can ask to clear up your own confusion about subjects and verbs is this: *What do you do when the subject and predicate nominative are joined by a linking verb?* You know the answer: *Make the verb agree with the subject.*

The solution is longer study halls.
(*Is* agrees with *solution,* not *halls.*)

Longer study halls are the solution.
(*Are* agrees with *study halls,* not *solution.*)

Take a look at a recent composition to see if your subjects and verbs agree throughout. Correct any errors in subject-verb agreement.

● Practice Your Skills

Matching Subjects and Verbs

Read each sentence aloud. Decide whether the subject is singular or plural, and then choose the verb that agrees with the subject.

1. Frogs (was, were) on the earth fifty million years before dinosaurs.

2. A close relative of the frog (is, are) the toad.

3. These small creatures (has, have) huge appetites.

4. A toad (eats, eat) about one hundred insects every day.

5. Toads (catches, catch) insects with their long, sticky tongues.

6. The longest leap by a frog (was, were) more than seventeen feet.

7. Many people (collects, collect) frog figures.

8. One frog balloon (was, were) huge.

9. People (runs, run) frog farms in marshes and swamps.

10. Frogs' legs (is, are) popular appetizers in some restaurants.

● Practice Your Skills

Making Subjects and Verbs Agree

Write each word or words in the **Subjects** column that agrees in number with the verb in the **Verbs** column.

Subjects	Verbs
1. stores, house, monuments, shed	stands
2. friends, Luisa, Dad, leader	talks
3. minerals, rocks, metal, gem	is
4. planes, kites, pilot, flag	fly
5. puppy, kittens, baby, men	sleeps
6. cars, boat, bicycle, train	moves
7. leaves, bark, plants, tree	grow
8. Mother, artists, guard, teachers	study
9. stars, diamond, light, silver	twinkle
10. tadpoles, Alex, rabbits, child	hop

Making Subjects and Verbs Agree

Write each sentence, changing the verb to agree with the subject. If the verb in a sentence is correct, write **C**.

1. Red-spotted toads lives in the desert.

2. They make sounds like the chirp of a cricket.

3. Rocks provides cool shelters for them on hot days.

4. A summer thunderstorm bring them out.

5. A toad's diet consists mostly of insects.

✔ Check Point: Mixed Practice

Write the appropriate form of the verb in parentheses.

1. Alonzo Clemens (has, have) a brain disorder.

2. Many everyday activities (is, are) hard for him.

3. Nevertheless, he (make, makes) extraordinary animal sculptures.

4. This unusual artist (is, are) able to sculpt any animal he sees.

5. A very short glimpse (tells, tell) him all he needs to know.

6. Clemens's unusual memory (stores, store) every small detail.

7. Every muscle (stands, stand) out as in real life.

8. He (make, makes) wax sculptures in less than twenty minutes.

9. His unique talent (helps, help) him succeed.

10. Doctors (calls, call) people with his kind of memory *savants*.

11. *Savant* (come, comes) from the French word *savoir*.

12. *Savoir* (means, mean) "to know."

● *Connect to Writing:* Descriptive Paragraph

Subject and Verb Agreement

Your class is planning a booklet called "Interesting *B*s." Think about an interesting bird, butterfly, or bug you have seen. Write a paragraph that describes the animal. Be sure to explain how the animal looks and behaves. When you have finished, check that your subject and verb agree in each sentence.

Certain problems in making subjects and verbs agree arise more often than others. The following are some of the most common problems.

25 B Verb phrases, contractions, interrupting words, and sentences in inverted order can present agreement problems.

Verb Phrases

A **verb phrase** is the main verb plus one or more helping verbs. If a sentence has a verb phrase, the first helping verb must agree in number with the subject. In all of the following examples, subjects are underlined once, verbs are underlined twice, and the first helping verb is in bold type.

Singular	Mom **is** driving today.
	(*Mom* and the helping verb *is* agree because they are both singular.)
Plural	We **have** been taking the early bus.
	(*We* and the first helping verb *have* agree because they are both plural.)

25 B.1 The first helping verb must agree in number with the subject.

The following is a list of singular and plural forms of common helping verbs.

COMMON HELPING VERBS	
Singular	am, is, was, has, does
Plural	are, were, have, do

Singular	Angie **was** waiting for the bus.
	Briana **does** have a ride.
Plural	The buses **have** been running late today.
	The twins **are** riding their bikes.

Practice Your Skills

Making Subjects and Verbs Agree

Write each subject. Then write the helping verb in parentheses that agrees with the subject.

1. Automobiles (does, do) have a long and interesting history.
2. Inventors (has, have) been tinkering with vehicles for centuries.
3. A steam carriage (was, were) built in France in 1770.
4. Its passengers (was, were) barreling along at 2.5 mph.
5. An early steam carriage (has, have) been discovered recently.
6. A regular steam bus route (was, were) established in Britain by 1836.
7. Unfortunately, the railroad companies (was, were) opposed to the competition.
8. Laws (was, were) passed against the buses.
9. A man (was, were) required to walk in front of each bus.
10. Red danger flags (was, were) waved by the men.

Connect to Writing: Drafting

Making Subjects and Verbs Agree

Choose the verb form in parentheses that agrees with each subject. Then write a complete sentence for each item.

1. Today's cars (has, have) ____.
2. Most bicyclists (is, are) ____.
3. Our neighbors' daughter (was, were) ____.
4. The weather (is, are) becoming ____.
5. The children (was, were) looking ____.

Connect to Writing: Editing

Making Subjects and Verbs Agree

Rewrite the sentences in which the subjects and verbs do not agree. If a sentence is correct, write **C.**

1. The Japanese transit system have become one of the world's best.
2. The railway lines has been linking more and more cities together.
3. The first high-speed trains were launched in Japan in 1964.
4. Today's passengers is traveling at speeds around 140 mph.
5. Engineers has steadily improved the bullet trains.

Subject and Verb Agreement

Doesn't or Don't?

When contractions are used, agreement with a subject can be confusing. To check for agreement, always say the individual words of any contraction.

25 B.2 The verb part of a contraction must agree in number with the subject.

Incorrect	This <u>piece</u> **do**<u>n't</u> <u>fit</u> into the puzzle. (This piece *do* not fit into the puzzle.)
Correct	This <u>piece</u> **does**<u>n't</u> <u>fit</u> into the puzzle. (*Does* agrees with *piece*.)
Incorrect	<u>They</u> **does**<u>n't</u> <u>enjoy</u> puzzles. (They *does* not enjoy puzzles.)
Correct	<u>They</u> **do**<u>n't</u> <u>enjoy</u> puzzles. (*Do* agrees with *they*.)

The preceding rule applies to all contractions. Remember which contractions are singular and which are plural.

CONTRACTIONS	
Singular	**does**n't, **is**n't, **was**n't, **has**n't
Plural	**do**n't, **are**n't, **were**n't, **have**n't

You can learn more about contractions on pages 883–884.

● Practice Your Skills

Making Subjects and Contractions Agree

Write the contraction in parentheses that agrees with the subject.

1. Many Americans (hasn't, haven't) been to Canada.

2. At one time travelers from the United States (didn't, don't) need passports to cross the border into Canada.

3. The Canadian dollar (isn't, aren't) the same as the U.S. dollar.

4. Danielle (wasn't, weren't) aware that Quebec is a city and a province.

5. Quebec City (don't, doesn't) lie too far from the Maine border.

6. Amy's family (wasn't, weren't) from Quebec.

7. Her parents (isn't, aren't) able to speak French.

8. They (wasn't, weren't) of French heritage.

9. Amy (hasn't, haven't) studied French yet.

10. She (isn't, aren't) able to speak or understand the language easily.

Making Subjects and Contractions Agree

Use each of the following word combinations to write a sentence.

1. don't want

2. aren't here

3. wasn't lost

4. haven't stopped

5. isn't waiting

➤ Interrupting Words

Words, such as prepositional phrases, can come between a subject and its verb. When this happens, a mistake in agreement is easy to make. Sometimes the verb is mistakenly made to agree with a word that is closer to it, rather than with the subject.

25 B.3 The agreement of a verb with its subject is not changed by any interrupting words.

In the following examples, notice that each subject and verb agree in number—despite the words that come between them. The best way to find the correct agreement in these sentences is to mentally take out all of the prepositional phrases. Then it is easy to see the remaining subject and verb.

Singular   The juice from these oranges is sour.

(*Is* agrees with the subject *juice,* not with the object of the preposition *oranges*—even though *oranges* is closer to the verb.)

Plural   The fruits in this beverage are oranges and raspberries.

(*Are* agrees with the subject *fruits,* not with the object of the preposition *beverage*—even though *beverage* is closer to the verb.

Compound prepositions, such as *in addition to, as well as,* and *along with,* often begin interrupting phrases. Make sure the verb always agrees with the subject, not the object of the preposition.

Blackberry pie, as well as several other desserts, was on the menu.

(*Was* agrees with the subject *pie*—not with *desserts,* the object of the preposition *as well as.*)

Cinnamon and mocha ice cream flavors, in addition to vanilla, were available.

(*Were* agrees with the subject *flavors*—not with *vanilla,* the object of the preposition *in addition to.*)

You can learn more about prepositional phrases on pages 547–548.

● *Connect to Speaking and Writing:* **Grammar Vocabulary**

Understanding Interrupting Prepositions

With a partner, discuss what you have learned about the influence of prepositions and prepositional phrases on subject-verb agreement. Share an example with each other. Then say the sentences below aloud and discuss how you would make each subject and verb agree. Write your corrected sentences, and read them aloud.

1. Artisans from all over the country was preparing for the art festival.

2. Those with fragile items or perishable goods has an earlier set-up time.

3. Any art collector with a ticket in hand are able to make an offer.

4. The art festivals that are most popular takes place near Phoenix and Sedona.

● **Practice Your Skills**

Making Interrupted Subjects and Verbs Agree

Write each subject. Then write the verb form in parentheses that agrees with the subject.

1. The Museum of American Arts and Crafts (cover, covers) an entire block.

2. The cases in the Native American Hall (holds, hold) ancient craft items.

3. The display of Native American baskets (has, have) been recently added.

4. The materials in the baskets (is, are) mostly plant stems or split reeds.

5. Different techniques of weaving (was, were) used to make baskets, mats, and bags.

6. Native American artists (says, say) that women did most of the weaving.

7. Women of the far North (was, were) known for their delicate baskets.

8. Expert needlework with colored silks (creates, create) pretty patterns.

9. Cradles for children (was, were) woven by the men in some regions.

10. The plaque next to these items (identifies, identify) them as fishing baskets.

➤ Inverted Order

In a sentence's natural order, the subject comes before the verb. In a sentence that is in **inverted order,** the verb or part of the verb phrase comes before the subject. A verb always agrees with its subject, whether the sentence is in natural order or in inverted order.

25 B.4   The subject and the verb of an inverted sentence must agree in number.

To find the subject of an **inverted sentence**, turn the sentence around to its natural order.

Inverted Order	On the glacier were two penguins.
Natural Order	Two penguins were on the glacier.
Question	Can these large birds fly?
Natural Order	These large birds can fly.
Sentence Beginning with *Here*	Here is the penguins' nesting colony.
Natural Order	The penguins' nesting colony is here.
Sentence Beginning with *There*	There were no babies in the nest.
Natural Order	No babies were in the nest.
	(Sometimes *here* or *there* must be dropped to make a sentence sound right.)

Remember that the words *here* and *there* are never the subject of a sentence.

When You Speak and Write

"Think before you speak" is an especially good policy when you begin sentences with the contractions *there're (there are)* and *there's (there is)*. A common mistake is to use a sentence such as "There's more people using public transportation" because you didn't pause to think about the meaning of the contraction. Your ear can tell you that "There is people" sounds wrong before you utter the words.

Look over a recent composition for any mistakes you may have made in using *there're* and *there's*.

● **Practice Your Skills**

Making Subjects and Verbs in Inverted Order Agree

Write each subject. Then write the verb form in parentheses that agrees with the subject.

1. There (is, was) a national historical landmark in San Angelo, Texas.

2. Here (is, are) the best preserved frontier outpost in the United States.

3. At the top of that pole (fly, flies) the Lone Star flag.

4. (Was, Were) this fort established before or after the Civil War?

5. Not far from the fort (was, were) the junction of two rivers.

6. (Wasn't, Weren't) Fort Concho established in 1867?

7. There (was, were) many cavalry and infantry units stationed here.

8. Among the companies (was, were) the Buffalo Soldiers.

9. (Wasn't, Weren't) that the name the Native Americans gave the African American soldiers?

10. There (is, are) a buffalo on the crest of the Tenth Cavalry today.

● *Connect to Writing:* **Drafting**

Writing Sentences Using Subject and Verb Agreement

Write five sentences, following the instructions below.

1. Write a sentence that includes *the students in our school* as the subject. Use a present-tense verb.

2. Write a sentence that includes *the street by my home* as the subject. Use a present-tense verb.

3. Write a sentence in inverted order that includes the verb phrase *were sitting*.

4. Write a question that begins with *Has*.

5. Write a sentence that begins with *There are*.

● *Connect to Writing:* **Editing**

Making Interrupted or Inverted-Order Subjects and Verbs Agree

Rewrite each sentence, using the correct verb form. If a verb form is correct, write **C.**

1. Twenty-three buildings on the site has been restored.

2. In the men's barracks are stored the equipment of the infantry soldiers.

3. There is an outstanding living history program at Fort Concho.

4. Isn't there historical reenactments at the fort on weekends?

5. Volunteers from the community dress in authentic historical costumes.

✔ Check Point: Mixed Practice

Write the appropriate form of the verb in parentheses.

1. (Doesn't, Don't) this game take hours to play?

2. The objects of the game (is, are) to find the secret chamber and locate the treasure chest.

3. There (is, are) a gold-and-silver crown inside the chest.

4. Here (is, are) the first of your choices.

5. Which one of these doors (seem, seems) the most promising?

6. Behind one of the doors (is, are) the first important clue.

7. There (is, are) many misleading clues, however.

8. (Isn't, Aren't) there hazards to look out for?

9. Sometimes the long corridors of the castle (doesn't, don't) go anywhere.

10. At the end of some passages (is, are) trapdoors into the dungeons.

Connect to Writing: Drafting

Analyzing Subject-Verb Agreement

When there are several shifts between singular and plural subjects within a paragraph, writers must stay alert to keep their verbs in agreement. The following passage is from a memoir written by a woman who lived in the Southwest in the late 1800s. Read the paragraph and then follow the directions.

> We <u>were walking</u> single file, John first, I next, and Mother bringing up the rear. We had gone a little way, when mother called John. I had stepped right over a snake that <u>was crawling</u> across our path. It <u>was</u> not a rattle snake, however, tho' quite as exciting. As we <u>were returning</u>, we <u>were startled</u> by the real thing. On the opposite side of a bush—his head at least two feet in the air—<u>was</u> a rattler—coiled ready to strike. Mother and I stood guard until John secured a shovel to kill it.
>
> —Sadie Martin, *My Desert Memories*

- Write the underlined verbs and verb phrases in the passage. Then write the subject that each one agrees with.

- Find the verb phrase *was crawling*. Why did the writer choose the singular verb *was* instead of the plural verb *were*?

- Which sentence is in inverted order? Why do you think the writer chose to put the subject near the end of the sentence?

Certain other subjects and verbs require special attention as well.

25 C   **Compound subjects** and **collective nouns** can present agreement problems.

➤ Compound Subjects

A **compound subject** is two or more subjects that have the same verb. A compound subject is usually joined by the conjunction *and* or *or,* but a compound subject can also be joined by the pairs of conjunctions *and/or, both/and, either/or,* or *neither/nor.* When you write a sentence with a compound subject, you need to remember two agreement rules.

25 C.1   When subjects are joined by *and* or *both/and,* the verb is usually plural.

And indicates more than one. When a subject is more than one, it is plural. The verb, therefore, must also be plural to agree with the subject.

> **Plural Verb**
>
> Jordan **and** Hannah **are** sketching the lake in their artist's tablets.
>
> **Both** the tablet **and** the pencils **belong** to Hannah.

When a compound subject is joined by *or, either/or,* or *neither/nor,* agreement between the subject and the verb follows a different rule.

25 C.2   When subjects are joined by *or, either/or,* or *neither/nor,* the verb agrees with the closer subject.

> **Singular Verb**
>
> **Either** Julia **or** the teacher **has** left this tablet behind.
> (The verb is singular because *teacher,* the subject closer to it, is singular.)
>
> **Plural Verb**
>
> Charcoal **or** pastels **are** best for this purpose.
> (The verb is plural because *pastels,* the subject closer to it, is plural.)

This rule is especially important to keep in mind when one subject is singular and the other is plural.

Singular Verb	**Neither** the two <u>boys</u> **nor** <u>Sarah</u> **has** <u>brought</u> an easel.
	(The verb is singular because *Sarah,* the subject closer to it, is singular.)
Plural Verb	**Neither** the <u>tree</u> **nor** the <u>ducklings</u> <u>**were**</u> in Sarah's picture.
	(The verb is plural because *ducklings,* the subject closer to it, is plural.)

● **Practice Your Skills**

Making Verbs Agree with Compound Subjects

Write the correct form of the verb in parentheses.

1. Ronnie and Christine (is, are) eating at Carmen's Café.
2. Neither Paul nor his parents (has, have) eaten there before.
3. The twins and their cousin (is, are) meeting them here.
4. Neither the counter nor the tables (has, have) room for a party of five.
5. Both Emily and Nita (eats, eat) here often.
6. Either Carmen or Sunny (waits, wait) on the tables.
7. Salsa and chips (was, were) brought to the table.
8. Both the chili and burrito (costs, cost) $3.50.
9. Neither the bean burrito nor the cheese enchilada (contains, contain) meat.
10. Beef, chicken, or cheese (is, are) used in the enchiladas.
11. Both Carmen and Joshua (cooks, cook) during the lunch hour.
12. Two rell=os or the combination plate (is, are) what Brandon wants.
13. Neither April nor her cousin (likes, like) the shrimp dishes.
14. Rice, beans, and a salad (comes, come) with all the dinners.
15. A soup or salad (is, are) included in the price of the dinner.

● *Connect to Writing:* **Editing**

Making Verbs Agree with Compound Subjects

Rewrite each sentence, using the correct verb form. If a verb form is correct, write **C.**

1. Sonia and her friends wants to grab a snack.
2. Either Chinese food or Mexican food are fine with her.
3. Neither Melissa nor the boys walks far.
4. Minh and Sonia discuss their food choices.
5. Neither Broadway nor Third Avenue have a Chinese restaurant.
6. Hamburgers or a pizza sound great to Juan.

Collective Nouns

In Chapter 14 you learned that a **collective noun** names a group of people or things.

COMMON COLLECTIVE NOUNS			
band	congregation	flock	orchestra
class	crew	group	swarm
committee	crowd	herd	team
colony	family	league	tribe

The way a collective noun is used determines its agreement with the verb.

25 C.3   Use a singular verb with a collective-noun subject that is thought of as a unit. Use a plural verb with a collective-noun subject that is thought of as individuals.

The <u>team</u> **is** playing in the Memorial Day game.
(The team as a whole—as one unit—is playing in the game. Therefore, the verb is singular.)

The <u>team</u> **are** unable to agree on new uniforms.
(The individuals on the team are acting separately. Therefore, the verb is plural.)

To make the second sentence clearer—and less awkward—you could add the word *members* after *team*.

The team <u>members</u> **are** unable to agree on new uniforms.

● Practice Your Skills

Making Verbs Agree with Collective Nouns

Write the correct form of the verb in parentheses.

1. The crowd (is, are) the largest of the season.
2. The orchestra (was, were) tuning up their instruments.
3. The band (was, were) in their new uniforms.
4. The audience (was, were) filing out through the emergency exits.
5. The team (heads, head) to the new restaurant.

6. The Yien family (meet, meets) us there.

7. The committee (has, have) been holding its meetings before the show.

Connect to Writing: Editing

Making Verbs Agree with Collective Nouns

Rewrite each sentence, using the correct verb form. If a verb form is correct, write **C.**

1. The Scout Troop have eighteen members.

2. The flock were scattered by the barking dogs.

3. The congregation was shaking the pastor's hand.

4. The public was sending letters to the editor of the newspaper.

5. The league are holding tryouts next week.

Check Point: Mixed Practice

Write each verb. If a verb does not agree with the subject, write the correct form of the verb. If a verb is correct, write **C.**

1. Amanda, Jeff, and Jordan is on the same Little League team.

2. The team are called the Giants.

3. The league are made up of eight teams from the Garden Grove area.

4. Either Jordan's team or his brother's team were the winner of the championship.

5. Jeff, Amanda, or Kai are pitching in the first inning.

6. The team has invited their parents to the play-offs.

7. Jeff's family always watches him.

8. Amanda's mother or Jeff's parents is taking videos of the game.

9. Neither Jeff nor his two best friends has made it into the all-star game.

10. Don't your sister or your cousins play for Little League?

Connect to Writing: Critical Review

Making Verbs Agree with Collective Nouns

Write a review of a musical production or performance for your school newspaper. It can be one that you have seen live or one that you have seen on TV. In your review, use at least three of these words as the subject of a sentence: *orchestra, band, cast, crew, audience,* or *public.* Use at least one compound subject joined by *either/or* or *neither/nor.*

Lesson 4

When certain pronouns are used as subjects, they can present some subject-verb agreement problems.

25 D   The pronouns *you* and *I* and indefinite pronouns can present agreement problems.

➤ *You* and *I* as Subjects

The pronouns *you* and *I* do not follow the rules for agreement that you just learned. *You* is always used with a plural verb—whether *you* refers to one person or more than one person.

25 D.1   Use a plural verb with *you* whether it refers to one person or more than one person.

Plural Verbs	Martina, you are an excellent poet.
	Students, you write very well.
	You have many good ideas.

Although *I* refers to one person, it takes a plural verb. The only exceptions are the *be* forms *am* and *was*.

25 D.2   Except for the forms of *be (am* and *was)*, use a plural verb with *I*.

Plural Verbs	I write poetry.
	I have Dickinson's *Collected Poems*.
	I like Dickinson's poetry style.
Singular Verbs	I am a poet.
	I was in the Corner Book Shop yesterday.

When *I* is part of a compound subject connected with *and,* the *be* verbs become plural, just as they would with any compound subject.

Jordan **and** I are poets.

Miriam **and** I were the readers of the poems.

CHAPTER 25

● **Practice Your Skills**

Making Verbs Agree with **You** *and* **I**

Write the correct form of the verb in parentheses.

1. I (intends, intend) to rehearse my parts of the performance.

2. Marisa, you (sounds, sound) a little flat.

3. You two boys (has, have) to sing louder.

4. I (don't, doesn't) hear you singing, Angela.

5. You (was, were) a little slow at the start of the first song.

6. I (was, were) thinking about the rhythm.

7. You (come, comes) in with the response immediately.

8. Boys, you (sings, sing) that line more loudly than the other line.

9. (Hasn't, Haven't) you and Beth learned your parts?

10. Mr. Jamison and I (am, are) scheduling an extra rehearsal on Friday.

● *Connect to Writing:* **Editing**

Making Verbs Agree with **You** *and* **I**

Rewrite each sentence, using the correct verb form. If a verb form is correct, write **C**.

1. I were out front in the audience.

2. You has all deserved those cheers.

3. I applaud your best performance ever.

4. You three waits here for the curtain call.

5. I expects good reviews in tomorrow's newspaper.

➤ **Indefinite Pronouns**

An indefinite pronoun can be the subject of a sentence. Some indefinite pronouns are singular, some are plural, and some can be either singular or plural.

25 D.3   A verb must agree in number with an indefinite pronoun used as a subject.

The following is a list of common indefinite pronouns.

COMMON INDEFINITE PRONOUNS	
Singular	anybody, anyone, each, either, everybody, everyone, neither, nobody, no one, one, somebody, someone
Plural	both, few, many, several
Singular/Plural	all, any, most, none, some

Singular	Someone **has** called you on the telephone two times.
	(*Has* agrees with the singular indefinite pronoun *someone*.)
	Neither of the messages is very clear.
	(*Is* agrees with the singular indefinite pronoun *neither,* not with the object of the preposition *messages*.)
Plural	Both **are** ringing.
	(*Are* agrees with the plural indefinite pronoun *both*.)
	Few of the calls were for me.
	(*Were* agrees with the plural indefinite pronoun *few*, not with the object of the preposition *calls*.)

All, any, most, none, and *some* can be either singular or plural. The number of each of these pronouns is determined by the object of the preposition that follows it.

Singular	All of his **communication** was by phone.
	(Since *communication* is singular, *was* is also singular.)
Plural	All of the **calls** were in the morning.
	(Since *calls* is plural, *were* is also plural.)

You can learn more about indefinite pronouns on page 498.

● **Practice Your Skills**

Making Verbs Agree with Indefinite Pronouns

Write the correct form of the verb in parentheses.

1. Everyone in my homeroom (was, were) present yesterday.

2. All of the math classes (has, have) the same assignment.

3. Each of the crossing guards (wears, wear) a badge.

4. Neither of the boys on the bicycles (have, has) left yet.

5. All of the broken glass (has, have) been cleared from the walkway.

6. Several of the students (was, were) on their way to the cafeteria.

7. None of the milk (was, were) delivered on time.

8. One of my friends always (brings, bring) her own lunch.

9. Many of the teachers (dislike, dislikes) cafeteria duty.

10. Anyone with a lunch ticket (gets, get) food first.

✓ Check Point: Mixed Practice

Write the appropriate form of the verb in parentheses.

1. I (has, have) to help my family clean the garage today.

2. (Does, Do) you want some of this junk?

3. Most of it (is, are) no longer useful to us.

4. No one (wants, want) those stacks of old magazines.

5. All of them (is, are) going to the recycling center.

6. (Does, Do) anyone want these rackets?

7. Several (is, are) missing strings.

8. (Is, Are) you keeping those two dusty green skateboards?

9. Both (seems, seem) to have jammed wheels.

10. I (was, were) fixing them last week.

11. Most of this camping equipment (is, are) in good shape.

12. Perhaps someone (has, have) a use for it.

13. I (am, are) donating the sleeping bag and the tent to the thrift store.

14. Domingo, you (has, have) been a great help.

15. Everyone (deserves, deserve) the rest of the day off.

● *Connect to Writing:* Dialogue

Making Verbs Agree with Pronouns

Write a short dialogue between two friends who are discussing their feelings about snakes. Be sure to include both the dangers and the benefits of snakes. Use at least two indefinite pronouns as subjects, along with the pronouns *I* and *you*.

Assess Your Learning

Making Subjects and Verbs Agree

Write the verb form in parentheses that agrees with each subject.

1. The weight of those rocks (is, are) about five hundred pounds.
2. None of these instructions (makes, make) sense.
3. The common length of most lightning bolts (is, are) about half a mile.
4. (Is, Are) you trying out for the track team?
5. The boys in the shop (plays, play) baseball at lunchtime.
6. You (hasn't, haven't) received mail today.
7. As the football flies through the uprights, the crowd (cheers, cheer).
8. Some swans (carries, carry) their young on their backs.
9. A few of my friends (has, have) called about the party.
10. There (is, are) twelve letters in the Hawaiian alphabet.

Making Subjects and Verbs Agree

Find and write the verbs that do not agree with their subjects. Then write each sentence correctly. If the sentence is correct, write **C**.

1. The rich mud of drained swamps make good farmland.
2. Neither Don nor Chris were chosen as an actor.
3. No one on the front steps was waiting for a bus.
4. Have one of the actors forgotten his lines?
5. There are 35 million digestive glands in the stomach.
6. Don't Jerry have his jacket with him?
7. You was smiling in the photograph.
8. Each of the Miller children have a calf and a pig.
9. Does your family like Thanksgiving?
10. The grandfather clock chime beautifully.

CHAPTER 25

■ Editing for Subject and Verb Agreement

Write the following paragraphs, correcting each verb that does not agree with its subject.

Trees are green plants. A tree, like other green plants, have roots, stems, leaves, and seeds. Trees, however, are the oldest of all plants. Some of the sequoia trees of the northwestern United States is more than 4,000 years old. These giants were here before Columbus.

The age of trees are recorded in their rings. There is rings in the cross section of most kinds of tree trunks. Each of the rings represent one year of the tree's life.

■ Using Subject–Verb Agreement

Using the present tense, write five sentences that follow the directions below.

Write a sentence that . . .

1. begins with the word *Doesn't*.

2. begins with the word *There*.

3. includes *my brother and sister* as the subject.

4. includes *either Brad or his brothers* as the subject.

5. includes *band* as the subject.

Subject and Verb Agreement: Posttest

Directions

Write the letter of the best way to write each underlined word or words. If an underlined part contains no error, write **D**.

Mary Shelley and Bram Stoker **(1)** <u>was</u> novelists in the Gothic tradition. **(2)** <u>Wasn't</u> they writing nearly a century apart? There **(3)** <u>was</u> several movies based on their novels. Mary Shelley's famous novel about a scientist and his creation **(4)** <u>resemble</u> science fiction. Some of the best Gothic writers **(5)** <u>was</u> women. My mother's book club **(6)** <u>admires</u> Ann Radcliffe. Neither she nor Mary Shelley **(7)** <u>are</u> particularly well known. However, both **(8)** <u>have given</u> us classics in the genre. **(9)** <u>Hasn't</u> you read *The Mysteries of Udolpho?* That Radcliffe novel from the late eighteenth century still **(10)** <u>seem</u> scary today.

1. **A** is
   B were
   C has been
   D No error

2. **A** Weren't
   B Was
   C Hasn't
   D No error

3. **A** has been
   B is
   C were
   D No error

4. **A** resembles
   B are resembling
   C have resembled
   D No error

5. **A** is
   B were
   C has been
   D No error

6. **A** admire
   B are admiring
   C were admired
   D No error

7. **A** are being
   B were
   C is
   D No error

8. **A** is giving
   B gives
   C has given
   D No error

9. **A** Has
   B Haven't
   C Doesn't
   D No error

10. **A** seems
    B are seeming
    C have seemed
    D No error

Writer's Corner

Snapshot

25 A   A verb must agree with its subject in **number.** (pages 736–740)

25 B   Verb phrases, contractions, interrupting words, and sentences in inverted order can present agreement problems. (pages 741–748)

25 C   **Compound subjects** and **collective nouns** can present agreement problems. (pages 749–752)

25 D   The pronouns *you* and *I* and indefinite pronouns can present agreement problems. (pages 753–756)

Power Rules

Be sure that you have **subject-verb agreement** in your sentences. (pages 736–738 and 749–750)

Before Editing	After Editing
The whole team *travel* to the school.	The whole team *travels* to the school.
Maria, as well as her two sisters, *have* many hobbies.	Maria, as well as her two sisters, *has* many hobbies.
Neither Asami nor her sisters *has heard* of the party.	Neither Asami nor her sisters *have heard* of the party.
Neither of the boys *are* old enough to drive.	Neither of the boys *is* old enough to drive.

Check that you use **subject pronouns** in the subject's place. (pages 708–709 and 753–755)

Before Editing	After Editing
Her and Ciara study together.	*She and Ciara* study together.

Check that you use **object pronouns** in the object's place. (pages 712–717 and 755–756)

Before Editing	After Editing
Jo made a pie for *she* and the boys.	Jo made a pie for *her* and the boys.

Editing Checklist

Use this checklist when editing your writing.

✓ Did I make sure that all my verbs and subjects agree in number? (See pages 736–740.)

✓ Did I use the plural form of the verb where necessary? (See pages 741–744.)

✓ Did I use the singular form of the verb where necessary? (See pages 741–744.)

✓ Did I use the correct verb form with *both/and, either/or,* and *neither/nor?* (See pages 749–750.)

✓ Did I use the correct form of the verb with the pronoun *I?* (See pages 753–754.)

Use the Power

Press the "Right!" or "Wrong!" button after each sentence to indicate whether the subject and verb agreement is correct or incorrect. Correct any wrong sentence on another piece of paper.

We are going to the movies tomorrow.	Right!	Wrong!
We plan to see the new action adventure.	Right!	Wrong!
Greta want to see that movie, too.	Right!	Wrong!
She say that she will meet us at the theater.	Right!	Wrong!
Maybe all of us can goes for pizza after the show.	Right!	Wrong!

Write a similar Right/Wrong exercise for a student in another grade who might be having trouble with subject-verb agreement. Create sentences that will interest this student, and make the buttons as colorful and interactive as you can.

CHAPTER 25

Using Adjectives and Adverbs

How can you create colorful prose with adjectives and adverbs?

Using Adjectives and Adverbs: Pretest 1

The following first draft about the artist Sofonisba Anguissola contains errors in using adjective and adverbs. The first error has been corrected. Revise the draft so that all adjectives and adverbs are used correctly.

> Sofonisba Anguissola was a Renaissance painter whose parents allowed her to study art at a time when ~~little~~ *few* women were educated. She painted this portrait of her father, sister, and brother round the year 1559. Anguissola was the first woman of the Renaissance to become internationally known. While in her latest twenties, Anguissola became court painter to King Phillip II of Spain. As a lady-in-waiting in the court of Phillip II, Anguissola painted portraits of the royal family that exemplify the most liveliest aspects of the Italian Renaissance tradition of honest and truthful realism. Her success was very much important to many gifted women who came after her, in Italy and throughout Europe.

Using Adjectives and Adverbs: Pretest 2

Directions

Read the passage and choose the word or group of words that belongs in each underlined space. Write the letter of the correct answer.

Mercury is by far the ___(1)___ of the planets. It speeds around the sun in ___(2)___ time than it takes for a single growing season on Earth. Mercury does not have ___(3)___ air to trap heat, so it is very cold at night. Venus, which is not as close to the sun, is hotter than ___(4)___ planet.

Nothing ___(5)___ live on Saturn—it has no water or oxygen. Saturn's day is ten hours long—far ___(6)___ than ours on Earth. Its trip around the sun, however, takes twenty-nine years. Even at that pace, Saturn revolves ___(7)___ than Uranus or Neptune. Those planets travel ___(8)___ distances than Saturn, so it makes sense that they are ___(9)___. Pluto, no longer considered a planet, still moves at a pretty ___(10)___ speed.

1. **A** swiftest
   B swifter
   C most swift
   D swift

2. **A** least
   B less
   C little
   D leastest

3. **A** no
   B none
   C any
   D nothing

4. **A** other
   B anyone else
   C any
   D any other

5. **A** can
   B can't
   C doesn't
   D cannot

6. **A** more shorter
   B short
   C shorter
   D shortest

7. **A** rapidly
   B more rapidly
   C most rapidly
   D more rapidlier

8. **A** long
   B longer
   C longest
   D more long

9. **A** the most slowest
   B more slower
   C slowest
   D slower

10. **A** better
    B well
    C best
    D good

Comparison of Adjectives and Adverbs

When you write, you often compare one thing with another. Adjectives and adverbs generally have three forms that are used for comparisons. These forms are called **degrees of comparison.**

26 A Most adjectives and adverbs have three degrees of comparison: **the positive, the comparative,** and **the superlative.**

The **positive degree** is used when no comparison is being made.

> **Adjective** The tiger is **big.**
> **Adverb** A giraffe runs **swiftly.**

The **comparative degree** is used when two people, things, or actions are being compared.

> **Adjective** Obviously, an elephant is even **bigger** than a tiger.
> **Adverb** A giraffe can run **more swiftly** than a zebra.

The **superlative degree** is used when more than two people, things, or actions are being compared.

> **Adjective** The blue whale is the **biggest** animal of all.
> **Adverb** Of all animals, the cheetah runs **most swiftly.**

You can learn more about adjectives and adverbs in Chapter 16.

● Practice Your Skills

Identifying Degrees of Comparison

Label each underlined adjective or adverb *P* for positive, *C* for comparative, or *S* for superlative.

1. This winter has been the <u>rainiest</u> winter of the last ten years.
2. I would <u>gladly</u> never see another winter like that one.
3. The days are growing <u>longer</u> now that spring is here.
4. The winds have been blowing <u>more gently</u> today than yesterday.
5. Yesterday must have been the <u>warmest</u> day of the year.
6. It was <u>hazier</u> this morning than it was yesterday.

7. The haze has been burning off <u>more slowly</u> this month than last.

8. Today will be <u>muggy</u>.

9. Monday was the <u>clearest</u> day of the week.

10. Next week's weather should be <u>drier</u> than this week's weather.

➤ Regular Comparison

Most adjectives and adverbs form the comparative and superlative degrees in a regular manner. The form often depends on the number of syllables in the modifier.

26 A.1   Add *-er* to form the comparative degree and *-est* to form the superlative degree of one-syllable modifiers.

ONE-SYLLABLE MODIFIERS			
	Positive	Comparative	Superlative
Adjective	bright	bright**er**	bright**est**
	sad	sad**der**	sad**dest**
Adverb	soon	soon**er**	soon**est**

A spelling change sometimes occurs when *-er* or *-est* is added to certain modifiers, such as *sad*. Check the spelling in the dictionary if you are not sure of it.

Many two-syllable modifiers are formed exactly like one-syllable modifiers. A few two-syllable modifiers, however, would be difficult to pronounce if *-er* or *-est* was added. "Usefuler" and "usefulest" for instance, sound awkward. For such two-syllable modifiers, *more* and *most* are used to form the comparative and superlative forms. Also, *more* and *most* are usually used with adverbs ending in *-ly*.

26 A.2   Use *-er* or *more* to form the comparative degree and *-est* or *most* to form the superlative degree of two-syllable modifiers.

TWO-SYLLABLE MODIFIERS			
	Positive	Comparative	Superlative
Adjective	funny	funn**ier**	funn**iest**
	cheerful	**more** cheerful	**most** cheerful
Adverbs	early	earl**ier**	earl**iest**
	quickly	**more** quickly	**most** quickly

Notice that a spelling change occurs in modifiers that end in *y,* such as *funny* and *early*. The *y* changes to *i* before *-er* or *-est* is added.

When You Write

Many two-syllable modifiers are heard so often that you automatically know which comparative form to use. Occasionally both forms may sound right. That may be because the comparative degrees of some two-syllable modifiers—such as *handsome, common,* and *lovely*—are correctly written either way. Consult an unabridged dictionary whenever you are in doubt about a comparative form. If you have a choice, choose the form that sounds best in the sentence you are writing.

Look back at a recent composition and be sure that you have used comparisons correctly.

All modifiers with three or more syllables form their comparative and superlative degrees by using *more* and *most.*

26 A.3 Use *more* to form the comparative degree and *most* to form the superlative degree of modifiers with three or more syllables.

THREE-SYLLABLE MODIFIERS		
Positive	**Comparative**	**Superlative**
Adjective difficult	**more** difficult	**most** difficult
Adverb frequently	**more** frequently	**most** frequently

● **Practice Your Skills**

Forming Regular Comparisons

Read each sentence aloud, trying each form in parentheses. Choose the correct form and then read the sentence aloud again.

1. Pyrotechnicians have one of the (thrillingest, most thrilling) jobs available.
2. Creating fireworks displays is (riskier, more risky) than most other jobs.
3. Independence Day is the (busiest, most busy) day of the year for pyrotechnicians.
4. Each year they stage (beautifuler, more beautiful) displays than the year before.
5. Displays in the past were (dangerouser, more dangerous) than displays are now.
6. The experts lit a fuse and ran away (faster, more fast) than the speed of fire.
7. Today, launching rockets is (safer, more safe) than it was fifty years ago.
8. Computerization allows the technicians to stand (farther, more far) away.

CHAPTER 26

766 Using Adjectives and Adverbs

9. The (latest, most late) technology times each explosion down to a millisecond.

10. The (creativest, most creative) task is planning the displays.

● **Practice Your Skills**

Forming Comparative and Superlative Modifiers

Write each modifier. Then write its comparative and superlative forms.

1. restless   **9.** often

2. late   **10.** wonderful

3. hard   **11.** happy

4. safe   **12.** high

5. pretty   **13.** carefully

6. fast   **14.** athletic

7. narrow   **15.** easily

8. dark

● **Practice Your Skills**

Using the Correct Form of Modifiers

Write the correct modifier in each sentence.

1. Pyrotechnicians are (more skillful, most skillful) than you might think.

2. The (more scientific, most scientific) part of their jobs is making the fireworks.

3. Their knowledge of chemistry is (deeper, deepest) than that of most people.

4. Colors of today glow (redder, reddest) than before.

5. Colors are (brighter, brightest) than ever.

# Irregular Comparison

A few adjectives and adverbs are compared in an irregular manner. You should learn the comparative and superlative forms of the following modifiers so that you can use them correctly in your writing.

IRREGULAR MODIFIERS		
Positive	**Comparative**	**Superlative**
bad/badly	worse	worst
good/well	better	best
little	less	least
much/many	more	most

Positive	Yesterday's storm was **bad.**
Comparative	It was **worse** than the storm last week.
Superlative	In fact, it was the **worst** storm of the summer.

When You Speak and Write

You will never hear a careful speaker call something "the most unique" of its kind. Some adjectives have no degrees of comparison. *Unique, universal, perfect, infinite,* and their adverb forms, describe a quality of being complete or perfect. They need no modifiers. Be sure you use them correctly in your writing.

● Practice Your Skills

Forming Irregular Comparisons

Read each sentence aloud, trying out each word in parentheses. Choose the correct word and then read the sentence aloud again.

1. Medieval people didn't have (much, many) variety in their winter diets.

2. For (much, many) months there was no fresh meat or fish.

3. The winter was the (worse, worst) time of the year for fishing.

4. There was very (little, less) fodder for farm animals.

5. (More, Most) peasants sold or slaughtered their stock in the fall.

6. It was (good, better) to do this than to have the animals starve.

7. Beef and pork kept (bad, badly), even in cold climates.

8. The (better, best) solution was to salt or dry meats.

9. Vegetables were (less, least) important in the diet than meat.

10. Only dried beans and some root vegetables stored (well, best).

● **Practice Your Skills**

Supplying the Correct Form of Modifiers

Read the first sentence in each group. Then write the comparative and superlative forms of the underlined modifier in the two sentences below it.

1. Vegetables were not a <u>good</u> source of natural salt.

Cooked meat was a ____ source.

Raw meat was the ____ source but it was unsafe to eat.

2. <u>Many</u> people preferred the brine salt from salt springs.

____ people could afford seawater salt.

____ people bought cheaper salt from the mines.

3. Preserving fish by drying worked <u>well</u>.

It worked ____ in drier climates.

It worked ____ in areas that were both dry and windy.

4. Dried meat was not too <u>bad</u> for the people's health.

Heavily salted meat was ____ for them.

Heavily salted, half-spoiled meat was ____ of all.

5. A <u>little</u> fresh game usually appeared on the menus of the wealthy.

A craftsperson's menu contained ____ meat.

A peasant's menu contained the ____ meat of all.

● *Connect to Writing:* **Editing**

Correcting the Form of Modifiers

If the underlined adjective or adverb in a sentence is incorrect, replace it with the correct word. If it is correct, write **C.**

1. The wealthy liked elaborate dishes <u>better</u> of all.

2. Their cooks used sauces far <u>much</u> than we do today.

3. Sauces made meats taste <u>least</u> salty than they would have otherwise.

4. Some of the sauces were <u>much</u> like today's curries.

5. Meats were the basis of <u>more</u> dishes on a banquet menu.

6. <u>Much</u> different meats were served in one course.

7. The roasts of fresh meat would taste <u>better</u> to us today.

8. Cod liver pastries might not be as <u>worse</u> as they sound.

9. One of the <u>less</u> appealing dishes of all was simmered eels.

10. I can't imagine anything <u>worst</u> than songbirds cooked whole.

✔ *Check Point:* **Mixed Practice**

Find and write each incorrect modifier. Then write it correctly. If a sentence is correct, write **C.**

1. The landmarks tour is the better thing to do on a Sunday.

2. The courthouse is the most old building in the city.

3. The more famous landmark in the county is the mission.

4. Rancho de los Alamedas was largest than the mission property.

5. There were many people on the ranches than in the village.

6. The village's faster growth took place after 1865.

7. Frame houses were built more often than brick houses.

8. Wood cost lesser than bricks after the railroad came through.

9. The Morrison house is the more interesting one on the whole tour.

10. It was most expensive to build than any other house of its time.

● *Connect to Writing:* **Persuasive Letter**

Using Forms of Modifiers

Suppose that a scientist has made time travel possible. The scientist has given you a choice of time periods in which to live—now, in medieval times, or in the future. Write a letter asking the scientist to let you live in the time period you prefer. Tell why you choose this era. Use a variety of complete sentences that include both comparative and superlative forms of adjectives and adverbs. Be prepared to identify the forms you use.

26 B   Avoid confusing certain adjectives and adverbs, comparing a thing with itself, and using **double comparisons** and **double negatives**.

Other and Else

Do not make the mistake of comparing one thing with itself when it is part of a group. You can avoid this by adding the word *other* or *else* to your comparison.

26 B.1   Add *other* or *else* to avoid comparing a thing with itself.

Incorrect	Dan is taller than any student in the eighth grade. (Dan is being compared to all the students in the eighth grade. This means he is also being compared to himself because he is in the eighth grade, too.)
Correct	Dan is taller than any **other** student in the eighth grade. (Now he's compared only with the other students, not with himself.)
Incorrect	Beth runs faster than anyone in her class. (Since Beth is in the class, she is also being compared with herself.)
Correct	Beth runs faster than anyone **else** in her class. (Now she is being compared only to the rest of the class, not to herself.)

● Practice Your Skills

Using Other *and* Else *Correctly*

Write the word or words in parentheses that make the most sense in each sentence.

1. I know more about dogs than (anyone, anyone else) in my class does.

2. I like Labradors better than (any, any other) dog I've seen.

3. A Labrador is smarter than (any, any other) spaniel or Dalmatian.

4. Our dog Ginger would rather be with me than (anyone, anyone else) in our family.

5. Ginger prefers Skippers to (any, any other) pet food she's eaten.

6. She'd rather eat our sandwiches than (any, any other) dog food we give her.

7. She barks more at the new meter reader than at (anyone, anyone else).

8. Our neighbor's cat is meaner than (any, any other) dog in our neighborhood.

CHAPTER 26

Correcting Comparisons with Other and Else

Rewrite each incorrect sentence. If a sentence is already correct, write **C.**

1. Fish are easier to care for than any animal in the pet shop.

2. Kahn's Pet Store has more kinds of fish than any shop in town.

3. An angelfish is much prettier than any goldfish.

4. The animals are healthier here than anywhere I've been.

5. The puppy likes the rubber bone better than any toy he has.

6. I want this puppy more than any puppy I've seen.

➤ Double Comparisons

Use only one method to form the comparative or the superlative of a modifier. Using *-er* and *more* together, for example, produces a **double comparison,** which is incorrect.

26 B.2   Do not use both *-er* and *more* to form the comparative degree, or both *-est* and *most* to form the superlative degree.

Double Comparison	Can you work **more quicklier?**
Correct	Can you work **more quickly?**
Double Comparison	This project is the **most hardest** one we've worked on.
Correct	This project is the **hardest** one we've worked on.

● **Practice Your Skills**

Identifying Double Comparisons

Write *I* if a sentence contains double comparisons. Write **C** if a sentence is correct.

1. There were no flowers among the world's most earliest plants.

2. Bees are attracted to the most lightest flowers on plants.

3. Orchid blossoms last more longer than those of most other plants.

4. Succulents can live in a drier climate than many other plants.

5. A ten-ton saguaro cactus is more taller than many trees.

6. Among the most oddest plants are those that feed on insects.

7. The eucalyptus is the most tallest Australian tree.

8. The most rarest forget-me-not is found on only one Pacific Island.

9. Sequoias are more older than any other American trees.

10. The plant with the longest life span is the yucca.

Double Negatives

The following is a list of common negative words.

COMMON NEGATIVES		
no	nobody	none
not	no one	never
-n't	nothing	hardly

Two negative words should not be used together to express the same idea. When they are, the result is a **double negative.**

26 B.3   Avoid using a double negative.

Double Negative	We did**n't** swim **no** laps today.
Correct	We did**n't** swim any laps today.
Correct	We swam **no** laps today.
Double Negative	Carmen did**n't hardly** practice last week.
Correct	Carmen **hardly** practiced last week.

● **Practice Your Skills**

Identifying Double Negatives

Write *I* if a sentence contains a double negative. Write **C** if a sentence is correct.

1. Many people don't know nothing about turtles.
2. Hardly anything was known about the Rancho del Oso Park turtles.
3. Researchers hadn't never been able to track the turtles' movements.
4. They couldn't see no reason against equipping turtles with beepers on their backs.
5. The transistors on their backs didn't hardly bother the turtles at all.
6. A turtle doesn't like anything better than basking on a sunny log.
7. Female turtles don't like no one near their nests.
8. Their nests couldn't never be found by most researchers.
9. Even with beepers, the researchers still couldn't hardly track the turtles.
10. They don't know how young turtles find their way to water.

Good or Well?

Good is always used as an adjective. *Well* is usually used as an adverb. When *well* means "in good health," it is used as an adjective. Remember that adjectives can follow linking verbs.

Adjective	The story was **good.**
	(*Good* is a predicate adjective that describes *story*.)
Adverb	Michael read the story **well.**
	(*Well* is an adverb that tells how Michael read.)
Adjective	I don't feel **well** today. (in good health)

You can learn more about predicate adjectives and linking verbs on pages 514–516 and 571–572.

Power Your Writing: Speak Volumes

A single descriptive word can sometimes speak volumes about a character, a place, a mood, or an event. In the following excerpt from *Rascal* by Sterling North, the dog Wowser is surprised by a raccoon. Notice how the author uses adjectives to intensify the action.

> But we couldn't have been more surprised when a **furious** mother raccoon exploded from her lair screaming her rage and dismay. Wowser nearly fell over backward to avoid the **flying** claws and **slashing little** teeth. A moment later, the **big** raccoon had racked her way up a **slender** oak tree.

Compare the plain versions stripped of adjectives and other descriptive words to the actual passages from *Rascal*.

Plain	After being challenged . . . he would turn and look at the racoon.
Vivid	After being challenged . . . he eventually would turn his worried face and great sad eyes upon his tormentor.
Plain	Wowser was a Saint Bernard.
Vivid	Wowser was an affectionate, perpetually hungry Saint Bernard.

Look back at a recent composition, and strive to include adjectives that supply vivid details to your writing.

Practice Your Skills

Using Good and Well

Write either *good* or *well* to correctly complete each sentence.

1. Ted swims ___.

2. The warm water at the beach felt ___.

3. The loud pounding of the surf sounds ___ to me.

4. Dad's cold is gone, so he finally feels ___.

5. Sandy surfs ___.

6. Our car worked ___ on the way to the beach.

7. Ice cream tastes ___ on a warm day.

8. After eating the greasy fried food, Bert did not feel ___.

9. I did ___ at my first diving lesson with my new coach.

10. The popcorn from the boardwalk stand smelled ___.

Connect to Writing: Editing

Correcting Errors with Good or Well

Rewrite the following sentences if they contain errors with *good* or *well*. If a sentence is correct, write **C.**

1. Can young children learn to swim good?

2. Many good instructors say *yes*.

3. Why should little children learn to swim good?

4. Some youngsters swim well, and that makes pools safer for them.

5. Children who cannot swim good die every year.

Connect to Writing: Personal Assessment

Problem Modifiers

Write an assessment for yourself of the progress you've made in the last year in one of your activities. Describe the activity and compare the skills you had before to the ones you have now. When you have finished, check to make sure you have used all modifiers correctly.

Find the error in each sentence. Then write the sentence correctly.

1. The anaconda is longer and bigger than any kind of snake.

2. The cobra is one of the three most largest snakes.

3. Rattlesnakes are the most deadliest snakes in the far West.

4. You won't never see copperheads in the western states.

5. There aren't no snakes at all in Iceland and Ireland.

6. Cobra family members are more common in Australia than any snake.

7. The most greatest number of snake species live in the tropics.

8. Snakes don't eat nothing but animal food.

9. Snakes that hunt in the daytime can see good.

10. A snake's sense of smell is better than that of almost any animal.

11. The most fastest snake of all is probably the black mamba of Africa.

12. The snake that is smaller than any snake is the Braminy blind snake.

13. Young snakes shed their skins more oftener than old snakes.

14. Most snakes cannot focus their eyes good.

15. Snakes actually move most slowly than many other animals.

Assess Your Learning

▨ Using the Correct Form of Modifiers

Write the correct word or words in parentheses.

1. Your book report sounded (good, well).

2. Which shines (more, most) brightly, gold or silver?

3. Craig didn't know (nothing, anything) about the ring.

4. My three aunts held the baby, but Aunt Carrie was the (more, most) nervous.

5. Is Daniel (taller, more taller) than you?

6. There aren't (no, any) seats left in the theater.

7. Which of these three snakes is the (deadlier, deadliest)?

8. Susan worked harder than (anyone, anyone else) on the committee.

9. Who made the (wiser, wisest) choice, Jerry or Pat?

10. Which television set has a (worse, worst) picture, mine or yours?

▨ Correcting Errors with Modifiers

Write the following sentences, correcting each error. If a sentence is correct, write **C.**

1. Which of the six New England states is smaller?

2. There aren't no oars in this boat.

3. In some science fiction stories, spaceships travel more faster than the speed of light.

4. I don't know who was coldest, you or I.

5. Of the two cars, this one is more reliable.

6. Haven't you seen none of my pictures?

7. That tree is healthier than any tree in the garden.

8. Our twelve-year-old dog doesn't see very good.

9. This coat looks more better on you than on me.

10. I did well on my lifesaving test at the YMCA.

Forming Comparatives and Superlatives

Write the form indicated below for each modifier. Then use that form in a sentence.

1. the comparative of *wisely*
2. the comparative of *keen*
3. the superlative of *good*
4. the comparative of *useful*
5. the comparative of *scary*
6. the superlative of *much*
7. the superlative of *smooth*
8. the comparative of *cautiously*
9. the superlative of *dangerous*
10. the comparative of *comfortable*

Using Adjectives and Adverbs

Write eight sentences that follow the directions below.

Write a sentence that . . .

1. compares two friends.
2. compares three desserts.
3. uses a form of *large* to compare three states.
4. uses a form of *easily* to compare two chores.
5. uses a form of *good* to compare two movies.
6. uses a form of *little* to compare three school subjects.
7. uses *other* in a comparison.
8. uses *else* in a comparison.

Using Adjectives and Adverbs: Posttest

Directions

Read the passage and choose the word or group of words that belongs in each underlined space. Write the letter of the correct answer.

Aerobic conditioning has become one of the __(1)__ of all forms of exercise. Nobody __(2)__ go without some form of aerobics. Some aerobic exercises are cycling, dancing, jogging, jumping rope, swimming, tennis, and basketball. Of these, jumping rope may be the __(3)__. It doesn't require fancy shoes or equipment, and it takes up __(4)__ room than __(5)__ sport.

Warming up is __(6)__ no matter what exercise you do. If you are jumping rope, begin by jogging in place until your heart beats __(7)__ than it does at rest. Then do some warm-up jumps before proceeding to your basic jumps. You are doing __(8)__ if you can jump seventy-five jumps per minute. However, even if you jump __(9)__ than __(10)__ in your class, you are still helping your heart and lungs.

1. A popular	**6. A** good
B more popular	**B** well
C most popular	**C** better
D popularest	**D** best
2. A shouldn't	**7. A** fast
B should	**B** more fast
C cannot	**C** fastest
D doesn't	**D** faster
3. A cheap	**8. A** good
B cheaper	**B** well
C cheapest	**C** finely
D most cheapest	**D** more better
4. A little	**9. A** the most slowest
B less	**B** more slower
C lesser	**C** slowest
D least	**D** slower
5. A any	**10. A** anyone
B other	**B** any other
C any other	**C** anyone else
D anybody else	**D** everyone

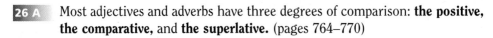

Writer's Corner

Snapshot

26 A Most adjectives and adverbs have three degrees of comparison: **the positive, the comparative,** and **the superlative.** (pages 764–770)

26 B Avoid confusing certain adjectives and adverbs, comparing a thing with itself, and using **double comparisons** and **double negatives.** (pages 771–776)

Power Rules

Use only one **negative form** for a single negative idea. (page 773)

Before Editing	**After Editing**
Nobody never goes to that part of the park.	*Nobody ever* goes to that part of the park.
Rachel *didn't hardly say* a word.	Rachel *hardly said* a word.

Be sure that when you use **helping verbs with negatives,** such as *not* and *n't,* you use the proper form of the helping verb. (page 512)

Before Editing	**After Editing**
They *hasn't read* that book.	They *haven't read* that book.
I *isn't going* to that summer camp.	*I'm not going* to that summer camp.

Use **subject forms** of pronouns in the subject position. Use the **object form** when the pronoun is a direct object, indirect object, or object of a preposition. (pages 712–716)

Before Editing	**After Editing**
Pat and *him* like baseball.	Pat and *he* like baseball.
Mr. Lee gives Al and *we* extra homework.	Mr. Lee gives Al and *us* extra homework.

Editing Checklist

Use this checklist when editing your writing.

- ✓ Did I use the correct degree of comparison? (See pages 764–770.)
- ✓ Did I add *-er* and *-est* correctly to the modifiers? (See pages 764–770.)
- ✓ Did I use *more* and *most* correctly with the modifiers? (See pages 764–767.)
- ✓ Did I avoid using double negatives? (See page 773.)
- ✓ Did I use *well* and *good* correctly? (See pages 774–775.)
- ✓ Did I add *other* or *else* when comparing a member of a group to the rest of the group? (See pages 771–772.)

Use the Power

Create charts such as these to help you form comparative and superlative adjectives and adverbs. If you're not sure which word to use, think about what sounds the most familiar.

Adjectives	Comparative (Add *-er* or *more*)	Superlative (Add *-est* or *most*)
beautiful	more beautiful	most beautiful
silly	sillier	silliest
strange	stranger	strangest

Adverbs	Comparative (Add *-er* or *more*)	Superlative (Add *-est* or *most*)
carefully	more carefully	most carefully
soon	sooner	soonest
quickly	more quickly	most quickly

Add color to a recent composition by adding at least three adjectives and at least three adverbs.

A Writer's Glossary of Usage

While the last four chapters dealt with the basic elements of usage, this section covers specific areas of difficulty. As you study A Writer's Glossary of Usage, pay attention to the various levels of language, including standard English and nonstandard English.

Standard English refers to the rules and conventions of usage most often accepted and used by English-speaking people throughout the world. **Nonstandard English** does not follow these conventions. The differences in regions and dialect, including current slang, account for the variations in nonstandard English. Using nonstandard English, although not always wrong, is unacceptable in certain circumstances. Because nonstandard English lacks uniformity, be sure to use standard English when you write or speak in formal situations, such as in school assignments.

You will find references to formal and informal English in the glossary. **Formal English** follows conventional rules for grammar, usage, and mechanics. Business letters, technical reports, and well-written compositions are typical examples of formal English usage. In magazines, newspapers, and fiction, however, informal English is often used. Although it may follow some of the conventions of standard English, **informal English** often includes words and phrases that would sound inappropriate in a formal piece of writing.

So that you can use this glossary more easily, the words appear in alphabetical order.

a, an Use *a* before words beginning with consonant sounds and *an* before words beginning with vowel sounds.

> Matt has **a** soccer game tonight.
>
> He'll have to eat **an** early dinner.

accept, except *Accept* is commonly a verb that means "to receive with consent." *Except* is usually a preposition that means "but" or "other than."

> I will **accept** Jennifer's invitation to the dance.
>
> I would call her tonight to tell her **except** I have to study for a test.

affect, effect *Affect* is a verb that means "to influence" or "to act upon." *Effect* is usually a noun that means "a result" or "an influence." As a verb, *effect* means "to accomplish" or "to produce."

> How did the news **affect** Rachel?
>
> It had a pleasing **effect** on her.
>
> I'm glad it **effected** a positive improvement in her attitude.

all ready, already *All ready* means "completely ready." *Already* means "previously."

> If we are **all ready,** we'll leave for the football game.
>
> Jan **already** said that she is waiting for us.

a lot People very often write these two words incorrectly as one. There is no such word as "alot." *A lot*, even as two words, should be avoided in formal writing.

> **Informal**   You'll have **a lot** of fun at the springs.
>
> **Formal**   You'll have a great deal of fun at the springs.

among, between These words are both prepositions. *Among* is used when referring to three or more people or things. *Between* is used when referring to two people or things.

> Please divide your time **among** the whole family.
>
> Tomorrow we can have a talk just **between** you and me.

amount, number *Amount* refers to a singular word. *Number* refers to a plural word.

> The **amount** of time Lenny spent on the computer last week is more than the **number** of hours he worked on his homework.

anywhere, everywhere, nowhere, somewhere Do not add *-s* to any of these words.

> Don't go **anywhere** until I return.
>
> We went **nowhere** on Saturday.
>
> I looked **everywhere** for my glasses.

at Do not use *at* after *where*.

> **Nonstandard** **Where** they're **at** really isn't our business.
>
> **Standard** **Where** they are really isn't our business.

● *Connect to Writing:* Editing

Recognizing Correct Usage

Write each underlined word. If the word is used correctly, write **C** beside it. If the word is used incorrectly, write the correct form of the word.

In the early 1800s, almost <u>nowheres</u> was nursing considered <u>a</u> honorable profession. The person who <u>affected</u> a change was Florence Nightingale. She was known as "The Lady with the Lamp" because she carried a lamp to light her way when she walked <u>between</u> her patients at night. The <u>number</u> of countries where she trained <u>at</u> included England, Egypt, and Germany. Rumors of the terrible medical conditions of the Crimean War in 1854 <u>affected</u> her greatly. <u>Already</u> to volunteer her nursing services, she was appointed to lead the entire reform effort. Her bravery and compassion established modern nursing as <u>a</u> profession of honor.

bad, badly *Bad* is an adjective and often follows a linking verb. *Badly* is used as an adverb. In the first two examples, *tastes* is a linking verb.

> **Nonstandard** The food tastes **badly** to me.
>
> **Standard** The food tastes **bad** to me.
>
> **Standard** Mother **badly** wanted to throw it away.

You can learn more about using adjectives and adverbs in Chapter 16.

bring, take *Bring* indicates motion toward the speaker. *Take* indicates motion away from the speaker.

> Won't you **bring** me a clean plate?
>
> Yes, after I **take** the dirty one to the kitchen.

You can learn more about using bring *and* take *on pages 683–684.*

can, may *Can* expresses ability. *May* expresses possibility or permission.

> Holly **can** speak French fluently.
>
> When she visits, **may** I ask her to teach me?

doesn't, don't *Doesn't* is singular and must agree with a singular subject. *Don't* is plural and must agree with a plural subject or with the singular pronouns *I* or *you*.

> The new singer **doesn't** have a large following yet.
>
> The new singers **don't** have a large following yet.

double negative Words such as *but* (when it means "only"), *hardly, never, no, none, no one, nobody, not* (and its contraction *n't*), *nothing, nowhere, only, barely,* and *scarcely* are all negatives. Avoid using these words with other negative words in writing and speaking.

> **Nonstandard**   **Nothing never** upsets Katie.
>
> **Standard**   **Nothing ever** upsets Katie.
>
> **Standard**   **Nothing** upsets Katie.

You can learn more about double negatives on page 773.

fewer, less *Fewer* is plural and refers to things that can be counted. *Less* is singular and refers to quantities and qualities that cannot be counted.

> You will have **fewer** clothes after cleaning out your closet.
>
> It will take **less** effort to put everything back in order.

good, well *Good* is an adjective and often follows a linking verb. *Well* is an adverb and often follows an action verb. However, when *well* means "in good health" or "satisfactory," it is used as an adjective.

> Don't you think the band sounds **good?** (adjective)
>
> The lead guitarist plays **well.** (adverb)
>
> I'm glad I felt **well** enough to attend the concert.
>
> (adjective meaning "in good health")

You can learn more about using good *and* well *on pages 774–775.*

have, of Never substitute *of* for the verb *have*. When speaking, many people make a contraction of *have*. For example, they might say, "We should've gone." Because *'ve* sounds like *of*, *of* is often mistakenly substituted for *have* in writing.

> **Nonstandard**   Tell them they should **of** waited for us.
>
> **Standard**   Tell them they should **have** waited for us.

in, into Use *into* when you want to express motion from one place to another.

> The stained glass window **in** the cathedral is beautiful.
>
> Can you see it when you first walk **into** the vestibule?

its, it's *Its* is a possessive pronoun and means "belonging to it." *It's* is a contraction for "it is."

> To learn about **its** significance, we studied a unit on the flag.
>
> **It's** surprising how much we already knew about **its** history.

When You Write

A contraction, which **always** contains an apostrophe, stands for two words. When trying to decide correct usage between the possessive pronoun *its* and the contraction *it's* (it is), simply say *it is* in the sentence. The correct usage will immediately become obvious.

It's a symbol of freedom.

It is a symbol of freedom.

● *Connect to Writing:* Revising

Writing Negatives Correctly

Rewrite each sentence so that there are no double negatives.

1. Before the frontier days, almost no one never heard a tall tale.

2. Tall tales hadn't hardly been written at that time.

3. Of course, tall tales don't never tell a straight story.

4. In most tall tales, scarcely no one speaks without using dialect.

5. Naturally, not none of these stories is believed.

learn, teach *Learn* means "to gain knowledge." *Teach* means "to instruct."

I will **learn** how to play the piano this year.

Will you **teach** me how to play the piano after our last class is over?

You can learn more about using the verbs learn *and* teach *on pages 685–686.*

leave, let *Leave* means "to depart" or "to go away from." *Let* means "to allow" or "to permit."

Nonstandard	Will you **leave** me finish the dishes?
Standard	Will you **let** me finish the dishes?
Standard	I won't **leave** until you're through cleaning the kitchen.

You can learn more about using the verbs leave *and* let *on pages 687–688.*

lie, lay *Lie* means "to rest or recline." *Lie* is never followed by a direct object. Its principal parts are *lie, lying, lay,* and *lain. Lay* means "to put or set (something) down." *Lay* is usually followed by a direct object. Its principal parts are *lay, laying, laid,* and *laid.*

Lie	When I want to think quietly, I **lie** on the beach.
	I wish I were **lying** there today.
	Last week I **lay** near the pier.
	I have **lain** there peacefully many times.
Lay	**Lay** the books on the desk. (*Books* is the direct object.)
	Are you **laying** the books on the corner of your desk?
	When one student **laid** some books on the corner, they fell.
	I have carefully **laid** my books in the middle of my desk.

You can learn more about using problem verbs on pages 683–688.

passed, past *Passed* is the past tense of the verb *pass*. As a noun, *past* means "a time gone by." As an adjective, *past* means "just gone" or "elapsed." As a preposition, *past* means "beyond."

> The surveyors often **passed** this street.
>
> (*passed* as a verb)
>
> In the **past,** our property was surveyed only when Father decided to plant trees.
>
> (*past* as a noun)
>
> In the **past** two hours, they have walked **past** our house twice.
>
> (*past* as an adjective and then as a preposition)

rise, raise *Rise* means "to move upward" or "to get up." *Rise* is never followed by a direct object. Its principal parts are *rise, rising, rose,* and *risen. Raise* means "to lift (something) up," "to increase," or "to grow something." Raise is usually followed by a direct object. Its principal parts are *raise, raising, raised,* and *raised.*

> Mother always said that we should **rise** and shine in the morning.
>
> I would always **raise** the sheet over my head.
>
> (*Sheet* is the direct object.)

When You Write

To avoid confusion between these two verbs and their principal parts, notice that all principal parts of *raise* retain the same *a* spelling as the base word: raise, raising, raised, and raised. For the word *rise,* neither the base word nor any of its principal parts contain the letter *a.*

shall, will Formal English uses *shall* with first person pronouns and *will* with second and third person pronouns. Today *shall* and *will* are used interchangeably with *I* and *we,* except that *shall* is used with *I* and *we* for questions.

> **Shall** we have lunch together?
>
> Yes, Elizabeth **will** join us also.
>
> I **will** be fifteen minutes late.

sit, set *Sit* means "to rest in an upright position." *Sit* is never followed by a direct object. Its principal parts are *sit, sitting, sat,* and *sat*. *Set* means "to put or place (something)." *Set* is usually followed by a direct object. Its principal parts are *set, setting, set,* and *set*.

> I'll **set** the time for the luncheon. (*Time* is the direct object.)
>
> Please **sit** down and relax while waiting for the team to arrive. (no direct object)

suppose to, supposed to Be sure to add the *d* to *suppose* when it is followed by *to*.

> **Nonstandard**   We were **suppose to** clean this room yesterday.
>
> **Standard**   We were **supposed to** clean this room yesterday.

than, then *Than* is a subordinating conjunction and is used for comparisons. *Then* is an adverb and means "at that time" or "next." *Than* should not be used with *different*, which requires the word *from:* This sweater is *different from* my old one.

> **Nonstandard**   Did you meet the quarterback who is taller **then** the coach?
>
> **Standard**   After the coach acknowledged that Jim was taller **than** he was, the coach **then** introduced the other players.

that, which, who As relative pronouns, *that* refers to people, animals, or things; *which* refers to animals or things; and *who* refers to people.

> The books **that** I found in the attic were very old.
>
> The photo album, **which** was in the trunk, contained faded pictures.
>
> I thought it must have belonged to my aunt, **who** used to live with us.

Connect to Writing: Editing

Recognizing Correct Usage

Write each underlined word. If the word is used correctly, write **C** beside it. If the word is used incorrectly, write the correct form of the word.

Students <u>learn</u> that band practice often requires more practice <u>then</u> many sports. They sometimes <u>raise</u> early to attend rehearsals before school. Band performances, <u>who</u> are played on various wind and percussion instruments, are popular events. When the band director <u>raises</u> the baton, it <u>then</u> signals the start of the program. Before a marching performance, band members <u>that</u> have <u>passed</u> inspection experience relief. Many parents experience pride when the school band marches <u>passed</u> them in a parade. During a concert program, students must <u>sit</u> attentively and watch for the band director's cues, <u>which</u> <u>set</u> the music's tempo. Performances at elementary schools <u>shall</u> often help recruit future members.

their, there, they're *Their* is a possessive pronoun. *There* is usually an adverb, but sometimes it begins an inverted sentence. *They're* is a contraction for *they are*.

> Can we get **their** autographs?
>
> **There** is usually time before the game.
>
> **They're** in a hurry today because the bus was late.

theirs, there's *Theirs* is a possessive pronoun. *There's* is a contraction for *there is*.

> Our breakfast is delicious; I wonder if **theirs** is also.
>
> If **there's** time, I'll ask them before we leave.

them, those Never use *them* as a subject or a modifier.

Nonstandard	**Them** are the new neighbors. (subject)
Standard	**Those** are the new neighbors.
Nonstandard	Have you met **them** people? (adjective)
Standard	Have you met **those** people?

this here, that there Avoid using *here* or *there* in addition to *this* or *that*.

Nonstandard	I like **that there** frozen dessert.
Standard	I like **that** frozen dessert.

to, too, two *To* is a preposition. *To* also begins an infinitive. *Too* is an adverb that modifies a verb, an adjective, or another adverb. *Two* is a number.

> Is Daniel going **to** the backyard **to** jump on the trampoline?
> (preposition, infinitive)
>
> It's **too** late; only **two** can jump at one time.
> (adverb, number)
>
> He can participate **too** when one person gets down.
> (adverb)

use to, used to Be sure to add the *d* to *use* when it is followed by *to*.

> **Nonstandard**   When I was younger, I **use to** jump rope.
>
> **Standard**   When I was younger, I **used to** jump rope.

way, ways Do not substitute *ways* for *way* when referring to a distance.

> **Nonstandard**   She drove a long **ways** to buy groceries.
>
> **Standard**   She drove a long **way** to buy groceries.

where Do not substitute *where* for *that*.

> **Nonstandard**   Did you read *where* school starts earlier?
>
> **Standard**   Did you read *that* school starts earlier?

who, whom *Who,* a pronoun in the nominative case, is used as either a subject or a predicate nominative. *Whom,* a pronoun in the objective case, is used as a direct object, an indirect object, or an object of a preposition.

> **Who** gave you the new bicycle? (subject)
>
> From **whom** did your sister buy it? (object of a preposition)

whose, who's *Whose* is a possessive pronoun. *Who's* is a contraction for *who is*.

> **Whose** party are you going to attend?
>
> **Who's** going to take you home?

your, you're *Your* is a possessive pronoun. *You're* is a contraction for *you are*.

> **Your** idea is the best.
>
> We think **you're** going to win first place.

Connect to Writing: Composing Sentences

Using Pronouns

The words *who, whom, whose,* and *who's* can be confusing to use. Work with a partner to write original, creative sentences for each of these four pronouns. Discuss with one another why you are choosing this particular pronoun for each sentence. Then read your sentences aloud to one another. Offer ways to improve any sentence in which the pronoun is not used correctly.

Finding the Correct Word

Write the word in parentheses that correctly completes each sentence.

1. When (your, you're) in eighth grade, you might go on a special class trip.
2. Parents and students (who, whom) express interest are invited (to, too, two) an informational meeting.
3. At (this, this here) meeting, a video usually describes the trip.
4. Most class trips are designed (to, too, two) provide students with insight into a subject (their, there, they're) currently studying.
5. The nation's capital is one of (them, those) popular and relevant sites.
6. (Theirs, There's) usually a need for parent chaperones for the trip (to, too, two).
7. (Theirs, There's) is an important job because they assist students (who, whom) are traveling without family.
8. Some students are not (use to, used to) being a long (way, ways) from home.
9. Teachers usually give at least one or (to, too, two) assignments that connect the class trip to what the students are studying.
10. (Your, You're) assignment might range from answering specific questions to keeping a journal.
11. (Whose, Who's) interested in touring our nation's Capitol building?
12. (Theirs, There's) an interesting story concerning the completion of the dome.

● *Connect to Writing:* Revising

Recognizing Correct Usage

Write each underlined word. If the word is used correctly, write **C** beside it. If the word is used incorrectly, write the correct form of the word.

Many students are looking forward to <u>they're</u> trip to the nation's capital. Headphones, MP3 players, books, and games make the bus ride <u>there</u> enjoyable <u>too</u>. <u>Whose</u> going to room together and <u>who's</u> travel "buddy" you'll be are important. <u>Those</u> not from a large city will notice <u>where</u> the traffic in Washington is bad. <u>Theirs</u> a variety of tours available. <u>Your</u> sure to enjoy a dinner cruise on the Potomac River. On the walking tour in the National Mall, <u>your</u> guide will point out famous landmarks. <u>Too</u> important sites that you should not miss are the Smithsonian Institution and the National Gallery of Art. There are also many statues in the Hall of Presidents in <u>that there</u> Capitol building. Interesting facts will be revealed to you, for example from <u>who</u> the United States received the gift of cherry trees.

The spell check feature on your word processing or e-mail software can be very helpful. It can help you check your spelling as you compose or edit your writing. Be careful, however, because a spelling check will not edit your work. For example, spell check will not flag your writing if you incorrectly use *affect* when *effect* is the right choice. You can usually find the spelling feature in the Edit or the Tools menu of your software. You can also set most current programs to mark misspelled words as you type. Look in the Preferences menu to activate this feature.

✓ Check Point: Mixed Practice

Write the word in parentheses that correctly completes each sentence.

1. Many history lessons await students (who, whom) visit Washington, D.C.

2. The (amount, number) of information that (can, may) be learned is substantial.

3. Three of the most historic sites you (can, may) want to visit are located on the National Mall.

4. In 1848, workers (lay, laid) the cornerstone for Washington Monument, after the project (passed, past) government approval.

5. (Its, It's) in the shape of an obelisk, a design that (use to, used to) be prevalent in ancient Egypt.

6. From the top of (this, this here) monument, a view of the city (lays, lies) before you.

7. (Than, Then) you might visit the Jefferson Memorial, dedicated to the main author of the Declaration of Independence.

8. Built in the classic tradition, (its, it's) design is similar to that of Monticello, Jefferson's home.

9. A large statue of Jefferson and excerpts from his many writings are (in, into) the memorial.

10. (Nowhere, Nowheres) can you find a better view of the cherry trees in bloom.

● *Connect to Writing:* Writing a Narrative

Using Glossary Words

Read over the Writer's Glossary of Usage on pages 782-791, paying particular attention to items that give you trouble in your writing. Then write a short account of things you do or would like to do with a pet. Describe the setting and recreate the action. Try to use as many of the words you find troublesome as you can. Read your narrative to a friend.

Unit 6

Mechanics

When you write, you are a composer. You tell your readers how to "play" or "sing" your composition. When should they read quietly, and when should they belt it out? When should one clause flow into the next, and when should another end abruptly? When should your readers question, and when should they declare? Only the composer, the one who imagined and created the piece, can guide the way.

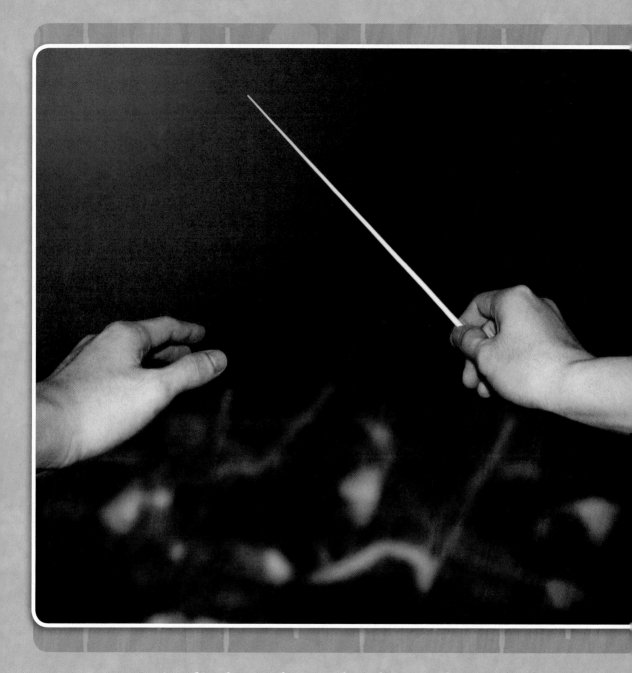

Punctuation herds words together, keeps others apart.
Punctuation directs you how to read, in the way musical
notation directs a musician how to play. —Lynne Truss

Capital Letters

David Hockney in front of one of his large landscapes

How can you use capital letters to clarify your writing?

Capital Letters: Pretest 1

The following first draft about the artist David Hockney contains several errors in capitalization. The first error has been corrected by putting three lines under the small *b* to indicate a capital *B* in the word *British*. Revise the rest of the draft so that capitalization is used correctly.

David Hockney is a noted british artist. He is a painter, a printer, a graphic designer, a photographer, and a Stage designer. Hockney began his career as a Pop artist, a painter of popular objects. Hockney's early paintings are said to have started the pop movement in England in the late 1950s. He began creating photographic collages and using photocopiers in his artworks in the 1980s. Recently, he has returned to his birthplace in northern england to paint landscapes of yorkshire. The painting above shows Hockney with one of these Vibrant paintings.

Capital Letters: Pretest 2

Directions

Read the passage and decide which underlined word should be capitalized. Write the letter of the correct answer.

(1) Mohandas Gandhi was an <u>important indian national and spiritual</u> leader. **(2)** Gandhi was <u>born to a hindu family in the year</u> 1869 and educated abroad. **(3)** <u>on his return to India, he worked on campaigns for workers' rights</u>. At the time, the **(4)** <u>country was controlled by the British government in a rule known as the "raj."</u> Gandhi joined the major **(5)** <u>political party, the Indian National congress.</u>

1. A Important
   B Indian
   C National
   D Spiritual

2. A Born
   B Hindu
   C Family
   D Year

3. A On
   B Campaigns
   C Workers'
   D Rights

4. A Country
   B Government
   C Rule
   D "Raj"

5. A Political
   B Party
   C The
   D Congress

Capital letters can be as important to writing as the words themselves. A capital letter clearly marks the beginning of a new idea. Correct capitalization is important in any writing you do, be it a sentence, a line of poetry, or an outline.

27 A   **Capitalize first words and the pronoun *I*.**

Sentences and Poetry

A capital letter always tells readers that a new sentence or a new line of poetry has begun.

27 A.1   Capitalize the first word of a sentence and the first word of a line of poetry.

Sentence	**T**here are about twenty-five species of apples.
Lines of Poetry	**O**f Jonathan Chapman **T**wo things are known, **T**hat he loved apples, **T**hat he walked alone.
	— *Stephen Vincent Benét,* "Johnny Appleseed"

Some modern poets purposely misuse capital letters or do not use any capitals at all in their poetry. When you quote such a poem, copy it exactly as the poet wrote it.

Parts of Letters

Certain parts of a letter stand out because they begin with a capital letter.

27 A.2   Capitalize the first word in the greeting of a letter and the first word in the closing of a letter.

GREETINGS AND CLOSINGS	
Greeting	**D**ear Mr. Chapman,
Closing	**S**incerely yours,

Outlines

Capital letters make parts of an outline stand out.

27 A.3   Capitalize the first word of each item in an outline and the letters that begin major subsections of the outline.

     I.   **A**pple production in the U. S.

    II.   **H**ow apple trees and apples are used

         A.   **F**oods and beverages prepared from apples

         B.   **T**he uses of apple wood

            1. **U**ses in manufacturing

            2. **U**se for smoking meats

         C.   **O**rnamental uses of trees

The Pronoun *I*

The pronoun *I* is always capitalized.

27 A.4   Capitalize the pronoun *I*, both alone and in contractions.

Alone   Yesterday **I** bought a pound of apples.

Contraction   Today **I**'m going to make a pie.

You can learn about using capital letters with direct quotations on pages 862–863.

● *Connect to Writing:* **Composing a Letter**

Using Capital Letters

Find a short poem you like. Write a letter to a friend, telling him or her why the poem appeals to you. Quote some lines from the poem to get your point across. Be sure that you correctly capitalize the word *I*, the greeting and closing of your letter, the first word in each sentence, and the first word in each line of the poem.

Capitalizing First Words and I

Write the words and letters that should be capitalized in each item below.

1. Poem

> red sky at morning,
> sailors take warning.
> red sky at night,
> sailors delight.

2. Outline

> I. weather lore
>> a. natural signs of weather changes
>>> 1. changes in animal behavior
>>> 2. environmental changes
>> b. superstitions about the weather

3. Letter

dear Anna,

> my uncle has been letting me help at the weather station, so i'm having a wonderful time. When I come home, i'll tell you all about it.

> your friend,

> Katy

Connect to Writing: Editing

Correcting Errors in Capitalization

Rewrite the following paragraph, adding capital letters where needed.

(1) there is no school today. **(2)** I wonder what i should do. **(3)** for several days i've been meaning to write to my grandparents. **(4)** I think i will do that. **(5)** sooner or later, though, i'll have to give the dog a bath. **(6)** there's also that new magazine i've been wanting to read. **(7)** oh, well. i think i will just sit down for a while and rest until i make up my mind.

Connect to Writing: Peer Consultation

Using Capitals in an Outline

With a partner, write an outline for a short skit you would like to perform. Talk about what you will include in the skit, and then work on the outline together. Use capital letters correctly when creating your outline.

Proper Nouns Lesson 2

A **proper noun** is the name of a particular person, place, thing, or idea. A proper noun begins with a capital letter.

COMMON AND PROPER NOUNS			
Common Nouns	boy	park	cat
Proper Nouns	Daniel Lopez	Big Bend National Park	Smoky

27 B Capitalize proper nouns and their abbreviations.

Study the following rules for capitalizing proper nouns. Then refer to them when you edit your writing.

Names of persons and animals should be capitalized. Also capitalize the initials that stand for people's names.

NAMES OF PERSONS AND ANIMALS	
Persons	Kayla, V. H. Tang, James R. Ricco, Jr.
Animals	Max, Ginger, Rocky, Miss Kitty

You can learn more about nouns on pages 488–493 and about punctuating people's titles on pages 824–825.

● **Practice Your Skills**

Capitalizing the Names of Persons and Animals

Write correctly each word that should be capitalized.

1. My real name is hee sook park, but my friends call me suki.

2. I have a dog named grumpy and a cat named sneezy.

3. My street was named after the explorer ferdinand magellan.

4. My best friend's full name is jacob joseph venturi.

5. He dreams of owning a horse called silver blaze.

6. I met my friend rachel berg at camp.

7. She wants to sing like judy garland, a well-known singer from long ago.

8. My friend taylor johnson lives next door.

Geographical names of particular places and bodies of waters are capitalized. Do not capitalize prepositions, articles, or the conjunction *and* in geographical names.

GEOGRAPHICAL NAMES	
Streets, Highways	Avery Road (**Rd.**), Ohio Turnpike (**Tpk.**), Route (**Rt.**) 128, Fifty-sixth Street (**St.**) (The second part of a hyphenated numbered street is not capitalized.)
Cities, States	Los Angeles, California (**CA**); Plano, Texas (**TX**)
Counties, Parishes	Medina County (**Co.**), Acadia Parish
Countries	United States of America (**U.S.A.**), Czech Republic, Egypt, Brazil
Continents	North America, Africa, Antarctica
World Regions	Western Hemisphere, Pacific Rim, North Pole
Islands	South Padre Island, Long Island
Mountains	Rocky Mountains, Mount (**Mt.**) Hood
Forests and Parks	Superior National Forest, Great Basin National Park
Bodies of Water	Po River, Lake Ontario, Pacific Ocean, Gulf of Mexico
Sections of the Country	the South, the West Coast, New England (Simple compass directions are not capitalized. *Go south on Main Street.*)

Words such as *Street, Lake, Ocean,* and *Mountain* are capitalized only when they are part of a proper noun.

> We live near **m**ountains, but they are small compared to the **R**ocky **M**ountains.

When You Write

In geography class you might say a sentence like this: "The Isthmus of Panama lies between the **A**tlantic **O**cean and the **P**acific **O**cean."

You can shorten the sentence by changing it to the following: "The Isthmus of Panama lies between the **A**tlantic and the **P**acific oceans."

In the second sentence the word *oceans* is not capitalized because it is no longer a part of a proper name. *Isthmus of Panama* is capitalized because it is a particular strip of land.

Practice Your Skills

Using Capital Letters in Geographical Names

Write *a* or *b* to indicate which item is correctly capitalized.

1. a. a park in Denver
b. a Park in Denver

2. a. Moosehead lake
b. Moosehead Lake

3. a. niagara falls
b. Niagara Falls

4. a. Indian ocean
b. Indian Ocean

5. a. the Frozen North
b. the frozen North

6. a. a store on Forty-fifth Street
b. a store on Forty-Fifth street

7. a. made in the u.s.a.
b. made in the U.S.A.

8. a. a port on lake Michigan
b. a port on Lake Michigan

Practice Your Skills

Capitalizing Proper Nouns and Their Abbreviations

Write correctly each word that should be capitalized.

(1) in 1812, robert stuart led settlers across the continental divide. **(2)** this group may have crossed near south pass, today known as an important gateway to the west. **(3)** a trapper's meeting place was established on the green river. **(4)** john coulter explored the area of wyoming that later became yellowstone national park. **(5)** esther hobart morris of tioga county, in new york, was another early settler in wyoming. **(6)** wyoming became a state in 1890. **(7)** mrs. nellie taylor ross became governor of wyoming in 1925. **(8)** she was the first female governor in the united states.

Connect to Writing: Editing

Correcting Proper Nouns and Their Abbreviations

Rewrite the following paragraph, adding capital letters where needed.

(1) The third-largest country in the world is china. **(2)** On the east, it is bounded by the yellow sea, the east china sea, and the west china sea. **(3)** All three are part of the pacific ocean. **(4)** Also to china's east lie japan, korea, and the philippine islands. **(5)** The himalaya mountains form a boundary between the qing zang plateau and the countries of nepal, india, and bangladesh. **(6)** The highest mountain in the himalayas, mt. everest, is actually on the nepal-tibet side of the border.

Nouns of historical importance should be capitalized. Capitalize the names of historical events, periods, and documents and their associated initials and acronyms.

HISTORIC NAMES	
Events	the French Revolution, the Battle of Hastings, World War II (**WWII**)
Periods of Time	the Victorian Era, the Space Age, the Dark Ages
Documents	the Declaration of Independence, the Articles of Confederation, the Mayflower Compact

Do not capitalize prepositions such as *of* in the names of events and documents.

Names of groups and businesses begin with capital letters. These include the names of organizations, businesses, institutions, teams, and government entities.

NAMES OF GROUPS	
Organizations	Little League, the National Organization for Women (**NOW**), American Medical Association (**AMA**)
Businesses	Casper's Market, F. Rosenberg & Company (Co.), the Westward Corporation (Corp.)
Institutions	Glover Memorial Hospital, Wayne Middle School, the University of California at Los Angeles (**UCLA**)
Teams	the Dallas Cowboys, the Bayside Tigers, the Minnesota Twins
Government Bodies and Agencies	the Senate, Congress, the Federal Trade Commission (**FTC**), the Supreme Court
Political Parties	Democratic Party, a Republican, a Democrat

Specific time periods and events begin with capital letters. Capitalize the days of the week, the months of the year, civil and religious holidays, and special events. Also capitalize the abbreviations used in giving dates and the time of day.

TIME PERIODS AND EVENTS	
Days, Months	Monday (Mon.), Tuesday (Tues.), February (Feb.), March (Mar.)
Holidays	Martin Luther King, Jr., Day, Presidents' Day, the Fourth of July
Special Events	the New York Marathon, the Festival of Roses
Time Abbreviations	A.D. 466, 100 B.C., 100 B.C.E., 6:30 AM or 6:30 a.m., 9:00 PM or 9:00 p.m.

Do not capitalize the seasons of the year unless they are part of a specific name.

> Each summer the library runs a special reading program.
>
> Here is a flyer about the library's Summer Festival of Books.

You can learn more about punctuating abbreviations on pages 824–826.

● Practice Your Skills

Using Capital Letters for Proper Names

Write correctly each word that should be capitalized. If a sentence is correct, write **C.**

1. The two houses of congress are the senate and the house of representatives.
2. Many cornell university graduates have served in the peace corps.
3. The smithsonian institution is our nation's most famous museum.
4. The boston tea party was one of the acts of rebellion that led to the american revolution.
5. The dallas cowboys defeated the buffalo bills by a score of 14–0.
6. The prosperous 1920s were known as the roaring twenties.

● Practice Your Skills

Using Capital Letters for Specific Time Periods and Events

Write *a* or *b* to indicate which item is correctly capitalized.

1. **a.** an Independence Day celebration
   b. an Independence Day Celebration
2. **a.** the last Saturday in August
   b. the last saturday in August
3. **a.** the New York world's fair of 1939
   b. the New York World's Fair of 1939
4. **a.** a mother's day surprise
   b. a Mother's Day surprise
5. **a.** a 9:00 am class
   b. a 9:00 AM class
6. **a.** the Rose Bowl parade
   b. the Rose Bowl Parade
7. **a.** in approximately 200 B.C.
   b. in approximately 200 b.c.
8. **a.** february 14, Valentine's day
   b. February 14, Valentine's Day

Practice Your Skills

Capitalizing Proper Names

Write correctly each word that should be capitalized.

1. A very ancient law code, the code of hammurabi, was created before 1750 b.c.
2. The gilded age was a period of gross materialism in the 1870s.
3. We celebrate labor day on the first monday in september.
4. Until 1953, armistice day was celebrated in november to commemorate the end of world war I.
5. In june, the red earth pow wow is held in oklahoma city.
6. The u.s. marine corps band played in a concert on presidents' day.
7. Our town holds its may day celebration every spring.
8. The emoryville environment club sent for information from the u.s. department of forestry.
9. The delicatessen on vine street is very busy just before each baseball game.
10. The redwing bicycle company sponsored a team called the rockets in last summer's little league games.

Connect to Writing: Editing

Correcting Sentences with Proper Nouns

Rewrite the following paragraph, adding capital letters where needed.

(1) The american civil war came to a weary end in the spring of 1865. (2) By march the confederates were outnumbered 2–1 by the union troops. (3) Then, on april 1, General sheridan's victory in the battle of five forks spurred ulysses s. grant to conquer petersburg and richmond. (4) The army of the potomac closed in on the confederates. (5) They were starving because the confederate commissary department could not get supplies through the union lines. (6) At 5:00 p.m. on april 7, grant sent robert e. lee a note. (7) The note asked him to surrender. (8) On april 9, lee and grant met and agreed upon the terms of surrender shortly before 4:00 p.m.

Connect to Speaking and Writing: Travel Magazine Article

Capitalizing Geographical Names

With your classmates, talk about the places listed on page 802. Have you visited any of them? Share information about a place on the list you have visited or one you would like to visit. Then collaborate on an illustrated travel magazine article that describes the features of this location. Finally, proofread your article to be sure that you have capitalized all the proper nouns.

Names of nationalities and ethnicities should be capitalized.

NATIONALITIES AND ETHNICITIES	
Nationalities	a Nigerian, a German, a Bulgarian, Chinese, Cuban, a Canadian
Ethnic Groups	Basque, Sherpa, Hmong, Cornish, Cree, Hispanic

Religions, religious references, and religious holidays and holy days begin with capital letters.

RELIGIOUS NAMES	
Religions	Catholicism, Buddhism, Judaism, Islam
Religious Holidays and Holy Days	Hanukkah, Christmas, Ramadan, Epiphany, Yom Kippur, Palm Sunday, St. Michael's Day
Religious References	God, the Almighty, the Old Testament, the Talmud, the Koran, the Vedas

The word *god* is not capitalized when it refers to polytheistic gods. Their proper names, however, are capitalized.

The Greek god who gave fire to mortals was Prometheus.

● **Practice Your Skills**

Using Capital Letters Correctly

Write correctly each word that should be capitalized.

1. On ash wednesday, christians begin the period called lent.

2. They prepare for easter.

3. On the day called qing ming, the chinese visit cemeteries.

4. Some buddhists make pilgrimages to honor the buddha during magha puja.

5. In the city of caracas, the children of venezuela roller-skate to the daily "christmas carol mass" between december 16 and 24.

6. On the jewish holiday purim, a family member reads aloud the book of esther.

7. The muslims celebrate awwal muharram.

8. This is the day that the religion of islam began.

Names of planets, moons, stars, and constellations are capitalized. Do not capitalize the words *sun* and *moon.*

ASTRONOMICAL NAMES	
Planets and Moons	Mercury, Uranus, Neptune, Ganymede
Stars	the North Star, Sirus, Canopus
Constellations	Big Dipper, Orion, Ursa Major

Do not capitalize *earth* if *the* comes before it.

Capital	Is Venus larger or smaller than **E**arth?
No Capital	Six billion people live on *the* **e**arth.

Languages and specific school courses followed by a number are capitalized.

LANGUAGES AND SCHOOL COURSES	
Languages	English, Turkish, Russian, Spanish, French
Computer Languages	Java, Cobal, Visual Basic
Numbered Courses	Art II, Algebra I, Biology II

Course names such as *history, math, science,* and *physical education* are not capitalized.

Other proper nouns should also begin with capital letters.

OTHER PROPER NOUNS	
Awards	Nobel Peace Prize, World Cup, Grammy Award
Brand Names	Ultrasheen shampoo, Sunrise orange juice, Roadrunner vans (The product itself—such as *shampoo, orange juice,* and *vans*—is not capitalized.)
Bridges, Buildings	Brooklyn Bridge, Empire State Building, World Trade Center, Windsor Castle
Monuments, Memorials	Gateway Arch, Pearl Harbor Memorial, Washington Monument
Technological Terms	the Internet, the Web, World Wide Web, Web page,
Vehicles	the *Queen Mary, Apollo V, Air Force One*

● **Practice Your Skills**

Capitalizing Proper Nouns

Write *a* or *b* to indicate the sentence in each pair that is correctly written.

1. a. In our Astronomy class, we will take a field trip to the yerkes observatory.

   b. In our astronomy class, we will take a field trip to the Yerkes Observatory.

2. a. One of the apollo spacecraft carried the first men to walk on the Moon.

   b. One of the Apollo spacecraft carried the first men to walk on the moon.

3. a. I could see the planet Venus through my new Star Gazer telescope.

   b. I could see the Planet Venus through my new Star Gazer Telescope.

4. a. The Voyager spacecraft was the first to photograph Jupiter's moon Europa.

   b. The Voyager Spacecraft was the first to photograph Jupiter's Moon Europa.

5. a. In science class we learned about Nobel Prize-winning physicists.

   b. In Science Class we learned about Nobel Prize-winning physicists.

● **Practice Your Skills**

Using Capital Letters

Write the following items, using capital letters where needed.

1. the classroom for geometry 1

2. the planet neptune

3. the golden gate bridge

4. the flight of the *spirit of st. louis*

5. the pulitzer prize

✓ *Check Point:* **Mixed Practice**

Write each word that should begin with a capital letter. Then answer as many of the questions as you can.

1. who wrote the declaration of independence?

2. who wins the stanley cup, a football team or a hockey team?

3. who was the first person to fly solo across the atlantic ocean?

4. who won the first world series, new york or boston?

5. which country launched sputnik I, the world's first artificial satellite?

6. who was the first american to orbit the earth, john glenn or alan shepard?

There are other uses for capital letters

27 C   **Some proper adjectives and the titles of artworks and certain people are capitalized.**

➤ Proper Adjectives

Like proper nouns, almost all proper adjectives begin with a capital letter.

27 C.1   Capitalize most proper adjectives.

PROPER NOUNS AND ADJECTIVES

Proper Noun	Proper Adjective
Asia	Asian art
Canada	Canadian provinces
Rome	Roman baths
Copernicus	Copernican theory
South America	South American rivers
Florida	Florida oranges

A cookbook may refer to both *French food* and *french fries*. Some words or phrases from proper nouns become so common that they are written entirely in lowercase letters.

SOME ADJECTIVES NO LONGER CAPITALIZED

Proper Noun	Adjective
Brussels	brussels sprouts
Dutch	dutch oven
India	india ink
Manila	manila envelope
Venice	venetian blinds

When you use words like these, check a dictionary to see whether you should use a capital letter or not.

Capitalizing Proper Adjectives

Write *a* or *b* to indicate which item is correctly capitalized. You may use a dictionary.

1. a. new england seafood
   b. New England seafood

2. a. an australian movie
   b. an Australian movie

3. a. victorian literature
   b. Victorian literature

4. a. Italian scientists
   b. italian scientists

5. a. American History
   b. American history

6. a. congressional committee
   b. Congressional committee

7. a. British seaports
   b. british seaports

8. a. a french restaurant
   b. a French restaurant

● *Connect to Writing:* **Editing**

Correcting Sentences with Proper Adjectives

Rewrite each sentence, adding capital letters where needed.

1. what replaced the julian calendar?
2. who was the last hawaiian royal ruler?
3. what is the british term for elevator?
4. why isn't basque a true spanish language?
5. what bodies of water lie off the vietnamese coast?

CHAPTER 27

➤ Titles

Capital letters are used in the titles of people, written works, and other works of art.

27 C.2   Capitalize the titles of people and works of art.

Titles Used with Names of Persons

Capitalize a title showing office, rank, or profession when it comes before a person's name. The same title is usually not capitalized when it follows a name.

Before a Name   That woman is **C**olonel Hanks.

After a Name   When was Ann promoted to **c**olonel?

Titles Used in Direct Address

A noun of **direct address** is used to call someone by name. Capitalize a title used alone, instead of a name, in direct address.

> **Direct Address**   What is your opinion, **P**rofessor?
>
>   What, **S**enator, do you think about a possible tax increase?

You can learn more about commas with titles used in direct address on pages 838–839.

Titles Showing Family Relationships

Capitalize titles showing family relationships when the titles come before people's names, and when they are used instead of names or in direct address.

> **Before a Name**   Is **U**ncle David staying for dinner?
>
> **As a Name**   Yesterday **M**om helped with my homework.
>
> **Direct Address**   Thanks for the ride, **D**ad.

When a possessive noun or pronoun comes before a title showing a family relationship, do not capitalize the title—unless it is considered part of the person's name.

> **No Capital**   *My* aunt is talking to *Linda's* uncle.
>
> **Capital**   Is *your* **A**unt Harriet from Arizona visiting?

You can learn about the use of possessive nouns with apostrophes on pages 878–880 and about the use of possessive pronouns on pages 881–882.

● Practice Your Skills

Capitalizing Titles Used with Names of People

Write correctly each word that should be capitalized.

1. have you seen the governor of our state on television?

2. i think, sis, that we should visit the capital.

3. can carmen's mother arrange a tour for us, mom?

4. she knows the representative from hidalgo county.

5. let's ask dad if we can go.

6. last fall grandma solano invited us to austin.

Correcting Titles Used with Names of People

Rewrite the following story, adding capital letters where needed.

> **(1)** Tyler asked, "Is there something special we can do for grandma's birthday, dad?"
> **(2)** In no time, mom, dad, my brother, and I were planning a surprise party.
> **(3)** Fortunately, aunt elena brought the food, and my uncle joe supervised the barbecue.
> **(4)** Altogether, it was a wonderful party. **(5)** Grandma was especially surprised to see uncle tony. **(6)** He had flown in from chicago.

Titles of Written Works and Other Works of Art

Capitalize the first word, the last word, and all important words in the titles of books, newspapers, magazines, stories, poems, movies, plays, musical compositions, and other works of art. Do not capitalize a short preposition, a coordinating conjunction, or an article unless it is the first or last word in a title.

Books and Chapter Titles	I am reading the chapter "**P**eople and **L**and" in our textbook *The Geography of the World.*
Short Stories	Have you read Arthur Conan Doyle's story "**T**he **H**ound of the **B**askervilles"?
Poems	Edgar Allan Poe wrote a poem called "**T**o **M**y **M**other."
Magazines and Magazine Articles	He found the facts in an article called "**A**re **C**ats **S**mart?" in *Discover* magazine.
Newspapers and Newspaper Articles	My sister wrote "**N**ew **D**igs for **D**inosaur **B**ones" for the *Valley Banner.* (The word *the* is not usually capitalized before the title of a newspaper. One exception is *The New York Times.*)
Television Series	She tapes the *Wild World* programs to watch later.
Musical Compositions	Have you heard **B**eethoven's **F**ifth **S**ymphony?
Movies	Most people are surprised by the ending of *Citizen Kane.*

You can learn about the punctuation of titles on pages 854–859.

Practice Your Skills

Capitalizing Titles of Things

Write **C** if an item is correctly capitalized. Write *I* if it is incorrectly capitalized.

1. a newspaper named *The Oakland Daily times*

2. a newspaper article entitled "It's a dog's life"

3. Thurber's short story "The Night the Ghost Got In"

4. the Western song "home on the range"

5. Shakespeare's play *the Taming of the Shrew*

6. Shelley's poem "Ode to the west wind"

7. Debussy's composition *sonata for piano and cello*

8. a book called *The ABC's of the Human Body*

9. the TV series *the adventures of sherlock holmes*

10. the movie *Back to the Future*

Connect to Writing: Creating a List

Using Capital Letters

Imagine that you are going to stay at the South Pole for several months. You can take along books, videos, music CDs, and magazines to entertain yourself. Using what you have read about how to capitalize titles, list ten of these items that you would take with you.

Check Point: Mixed Practice

Write correctly each word that should be capitalized. Then answer as many of the questions as you can.

1. what were lewis and clark sent to explore, the mississippi river or the louisiana territory?

2. was the famous painter picasso french or spanish?

3. what is the name of the author of *dr. jekyll and mr. hyde,* mark twain or robert louis stevenson?

4. what time is it in los angeles when it is 1:00 p.m. in new york city?

5. what is the name of dorothy's dog in the movie *the wizard of oz,* toto or lassie?

Assess Your Learning

▦ Using Capital Letters

Write each word that should begin with a capital letter.

1. saturn has twenty moons, but earth has only one.

2. the supertanker *seawise giant* can carry a total load of over 560,000 tons.

3. do your mom and dad subscribe to the *tribune?*

4. the aardvark, an african mammal, eats termites.

5. the month of july was named after julius caesar.

6. does haver's hardware store rent clark tools, uncle ed?

7. the united states air force academy is located in colorado springs.

8. tasmania, a small island, is south of australia.

9. the song "happy birthday to you" was written by two sisters in 1936.

10. the red sea separates egypt from saudi arabia.

▦ Using Capital Letters

Write each word that should begin with a capital letter.

1. if all the world's ice melted, cities such as london and paris would be underwater.

2. is your brother taking algebra II or geometry?

3. medieval knights were specially trained soldiers.

4. uncle george and aunt martha live in the south.

5. the temperature on venus is hotter than it is on mercury, the planet closest to the sun.

6. i memorized "casey at the bat," a poem by ernest l. thayer.

■ Editing for Proper Capitalization

Write each word that should begin with a capital letter. Do not include words that are already capitalized.

(1) Early in the morning of monday, april 15, 1912, the *titanic,* a great ocean liner, struck an iceberg and sank off the coast of newfoundland. **(2)** The ship was on a voyage from england to new york city.

(3) In 1985, the ship was discovered on the floor of the atlantic ocean. **(4)** Finding the ship had been a joint effort of the united states and france. **(5)** Using sonar, a french research ship scanned the ocean bottom. **(6)** When the wreck was found, scientists from the woods hole oceanographic institute in massachussetts sent down a submersible underwater sled named *argo.* **(7)** Attached to the sled were lights and television cameras. **(8)** After seventy-three years, the great ship had been found in its resting place.

■ Writing Sentences

At the library or media center, find and write a one-sentence fact about each of the following topics. Each fact should include a proper noun, a proper adjective, or a title.

1. geography
2. government official
3. the presidency
4. astronomy
5. national business
6. brand name
7. holidays
8. social studies
9. space exploration
10. languages

Capital Letters: Posttest

Directions

Read the passage and decide which underlined word should be capitalized. Write the letter of the correct answer.

The space shuttle **(1)** columbia has flown several missions and been piloted by several commanders. Other **(2)** female astronauts include Valentina Tereshkova, who orbited earth in a capsule in 1963. Sally Ride, who blasted off in the **(3)** year 1983, was the first american woman in space. However, Air Force **(4)** lieutenant Colonel Eileen Collins was our first female space shuttle pilot. As a girl, Collins loved Star **(5)** trek and other science fiction, but it was reading about famous women aviators that led her to get her license to fly.

1. A Columbia
   B Missions
   C Piloted
   D Commanders

2. A Female
   B Astronauts
   C Earth
   D Capsule

3. A Year
   B American
   C Woman
   D Space

4. A Lieutenant
   B Space
   C Shuttle
   D Pilot

5. A Trek
   B Science Fiction
   C Aviators
   D License

Writer's Corner

Snapshot

27 A Capitalize first words and the pronoun *I*. (pages 798–800)

27 B Capitalize proper nouns and their abbreviations. (pages 801–809)

27 C Some proper adjectives and the titles of certain artworks and people are capitalized. (pages 810–814)

Power Rules

 Every statement that begins with a capital letter should be a **complete sentence**, not a sentence fragment. (pages 656–661)

Before Editing	After Editing
The weather today. Is lovely.	The weather today is lovely.
The baby cries. When the dog barks.	The baby cries when the dog barks.

Check for **run-on sentences** and separate them by capitalizing the first word of the second sentence or adding a conjunction and/or punctuation. (pages 81 and 663)

Fused Sentence

He rides his bike his dog Charley sits in the basket.

After Editing

He rides his bike, *and* his dog Charley sits in the basket.

He rides his bike. His dog Charley sits in the basket.

Comma Splices

It began to rain, we went inside.

She baked a pie, it was delicious.

After Editing

It began to rain, *so* we went inside.

She baked a pie. *It* was delicious.

She baked a pie, *and* it was delicious.

Editing Checklist ✓

Use this checklist when editing your writing.

- ✓ Did I capitalize the first words in all my sentences? (See page 798.)
- ✓ Did I capitalize the pronoun *I* everywhere it appears? (See pages 799–800.)
- ✓ Did I capitalize proper nouns and abbreviations? (See pages 801–809.)
- ✓ Did I capitalize all proper adjectives, titles of people, and titles of works of art? (See pages 810–814.)

Use the Power

Think about the rules for capitalizing that you learned in this chapter. Then decide which letter should be part of the words in the passage below. If you are not sure how to answer, go back and check in the previous pages.

(D/d)ear (M/m)rs. (R/r)edding,

(T/t)hank you very much for the lovely scarf. (I/i) know that it will keep me very warm this (W/w)inter. The colors remind (M/m)e of the painting <u>(W/w)ater (L/l)ilies</u> by the (F/f)rench painter (C/c)laude (M/m)onet.

(I/i)t means so much to me that (Y/y)ou knitted it yourself with me in mind.

(S/s)incerely,

(D/d)oreen

Now write a letter to a friend or relative who has done something nice for you. Be sure to use capital letters correctly.

End Marks and Commas

How can you create meaning through the careful use of end marks and commas?

End Marks and Commas: Pretest 1

The following draft paragraph about the artist Elizabeth Catlett has errors in end marks and commas. The first error is corrected. Revise the draft to correct all remaining errors.

Elizabeth Catlett is widely known for her sculpture and graphic art, which often depicts her African American heritage. Born in Washington D.C. Catlett began her art training at Howard University and continued at the University of Iowa There, Grant Wood encouraged her work in sculpture. She moved to Mexico in the 1940s and she eventually became a Mexican citizen. In 1958, Catlett became the first female professor of art at the National Autonomous University of Mexico. Her art reflects the influence of Mexican murals pre-Columbian sculpture, and African art. Catlett uses hard wood to create sculpture that looks soft and perhaps even warm She achieves a sense of dignity and emotion in her work through the coalescence of her medium her artistic impulse and her humanity

Directions

Read the passage. Write the letter of the best way to write each underlined part. If the underlined part contains no error, write *D*.

(1) On February 12 1908 a difficult automobile race was in progress. Six cars left New York for Paris in a route that included the United States, Japan, Russia, Poland, **(2)** Germany and part of France Met by **(3)** blizzards and other dangers the **(4)** racers nevertheless kept on. The German entry reached Paris five months **(5)** later, and the American entry **(6)** followed Although the German car **(7)** came in first, it was given a penalty. As a **(8)** result of this decision the American car won. The **(9)** car a Thomas Flyer had gone 13,400 miles in 168 days. What a race that **(10)** was

1. A On February 12, 1908,
  B On February 12 1908,
  C On February 12, 1908
  D No error

2. A Germany, and, part of France.
  B Germany and, part of France.
  C Germany, and part of France.
  D No error

3. A blizzards, and other dangers,
  B blizzards, and other dangers
  C blizzards and other dangers,
  D No error

4. A racers, nevertheless, kept
  B racers nevertheless, kept
  C racers, nevertheless kept
  D No error

5. A later and the
  B later and, the
  C later, and, the
  D No error

6. A followed, Although
  B followed. Although
  C followed. Although,
  D No error

7. A came in, first, it was
  B came in first it was
  C came in, first it was
  D No error

8. A result, of this decision,
  B result, of this decision
  C result of this decision,
  D No error

9. A car, a Thomas Flyer,
  B car a Thomas Flyer,
  C car, a Thomas Flyer
  D No error

10. A was!
  B was.
  C was?
  D No error

28 A An **end mark** is a mark of punctuation at the end of a sentence. You may recall that the purpose of a sentence determines its end mark.

28 A.1 Place a **period** after a statement, after an opinion, and after a command or request made in a normal tone of voice.

Periods

I want to be a forest ranger. (statement)

The wilderness is peaceful. (opinion)

Sign up for the career workshop. (command)

28 A.2 Place a **question mark** after a sentence that asks a question.

Question Mark Would you like to work outdoors?

28 A.3 Place an **exclamation point** after a sentence that expresses strong feeling or after a command or request that expresses great excitement.

Exclamation Points

The fire is spreading through the woods!

Listen to that roar!

You can learn more about kinds of sentences on pages 477–478. You can learn about using end marks with direct quotations on pages 864–867.

● **Practice Your Skills**

Using End Marks

Write the correct end mark for each sentence.

1. Should we take the train or the bus to Rock Island

2. I think trains are more comfortable than buses

3. The bus, however, is faster

4. Where do I buy a ticket

5. Go over to that booth

6. The line has twenty-five people in it

7. We'll miss the train

8. Don't panic

CHAPTER 28

Adding End Marks to Sentences

Rewrite the following paragraphs, adding the correct end marks where needed.

(1) Do you think electric cars are a new development **(2)** Think again **(3)** The first practical electric cars were on the roads by the late 1880s **(4)** By 1917, more than eleven million people per year in the United States were traveling by electric cars **(5)** Does this fact puzzle you **(6)** If it does, you're probably thinking along the wrong lines **(7)** You're thinking of electric automobiles **(8)** The electric cars of the past were actually streetcars, or trolleys

(9) Trolleys can run only on tracks **(10)** They are powered by electricity **(11)** Where does the power come from **(12)** The trolleys are connected to overhead lines that conduct electricity **(13)** Unfortunately, their need to run on tracks limits their use **(14)** That's why inventors are trying to perfect electric automobiles **(15)** These cars don't pollute the environment, and they can be run on electricity generated from water, solar power, and wind power **(16)** Perhaps in a few decades, you won't have to step on the gas to start a car **(17)** You'll just switch on the power

CHAPTER 28

● *Connect to Speaking, Listening, and Writing:* **Peer Interaction**

Speaking with Inflections

Play an inflection game with a partner. You use inflection when you change the pitch or loudness of your voice. Both of you write three or four sentences, such as "This is fantastic" or "Are you ready to go." Say each sentence in one of three ways: as a statement with no inflection, as a question with inflection at the end, and as an exclamation with excitement in your voice. Your partner must write the sentence using the correct end mark and then read it aloud.

Other Uses of Periods  Lesson 2

28 B   Periods are also used in abbreviations and outlines.

➤ Periods with Abbreviations

Abbreviations are handy shortcuts when you are writing messages or taking notes in class. Most abbreviations should not be used in formal writing such as letters or reports.

28 B.1   Use a period with most abbreviations.

Below is a list of common abbreviations. For the spelling and the punctuation of other abbreviations, look in a dictionary. Most dictionaries have a special section that lists abbreviations.

COMMON ABBREVIATIONS	
Days	Sun. Mon. Tues. Wed. Thurs. Fri. Sat.
Months	Jan. Feb. Mar. Apr. Aug. Sept. Oct. Nov. Dec. (May, June, and July should not be abbreviated.)
Addresses	Ave. Blvd. Dr. Hwy. Pl. Rd. Rt. St. Apt.
Titles with Names	Mr. Mrs. Ms. Dr. Rev. Gen. Sgt. Lt. Jr. Sr. Pres.
Initials for Names	R. L. Rosen Kenneth A. Brevik L. Elizabeth Page
Times with Numbers	6:45 a.m. OR 6:45 AM (*ante meridiem*—before noon) 9:00 p.m. OR 9:00 PM (*post meridiem*—after noon) (A colon (:) goes between the hour and the minutes when time is written in numbers.) 200 B.C. (before Christ) OR 200 B.C.E. (before the Common Era) A.D. 900 (*anno Domini*—in the year of the Lord) OR 900 C.E. (Common Era)
Companies	Assoc. Co. Corp. Dept. Inc. Ltd.

CHAPTER 28

Most abbreviations that stand for the full names of organizations do not include periods. Always check a dictionary if you are not sure whether an abbreviation needs periods.

ABBREVIATIONS WITHOUT PERIODS

UN = United Nations	CD = compact disc
CIA = Central Intelligence Agency	ATM = automated teller machine
IQ = Intelligence Quotient	FAX = facsimile
km = kilometer	l = liter

The post office's two-letter state abbreviations do not include periods. A list of these abbreviations usually can be found in the front of a telephone book. Here are a few examples.

STATE ABBREVIATIONS

AL = Alabama	MD = Maryland	OH = Ohio
AK = Alaska	NV = Nevada	TX = Texas
HI = Hawaii	NY = New York	UT = Utah

When You Write

When a sentence ends with an abbreviation ending in a period, use only one period. It serves as both the period for the abbreviation and the end mark for the sentence.

The man in the brown suit is Michael Alvarez, Jr.

Periods with Outlines

28 B.2   Use a period after each number or letter that shows a division in an outline.

I. Routes to Oregon in the early 1800s
   A. Oregon Trail blazed in 1812 by fur traders
      1. Steamship from St. Louis to Independence
      2. Covered wagons to plains and Rockies
   B. The journey around Cape Horn
II. New routes to California

Writing Abbreviations

Write the correct abbreviation in parentheses for each item.

1. Monday (Mon. *or* Mon)

2. September (Septr. *or* Sept.)

3. centimeter (cm *or* cm.)

4. Mister (Mr *or* Mr.)

5. quart (qt. *or* qt)

6. post meridiem (pm *or* p.m.)

7. Route (Rt. *or* Rt)

8. United Nations (UN *or* U.N.)

9. before the Common Era (bce *or* B.C.E.)

10. Michigan (MI. *or* MI)

● *Connect to Writing:* **Editing**

Using Periods

Rewrite the following items, adding periods where needed.

1. Fri, Sept 8, 2000

2. Abrams and Patel, Inc

3. Rev R J Wong

4. a new CD by P J Smith

5. Ms Elizabeth C Boxer

6. Sun, July 17, at Moore Corp

7. Dr Lee T Silveira, Jr

8. AD 250

● *Connect to Writing:* **Friendly E-mail**

Using Abbreviations

Write an informal e-mail to a friend that you are planning to visit. Tell your friend when you will be arriving and what you would like to do during your visit. Use as many abbreviations as you can, such as for dates, times, addresses, initials, and so on.

Commas That Separate

Commas are punctuation marks that are used to keep similar items from running into each other and to prevent misunderstanding by the reader.

28 C One function of commas is to separate elements in a sentence.

➤ Items in a Series

A **series** is three or more similar words or groups of words listed one after another. Commas are used to separate the items in a series.

28 C.1 Use commas to separate items in a series.

Words	We saw crabs, pelicans, and sandpipers. (nouns)
	Their new sailboat is lean, sleek, and swift. (adjectives)
	We found seashells, starfish, and seaweed. (compound words)
Groups of Words	We will pack a lunch, walk to the dunes, and look for shells. (complete predicates)
	Paul is either on the beach, in the bait shop, or on his way to the pier. (prepositional phrases)

If a conjunction such as *and* or *or* connects all the items in a series, no commas are needed.

Swimming and boating and hiking are fun beach activities.

When You Write

When you list three or more items in a series, use the same part of speech or parallel structure for each of the items. This is called *parallelism*.

Not Parallel	My aunt is a talented violinist, a generous friend, and good at cooking.
Parallel	My aunt is a talented violinist, a generous friend, and a good cook.

Look back at two recent compositions, and check to be sure you have used parallel construction in your writing.

Using Commas in a Series

Write *a* or *b* to indicate the sentence in each pair that is correctly punctuated.

1. a. Cape Hatteras Cape Lookout Assateague Island, and Cape Cod are the names of four national seashores on the East coast.

   b. Cape Hatteras, Cape Lookout, Assateague Island, and Cape Cod are the names of four national seashores on the East coast.

2. a. Waves wash over the beach, pick up sand, and drag it back into the sea.

   b. Waves wash over the beach, pick up sand, and, drag it back into the sea.

3. a. The driftwood was dry smooth and silvery.

   b. The driftwood was dry, smooth, and silvery.

4. a. Look for rocks or worn pebbles or sand dunes.

   b. Look for rocks, or worn pebbles, or sand dunes.

5. a. Scrubby plants grow near the dunes, next to the seawall, and, up the cliff.

   b. Scrubby plants grow near the dunes, next to the seawall, and up the cliff.

● *Connect to Writing:* **Editing**

Using Commas in a Series

Rewrite the following sentences, adding commas where needed. If a sentence is correctly punctuated, write **C**.

1. A sandpiper scurries along the beach probes the wet sand and pulls out a mole crab.

2. The strange body of the mole crab is smooth shiny and pale.

3. What lives in tide pools under rocks and in the sand?

4. You might see a ghost shrimp or an oliveshell snail or a razor clam in the sand.

5. Earwigs and flies and mole crickets hide under wood.

6. The highest monthly tide rises up past the rockweed zone past the barnacle zone and up to the periwinkle zone.

7. A barnacle may fall prey to a starfish a marine worm or a carnivorous snail.

8. Sea hares swim to the shore browse on the seaweed and lay stringy eggs.

9. A beadlet anemone may be green red or amber.

10. Starfish eat little mollusks and shore worms and brittle stars.

Adjectives Before a Noun

You have just learned that commas are needed between three or more adjectives in a series. If you have only two adjectives before a noun, however, you may or may not need a comma.

A comma is needed between two adjectives if it is replacing the word *and* between the two adjectives.

> I read new, unusual facts about Juana Briones de Miranda.
>
> (The facts were new *and* unusual.)

28 C.2   Use a comma sometimes to separate two adjectives that precede a noun and are not joined by a conjunction.

Sometimes a comma is not needed between two adjectives. To decide if a comma is needed, read the sentence with the word *and* between the two adjectives. If the sentence makes sense, use a comma. If it sounds awkward, do not.

> **Comma Needed**   She was a strong, remarkable woman.
> (*A strong and remarkable woman* reads well.)
>
> **Comma Not Needed**   She was a strong pioneer woman. (Since *a strong and pioneer woman* sounds awkward, no comma is used.)

Usually, no comma is used after a number or after an adjective that refers to size, shape, or age.

ADJECTIVE EXPRESSIONS	
six e-mail messages	a young black cat

● Practice Your Skills

Using Commas with Adjectives

Write *a* or *b* to indicate the sentence in each pair that is correctly punctuated.

1. a. Juana's parents were brave Spanish colonists.
    b. Juana's parents were brave, Spanish colonists.

2. a. They lived in a small unimportant town.
    b. They lived in a small, unimportant town.

3. a. Today this town is the large urban city of San Francisco.
    b. Today this town is the large, urban city of San Francisco.

4. a. Juana married a young rash soldier.
    b. Juana married a young, rash soldier.

● *Connect to Writing:* **Editing**

Using Commas with Adjectives

Write the following sentences, adding commas where needed. If a sentence is correct, write **C.**

1. Juana Briones bought a vast fertile rancho south of San Francisco.
2. She was a clever practical businesswoman.
3. She held onto her land through two dramatic changes in government.
4. This was an unusual resourceful accomplishment.
5. Juana was also a sincere kind woman.
6. She raised five orphaned children.
7. She was also an unselfish fearless nurse.
8. She took care of her community during a deadly smallpox epidemic.
9. A memorial to her stands in a small popular park in San Francisco.

☑ *Check Point:* **Mixed Practice**

Rewrite the following sentences, adding commas where needed.

1. The most valuable animals in the Old West were small dependable burros.
2. They plodded steadily across deserts over mountains and through creeks.
3. They could survive long journeys in which food water and rest were scarce.
4. The ranchers miners and soldiers all praised burros.
5. Is the burro the strongest bravest domestic animal?
6. Burros have soft trustful eyes.
7. However, a burro will fight a wild stallion a bull or even a grizzly bear.
8. They quickly recognize danger dodge it fast and keep their heads.
9. A threatened burro will halt turn around and kick.
10. A burro's hooves are hard sharp and very dangerous.

● *Connect to Speaking, Listening, and Writing:* **Cultural History**

Using Commas that Separate

Talk to a partner about your family history and culture. Then interview an older family member, friend, or neighbor who has struggled through hard times. Record this person's remarks, if possible. Write a paragraph to share with your classmates. Describe the person and what he or she accomplished. Use commas to separate items in a series and to separate adjectives before a noun. Try to use quotations also.

830 End Marks and Commas

Compound Sentences

A comma and a conjunction often separate the independent clauses in a compound sentence. *And, but, or, nor,* and *yet* are commonly used conjunctions.

28 C.3   Use a comma to separate the independent clauses of a compound sentence if the clauses are joined by a conjunction.

In the following examples, notice that the comma comes before the conjunction.

> Many animals are plant eaters, and a few plants are animal eaters.
>
> Most soils nourish plants, but the soil in bogs may lack nitrogen.

Keep in mind the difference between a compound sentence and a simple sentence that has a compound verb.

> **Compound Sentence**   Bog plants attract insects, and the insects provide necessary nutrients. (A comma is needed because there are two sets of subjects and verbs.)
>
> **Compound Verb**   Bog plants attract insects and get nutrients from them. (No comma is needed with a compound verb.)

Using a comma and a conjunction together is one way to correct a run-on sentence.

> **Run-on Sentence**   Carnivorous plants can survive without insects, they grow better with insects in their diet.
>
> **Corrected Compound Sentence**   Carnivorous plants can survive without insects, **but** they grow better with insects in their diet.

You can learn more about compound sentences on pages 642–646 and 887–888. You can learn about other ways to correct run-on sentences on page 663.

● **Practice Your Skills**

Using Commas with Compound Sentences

Write **C** if a sentence is punctuated correctly. Write **I** if a sentence is punctuated incorrectly. Remember that a compound sentence needs a comma, but a compound verb does not.

1. The cobra lily is the best-known carnivorous plant in the United States and it is found in California and Oregon.
2. It is also known as the California pitcher plant and its scientific name is *Darlington californica*.
3. It has a hooded head and looks like a colorful speckled snake.
4. The roof of its hood is called a *dome* and its forked tongue is called a *fishtail*.
5. The dome has windows and these let in light.
6. Insects are attracted by the light and do not realize it is a trap.
7. The pitcher and tongue produce nectar and attract many different insects.
8. Insects fly inside the pitcher and then are unable to escape.
9. They may fly up toward the light but then they slip down into the pitcher.
10. The water at the bottom dampens their wings and they are unable to fly out.

● *Connect to Writing:* **Editing**

Punctuating Compound Sentences

Rewrite each incorrect sentence from the preceding exercise, adding commas where needed.

➤ Introductory Structures

A comma follows certain words and groups of words at the beginning of a sentence.

28 C.4   Use a comma after certain introductory structures.

A comma sometimes separates an interjection from the rest of a sentence. Words such as *no, now, oh, well, why,* and *yes* can be used as interjections.

| **Words** | **Yes,** I really do enjoy hiking. |
| | **Well,** my last hike was a real disaster! |

An interjection can also be followed by an exclamation point.

Interjection   **Oh!** I almost forgot my compass.

A comma follows two or more prepositional phrases that come at the beginning of a sentence. A comma also follows one introductory prepositional phrase that has four or more words.

Prepositional   **With a map in my pocket,** I started out.
Phrases   (two prepositional phrases)

                     Inside the dense forest, the trail forked in two directions.
                     (one prepositional phrase with four words)

You can learn more about prepositional phrases on pages 547–548.

A comma follows a participial phrase that comes at the beginning of a sentence.

Participial   **Looking at my map,** I could not find this fork.
Phrases   **Bubbling and murmuring,** the stream rushed down
                   the hillside.

You can learn more about participial phrases on pages 606–611.

A comma follows an infinitive phrase that comes at the beginning of a sentence.

Infinitive   **To make up my mind,** I decided to flip a coin.
Phrases   **To take me to my destination,** the trail had to cross
                  the stream.

You can learn more about infinitive phrases on pages 615–618.

A comma follows an adverbial clause when it comes at the beginning of a sentence.

Adverbial   **If I chose the right fork,** I'd be at the ranger station in
Clauses   an hour.
                 When I set out on my journey, the sun was in the east.

You can learn more about adverbial clauses on pages 632–634.

● **Practice Your Skills**

Identifying Introductory Structures

Identify and write the word or words that serve as the introductory element in each sentence. Be prepared to tell where you would insert a comma.

1. Looking back on my hike I didn't make too many mistakes.

2. For my last birthday my family had given me sturdy hiking boots.

3. To prepare for my hike I had packed a map and compass.

4. To protect me from sudden storms a garbage bag went into my pack.

5. Well maybe it was a mistake to go hiking alone.

6. If I had hiked with Emily she might have kept us on the right path.

7. During the previous year our hiking group had taken that route only twice.

8. Between the two of us we might have figured out our location.

9. Seeing a stream that deep Emily would not have tried to cross it.

10. When I slipped on the stones my pack fell off.

● *Connect to Writing:* **Editing**

Using Commas with Introductory Structures

Rewrite each sentence, adding commas where needed.

1. As soon as my pack fell into the stream I jumped in after it.

2. Rapidly rushing down the mountain the stream carried my knapsack away.

3. Oh what a disaster it was to lose my compass and map of the terrain!

4. Preparing us for this situation our hike leader had given us good advice.

5. To find your way back to civilization follow a stream downhill.

6. Squishing along in wet boots I followed the stream.

7. After I had hiked for an hour the ground became soft and mushy.

8. No I did not try to cross the bog.

9. At the end of the day two rangers found me.

10. Boy was I glad I'd checked in with them before I started out!

Commonly Used Commas

You will use some commas more often than others. On the following pages are some examples of the most common uses of commas.

With Dates and Addresses

Commas are commonly used between the parts of a date or an address.

28 C.5   Use commas to separate elements in dates and addresses.

In the following examples, notice that when a date or an address comes within a sentence, another comma is used at the end to separate it from the rest of the sentence.

Dates	On Tuesday, December 7, 1999, our voyage began. (No comma is used between the month and the day, but a comma is used after the year to separate the date from the rest of the sentence.)
	We arrived home in January 2001. (No comma is used between the month and the year if no day is given.)
Addresses	Write to us in care of Anna Melon, 791 Reata Lane, Arizona City, Arizona 85223, until March 4. (No comma is used between the state and the ZIP Code, but a comma is used after the ZIP code to separate the address from the rest of the sentence.)
	We live at 18 Elgin Street **in** Boston, Massachusetts. (A preposition can take the place of a comma between parts of an address.)

In Letters

Commas are commonly used after parts of a letter.

28 C.6   Use a comma after the salutation of a friendly letter and after the closing of all letters.

OPENINGS AND CLOSINGS		
Openings	Dear Aunt Chris,	Dear Dad,
Closings	Yours truly,	Sincerely yours,

● **Practice Your Skills**

Using Commas That Separate

Write *a* or *b* to indicate the sentence in each pair that is correctly punctuated.

1. a. On May 1, 1884, construction was begun in Chicago, Illinois, on the first American skyscraper.

   b. On May 1 1884, construction was begun in Chicago, Illinois on the first American skyscraper.

2. a. The National Baseball Hall of Fame and Museum is at 25 Main Street, Cooperstown, NY 13326.

   b. The National Baseball Hall of Fame and Museum is at 25 Main Street, Cooperstown, NY, 13326.

3. a. In December 1886, Josephine Cochrane of Shelbyville, Illinois, patented a dishwasher.

   b. In December 1886, Josephine Cochrane of Shelbyville, Illinois patented a dishwasher.

4. a. On March 10 1876, Alexander Graham Bell's home at 5 Exeter Place Boston, Massachusetts was the site of the first successful phone call.

   b. On March 10, 1876, Alexander Graham Bell's home at 5 Exeter Place, Boston, Massachusetts, was the site of the first successful phone call.

5. a. Dear Lily,

    We stayed at this park. I can't wait to tell you about it.

                      Your friend,

                      Amanda

   b. Dear Lily.

    We stayed at this park. I can't wait to tell you about it.

                      Your friend.

                      Amanda

● *Connect to Writing:* **Invitation**

Using Commas That Separate

Imagine that your family is going to have a special celebration. You are allowed to invite one friend to this special family party. Write an invitation to your friend, describing the celebration. Give your friend details about the location and date of the party. When you have finished, check to make sure that you have used commas correctly.

Connect to Writing: Editing

Using Commas That Separate

Rewrite each sentence, adding commas where needed.

1. San Francisco's famous cable cars were first put into service on August 1 1893.
2. In 1872 the first mail-order house was established at 825 North Clark Street Chicago Illinois.
3. On December 25 1777 Captain Cook landed on Christmas Island.
4. Before August 1 1958 a first-class stamp cost only three cents.
5. On May 30 1793 the first daily newspaper in America was published in Philadelphia Pennsylvania.
6. President George Washington went to Philadelphia Pennsylvania on April 22 1793 to visit the first American circus.
7. On December 11 1882 the Bijou Theater at 545 Washington Street in Boston Massachusetts became the first theater with electric lights.
8. In October 1797 the first parachute jump was made from a hot-air balloon over Paris France.
9. The first hotel elevator was installed on August 23 1859 in the Fifth Avenue Hotel in New York City.
10. You can write to 123 North Center Street Mount Olive North Carolina 28365 to find out about the North Carolina Pickle Festival.

Check Point: Mixed Practice

Rewrite each sentence, adding commas where needed.

(1) While I was researching skateboards I found an interesting old newspaper story. (2) In the June 29 1999 edition of the *Mercury* there was an article on skateboarding. (3) Some scientists in San Francisco California filmed skateboarders in action. (4) As they studied the film they noticed some rules of science at work. (5) To be a good skater you have to follow safety rules. (6) Yes skateboarding is not only a sport but a science. (7) When you balance on a skateboard there are three forces at work. (8) The weight of the rider is one force and gravity is another. (9) Pushing up against the skateboard the ground also acts as a force. (10) According to the laws of physics these three forces must balance out to zero. (11) When one force changes the others must also be adjusted. (12) If they want to jump high skaters have to be going fast. (13) Before they roll onto a ramp the skaters crouch. (14) At the beginning of a ramp the skaters rise suddenly. (15) The action is called *pumping* and it increases the skaters' speed.

When you read a sentence aloud, you naturally pause before and after an interrupting expression. Commas are placed where these pauses would occur. If you remove an interrupter from a sentence, the sentence will still make sense.

28 D   Commas are used to enclose words that interrupt the main idea of a sentence.

➤ Direct Address

In conversation people are often addressed by name. This kind of interrupter is called a **noun of direct address**. Since nouns of direct address interrupt the flow of a sentence, they should be set off by commas.

28 D.1   Use commas to set off **nouns of direct address**.

> The community picnic, **Brian,** will start at 11:00 A.M.
> (The noun of direct address, *Brian*, could be removed.)
>
> Please help me, **Dana and James,** pack the car.
> (More than one noun can be included in direct address. *Dana and James* could be removed.)
>
> Close the door, **kids,** behind us.
> (Direct address might include a noun that is not a proper noun.)

In the following examples, only one comma is needed because the noun of direct address comes at the beginning or at the end of the sentence.

> **Mom,** where is our ice chest?
>
> May we borrow your canvas chairs, **Mrs. Anders?**

● Practice Your Skills

Using Commas with Direct Address

Write the word or words that should be set off by a comma or commas.

1. Tell me Reverend Dixon where to find the grill.

2. Let me give you a hand with the cooler Brandon.

3. Wait Isaac and I'll give you some plates to carry.

4. Do you need help moving the tables Mrs. Aylard?

5. Yes Tyler I can use your help.

6. Mr. Mott is here Dad and is looking for you.

7. The food Giselle should be put out on the tables.

8. Tell Mom Matt that we brought more hamburgers.

9. No Spot get your nose out of that basket!

10. Hey Jenna catch that dog!

● *Connect to Writing:* **Editing**

Using Commas with Direct Address

Rewrite each sentence, adding commas where needed.

1. Please Mrs. Hernandez may I have another helping?

2. Surely Ryan you aren't going to eat all that.

3. Well Lonnie you ate at least three hot dogs.

4. Excuse me sir but have you seen a little boy with red hair?

5. Oh Angelica your brother is with your mom.

● *Connect to Writing, Speaking, and Listening:* **Peer Review**

Reading Dialogue Aloud

To understand and use what you've learned about direct address, try this idea: Write a scene containing dialogue between two people. Read your dialogue to a partner. As you read, say the punctuation marks aloud. For example, "Well [comma] Cynthia [comma] you've really done it this time [exclamation point]." The listener must catch any errors and help the author rewrite the dialogue.

Parenthetical Expressions

One type of interrupter is called a **parenthetical expression**. The following parenthetical expressions should be enclosed in commas.

COMMON PARENTHETICAL EXPRESSIONS			
after all	for instance	I hope (know)	of course
at any rate	generally speaking	in fact	on the contrary
by the way	however	in my opinion	on the other hand
consequently	I believe	moreover	to tell the truth
for example	I guess	nevertheless	

Use commas to set off **parenthetical expressions.**

> Soccer **,** in fact **,** is preferred to baseball in many countries.
>
> (*In fact* could be removed without affecting the meaning of the sentence.)

In the following examples, only one comma is needed because the parenthetical expression comes at the beginning or at the end of the sentence.

> **In my opinion,** soccer is more fun than baseball.
>
> Soccer is a much more active game **,** **at any rate.**

When You Write

When the words *I believe, I hope,* or *I think* appear at the beginning of a sentence, they are never parenthetical. In a sentence that begins with *I, I* is always the subject or part of the subject. Note the difference between these two sentences.

> I hope John will come tomorrow.
>
> John will come tomorrow **,** **I hope.**

In the second sentence, the subject is *John* and the main idea is that John is coming. *I hope* is only an afterthought.

Look over a recent composition and be sure you have used commas with all parenthetical phrases.

● Practice Your Skills

Using Commas with Parenthetical Expressions

Write *I* if a parenthetical expression is incorrectly punctuated. Write **C** if it is correctly punctuated.

1. To tell the truth, the Masters Golf Tournament isn't very interesting to me.

2. Golf, I suspect is more fun for the player than the spectator.

3. Golf requires considerable skill of course.

4. This sport after all, requires the ability to aim very accurately.

5. Without a doubt, players must know exactly how to strike a ball.

6. Tennis matches on the other hand, fascinate me.

7. Consequently I prefer to watch a Davis Cup match.

Using Commas with Parenthetical Expressions

Rewrite the incorrect sentences from the preceding exercise, adding commas where needed.

➤ Appositives

An **appositive** is a word or group of words that identifies or adds identifying information to a preceding noun or pronoun in a sentence. Usually an appositive comes immediately after that noun or pronoun and is written with modifiers. Because they interrupt the sentence, appositives should be set off by commas.

28 D.3   Use commas to set off most **appositives** and their modifiers.

Texas**,** **my home state,** has an interesting history.

(The appositive, *my home state*, could be removed.)

In the following example, only one comma is needed because the appositive comes at the end of the sentence.

La Salle established Fort St. Louis**,** **the first French settlement here.**

Commas are *not* used if an appositive identifies a person or thing by clarifying, or naming, which one or ones are meant.

A street has been named after the explorer **La Salle.**

You can learn more about appositives on pages 592–594.

● *Connect to Writing:* **Description**

Using Commas with Parenthetical Expressions

In the Practice Your Skills on the previous page, the writer expresses the opinion that golf is more fun for the player than the spectator. Think of an activity or sport that, for you, is more fun to do than to watch. Describe the activity and how it bores you to watch it, while at the same time, it excites you to actually participate in it. Use phrases, clauses, and appositives in your description, employing commas where needed.

Classifying Appositives

Identify the appositive in each sentence. Then tell if it is necessary or unnecessary.

1. The Caddo, a Native American group, lived in East Texas.
2. They were the leaders of the Caddo Confederacy, a group that included the Wichita and Waco nations.
3. Cabeza de Vaca, a Spanish explorer, was shipwrecked on the Texas coast in 1528.
4. His companion Estevanico was probably the first African American seen by Native Americans.
5. In 1689, Mexican explorer Alonso de Leon found Ft. St. Louis abandoned.
6. A city grew up around San Antonio Mission, one of many missions established in the early 1700s.
7. Spain's claim to Texas was surrendered to the newly independent nation Mexico.
8. Stephen Austin, spokesman for three hundred families, received permission to settle in Texas.
9. In 1821, the families began settling in a region near the Brazos, a river in northern Texas.

● *Connect to Writing:* **Editing**

Using Commas with Appositives

Rewrite each sentence, adding commas where needed. If a sentence is correct, write **C**.

1. Mexico's dictator Santa Anna forbade further colonization.
2. In 1835, Anglo-American Texans captured San Antonio a Mexican stronghold.
3. Members of the Convention of 1836 a revolutionary group signed the Texas Declaration of Independence.
4. Texas was declared an independent republic on March 2, 1836 Sam Houston's birthday.
5. Mexican forces recaptured San Antonio in the Battle of the Alamo one of the best-known events in Texas history.
6. Commander-in-Chief Sam Houston defeated the Mexican army and captured Santa Anna in 1836.

7. In 1845 James Knox Polk the president of the United States signed a law making Texas our twenty-eighth state.

8. The Rio Grande a river that flows into the Gulf of Mexico was established as the Mexico-Texas boundary in 1846.

9. Confederacy supporters mostly colonists from the South caused Texas to secede during the Civil War.

10. Republican Edmund Davis became governor in 1870 and Texas was readmitted to the Union.

✔ Check Point: Mixed Practice

Rewrite the following paragraphs, adding commas where needed.

(1) Noise can be harmful to your health. **(2)** In fact loud sounds can cause earaches and persistent noise can give some people headaches. **(3)** Worst of all however it can cause hearing loss in some people.

(4) Measured in units called decibels noise can be monitored. **(5)** A classroom discussion one type of ordinary conversation hovers around 60 decibels. **(6)** Popular music however can reach 110–120 decibels. **(7)** Any noise over 70 decibels by the way can be dangerous.

(8) For more information about noise write to the Noise Center of the League for the Hard of Hearing at 71 West 23rd Street New York New York 10010-4162.

➤ Nonrestrictive Elements

Like parenthetical expressions, entire phrases and clauses can interrupt a sentence. These phrases and clauses are called **nonrestrictive** or **nonessential**.

A **nonrestrictive** or **nonessential** phrase or clause can be removed from a sentence, and the sentence would still make complete sense. A comma goes before and after a nonrestrictive phrase or clause to show that the phrase could be removed.

28 D.4   Use commas to set off nonrestrictive participial phrases and clauses.

A participial phrase is nonessential if it provides extra, unnecessary information.

Nonrestrictive Participial Phrase	Outdoor games**,** **played in most cultures,** are enjoyed by old and young alike.

If the nonrestrictive participial phrase were dropped, the main idea of the sentence would not be changed.

> Outdoor games are enjoyed by old and young alike.

You can learn more about participial phrases on pages 606–611.

Likewise, an adjectival clause is nonrestrictive if it provides extra, unnecessary information.

> **Nonrestrictive Adjectival Clause**   Tug-of-war**,** **which is played in many cultures,** can be a team sport or a two-player contest.

If the nonrestrictive adjectival clause were dropped, the basic meaning of the sentence would not be changed.

> Tug-of-war can be a team sport or a two-player contest.

You can learn more about adjectival clauses on pages 635–638.

A participial phrase or an adjectival clause is sometimes essential, or restrictive. If a restrictive phrase or clause were dropped, the meaning of the sentence would be incomplete. **Restrictive phrases and clauses** usually identify a person, place, or thing and answer the question *Which one?* When a phrase or clause is essential, no commas are used.

> **Restrictive Participial Phrase**   Games **played in the ancient world** were often taken seriously. (Without the phrase, the sentence would read *Games were often taken seriously.* The reader would not know which games.)
>
> **Restrictive Adjectival Clauses**   Adults in ancient cultures participated in sports **that developed necessary skills.** (Without the clause, the sentence would read *Adults in ancient cultures participated in sports.* The reader would not know which sports are meant.)
>
> Ancient hunters enjoyed games **that developed marksmanship.** (Without the clause, the sentence would read *Ancient hunters enjoyed games.* The reader would not know which games are meant.)

Identifying Restrictive and Nonrestrictive Elements

Write **R** if the underlined words in a sentence are restrictive or **N** if they are nonrestrictive. Be prepared to explain your answer.

(1) People <u>living in today's world</u> seldom recognize the value of board games. (2) *Chaturanga,* <u>developed in seventh-century India,</u> taught players to think ahead. (3) A great leader <u>who commanded armies</u> had to be able to anticipate the future. (4) This complex game, <u>renamed *chess* by the Europeans,</u> was very popular in medieval times. (5) The Europeans substituted the word *king* for the word *shah,* <u>which was used by the Persians for their ruler.</u> (6) The word *checkmate* comes from *shat-mat,* <u>which means "the shah is helpless."</u> (7) A similar battle-tactics game is *Go,* <u>brought to Japan from China.</u> (8) Until A.D. 1600, students <u>studying in military schools</u> were required to play *Go.* (9) The game *Wari,* <u>which also goes by other names,</u> is a game of strategy in Africa. (10) Each player tries to capture the stones <u>that sit in the other player's compartments.</u>

● Practice Your Skills

Classifying Nonrestrictive Elements

Write **N** if a sentence has a nonrestrictive element that needs a comma or commas. Write **C** if a sentence is correct.

1. Nine Men's Morris little known in the United States is one of the oldest games in the world.
2. Archeologists have found a Nine Men's Morris board that was used in Egypt in 1400 B.C.
3. Each player gets nine men which look like checkers.
4. Checkers was created from backgammon pieces and the board used for chess.
5. Polish checkers which is one of many variations is played on a board of one hundred squares.
6. Few people have heard of the game of *halma* which gets its name from the Greek word for *jump.*
7. A new variation of it was developed in 1880 in Sweden where it became very popular.
8. People who play the game in the United States call it *Chinese checkers.*
9. From England comes the hunt game *Fox and Geese* which was a favorite of Queen Victoria.
10. The fox which gets the first turn in the game has only one game piece.

● **Connect to Writing:** **Editing**

Using Commas with Nonrestrictive Elements

Rewrite the incorrect sentences from the preceding exercise, adding commas where needed.

✔ **Check Point:** **Mixed Practice**

Rewrite the following paragraphs, adding commas where needed.

(1) I can walk to the Westside Pool which is quite near my home. **(2)** Consequently my friend Scott and I go there often in the summer. **(3)** Whitney and Ryan bicycling over from their own homes often meet us there.

(4) As far as we're concerned the best time to get there is 9:00 A.M. **(5)** The pool which gets very crowded by noon is almost empty in the morning. **(6)** Little children aren't there because they must be brought by their parents who have errands to do in the morning. **(7)** The lifeguard a friend of Ryan's sister lets us play games that aren't allowed in a crowded pool. **(8)** We don't have to worry about splashing or running into other swimmers.

(9, 10) For example we have made up our own form of water polo which is played with two people on each side. **(11)** Our ball borrowed from my little sister is a soft beach ball. **(12)** What is most fun about our game in my opinion is changing the rules. **(13)** Our most important rule which never changes is that the team who scores a goal gets to make up one new rule.

● **Connect to Writing:** **Directions**

Using Commas That Enclose

Your class is putting together a book of games for middle school students. Write brief directions for a board game that you enjoy or for an imaginary board game. Be sure to include answers to the following questions.

• How do the pieces move?

• What is the goal of the game?

• What strategies can players use to win?

As you write the directions, try to include some essential and nonessential elements. When you have finished, check to make sure that you have used commas correctly.

Assess Your Learning

Using End Marks and Commas Correctly

Write each sentence, adding end marks and commas where needed.

1. The fascinating famous magician Houdini was born in Wisconsin
2. Queens workers and drones are three classes of bees.
3. On the calendar several dates were circled but I didn't know why.
4. To begin the game on time the players will have to be here soon
5. Before Columbus traveled to the Americas tomatoes and corn were unknown in Europe
6. On August 1 1918 the Pirates and the Braves played twenty scoreless innings.
7. The first cold spell of course killed our plants
8. Does Mark collect editions of the novel *Robin Hood*
9. Watch out Pam for those rocks
10. Mars which is the fourth planet from the sun is much smaller than Earth.

Using End Marks and Commas Correctly

Write each sentence, adding end marks and commas where needed. If a sentence does not need any changes, write **C.**

1. A star of course shines for millions of years
2. To finish her test quickly Amanda wrote less neatly than usual.
3. On the beach at Atlantic City we found unusual shells
4. My brother Sam pitches for the varsity team.
5. *Black Beauty* is about a horse and is set in England.
6. Air contains three gases: oxygen nitrogen and argon.
7. Write to Pride and Sons 4290 Peach Tree Pkwy Atlanta GA 30341 for a free catalog.
8. Philadelphia Benjamin Franklin's birthplace is one of the country's major convention centers.
9. Standing on the stage the mayor read the short startling proclamation.
10. Did Liz bring the eggs milk cheese and English muffins

Using Commas

Write sentences that follow the directions below.

Write a sentence that . . .

1. includes a series of nouns.
2. includes two adjectives before a noun.
3. has two independent clauses joined by a coordinating conjunction.
4. includes a participial phrase at the beginning.
5. includes an adverbial clause at the beginning.
6. includes direct address.
7. includes a parenthetical expression.
8. includes an appositive.
9. includes a nonrestrictive adjectival clause.
10. includes a street number and name, city, state, and ZIP code.

End Marks and Commas: Posttest

Directions

Read the passage. Write the letter of the best way to write each underlined part. If the underlined part contains no error, write **D**.

Albert Einstein, a **(1)** <u>world-famous mathematician</u> was born in Bavaria in 1879. He acquired Swiss nationality **(2)** <u>in 1901 and</u> he began working at the Swiss patent office the next year. Einstein **(3)** <u>was however also</u> publishing papers in physics. He became famous for his theories of **(4)** <u>relativity and won</u> the 1921 Nobel Prize for physics. To educate others about his **(5)** <u>theories Einstein</u> held some teaching positions. These positions were in **(6)** <u>Switzerland Prague</u> and Germany. After Hitler's rise to **(7)** <u>power Einstein</u> came to the United States. He lectured at Princeton University in **(8)** <u>Princeton NJ</u> This **(9)** <u>brilliant creative</u> man became a U.S. citizen in 1940. He is my **(10)** <u>hero</u>

CHAPTER 28

1. **A** world-famous, mathematician
   B world-famous, mathematician,
   C world-famous mathematician,
   D No error

2. **A** in 1901 and,
   B in 1901, and
   C in 1901, and,
   D No error

3. **A** was, however, also
   B was however, also
   C was, however also
   D No error

4. **A** relativity, and won
   B relativity and, won
   C relativity, and, won
   D No error

5. **A** theories, Einstein
   B theories, Einstein,
   C theories Einstein,
   D No error

6. **A** Switzerland, Prague,
   B Switzerland Prague,
   C Switzerland, Prague
   D No error

7. **A** power Einstein,
   B power, Einstein,
   C power, Einstein
   D No error

8. **A** Princeton N.J.
   B Princeton, NJ.
   C Princeton, NJ
   D No error

9. **A** brilliant, creative
   B brilliant, creative,
   C brilliant creative,
   D No error

10. **A** hero?
    B hero!
    C hero,
    D No error

End Marks and Commas: Posttest **849**

Writer's Corner

Snapshot

28 A   **End marks,** including **periods, question marks,** and **exclamation points**, signal the end of a sentence. (pages 822–823)

28 B   **Periods** are also used in **abbreviations** and **outlines.** (pages 824–826)

28 C   One function of **commas** is to **separate elements** in a sentence. (pages 827–837)

28 D   **Commas** are also used to **enclose words that interrupt** the main idea of a sentence. (pages 838–846)

Power Rules

 Be sure that your sentences are complete and not **sentence fragments.** (pages 656–661)

Before Editing	**After Editing**
When we travel. We carry many suitcases.	When we travel, we carry many suitcases.
There are many buildings. On the left.	There are many buildings on the left.

 Check that **fused sentences** and **comma splices** are joined with a coordinating conjunction and/or proper punctuation. (pages 81 and 663)

Before Editing	**After Editing**
The tree grows leaves the flowers bloom.	The tree grows leaves, *and* the flowers bloom
It started snowing, I put on my hat.	It started snowing, *so* I put on my hat.
	It started snowing. I put on my hat.

Editing Checklist

Use this checklist when editing your writing.

✓ Did I include the correct end marks at the end of each of my sentences? (See pages 822–823.)
✓ Did I use periods at the end of the abbreviations? (See pages 824–825.)
✓ Did I use commas to separate items in a series? (See pages 827–828.)
✓ Did I use commas between adjectives when necessary? (See pages 829–830.)
✓ Did I make sure to use commas to set off parenthetical expressions, appositives and their modifiers, and nonessential participial phrases and clauses? (See pages 839–846.)

Use the Power

Choose one of the marks of punctuation to go in each blank in the sentences below.

Period **.**
Exclamation Point **!**
Question Mark **?**
Comma **,**

I'm so excited ____ I will be going to space camp next summer ____ Have you ever heard of space camp ____ I will live like a real astronaut ____ eating the same food and doing the same exercises ____ You should apply to space camp too ____ Wouldn't it be great to go together ____

Write a paragraph or two about something you would like to do this summer. Be sure to use the correct end marks and commas where needed.

CHAPTER 29

Italics and Quotation Marks

How can you use italics and quotation marks to communicate clearly and expertly?

Italics and Quotation Marks: Pretest 1

The following first draft about political cartoons contains errors in the use of italics and quotation marks. The first error has been corrected. Revise the draft so that no errors in italics or quotation marks remain.

The humorist Will Rogers once said, "I don't make jokes. I just watch the government and report the facts. Like Will Rogers, editorial cartoonists throughout history have reported on political goings-on from a humorous perspective. Newspapers like The New York Times and the Boston Globe have published editorial cartoons featuring politicians from city mayors to commanders in chief. The cartoon above, from 1865, is titled The Rail Splitter Repairing the Union." In the cartoon, Andrew Johnson warns, Take it quietly, Uncle Abe, and I will draw it closer than ever. Abraham Lincoln replies, "A few more stitches, Andy, and the good old Union will be mended.

Italics and Quotation Marks: Pretest 2

Directions

Read the passage and choose the best way to write each underlined part. Write the letter of the correct answer. If the underlined part contains no error, write *D*.

Jo **(1)** said I learned crickets are like **(2)** grasshoppers." **(3)** Well, I always thought," said **(4)** Jamal that crickets and grasshoppers were the same." **(5)** No she replied but they are related. I looked up **(6)** cricket and *grasshopper* in **(7)** "Encyclopedia Britannica." "Are there different kinds of crickets?" **(8)** Jamal asked Jo **(9)** replied there are four main types of crickets." **(10)** Yes he agreed "I think I heard that."

1. A said, "I
   B said. "I
   C said, I
   D No error

2. A grasshoppers".
   B grasshoppers.
   C grasshoppers,"
   D No error

3. A *Well,*
   B "Well,"
   C "Well,
   D No error

4. A Jamal, "That
   B Jamal, "that
   C Jamal "that
   D No error

5. A "No," she replied, "but
   B "No," she replied, "But
   C "No" she replied, "but
   D No error

6. A cricket and
   B *"cricket"* and
   C *cricket* and
   D No error

7. A Encyclopedia "Britannica."
   B *Encyclopedia Britannica."*
   C "Encyclopedia Britannica".
   D No error

8. A Jamal asked.
   B Jamal asked?
   C Jamal asked."
   D No error

9. A replied "There
   B replied, "There
   C replied, "there
   D No error

10. A "Yes," he agreed,
    B "Yes" he agreed,
    C Yes, "he agreed,"
    D No error

Italics (Underlining)

A special kind of slanted print called *italics* is used when certain titles, letters, numbers, and words appear in a book. *Italics is the print used in this sentence.* When writing longhand, you should substitute underlining wherever italics are needed. When you use a computer, highlight the words you want to italicize. Then use the command for italics.

Italics	Have you ever read the book *Dragonwings* by Laurence Yep?
Underlining	Have you ever read the book Dragonwings by Laurence Yep?

29 A   **Italics (underlining) are used to set off titles and certain numbers, words, and letters.**

Certain letters, numbers, words, and titles should be italicized or underlined.

29 A.1   Italicize (or underline) letters, numbers, and words when they are used to represent themselves.

Letters	His *I*'s look like *L*'s. I got all *B*s on my report card.
Numbers	Does your telephone number have a *3* in it?
Words	The word *paint* can be a noun, adjective, or verb.

In the first example, notice that only the *I* and the *L* are underlined (or italicized), not the apostrophe or the *s*.

You can learn about the use of apostrophes on pages 878–886.

29 A.2   Italicize (underline) the titles of long written or musical works that are published as a single unit. Also italicize (underline) the titles of paintings and sculptures and the names of vehicles.

Italicize separately published works that include books, magazines, newspapers, full-length plays, movies, and very long poems. Long musical works include operas, symphonies, ballets, and album or CD titles. Names of vehicles include the proper names of airplanes, ships, trains, and spacecraft. The titles of radio and television series are also italicized (or underlined).

Books	After I have finished reading *Robinson Crusoe*, I'm going to read *Hatchet*.
Magazines	I used *National Geographic* magazine for my research.

Newspapers	The <u>Chicago Tribune</u> is delivered to our house every day. (The word *the* is not considered part of the title of a newspaper or magazine except in the case of *The New York Times*.)
Plays, Movies	In 1999, *Titanic* won the Academy Award for the best picture. *Cats* is one of the longest-running Broadway musicals.
TV Series	One of the longest-running TV series is <u>60 Minutes</u>.
Works of Art	Edward Hopper painted *Railroad Sunset*.
Names of Vehicles	An Agatha Christie mystery is set on the <u>Orient Express</u>. (The word *the* is not considered part of the title of a vehicle.)

You can learn about the capitalization of titles on pages 811–814.

● **Practice Your Skills**

Using Italics (Underlining)

Write *a* or *b* to indicate the item in each pair that is correctly underlined. In newspapers and magazines, the word *the* is not usually part of the title.

1. a. the <u>Greek</u> word chron
   b. the Greek word <u>chron</u>

2. a. the painting <u>Washington Crossing</u> the <u>Delaware</u>
   b. the painting <u>Washington Crossing the Delaware</u>

3. a. the newspaper the <u>Miami Herald</u>
   b. the newspaper the Miami <u>Herald</u>

4. a. the film <u>The Bridge on the River Kwai</u>
   b. the film The <u>Bridge on the River Kwai</u>

5. a. the word <u>happiness</u>
   b. the <u>word</u> happiness

6. a. the number <u>2</u>
   b. the <u>number</u> 2

7. a. <u>Good Housekeeping</u> magazine
   b. <u>Good Housekeeping magazine</u>

● *Connect to Writing and Speaking:* **Peer Consultation**

Using Italics

Write a paragraph about the books, magazines, films, and music you most enjoy. Then consult with a partner about your preferences. Together, write a new paragraph that combines examples that you both agree are of the highest caliber. Be sure your examples are correctly italicized. Read your paragraph for the class.

● *Connect to Writing:* **Editing**

Using Italics (Underlining) Correctly

Rewrite each sentence, underlining where needed.

1. The 1961 Newbery Medal book was Island of the Blue Dolphins.
2. John Paul Jones sailed on a ship called the Bonhomme Richard.
3. The words broccoli and zucchini both have two c's.
4. The smallest plane ever built was called the Stits Skybaby; it was half as long as an average car.
5. The word quark was taken from the book Ulysses.
6. The two most successful newsmagazines are Time and Newsweek.
7. The word unquestionably contains all five vowels and the letter y.
8. Bertolt Brecht wrote The Threepenny Opera.
9. The numbers 3, 5, and 7 are prime numbers.
10. During the Old English period, storytellers recited long poems such as Beowulf.
11. The radio play Sorry, Wrong Number is a classic mystery.
12. The musical titled Man of La Mancha is based on the Spanish novel Don Quixote.
13. Russian astronaut Valentina V. Tereshkova rode in a spacecraft called Vostok 5 in 1963.
14. One of the many phrases people use for the rolls of dust that collect under furniture is dust bunnies.

● *Connect to Speaking and Writing:* **Interview**

Italics (Underlining)

Interview one of your classmates to find out his or her five favorite television shows. Ask why he or she likes each favorite. Then write a paragraph naming and describing your classmate's favorites and what your classmate finds most interesting about each of them. Be sure to italicize or underline each title correctly.

Quotation Marks  Lesson 2

Quotation marks (**" "**) are punctuation marks that always come in pairs. They are used to enclose certain titles, and they are used to enclose a person's exact words. Without quotation marks, a conversation between the people in a story would be difficult to read or understand.

> **29 B** **Quotation marks** are used to enclose the titles of short works and parts of longer works and to set off a speaker's exact words.

➤ Quotation Marks with Titles

Long works are italicized (or underlined). Many long works are made up of smaller parts. A book, for example, might contain short stories, poems, or titled chapters. The titles of these smaller parts are enclosed in quotation marks. Commas and periods that follow immediately after a title are always placed inside the quotation marks.

> **29 B.1** Use quotation marks to enclose the titles of chapters, articles, stories, one-act plays, short poems, and songs.

Chapters in Books	Our assignment is to read the chapter "The Disappearing Frontier" in our history book, *American History*.
Articles in Magazines and Newspapers	The lead story in this week's <u>Newsweek</u> is "DNA Solves Crimes."
	The Sunday *Salem News* had a feature called "Garbage Gardening."
Short Stories in Books and Magazines	I liked the short story "The Ransom of Red Chief" in our literature book <u>Discoveries</u>.
	Did you read the story "Ticket to Saturn" in the last issue of *Galaxy* magazine?
Short Poems	I memorized the poem "O Pioneers" from the book <u>From Sea to Shining Sea</u>.
Songs	The old song "All You Need Is Love" is my mother's favorite.

Practice Your Skills

Using Quotation Marks

Write C if quotation marks are used correctly. Write I if the punctuation is used incorrectly.

1. *Does Your Chewing Gum Lose Its Flavor on the Bedpost Overnight* was once a popular song.
2. John McCrae wrote the patriotic "poem In Flanders Fields" during World War I.
3. The song *The Lonely Goatherd* was written for the Broadway musical "The Sound of Music."
4. My favorite chapter in the book *The Wind in the Willows* is called "The Further Adventures of Toad."
5. The newspaper article "A Fair to Remember" described events at the Ohio State Fair.
6. The article *Breaking the Record* was in the September issue of "Sports Illustrated."
7. Escape from the Sea is the first chapter in the novel *Agents of Destiny*.
8. In our textbook *Discovering Literature*, we read the poem "The Base Stealer" by Robert Francis.
9. *Drought Predicted* was today's lead story in our newspaper, the "Des Moines Register."
10. "Those Were the Days" was the theme song for the long-running television series *All in the Family*.
11. This month's issue of *National Geographic* includes an article titled *The Brothers Grimm*.
12. *The Star-Spangled Banner* was written by Francis Scott Key.

Connect to Writing: Editing

Correcting Punctuation of Titles

Rewrite the incorrectly punctuated sentences from the preceding exercise, using underlining and quotation marks correctly.

Rewrite each sentence, using quotation marks and italics (underlining) where needed.

1. The word nevermore appears ten times in the poem The Raven.
2. The Oxford English Dictionary lists 194 meanings for the word set.
3. The tune of Happy Birthday to You was written by two sisters, Mildred and Patty Hill.
4. Rod McKuen said he rewrote his book The Sound of Solitude thirty-four times.
5. The TV series I Love Lucy has remained popular since the 1950s.
6. My favorite painting is van Gogh's Sunflowers.
7. Some buildings give the floor just after the twelfth floor the number 14 because of superstitions about the number 13.
8. The article An Underground Railroad in Boston was a feature in Scientific American magazine in 1849.
9. The word chortled first appeared in the poem Jabberwocky by Lewis Carroll.
10. An article in the Chicago Tribune described an exhibit of artifacts recovered from the Titanic.

● *Connect to Writing:* **Bibliography**

Titles

Imagine that you are collecting materials to publish in an anthology about the sea. Your plan is to reprint magazine articles, poems, stories, songs, and chapters from books about the sea. Create a bibliography of at least five materials that you might include in your book. Be sure to give complete information about the materials. For example, list not only a poem but the name of a book where you found it. Remember to use italics (or underlining) and quotation marks correctly.

● *Connect to Speaking and Listening:* **Comprehension**

Using New Vocabulary

So far in this chapter, you have learned and applied the terms *italics, underlining,* and *quotation marks.* Explain to a partner what these terms mean and how you have used them in your writing. Then give your partner a test by writing sentences that require italics (or underlining) and quotation marks. Go over the test you have devised with your partner and have your partner go over the test that was given to you. Together, discuss any mistakes that were made, and correct them.

Quotation Marks with Direct Quotations

Quotation marks are used to enclose a **direct quotation,** the exact words of a person.

29 B.2 Use quotation marks to enclose a person's exact words.

> Scott said, "I rowed across the harbor."
>
> "The sea was very calm," he added.

Quotation marks do not enclose an **indirect quotation,** a rephrasing of a person's exact words.

> Scott said he rowed across the harbor.
>
> He added that the sea was very calm.

A direct quotation that is a single sentence can be written in various ways. It can appear before or after a **speaker tag** such as *she answered* or *he stated*. It can also be interrupted by a speaker tag. In every case, quotation marks enclose only the person's exact words, not the speaker tag.

Before	"The tide comes in at six o'clock tonight," he said.
After	He said, "The tide comes in at six o'clock tonight."
Interrupted	"The tide," he said, "comes in at six o'clock tonight." (Two sets of quotation marks are needed because the speaker tag interrupts the direct quotation.)

Use only one set of quotation marks to set off two or more sentences in a direct quotation if the sentences are not interrupted by a speaker tag.

> He said, "The tide tonight comes in at six. The ship will sail then."
> (Quotation marks come only before *The* and after *then*.)

Using Quotation Marks with Direct Quotations

Write *a* or *b* to indicate the item in each pair that uses quotation marks correctly.

1. **a.** "The earliest ancestor of bubble gum was created in 1906," said Ken.
   b. "The earliest ancestor of bubble gum was created in 1906, said Ken."

2. **a.** He continued, Unfortunately, the gum had a lot of problems.
   b. He continued, "Unfortunately, the gum had a lot of problems."

3. **a.** His friend, Victoria, asked him what he meant by that.
   b. His friend, Victoria, asked him "what he meant by that."

4. **a.** He told her that the gum was too sticky and brittle.
   b. He told her "that the gum was too sticky and brittle."

5. **a.** "Besides," he added, "it had a terrible name."
   b. "Besides, he added, it had a terrible name."

● *Connect to Writing:* **Editing**

Using Quotation Marks with Direct Quotations

Rewrite each sentence, adding or taking out quotation marks where needed. If you are using a quotation mark to enclose a group of words that ends with a comma or a period, put the quotation marks after the comma or period.

1. Ken explained "that the original name of the gum was Blibber-Blubber."

2. "In 1928, Ken continued, the gum company was still working on a formula for bubble gum."

3. "This is the story I read about Blibber-Blubber, Ken went on. A young man named Walter Diemer kept experimenting with different mixes. Then one day he found the perfect mix."

4. "When Diemer found the correct formula, Ken said with a smile, he started dancing all over his office."

5. "Unfortunately, Ken added," the gum wouldn't work the next day.

6. "So, he experimented for another four months until the formula was just right, said Ken."

7. Eve asked Ken "what color the first bubble gum was."

8. "Ken smiled and said, There's a funny story about that." Diemer made the gum pink because pink was the only food coloring he had on hand.

9. "So that's why bubble gum is usually pink, Ken concluded."

10. "I think I have seen bubble gum in other colors as well, Eve said."

Capital Letters with Direct Quotations

You know that a capital letter begins a sentence. It is natural, therefore, for a capital letter to begin a direct quotation.

29 B.3   Begin each sentence of a direct quotation with a capital letter.

> **"L**ast summer we went to Minnesota," she said.
>
> She said, **"L**ast summer we went to Minnesota."
>
> **"L**ast summer," she said, **"w**e went to Minnesota."

Notice that in the last example the word *we* does not begin with a capital letter because it is in the middle of a one-sentence direct quotation. In the following examples, however, a capital letter is used to begin a new sentence.

> She said, **"L**ast summer we went to Minnesota. **I**t was an interesting trip."
>
> **"L**ast summer we went to Minnesota," she said. **"I**t was an interesting trip."

● Practice Your Skills

Using Capital Letters with Direct Quotations

Write *a* or *b* to indicate the item in each pair that is correctly capitalized.

1. a. "We saw some gigantic wooden statues along the roadside in Minnesota!" exclaimed Angelica.

   b. "we saw some gigantic wooden statues along the roadside in Minnesota!" Exclaimed Angelica.

2. a. "There are many statues of Paul Bunyan in Minnesota," said Ty. "did you see any of them?"

   b. "There are many statues of Paul Bunyan in Minnesota," said Ty. "Did you see any of them?"

3. a. "We saw Paul Bunyan frequently," Angelica responded, "along with Babe the Blue Ox."

   b. "We saw Paul Bunyan frequently," Angelica responded, "Along with Babe the Blue Ox."

4. a. She remarked, "one of the funniest statues we saw was a huge mouse and cheese near Lindstrom, Minnesota."

b. She remarked, "One of the funniest statues we saw was a huge mouse and cheese near Lindstrom, Minnesota."

5. a. "the most impressive statue," added Angelica, "Was the enormous wooden one of Smokey the Bear at International Falls."

b. "The most impressive statue," added Angelica, "was the enormous wooden one of Smokey the Bear at International Falls."

● *Connect to Writing:* **Editing**

Using Capital Letters with Direct Quotations

Rewrite each sentence, adding capital letters where needed.

1. "wasn't Smokey the Bear just a cartoon character?" James asked.

2. "no, he was also a real bear," Ms. Low responded.

3. "rangers rescued him," she continued, "in New Mexico."

4. Tony asked, "why did Smokey need to be rescued?"

5. Ms. Low answered, "he was orphaned in a forest fire. the rangers found him clinging to a charred tree."

6. "when his burns healed," continued Ms. Low, "he was taken to the National Zoo in Washington, D.C."

7. "this bear became the symbol in a campaign to fight forest fires," she said.

Commas with Direct Quotations

Commas are used to separate direct quotations from speaker tags.

29 B.4   Use a comma to separate a direct quotation from a speaker tag.

Commas and periods are always placed inside quotation marks. Look at the examples below to see how placement and punctuation of the speaker tag can vary.

"A penny saved is a penny earned," said Ben Franklin.

Ben Franklin said, "A penny saved is a penny earned."

"A penny saved," said Ben Franklin, "is a penny earned."

In the third sentence, two commas are needed to separate the speaker tag from the direct quotation—one before the speaker tag and one after it.

Using Commas with Direct Quotations

Write **C** if commas are used correctly in a sentence. Write **I** if commas are used incorrectly.

1. Mark Twain said "If you tell the truth, you don't have to remember anything."
2. "Prejudice is an unwillingness to be confused by facts", remarked H. L. Mencken.
3. "False words are not only evil in themselves," Plato told his students "but they infect the soul with evil."
4. A Spanish proverb says "Those who give quickly, give twice."
5. "The weak can be terrible" commented Rabindranath Tagore, "because they try furiously to be strong."
6. Picasso once said, "Art is a lie which makes us see the truth."
7. "Those who have the power to control themselves are the most powerful of all people," wrote Seneca.
8. "The art of writing" said Mary Heaton Vorse, "is the act of applying the seat of the pants to the seat of the chair."
9. "Tell me what company you keep," wrote Miguel de Cervantes, "and I'll tell you who you are."
10. "Civility costs nothing", remarked Mary Wortley Montagu, "and buys everything."

● *Connect to Writing:* Editing

Using Commas with Direct Quotations

Rewrite the incorrectly punctuated sentences from the preceding exercise, using commas correctly.

End Marks with Direct Quotations

A period is used at the end of a sentence—whether it is a regular sentence or a direct quotation. The period goes *inside* the closing quotation marks when the quotation ends the sentence.

29 B.5   Place a period inside the closing quotation marks when the end of the quotation comes at the end of the sentence.

She said, "The storm has grown much fiercer."

"The storm," she said, "has grown much fiercer."

Usually question marks and exclamation points, like periods, go inside the closing quotation marks.

> He yelled, **"**The lightning struck nearby**!"**
>
> She asked, **"**Where did it strike**?"**
>
> (In both examples, the end marks go *inside* the closing quotation marks.)

When a question mark or exclamation point comes just before a speaker tag, the mark is still placed inside the closing quotation marks.

> **"**The lightning hit a tree**!"** Chris exclaimed.
>
> **"**Did it hit the pine on the hill**?"** asked Hannah.

● *Connect to Writing:* **Comic Strip**

End Marks in Quotations

Find a comic strip. Change the speech inside the balloons into direct quotations with speaker tags. For example: "Why are you always so mean to me?" Charlie Brown asked Lucy. Be sure you use end marks correctly in your quotations.

● *Connect to Writing:* **Peer Project**

Using Quotations

With three other classmates, create a mural entitled "Words of Wisdom." Collect quotations that you feel are truthful and relevant to life today. Then use your drawing and painting skills to illustrate the quotations you collect. Use the largest sheet of heavy paper you can find. You may want to incorporate collage elements and other media techniques, but draw a rough sketch before you begin the process of creating your mural. Be sure all quotations are spelled and punctuated correctly.

● **Practice Your Skills**

Using End Marks with Direct Quotations

Write *a* or *b* to indicate the item in each pair that is punctuated correctly.

1. a. Mr. Ott said, "Some legends tell about dragons".

　　b. Mr. Ott said, "Some legends tell about dragons."

2. a. "Do you mean fire-breathing dragons?" asked Liz.

　　b. "Do you mean fire-breathing dragons," asked Liz?

3. a. "Yes, Mr. Ott answered, "and there is an iguana that resembles that
kind of dragon"

　　b. "Yes," Mr. Ott answered, "and there is an iguana that resembles that
kind of dragon."

4. a. "That iguana is about four feet long." he added

　　b. "That iguana is about four feet long," he added.

5. a. "I hope I never run into one in my neighborhood!" Jeff exclaimed.

　　b. "I hope I never run into one in my neighborhood," Jeff exclaimed!

● *Connect to Writing:* **Editing**

Using End Marks with Direct Quotations

Rewrite each sentence, adding periods, question marks, and exclamation points
where needed.

1. Bria said, "My topic is the Middle Ages in England"

2. Ms. Rayburn asked, "Who were the educated people at that time"

3. "The priests were the educated ones," responded Bria, "and they wrote in
Latin or Greek"

4. "Why didn't they use English" asked Nelson "Didn't most people speak
English"

5. "The common people spoke English," Bria explained, "but scholars looked
down on it"

Check Point: Mixed Practice

Rewrite the following quotations, adding quotation marks, commas, end marks, and capital letters where needed.

1. how much of the earth is covered by ocean water asked Mr. Ames

2. More than half the earth is covered Tracy answered

3. Mr. Ames responded ocean water actually covers three fourths of the earth's surface

4. that doesn't leave much room for land Brad exclaimed

5. how deep is the deepest ocean Julie asked

6. the average depth of the world's oceans Mr. Ames replied is about three miles

7. Brad asked how high can waves get

8. Mr. Ames answered in a severe storm, some waves are forty-nine feet high. they travel at fifty miles an hour

 ## Other Uses of Quotation Marks

What you have just learned about punctuating direct quotations can now be applied in the following situations.

Writing Dialogue

A **dialogue** is a conversation between two or more persons. The way it is written shows who is speaking.

`29 B.6` When writing dialogue, begin a new paragraph each time the speaker changes.

In the following dialogue between Miguel and Lisa, a new paragraph begins each time the speaker changes.

> Miguel asked, "How long have you been helping at the computer club?"
> "I started last year," Lisa answered.
> "I'm thinking of joining the club, but I don't know if I should," he told her.
> Lisa answered, "Oh, I think you should. It's fun."

Practice Your Skills

Reading Dialogue

Read aloud the following dialogue between Miguel and Lisa. Identify each place where a new paragraph should begin.

> Miguel asked, "Do you need to have a computer at home to be a member?" "You don't have to," Lisa answered. "That's good because I don't have one. I am going to get one soon for my birthday," he told her. Lisa added, "I don't have one of my own either. I use my sister's."

Connect to Writing: Editing

Correcting the Paragraphing in a Dialogue

Rewrite the preceding dialogue correctly, beginning a new paragraph each time the speaker changes.

Quoting Long Passages

When you write a report, sometimes you need to support your own points with quotations by experts. If any of those quotations are more than a paragraph long, there is a special way to write them. There is also a special way to handle text that you omit from these paragraphs.

29 B.7 When quoting a passage of more than one paragraph, place quotation marks at the beginning of each paragraph—but at the end of *only* the last paragraph. Use an ellipsis (. . .) to indicate where text is left out.

You omit the closing quotation marks at the end of each paragraph except the last one as a signal to a reader that the quotation is continuing. Look at the following example.

> "Goats were probably first used as domestic animals in Asia, about nine thousand years ago. Today there are about five species of goats, including both wild and domesticated ones.
>
> "Among the domestic goats, there are more than two hundred breeds. A few, like the Angora and Kashmiri goats, are grown for their soft fleece. . . . The rest are used for meat and milk."

When You Write

A long quoted passage may also be set off from the rest of the text by indenting both the left and right margins. When you use this method—called a block quote—no quotation marks are needed.

Practice Your Skills

Quoting Long Passages

In a report on how to improve one's study skills, a student quotes the following passage. Add quotation marks correctly.

To help remember facts, try to make a connection with something you already know. Suppose you wanted to remember that warm air rises. If you live in a house with more than one story, you know that the top floor is the hottest place. The basement is the coolest. Use these facts to recall that warm air rises.

Another good idea is to count the items you need to remember. That way, you'll always know whether you have remembered the whole list or left something out.

It is also smart to break a long list into shorter parts. It is easier to learn two or three items at a time. If you need to memorize six things, memorize the first three; then memorize the last three. Finally, put the whole list together.

✔ Check Point: Mixed Practice

Rewrite each sentence, adding underlining, quotation marks, commas, capital letters, and end marks where needed. Remember that only a sentence with a speaker tag should be considered a direct quotation.

1. too often we enjoy the comfort of opinion without the discomfort of thought said John F. Kennedy

2. the article called A Persistent Rebel in American History magazine told about Elizabeth Blackwell

3. My favorite song from the musical My Fair Lady is The Rain in Spain.

4. Education costs money, observed St. Claus Moser, but then so does ignorance

5. Carl Sandburg's book Slabs of the Sunburnt West contains his poem Primer Lesson

6. Alfred Adler once remarked it is easier to fight for one's principles than to live up to them

7. how many r's are in the word February asked Ty

Analyzing Dialogue

You will notice, as you read short stories and novels, that writers usually put brief descriptions of a character's actions in the same paragraph with the direct quotations. In the following excerpt from a novel, the narrator describes the efforts of his father, a teacher, to lure a goat off the schoolhouse fire escape. Billy Joe, one of the father's pupils, offers the goat bait.

> "They gave me some stuff for the goat to eat," Billy Joe said.
>
> "What have you got?"
>
> He opened the bag and peeped. "Got some turnips here and some broccoli and a pretty good bunch of carrots."
>
> "Broccoli?" my father said. "I hate that stuff. I don't think that even a goat could choke down broccoli. Let's try the carrots."
>
> "Here you go." He offered to toss the bag up to him.
>
> "Just the carrots," he said. "The paper makes too much noise. Don't want to scare him off."
>
> —Fred Chappell, *Brighten the Corner Where You Are*

- As you can see, the pronoun *he* is used for both characters. How can you tell which character is speaking or acting?

- Who speaks first? How can you tell?

- Who finishes the dialogue?

- What would happen if the paragraph beginning with the word **broccoli** were missing?

Assess Your Learning

Punctuating Titles

Write each sentence, adding quotation marks and underlining where needed.

1. Is Phantom of the Opera a classic horror film?
2. In our textbook New Poetry, I read the poem Dreams.
3. The word typewriter uses only the top row of letters on a typewriter.
4. Is Guy de Maupassant's short story The Necklace considered tragic?
5. Charles Lindbergh's plane, Spirit of St. Louis, had no radio receiver or transmitter.
6. I read the article Sports Greats in this issue of Life.
7. The shortest word containing all five vowels is euphoria.
8. Twelve Angry Men, a three-act play, is also a movie.
9. Circle of Life is one song from The Lion King.
10. Sarah Bernhardt, a French actress, once played the prince's part in Shakespeare's Hamlet.

Punctuating Direct Quotations

Write each direct quotation, adding capital letters, quotation marks, and other punctuation marks where needed.

1. what time do you want to get up Mom asked
2. a baby gazelle can outrun a horse he explained
3. this book Mom said must be returned to the library
4. you're out shouted the umpire
5. Dad asked do we have another gallon of paint
6. the coach asked which is the third-most popular sport
7. the humpback whale Mr. Keating said often covers more than four thousand miles in a single year
8. Karen cried out I've burned my finger
9. Mr. Andrews said the bell just rang
10. I just finished lunch she said it was delicious

Punctuating Direct Quotations

Write each direct quotation, adding quotation marks, other punctuation marks, and capital letters where needed.

1. a female whale weighs as much as thirty elephants he stated

2. have you ever visited New York City Pat asked

3. Ms. Marsh said the piano pieces by Mozart were composed for pianos with only five octaves

4. I smell smoke Shelley screamed

5. Mrs. Jones asked who is going on the field trip

6. lobsters are so small at birth he explained that hundreds could fit in the palm of your hand

7. Andrew exclaimed I just won a free trip to Mexico

8. work on the book reports that are due on Friday Mrs. Keaton stated

9. Thomas Edison invented the electric voting machine she said it was never used until twenty-three years later.

10. Ben asked are you cold shall I turn up the heat

Using Quotation Marks

Follow the directions below.

1. Write an imaginary dialogue between you and your favorite singer or actor. Punctuate the dialogue correctly.

2. After writing an introductory paragraph, quote a long passage from a nonfiction book.

Directions

Read the passage and choose the best way to write each underlined part. Write the letter of the correct answer. If the underlined part contains no error, write **D.**

Mr. Cyr read about block parties in the article **(1)** <u>Know Your Neighbors</u>. On our street all addresses start with **(2)** <u>2's or 4's</u>. Mom **(3)** <u>said that</u> Mr. Cyr is in charge. "Let's enter the cake-baking **(4)** <u>contest said</u> Bonnie. "Will a police officer speak about **(5)** <u>safety asked Lon</u> "The article," continued **(6)** <u>Mr. Cyr says</u> that neighbors should know each other." I asked, "Does that increase **(7)** <u>safety?</u> **(8)** <u>Yes answered</u> Mr. Cyr. A sign on our street now reads **(9)** <u>Crime Watch Area</u>. No one wants to yell, **(10)** <u>Help! Robbery!</u>

1. A *Know Your Neighbors.*
   B Know Your Neighbors.
   C "Know Your Neighbors."
   D No error

2. A "2"'s or "4"'s
   B *2*s or *4*s
   C "2s" or "4s"
   D No error

3. A said, "That
   B said, that,
   C said "that
   D No error

4. A contest." Said
   B contest", said
   C contest," said
   D No error

5. A safety" asked Lon?
   B safety?" asked Lon.
   C safety"? asked Lon!
   D No error

6. A Mr. Cyr "says
   B Mr. Cyr, "says
   C Mr. Cyr, "Says
   D No error

7. A safety?"
   B safety"?
   C safety?".
   D No error

8. A Yes, answered
   B "Yes," answered
   C Yes, "Answered
   D No error

9. A *Crime Watch Area.*
   B *"Crime Watch Area."*
   C "Crime Watch Area."
   D No error

10. A "Help! Robbery!"
   B "Help! Robbery"!
   C *Help! Robbery!*
   D No error

Writer's Corner

Snapshot

29 A   **Italics (underlining)** are used to set off titles and certain numbers, words and letters. (pages 854–856)

29 B   **Quotation marks** are used to enclose the titles of short works and parts of longer works and to set off a speaker's exact words. (pages 857–870)

Power Rules

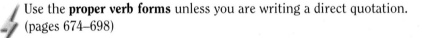 Avoid **sentence fragments** unless you are writing dialogue. (pages 656–661)

Before Editing	**After Editing**
Tomorrow afternoon.	The trip is tomorrow afternoon.
	"Ms. Connor, when are we going to the museum?"
	"Tomorrow afternoon."

Use the **proper verb forms** unless you are writing a direct quotation. (pages 674–698)

Before Editing	**After Editing**
They *hasn't* got a dog.	They *haven't* got a dog.
	"They hasn't got a dog," said the little girl.

Editing Checklist

Use this checklist when editing your writing.

✓ Did I italicize or underline letters, numbers, and words when they are used to represent themselves? (See page 854.)

✓ Did I italicize or underline titles of long written or musical works, titles of artwork, and names of vehicles? (See pages 854–855.)

✓ Did I use quotation marks around titles of chapters, articles, stories, one-act plays, short poems, songs, and around the exact words of speakers? (See pages 857–861.)

✓ Did I make sure to use capital letters and punctuation correctly within quotation marks? (See pages 862–867.)

✓ Did I create a new paragraph each time the speaker changed? (See pages 867–870.)

Use the Power

Quotation marks are like the speech bubbles in cartoons. They show us what is being said. The speaker tags (*he said, she whispered, they yelled*) in writing are like the tails on the speech bubbles, connecting the words to the speaker.

Write a discussion between two friends. Use quotation marks to indicate their dialogue.

Quotation marks are useful.

Yes. They help us know when someone is speaking.

Other Punctuation

How can you use apostrophes and other punctuation to communicate precisely?

Other Punctuation: Pretest 1

The following first draft contains errors in various kinds of punctuation. The first error, in which a word needs an apostrophe, has been corrected. Revise the draft so that dashes, hyphens, apostrophes, colons, and semicolons are applied correctly. One of the errors has been corrected.

> Isn't the quilt above colorful and varied? Quilting has been an American tradition throughout our history it is said to symbolize a coming together of African and American cultures. Quilts have come to represent the following heritage, history, family, comfort, and love. The memorial quilt above similar to quilts made for the NAMES Project Foundation is a world class creation meant to foster healing and inspire individual's to work together in the struggle against HIV and AIDS. If youd like to learn more about what such quilts represent, visit http://www.aidsquilt.org.

Other Punctuation: Pretest

Directions

Each sentence is missing one type of punctuation. Write the letter of the punctuation that correctly completes each sentence.

(1) Do you wear red on Valentines Day?

(2) We set up a self serve buffet on the Fourth of July.

(3) Everyones house is decorated for Christmas.

(4) I sent Easter cards to Topeka, Kansas Duluth, Minnesota and Salt Lake City, Utah.

(5) Doesnt anyone in your family like eggnog?

(6) How many *as* are in *Kwanzaa?*

(7) My most memorable birthday party was in 07.

(8) I always stay up at least until midnight on New Year's Eve I sleep late the next day.

(9) I need the following gift wrap, boxes, and tape.

(10) It is twenty two days until April Fool's Day.

1. A apostrophe
  B semicolon
  C colon
  D hyphen

2. A apostrophe
  B semicolon
  C colon
  D hyphen

3. A apostrophe
  B semicolon
  C colon
  D hyphen

4. A apostrophe
  B semicolon
  C colon
  D hyphen

5. A apostrophe
  B semicolon
  C colon
  D hyphen

6. A apostrophe
  B semicolon
  C colon
  D hyphen

7. A apostrophe
  B semicolon
  C colon
  D hyphen

8. A apostrophe
  B semicolon
  C colon
  D hyphen

9. A apostrophe
  B semicolon
  C colon
  D hyphen

10. A apostrophe
  B semicolon
  C colon
  D hyphen

30 A   An **apostrophe** (') is used to show possession. It is also used to form a contraction.

Apostrophes to Show Possession

You see apostrophes used most often to show that a person or thing owns or has something.

> Paul**'s** shirt = the shirt that belongs to Paul
>
> the shirt**'s** buttons = the buttons that the shirt has

The Possessive Forms of Singular Nouns

To form the possessive of a singular noun, write the noun but do not add or omit any letters. Then add an apostrophe and an *s*.

30 A.1   Add **'**s to form the possessive of a singular noun.

> Nick + **'s** = Nick**'s**   Is that Nick**'s** green backpack?
>
> backpack + **'s** = backpack**'s**   The backpack**'s** zipper is broken.
>
> teacher + **'s** = teacher**'s**   That notebook is the teacher**'s.**
>
> class + **'s** = class**'s**   The class**'s** assignment is on the board.
>
> box + **'s** = box**'s**   The box**'s** flaps were torn.

● **Practice Your Skills**

Forming Possessive Singular Nouns

Rewrite the following expressions, using the possessive form.

1. core of an apple   **6.** handbook of a scout

2. fender of a bus   **7.** job of my mother

3. song of a bird   **8.** cubs of a lioness

4. chair of a dentist   **9.** edge of a river

5. sister of Rose   **10.** bat belonging to James

The Possessive Forms of Plural Nouns

There are two rules to follow when forming the possessive of plural nouns.

30 A.2   Add only an apostrophe to form the possessive of a plural noun that ends in *s*.

boys + **'** = boy**s'**	The two boy**s'** pets are dogs.
dogs + **'** = dog**s'**	The dog**s'** tails are bushy.

30 A.3   Add **'**s to form the possessive of a plural noun that does not end in **s**.

men + **'s** = men**'s**	The men**'s** cars are red.
sheep + **'s** = sheep**'s**	The sheep**'s** coats are wool.

Deciding which rule to follow is easy if you take two steps. First, write the plural of the noun—as it is. Second, look at the ending of the word. If the word ends in an *s*, add only an apostrophe. If it does not end in *s*, add an apostrophe and an *s*.

FORMING THE POSSESSIVE OF PLURAL NOUNS

Plural	Ending	Add	Possessive
lions	*s*	**'**	lion**s'** roars
cats	*s*	**'**	cat**s'** whiskers
mice	no *s*	**'s**	mice**'s** tails
deer	no *s*	**'s**	deer**'s** antlers

When You Write

Have you ever seen a sign that advertised "Orange's and Peach's"? The sign should have said "Oranges and Peaches." The sign maker got confused and used *'s* to form the plurals of nouns. Do not use an apostrophe to form the plural of a noun.

Look critically at a recent composition to be sure you have used apostrophes only to show possession and not to form plurals.

Practice Your Skills

Forming Possessive Plural Nouns

Rewrite the following expressions, using the possessive form.

1. work of students
2. honks of geese
3. lease of two years
4. worth of six dollars
5. farm of grandparents

6. first names of men
7. cars of women
8. harnesses of oxen
9. barking of dogs
10. ideas of both girls

Practice Your Skills

Forming Singular and Plural Possessive Nouns

Decide whether each underlined noun is singular or plural. Then write its correct possessive form.

1. job of my <u>sister</u>
2. prices of the <u>dresses</u>
3. names of my <u>sisters</u>
4. notice of one <u>month</u>
5. age of the <u>child</u>

6. notice of two <u>months</u>
7. ages of the <u>children</u>
8. den of the <u>wolf</u>
9. price of the <u>dress</u>
10. leader of the <u>wolves</u>

Connect to Writing: Editing

Correcting Sentences with Possessive Nouns

Rewrite each sentence, correcting the possessive form. If the possessive form is correct, write **C.**

1. Charlenes' library book is about the history of domesticated animals.
2. People's first domesticated animal was the dog.
3. Dogs's instincts attracted them to human's leftovers.
4. Sheeps' meat helped people survive when there were few animals to hunt.
5. Tending sheep was often children's work.
6. According to many experts' conclusions, cattle were next to be tamed.

The Possessive Forms of Pronouns

Personal pronouns do not use an apostrophe to show possession the way nouns do. Instead, they change their form.

POSSESSIVE PERSONAL PRONOUNS	
Singular	my, mine, your, yours, his, her, hers, its
Plural	our, ours, your, yours, their, theirs

30 A.4   Do not add an apostrophe to form the possessive of a personal pronoun.

> **Personal Pronouns**   The bicycle is **hers.**
> The spider spun **its** web.

Singular indefinite pronouns, however, form the possessive by adding *'s.*

COMMON INDEFINITE PRONOUNS	
Singular	anybody, anyone, each, either, everybody, everyone, neither, nobody, no one, one, somebody, someone
Plural	both, few, many, several

30 A.5   Add *'s* to form the possessive of an indefinite singular pronoun.

> **Indefinite Pronouns**   She asked for everyone**'s** opinion.
> Someone**'s** wallet was found on the floor.

● **Practice Your Skills**

Using Possessive Pronouns

Rewrite the following expressions, using the possessive form of each underlined pronoun.

1. bike belonging to <u>him</u>
2. front wheel of <u>it</u>
3. house belonging to <u>us</u>
4. bedroom belonging to <u>me</u>
5. coat of <u>anybody</u>

6. first choice of <u>no one</u>
7. sister of <u>you</u>
8. good idea of <u>someone</u>
9. watch belonging to <u>her</u>
10. skateboards belonging to <u>them</u>

● *Connect to Writing:* **Editing**

Correcting Sentences with Possessive Pronouns

Rewrite each sentence, using the correct possessive pronoun. If a sentence is correct, write **C**.

1. I have been working very hard on our school's Web site.

2. It's name is School Daze.

3. Everyones suggestions have been both thoughtful and useful.

4. The idea for the design was her's.

5. I have spent my time organizing more than twenty volunteers.

6. Tony and Emma have offered they're help.

✓ *Check Point:* **Mixed Practice**

Write the possessive form of each phrase in parentheses.

1. I enjoy (the class of Ms. Tahaku) in Japanese brush painting.

2. We use only black ink and brushes for (the drawings belonging to us).

3. My teacher was taught the art by (the uncle belonging to her).

4. Brush painting has been practiced in (the family of my teacher) for many generations.

5. (The techniques of the painters) were inspired by ancient thinkers.

6. (The goals of the thinkers) were to have an uncluttered mind and to appreciate the simple beauty of nature.

7. The painters want (the work that belongs to them) to suggest a great deal in just a few brush strokes.

8. To do (the job of it), each brush stroke must be graceful and perfectly placed.

Apostrophes with Contractions

Besides showing possession, an apostrophe is used in contractions. Two or more words are combined to form a contraction. The apostrophe replaces one or more missing letters.

CONTRACTIONS	
is not = isn**'t**	let us = let**'s**
who is = who**'s**	there is = there**'s**
I am = I**'m**	of the clock = **o'**clock
he is *or* has = he**'s**	she had *or* would = she**'d**

30 A.6   Use an apostrophe in a contraction to show where one or more letters have been omitted.

Do not confuse contractions with possessive pronouns, which have no apostrophe. When you are wondering whether to use an apostrophe, mentally say the individual words of a contraction.

Contractions

it**'s** = it is

you**'re** = you are

they**'re** = they are

there**'s** = there is *or* there has

who**'s** = who is or who has

Possessive Pronouns

its = belonging to it

your/yours = belonging to you

their/theirs = belonging to them

whose = belonging to whom

When You Write

In everyday speech you probably make contractions using nouns. You may say, "Aaron's waiting in the car" instead of "Aaron is waiting in the car" or "The dog's chewed up your mitt" instead of "The dog has chewed up your mitt." When you write, these colloquial contractions are appropriate only in story dialogue. They are not acceptable in any form of formal writing.

Practice Your Skills

Writing Contractions

Write the contraction for each pair of words.

1. have not	**6.** you have	**11.** we will
2. I am	**7.** that is	**12.** you are
3. they are	**8.** was not	**13.** who is
4. did not	**9.** would not	**14.** I have
5. she is	**10.** are not	**15.** we are

Practice Your Skills

Distinguishing Between Contractions and Possessive Pronouns

Write the correct word in parentheses.

1. (Who's, Whose) ready to go?

2. (Who's, Whose) name is on the class list for the first bus?

3. (It's, its) going to be late because (it's, its) tires needed more air.

4. (They're, Their) leaving now because (they're, their) bus has arrived.

5. (There's, Theirs) another bus arriving behind (there's, theirs).

6. (You're, your) going to be left behind if you don't find (you're, your) bus.

7. I can't tell (who's, whose) bus this is or (who's, whose) driving it.

8. I can see (it's, its) number; (it's, its) the bus for your group.

9. (There's, Theirs) plenty of time to find a seat.

10. Wait until others have found (there's, theirs).

Connect to Writing: Editing

Correcting Sentences with Contractions

Rewrite each sentence, using the correct contraction or possessive pronoun. If a sentence is correct, write **C.**

1. Their getting off the bus now.

2. It's time for everyone to choose a partner.

3. Your starting your tour of the wildlife park now.

4. Theirs a new trail here I'd like to try.

5. Their starting a clean-up program on this trail.

6. A class comes and cleans it's part of the trail.

Apostrophes with Certain Plurals

To prevent confusion, certain items form their plurals by adding 's.

30 A.7 Add 's to form the plurals of all lowercase letters, some capital letters, and some words used as words that might otherwise be misread.

Lowercase Letters	My *u*'s and *i*'s look too much alike.
Capital Letters	How many *A*'s did you write on your paper?
Words Used as Words	Our *hi*'s echoed down the hallway.
	(Without the apostrophe, you might think that the word was *his*.)

Remember that the numbers, letters, symbols, and words used as words are themselves italicized (underlined) but that the apostrophe and the *s* are not.

The plurals of most other capital letters, symbols, numerals, and words used as words can be formed by adding just an *s*.

Capital Letters	How many *T*s did you have in your answers for the test?
Symbols	I used *s to mark the important information.
Numerals	There are three *2*s in her phone number.
Words Used as Words	Don't use too many *and*s in your sentences.

You can learn more about using apostrophes for plurals on pages 879–880.

Apostrophes in Certain Dates

An apostrophe is also used when numbers are dropped from a date.

30 A.8 Use an apostrophe to show that numbers have been left out of a date.

My sister will graduate from college in '16. (2016)

The Blizzard of '88 was a major disaster in the Northeast. (1988)

The apostrophe is not used to form the plural of years in a decade. Add just an *s*.

> I listen to some old bands from the 1960s.

Practice Your Skills

Using Apostrophes

Rewrite each phrase, adding an apostrophe if one is needed.

1. the Stock Market Crash of 29

2. a word with three *a*s in it

3. people born in the 1980s

4. the Spirit of 76

5. an address with three *6*s

6. two *r*s in February

7. replace *and*s with *&*s

8. the *ha-ha*s for laughter

9. too many *like*s in his sentences

10. learning one's *ABC*s

✔ Check Point: Mixed Practice

Write each word that is missing an apostrophe and add the apostrophe in the proper place.

1. Polar bears fur is not white but clear, and their skin is black.

2. The Statue of Libertys tablet is two feet thick.

3. There are two *c*s and two *m*s in the word *accommodate*.

4. Colonists declared independence from Great Britains empire in 1776.

5. Cats were adored in ancient Egypt, but theyre not mentioned in the Bible.

6. Whenever you see one of these #s, youre likely to call it the "number sign" or the "pound sign."

7. The country of Nauru doesnt have an official capital city; however, its government is based in Yaren.

8. During the Gold Rush, many of the first 49ers came from Mexico, Peru, and Chile.

9. Congress didnt vote to admit Ohio to the Union until the 1950s.

10. Its possible to housebreak an armadillo.

Connect to Writing: Friendly Letter

Using Apostrophes

Write a letter to a friend about your favorite hobby or collection. Describe what you enjoy about this hobby or the objects you collect. Use apostrophes in three contractions and in one date, and to show possession of two items.

30 B A **semicolon** (**;**) is used between the parts of some compound sentences and to avoid confusion when items in a series contain commas.

➤ Semicolons with Compound Sentences

A **compound sentence** has two or more independent clauses. These clauses can be joined by a comma and a coordinating conjunction or by a semicolon.

30 B.1 Use a semicolon between the clauses of a compound sentence that are not joined by a coordinating conjunction. Coordinating conjunctions include *and, but, or,* and *yet.*

Comma and Coordinating Conjunction	My sister's hair is red**, but** mine is blond.
	My father's ancestors came from Ireland**, and** my mother's ancestors were Swedish.
Semicolon	My sister's hair is red**;** mine is blond.
	My father's ancestors came from Ireland**;** my mother's ancestors were Swedish.

You can learn more about compound sentences on pages 642–646.

When You Write

You can use a semicolon to correct a run-on sentence.

Run-on	Everyone in my family is tall, my brother, for example, is six feet tall.
Correct	Everyone in my family is tall**;** my brother, for example, is six feet tall.

Look back at a recent composition, and check for run-on sentences. Correct any you find by using semicolons.

You can learn more about run-on sentences on pages 662–663.

Practice Your Skills

Using Commas and Semicolons with Compound Sentences

Write **C** if a sentence is punctuated correctly. Write **I** if a sentence is punctuated incorrectly.

1. Our bodies are made up of cells, and different types of cells have different functions.

2. A control center is at the heart of each cell, it is called a nucleus.

3. Each nucleus contains forty-six threadlike parts; and these are our chromosomes.

4. These chromosomes are very small, but there is something else even tinier.

5. Each chromosome is made up of thousands of genes, a gene is too small to be seen.

6. Our bodies are made up of many types of protein; genes carry the commands to make this protein.

7. Genes come in pairs, we have one pair of genes for each of our physical characteristics.

8. One pair of genes determines the color of our hair, another pair determines the color of our eyes.

9. Brothers and sisters have the same parents, yet only identical twins have the same genes.

10. There are thousands of genes in a chromosome; and there are billions of possible combinations of the genes from just two parents.

Connect to Writing: Editing

Punctuating Compound Sentences

Rewrite the incorrectly punctuated sentences from the preceding exercise, using commas and semicolons correctly.

Connect to Speaking and Listening: Peer Interaction

Listening for Commas and Semicolons

A good way to learn when to use commas and semicolons is to acquire an ear for their use. With a partner, practice reading some of the examples in this lesson. Then write new compound sentences that need commas and semicolons. Read your new sentences aloud, saying the word *comma* or *semicolon* where each would appear. Examples: "I want to go [comma] but my parents won't allow it." "I am so excited [semicolon] this school year is going to be the best!"

Semicolons with Conjunctive Adverbs and Transitional Words

Another way to combine independent clauses in a compound sentence is to use a semicolon along with one of the following **conjunctive adverbs** or **transitional words**.

COMMON CONJUNCTIVE ADVERBS		
accordingly	furthermore	otherwise
also	hence	similarly
besides	however	still
consequently	instead	therefore
finally	nevertheless	thus
COMMON TRANSITIONAL WORDS		
as a result	in addition	in other words
for example	in fact	on the other hand

30 B.2 Use a semicolon between clauses in a compound sentence that are joined by certain **conjunctive adverbs** or **transitional words**.

Notice in the following examples that the conjunctive adverb *therefore* and the transitional words *in fact* are preceded by a semicolon and followed by a comma.

Kim practiced repeatedly**;** **therefore,** she played well at the recital.

She had worried about stage fright**;** **in fact,** she performed calmly.

When You Write

Some conjunctive adverbs and transitional words can also be used as parenthetical expressions within a single clause. When you use them as parenthetical expressions, you use commas—not a semicolon—to set them off.

Joining Clauses	I play the guitar**;** **however,** I have never performed in public.
Within a Clause	My brother, **however,** has played in several concerts.

You can learn more about punctuating parenthetical expressions on pages 839–841 and 901–903.

Punctuating Sentences

Write **C** if a sentence is punctuated correctly. Write **I** if a sentence is punctuated incorrectly.

1. Your body needs special cells to fight germs; otherwise you would be overcome by viruses and bacteria.
2. Every day; in fact, your body makes billions of white blood cells.
3. These defender cells travel throughout your bloodstream; consequently, they can attack germs anywhere in your body.
4. Some white cells will attack any germ along the way, however, these cells often die quickly.
5. Other white cells attack only a specific type of germ, in fact, they carry special weapons called antibodies.
6. Antibodies stick to the germs; in addition other defenders destroy damaged cells.
7. Antibodies are very strong; furthermore, they even have a kind of memory.
8. They will, in other words, attack that kind of germ the next time.
9. Your defender cells; however, sometimes need help from outside the body.
10. Vaccinations are harmless germs; consequently, your cells make antibodies against them.

Connect to Writing: Editing

Correcting Compound Sentences

Rewrite the incorrect sentences from the preceding exercise, using commas and semicolons correctly.

Connect to Writing: Drafting

Writing Sentences

Write four sentences, following the directions for each given below.

1. Write a compound sentence joined by a comma and the conjunction *and*.
2. Write a compound sentence joined by a semicolon.
3. Write a compound sentence joined by *however*.
4. Write a compound sentence joined by *in fact*.

Semicolons to Avoid Confusion

Occasionally a semicolon will be used in place of a comma to eliminate any possible confusion in a sentence.

30 B.3 Use a semicolon instead of a comma between the clauses of a compound sentence if there are commas within a clause.

In the following sentences, the first independent clause has commas in it. Therefore, a semicolon is used between that clause and the second clause.

> Matt grew healthy tomatoes, lettuce, and peppers; but his melons were a failure.
>
> In the Southern states, summers are hot, dry, and long; and this climate is ideal for growing melons.

When You Write

If a compound sentence still seems confusing even when you use a semicolon, you may be better off rewriting it as two or more sentences.

> Summers are hot, dry, and long in the Southern states. This climate is ideal for growing melons.

A semicolon also can take the place of a comma in certain sentences that consist of only one independent clause.

30 B.4 Use a semicolon instead of a comma between the items in a series if the items themselves contain commas.

In the following examples, a comma is needed between the cities and states. Normally a comma also would be placed between each item in a series. If all of those commas were put in, however, the second sentence would become very confusing to read. Therefore, semicolons are used between the items in a series when the items themselves contain commas.

Sentence with No Series	They stayed in Jacksonville, Florida, and two other large cities.
Sentence with a Series	They stayed in Jacksonville, Florida; Albany, Georgia; and Mobile, Alabama.

You can learn more about items in a series on pages 827–828 and 887.

Using Semicolons to Avoid Confusion

Write **C** if a sentence is punctuated correctly. Write **I** if a sentence is punctuated incorrectly.

1. The three largest cities in the United States are New York New York, Los Angeles California, and Chicago Illinois.

2. New York City has many art galleries, museums, and colleges, its opera and ballet companies are famous.

3. The four island boroughs of New York City are Manhattan, Brooklyn, Queens, and Staten Island, and only the Bronx is on the mainland.

4. Los Angeles is a national center of manufacturing, finance, and transportation and its mass media industry is one of the largest in the world.

5. The Los Angeles metropolitan area, which includes Long Beach, covers an area of more than 460 square miles.

6. Los Angeles's museums include the County Museum of Natural History, with exhibits relating to California history; the Southwest Museum, where Native American arts are on display; and the California Museum of Science and Industry.

7. Chicago was the birthplace of a modern school of architecture, and the city has buildings designed by great architects such as Frank Lloyd Wright, Louis Henry Sullivan, and William Le Baron Jenney.

8. Chicago is home to the Cubs, a baseball team, the White Sox, a baseball team, and the Bulls, a basketball team.

● *Connect to Writing:* **Editing**

Punctuating Sentences with Semicolons

Rewrite the incorrectly punctuated sentences from the preceding exercise.

● *Connect to Writing:* **Guidebook Entry**

Semicolons

Research the Chicago School of Architecture. Then use the facts you uncover to write a paragraph for a guidebook to Chicago. Use at least two sentences that contain semicolons in your paragraph.

30 C   A **colon** (:) is used to introduce a list of items, between hours and minutes and Biblical chapter and verse, and at the end of the salutation in a business letter.

30 C.1   Use a colon before most lists of items, especially when the list comes after an expression like *the following*.

Notice that commas are used between the items in each series.

> I am very interested in three subjects: biology, geography, and geology.
>
> The test will cover the following periods: the Jurassic, the Triassic, and the Permian.

You can learn more about commas with items in a series on pages 827–828.

A colon is not needed between a verb and its complement or directly after a preposition.

> **Incorrect**   The earth's four main layers include: the inner core, outer core, mantle, and crust.
>
> **Correct**   The earth's four main layers include the inner core, outer core, mantle, and crust.
>
> **Correct**   The earth consists of four main layers: the inner core, outer core, mantle, and crust.
>
> **Incorrect**   The earth's mantle consists mainly of: silicon dioxide, magnesium oxide, and iron oxide.
>
> **Correct**   The earth's mantle consists mainly of silicon dioxide, magnesium oxide, and iron oxide.
>
> **Correct**   The earth's mantle consists mainly of three materials: silicon dioxide, magnesium oxide, and iron oxide.

There are a few other situations that require colons.

30 C.2 Use a colon to write hours and minutes, Biblical chapters and verses, and salutations in business letters.

COLON USAGE	
Hours and Minutes	6:30 AM OR 6:30 a.m.
Biblical Chapters and Verses	Job 28:18
Salutations in Business Letters	Dear Sir:

● Practice Your Skills

Using Colons

Write **C** if a sentence is punctuated correctly. Write *I* if a sentence is punctuated incorrectly.

1. In the past ten years, my family has lived in three cities Memphis, Charlottesville, and Atlanta.

2. The movie at Cinema II starts at 720 p.m.

3. The verse read by the minister was John 10:9.

4. Animals with horns include these six: giraffes, deer, cattle, antelopes, sheep, and goats.

5. California borders three other states Arizona, Nevada, and Oregon.

6. We are waiting for: Pat, Dylan, Chico, and Charlene.

7. By 1944, Americans could buy the following frozen foods: meats, vegetables, fish, and dairy products.

8. The bus stops here at 230 and 430.

9. The three most heavily consumed food items in the United States are milk, potatoes, and beef.

10. Dear Ms. Anderson I am writing to apply for a summer job.

● *Connect to Writing:* Editing

Correcting Sentences with Colons

Rewrite the incorrect sentences from the preceding exercise, punctuating them correctly.

Rewrite each sentence, adding semicolons or colons where needed.

1. Fruits that are purple include blueberries, plums, and figs but no fruits are a true blue color.

2. A green color is a sign of ripeness in the following fruits kiwis, limes, and honeydew melons.

3. Some color names come from the names of fruit peach, apricot, orange, melon, and lime green.

4. A painter's palette may contain violet, rose, lavender, pink, buttercup, and goldenrod and a garden may contain flowers with the same names.

5. The green violet has green petals otherwise most violets are violet or purple.

● *Connect to Writing:* **Summary**

Colons

As a study aid for yourself, write a summary of the most important facts you have been studying recently in your science or social studies class. Include at least three lists that are introduced by colons.

30 D A **hyphen (-)** is used to divide words and in the spelling of certain numbers and words.

Hyphens with Divided Words

30 D.1 Use a hyphen to divide a word at the end of a line.

The following are some guidelines for dividing a word at the end of a line.

GUIDELINES FOR DIVIDING WORDS
1. Divide words only between syllables.
pro·duc·tion   pro-duction or produc-tion
2. Never divide a one-syllable word.
Do Not Break   dine   cheap   strength
3. Do not divide a word after the first letter.
Do Not Break   omit   able   enough
4. Divide hyphenated words only after the hyphens.
sister-in-law   maid-of-honor   side-by-side

If you are not certain where the syllables break in a word, look the word up in a dictionary.

● Practice Your Skills

Using Hyphens to Divide Words

Add a hyphen or hyphens to show where each word can be correctly divided. If a word should not be divided, write *no* after the word.

1. occasion	**6.** fleet	**11.** question
2. prince	**7.** evict	**12.** ocean
3. repeat	**8.** middle	**13.** sponge
4. summer	**9.** amazement	**14.** silent
5. around	**10.** milk	**15.** aboard

Correcting Sentences with Hyphens

Rewrite the following paragraph, correcting the incorrect use of hyphens. If a word can be hyphenated, move the hyphen to an appropriate place. If a word cannot be hyphenated, write it as one word.

    The hour of the day is determined a-
ccording to the position of the sun. This means that clocks in different regions show different hours at the same moment in time. Up until the 1800s, it was never necessary for Americans to know exactly what h-
our it was in places far from their own homes.

    In those days, travel was so slow and unr-
eliable that people measured long trips in days,
not in hours. They were wil-
ling to set their watches according to the clocks where they were. With the coming of railroads and rapid travel, however, Americans found that it was necessary
for train station clocks to agree with other clocks in a region for the times of arr-
ivals and departures.

When You Write

When using a word processor, be sure to make a distinction between a hyphen and a dash. A hyphen (-) is shorter than a dash, and it is primarily used to divide words. The most common versions of the dash are the en dash (–), which is used to indicate range, as in *pages 6–10,* and the em dash (—), which is used for parenthetical ideas—something like this—that interrupt a sentence.

CHAPTER 30

➤ Other Uses of Hyphens

A hyphen is used in spelling certain words, as well as in certain numbers, fractions, and compound nouns.

Hyphens with Certain Numbers

A hyphen is used in most numbers when they are written out in a report or story.

30 D.2 Use a hyphen when writing out the numbers twenty-one through ninety-nine.

> "Sixty-four" is the answer to the math problem.
>
> Twenty-five problems were on the test.

If a number is the first word of a sentence, it must *always* be written out.

> There were **164** students taking the test.
>
> **One hundred sixty-four** students were taking the test.

Hyphens with Certain Fractions

When a fraction is used as an adjective, it is written with a hyphen.

30 D.3 Use a hyphen when writing out a fraction used as an adjective.

> **Hyphen** A **three-fourths** majority is needed to pass the amendment.
> (*Three-fourths* is an adjective that describes *majority*.)
>
> **No Hyphen** **Three fourths** of the members were present.
> (*Three fourths* is a noun used as the subject.)

Hyphens with Some Compound Nouns

A **compound noun** is a noun that is made up of two or more words. The words in a compound may be written in one of three ways: (1) together as one word, (2) as two separate words, or (3) as two words joined with a hyphen.

30 D.4   Use a hyphen to separate the parts of some compound words.

COMPOUND WORDS	
One Word	birdlike, worldwide, crossroads, supermarket, grandmother
Two Words	all right, grocery store, dump truck, air conditioning
Hyphenated	great-grandmother, first-class, cross-examine

You can learn more about compound nouns on page 490.

● **Practice Your Skills**

Using Hyphens

Rewrite each phrase, adding hyphens where needed. If a phrase does not need a hyphen, write **C**. Use a dictionary to look up words you are unsure of.

1. the twenty four members of the steering committee

2. a noisy jack-in-the-box

3. three eighths of an apple pie

4. a trade in on a sports car

5. a children's merry go round

6. a first class campground

7. a one tenth share of the profits

8. the fifty first skydiver

✔ *Check Point:* Mixed Practice

Rewrite the following paragraphs, adding apostrophes, semicolons, and colons where needed.

Streetcars were a very common sight in the early 1900s. Maybe youve seen them in photographs or films. Perhaps youve actually ridden on one.

A streetcars power came from electricity. Europes streetcars were powered by two overhead wires however, most early streetcars in the United States were powered by one wire and one electrified track. Europe got its first streetcar system in 1881 the United States followed four years later.

Streetcars are used today in the following European countries Germany, Austria, and Switzerland. They are almost extinct in the United States. A few lines have been revived in such cities as Portland, Oregon, Buffalo, New York, and Sacramento California.

● *Connect to Writing:* Descriptive Paragraph

Hyphens

What would a meal made of your favorite foods consist of? Write a description to share with your parents. Use vivid adjectives to describe the appearance, taste, and smell of the dishes on the menu. Use at least three words that contain hyphens.

30 E   **Parentheses, dashes, brackets,** and **ellipses** are used when a sentence either contains extra information or leaves something out.

Parentheses

Parentheses separate additional information, or an explanation that is added but not needed, from the rest of the sentence. Definitions and dates, for example, are sometimes put in parentheses. When using parentheses, remember that they come in pairs.

30 E.1   Use **parentheses ( )** to enclose information that is not related closely to the meaning in the sentence.

To decide whether or not you should use parentheses, read the sentence without the parenthetical material. If the meaning and structure of the sentence are not changed, then add parentheses. Just keep in mind that parenthetical additions to sentences slow readers down and interrupt their train of thought. Limit your use of parentheses to times when it is really necessary.

> Tony Hawk was the first skateboarder to land a "900" **(**a 900-degree turn, or two and a half revolutions**)**.

When the closing parenthesis comes at the end of a sentence, the end mark usually goes outside of the parenthesis.

> Born in California, Hawk became a professional skateboarder at the age of 14 **(in 1982)**.

Occasionally the end mark goes inside the parenthesis if the end mark actually belongs with the parenthetical material.

> When Hawk was nine years old, his brother gave him his first skateboard. **(**It was a used board.**)**

CHAPTER 30

➤ Dashes

The **dash** indicates a greater separation between words than a comma.

30 E.2   Use the **dash (—)** to set off an abrupt change in thought; to set off an appositive that contains introductory words such as *for example, that is,* and *for instance;* and to set off a parenthetical expression or an appositive that contains commas.

Abrupt Change in Thought	The Caspian Sea—the name *sea* is misleading—is by far the largest lake in the world.
Appositive with Introductory Words	Some family names—for example, Baker, Butler, and Miller—come from occupations.
	Some plants—for instance, the pitcher, the sidesaddle, and the sundew—devour insects.
Parenthetical Expression or Appositive with Commas	Thomas Jefferson—scientist, architect, philosopher—was truly a great person.
	Three scientists—Finlay, Reed, and Theiler—are responsible for conquering yellow fever.

If you do not know how to make a dash on the computer, you can place two hyphens together. Do not leave space before or after the hyphens.

➤ Brackets

When you use quoted passages, you may need to use **brackets**.

30 E.3   Use **brackets [ ]** to enclose an explanation within quoted material that is not part of the quotation.

According to the official Tony Hawk Web site, "Frank [Tony's father] drove Tony up and down the coast of California for skate contests, built innumerable skate ramps over the years, and when he grew dissatisfied with the competitive organizations, founded both the California Amateur Skateboard League and the National Skateboard Association."

The following summary may help you decide when to use certain kinds of punctuation.

PUNCTUATING PARENTHETICAL INFORMATION

Parenthetical (nonessential) information is always set off from the rest of the sentence by special punctuation. Depending on how important the parenthetical material is, use one of the following marks of punctuation.

- Use commas to enclose information that is loosely related to the rest of the sentence yet is nonessential. This method is the most common.
- Use parentheses **( )** to enclose information that is not essential to the meaning of the sentence but that adds an interesting point.
- Use dashes **—** to signal a break in the train of thought.
- Use brackets **[ ]** to enclose your own words inserted into a quotation.

● Practice Your Skills

Using Parentheses and Brackets

Rewrite each sentence, using parentheses, dashes, or brackets to enclose the underlined words.

1. Clara's report stated, "Both sports <u>skateboarding and skiing</u> require fearlessness and agility."

2. We saw thirteen <u>yes, we counted them</u> reporters at the opening of the skate park.

3. The article about the new skate park reported, "Students there <u>Chicago</u> raised more than $700 for construction costs."

4. Jim said he likes skateboarding <u>but not rollerblading</u>.

5. Several sports <u>for example, snowboarding and skateboarding</u> have great appeal to younger athletes.

6. Unlike vertical skating <u>performed on structures built specifically for the sport</u>, street skating takes place anywhere kids find a place to skate.

7. A recent study showed a "significant reduction in the number of injuries among those who wear protective gear, including helmets, when participating in this sport <u>skateboarding</u>."

8. The ollie <u>as any skateboarder will tell you</u> is one of the most important skateboarding tricks.

 **Ellipses**

An **ellipsis** is used most often to show that part of a complete quotation has been dropped.

> **30 E.4**   Use an **ellipsis . . .** to indicate any omission in a quoted passage or a pause in a written passage.

Original Passage

"We choose to go to the moon. We choose to go to the moon in this decade and do the other things, not because they are easy, but because they are hard, because that goal will serve to organize and measure the best of our energies and skills, because that challenge is one that we are willing to accept, one we are unwilling to postpone, and one we intend to win, and the others, too." (John F. Kennedy's exact words in a 1962 speech at Rice University)

Quoted Passage

"We choose to go to the moon **. . .** because that challenge is one that we are willing to accept, one we are unwilling to postpone, and one which we intend to win **. . . .**"
(The first set of ellipsis points indicates where some of Kennedy's words have been left out. The second set of ellipsis points indicates that more of Kennedy's words follow in the original sentence. This set ends with a period.)

Written Passage

"Well **. . .** Let me think about it," I said.
(The ellipsis points here indicate that the speaker paused.)

● **Practice Your Skills**

Using Ellipsis Points

Rewrite the following paragraph from a 2009 speech by Barack Obama, omitting the underlined portions and inserting ellipsis points as needed.

Thanks to our recovery plan, we will double this nation's supply of renewable energy in the next three years. We've also made the largest investment in basic research funding in American history — <u>an investment that will spur not only new discoveries in energy, but breakthroughs in medicine, science, and technology</u>. We will soon lay down thousands of miles of power lines that can carry new energy to cities and towns <u>across this country</u>. And we will put Americans to work making our homes and buildings more efficient so that we can save billions of dollars on our energy bills. But to truly transform our economy, <u>to protect our security, and save our planet from the ravages of climate change,</u> we need to ultimately make clean, renewable energy the profitable kind of energy.

Assess Your Learning

Punctuating Correctly

Write each sentence, adding apostrophes, semicolons, colons, and hyphens where needed. If a sentence is correct, write C.

1. Some restaurants serve frogs legs.

2. Theirs cant be the house with the shutters.

3. Turtles have no teeth instead, they have sharp beaks.

4. A honeybees stinger has a hook at the end.

5. "A one fifth share of the profits sounds good to me," said the board member whom we had just elected.

6. We steamed twenty five ears of corn as part of someones catering order.

7. Dad travels to these cities Tulsa, Oklahoma Tucson, Arizona Las Vegas, Nevada and Detroit, Michigan.

8. Vermont was not one of the original thirteen colonies it became the fourteenth state in 1791.

9. Womens coats are on sale at the mall.

10. Do you know the following computer terms *bit, byte,* and *bug?*

Punctuating Correctly

Write each sentence, adding apostrophes, semicolons, colons, and hyphens where needed. If a sentence is correct, write **C.**

1. Thirty five billion pounds of potatoes are consumed by Americans each year.

2. An elephant's trunk is actually its nose and upper lip.

3. After eight hours work, Mom finished her painting.

4. Tendons connect muscles to bones ligaments link the bones of ankles, knees, and elbows.

5. Well have to take the early train in order to get to everyones appointments on time.

6. I missed the bus otherwise, I had a wonderful day.

7. My parents birthday present to me was a down vest stitched with a pattern of ss.

8. I wrote down the time of the sunrise, 617 am the time of the sunset 720 pm and the days average temperature.

9. A small plane has three main controls a throttle lever, a control column, and a rudder bar.

10. The men's soccer team is practicing for the Olympics.

Using Punctuation Marks

Write sentences that follow the directions below.

Write a sentence that . . .

1. includes the possessive form of the noun *uncle*.

2. includes the possessive form of the noun *grandparents*.

3. includes the possessive form of the noun *children*.

4. includes the possessive form of the pronoun *no one*.

5. includes the words *you're* and *your*.

6. includes the plural of *no*.

7. includes two independent clauses joined by only a semicolon.

8. includes the word *nevertheless* between two independent clauses in a compound sentence.

9. includes a series of dates (day, month, and year).

10. includes *two-thirds* as an adjective.

When you are finished, make sure you have used all punctuation correctly.

Other Punctuation: Posttest

Directions

Each sentence is missing one type of punctuation. Write the letter of the punctuation that correctly completes each sentence.

(1) The pet stores shelves were filled with items I wanted for my pets. **(2)** At this store, youre invited to bring your pet inside. **(3)** I didn't bring Whiskers, my older cat, or Bobtail, my younger cat but I did bring Rascal, my dog. **(4)** An announcement came over the loudspeaker saying that the store would stay open until 830 tonight. **(5)** I walked through the store with a basket I gradually filled the basket with items. **(6)** I remembered that my two cats scratching post was broken. **(7)** I asked someones help in getting a new scratching post from a high shelf. **(8)** After paying the cashier, I was down to my last dollar however, I was glad I had made the purchases. **(9)** I had bought the following items dog biscuits, catnip, a scratching post, and chew toys. **(10)** The narrow receipt divided the word *customer* as *cus tomer*.

1. A apostrophe
   B semicolon
   C colon
   D hyphen

2. A apostrophe
   B semicolon
   C colon
   D hyphen

3. A apostrophe
   B semicolon
   C colon
   D hyphen

4. A apostrophe
   B semicolon
   C colon
   D hyphen

5. A apostrophe
   B semicolon
   C colon
   D hyphen

6. A apostrophe
   B semicolon
   C colon
   D hyphen

7. A apostrophe
   B semicolon
   C colon
   D hyphen

8. A apostrophe
   B semicolon
   C colon
   D hyphen

9. A apostrophe
   B semicolon
   C colon
   D hyphen

10. A apostrophe
   B semicolon
   C colon
   D hyphen

Writer's Corner

Snapshot

30 A An **apostrophe (')** is used to show possession. It is also used to form possessives, contractions and plurals of certain numbers and words. (pages 878–886)

30 B A **semicolon (;)** is used between the parts of a compound sentence, and to avoid confusion when items in a series contain commas. (pages 887–892)

30 C A **colon (:)** is used to introduce a list of items; to separate hours and minutes and Biblical chapter and verse; and it is also used at the end of the salutation in a business letter. (pages 893–895)

30 D A **hyphen (-)** is used to divide words and in the spelling of certain numbers and words. (pages 896–900)

30 E **Parentheses, dashes, brackets,** and **ellipses** are used when a sentence either contains extra information or leaves something out. (pages 901–904)

Power Rules

 Be sure that you use **apostrophes** correctly to show the **possessive form** of a noun. (pages 878–880)

Before Editing	**After Editing**
Franks cat can meow loudly.	*Frank's* cat can meow loudly.
The *childrens* schedule is very busy.	The *children's* schedule is very busy.
The *cities* buildings are similar to each other.	The *cities'* buildings are similar to each other.

 Use apostrophes correctly to show where letters have been omitted from words. (pages 883–884)

Before Editing	**After Editing**
I *have'nt* finished with the newspaper yet.	I *haven't* finished with the newspaper yet.
Theyr'e very nice people.	*They're* very nice people.

Editing Checklist

Use this checklist when editing your writing.

✓ Did I use apostrophes correctly in contractions, to show possession, and with certain plurals? (See pages 878–884.)

✓ Did I use semicolons between clauses of a compound sentence that are not joined by a coordinating conjunction? (See pages 887–888.)

✓ Did I use semicolons between items in a series when the items themselves contain commas? (See pages 891–892.)

✓ Did I use a colon before a list of items? (See pages 893–895.)

✓ Did I make sure to use hyphens when I divide a word at the end of a line of text? (See pages 896–897.)

✓ Did I use hyphens where they are needed in some numbers and compound words? (See pages 898–900.)

Use the Power ⚡

Use the table below to review the use of these punctuation marks.

Apostrophe '	Are you going to Gabrielle's house to study?
Dash —	Her brother Jackson—he's majoring in English at Indiana University—is going to help us study for the exam.
Semicolon ;	Before choosing to go to school in Indiana, Jackson visited schools in Evanston, Illinios; Grand Rapids, Michigan; and Madison, Wisconsin.
Colon :	This semester, he's studying the following authors: Ernest Hemingway, F. Scott Fitzgerald, and William Faulkner.
Hyphen -	He'll graduate when he's twenty-one.
(Parentheses)	The professor assigned Chapter 2 (pages 56–89) for homework.
[Brackets]	"Maria [Gabrielle's sister] is going to France this summer."
Ellipsis . . .	"I'm sorry . . . I didn't see you there," she said.

Write eight sentences, each of which uses one of the punctuation marks in the chart above. Try to make your sentences light and breezy but meaningful.

Spelling Correctly

How can you communicate your message effectively by using accurate spelling?

Spelling Correctly: Pretest 1

This first draft below about the artist Janet Fish contains several spelling errors. The first error has been corrected. Revise the paragraph so that all spelling errors are corrected.

Janet Fish, who was born in 1938, ~~new~~ *knew* as a child that she wanted to be an artist. She was influenced buy her mother, a sculptor, and buy her grandfather, a painter. Although her earlyer workes were in the Abstract Expressionist style, she now perfers to paint realistic images. Fish says, "I chose to be faithful to what I see."

Spelling Correctly: Pretest 2

Directions

Read the passage and write the letter of the answer that correctly spells each underlined word. If the underlined word is correct, write *D.*

It is hard to **(1)** believe that the voice of a skilled ventriloquist's puppet comes from the human **(2)** purformer. Yet learning to speak without **(3)** moveing your lips does not present much **(4)** difficulty. Only five letters—*b, f, m, p,* and *v*— **(5)** require lip movement. You can avoid words with **(6)** troublsome letters, or a **(7)** similar sound, such as an *n* for an *m*, can be used. A **(8)** majorety of the audience won't **(9)** notise. If you **(10)** practice often, you can become a ventriloquist.

1. **A** beleive
   B believ
   C beelieve
   D No error

2. **A** performur
   B preformer
   C performer
   D No error

3. **A** mooving
   B moving
   C moveng
   D No error

4. **A** difficulte
   B dificulty
   C difficultie
   D No error

5. **A** reqire
   B requir
   C reequire
   D No error

6. **A** troublesome
   B trublesome
   C troublesume
   D No error

7. **A** simular
   B simelar
   C similer
   D No error

8. **A** majarity
   B mejority
   C majority
   D No error

9. **A** notice
   B notuce
   C notuse
   D No error

10. **A** practise
    B practis
    C practus
    D No error

Strategies for Learning to Spell

The senses of hearing, sight, and touch are useful tools for learning to spell correctly. Try this five-step strategy that helps many people spell unfamiliar words.

1 Auditory

Say the word aloud. Answer these questions.

- Where have I heard or read the word before?
- What was the context in which I heard or read the word?

2 Visual

Look at the word. Answer these questions.

- Does this word divide into parts? Is it a compound word? Does it have a prefix or a suffix?
- Does this word look like any other word I know? Could it be part of a word family I would recognize?

3 Auditory

Spell the word to yourself. Answer these questions.

- How is each sound spelled?
- Are there any surprises? Does the word follow spelling rules I know, or does it break the rules?

4 Visual/Kinesthetic

Write the word as you look at it. Answer these questions.

- Have I written the word clearly?
- Are my letters formed correctly?

5 Visual/Kinesthetic

Cover up the word. Visualize it. Write it. Answer this question.

- Did I write the word correctly?
- If the answer is no, return to step 1.

Spelling Strategies

Misspelled words, whether in a composition for school or in a letter to a friend, call attention to themselves. Unfortunately, that means they are likely to distract readers from the thoughts being expressed. This chapter will introduce you to strategies and generalizations to help you improve your spelling.

Use a dictionary. If you're not sure how to spell a word, or if a word doesn't "look right," check its spelling in a dictionary. Don't rely on guessing to help you spell accurately.

Proofread your writing carefully. If you use a computer, do not rely on your word processing program to catch spelling errors. When you type the word *strait,* the computer can't know that you really meant to type *straight, trait,* or even *strain.*

Be sure you are pronouncing words correctly. "Swallowing" syllables or adding extra syllables can cause you to misspell a word.

Make up mnemonic devices. Look for memorable small words or word patterns in difficult words: "It is un**clear** to me what nu**clear** energy is" or "The first *two* syllables of *Antarctica* begin with *a*'s followed by *two* consonants." Inventing a sentence like "**Re**placing **cur**tains **ren**ovates **ce**llars" can help you remember the letter groups in *recurrence.*

Keep a spelling journal. Use it to record the words you have had trouble spelling. Here are some suggestions for organizing your spelling journal.

- Write the word correctly.
- Write the word again, underlining or circling the part of the word that gave you trouble.
- Write a tip that will help you remember how to spell the word in the future.

stationery	stationery	A writer writes on stationery. (An artist needs a stationary model.)
accidentally	accidentally	The first and last consonants are doubled; the consonants in the middle are single.

Practice Your Skills

Recognizing Misspelled Words

Write the letter of the misspelled word in each set. Then write the word correctly.

1. (a) absence   (b) villain   (c) sergent
2. (a) exceed   (b) occured   (c) vacuum
3. (a) picniced   (b) receipt   (c) leisurely
4. (a) exshaust   (b) gauge   (c) fascinate
5. (a) cemetery   (b) fourty   (c) foreign
6. (a) echoes   (b) specialty   (c) privelege
7. (a) achievement   (b) likeble   (c) quotation
8. (a) prefered   (b) discipline   (c) procedure
9. (a) existance   (b) condemn   (c) conscience

Practice Your Skills

Pronouncing Words

Practice saying each syllable in the following words to help you spell the words correctly.

1. re•al•is•tic
2. cus•to•mar•y
3. re•cur•rence
4. nu•cle•ar
5. in•ter•fere
6. coun•ter•feit
7. Ant•arc•ti•ca
8. se•cur•i•ty
9. nat•ur•al•ly
10. di•a•per

11. ex•pe•di•tion
12. prac•ti•cal•ly
13. va•ca•tion
14. res•i•dence
15. e•qual•ly
16. pre•de•ter•mine
17. de•fi•cient
18. par•lia•ment
19. guar•an•tee
20. qual•i•fi•ca•tion

Some people are naturally good spellers. They can "see" the correct spelling of a word in their minds, or they can "hear" the word, remembering how the syllables sound. There are also those for whom spelling is very difficult, no matter what method they use. These people are bright, and they are quick to learn other subjects, but spelling is a challenge for them. If you are not a naturally good speller, learning some generalizations should make spelling easier for you.

31 A **Some spelling generalizations are based on the patterns of letters. Two common patterns are found in words spelled with *ie* or *ei* and in words that end with the *seed* sound.**

Words with *ie* and *ei*

Words with *ie* and *ei* often cause confusion. Use the following familiar rhyme to help you spell such words.

> Put *i* before *e*
> Except after *c*
> Or when it sounds like long *a*
> As in *neighbor* and *weigh*.

31 A.1 When you spell words with *ie* or *ei*, *i* frequently comes before *e* except when the letters follow *c* or when they stand for the long *a* sound.

The following examples show this generalization.

IE AND EI					
I Before E	belief	achieve	niece	piece	field	brief
Except After C	ceiling	conceit	deceive	perceive	receipt	receive
Sounds Like A	eight	reins	sleigh	veil	weight	feign

These words do not follow the pattern.

EXCEPTIONS			
either	foreign	height	ancient
sufficient	species	forfeit	conscience
glacier	weird	their	leisure

When you look at exceptions to spelling generalizations, ask yourself if you can see patterns in them. For example, you might notice that *c* is followed by *ie* in words like *ancient*, *conscience*, and *sufficient*. Figuring out that *ie* follows *c* in the suffixes *-cient* and *-cience* can help you spell similar words.

Words Ending in *-cede*, *-ceed*, or *-sede*

Some other words that cause problems are those that end with a "seed" sound. This sound can be spelled *-cede*, *-ceed*, or *-sede*. Most words that end with this sound are spelled *-cede*.

31 A.2   In all but four words that end with the "seed" sound, this sound is spelled *-cede*.

-CEDE			
precede	recede	concede	intercede

You'll have no trouble spelling these words if you memorize the four exceptions.

-CEED AND -SEDE			
exceed	proceed	succeed	supersede

● **Practice Your Skills**

Identifying Spelling Patterns

Write each word correctly, adding *ie* or *ei*.

1. r ⬜ gn

2. shr ⬜ k

3. ⬜ ghty

4. th ⬜ f

5. br ⬜ f

6. p ⬜ rce

7. pr ⬜ st

8. h ⬜ ght

9. sh ⬜ ld

10. w ⬜ ghty

11. forf ⬜ t

12. rel ⬜ ve

13. c ⬜ ling

14. retr ⬜ ve

15. for ⬜ gn

16. n ⬜ ghborhood

17. front ⬜ r

18. n ⬜ ther

19. effic ⬜ nt

20. consc ⬜ nce

CHAPTER 31

● Practice Your Skills

Write each word, adding *-sede, -ceed,* or *-cede.*

1. re ▨   **6.** suc ▨

2. ex ▨   **7.** pro ▨

3. ac ▨   **8.** con ▨

4. se ▨   **9.** inter ▨

5. pre ▨   **10.** super ▨

● *Connect to Writing:* Editing

Using Spelling Patterns

Find and rewrite the ten words that have been spelled incorrectly.

An anceint Greek myth tells the story of Jason and the Golden Fleece. His uncle had agreed to act briefly as king. Then he would conceed the throne when Jason was old enough to regn. His deceitful uncle wasn't ready to yeild the crown, however. To get Jason out of the way, his uncle succeded in persuading him to go on a quest to the neghboring kingdom of Colchis. Jason was determined to retreive the Golden Fleece from there. He believed his family was its heirs. He proceded to have a ship built. Then, to the releif of his uncle, Jason wieghed anchor and set out on the voyage.

When You Use Technology

You can use the spelling check features of your word processing and e-mail software to help you as you compose or edit on a computer. Be careful. A spelling checker will not edit your work. For example, spell check will not tell you that you incorrectly used the word *herd* for *heard,* or point out that you used *principal* where you should have used *principle.* You can usually find the spelling feature in the Edit or the Tools menu of your software. You can also set most modern programs to mark misspelled words as you type. Look in the Preferences menu to turn on this feature.

Forming Plurals   Lesson 2

The following generalizations will help you spell the plurals of nouns correctly.

31 B   **To form the plural of most nouns, add *s* or *es*. Some nouns are exceptions.**

Regular Nouns

31 B.1   To form the plural of most nouns, simply add *s*.

MOST NOUNS				
Singular	moon	moth	nova	age
Plural	moons	moths	novas	ages

31 B.2   If a noun ends in *s, ch, sh, x,* or *z,* add *es* to form the plural.

S, CH, SH, X, OR Z					
Singular	lens	peach	blush	box	chintz
Plural	lenses	peaches	blushes	boxes	chintzes

Follow the same generalizations to make proper nouns plural.

    the Garcia family = the Garcias

    the James family = the Jameses

    the Walsh family = the Walshes

An apostrophe is never used to make the plural form of proper nouns. It is used to show possession.

Nouns Ending in *y*

31 B.3   Add *s* to form plurals of nouns ending in a vowel and *y*.

VOWELS AND Y				
Singular	decoy	alley	delay	chimney
Plural	decoys	alleys	delays	chimneys

31 B.4   Change the *y* to *i* and add *es* to a noun ending in a consonant and *y*.

CONSONANTS AND Y				
Singular	gala**xy**	recove**ry**	pad**dy**	balco**ny**
Plural	gala**xies**	recove**ries**	pad**dies**	balco**nies**

● **Practice Your Skills**

Forming Plurals

Write the plural form of each noun.

1. hitch
2. loss
3. factory
4. essay
5. ploy
6. duplex
7. flash

8. history
9. focus
10. mouth
11. nursery
12. sketch
13. brick
14. barbecue

15. hoax
16. waltz
17. injury
18. kidney
19. atlas
20. Holmes

● *Connect to Writing:* **Editing**

Spelling Plural Nouns

Rewrite each sentence, changing the underlined nouns from singular to plural.

1. The diet of ancient people included many <u>variety</u> of <u>berry</u> from <u>bush</u> in the wild.

2. They foraged for the <u>bulb</u> of <u>lily</u>, <u>tulip</u>, and other plants.

3. Necessary <u>starch</u> were also provided by cassava <u>root</u> and <u>salsify</u>.

4. Successful <u>search</u> for food would have turned up tiny <u>bunch</u> of wild <u>grape</u>.

5. <u>Gourd</u>, used both as food and <u>container</u>, were a welcome addition to the pantry.

6. The first <u>agriculturist</u> probably cultivated root <u>plant</u> like <u>turnip</u> and <u>radish</u>.

7. Today's different <u>barley</u> are the <u>descendant</u> of the first wild <u>grass</u>.

8. The <u>seed</u> of some plants might be considered <u>delicacy</u>.

9. The large <u>seed</u> of <u>pumpkin</u>, <u>sunflower</u>, and <u>lotus</u> are eaten as <u>snack</u> today.

10. Modern <u>cook</u> often sprinkle baked <u>good</u> with the <u>seed</u> of <u>poppy</u> and sesame <u>flower</u>.

Nouns Ending in *o*

31 B.5 Add *s* to form the plural of a noun ending with a vowel and *o*.

VOWELS AND *O*				
Singular	ratio	cameo	embryo	taboo
Plural	ratios	cameos	embryos	taboos

31 B.6 Add *s* to form the plural of musical terms ending in *o*.

MUSICAL TERMS WITH *O*				
Singular	trio	soprano	piccolo	tango
Plural	trios	sopranos	piccolos	tangos

31 B.7 Add *s* to form the plural of words that were borrowed from the Spanish language.

SPANISH WORDS				
Singular	lasso	rodeo	pinto	presidio
Plural	lassos	rodeos	pintos	presidios

31 B.8 The plurals of nouns ending in a consonant and *o* do not follow a regular pattern.

CONSONANTS AND *O*				
Singular	yo-yo	silo	veto	echo
Plural	yo-yos	silos	vetoes	echoes

When you are not sure how to form the plural of a word that ends in *o*, consult a dictionary. Sometimes you will find that either spelling is acceptable. In this case, use the first form given. If the dictionary does not give a plural form, the plural is usually formed by adding *s*.

Nouns Ending in *f* or *fe*

31 B.9 To form the plural of some nouns ending in *f* or *fe*, just add *s*.

F OR *FE*				
Singular	belief	staff	giraffe	carafe
Plural	belie**fs**	staf**fs**	giraffe**s**	carafe**s**

31 B.10 For some nouns ending in *f* or *fe*, change the *f* to *v* and add *es* or *s*.

F OR *FE* TO *V*				
Singular	calf	scarf	thief	life
Plural	cal**ves**	scar**ves**	thie**ves**	li**ves**

Because there is no sure way to tell which generalization applies, consult a dictionary to check the plural form of a word that ends with *f* or *fe*.

CHAPTER 31

● **Practice Your Skills**

Forming Plurals

Write the plural form of each noun.

1. potato	**6.** loaf	**11.** chef	**16.** curio
2. alto	**7.** oaf	**12.** armadillo	**17.** carafe
3. knife	**8.** dwarf	**13.** skiff	**18.** foodstuff
4. taco	**9.** kazoo	**14.** portfolio	**19.** yourself
5. gulf	**10.** concerto	**15.** patio	**20.** tariff

● *Connect to Writing:* **Editing**

Spelling Plural Nouns

Rewrite this paragraph, changing the underlined nouns from singular to plural.

These photo of ancient Roman houses are memento of our trip to Italy. The buildings' roof have been replaced. The fresco have been restored to suggest how they looked centuries ago. Most homes had central patio. Motif about nature were popular in their art. My favorite fresco shows houses on cliff above the sea. I also saw a harbor scene with busy wharf and small skiff. I could almost hear the echo of the past.

Compound Words

Most compound nouns are made plural by adding an *s* or the letters *es* at the end. However, it sometimes makes more sense to add the ending to the first word.

31 B.11 The letter *s* or *es* are added to the end of most compound nouns.

COMPOUND NOUNS				
Singular	teammate	dragonfly	tryout	bathing suit
Plural	teammate**s**	dragonfl**ies**	tryout**s**	bathing suit**s**

31 B.12 When the main word in a compound noun appears first, that word is made plural.

EXCEPTIONS				
Singular	attorney general	father-in-law	part of speech	passerby
Plural	attorney**s** general	father**s**-in-law	part**s** of speech	passer**s**by

Numerals, Letters, Symbols, and Words as Words

31 B.13 To form the plurals of most numerals, letters, symbols, and words used as words, add an *s*.

Those *8***s** look too much like *B***s**.

The 1870**s** and 1880**s** were called the Gilded Age.

Proofreaders' #**s** tell printers to add space.

To prevent confusion, it's best to use an apostrophe and *s* with lowercase letters, some capital letters, and some words used as words. However, when you use this method to create the plural of italicized letters or words, you do not italicize the apostrophe and *s*.

How do you pronounce the *o***'s** in *footstool?*

There are a lot of *I***'s** in his conversation.

These two *theirs***'s** should be *they're***'s**.

WORD ALERT

Remember to use the apostrophe when writing letters as plurals to avoid confusion in content. Otherwise, plural letters might be mistaken for words such as *is, as,* and *us.*

Confusing	*is*	*as*	*us*
Clear	*i*'s	*a*'s	*u*'s

You can learn about the use of italics on pages 854–856.

Practice Your Skills

Forming Plurals

Write the plural form of each noun.

1. *12*	**8.** snackbar	**15.** assistant coach
2. member at large	**9.** 1930	**16.** pilot-in-command
3. handout	**10.** *e*	**17.** *p* and *q*
4. *ABC*	**11.** +	**18.** 1400
5. son-in-law	**12.** boiling point	**19.** play-off
6. solar system	**13.** forget-me-not	**20.** *R*
7. *hurray*	**14.** *pro* and *con*	

Connect to Writing: Editing

Spelling Plural Nouns

Write the underlined items as plurals.

1. The center of balance in men and women are in different parts of their bodies.
2. The only word with six *i* and no other vowels is *indivisibility.*
3. In German, *zwei* means "two," but you will hear *zwo* when Germans give addresses with 2 in them.
4. A were first called *alephs.*
5. Our speech is full of *and, of,* and *in.*
6. The cost of living in Hong Kong and Tokyo are high.
7. *Gee* and *haw* tell sled dogs to turn left or right.
8. The two runner-up in the Olympics receive silver and bronze medals.
9. The 1900 have been referred to as the Age of Anxiety.
10. Most legal documents must be signed in the presence of lawyers or notary public.

Other Plural Forms

31 B.14 Irregular plurals are not formed by adding *s* or *es*.

IRREGULAR PLURALS		
foot, f**ee**t	wom**a**n, wom**e**n	child, child**ren**
g**oo**se, g**ee**se	m**ou**se, m**i**ce	die, di**ce**

31 B.15 Some nouns have the same form for singular and plural.

SAME SINGULAR AND PLURAL		
Swiss	sheep	pliers
moose	species	politics

● **Practice Your Skills**

Forming Plurals

Write the plural form of each noun. Some words are already plural.

1. square foot	**6.** trout	**11.** measles	**16.** advice
2. series	**7.** eyetooth	**12.** pants	**17.** snow goose
3. musk ox	**8.** schoolchild	**13.** walrus	**18.** louse
4. toothbrush	**9.** physics	**14.** nobleman	**19.** mongoose
5. homework	**10.** dormouse	**15.** equipment	**20.** policewoman

● *Connect to Writing:* **Journal Entry**

Plurals

Among the first European settlers in the Old West were pioneers from Mexico and Spain. Many established great ranches in the rolling foothills of California. Put yourself in the place of a first-time visitor to the area. Record your thoughts in a journal. Use at least ten plural nouns in your entry. Try to use at least one word from Spanish and at least one noun with an irregular plural.

Connect to Writing: Editing

Spelling Plural Nouns

Rewrite each sentence, changing the underlined nouns from singular to plural. If the plural form of a word is the same as the singular, simply write the word again as it is written.

1. John Steinbeck wrote the novel *Of Mouse and Man*.
2. Farley Mowat wrote *Person of the Deer* about an Inuit group's struggle to survive.
3. Thornton Wilder's play *The Skin of Our Tooth* won a Pulitzer Prize.
4. *The Earth Beneath Sky Bear's Foot* is a collection of Native American nature poems.
5. *Hamadi & the Stolen Cattle* is a children's story by an African author.
6. Euripides's play *The Trojan Woman* is about the brutality of war.
7. Folktales of the Canadian north have been collected in *The Girl Who Dreamed Only Goose*.
8. One of Gertrude Atherton's most popular books was *Black Ox*.
9. *The Child of Sanchez* is a famous book about a poor family in Mexico.
10. *How the Irish Saved Civilization* is a book about European history.

Check Point: Mixed Practice

Write the plural form of each word. Use a dictionary whenever necessary.

1. proof	**8.** hockey	**15.** twenty
2. rancho	**9.** Jones	**16.** good-bye
3. relish	**10.** leaf	**17.** cello
4. lullaby	**11.** right-of-way	**18.** hoof
5. pathway	**12.** strike-out	**19.** buoy
6. batch	**13.** video	**20.** prefix
7. echo	**14.** 20	

31 C   Adding a prefix does not change the spelling of the base word. When you add
a suffix, you may need to change the spelling of the base word.

Adding Prefixes

A **prefix** is one or more syllables placed in front of a base word to form a new word.
When you add a prefix, the spelling of the base word does not change.

in + sincere = **in**sincere	**im** + patient = **im**patient
pre + caution = **pre**caution	**over** + rated = **over**rated
dis + honest = **dis**honest	**mis** + heard = **mis**heard
re + arrange = **re**arrange	**un** + noticed = **un**noticed
ir + resistible = **ir**resistible	**il** + legible = **il**legible

Occasionally, it is necessary to add a hyphen after a prefix to avoid confusing your reader.
Check a dictionary if you are in doubt.

HYPHENATED PREFIXES	
re-cover	**semi**-independent

WORD ALERT

It's easy to leave out one of the *r*'s in
irresistible or *overrated* if you forget that
the words are created by adding prefixes
to base words. Neither changes when you
combine the two. If you're not sure whether
a word has double letters in the beginning,
ask yourself whether it could be one of these
prefix-base word combinations.

Adding Suffixes

A **suffix** is one or more syllables placed after a base word to change its part of speech and possibly also its meaning.

31 C.1 In many cases, especially when the base word ends in a consonant, you simply add the suffix.

SUFFIXES	
eager + **ness** = eager**ness**	right + **ful** = right**ful**
treat + **ment** = treat**ment**	vague + **ly** = vague**ly**

In other cases you must change the spelling of the base word before you add the suffix.

Words Ending in *e*

31 C.2 Drop the final *e* before adding a suffix that begins with a vowel.

VOWELS AND *E*	
pause + **ing** = paus**ing**	size + **able** = siz**able**
narrate + **ion** = narrat**ion**	universe + **al** = univers**al**

31 C.3 Keep the final *e* in words that end in *ce* or *ge* if the suffix begins with an *a* or *o*. The *e* keeps the sound of the *c* or *g* soft before these vowels.

CE AND *GE*	
manage + **able** = manage**able**	outrage + **ous** = outrage**ous**
replace + **able** = replace**able**	knowledge + **able** = knowledge**able**

31 C.4 Keep the final *e* when adding a suffix that begins with a consonant.

CONSONANTS AND *E*		
Examples	peace + **ful** = peace**ful**	wise + **ly** = wise**ly**
	amuse + **ment** = amuse**ment**	same + **ness** = same**ness**
Exceptions	wise + **dom** = wis**dom**	argue + **ment** = argu**ment**
	judge + **ment** = judg**ment**	awe + **ful** = aw**ful**
	true + **ly** = tru**ly**	

Exceptions can be difficult to remember. Take the time now to create your own mnemonic aid.

Jan **u**sually **d**oesn't **g**reet **m**y **e**xceptionally **n**ervous **t**iger. = judgment

Millie **i**s **l**osing **e**very **a**fternoon **g**ym **e**vent. = mileage

Practice Your Skills

Adding Suffixes

Combine the base words and suffixes. Remember to make any necessary spelling changes.

1. rotate + ion	**11.** idle + ness
2. dense + ly	**12.** judge + ment
3. admire + er	**13.** blue + ish
4. true + ly	**14.** separate + ion
5. rhyme + ing	**15.** courage + ous
6. continue + al	**16.** pronounce + able
7. solve + able	**17.** settle + ment
8. tense + ion	**18.** endure + ance
9. spire + al	**19.** adore + able
10. mature + ity	**20.** knowledge + able

Connect to Writing: Editing

Spelling Words with Prefixes and Suffixes

Rewrite the underlined words in the following paragraphs, correctly spelling those that are incorrect.

The singing sands of the Bay of Laig in Scotland are <u>remarkable</u>. If you walk on the sand, it emits sounds with <u>noticably</u> strong <u>resemblences</u> to the string instruments of an orchestra. The <u>tuneful</u> sounds range from basses to sopranos.

Scientists have <u>carefully</u> <u>investigated</u> the mystery and found the answer. Tiny grains of <u>unpolished</u> quartz have the <u>noteable</u> <u>ability</u> to transfer <u>vibrations</u>. This means that the sand <u>naturaly</u> produces <u>contineuous</u> sounds. <u>Interestingly</u>, laboratory <u>experimentation</u> has shown that the transmission can be <u>interrupted</u> when the sand is not <u>completly</u> clean.

CHAPTER 31

Words Ending in y

31 C.5 To add a suffix to most words ending in a vowel and *y*, keep the *y*.

VOWELS AND Y		
Examples	play + **able** = play**able**	enjoy + **ment** = enjoy**ment**
	mislay + **ing** = mislay**ing**	replay + **ed** = replay**ed**
Exceptions	day + **ly** = dai**ly**	gay + **ly** = gai**ly**

31 C.6 To add a suffix to most words ending in a consonant and *y*, change the *y* to *i* before adding the suffix. However, do not drop the *y* when adding *-ing*.

CONSONANTS AND Y		
Examples	envy + **able** = env**iable**	dreary + **ness** = drear**iness**
	bounty + **ful** = bount**iful**	mercy + **ful** = merc**iful**
	thrifty + **ly** = thrift**ily**	
Exception	identify + **ing** = identif**ying**	

WORD ALERT

One-syllable words that end in *y* pronounced long *i* do not change their spellings when the suffixes *-ness* or *-ing* are added. They *do* change their spellings when the suffix *-ed* is added.

shy + **ness** = shy**ness**	dry + **ed** = dr**ied**
dry + **ing** = dry**ing**	pry + **ed** = pr**ied**
sly + **ness** = sly**ness**	spy + **ed** = sp**ied**

Doubling the Final Consonant

Sometimes the final consonant in a word is doubled before a suffix is added.

31 C.7   Double the final consonant in a word before adding a suffix only when all three of the following conditions are met:

(1) The suffix begins with a vowel.

(2) The base word has only one syllable or is stressed on the last syllable.

(3) The base word ends in one consonant preceded by a vowel.

DOUBLE CONSONANTS		
One-Syllable Words	plot + **ing** = plot**ting**	trap + **er** = trap**per**
	char + **ed** = char**red**	mad + **est** = ma**ddest**
Final Syllable Stressed	befit + **ing** = befi**tting**	rebut + **al** = rebu**ttal**
	transfer + **ed** = transfe**rred**	recur + **ence** = recu**rrence**

Don't double the final *r* in words that end in *fer* when you add the suffix *-ence* or *-able*. Notice how the pronunciation of the base word changes when the suffix is added. This is your clue that only one *r* is needed.

FINAL *R*	
refer + **ence** = refe**rence**	defer + **ence** = defe**rence**
infer + **ence** = infe**rence**	transfer + **able** = transfe**rable**

Be sure not to double the final letter if it is preceded by two vowels.

TWO VOWELS	
creep + **ing** = cree**ping**	seat + **ed** = sea**ted**
train + **er** = trai**ner**	proud + **est** = prou**dest**

Connect to Reading and Writing: Classroom Vocabulary

English Vocabulary and Spelling

This chapter has introduced you to new terms that will be used often in your study of English grammar. To keep track of these new words, such as *plurals*, *prefixes*, and *suffixes*, make a booklet that lists and tells about them. Include all the rules that apply and give your booklet a title.

Practice Your Skills

Adding Suffixes

Combine the base words and suffixes. Remember to make any necessary spelling changes.

1. deter + ed

2. cram + ed

3. day + ly

4. weak + en

5. plenty + ful

6. unnecessary + ly

7. strut + ing

8. comply + ance

9. hot + est

10. snob + ism

11. timid + est

12. annoy + ance

13. trek + ed

14. employ + able

15. infer + ing

16. study + ing

17. survey + ing

18. justify + able

19. incur + ing

20. drowsy + ness

21. confer + ence

22. drain + ed

Connect to Writing: Editing

Spelling Words with Prefixes and Suffixes

Rewrite the underlined words in the following paragraph, correctly spelling those that are incorrect.

We take household <u>applyances</u> for granted. We don't <u>ordinarily</u> give any thought to their <u>fascinateing</u> history. Among the <u>earilest</u> "irons," for example, were the glass linen smoothers. They were used by tenth-century Vikings. Later, European servants <u>wearly</u> <u>emploied</u> flat mallets to beat fabric smooth. By the 1500s, the <u>exhausted</u> servants were <u>clumsily</u> using flat metal boxes filled with hot charcoal. These <u>primateive</u> contraptions were <u>undeniablely</u> dangerous to use. They sometimes <u>chared</u> and <u>spoilled</u> the linen. When stoves replaced open fireplaces, these fabric smoothers could be made of solid cast iron. They were <u>readily</u> <u>heatted</u> on the stove. They cooled quickly once off the stove and required <u>heatting</u> over and over again. By the late 1800s, the dreary <u>busyness</u> of <u>ironing</u> was made <u>easyier</u> by the development of fuel-powered irons. Gasoline, alcohol, and gas irons were <u>fited</u> with long tubes. The tubes were <u>connected</u> to fuel tanks. They stayed hotter longer, but they were <u>necessarilly</u> awkward to use.

✔ *Check Point:* **Mixed Practice**

Add the prefix and/or suffix to each base word and write the new word.

1. ideal + ly
2. trek + ed
3. argue + ment
4. re + play + able
5. out + wit + ing
6. transfer + able
7. value + able
8. rely + ance
9. change + able
10. terse + ly
11. admire + ation
12. duty + ful
13. service + able
14. refer + ing
15. ally + ance
16. ir + response + ible
17. program + ed
18. un + necessary + ly
19. occur + ence
20. dis + advantage + ous

● *Connect to Writing:* **Advertisement**

Suffixes

Write an advertisement for a kitchen appliance. Choose any appliance, describe it, and explain why someone should have one. Make your advertisement convincing. Use at least five of the following words with suffixes in your ad.

- handy + er, est, or ly
- rely + able or ance
- dirty + er or est
- equip + ed or ing
- day + ly
- plug + ed or ing
- sturdy + er, est, or ly
- cook + ed or ing

When You Use Technology

Most word-processing programs come with spell check capabilities. Some also come with an electronic dictionary and a thesaurus. To use the dictionary, highlight the word in question and select Dictionary from the appropriate menu. The definition of the word will show in a window along with some related words. Selecting Thesaurus can also help you find the spelling of a word. For example, if you forgot how to spell *aisle*, you can enter the word *passageway* and the word *aisle* will appear as one of the synonyms in the thesaurus.

Make it your goal to learn to spell these fifty words this year. Use them in your writing and practice writing them until spelling them comes automatically.

accelerate	counterfeit	pageant
accessory	defendant	paralysis
accommodate	defiance	physics
accumulate	dissatisfied	pneumonia
acquaintance	efficient	possibility
admittance	existence	precipitation
advisable	exquisite	preference
alliance	furlough	recruit
appreciation	hygiene	regrettable
ascend	ingredient	siege
carburetor	intercede	stationary
circuit	irregular	stationery
coincidence	liable	succession
committee	maneuver	tariff
conceit	miscellaneous	temporary
consequence	noticeable	vacuum
convenience	occurrence	

Assess Your Learning

▓ Applying Spelling Generalizations

Write the letter of the misspelled word in each group. Then write the word, spelling it correctly.

1. (a) calfs (b) sheriffs (c) dollar signs
2. (a) sharing (b) appling (c) receive
3. (a) busily (b) foreign (c) hankerchief
4. (a) solos (b) mouses (c) discouraged
5. (a) desparate (b) Internet (c) resentful
6. (a) siegh (b) portraying (c) happiest
7. (a) proofs (b) complexs (c) casually
8. (a) trader (b) misplace (c) horrifyed
9. (a) plainess (b) kangaroos (c) hastily
10. (a) singular (b) nineth (c) commanders-in-chief
11. (a) ambushes (b) sameness (c) mistatement
12. (a) vetos (b) succeed (c) carrying
13. (a) joys (b) puppyes (c) blitzes
14. (a) yeild (b) insane (c) placement
15. (a) altoes (b) field (c) craftiness
16. (a) replied (b) intersect (c) unatural
17. (a) pigment (b) speceis (c) dissatisfied
18. (a) assured (b) realize (c) poletics
19. (a) wierd (b) ranches (c) efficient
20. (a) dutyful (b) finally (c) blindness

Directions

Write the letter of the answer that correctly spells the underlined word. If the underlined word is correct, write *D*.

   If you are **(1)** <u>adventurous</u>, try **(2)** <u>rideing</u> the swift-moving waves at the beach with a surfboard. A fast-paced volleyball game can provide both **(3)** <u>eggercise</u> and **(4)** <u>excitment</u>. Additionally, a **(5)** <u>skillful</u> cast of a net might bring a reward of live bait. **(6)** <u>Nothing</u> is more challenging than battling the surf to reel in a fish. All ages **(7)** <u>injoy</u> the task of building a mighty sand castle before the tide **(8)** <u>washes</u> it away. With so many exciting things to do, it's almost **(9)** <u>imposible</u> to **(10)** <u>expereince</u> boredom at the beach.

1. A adventureous
   B aventurous
   C adventureus
   D No error

2. A ridding
   B rideng
   C riding
   D No error

3. A exersize
   B exercise
   C egercise
   D No error

4. A exsitement
   B excitement
   C excitemint
   D No error

5. A skillfull
   B skillfule
   C skilfull
   D No error

6. A Nuthing
   B No thing
   C Notthing
   D No error

7. A enjoy
   B ennjoy
   C innjoy
   D No error

8. A washs
   B waches
   C wasches
   D No error

9. A impossable
   B imposable
   C impossible
   D No error

10. A experience
   B experiense
   C expereinse
   D No error

Writer's Corner

Snapshot

31 A Some **spelling generalizations** are based on the **patterns of letters** in words. You can find certain common patterns in words spelled with *ie* or *ei* and in words that end with the "seed" sound. (pages 915–917)

31 B To form the **plural** of most nouns, add *s* or *es*. Some nouns are exceptions. (pages 918–925)

31 C Adding a **prefix** does not change the spelling of the base word. When you add a **suffix,** you may need to change the spelling of the base word. (pages 926–932)

Power Rules

 Check the spelling of words that sound like other words. (pages 719–720)

Before Editing	**After Editing**
I hope it won't *reign* during the parade.	I hope it won't *rain* during the parade.
I will not *except* that as the truth.	I will not *accept* that as the truth.

Be sure that when a word has an *ie* or an *ei* in it, you remember the rule that *i* comes before *e* except when it follows *c* or when it has the long *a* sound. Learn exceptions to the rule. (pages 915–916)

Before Editing	**After Editing**
We will visit our *nieghbor* tomorrow.	We will visit our *neighbor* tomorrow.
I am in a *wierd* mood.	I am in a *weird* mood.

Editing Checklist

Use this checklist when editing your writing.

✓ Did I spell words with *ie* and *ei* correctly? (See pages 915–916.)

✓ Did I use *s* and *es* correctly to make the plural form? (See pages 918–925.)

✓ Did I make sure to recognize irregular plural words and spell them correctly? (See page 924.)

✓ Did I make sure to recognize words that have the same singular and plural forms? (See page 924.)

✓ Did I spell words correctly after adding a suffix? (See pages 927–932.)

Use the Power

Think about the rules you learned in this chapter. Then look at the words in the first column. Try to spell each word by combining it with a prefix or suffix in the second column. Note that not all combinations will work.

Word	Prefix / Suffix
month	*-s/-es*
bush	*in-*
monkey	*im-*
fish	*-ly*
sincere	*dis-*
patient	*-ing*
honest	
pause	
amuse	

Language QuickGuide

QUICKGUIDE

The Power Rules

Researchers have found that certain patterns of language used offend educated people more than others and therefore affect how people perceive you. Since these patterns of language use have such an impact on future success, you should learn how to edit for the more widely accepted forms. The list below identifies ten of the most important conventions to master the Power Rules. Always check for them when you edit.

1. **Use only one negative form for a single negative idea.** (See page 773.)

Before Editing	After Editing
You don't got *nothing*.	You don't have *anything*.
I didn't do *nothing*.	I didn't do *anything*.

2. **Use mainstream past-tense forms of regular and irregular verbs.** (See pages 674–682.) You might try to recite and memorize the parts of the most common irregular verbs.

Before Editing	After Editing
I *play* that song two minutes ago.	I *played* that song two minutes ago.
We *was* chilling.	We *were* chilling.
Consuelo *come* to the game last night.	Consuelo *came* to the game last night.
Y'all should have *went* home.	Y'all should have *gone* home.
They *done brung* me to the concert.	They *brought* me to the concert.

3. **Use verbs that agree with the subject.** (See pages 736–740.)

Before Editing	After Editing
Shamique usually *clean* her plate.	Shamique usually *cleans* her plate.
The cat and the dog *gets* along well.	The cat and the dog *get* along well.
Either the chipmunks or the squirrel *eat* the walnut.	Either the chipmunks or the squirrel *eats* the walnut.
Neither the biscuit nor the muffins *is finished* baking.	Neither the biscuit nor the muffins *are finished* baking.

4. Use subject forms of pronouns in subject position. Use object forms of pronouns in object position. (See pages 706–716.)

Before Editing

Her and her backpack are inseparable.
Him and his problems are none of my business.
Her and *me* had lunch at Murray's Deli.

After Editing

She and her backpack are inseparable.
He and his problems are none of my business.
She and *I* had lunch at Murray's Deli.

5. Use standard ways to make nouns possessive. (See pages 878–880.)

Before Editing

Who is the *dogs* owner?
Who broke the *cars* window?
Horace mounted the *horses* back.
Both *dogs* barking kept me awake.

After Editing

Who is the *dog's* owner?
Who broke the *car's* window?
Horace mounted the *horse's* back.
Both *dogs'* barking kept me awake.

6. Use a consistent verb tense except when a change is clearly necessary. (See pages 689–694.)

Before Editing

The bell *rings* when the class ended.
After the boring movie, I *yawn* and gave it thumbs down.

After Editing

The bell *rang* when the class ended.
After the boring movie, I *yawned* and gave it thumbs down.

7. Use sentence fragments only the way professional writers do, after the sentence they refer to and usually to emphasize a point. Fix all sentence fragments that occur before the sentence they refer to and ones that occur in the middle of a sentence. (See page 656.)

Before Editing

Today. I will ace the test.
Trying to build a boat. *While sailing it is hard.* So we try to build it ahead of time.
I released the healed robin Into the wild. *The reason being that I wanted it to be free.*

After Editing

Today, I will ace the test.
Trying to build a boat *while sailing it is hard,* so we try to build it ahead of time.
I released the healed robin into the wild *because I wanted it to be free.*

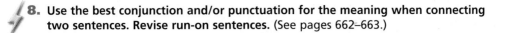

8. Use the best conjunction and/or punctuation for the meaning when connecting two sentences. Revise run-on sentences. (See pages 662–663.)

Before Editing	After Editing
We turned on the faucet, brown water came out.	*When we turned on the faucet,* brown water came out.
I went to summer school, I didn't go on vacation.	I went to summer school, *so* I didn't go on vacation.
Preston ironed his shirt, he polished his shoes.	Preston ironed his shirt, *and* he polished his shoes.

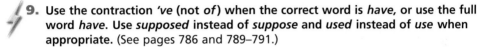

9. Use the contraction *'ve* (not *of*) when the correct word is *have,* or use the full word *have.* Use *supposed* instead of *suppose* and *used* instead of *use* when appropriate. (See pages 786 and 789–791.)

Before Editing	After Editing
They should *of* elected me president.	They should *have* elected me president.
We might *of* underestimated her ability.	We might *have* underestimated her ability.
The banana would *of* tasted better if we hadn't let it turn brown.	The banana would *have* tasted better if we hadn't let it turn brown.
We were *suppose* to turn off the lights.	We were *supposed* to turn off the lights.
Pedro *use* to be wasteful, but he now recycles his cans and bottles.	Pedro *used* to be wasteful, but he now recycles his cans and bottles.

10. For sound-alikes and certain words that sound almost alike, choose the word with your intended meaning. (See pages 782–791.)

Before Editing	After Editing
We are going *too* quit watching so much TV. (*too* means *also* or *in addition*)	We are going *to* quit watching so much TV. (*to* is part of the infinitive form of the verb *to quit*)
I will put *to* slices of tofu on each sandwich. (*to* means in the direction of)	I will put *two* slices of tofu on each sandwich. (*two* is a number)
Was that *you're* seat I took? (*you're* is a contraction of *you are*)	Was that *your* seat I took? (*your* is the possessive form of *you*)
They're idea is worth considering. (*they're* is a contraction of *they are*)	*Their* idea is worth considering. (*their* is the possessive form of *they*)
I'd like the table placed *their.* (*their* is the possessive form of *they*)	I'd like the table placed *there.* (*there* means in that place)
Its a shame I ran out of zucchini. (*its* is the possessive form of *it*)	*It's* a shame I ran out of zucchini. (*it's* is a contraction of *it is*)

QUICKGUIDE

Nine Tools for Powerful Writing • • • • • • • • • • • • •

Besides knowing the Power Rules that will help you avoid errors, you can also use the following nine tools to turn your good writing into powerful writing.

1. Write **in living color** with strong verbs. (See page 202.)

Here's how a statement might look in "black and white."

> The boy ate the meal.

Strengthen the verb, though, and suddenly the scene takes on color.

> The boy **devoured** the meal.

2. Answer the question **What kind?** by using descriptive **adjectives.** (See page 139.)

Vivid adjectives can intensify action or mood. They also can add colorful details about characters, things, and places.

> The boy, **ravenous** and **eager,** devoured **his favorite** meal, a **delectable steaming** plate of chicken and rice.

3. **Set the scene** with adverbial clauses and prepositional phrases. (See pages 49 and 320.)

Begin your sentence with a clause that provides meaningful and descriptive details. Adverbial clauses help you explain when, where, why, or how something happens. They begin with a subordinating word like *when, if, because, until, while,* or *since.* Remember that a subordinate clause must be attached to an independent clause.

> **Although he had snacked just an hour ago,** the boy devoured the meal.

You can also set the scene with details in the form of a prepositional phrase. Use a preposition, followed by its object and any word that describes the object.

> **In his aunt's warm dining room on that cool fall day,** he joined his family.

4. **Get into the action** with participial phrases. (See page 266.)

You can pack a lot of action into your sentences if you include an *–ing* verb, or "*–ing* modifier." Formally called a *present participial phrase,* these *–ing* modifiers describe a person, thing, or action in a sentence.

> **Smiling broadly,** he looked at the steaming food, **inhaling its aroma.**

5. Elaborate by **explaining who or what with appositives.** (See page 165.)

Details that elaborate on a person, place, or thing that may be unknown to your reader will strengthen your writing. You can add such details in the form of an appositive. An appositive is a noun or pronoun phrase that identifies or adds identifying information to the preceding noun.

> The meal, a **chicken smothered in a sweet and sour sauce and served with vegetables and rice,** had been a family favorite for generations.

6. Create emphasis **by dashing it all.** (See page 120.)

When you are writing informally, dashes can create abrupt breaks that emphasize a word or group of words. Use one dash to set off words at the end of a sentence. Use a pair of dashes to set off words in the middle of a sentence.

> After he thought he could eat no more, she set down the final and most anticipated part of the meal—**a four-layer chocolate cake.**

> The boy—**he had not realized how hungry he was**—devoured the entire meal in less than ten minutes.

7. **Tip the scale** with clauses. (See page 237.)

In persuasive writing, use a subordinate clause to acknowledge opposing viewpoints. This will tip the scale toward your own viewpoint, which remains in the main clause.

> **While some people may say this dish has too many calories,** I remind them that it is only eaten on special occasions.

8. Use the **power of 3s** to add style and emphasis with **parallelism.** (See page 78.)

One way to add power is to use a writing device called parallelism. Parallelism is the use of the same kind of word or group of words in a series of three or more.

> Years later he can still **smell the** tangy sauce, **taste the** tender meat, and **feel the** delicate texture of the cake.

9. Write with variety and coherence and **let it flow.** (See page 97.)

Vary the length, structure, and beginnings of your sentences and use connecting words to help your writing flow smoothly.

> One year the boy's family gathered at his aunt's house to celebrate his birthday. He was ten. He remembers the day with all his senses. Joining his family in his aunt's warm dining room on that fall day, he had smiled at the steaming food. The main dish, a chicken smothered in a sweet and sour sauce and served with vegetables and rice, had been a family favorite for generations. He can still smell the tangy sauce, taste the tender meat, and feel the delicate texture of the meal's highlight—a four-layer chocolate cake.

Nine Tools for Powerful Writing   **943**

This section presents an easy-to-use reference for the definitions of grammatical terms. The number on the colored tab tells you the chapter covering that topic. The page number to the right of each definition refers to the place in the chapter where you can find additional instruction, examples, and applications to writing.

13 The Sentence

How can you use sentences to paint powerful images and to tell interesting stories?

A Sentence

Subjects

Predicates

QUICKGUIDE

Different Positions of Subjects

Compound Subjects and Predicates

Kinds of Sentences

14 Nouns and Pronouns

How can you use nouns and pronouns to create lively and precise prose?

Nouns

QUICKGUIDE

15 Verbs

How can you make you make your writing sing by adding just the right verbs?

Action Verbs

Transitive and Intransitive Verbs

Helping Verbs

Linking Verbs

16 Adjectives and Adverbs

How can you add interest and detail to your writing with adjectives and adverbs?

Adjectives

Adverbs

17 Other Parts of Speech and Review

How can you create fluency in your writing by using prepositions and conjunctions to join ideas and sentences?

Prepositions

Conjunctions and Interjections

QUICKGUIDE

Parts of Speech Review

18 Complements

How can you use complements, or completers, to focus your writing?

Kinds of Complements

Direct Objects

Indirect Objects

Predicate Nominatives

Predicate Adjectives

19 Phrases

How can you use phrases to add variety and detail to your writing?

Prepositional Phrases

Appositives and Appositive Phrases

20 Verbals and Verbal Phrases

How can you add details and a sense of action to your writing with verbals and verbal phrases?

Participles and Participial Phrases

Gerunds and Gerund Phrases

Infinitives and Infinitive Phrases

QUICKGUIDE

21 Clauses

How can you use clauses to connect related ideas and to add interest to your writing?

Independent and Subordinate Clauses

Uses of Subordinate Clauses

Kinds of Sentence Structure

22 Sentence Fragments and Run-ons

How can you clarify your meaning and add sentence variety by fixing unintended sentence fragments and run-ons?

Sentence Fragments

Phrase Fragments

22 B A **phrase fragment** is a group of words that is incorrectly punctuated   657
as a sentence but is missing a subject and a verb.

Clause Fragments

22 C A **clause fragment** is a subordinate clause that is incorrectly written as   660
a sentence.

Run-on Sentences

22 D A **run-on sentence** is two or more sentences that are written together   662
and are separated by a comma or no mark of punctuation at all.

This section presents an easy-to-use reference for the explanations of how various grammatical elements are and should be used. The number on the colored tab tells you the chapter covering that topic. The page number to the right of each definition refers to the place in the chapter where you can find additional instruction, examples, and applications to writing. You can also refer to the Writer's Glossary of Usage (pages 782–793) for help with commonly confused usage items.

23 Using Verbs

How can understanding how to use verbs help you improve your writing?

The Principal Parts of Verbs

Six Problem Verbs

Verb Tense

Active Voice and Passive Voice

24 Using Pronouns

How can you use pronouns to make your writing flow smoothly?

The Cases of Personal Pronouns

Pronoun Problem: *Who* or *Whom?*

Pronouns and Their Antecedents

25 Subject and Verb Agreement

How can you make your subjects and verbs work together so that your ideas are clear?

Agreement of Subjects and Verbs

Common Agreement Problems

QUICKGUIDE

26 Using Adjectives and Adverbs

How can you create colorful prose with adjectives and adverbs?

Comparison of Adjectives and Adverbs

| 26 A.2 | Use *-er* or *more* to form the comparative degree and *-est* or *most* to form the superlative degree of two-syllable modifiers. | 765 |
| 26 A.3 | Use *more* to form the comparative degree and *most* to form the superlative degree of modifiers with three or more syllables. | 766 |

Problems with Modifiers

26 B	Avoid confusing certain adjectives and adverbs, comparing a thing with itself, and using **double comparisons** and **double negatives.**	771
26 B.1	Add *other* or *else* to avoid comparing a thing with itself.	771
26 B.2	Do not use both *-er* and *more* to form the comparative degree, or both *-est* and *most* to form the superlative degree.	772
26 B.3	Avoid using a double negative.	773

Mechanics QuickGuide ● ● ● ● ● ● ● ● ● ● ● ● ● ● ● ● ● ●

This section presents an easy-to-use reference for the mechanics of writing: capitalization, punctuation, and spelling. The number on the colored tab tells you the chapter covering that topic. The page number to the right of each definition refers to the place in the chapter where you can find additional instruction, examples, and applications to writing.

27 Capital Letters

How can you use capital letters to clarify your writing?

First Words and the Pronoun *I*

Proper Nouns

Other Uses of Capital Letters

QUICKGUIDE

28 End Marks and Commas

How can you create meaning through the careful use of end marks and commas?

End Marks

28 A   An **end mark** is a mark of punctuation at the end of a sentence. You may recall that the purpose of a sentence determines its end mark.   822

     28 A.1   Place a **period** after a statement, after an opinion, and after a command or request made in a normal tone of voice.   822

     28 A.2   Place a **question mark** after a sentence that asks a question.   822

     28 A.3   Place an **exclamation point** after a sentence that expresses strong feeling or after a command or request that expresses great excitement.   822

Other Uses of Periods

28 B   Periods are also used in abbreviations and outlines.   824

     28 B.1   Use a period with most abbreviations.   824

     28 B.2   Use a period after each number or letter that shows a division in an outline.   825

Commas That Separate

28 C   One function of commas is to separate elements in a sentence.   827

     28 C.1   Use commas to separate items in a series.   827

     28 C.2   Use a comma sometimes to separate two adjectives that precede a noun and are not joined by a conjunction.   829

     28 C.3   Use a comma to separate the independent clauses of a compound sentence if the clauses are joined by a conjunction.   831

     28 C.4   Use a comma after certain introductory structures.   832

     28 C.5   Use commas to separate elements in dates and addresses.   835

     28 C.6   Use a comma after the salutation of a friendly letter and after the closing of all letters.   835

Commas That Enclose

28 D   Commas are used to enclose words that interrupt the main idea of a sentence.   838

QUICKGUIDE

29 Italics and Quotation Marks

How can you use italics and quotation marks to communicate clearly and expertly?

Italics (Underlining)

Quotation Marks

30 Other Punctuation

How can you use apostrophes and other punctuation to communicate precisely?

Apostrophes

Semicolons

Colons

Hyphens

Parentheses, Dashes, Brackets, and Ellipses

31 Spelling Correctly

How can you communicate your message effectively by using accurate spelling?

Spelling Patterns

Forming Plurals

Prefixes and Suffixes

Glossary

English

A

abbreviation shortened form of a word that generally begins with a capital letter and ends with a period.

abstract noun noun that cannot be seen or touched, such as an idea, quality, or characteristic.

acronym an abbreviation formed by using the initial letters of a phrase or name (CIA—Central Intelligence Agency).

action verb verb that tells what action a subject is performing.

active voice voice the verb is in when it expresses that the subject is performing the action.

adjective word that modifies a noun or a pronoun.

adjectival clause subordinate clause used to modify a noun or pronoun.

adjectival phrase prepositional phrase that modifies a noun or a pronoun.

adverb word that modifies a verb, an adjective, or another adverb.

adverbial clause subordinate clause that is used mainly to modify a verb.

Español

abreviatura forma reducida de una palabra que generalmente comienza con mayúscula y termina en punto.

austantivo abstracto sustantivo que no puede verse ni tocarse, como una idea, una cualidad o una característica.

acrónimo abreviatura que se forma al usar las letras iniciales de una frase o de un nombre (CIA—Central Intelligence Agency [Agencia Central de Inteligencia]).

verbo de acción verbo que indica qué acción realiza el sujeto.

voz activa voz en que está el verbo cuando expresa que el sujeto está realizando la acción.

adjetivo palabra que modifica a un sustantivo o a un pronombre.

cláusula adjetiva cláusula subordinada utilizada para modificar a un sustantivo o a un pronombre.

frase adjetiva frase preposicional que modifica a un sustantivo o a un pronombre.

adverbio palabra que modifica a un verbo, a un adjetivo o a otro adverbio.

cláusula adverbial cláusula subordinada que se utiliza principalmente para modificar a un verbo.

English	Español
adverbial phrase prepositional phrase that is used mainly to modify a verb.	**frase adverbial** frase preposicional que se utiliza principalmente para modificar a un verbo.
analogy logical relationship between a pair of words.	**analogía** relación lógica entre una pareja de palabras.
antecedent word or group of words to which a pronoun refers.	**antecedente** palabra o grupo de palabras a que hace referencia un pronombre.
antonym word that means the opposite of another word.	**antónimo** palabra que significa lo opuesto de otra palabra.
appositive noun or pronoun that identifies or explains another noun or pronoun in a sentence.	**aposición** sustantivo o pronombre que especifica o explica a otro sustantivo o pronombre en una oración.
audience person or persons who will read your work or hear your speech.	**público** persona o personas que leerán tu trabajo o escucharán tu discurso.

B

bandwagon statement appeal that leads the reader to believe that everyone is using a certain product.	**enunciado de arrastre** enunciado apelativo que lleva al lector a creer que todos usan cierto producto.
bibliographic information information about a source, such as author, title, publisher, date of publication, and Internet address.	**información bibliográfica** datos sobre una fuente: autor, título, editorial, fecha de publicación, dirección de Internet, etc.
body one or more paragraphs composed of details, facts, and examples that support the main idea.	**cuerpo** uno o más párrafos compuestos de detalles, hechos y ejemplos que apoyan la idea principal.

brackets punctuation marks [ ] used to enclose information added to text or to indicate new text replacing the original quoted text; always used in pairs.

brainstorming prewriting technique of writing down ideas that come to mind about a given subject.

business letter formal letter that asks for action on the part of the receiver and includes an inside address, heading, salutation, body, closing, and signature.

C

case form of a noun or a pronoun that indicates its use in a sentence. In English there are three cases: the nominative case, the objective case, and the possessive case.

chronological order the order in which events occur.

citation note that gives credit to the source of another person's paraphrased or quoted ideas.

clarity the quality of being clear.

clause group of words that has a subject and verb and is used as part of a sentence.

close reading reading carefully to locate specific information, follow an argument's logic, or comprehend the meaning of information.

corchetes signos de puntuación [ ] utilizados para encerrar la información añadida al texto o para indicar el texto nuevo que reemplaza al texto original citado; siempre se usan en parejas.

intercambio de ideas técnica de preparación para la escritura que consiste en anotar las ideas que surgen sobre un tema.

carta de negocios carta formal que solicita al destinatario que realice una acción e incluye dirección del destinatario, membrete, saludo, cuerpo, despedida y firma.

caso forma de un sustantivo o de un pronombre que indica su uso en una oración. En inglés hay tres casos: nominativo, objetivo y posesivo.

orden cronológico orden en el que ocurren los sucesos.

cita nota que menciona la fuente de donde se extrajeron las ideas, parafraseadas o textuales, de otra persona.

claridad cualidad de un texto de ser claro.

cláusula grupo de palabras que tiene sujeto y verbo y se utiliza como parte de una oración.

lectura atenta lectura minuciosa para identificar información específica, seguir un argumento lógico o comprender el significado de la información.

GLOSSARY

clustering visual strategy a writer uses to organize ideas and details connected to the subject.	**agrupación** estrategia visual que emplea un escritor para organizar las ideas y los detalles relacionados con el tema.
coherence logical and smooth flow of ideas connected with clear transitions.	**coherencia** flujo lógico de ideas que discurren conectadas con transiciones claras.
collaboration in writing, the working together of several individuals on one piece of writing, usually done during prewriting, including brainstorming, and revising.	**colaboración** en el ámbito de la escritura, el trabajo en común de varios individuos en un texto, usualmente durante la etapa de preparación para la escritura, incluida la técnica de intercambio de ideas y la tarea de revisión.
collective noun noun that names a group of people or things.	**sustantivo colectivo** sustantivo que designa un grupo de personas o cosas.
colloquialism informal phrase or colorful expression not meant to be taken literally but understood to have particular non-literal meaning.	**coloquialismo** frase informal o expresión pintoresca que no debe tomarse literalmente, pues tiene un significado figurado específico.
complement word or group of words used to complete a predicate.	**complemento** palabra o grupo de palabras utilizadas para completar un predicado.
complete predicate all the words that tell what the subject is doing or that tell something about the subject.	**predicado completo** todas las palabras que expresan qué hace el sujeto o dicen algo acerca del sujeto.
complete subject all the words used to identify the person, place, thing, or idea that the sentence is about.	**sujeto completo** todas las palabras utilizadas para identificar la persona, el lugar, la cosa o la idea de la que trata la oración.
complex sentence sentence that consists of a dependent and an independent clause.	**oración compleja** oración que consiste de una cláusula dependiente y una independiente.

English	Español
composition writing form that presents and develops one main idea.	**composición** tipo de texto que presenta y desarrolla una idea principal.
compound noun a single noun comprised of several words.	**sustantivo compuesto** sustantivo individual formado por varias palabras.
compound sentence consists of two simple sentences, usually joined by a comma and the coordinating conjunction *and, but, or,* or *yet.*	**oración compuesta** consiste de dos oraciones simples, unidas generalmente por una coma y la conjunción coordinante and (y), but (pero), or (o) y yet (sin embargo).
compound subject two or more subjects in a sentence that have the same verb and are joined by a conjunction.	**sujeto compuesto** dos o más sujetos en una oración que tienen el mismo verbo y están unidos por una conjunción.
compound verb two or more verbs in one sentence that have the same subject and are joined by a conjunction.	**verbo compuesto** dos o más verbos en una oración que tienen el mismo sujeto y están unidos por una conjunción.
concluding sentence a strong ending added to a paragraph that summarizes the major points, refers to the main idea, or adds an insight.	**oración conclusiva** un final que se añade a un párrafo y que resume los puntos principales, se refiere a la idea principal o añade una reflexión.
conclusion a strong ending added to a paragraph or composition that summarizes the major points, refers to the main idea, and adds an insight.	**conclusión** un final fuerte que se añade a un párrafo o a una composición y que resume los puntos principales, se refiere a la idea principal y añade una reflexión.
concrete noun person, place, or thing that can be seen or touched.	**sustantivo concreto** una persona, un lugar o una cosa que puede verse o tocarse.
conjunction word that joins together sentences, clauses, phrases, or other words.	**conjunción** palabra que une dos oraciones, cláusulas, frases u otras palabras.
conjunctive adverb an adverb used to connect two clauses.	**adverbio conjuntivo** adverbio utilizado para conectar dos cláusulas.

connotation meaning that comes from attitudes attached to a word.

contraction word that combines two words into one and uses an apostrophe to replace one or more missing letters.

coordinating conjunction single connecting word used to join words or groups of words.

count noun a noun that names an object that can be counted (grains of rice, storms, songs).

counter-argument argument offered to address opposing views in a persuasive composition.

creative writing writing style in which the writer creates characters, events, and images within stories, plays, or poems to express feelings, perceptions, and points of view.

connotación significado que proviene de los valores vinculados a una palabra.

contracción palabra que combina dos palabras en una y utiliza un apóstrofo en lugar de la(s) letra(s) faltante(s).

conjunción coordinante palabra de conexión usada para unir palabras o grupos de palabras.

sustantivo contable sustantivo que designa un objeto que se puede contar (granos de arroz, tormentas, canciones).

contraargumento argumento que se ofrece para tratar las opiniones contrarias en una composición persuasiva.

escritura creativa estilo de escritura en cual el escritor crea los personajes, los sucesos y las imágenes de cuentos, obras de teatro o poemas para expresar sentimientos, percepciones y puntos de vista.

D

declarative sentence a statement or expression of an opinion. It ends with a period.

demonstrative pronoun word that substitutes for a noun and points out a person or thing.

denotation literal meaning of a word.

oración enunciativa enunciado o expresión de una opinión. Termina en punto.

pronombre demostrativo palabra que está en lugar de un sustantivo y señala una persona o cosa.

denotación significado literal de una palabra.

GLOSSARY

descriptive writing writing that creates a vivid picture of a person, an object, or a scene by stimulating the reader's senses.

dialogue conversation between two or more people in a story or play.

direct object noun or a pronoun that answers the question *What?* or *Whom?* after an action verb.

direct quotation passage, sentence, or words stated exactly as the person wrote or said them.

documentary images, interviews, and narration put together to create a powerful report.

double negative use of two negative words to express an idea when only one is needed.

drafting stage of the writing process in which the writer expresses ideas in sentences, forming a beginning, a middle, and an ending in a composition.

texto descriptivo texto que crea una imagen vívida de una persona, un objeto o una escena estimulando los sentidos del lector.

diálogo conversación entre dos o más personas en un cuento o en una obra de teatro.

objeto directo sustantivo o pronombre que responde la pregunta ¿Qué? *(What?)* o ¿Quién? *(Whom?)* después de un verbo de acción.

cita directa pasaje, oración o palabras enunciadas exactamente como la persona las escribió o las dijo.

documental imágenes, entrevistas y narración que se combinan para crear un informe poderoso.

negación doble uso de dos palabras negativas para expresar una idea cuando sólo una es necesaria.

borrador etapa del proceso de escritura en la cual el escritor expresa sus ideas en oraciones que forman el principio, el medio y el final de una composición.

E

editing stage of the writing process in which the writer polishes his or her work by correcting errors in grammar, usage, mechanics, and spelling.

edición etapa del proceso de escritura en la cual el escritor mejora su trabajo y corrige los errores de gramática, uso del lenguaje, aspectos prácticos y ortografía.

elaboration addition of explanatory or descriptive information to a piece of writing, such as supporting details, examples, facts, and descriptions.

explicación agregar información explicativa o descriptiva a un texto, como detalles de apoyo, ejemplos, hechos y descripciones.

electronic publishing various ways to present information through the use of technology. It includes desktop publishing (creating printed documents on a computer), audio and video recordings, and online publishing (creating a Web site).

publicación electrónica o Ciberedición varias maneras de presentar la información por el uso de la tecnología. Incluye la autoedición (crear documentos impresos en una computadora), las grabaciones de audio y video y la publicación en línea (crear un sitio web).

ellipses punctuation marks (. . .) used to indicate where text has been removed from quoted material or to indicate a pause or interruption in speech.

puntos suspensivos signos de puntuación (. . .) utilizados para indicar dónde se ha quitado parte del texto de una cita o para indicar una pausa o una interrupción en el discurso.

e-mail electronic mail that can be sent all over the world from one computer to another.

correo electrónico mensaje electrónico que puede enviarse a cualquier lugar del mundo desde una computadora a otra.

essay composition of three or more paragraphs that presents and develops one main idea.

ensayo composición de tres o más párrafos que presenta y desarrolla una idea principal.

exclamatory sentence expression of strong feeling that ends with an exclamation point.

oración exclamativa expresión de sentimiento intenso que termina con signo de exclamación.

external coherence organization of the major components of a written piece (introduction, body, conclusion) in a logical sequence and flow, progressing from one idea to another while holding true to the central idea of the composition.

coherencia externa organización de las partes principales de un trabajo escrito (introducción, cuerpo, conclusión) en una secuencia lógica que presenta fluidez y avanza de una idea a otra, pero sustentando la idea central de la composición.

English	Español
F	
fable story in which animal characters act like people to teach a lesson or moral.	**fábula** relato en cual los personajes son animales que actúan como personas para enseñar una lección o una moraleja.
fact statement that can be proven.	**hecho** enunciado que puede probarse.
fiction prose works of literature, such as short stories and novels, which are partly or totally imaginary.	**ficción** obras literarias en prosa, como cuentos y novelas, que son parcial o totalmente imaginarias.
figurative language language that uses such devices as imagery, metaphor, simile, hyperbole, personification, or analogy to convey a sense beyond the literal meaning of the words.	**lenguaje figurado** lenguaje que emplea recursos tales como imágenes, metáforas, símiles, hipérboles, personificación o analogía para transmitir un sentido que va más allá del sentido literal de las palabras.
folktale story that was told aloud long before it was written.	**cuento folclórico** relato que se contaba en voz alta mucho antes de que fuera puesto por escrito.
fragment group of words that does not express a complete thought.	**fragmento** grupo de palabras que no expresa un pensamiento completo.
freewriting prewriting technique of writing freely without concern for mistakes made.	**escritura libre** técnica de preparación para la escritura que consiste en escribir libremente sin preocuparse por los errores cometidos.
friendly letter writing form that may use informal language and includes a heading, greeting (salutation), body, closing, and signature.	**carta amistosa** tipo de texto que puede usar un lenguaje informal e incluye membrete, saludo, cuerpo, despedida y firma.
G	
generalization a conclusion based on facts, examples, or instances.	**generalización** conclusión basada en hechos, ejemplos o casos.

English	Español
generalizing forming an overall idea that explains something specific.	**generalizando** formar una idea general que explica algo específico.
genre a distinctive type or category of text, such as personal narrative, expository essay, or short story.	**género** tipo distintivo o categoría de texto, como la narración personal, el ensayo expositivo o el cuento.
gerund verb form ending in *–ing* that is used as a noun.	**gerundio** forma verbal que termina en –ing y puede usarse como sustantivo.
glittering generality word or phrase that most people associate with virtue and goodness that is used to trick people into feeling positively about a subject.	**generalidad entusiasta** palabra o frase que la mayoría de la gente asocia con la virtud y la bondad, y que se utiliza con el fin de engañar a las personas para que tengan una reacción positiva respecto de cierto tema.
graphic elements (in poetry) use of word position, line length, and overall text layout to express or reflect meaning.	**elementos gráficos (en la poesía)** el uso de la ubicación de las palabras, la extensión de los versos y la disposición general del texto para expresar o mostrar el significado.

H

English	Español
helping verb auxiliary verb that combines with the main verb to make up a verb phrase.	**verbo auxiliar** verbo que se emplea junto con el verbo principal para formar una frase verbal.
homographs words that are spelled alike but have different meanings and pronunciations.	**homógrafos** palabras que se escriben de igual manera, pero tienen significados y pronunciaciones diferentes
homophones words that sound alike but have different meanings and spellings.	**homófonos** palabras que suenan de igual manera, pero tienen significados diferentes y se escriben de manera distinta.

English	Español

imperative sentence a request or command that ends with either a period or an exclamation point.

indefinite pronoun word that substitutes for a noun and refers to unnamed persons or things.

independent clause group of words that can stand alone as a sentence because it expresses a complete thought.

indirect object noun or a pronoun that answers the question *To or from whom?* or *To or for what?* after an action word.

infinitive verb form that usually begins with *to* and can be used as a noun, adjective, or adverb.

informative writing writing that explains with facts and examples, gives directions, or lists steps in a process.

interjection word that expresses strong feeling.

internal coherence in a written piece, organization of ideas and/or sentences in a logical sequence and with a fluid progression.

Internet global network of computers that are connected to one another with high speed data lines and telephone lines.

oración imperativa pedido u orden que termina en punto con signo de exclamación.

pronombre indefinido palabra que sustituye a un sustantivo y alude a personas o cosas que no han sido identificadas.

cláusula independiente grupo de palabras que pueden formar por sí solas una oración porque expresan un pensamiento completo.

objeto indirecto nombre o pronombre que responde la pregunta ¿A quién o para quién? (*To or from whom?*) o ¿A qué o para qué? (*To or for what?*) después de una palabra de acción.

infinitivo forma verbal que generalmente empieza con *to* y se puede usar como sustantivo, adjetivo o adverbio.

texto informativo texto que explica algo con hechos y ejemplos, da instrucciones o enumera los pasos de un proceso.

interjección palabra que expresa un sentimiento intenso.

coherencia interna en un texto escrito, la organización de las ideas y/o de las oraciones en una secuencia lógica y con un desarrollo fluido.

internet red mundial de computadoras que están conectadas entre sí con líneas de datos y líneas telefónicas de alta velocidad.

interrogative pronoun pronoun used to ask a question.

pronombre interrogativo pronombre utilizado para hacer una pregunta.

interrogative sentence a question. It ends with a question mark.

oración interrogativa pregunta. Empieza y termina con signos de interrogación en español y termina con signo de interrogación en inglés.

intransitive verb action verb that does not pass the action from a doer to a receiver.

verbo intransitivo verbo de acción que no transfiere la acción del agente a un receptor.

introduction first paragraph of a composition that catches the reader's attention and states the main idea.

introducción primer párrafo de una composición que capta la atención del lector y enuncia la idea principal.

irregular verb verb that does not form its past and past participle by adding –ed or –d to the present tense.

verbo irregular verbo que no forma el pasado o el participio pasado al agregar –ed o –d al tiempo presente.

J

jargon specialized vocabulary used by a particular group of people.

jerga vocabulario especializado usado por un grupo específico de personas.

L

linking verb verb that links the subject with another word that renames or describes the subject.

verbo copulativo verbo que conecta al sujeto con otra palabra que vuelve a nombrar o describe al sujeto.

literary analysis interpretation of a work of literature supported with appropriate details and quotations from the work.

análisis literario interpretación de una obra literaria fundamentada con detalles apropiados y citas de la obra.

GLOSSARY

English	Español
loaded words words carefully chosen to appeal to one's hopes or fears rather than to reason or logic.	**palabras tendenciosas** palabras escogidas cuidadosamente para apelar a las esperanzas o los temores del destinatario, en lugar de la razón o la lógica.

M

modifier word that makes the meaning of another word more precise.	**modificador** palabra que hace más preciso el significado de otra palabra.

N

narrative writing writing that tells a real or an imaginary story with a clear beginning, middle, and ending.	**texto narrativo** texto que relata una historia real o imaginaria con un principio, un medio y un final.
network a system of interconnected computers.	**red** sistema de computadoras interconectadas.
noncount noun a noun that names something that cannot be counted (*health, weather, music*).	**sustantivo no contable** sustantivo que designa algo que no se puede contar (la salud, el clima, la música).
nonessential phrase phrase or clause that can be removed from a sentence without changing the meaning of the sentence.	**frase accesoria** frase o cláusula que puede eliminarse de una oración sin cambiar el significado de la oración.
nonfiction prose writing that contains facts about real people and real events.	**no ficción** texto en prosa que contiene hechos sobre gente real y sucesos reales.
nonstandard English less formal language used by people of varying regions and dialects; not appropriate for use in writing.	**inglés no estándar** lenguaje menos formal utilizado por personas de diversas regiones y dialectos; inapropiado para usarlo en la escritura.

noun a word that names a person, place, thing, or idea. A common noun gives a general name. A proper noun names a specific person, place, or thing and always begins with a capital letter. Concrete nouns can be seen or touched; abstract nouns can not.

sustantivo palabra que designa una persona, un lugar, una cosa o una idea. Un sustantivo común expresa un nombre general. Un sustantivo propio nombra una persona, un lugar o una cosa específica y siempre comienza con mayúscula. Los sustantivos concretos designan cosas que pueden verse o tocarse, mientras que los sustantivos abstractos no lo hacen.

noun clause a subordinate clause used like a noun.

cláusula nominal cláusula subordinada usada como sustantivo.

O

object word that answers the question *What?* or *Whom?*

objeto palabra que responde la pregunta ¿Qué? *(What?)* o ¿Quién? *(Whom?)*.

object pronoun type of pronoun used for direct objects, indirect objects, and objects of prepositions.

pronombre objeto tipo de pronombre utilizado para los objetos directos, objetos indirectos y objetos de preposiciones.

occasion motivation for composing; the factor that prompts communication.

ocasión motivación para componer; factor que da lugar a la comunicación.

online connected to the Internet via line modem connection.

en línea conectado a la Internet a través de una conexión de módem.

opinion a judgment or belief that cannot be absolutely proven.

opinión juicio o creencia que no se puede probar completamente.

order of importance or size way of organizing information by arranging details in the order of least to most (or most to least) pertinent.

orden de importancia o tamaño manera de organizar la información poniendo los detalles en orden de menor a mayor (o de mayor a menor) pertinencia.

GLOSSARY

English	Español
outline information about a subject organized into main topics and subtopics.	**esquema** información sobre un tema organizada en temas principales y subtemas.

P

English	Español
paragraph group of related sentences that present and develop one main idea.	**párrafo** grupo de oraciones relacionadas que presentan y desarrollan una idea principal.
parallelism repetition of two or more similar words, phrases, or clauses creating emphasis in a piece of writing and easing readability.	**paralelismo** repetición de dos o más palabras, frases o cláusulas similares que crea énfasis en un texto escrito y facilita su lectura.
parentheses punctuation marks ( ) used to enclose supplementary information not essential to the meaning of the sentence; always used in pairs.	**paréntesis** signos de puntuación ( ) utilizados para encerrar información adicional que no es esencial para el significado de la oración; se usan siempre en parejas.
parody humorous imitation of a serious work.	**parodia** imitación humorística de una obra seria.
participial phrase participle that works together with its modifier and complement as an adjective.	**frase participial** participio que funciona junto con su modificador y su complemento como adjetivo.
participle verb form that is used as an adjective.	**participio** forma verbal que se utiliza como adjetivo.
parts of speech eight categories into which all words can be placed: noun, pronoun, verb, adjective, adverb, preposition, conjunction, and interjection.	**categorías gramaticales** ocho categorías en las que pueden clasificarse todas las palabras: sustantivo, pronombre, verbo, adjetivo, adverbio, preposición, conjunción e interjección.
passive voice the voice a verb is in when it expresses that the action of the verb is being performed upon the subject.	**voz pasiva** voz en que está el verbo cuando expresa que la acción del verbo se realiza sobre el sujeto.

personal narrative narrative that tells a real or imaginary story from the writer's point of view.

narración personal narración que cuenta una historia real o imaginaria desde el punto de vista del escritor.

personal pronoun type of pronoun that renames a particular person or group of people. Pronouns can be categorized into one of three groups, dependent on the speaker's position: first person (I), second person (you), and third person (she/he/it).

pronombre personal tipo de pronombre que vuelve a nombrar a una persona o grupo de personas en particular. Los pronombres se pueden clasificar en tres grupos, según la posición del hablante: primera persona (I [yo]), segunda persona (you [tú]) y tercera persona (she/he/it [ella/él]).

personal writing writing that tells a real or imaginary story from the writer's point of view.

narración personal texto que cuenta una historia real o imaginaria desde el punto de vista del escritor.

personification giving human qualities to non-human subjects.

personificación atribuir cualidades humanas a sujetos no humanos.

persuasive writing writing that expresses an opinion and uses facts, examples, and reasons in order to convince the reader of the writer's viewpoint.

texto persuasivo texto que expresa una opinión y emplea hechos, ejemplos y razones con el fin de convencer al lector del punto de vista del escritor.

play a piece of writing to be performed on a stage by actors.

obra de teatro texto escrito para que los actores lo representen en un escenario.

plot sequence of events leading to the outcome or point of the story; contains a climax or high point, a resolution, and an outcome or ending.

argumento secuencia de sucesos que lleva a la resolución del relato o propósito del mismo; contiene un clímax o momento culminante y una resolución o final.

plural form of a noun used to indicate two or more.

plural forma del sustantivo utilizada para indicar dos o más personas o cosas.

poetry form of writing that uses rhythm, rhyme, and vivid imagery to express feelings and ideas.

poesía tipo de texto que utiliza ritmo, rima e imágenes vívidas para expresar sentimientos e ideas.

GLOSSARY

possessive pronoun a pronoun used to show ownership or possession.

predicate part of a sentence that tells what a subject is or does.

predicate adjective adjective that follows a linking verb and modifies, or describes, the subject.

predicate nominative noun or a pronoun that follows a linking verb and identifies, renames, or explains the subject.

prefix one or more syllables placed in front of a base word to form a new word.

preposition word that shows the relationship between a noun or a pronoun and another word in the sentence.

prepositional phrase a group of words made up of a preposition, its object, and any words that describe the object (modifiers).

prewriting invention stage of the writing process in which the writer plans for drafting based on the subject, occasion, audience, and purpose for writing.

principal parts of a verb the present, the past, and the past participle. The principal parts help form the tenses of verbs.

pronoun word that takes the place of one or more nouns. Three types of pronouns are personal, reflexive, and intensive.

pronombre posesivo pronombre utilizado para indicar propiedad o posesión.

predicado parte de la oración que indica qué es o qué hace el sujeto.

adjetivo predicativo adjetivo que sigue a un verbo copulativo y modifica, o describe, al sujeto.

predicado nominal sustantivo o pronombre que sigue a un verbo copulativo e identifica, vuelve a nombrar o explica al sujeto.

prefijo una o más sílabas colocadas adelante de la raíz de una palabra para formar una palabra nueva.

preposición palabra que muestra la relación entre un sustantivo o un pronombre y otra palabra de la oración.

frase preposicional grupo de palabras formado por una preposición, su objeto y todas las palabras que describan al objeto (modificadores).

preescritura etapa de invención del proceso de escritura en la cual el escritor planea un borrador basándose en el tema, la ocasión, el público y el propósito para escribir.

partes principales de un verbo presente, pasado y participio pasado. Las partes principales ayudan a formar los tiempos verbales.

pronombre palabra que está en lugar de uno o más sustantivos. Entre los tipos de pronombres están los pronombres personales, reflexivos y enfáticos.

GLOSSARY

proofreading carefully rereading and making corrections in grammar, usage, spelling, and mechanics in a piece of writing.

corregir relectura atenta de un texto y corrección de la gramática, del uso del lenguaje, de la ortografía y de los aspectos prácticos de la escritura.

publishing stage of the writing process in which the writer may choose to share the work with an audience.

publicar etapa del proceso de escritura en la cual el escritor puede escoger dar a conocer su trabajo a un público.

purpose reason for writing or speaking on a given subject.

propósito razón para escribir o hablar sobre un tema dado.

R

reader-friendly formatting page elements such as fonts, bullet points, line length, and heads adding to the ease of reading.

formato de fácil lectura elementos que se agregan a la página escrita, como tipo de letra, viñetas, extensión de los renglones y encabezados para facilitar la lectura.

reflexive pronoun pronoun formed by adding –self or –selves to a personal pronoun; it is used to refer to or emphasize a noun or pronoun.

pronombre reflexivo pronombre que se forma al agregar –self o –selves al pronombre personal; se usa para aludir a un sustantivo o a un pronombre o enfatizarlos .

regular verb verb that forms its past and past participle by adding –ed or –d to the present.

verbo regular verbo que forma el pasado o participio pasado al agregar –ed o –d al tiempo presente.

relative pronoun pronoun that begins most adjectival clauses and relates the adjectival clause to the noun or pronoun it describes.

pronombre relativo pronombre con el que comienza la mayoría de las cláusulas adjetivas y que relaciona la cláusula adjetiva con el sustantivo o pronombre que describe.

report a composition of three or more paragraphs that uses specific information from books, magazines, and other sources.

informe composición de tres o más párrafos que emplea información específica extraída de libros, revistas y otras fuentes.

GLOSSARY

English	Español
revising stage of the writing process in which the writer rethinks what is written and reworks it to increase its clarity, smoothness, and power.	**revisar** etapa del proceso de escritura en la cual el escritor vuelve a pensar en lo que ha escrito y lo adapta para mejorar su claridad, fluidez y contundencia.
rhetorical device a writing technique, often employing metaphor and analogy, designed to enhance the writer's message.	**recurso retórico** técnica de escritura, que suele emplear metáforas y analogías, destinada a realzar el mensaje del escritor.
root the part of a word that carries its basic meaning.	**raíz** parte de una palabra que lleva en sí lo esencial del significado de la palabra.
run-on sentence two or more sentences that are written as one sentence and are separated by a comma or have no mark of punctuation at all.	**oración sin final** dos o más oraciones escritas como una sola oración y separadas por una coma o escritas sin ningún signo de puntuación.

S

sensory details details that appeal to one of the five senses: seeing, hearing, touching, tasting, and smelling.	**detalles sensoriales** detalles que apelan a uno de los cinco sentidos: vista, oído, tacto, gusto y olfato.
sentence group of words that expresses a complete thought.	**oración** grupo de palabras que expresa un pensamiento completo.
sentence fragment group of words that does not express a complete thought.	**fragmento de oración** grupo de palabras que no expresa un pensamiento completo.
sequential order the order in which details are arranged according to when they take place or when they are done.	**orden secuencial** orden en que están organizados los detalles de acuerdo con el momento en que tienen lugar o cuándo se realizan.
setting the place and time of a story.	**ambiente** lugar y tiempo de un relato.

GLOSSARY

short story well-developed story about characters facing a conflict or problem.

simple predicate the main word or phrase in the complete predicate.

simple sentence a sentence that has one subject and one verb.

simple subject the main word in a complete subject.

slang nonstandard English expressions that are developed and used by particular groups.

spatial order the order in which details are arranged according to their physical location.

speaker tag in dialogue, text that indicates who is speaking; frequently includes a brief description of the manner of speaking.

standard English proper form of the language that follows a set pattern of rules and conventions.

style visual or verbal expression that is distinctive to an artist or writer.

subject (composition) topic of a composition or essay.

subject (grammar) word or group of words that names the person, place, thing, or idea that the sentence is about.

relato corto relato bien desarrollado sobre personajes que se enfrentan a un conflicto o problema.

predicado simple la palabra o la frase principal en el predicado completo.

oración simple oración que tiene un sujeto y un verbo.

sujeto simple la palabra principal en un sujeto completo.

argot expresiones propias del inglés no estándar desarrolladas y usadas por grupos específicos.

orden espacial orden en el cual los detalles se organizan de acuerdo con su ubicación física.

identificador del interlocutor en un diálogo, el texto que indica quién habla; suele incluir una breve descripción de la manera de hablar.

Inglés estándar forma correcta del lenguaje que sigue un patrón establecido de reglas y convenciones.

estilo expresión visual o verbal que es propia de un artista o escritor.

tema idea principal de una composición o ensayo.

sujeto palabra o grupo de palabras que nombran la persona, el lugar, la cosa o la idea de la que trata la oración

GLOSSARY

subordinate clause group of words that cannot stand alone as a sentence because it does not express a complete thought.

subordinating conjunction single connecting word used in a sentence to introduce a dependent clause which is an idea of less importance than the main idea.

suffix one or more syllables placed after a base word to change its part of speech and possibly its meaning.

supporting sentence sentence that explains or proves the topic sentence with specific details, facts, examples, or reasons.

synonym word that has nearly the same meaning as another word.

cláusula subordinada grupo de palabras que no puede funcionar por sí solo como una oración porque no expresa un pensamiento completo.

conjunción subordinante palabra de conexión usada en una oración para introducir una cláusula dependiente que expresa una idea de menor importancia que la idea principal.

sufijo una o más sílabas colocadas después de la raíz de una palabra para modificar su categoría gramatical y, posiblemente, su significado.

oración de apoyo oración que explica o prueba la oración principal con detalles específicos, hechos, ejemplos o razones.

sinónimo palabra que significa casi lo mismo que otra palabra.

T

tense the form a verb takes to show time. The six tenses are the present, past, future, present perfect, past perfect, and future perfect.

testimonial persuasive strategy in which a famous person encourages the purchase of a certain product.

tiempo verbal forma que toma un verbo para expresar el tiempo en que ocurre la acción. Los seis tiempos verbales son: presente, pasado, futuro, presente perfecto, pretérito perfecto y futuro perfecto.

testimonial estrategia persuasiva en cual una persona famosa alienta a comprar un cierto producto.

GLOSSARY

thesaurus online or print reference that gives synonyms for words.

tesauro (Diccionario de sinónimos) material de referencia en línea o impreso que ofrece alternativas para las palabras.

topic sentence a sentence that states the main idea of the paragraph.

oración principal oración que enuncia la idea principal del párrafo.

transitions words and phrases that show how ideas are related.

elementos de transición palabras y frases que muestran las ideas cómo están relacionadas.

U

understood subject a subject of a sentence that is not stated.

sujeto tácito sujeto de una oración que no está explícito.

unity combination or ordering of parts in a composition so that all the sentences or paragraphs work together as a whole to support one main idea.

unidad combinación u ordenamiento de las partes de una composición de tal manera que todas las oraciones o párrafos funcionen juntos como un todo para fundamentar una idea principal.

V

verb word used to express an action or state of being.

verbo palabra usada para expresar una acción o un estado del ser.

verb phrase main verb plus one or more helping verbs.

frase verbal verbo principal más uno o más verbos auxiliares.

verbal verb form that acts like another part of speech, such as an adjective or noun.

verbal forma del verbo que funciona como otra categoría gramatical, tal como un adjetivo o un sustantivo.

voice the particular sound and rhythm of the language the writer uses (closely related to tone).

voz sonido y ritmo particular del lenguaje que usa un escritor (estrechamente vinculado al tono).

English	Español
English	**Español**

World Wide Web network of computers within the Internet capable of delivering multimedia content and text over communication lines into personal computers all over the globe.

writing process recursive stages that a writer proceeds through in his or her own way when developing ideas and discovering the best way to express them.

red mundial de comunicación red de computadoras dentro de la Internet capaz de transmitir contenido multimedia y textos, a través de líneas de comunicación, a las computadoras personales de todas partes del mundo.

proceso de escritura etapas recurrentes que un escritor sigue a su manera cuando desarrolla ideas y descubre la mejor manera de expresarlas.

GLOSSARY

Index

Note: Italic locators (page numbers) indicate skill sets

INDEX

Note: Italic locators (page numbers) indicate skill sets

Note: Italic locators (page numbers) indicate skill sets

INDEX

Note: Italic locators (page numbers) indicate skill sets

Note: Italic locators (page numbers) indicate skill sets

Note: Italic locators (page numbers) indicate skill sets

INDEX

Formal English, 782
Formal outline. *See* Outline.
Formal speaking, 417-422. *See also* Speeches.
Forms
  business, 411-413
  of writing, 15
Fragment. *See* Sentence fragment.
Free-verse poem, 184-185
Freewriting
  as prewriting strategy, 88, 90, 115-116, 182, 195, 234
Friendly letter, 400-401
FTP, defined, 448
Future perfect tense, 690
Future tense, 690

G

Gathering evidence, 263-264
Gathering information
  for research report, 280-313
  for speech, 419-420
Gender
  agreement of pronoun and antecedent, 723-724
  defined, 723
Generalization
  explained, 73, 134
  forming plurals, 918
  spelling, 915-916, 936, 961
Genre, 16, 88
Gerund, 604, 612-613, 949
Gerund phrase, 613-614, 620, 949
Gestures, 177, 376, 421-422
Give, principal parts, 679, 691
Glossary, as research tool, 343
Glossary of usage, 171, 782-791
Go, principal parts, 681
Good, well, 774-775, 786
Grammar QuickGuide, 944-951
Graphic elements, 56, 186, 444
Graphic organizer, 48, 68, 72, 93, 133, 163, 201, 227, 264, 265, 268, 319, 344-346, 371
  defined, 345
Graphics
  charts and graphs, 437
  clip art, 436
  drawings, 436
  photographs, 437
  stand-alone, 438
  for Web site, 444-445
Group discussion
  guidelines for participating in, 416
Grow, principal parts, 679
Guide words, in dictionary, 384

H

Hasn't, haven't, 743
Have, as helping verb, 467, 512, 689, 741
Have, of, 786
Heading
  in a business letter, 407
  in a friendly letter, 400-401
  in a get-well letter, 403
  in an informational letter, 402
  in an invitation, 405
  in a letter of regret, 406
  on a note card, 294, 316, 318
  in an order letter, 410
  in a thank-you letter, 404
Helping verb, 467, 512-513, 515, 520, 533, 606, 674-677, 689, 741-742, 780, 946, 953
Hit, principal parts, 676
Home page, 445
  defined, 448
How-to writing, 37, 213
HTML, 445, 449
http, 449
Hyphen
  with compound noun, 490, 899
  with divided words, 383, 896, 908, 960
  with fractions, 898
  guidelines for usage, 120, 896-900, 926
  with numbers, 802, 898, 908, 960
  proofreading symbol, 11
Hypothesis, 246

I

Ideas for writing. *See also* Arranging ideas/information; Main idea; Order of ideas.
  brainstorming, 18, 47, 88, 90-93, 116, 182, 199, 234, 286, 371
  clustering, 18-19, 47, 88, 90, 116, 160, 182, 195, 234
  5W-How? questions, 19, 114
  freewriting, 88, 90, 115-116, 182, 195, 234
  observing, 96, 137
  personal experience, 23, 68, 110, 254, 257, 286
  for play, 174-180
  for poetry, 181-187
  prewriting techniques, 13-21, 116-120, 195-202, 234-237, 259-266

recalling, 102
  thinking, 12, 14, 22, 56, 104, 195, 209, 231, 340-375
Idioms, defined, 43
Ie, ei, spelling rule for, 915-916
Illustrations. *See* Graphics.
Imagery, 184, 186, 267-268
Imagining, 115
Imperative sentence, 477-478, 482, 945
Implicit theme, 177
Implied main idea, 22, 91-92
Implied meanings, 357
Impression
  lasting, 134, 243
  overall, 134-136
In, into, 786
In the Media
  Create a "How-to" Multimedia Presentation, 213
  Documentary, 331
  Evaluating Performances, 169
  Movie Review, 80
  Radio Advertising: Emotions and Audience, 233
  Screenplay, 274
  Sound Bites, 142
  Television Cartoons, 104
  Tourist Brochure, 46
In-camera editing, of video, 443
Indefinite pronoun
  agreement problems and, *753-756*, 760
  defined, 498, 946
  gender and, 725
  plural, *724-726*
  possessive, 881
  singular, *724-726*
Independent clause, 81, 236-237, 320, 630, 642-644, 661, 831, 887, 889, 891, 950, 957
Index, as research tool, 291, 293, 306, 310, 343, 473
Indirect object
  complement, 562
  compound, 565
  defined, 565, 580, 948
  diagraming, 575
  identifying, *565-566*
  pronoun and, 565, 580, 706, 712-713, 780
Indirect quotation, 860
Inferring, 94
Infinitive, 604, *615-618*, 621, 626, 833, 949
Infinitive phrase, 616-618, 621
Informal English, 782

Note: Italic locators (page numbers) indicate skill sets

Note: Italic locators (page numbers) indicate skill sets

Note: Italic locators (page numbers) indicate skill sets

Note: Italic locators (page numbers) indicate skill sets

Note: Italic locators (page numbers) indicate skill sets

INDEX

Note: Italic locators (page numbers) indicate skill sets

INDEX

Note: Italic locators (page numbers) indicate skill sets

Note: Italic locators (page numbers) indicate skill sets

Note: Italic locators (page numbers) indicate skill sets

Note: Italic locators (page numbers) indicate skill sets

INDEX

Note: Italic locators (page numbers) indicate skill sets

INDEX

Note: Italic locators (page numbers) indicate skill sets

INDEX

Note: Italic locators (page numbers) indicate skill sets

INDEX

INDEX

Verb tense *(continued)*
    past perfect, 689-693
    past perfect progressive, 695-696
    past progressive, 695-696
    present, 689-693
    present perfect, 689-693
    present perfect progressive,
        695-696
    present progressive, 695-696
    principal parts, 674-688
    progressive form, 695-696
    shift in, 102, 693-694
    uses of, *689-690, 692-694*
Verbal phrase, *602-604, 606-624*, 949
    and comma, 607
    defined, 604
    gerund phrase, 613-614, 618, 620,
        623, 949
    identifying, 605, 608-610, 612,
        614-615, 617, 623
    infinitive phrase, 604, 616-618,
        621, 623, 949
    participial phrase, 604, 606-611,
        618-619, 623, 949
Verbal strategies, 421-422
Verbals, *602-627*, 949
    defined, 604, 949
    gerund, 604, 612-614, 949
    infinitive, 604, 615-618, 949
    parallelism, 617
    participle, 604-606, 613, 949
Verb-subject agreement. *See*
    Agreement, subject-verb.
Vertical file, 310
Video files, on Web site, 444
Video production, 438-443
    assemble editing, 443
    background music, 443
    camera techniques, 441-442
    cutaway shot, 442
    dissolve, 443
    editing, 443
    establishing shot, 442
    fade, 443
    final cut, 443
    formats, 440
    in-camera editing, 443
    insert editing, 443
    panning, 441
    post-production, 443
    reaction shot, 442
    schedule, 440
    tracking, 441
    voiceover narration, 443
    zooming, 441

Viewing. *See* Listening and viewing.
Visual representations
    analyze, audience response, 419,
        441
    charts, 203, 326, 436-437
    creating a project, 243, 274,
        431-445, 419
    presenting a project, 421, 443
    reflecting critically on work
        produced, 291-292, 443
    using a variety of forms, 242-243,
        326, 377
    using a variety of technologies,
        242-243, 326, 377
Visuals, in research report, 326
Vivid words, 45-48
Vocabulary, 349, *378-397*. *See also*
    Word parts.
    acronyms, 380
    American dialects, 41
    analogies, 351-353
    antonyms, 349, 396
    base words, 393-395
    borrowed words, 379
    clichés, 50
    colloquialisms, 43
    compound words, 380-382
    connotations, 51
    context, 389, 391
    context clues, 391-392
    denotations, 51
    dialects, identifying, 41-42
    ethnic, 42
    exact words, importance of, 171,
        295, 857
    formal language, 43, 782
    growth of English language,
        378-383
    idioms, 43
    informal language, 43-44, 782
    jargon, 44
    meaning, from context, 365-366,
        390
    nonstandard American English,
        43, 782
    prefixes, 393-394
    slang, 44
    standard American English, 43, 782
    suffixes, 394-395
    synonyms, 349, 383, 389, 395
    tests, 349-361
    thesaurus, 309
    tired words, 50
    word origins, 379-381, 385
    words from names, 380

Voice
    active and passive, 697-702, 952
    analyzing, 6
    audience, 6, 40
    developing your writing voice,
        6, 40
    identifying, 6, 40, 334, 422, 697-
        698, 700
    purpose, 6, 40
    use of, 6, 40, 697
    using, 24, 40, 697
    volume, tone, and pitch, 422, 428

W

Way, ways, 791
Wear, principal parts, 681
Web 2.0, defined, 450
Web site. *See also* Internet; World
    Wide Web.
    blogs, 445
    building, 444-445
    drag and drop, 445
    HyperText Markup Language
        (HTML), 445, 449
    interfaces, 444
    Internet terminology, 448-450
    link, 449
    navigation, 445
    planning, 444-445
    site map, 445
    software, 445
    summary, 444-445
    WYSIWYG, 445
Where, that, 791
Who, whom, 721-722, 791
    in questions, 499
Whose, who's, 721-722, 791
Wiki, defined, 450
Wish, principal parts, 675
Wonder, principal parts, 675
Word division, 385-386, 388,
    393-394, 896, 926-927, 929-930
Word origins, 390
Word parts. *See also* Vocabulary.
    prefixes, 393, 926
    suffixes, 394, 927
Word web, 182
Wordiness, 30
Word-processing tools, in writing
    process, 33, 431-436, 445, 932.
    See also Computers.
Words. *See also* Prefixes; Suffixes;
    Vocabulary.
    meaning, 391-397
    often confused, 683, 719

Note: Italic locators (page numbers) indicate skill sets

Image Credits

Text Credits